The Silk Road

The Silk Road

Art and History

Jonathan Tucker

ART MEDIA RESOURCES

FOR JACK WILLIAM TUCKER

There I'll come when I'm a man
'With a camel caravan;'*

From the poem Travel, in A Child's Garden of Verses and Underwoods *by Robert Louis Stevenson (1850–94)

Source of Illustrations
As stated in the captions, except for:
Antonia Tozer– Figs. 1, 3, 29, 31, 32, 33, 44, 46, 48, 51, 60, 61, 63, 65, 66, 67, 68, 69, 70, 71, 72, 74, 75, 79, 83, 85, 86, 88, 89, 90, 93, 102, 103, 107, 114, 128, 131, 134, 135, 140, 141,142, 144, 148, 149, 151, 152, 168, 169, 170, 171, 175, 176, 181, 182, 183, 184, 185, 186, 188, 194, 196, 197, 198, 199, 200, 203, 207, 208, 210, 211, 212, 213, 220, 222, 223, 224, 225, 232, 235, 239, 240, 241, 242, 243, 246, 247, 248, 249, 250, 251, 252, 253, 254, 255, 256, 258, 259, 260, 261, 262, 263, 264, 266, 276, 277, 283, 287, 291, 294, 295, 296, 297, 298, 299, 301, 302, 303, 304, 305, 306, 307, 308, 310, 311, 312, 314, 315, 316, 318, 319, 320, 321, 323, 328, 331, 332, 335, 337, 338, 339, 340, 346, 351, 352, 354, 357, 358, 359, 360, 363, 365, 366, 367, 368, 369, 370, 371, 372, 373, 376, 377, 378, 380, 381, 382, 383, 384, 385, 386, 387, 388, 389, 390, 391, 393, 394, 395, 396, 397, 398, 399, 410, 413, 415, 418, 419, 423, 424, 425, 426, 427, 428, 429, 431, 432, 433, 434, 435 and 436.
Author – Figs. 2, 4, 8, 9, 18, 21, 25, 45, 62, 64, 73, 81, 92, 122, 132, 133, 150, 187, 206, 234, 237, 238, 244, 245, 267, 284, 289, 290, 292, 293, 309, 313, 317, 322, 326, 327, 333, 336, 341, 342, 343, 344, 349, 350, 362, 374, 379, 392, 412, 414 and 437.

Front Cover: Clockwise from top left: Fig. 149. Jiayuguan Fort, Gansu, China; Fig. 54. Gandhara stucco Buddha head;* Samarkand children, ca. 1900;* Afghan engineer in charge of rebuilding Emperor Babur's tomb, Kabul; Fig. 312. Beached ship, Aral Sea, Uzbekistan; Fig. 357. Remains of the Kharakhanid capital of Balasagun, Kyrgyzstan; Man and child with an eagle, Altai Region, Western Mongolia; (Centre) Fig. 369. Gonbad-e Kavus tomb tower, Golestan province, Iran, and (Background) Fig. 242. Hunza Valley, Northern Pakistan.

(All photographs by Antonia Tozer except for those marked with an asterisk)

Spine: Fig. 265. Limestone relief of Buddha with attendants.
Rear Cover: From left to right: Fig. 435. The Basilica Cistern (Yerebatan Saray), Istanbul; Fig. 422. The East Terrace, Nemrud Dagi, Turkey*; Sunset at Palmyra, Syria; Fig. 423. The Ishak Pasha Saray with the Silk Road beyond, Dogubeyazit, Turkey; Fig. 363. The Holy Shrine of Imam Reza, Masshad, Iran; Fig. 312. The Ships' Graveyard at Moynaq, formerly on the Aral Sea, Uzbekistan; Fig. 301. The East walls of the Ichan Kala, Khiva, Uzbekistan; Fig. 329. The Registan Square, Samarkand, Uzbekistan, ca. 1890*; Fig. 262. The mud walls of the Bala Hissar at Balkh, Northern Afghanistan; Fig. 70. The Great Buddha, Bamiyan, Afghanistan; Fig. 199. Mural of a goddess and a celestial musician, Kizil, Xinjiang province, China; Fig. 223. Remains of a Buddhist stupa, Niya, Xinjiang province, China; Fig. 180. Painted leaf from a Manichaean book, Gaochang (Khocho), near Turfan, Xinjiang province, China;* Fig. 161. Painted statue of Hong Bian, Dunhuang, Gansu province, China;* Fig. 134. Shandan Army Horse Ranch, Mount Yanzhi, Gansu province, China; Fig. 13. Bronze figure of a flying horse, Wuwei, Gansu province, China;* Fig. 135. General view of the Binglingsi Caves, Gansu province, China; Fig. 102. The Dayan (Great Goose) Pagoda, Xian, China; Fig. 109. Tri-colour glazed figure of a camel carrying a party of musicians, Zhongbao Village, Xian, China;* Fig. 85. Vairocana Buddha with a Bodhisattva and a disciple, Longmen caves, Henan province, China, and Fig. 81. Interior of Cave 6, Yungang caves, Shanxi province, China.

(All photographs by Antonia Tozer except for Fig. 81 [author] and those marked with an asterisk; see captions within text for more details)

Copyright © 2003 Jonathan Tucker

Published in 2003 by
Philip Wilson Publishers, 7 Deane House, 27 Greenwood Place
London NW5 1LB

Published in 2003 in North America by
Art Media Resources Ltd
1507 South Michigan Avenue, Chicago IL 60605

Designed by Peter Ling
Map artwork by Stephen Timson
Printed by Craft Print International Ltd., Singapore

ISBN 1 58886 022 1

CONTENTS

ACKNOWLEDGEMENTS

My wife Antonia Tozer, for her fortitude during three and a half years as a 'book widow', for her vitality and for her photographic skills. Without her this book would be a ten-page pamphlet!

Emmy Bunker for her enthusiasm, support and encouragement.

Philip Wilson, Cangy Venables, Peter Ling and Norman Turpin, for all of their hard work in the editing, design and production of this book.

My parents, Donald and Margaret Tucker, for 'babysitting' our business on two occasions while we sloped off along the Silk Road.

Dr M. Ashraf Khan and colleagues at the Taxila Museum.

Saeed Urrehman and Sher Muhammad for their help with our exploration of the sites along the Karakorum Highway.

Jamil Suliman, who guided us to and around what remains of Shah-ji-ki-Dheri in Peshawar.

M. Faheem Khan and Farid Sayed of the International Committee of the Red Cross in Peshawar.

Two anonymous friends, Mr P and Mr B, for their assistance in Pakistan and Afghanistan.

Zarif Maiwond, our courageous guide during an unforgettable morning in Kabul, when we succeeded in giving our Taleban minders the slip.

'The Professor', Amir Mohammad Shindandi, who guided us safely through Afghanistan with wit and patience.

Irina Bogoslovskaya for her assistance in Tashkent.

Dr Edvard Rtveladze at the Institute of Fine Arts, Tashkent for a fascinating morning spent with the treasures from the Soviet excavations in southern Uzbekistan.

Countess Patricia Jellicoe for her enthusiasm and encouragement.

Professor Marianne Yaldiz of the Museum für Indische Kunst, Berlin

Peter Scott, a former colleague at Spink, for his help and encouragement during the early stages of writing this book.

The staff at the Khotan Museum in Xinjiang.

Louise Firouz in Iran for her insightful remarks about ancient breeds of horse.

Mrs Fatima Farmanfarmaian for her helpful suggestions regarding classical Persian literature.

Jeffrey Moy and Shane Suvikapakornkul of Paragon Books.

Compiling over 400 images for this book was almost as arduous a process as the actual writing. I would like to thank the following people for their help in obtaining some of the more elusive images: Isao Kurita, Carol Michaelson of the British Museum, Edward Gibbs, Geoffrey King, Sarah Wong of Eskenazi Ltd and John Pett of Spink.

Finally, I would like to express my gratitude to the staff of the School of Oriental and African Studies Library at the University of London.

A note on the translation of the poetry and prose
contained in this book

When poetry and other forms of literature are translated from another language the quality of translation is almost as important as the original text. The interpretations of Chinese literature by Burton Watson, Arthur Waley and Vikram Seth, quoted in many places in this book, are superb. So, too, are the translations from the Persian by Gertrude Bell, Reuben Levy and A. J. Arberry and when several versions of the same text are available I have tried to use the one that is the most evocative and best captures the atmosphere of the time or place.

PREFACE

'When the towns go down there are stains of
Rust on the stone shores and illegible
Coins and a rhyme remembered of swans, say,
Or birds or leaves or a horse or fabulous
Bull forms or a falling of gold upon Softness.'

(Archibald MacLeish [1892–1982], '…& Forty-Second Street')

It would be no exaggeration if I were to tell you that my interest in the Silk Road borders on the obsessive, and has done so these past twenty years. The catalyst was the monumental Japanese TV documentary series *The Silk Road*, filmed when Central Asia was still firmly under Soviet control, China was grappling with the residual effects of the Cultural Revolution, and Afghanistan was – as it still is – embroiled in war. During the past ten years, perhaps for the first time since Genghis Khan and his descendants forcibly imposed the pax Mongolica on the lands between Eastern Europe and the Sea of Japan, it has been possible to travel the entire length of the old road in relative safety. In the khans' day it was said that 'a man might have journeyed from the land of sunrise to the land of sunset with a golden platter upon his head without suffering the least violence from anyone.' Today is a little different but I began, tentatively at first and then with growing confidence, to travel the old highways. In the beginning I journeyed alone but in recent years my long-suffering and ever-patient wife, Antonia Tozer, has accompanied me, carrying a large bag of camera equipment and (for the most part) a shared enthusiasm. We have visited the ancient places of the Silk Road and recorded what we saw; our journeys made to discover what remains and to record it before it is lost forever.

During the seven years it took to research and write this book there were times when my enthusiasm for the subject almost overcame me. The sheer beauty of the places I visited and the sense of freedom I felt produced an overwhelming desire to emulate Robert Browning's character Waring:

'What's become of Waring
Since he gave us all the slip,
Chose land-travel or seafaring,

Boots and chest or staff and scrip,
Rather than pace up and down
Any longer London town?'

(Robert Browning [1812–89], 'Waring'.)

Each time I returned to London's noise and drizzle, I sought solace among the aisles of the School of Oriental and African Studies library and discovered that its 850,000 books were filled with jewels. The standard texts on Asian art and history are there but so too are books by Victorian adventurers who rode bicycles to India, Edwardian hunters who trekked

Yanshui Gorge in snow
(Fig. 207)

* For more on Sir John Mandeville, see p. 225).

through the high passes of the Pamirs and Himalayas in search of game, and the accounts of some who wandered across Asia for decades and were just plain mad. Where else would one find a book called *Alone through the forbidden land: journeys in disguise through Soviet Central Asia* (by Gustav Krist), or one published in 1700 and concerning the fourteenth-century traveller (or according to many, the utter charlatan) Sir John Mandeville* (d. 1372) called *The travels and voyages of Sir John Mandevile, Knt.: containing an exact description of the way to Hierusalem, Great Caan, India, the country of Preston-John, and many other eastern countries: with an account of many strange monsters and whatever is curious and remarkable therein / carefully collected from the original manuscript, and illustrated with variety of pictures?*

These days, we are separated from most of the cities of the Silk Road by little more than a flight and an hour or two in a taxi, but it is still possible to follow the example of the great writers of history and learn to commune with the past. John Keats was stirred by literature – in his case it was Homer – while Edward Gibbon, author of *The History of the Decline and Fall of the Roman Empire*, drew inspiration from his surroundings:

> '*Much have I travell'd in the realms of gold,*
> *And many goodly states and kingdoms seen;*'

(John Keats (1795–1821), 'On first looking into Chapman's Homer')

> '*It was at Rome, on the 15th of October, 1764, as I sat musing amidst the ruins of the Capitol, while the barefoot friars were singing vespers in the Temple of Jupiter, that the idea of writing the decline and fall of the city first started to my mind.*'

(Edward Gibbon [1737–94], 'Autobiography')

The raw materials for this book, too – with all its faults and shortcomings – come from the Silk Road itself, from the histories of its states and their protagonists, and from the poetry and stories of the places that Tennyson called the 'ever-silent spaces of the East'.

INTRODUCTION

The past is closer than we think

'How worlds are spawned and where the dead gods go,
All shall be shard of broken memories.'

(Archibald MacLeish [1892–1982], 'Baccalaureate')

It is easy to forget that the great caravan cities of the Silk Road have, for the most part, been subjected to urban development and restoration projects only within the past fifty years. An examination of almost any pre-war photograph from China, Central Asia or the Middle East provides a glimpse of a lost era. There are people alive today who have looked upon the places of the Silk Road, albeit in a reduced and ruinous state, and seen pretty much what the contemporaries of Xuanzang or Timur would have seen. A

case in point would and should have been the inimitable Robert Byron (1905–41), whose occasionally tart observations of Persia and Afghanistan in *The Road to Oxiana* have entertained readers since they were written in 1937. Today, had the Second World War not claimed him, he would be a ninety-seven year old national treasure.

So, too, the indomitable missionaries Mildred Cable and Francesca French deserve a mention. The world they describe, of the old cities of the Silk Road before the advent of tourism; of journeys in western China requiring months instead of days to complete; and of traditions lost in antiquity but still practiced by the oasis-dwellers, occurred during the lifetime of our parents. Their classic, *The Gobi Desert*, for example, was published as recently as 1942.

And there is a country where even today, at the beginning of the third millennium, the Silk Road can still be seen in its

Fig.1 **An old caravanserai reverts slowly to dust on the road to Balkh. Near Andkhoi, Northern Afghanistan**
Probably Seljuk period, ca. 11th century
There is a sixteenth-century water tower at the site known as a *sardoba* (literally 'cold water'), a domed structure built at many places along the caravan routes to provide a supply of fresh water to travellers. Snow was sometimes packed into them during the winter months.

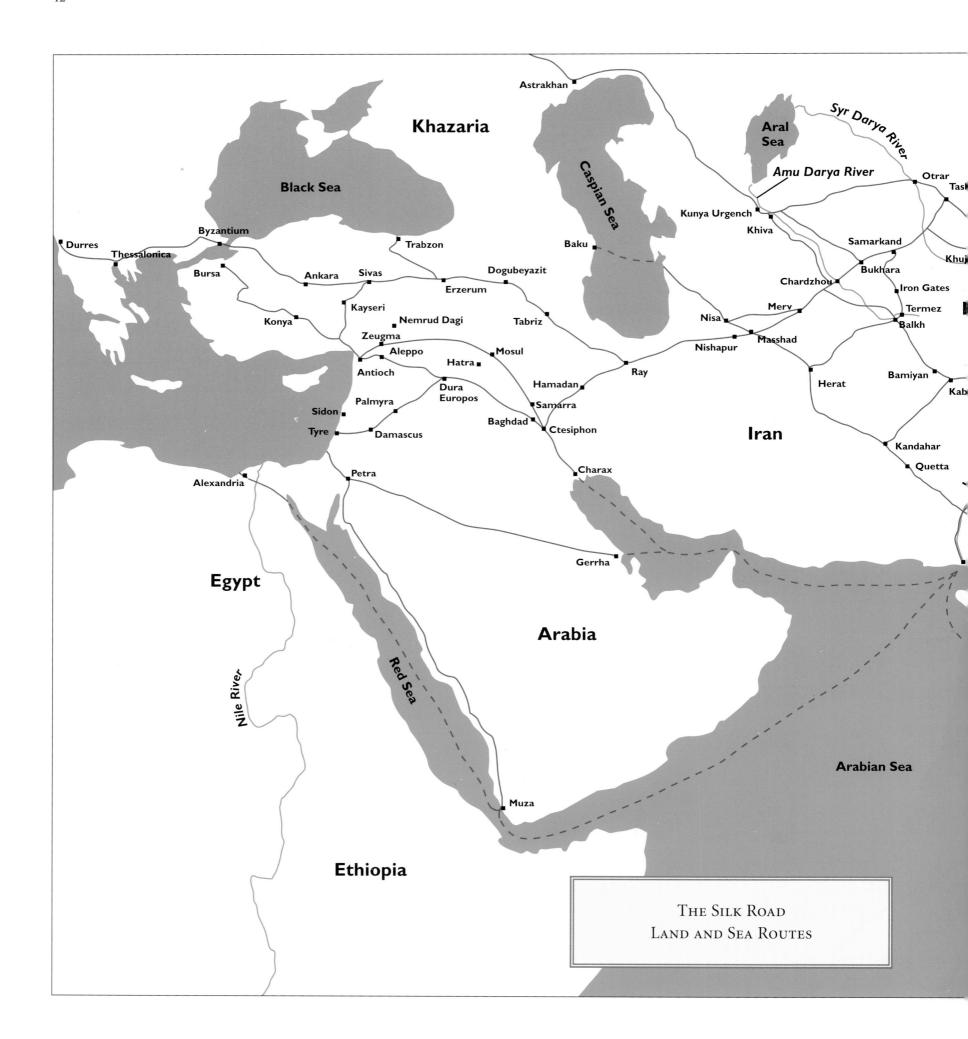

THE SILK ROAD
LAND AND SEA ROUTES

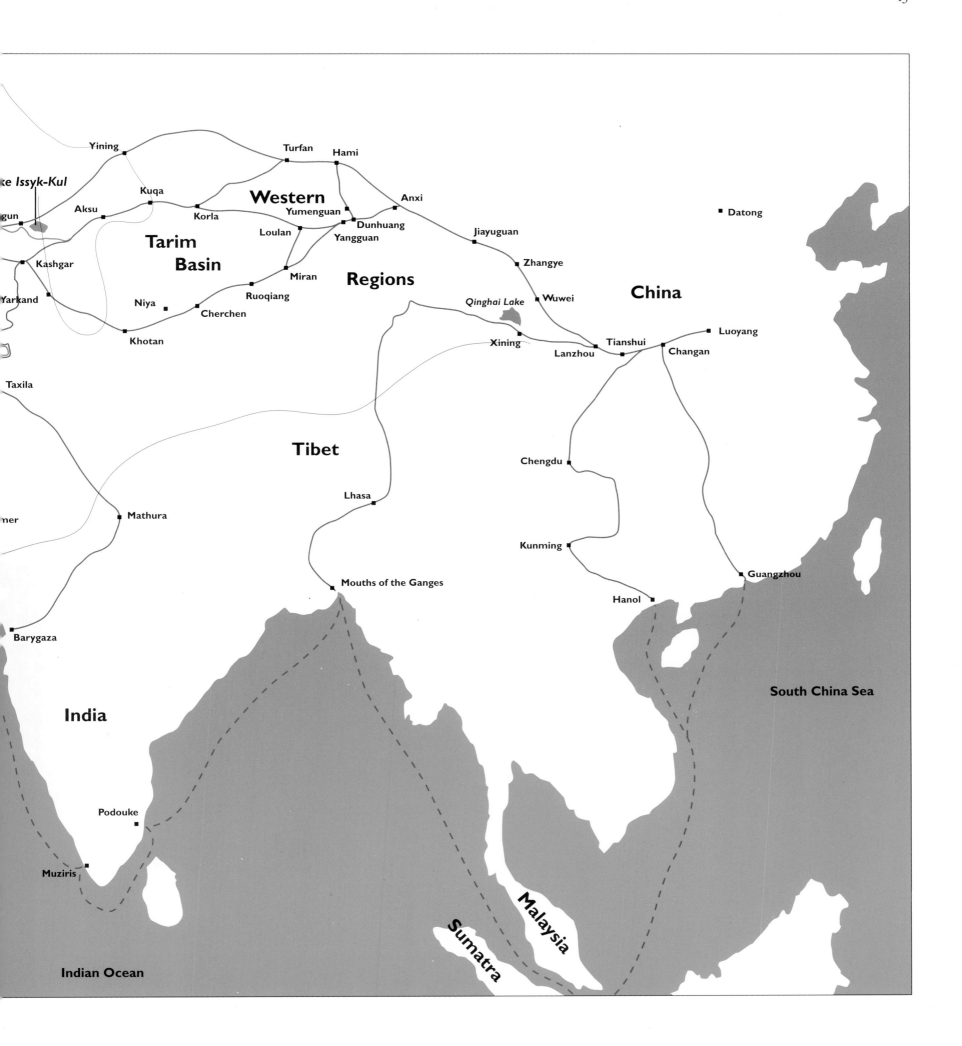

Figs. 2 and 3 **Silk and tea, two of the Silk Road's many commodities**

Silk Worms (*bombyx mori*) consuming mulberry leaves
(Suzhou Silk Museum, China)

Card players at a teahouse, Wuwei, Gansu Province, China

original state; where men still drag caravans of camels along disintegrating roads; where cities wrecked by Genghis and Timur still tower above the highway, and where ancient caravanserais revert slowly back to the dust from which they were built. In Afghanistan, the people of the backroads still live with few of the amenities of the modern world. Two decades of conflict have, if anything, left them with less and Afghanistan has reverted to a sort of pre-industrial twilight era. The one hundred hotels of 1970s Bamiyan are rubble and no tourists now explore the labyrinth of caves about the Buddhas. A new layer of archeology has been added to the country's past: mines by the million lie in strata like the layers of some ancient city; Taliban mines lie on Mujahadeen mines that lie on Soviet mines. Villages across this beautiful, blighted country, from Torkham to Turkmenistan, are ruined and abandoned and sometimes it is difficult to

distinguish an old ruin from a new one. Many of its great cities are damaged or destroyed: Bamiyan has been erased, Hadda is now little more than a mound of earth and Ai Khanum has been dug down to the bed rock by those in search of treasure. But Balkh (at least to date) is untouched and still stands, resplendent beside the old road. If one searches in every country today for the essence of the Silk Road, it to be found, like nowhere else, in Afghanistan.

The Swedish explorer Sven Hedin passed through Xinjiang, the cradle of the Chinese section of the Silk Road, in 1933–35. It was his last expedition and he carried with him dreams of reviving the old Silk Road as a great motorized highway linking China with Europe. China was in the grip of warlords and the old road was in a wretched state:

> '*We now saw the Silk Road at its lowest ebb, with dormant life and dying trade, the connecting towns and villages in ruins, and the population languishing in a state of permanent insecurity and miserable poverty.*'

(Sven Hedin in Hedin, 1938)

Its fortunes have since revived. It is now possible, more or less, to drive from Xian to the shores of the Atlantic Ocean without leaving a paved road, and even the remotest parts of Xinjiang have been opened up by the search for oil and other natural resources. Tourism has also arrived with a vengeance and the legendary travellers of old like Marco Polo and Xuanzang – were they to retread the ancient highways – would be severely challenged to recognize towns like Xian and Kashgar as they are today. The dangers now are not due to apathy and neglect – as they were in Hedin's day – although these problems still, of course, exist. Today it is China's phenomenal pace of economic development that threatens to submerge the old sites beneath an ocean of concrete. In Central Asia, too, the old caravan cities are threatened by urban expansion and, in some cases, by careless or excessive restoration. In twenty years time will Samarkand be a theme park? Will babes-in-arms live in fear of Timur once again, resurrected as some growling, posturing hologram? Among many of the countries along the Road, there already seems to be a headlong rush to sanitise the past, to recreate the old buildings with new materials and, on occasion, to appropriate the mantels of the great men of history for political ends.

Until *perestroika* there was little opportunity to explore the full extent of the Silk Road and in ten or twenty years, if this eagerness to restore and renew continues unabated, what will remain of the old road will be a pale, *ersatz* shadow of the way it really was. I hope that I will be proved wrong, but unless the nations of the Silk Road learn to preserve its cities and monuments with more patience and sensitivity, the four hundred or so photographs contained in this book may prove to be its epitaph.

Merchants, Monks and Migrants: The Traffic of the Silk Road

Baron Ferdinand Von Richtofen first coined the term 'Silk Road', or *Seidenstrasse,* in 1877, but it is a misnomer. It was not really a road at all; it was a vast network of land-based and maritime trade routes and the merchants who used it carried far, far more than just silk. The beginnings of land-based trade between Orient and Occident can probably be pinpointed to around 105 BC, when the Chinese Emperor Wudi (r. 140–87 BC) sent a group of Chinese emissaries to the court of Mithradates II (r. 123–88 BC), the Parthian ruler of Persia. Wudi's mission appears to have marked the beginnings of trade with Persia in 53 BC; the Persians unfurled dazzling silk banners during their battle with the Romans at Carrhae. The Romans are said to have fled in terror at the sight of the banners and were routed.

By 46 BC, however, Chinese silks had reached Rome. A triumphal procession for Julius Caesar in that year included silk canopies, and it was not long before the commentators of the day were lamenting the Romans' obsession with the new material and the drain it placed upon the economy. So pervasive was the new fashion that in 14 BC Rome's Senate was obliged to issue a ban against men 'disgracing themselves with the effeminate delicacy of silk apparel', but to little effect, it seems. The Roman commentator Seneca, writing in the first century AD, makes no attempt to hide his disapproval of women who wore silk:

> 'Silk garments provide no protection for the body, or indeed modesty, so that when a woman wears them she can scarcely…swear that she is not naked.'

(Seneca, 1st century AD, 'On Benefits')

During the first century AD, as trade increased between Rome and the East, many commentators criticised the apparently insatiable appetite among Romans for luxury goods:

> '…we have come now to see…journeys made to Seres* [China] to obtain cloth, the abysses of the Red Sea explored for pearls, and the depths of the earth scoured for emeralds. They have even taken up the notion of piercing the ears as if it were too small a matter to wear those gems in necklaces and tiaras unless holes were also made in the body into which to insert them…at the lowest computation, India and Seres and the [Arabian] Peninsula together drain our empire of one hundred million sesterces every year. That is the price that our luxuries and our womankind cost us.'

(Pliny the Elder, *Natural History*)

Trade between East and West was to continue, despite interruptions caused by wars and politics, until maritime routes pioneered by European explorers in the fifteenth and sixteenth centuries superseded the old highways. At different times and throughout its history, trading centres grew and prospered along the highways of the Silk Road. Great cities like the Abbasid capital of Baghdad, the Sogdian town of Samarkand and the Bactrian metropolis of Merv became dynamic entrepôts where goods were traded in both directions. Merchants did not lead their caravans across the whole route; they would transport their goods between two commercial centres and would then sell them on to other merchants. The caravan cities of the Silk Road benefited both from the trading of these goods and from the taxes and customs duties levied upon merchants. Along with trade goods came new ideas: religions, medical knowledge, scientific and technological innovations all passed in both directions and the Silk Road became a great network of veins and arteries, carrying the life blood of nations across the known world.

Silk Road commerce was driven by three basic factors: firstly, the obvious desire for profit; secondly, a fascination with the exotic; and thirdly, as a means to enhance the political power of a particular nation. All three issues will be discussed at length throughout this book. If anyone doubts that Silk Road commerce was truly global in nature, consider the following three items, each unearthed in distant corners of the earth in extraordinary circumstances: an Indian ivory mirror handle from the first century AD, found in the ruins of Pompeii, an Egyptian Pharaoh mask found in the thirteenth-century grave of a Mongol woman at Genghis Khan's capital of Karakorum in Mongolia and a seventh- or eighth-century bronze Buddha from Pakistan's Swat Valley, found in a Viking grave at Helgö in Sweden all reveal the extent to which the Silk Road disseminated its products. The notion that the peoples of ancient times seldom strayed from their home villages is a myth. People made journeys for the purpose of trade, to go on pilgrimages and, on occasion, for the sheer joy of travel.

As has already been mentioned, silk was the principal, but by no means the only commodity. A search through a substantial part of the extant literature on the Silk Road reveals literally dozens of different commodities and the following chart, which is by no means exhaustive, attempts to summarise the principal ones. There are also references throughout this book to the products of individual Silk Road cities, gleaned mainly from the writings of commentators of the time. Individual commodities are discussed in greater detail elsewhere in the book.

* Seres (the country of silk) was the name given by the Romans to China. Their notion of how silk was obtained was patchy at best: Pliny wrote, 'the Seres are famous for the wool of their forests. They remove the down from leaves with the help of water'; and Virgil thought that 'the Chinese comb off leaves their delicate down.'

SUMMARY OF TRADE GOODS FROM EAST AND WEST CARRIED BY LAND AND SEA

COMMODITIES FROM THE EAST

From India

Household slaves, pets and arena animals, exotic furs, cashmere wool, raw and finished cotton (cotton plants have been cultivated in India for 4,000 years), spinach (probably mainly from Nepal), sandalwood and other exotic woods, palm-oil, cane-sugar and perfumes (aromatics), gems (rubies, sapphires and emeralds although diamonds, surprisingly, were not prized by the Chinese).

From China

Silk, skins, iron, mirrors, weapons, porcelain (first manufactured around the 8th century), lacquerware, nephrite jade (from Khotan), rhubarb, tea.

Paper – traditionally thought to have been invented by the court eunuch Cai Lun in 105 AD.

Gunpowder, invented in China around the seventh century and first used by them for military purposes around the twelfth century. It reached Europe during the fourteenth century.

Medicines – Ephaedra (Chinese: *Mahuang* – used for millennia in China to treat respiratory diseases. Ephedrine – now synthesized – was originally made from ephaedra), Epsom salts, elixirs for immortality (which often shortened, rather than extended life), ginseng (the best was from Korea), snake bile (collected in Southern China and Indochina) and seaweed (a diuretic), among many other examples.

From various parts of Asia

Precious and semi-precious stones: including lapis lazuli (mined in Afghanistan), jadeite (from Burma), rock crystal, carnelians and other quartzes, rubies (from Sri Lanka and Southeast Asia), sapphires (from India, Southeast Asia and Sri Lanka).

Jewellery, ivory, tortoiseshell, rhinoceros horn, seashells and pearls.

Ornamental woods, gum resins and aromatics (camphor from China, Japan, Borneo and Indochina was highly coveted).

Silver and gold (especially from Southern China, Tibet and Indochina but also imported from many other parts of the world).

Spices (especially pepper, ginger, cardamom, turmeric, nutmeg and cloves and, from India, Sri Lanka and Southeast Asia – cinnamon).

Cochineal and indigo used for dyeing fabrics and cosmetics Minerals: sulphur (for elixirs, imported from Indonesia); realgar (or arsenic sulfide, found in many parts of the world – although the best comes from Hunan province in China – and used as an elixir, to treat skin diseases and, so it was believed, to convert copper into gold).

Ceramics.

Horses (Central Asian breeds were especially prized in China) and camels.

Flowers, including peonies, roses, camellias and chrysanthemums and tulips (tulips from Central Asia and Turkey first arrived in Europe in the 1550s and were so coveted in seventeenth-century Holland that a single bulb could sell for 5,000 guilders, more than the price of a house!).

Alfalfa for animal feed, millet.

Human beings: acrobats, Central Asian jugglers and musicians, Central Asian grooms, dwarves, household slaves, South Sea Island pearl divers, Southeast Asian dancers, foreign guards.

From Persia and the countries of the Middle East

Incense (from southern Arabia), dates, pistachios, peaches, walnuts, Tyrian purple (from the *Murex trunculus* shellfish) and indigo for dyeing; frankincense and myrrh; storax (an aromatic resin), muslin cloth, wines, glassware, olive oil and silver vessels (especially the work of the Sasanian craftsmen of Persia).

COMMODITIES FROM THE WEST

Merchants on the land routes and Roman ships, crewed by men from many nations, conveyed:
Wool and linen textiles, carpets, Baltic amber, Mediterranean coral, asbestos, bronze vessels, lamps, glass vessels and glass beads, wine and papyrus, huge quantities of coins and bullion, ambergris (from the sperm whale, used in the manufacture of perfume and collected along the African coast), entertainers, exotic animals and opium (opium poppies probably originated in the eastern Mediterranean and reached China in about the seventh century).

RELIGIONS
(SPREAD ALONG THE TRADE ROUTES IN ALL DIRECTIONS)

Buddhism (arose in India and spread in both directions as far east as Japan and as far west as modern day Turkmenistan).
Islam (founded in the seventh cenury, it spread in all directions and now attracts a worldwide following of more than one billion devotees).
Christianity (arose in the Eastern Mediterranean and spread throughout the Roman world. Nestorian Christianity spread eastwards after the expulsion of Nestorius, patriarch of Constantinople, during the fifth century. It reached China by 635).
Manichaeism (developed in the Middle East during the third century and reached China by the seventh or eighth century).
Zoroastrianism (the state religion of Persia until the arrival of Islam in the seventh century, it had spread eastwards to China and India by the seventh or eighth century).

TECHNOLOGY AND INNOVATIONS

Acquired by China from the lands to the west:
Harnesses, saddles and stirrups (from the steppe nomads), construction-methods for bridges and mountain roads, knowledge of medicinal plants and poisons, cultivation of cotton and seafaring techniques.

Acquired by the West from Asia:
Chinese inventions (summarized in the table below)
Medical techniques (especially from Arab scholars such as Ibn Sina)
Science and mathematics- algebra, astronomy and the Arab numerals that we use in the West today.
The use of passports (a Mongol innovation, known as the *paizi* or *gerege*)
Military techniques and strategies.
Architectural styles and devices (the Persian invention of the squinch allowed the addition of a dome and led to the construction of many of the world's great buildings).

The westward flow of Chinese technology occurred throughout the existence of the Silk Road. The renowned scholar Joseph Needham, in his monumental work *Science and Civilisation in China*, summarized the plethora of new inventions that reached Europe between the first and eighteenth centuries, often after a time lapse of several hundred years. There are many other examples, not listed below, such as the use of paper money, the abacus and the use of coal for fuel. The modern world owes a great debt to ancient China:

SUMMARY OF THE TRANSMISSION
OF MECHANICAL AND OTHER TECHNIQUES
FROM CHINA TO THE WEST

Type of device	Approximate timelag in centuries
SQUARE-PALLET CHAIN PUMP	15
EDGE-RUNNER MILL	13
EDGE-RUNNER MILL WITH APPLICATION OF WATER POWER	9
METALLURGICAL BLOWING ENGINES, WATER POWER	11
ROTARY FAN AND ROTARY WINNOWING MACHINE	14
PISTON BELLOWS	14 (approx.)
DRAW-LOOM	4
SILK-HANDLING MACHINERY (A FORM OF FLYER FOR LAYING THREAD EVENLY ON REELS APPEARS AROUND THE 11TH CENTURY AND WATER POWER IS APPLIED TO SPINNINGMILLS IN THE 14TH CENTURY)	3–13
WHEELBARROW	9–10
SAILING CARRIAGE	11
WAGON MILL	12
EFFICIENT HARNESS FOR DRAUGHT-ANIMALS: BREAST STRAP (POSTILION)	8
COLLAR	6
CROSSBOW (AS AN INDIVIDUAL ARM)	13
KITE	12 (approx.)
HELICOPTER TOP (SPUN BY CORD)	14
ZOETROPE (MOVED BY ASCENDING HOT-AIR CURRENT)	10 (approx.)
DEEP DRILLING	11
CAST IRON	10–12

'CARDAN SUPENSION'	8–9
SEGMENTAL ARCH BRIDGE	7
IRON-CHAIN SUSPENSION BRIDGE	10–13
CANAL LOCK-GATES	7–17
NAUTICAL CONSTRUCTION PRINCIPLES (INCLUDING WATERTIGHT COMPARTMENTS, AERODYNAMICALLY EFFICIENT SAILS AND FORE-AND-AFT RIGGING)	UP TO 10
STERN-POST RUDDER	4 (approx.)
GUNPOWDER	5–6
GUNPOWDER FOR MILITARY USE	4
MAGNETIC COMPASS (LODESTONE SPOON)	11
MAGNETIC COMPASS WITH NEEDLE	4
MAGNETIC COMPASS USED FOR NAVIGATION	2
PAPER	10
PRINTING (BLOCK)	6
PRINTING (MOVABLE TYPE)	4
PRINTING (METAL MOVABLE TYPE)	1
PORCELAIN	11–13

(Adapted from Joseph Needham, 1961)

The migration of peoples along the trade routes

There was considerable traffic in human beings in both directions along the Silk Road and there were also many instances of mass migration of entire communities. We will examine the migration of the Yuezhi, founders of the Kushan Empire, elsewhere in this book and also look briefly at the Europoid mummies of the Tarim Basin but perhaps the farthest wanderings of any single people are contained in the migration of the Roma, or Gypsies, who now number between eight- and twelve-million souls and reside mainly in Eastern Europe. The origin of the Roma is uncertain but there are linguistic similarities between the Romani language and some dialects of India. It appears that the Roma originated in northwestern India and departed from their homeland in about the ninth century. They moved slowly westwards through Iran and the Near East and by the fourteenth century were settled in the Balkans. Centuries of persecution and pogroms have caused the Roma to live in close-knit communities, often avoiding contact with non-Gypsies. The notion that contact with non-Gypsies, known as *Gorgio* to the Roma, is corrupting may originate in the group's Hindu origins.

Beginnings

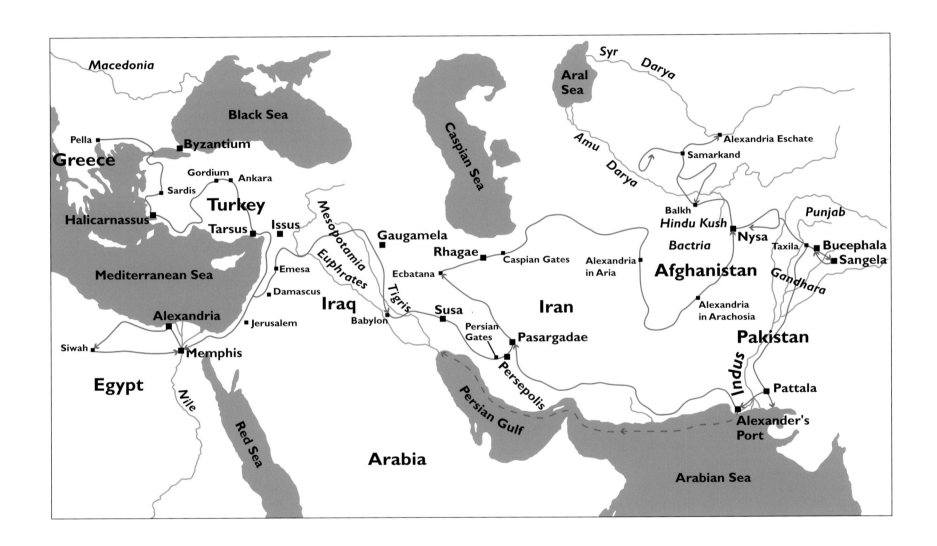

ALEXANDER THE GREAT'S JOURNEYS
AND THE EXTENT OF HIS EMPIRE

CHAPTER ONE

PRECURSORS OF THE SILK ROAD

Alexander the Great

The life and achievements of Alexander the Great (r. 336–23 BC) preceded the establishment of the Silk Road by some three centuries but the route that he followed approximates in many places to the highways that merchants of later years would come to use. His empire was vast but its existence was fleeting: within twelve years of embarking upon his conquest of Asia he lay dead in Babylon and his satraps began, almost immediately, to rebel. At the time of his death Alexander's empire encompassed all of the lands between Greece and India and the many cities that he founded became pockets of Greek culture that continued to exert a profound influence long after his passing. He took with him an army of up to 40,000 men and the soldiers that he left behind to garrison these new cities married local women. Greek ideas began to permeate through the societies of the East: religion, politics, medicine and the arts were all strongly affected by Alexander's legacy and the foundations for the subsequent development of the Silk Road were firmly laid. After Alexander's time it could never again be said that the Orient and Occident were two separate, unconnected worlds. A fully developed network of trade routes between Europe and Asia does not appear to have been in place until the first century BC but, in the years after Alexander's death, exotic goods are known to have reached the west in significant quantities. Ivory, spices and unusual pets (parrots and peacocks were especially prized) are all recorded among the possessions of the wealthy citizenry of ancient Athens.

Chinese Legend

The Travels of Emperor Mu, written around the third century BC, describe the exploits of King Mu of the Western Zhou dynasty (1050–771 BC). Emperor Mu is thought to have lived in around 1000 BC and the journeys ascribed to him are a mixture of legend and fact:

> '*Emperor Mu wished to satisfy his ambition by touring around the world and by marking the countries under the sky with the wheels of his chariots and the hoofs of his horses.*'

(From a commentary on 'Classic of Spring and Autumn', quoted in Franck and Brownstone, 1986)

Fig. 4 **Marble head of Alexander the Great**
Hellenistic period, first half of the 2nd century BC
H. 42 cm
From Pergamon (Bergama), Izmir province, Turkey
(Archeological Museum, Istanbul)

Emperor Mu is said to have departed from China through the Yumenguan (the Jade Gate) with an army and travelled in a jade-inlaid gold carriage to the lands of Central Asia. Legend has it that, after crossing the desert of the Taklamakan, he reached first the Pamirs and then journeyed through the Kunlun Mountains on the northern edge of the Tibet-Qinghai Plateau, the domain of Xi Wang Mu, the Queen Mother of the West (see p. 82). After presenting her with lavish gifts of jade and silk – the earliest mention of the precious commodity as tribute – he turned homeward, stopping en route to hunt. But Mu's exploits are legend. There are tantalising clues that the authors knew of the people of the Western Regions and had knowledge of their customs but the evidence is inconclusive. The only solid data for early Chinese contacts with the lands beyond its borders comes from studies of nomads and the processes of trade and tribute along what came to be known as the 'Steppe Route.'

CHAPTER TWO

NOMADS

'Sworn to sweep out the Huns
without regard for my own safety:
Five thousand sable hats and silk coats
Were lost in the border dust.
I grieve for those crumbling bones
scattered along the river bank of Wuding,
They are still in the hearts of lovers
Who dream of them in inner chambers.'

(Chen Tao [9th century], 'March on Western Lun', from Z. C. Tang, 1969. Western Lun, or Lung-Hsi was an outpost in Gansu)

* Sima Qian (c. 145–90 BC) was a descendant of the Qin family of nobles. Both he and his father, Sima Tan, held the post of Grand Historian and astrologer in the court of Emperor Wudi (r. 140–87 BC). He continued the work, begun by his father, of compiling a history of China and had unquestionably met many of the characters about whom he writes. Sim Qian travelled widely, including journeys to some of the new dominions of Wudi's expanded empire and appears to have read virtually all the extant Chinese literature, including documents in the Imperial archives. In 99 BC, Sima Qian's life took an appalling turn when an army led by the Chinese general Li Ning was defeated by the Xiongnu. Sima Qian attempted to defend Li Ning's capitulation to the nomads, but Wudi became enraged and ordered that he (Sima Qian) be arrested and sentenced to castration. He was subsequently rehabilitated and appointed to the post of palace secretary – a post open only to eunuchs, and this enabled Sima Qian to complete his history, *Shiji* ('Records of the Historian'). The *Shiji* is a huge work – 130 chapters and more than half a million characters – but is a veritable treasure trove of information about virtually every aspect of ancient Chinese history.

The Steppe Route

It is important to make brief mention here of what some scholars have termed the 'Steppe Route' and its relation to the Silk Road. The Steppe Route is not literally a route, since it does not follow a precise track in the way that the Silk Road does. Instead it covers a region as far west as the steppes of Southern Russia and the Danube, through the Kazakh Plain and Mongolia as far as the Great Wall of China. Nomadic equestrian tribes moved across the area in both directions in search of pasture for their cattle, horses and sheep, a practice that has been followed since Neolithic times. Because of their peripatetic lifestyle there are few remains of permanent settlements to be found and this makes identification of a precise route impossible. These nomadic groups (called *Hu* by the Chinese) conducted trade with neighbouring regions from a very early period, including the purchase of silks, bronze mirrors and weapons from China; furs and gold from Siberia; nephrite jade and wool from East Turkestan, and horses and wool from West Turkestan. The contents of *kurgans* (burial mounds) of the Scythian-Sakae period (sixth to fourth centuries BC), most notably at Pazyryk, show that contacts with the Chinese were taking place from an extremely early date. The Pazyryk mounds lie at a height of 1,600 metres above sea level in the Eastern part of the Altai, a range that begins 450 km south-east of Novosibirsk, and extends southwards through Kazakhstan, China and Mongolia. Among thousands of items unearthed at Pazyryk are Chinese bronze mirrors, woollen textiles that may come from Iraq, and a cream-coloured Chinese silk saddle cover, embroidered with phoenixes and birds (fig. 5).

By the time of the Western Han dynasty in China (206 BC–9 AD), there was a constant demand for Chinese silk, part of an essential barter process through which the Chinese obtained horses. An early description of this trade by a Chinese official reflects a belief that the Han were simultaneously receiving tribute and impoverishing the nomads. They did not regard it as trade.

'A piece of Chinese plain silk can be exchanged with the Hsiung-nu [Xiongnu] for articles worth several pieces of gold and thereby reduce the resources of our enemy. Mules, donkeys and camels enter the frontier in unbroken lines; horses, dapples and bays and prancing mounts, come into our possession. The furs of sables, marmots, foxes and badgers, coloured rugs and decorated carpets fill the imperial treasury, while jade and auspicious stones, corals and crystals become national treasures.'

(Ascribed to the Lord Grand Secretary of the Han Council in 81 BC and quoted in Franck and Brownstone, 1986)

The Xiongnu peoples, the most powerful and bellicose of all the *Hu* tribes, first appear in Chinese annals during the late fourth century BC, and come from the region between the Yellow River and the Yingshan Mountains. The term Xiongnu is extremely derogatory, meaning something along the lines of 'slave bastard' and reflects the contempt with which the Chinese regarded the nomadic peoples along their northern frontier. Sima Qian's *Shiji* ('Records of the Historian')* gives a fascinating account of the Xiongnu. He states that they had no walled cities or fixed dwellings and wandered from place to place in search of water and pasture for their animals. They did not engage in agriculture and had no means of writing. Their strength as warriors derives from the practice of training boys to hunt with bow and arrow from an early age. During times of peace, the Xiongnu were content to herd their flocks but, in time of war, they lived by 'plundering and marauding'. He describes them as being without honour: 'Their only concern is self-advantage, and they know nothing of propriety or righteousness'.

In recent years, historians have attempted to augment our knowledge of the Xiongnu and recent discoveries indicate that were a more highly developed society than Sima Qian's annals would lead us to believe. By the Warring States period (475–221 BC), the *Hu* peoples had established a strong, cohesive and prosperous society that posed a major threat to China's borders. The quality of their gold work suggests that the *Hu* had attained a high level of sophistication (fig. 6).

The Chinese adopted various methods to counter the threat from the *Hu*. Early Chinese accounts describe how, in 307 BC, King Wuling of Zhao State instructed his troops to adopt *Hu* dress and to change from a strategy of chariot warfare to one of fighting on horseback with bows. This enabled the Zhao to push back the *Hu* and to solidify their control of northern China by the mid-third century BC. Around 400 BC the Chinese had begun to erect an immense wall to keep out the nomads and the Zhao added sections of their own. The wall was strengthened and extended during the centuries that followed, most notably during the reign of Qin Shi Huangdi (r. 221–10 BC). During the Ming dynasty (1368–1644), the masonry and earth structure we know today as the Great Wall was completed.

Other strategies employed by the Chinese to contain the *Hu* included the payment of tribute and forging conjugal ties. By about 200 BC the Xiongnu were at the zenith of their power under the leadership of the chieftain (or *Shanyu*) Maodun. Maodun conquered the Ordos area to the south of the Yellow River as well as expanding his empire into Central Asia and defeating the *Yuezhi*, another of the Hu tribes. Attempts by the Chinese General Liu Bang, the founder of the Han dynasty, to attack the Xiongnu almost ended in disaster when his forces were cut off and surrounded by Maodun's army. A peace agreement was negotiated involving the payment of vast amounts of tribute in the form of silks and foodstuffs, a strategy that the Chinese continued to use for much of the Western Han dynasty (206 BC–9 AD). The Xiongnu Empire was formally recognized by the Han, who declared, according to Sima Qian, 'Let the state holding the bows beyond the Great Wall follow the rules of the *Shanyu* and let the Han govern the state of overcoat and hat, which lies inside the Great Wall.' Inscriptions on pottery architectural tiles unearthed at Baotou, Inner Mongolia, reveal the practice of exchanging marital ties in order to placate the Xiongnu (fig. 7).

Many of the Chinese women who were sent to marry nomads were extremely reluctant to go. A poem from around 107 BC describes the anguish of Liu Hsi-chun, a daughter of a disgraced prince of the Han ruling dynasty, sent to marry an ageing nomad chief:

Fig. 5 **Felt saddle blanket (shabrack) covered with Chinese silk**
Early nomadic culture, Scyth-Sakae, 6th to 4th century BC
L. 226 cm, W. 65 cm
Unearthed by S. I. Rudenko in 1949 at Pazyryk, Altai Region, Russia
(The State Hermitage Museum, St Petersburg)

Fig. 6 **Gold headdress**
Hu peoples
Warring States period (475–221 BC)
D. 16.5 cm
Discovered in 1973 at Aluchaideng in the Maowusu Desert, 40 km southeast of Hangjin Banner city, Ordos region of Inner Mongolia, China
(The Museum of the Inner Mongolia Autonomous Region, Hohhot)
This exquisite headdress consists of a skullcap with a depiction of four rams attacked by four wolves. The lower section is made up of three semicircular bands, each featuring a horse, a ram and a tiger with bared teeth. Atop the whole assemblage is an eagle with a head of turquoise. There is some disagreement as to whether the upper and lower parts of this object belong together.

Fig. 7 **Fragment of a gray architectural tile**
Western Han dynasty
(206 BC–9 AD)
D.15.5 cm
Unearthed from a tomb at the Zhaowan site in the suburbs of Baotou, Inner Mongolia
(The Museum of the Inner Mongolia Autonomous Region, Hohhot)
A moulded inscription in Chinese reads, 'Conjugal amity with the *Shanyu*' and commemorates marital ties between the Chinese and the Xiongnu (whose leader is known as the *Shanyu*).

'My family has married me
in this far corner of the world,
sent me to a strange land,
to the king of the Wu-sun.
A yurt is my chamber,
felt my walls,
flesh my only food,
kumiss to drink.
My thoughts are all of my homeland,
my heart aches within.
Oh to be the yellow crane
Winging home again!'

('Song of Sorrow', translated by Burton Watson in Watson, 1984)

It is quite clear from the excavation of burial mounds (known as *kurgans*), that the relationship between the Chinese and the Xiongnu was not merely adversarial, however. Excavations of the *kurgans* at the Noin-Ula site north of Ulan Bator in Mongolia, by Russian archeologists during the 1920s, reveal that there was a tremendous amount of

Fig. 8 **Lacquer bowl with Chinese inscription**
China, Han dynasty, dated 2 BC
From Noin-Ula, Mongolia
(Ulan Bator Museum)

interaction between the two groups. Fragments of bronze mirrors and lacquer bowls were discovered, all of Chinese manufacture, as well as a silk textile from Sichuan with tree and bird motifs. One of the lacquer bowls has a long inscription in Chinese which includes the date 2 BC and it seems likely that the site itself is of the same era (fig. 8).

Two large felt carpets were also found at Noin-Ula, decorated with the animal motifs common to the art of the steppes. Although the rugs appear to be of nomadic origin, one has a piece of Chinese silk sewn onto it (fig. 9).

Fig. 9 **Felt carpet with Chinese silk attached, depicting a gryphon attacking an elk**
Ca. 1st century AD
From Noin-Ula, Mongolia
(Ulan Bator Museum)

Zhang Qian

Despite their best efforts, Han strategies for pacifying the Xiongnu were ineffective and raiding continued unabated until the reign of Emperor Wudi (140–87 BC). Wudi's attempts to counter the Xiongnu threat were a pivotal event in the history and development of the Silk Road and are described at length by Sima Qian in *Records of the Historian*. After the death of the king of the Indo-Scythian Yuezhi peoples at the hands of the Xiongnu leader Maodun, they were driven westwards from the Gansu corridor to Bactria, in modern Afghanistan, where they eventually established the Kushan Empire (see chapter three). Emperor Wudi decided to send an envoy to the Yuezhi in the hope of persuading them to open a second front against the Xiongnu. He selected a palace courtier called Zhang Qian, together with a Xiongnu slave named Ganfu sent as interpreter. The expedition set out in 138 BC with over a hundred men. As it passed westwards through Xiongnu territory the party was taken hostage. Zhang was detained for more than ten years, taking a Xiongnu wife who bore him a son, but he eventually escaped and continued his journey to Bactria. He was unable to convince the somewhat indolent Yuezhi king to form an alliance against the Xiongnu and, after a year as their guest, he started for home. On the way back to China, Zhang was again captured by the Xiongnu and spent a further year with them before escaping with his Xiongnu wife and the slave Ganfu. Of the hundred men in his party only Zhang Qian and Ganfu returned safely to China.

Zhang's report to Emperor Wudi is recorded in the annals of Sima Qian. He describes the regions to the west of China including those of Dayuan (Ferghana, between the Oxus and the Jaxartes Rivers in present-day Uzbekistan and Kyrgyzstan), Daxia (Bactria) and Kangju (Transoxiana). He also related anecdotal information about more distant lands, describing 'a great shoreless lake' (probably the Caspian Sea), the Persian kingdom of Anxi (Parthia), where 'great birds lay eggs as big as pots' and the 'Western Sea' (possibly the Persian Gulf or the Red Sea). His descriptions of the land of Shendu (India) must have sounded outlandish to the Chinese:

'When I was in Daxia (Bactria)…I saw bamboo canes from Qiong and cloth made in the province of Shu' (Qiong and Shu are in the area of present day Sichuan, Guizhou and Yunnan provinces in southwestern China). He continues, 'When I asked the people how they had gotten such articles, they replied, "Our merchants go to buy them in the markets of Shendu"…. The region is said to be hot and damp. The inhabitants ride elephants when they go into battle. The kingdom is situated on a great river.'

Emperor Wudi immediately recognized an opportunity to increase trade with China's neighbours and to use that trade as an instrument of foreign policy to extend his dominions. Wudi was transfixed by accounts of the horses of Dayuan (Ferghana). Zhang Qian saw animals there that he described as having been foaled from those of heaven, and which sweated blood (probably the result of parasites). Wudi had consulted the oracle, the 'Book of Change', which warned that 'divine horses are due to appear from the northwest' and he believed the Ferghana animals to be the fulfilment of that prediction. Wudi's desire to acquire these horses may have been linked to his search for immortality and two poems (one quoted here) that survive from the Han dynasty were probably written to express the emperor's joy when he acquired some of them:

'From Great Unity heaven-sent,
The horse of heaven comes down,
Soaked with crimson sweat,
Froth flowing russet.
His courage is superb,
His spirit marvellous.
He prances through floating clouds,
Darkly racing upwards.
His body free and easy
Leaps across a myriad leagues.
Now who is his equal?
Dragons are his friends.'

(*The Horse of Heaven*, Anonymous, Han dynasty [206 BC–220 AD].
From Birrell, 1988)

Fig. 10 **Wall painting of Zhang Qian and his journey to the realm of the Yuezhi**
Tang dynasty (618–907)
Cave 323, Dunhuang, Gansu province, China

Fig. 11 **Birch-bark saddle
flap, painted with an image
of a heavenly horse**
Korea, Silla period,
ca. 6th century
H. 53 cm, W. 75 cm
From the Chonma-chong Tomb,
Kyongju, Korea
(Kyongju National Museum)

Fig. 12 **Przewalski's Horses**
(Photographed in Mongolia by an
unknown photogapher)

* Recent genetic research
suggests that Turcoman and
Caspian horses, and not Arab
breeds, may be ancestral to most,
if not all forms of oriental horse
(see p. 291).
† *Equus Przewalski* is the last
species of wild horse, first
identified by the Russian-Polish
explorer Colonel Nikolai
Przewalski in the Gobi desert in
1881. Attempts to breed this rare
animal in zoos failed and, by
1977, there were only about 300
animals left. A Dutch foundation
began a concerted campaign to
save the horse and reintroduce it
to the Mongolian steppe. The
project appears to have been a
success and, as of 1998, there
were a total of about 1500
examples, both in the wild and
in captivity.

The idea of the heavenly horse and its connection with dragons became embedded in the Chinese psyche. The Tang dynasty poet Li Bai (also known as Li Po, 701–62) has immortalized the way in which these horses were revered by the Chinese:

'The Horses of Heaven come out of the dens of the Kushanas [Yuezhi],
Backs formed with tiger markings, bones made from dragon wings.'

The legend of the heavenly horse also spread eastwards along the Silk Road to the kingdoms to the east (fig. 11).

Heavenly horses are popularly believed to have been Arab stallions,* now long disappeared, and were far superior in strength and endurance to the small local breeds used by the Chinese. The Chinese used the wild tarpan of the Asian steppe, identified as *Przewalski's Horse*† (fig. 12).

Ferghana horses, if they could be obtained in sufficient numbers, might enable the Chinese to subjugate the Xiongnu and missions were sent out to secure them, resulting in further contacts with neighbouring states and the establishment of routes which came to be known as the Silk Road. 'Heavenly Horses' figure in the art of the period again and again, the most sublime example being the celebrated 'Flying Horse of Gansu', unearthed at Wuwei in 1969 (fig. 13).

Sima Qian relates that Wudi sent Wang Ranyu, Bo Shichang and other envoys to search for a new route to Bactria via India, through the 'barbarian regions' of southwest China. The bellicosity of these tribes is described at length by Sima Qian. One of the groups he describes – the Dian peoples of Yunnan – are referred to as riders of elephants who traded with neighbouring states. Dian bronzes show that they wore the trousers and short tunics of the equestrian nomads of Central Asia. They produced intricate works of art, although their fondness for warfare is sometimes reflected in their choice of motif (fig. 14).

Attempts to establish a route to Bactria were unsuccessful and the project was abandoned but the Chinese continued to make contact with their neighbours. Zhang Qian's last expedition was to visit the Wusun people, who lived in the Ili River Valley south of Lake Balkash in modern-day Kazakhstan, to seek allies against the Xiongnu and to secure more 'heavenly horses' in fulfilment of Wudi's augury. Horses from Dayuan (Ferghana) were found to be even more robust than those supplied by the Wusun and Chinese trade with both states increased to the point where the Han began to construct fortifications along the route to protect travellers. By the time of Zhang Qian's death in 113 BC, he had become one of the most senior ministers of Wudi's court with the title of Grand Messenger. Sima Qian describes the return of envoys that Zhang Qian had dispatched to the kingdoms of Central Asia and the importance of this process to the development of China's relations with neighbouring countries. His words are a fitting valediction for a man who can safely be described as the father of the Silk Road:

'…for the first time relations were established between the lands of the northwest and the Han. It was Zhang Qian, however, who opened the way for this move, and all the envoys who journeyed to the lands in later times relied upon his reputation to gain them a hearing.'

A charming vignette about Emperor Wudi reveals that his long reign was not wholly devoted to military adventures. Wudi's mausoleum at Maoling, 40 km west of Xian, is the largest of all the Western Han tombs and is said to have taken fifty-three years to build. The attendant tombs contain the remains of important officials such as General Huo Qubing (see below). Nearby is the tomb of his favourite concubine,

Lady Li, an honour denied even to his two wives. She was a sister of the musician Li Yannian, who presented her to Wudi with a poem:

'There's a beauty in the north
Who stands alone in the world.
A smile from her would cause the fall of a city;
Another smile would ruin a country.
What do you care about the downfall of a city or a country?
A beautiful lady would be hard to meet again!'

(Quoted in He Zhenghuang, 1990)

A story from the time suggests that their love endured even after their deaths: whenever the moon rose, a thin thread of smoke would rise from Lady Li's tomb, circle round the mausoleum of Wudi and then disappear.

The long series of military campaigns that Wudi had begun in about 129 BC resulted in the gradual subjugation of the Xiongnu. One of Wudi's most celebrated and successful generals was Huo Qubing (140–117 BC), an acquaintance of Zhang Qian. Huo's mausoleum is adjacent

Fig. 14 **Bronze spearhead with hanging men**
Western Han dynasty
(206 BC – 9 AD)
H. 41.5 cm
Found in 1956 at Shizhaishan, Jinning county, Yunnan province
(Yunnan Provincial Museum, Kunming)

Fig. 13 **Bronze figure of a flying horse, one leg resting upon a swallow**
Eastern Han dynasty
(25–220 AD)
H. 34.5 cm, L. 45 cm
Unearthed at Leitai, Wuwei, Gansu in 1969
(Gansu Provincial Museum, Lanzhou)

Fig. 15 **Stone sculpture of a horse crushing a Xiongnu warrior**
Western Han dynasty, 117 BC
H. 168 cm, L. 190 cm
From the tomb of General Huo Qubing (140–117 BC), Maoling, Shaanxi province
The statues presiding over Huo Qubing's tomb are generally accepted as being the earliest stone sculptures in Chinese art.

to Wudi's and is presided over by spectacular life-size stone sculptures of horses, one of which tramples a Xiongnu warrior (fig. 15).

Huo Qubing was a gifted military strategist who was given command of his first army at the age of only eighteen. He was victorious in six consecutive campaigns against the Xiongnu and was honoured by Wudi who named him the 'swift Cavalry General. Sima Qian describes him as 'a man of few words…but…[that] he possessed great daring and initiative'. He is also described as having declined the Emperor's offer of a mansion, remarking that: 'While the Xiongnu have still not been wiped out there is no time to think about houses.' Another episode involving Huo occurred in 121 BC, when he led a force of 10,000 cavalrymen from Longxi in Gansu, about 500 km beyond Mt Yanzhi, to engage the Xiongnu. He killed or captured 18,000 of the Huns but, more significantly perhaps, is described by Sima Qian as having succeeded in defeating the Xiutu king – whose kingdom lay in the western part of Xiongnu territory – and '*seizing the golden man which he used in worshipping Heaven*'. There has been considerable speculation among

scholars that this incident marked China's first contact with Buddhism (see p. 36).

When Huo died in 117 BC at the age of only twenty-four, Wudi ordered that soldiers from the defeated Xiongnu tribes line the road to his mausoleum. His grave mound was constructed in the shape of the Qilian Mountains of Gansu, where many of his greatest victories had occurred.

The gradual reduction in the threat from the Xiongnu facilitated greater contacts with the lands to the west. It was not all plain sailing, however. By about 111 BC it seems that Emperor Wudi's desire for horses had exceeded the appetite of his neighbours for the goods he was offering in exchange. Returning emissaries had informed him that the horses of Ershi (Sutrishna), capital of the Dayuan region between Khujand (Khodjent) and Samarkand, were the most magnificent of all the Ferghana steeds. He sent a gift of a thousand gold coins and a golden horse and a request for some of the Ershi mounts. But Dayuan, by this time, 'was overflowing with Han goods' and the King felt sufficiently removed from Chinese influence to refuse to supply them. The incensed Han envoy smashed the golden horse and departed for Dayuan's eastern border. He and his party were overtaken, however, by agents of the king from the town of Yucheng and massacred.

Emperor Wudi was enraged by the murder of his envoys and dispatched Li Guangli, a second brother of his favourite concubine Lady Li, to exact revenge. In 104 BC, Li Guangli set off at the head of a force of 6,000 cavalry and 20,000 to 30,000 conscripts. As the army travelled west, the terrified occupants of the towns along the route barricaded themselves in and refused to supply provisions. By the time Li Guangli reached Yucheng he had lost all but a few thousand of his men and even they were exhausted. General Li attacked Yucheng but was beaten back and lost yet more men. He withdrew to Dunhuang, sending a message to Wudi to request permission to disband the army until reinforcements became available. Permission was refused and the troops were instructed to remain outside the Jade Gate (Yumenguan), China's western frontier. After some delay, a vast army of 60,000 men, 100,000 oxen and more than 30,000 horses was assembled and marched to Ershi with General Li in command. The town's water supply was diverted by the Chinese and after a siege of forty days it was on the verge of falling. Its occupants sought terms with the Chinese, who killed the king and yielded twenty or thirty of best horses as well as over 3,000 ordinary stallions and mares. Li Guangli's two campaigns had lasted four years and he acquired only a small number of 'heavenly horses.' But as he marched triumphantly back towards China the rulers of the small states he encountered on the way, having heard of the defeat of the Dayuan kingdom, swore loyalty to the Han and sent tribute to the court at Changan. This process enabled China to impose suzerainty on the entire Tarim Basin, thereafter known as Xinjiang ('New Dominion'). At about the same time, commanderies were established at Zhangye, Jiuquan, Dunhuang and Wuwei and a line of defensive fortifications built to protect the new routes to the West. This process of consolidation was completed by the formidable General Ban Chao (31–103 AD) who progressively subdued all of the kingdoms of the Tarim Basin and opened up the routes to the West (see p. 83).

A postscript to the story of China's perennial foe, the Xiongnu, was that their fortunes continued to decline long after the death of General Huo Qubing. In about 57 BC, riven by internal disputes, the Xiongnu Empire split into northern and southern factions. Following the death of the Northern Xiongnu ruler in 36 BC and a treaty agreed with the Southern leader, Huhanye, a long period of relative calm was achieved. Huhanye was presented with a Chinese concubine for a wife and was also paid generous annual tribute: the ensuing peace lasted well into the first century AD. By the end of that century the Xiongnu were thoroughly defeated and the remnants of their empire fled west into Central Asia or were transformed into fragmented, heavily sinocized communities in Gansu and Shaanxi. There they engaged in raising cattle and horses and were also recruited as mercenaries to fight for whichever Chinese ruler happened to hold power. The Xianbei (Toba) tribes were similarly occupied in parts of Hebei and Liaoning and both groups were subjected to discrimination and oppression by the Chinese. At the beginning of the fourth century, the nomads rose against their rulers and proclaimed independent kingdoms in northern China: the Xiongnu proclaimed independence in 304, first calling their new state the Han and later the Zhou (names taken from great Chinese dynasties). With their equestrian and archery skills, the Xiongnu proved unstoppable and, by 316, they had captured both Luoyang and Changan (Xian). There followed a period of civil war lasting nearly 150 years, in which various nomadic groups fought each other to create as many as sixteen different states, each as ephemeral as its predecessor. An enormous southward exodus of Chinese occurred and the country was effectively divided in two: the north was controlled by the nomads and the south by the Han. At the end of the fourth century the Toba (Xianbei) emerged as the most powerful force in North China and, in 386, established the Northern Wei dynasty (386–534) with their capital at Datong (see p. 69)

The Xiongnu were never again regarded as a serious and unified threat although another branch of the tribe – how distant a branch is hotly disputed – appears, also during the fourth century, on the southern plains of Eastern Europe. Contemporary accounts of the Huns leave little doubt that Europeans feared them as much as the Chinese feared the Xiongnu:

'Lo, suddenly messengers ran to and fro and the whole East trembled, for swarms of Huns had broken forth from the far distant Maeotis between the icy Tanais and the monstrous peoples of the Massagetae, where the Gates of Alexander pen in the wild nations behind the rocks of the Caucasus. They filled the whole earth with slaughter and panic alike as they flitted hither and thither on their swift horses…May Jesus avert such beasts from the Roman world in the future!'

(St Jerome, quoted in Sinor, 1990)

After the defeat of the Alani and the Goths, an immense confederation of Huns was created under the command of Attila, 'the scourge of God'. By 452 Attila had conquered Gaul and northern Italy but died unexpectedly of excessive feasting in 453. At his funeral, the Inner Asian traditions of the Huns were not forgotten: they slashed at their faces as a sign of mourning and raced horses around the coffin. After Attila's death the Hun tribes disintegrated and its members were eventually dispersed and absorbed into local populations.

THE KUSHAN EMPIRE:
TRADE ROUTES AND MAIN SITES

CHAPTER THREE

THE KUSHANS

Much of what we know about the Kushans comes from Chinese annals – especially Sima Qian's history – and from the study of coins. Sima Qian describes how the Yuezhi originally occupied an area in China's Gansu province, between the Tianshan (Heavenly) Mountains and Dunhuang. A once powerful nation, they were attacked and defeated by the Xiongnu leader Maodun, who killed the king of the Yuezhi and made his skull into a drinking vessel. After their defeat they were led westwards by the son of the slain king and conquered the kingdom of Daxia (Bactria), setting up their capital on the north bank of the Oxus, a region described as rich and fertile. The Han emissary Zhang Qian was unable to enlist the assistance of the Yuezhi king in fighting the Xiongnu; it seems that he felt no desire to avenge the death of his father.

The Yuezhi appear to have begun their migration in about 165 BC and arrived in Bactria in about 140 BC, thus migrating over a distance of more than 4,000 km within a single generation. They steadily extended their rule across Bactria and the Kabul region and, during the first century AD, into the Gandhara kingdom and the Punjab. Much of this was accomplished during the reign of Kujula Kadphises (r. ca. 30–80 AD)* thereby ending Parthian rule in the area. Kujula Kadphises unified the entire region, establishing the foundations for the Kushan Empire. Kujula issued coins that imitated the styles of the Scythians and Parthians who preceded him. Fascinatingly, some of these coins include depictions of the Roman Emperor, Augustus (r. 31 BC–14 AD), with modifications made to the design for his own use (fig. 16).

This is clear evidence that, even during this early stage of the Silk Road, Roman coins were already being imported into the area, via both land and through sea trade (see p. 329). A small number of examples have indeed been found. Other coins from Kujula's reign show Bactrian camels, perhaps symbolizing the Central Asian origins of the Kushans. It was not until the accession of Kujula's grandson Vima Kadphises that Kushan coinage appears. Vima appears to have embraced Hinduism and his coinage sometimes includes depictions of the Hindu god Siva with his vehicle, the Nandi bull (fig. 17).

By the early part of the second century AD the Kushan

Fig. 16 **Bronze coin of Kujula Kadphises (r. ca. 30–80 AD)**
Obverse: Bust of the Roman Emperor Augustus (r. 31 BC–14 AD), inscribed in Greek 'of Kujula Kadphises Kushan chieftain'
Reverse: Portrait of a king wearing a Kushan royal bonnet with an inscription in Indian (Kharosthi) script reading, 'Kujula Kadphises Kushan Chieftain, steadfast in the true law'
(British Museum. after Gardner, 1886)

Fig. 17 **Gold coin (double stater) of Kushan King Vima Kadphises (r. ca. 90–100 or 110–120 AD)**
Obverse: Bust of a king emerging from a mountain top
Reverse: Siva with erect phallus, holding a trident, a bull standing behind him. Inscribed in Kharosthi script with: 'of the King of Kings, Lord of the World, Great Lord, Vima Kadphises, the Great, the Saviour'
Note: there is some debate over whether the deity depicted is Lord Siva or the Wind god Vesho. The Kushans seem to have associated Vesho with both Siva and the Greek God Herakles.
(British Museum. after Gardner, 1886)

King Kanishka I (r. ca. 100–26 or 120–46 AD), son of Vima Kadphises, ruled an empire that extended from the Gangetic Plain of northern India to Sogdiana. Kushan rule brought prosperity and security and led to an increase in trade throughout the region. Kanishka was the greatest of all the Kushan rulers and the inscription found in 1993 at Rabatak, near Surkh Khotal, Baghlan Province, Afghanistan, describes his achievements (see note opposite). His empire encompassed part of Central Asia, Bactria (modern

* The line of succession and reign dates for the early Kushan kings are highly contentious issues. Important new evidence has recently come to light that has caused the generally accepted dates to be adjusted. On the face of a large limestone block, discovered in 1993 in the Rabatak region of Afghanistan, is a long Greek inscription that identifies Kanishka I as the son of Vima Kadphises and the grandson of a previously unknown ruler called Vima Tak [-to]. The scholars Nicholas Sims-Williams and Joe Cribb have, in turn, assessed the historical implications of the inscription and identified coins associated with Vima Tak [-to]. The result of their research is a new set of reign dates that I have followed in this book.

Fig. 18 **Red sandstone portrait statue of King Kanishka I**

Kushan period, Mathura

Ca. 100–146 AD

H. 185 cm

Inscribed: *Great King, the King of Kings, the Son of God, Kanishka.*

From Mat, Uttar Pradesh, India

(Archeological Museum, Mathura)

Fig. 19 **Gold coin (stater) of Kanishka I (r. ca. 110–26 AD or 120–46 AD)**

Obverse: Kanishka wearing a Kushan royal bonnet and diadem, holding a spear and elephant goad, inscribed in Bactrian (Greek script): *king of kings Kanishka Kushan*

Reverse: standing figure of Sakyamuni Buddha with his right hand raised in the gesture of reassurance (*abhayamudra*), inscribed in Bactrian: *BODDO* (Buddha)

(British Museum)

Afghanistan), Northwest India (modern Pakistan) and Northern India as far east as Bihar. Contemporary sources indicate that Kashmir was also part of his empire.

A closely related portrait sculpture from Surkh Khotal, one of the world's great works of art, was in the Kabul museum's collections. It survived the Russian occupation, civil war and looting, only to be destroyed in March 2001 by a Taliban official wielding a sledgehammer. Both images depict Kanishka in the guise of a warrior but he was also a man of great intellect with eclectic views on religion. His coins include depictions of almost the entire pantheon of Persian, Greek and Indian deities but it is the appearance of the Buddha image for the first time that has created such excitement among historians (fig. 19).

Depictions of the Buddha on Kushan coins are actually exceptionally rare; there are far more Zoroastrian deities shown. Only five or six examples in gold and approximately thirty-seven copper examples exist but they provide an essential resource for art historians, providing datable images of the Buddha in Gandhara style. Coins such as the one shown above are generally regarded as containing the first firmly dated depictions of the Buddha in human form. The earliest images of the Buddha are aniconic: a pair of footprints, an empty throne and the *chakra* – a discus or wheel which represents the *dharmachakra*, the wheel of the law set in motion by the Buddha during his First Sermon at the Deer Park in Sarnath. Such symbols are found on the great Buddhist monuments of Bharhut and Sanchi in Madhya Pradesh and at Amaravati in Andhra Pradesh. The reason for this early disinclination to show the Buddha Sakyamuni in human form seems to have been a belief that he was, himself, a reincarnation of Buddhas from previous aeons. Sakyamuni was therefore regarded as being eternal, like other Buddha incarnations, and not ephemeral like man. Depictions of the Buddha on coins from Kanishka's reign are of two types: standing images such as the example in the British Museum, illustrated above (fig. 19) and seated images of Maitreya. Maitreya is actually a Bodhisattva, the 'Buddha-to-be', but on these coins is depicted with the legend *Metrago Boud* (Maitreya Buddha) in Bactrian using Greek letters. He is commonly shown wearing heavy earrings and holding a water pot in his left hand. Kanishka may not have been a Buddhist himself but there is no doubt that he was a patron of the Buddhist faith. The construction of an immense stupa (a domed structure for relics), now destroyed, at his capital Kanishkapura or Purushapura (modern Peshawar), was accompanied by a surge in the activities of sculptors of Buddhist art.

The last of the great Kushan rulers was Vasudeva I (ca. 164–200 AD or 184–220 AD). The Kushan Empire, with its capital at Mathura, on the banks of the Yamuna River in modern Uttar Pradesh, northern India, had attained its apogee. Vasudeva's patronage of the Mathura style of art has endowed us with exquisite creations, most notably in the mottled red sandstone sculpture of the period (fig. 21). These sculptures reflect a time of great splendour and opulence.

A number of puzzling questions are raised by the existence of a Kharosthi inscription found at Ara, south of Attock (half way between Peshawar and Islamabad), near the Indus River. The inscription is dated to the year '41' of the Kanishka era, and was found on a stone used to mark the digging of a well. The legend refers to a Kanishka, son of Vajheshka (or Vasishka), who is accorded the following title: 'The Great King, King of Kings, Son of Heaven, Caesar' (*Maharajasa rajatirajasa devaputrasa kaisarasa*). There is

Fig. 20 **Grey schist frieze with depiction of a Kushan prince or king making offerings to the Bodhisattva Maitreya (the Buddha of the future)**
Kushan period, Gandhara
2nd or 3rd century AD
W. 84 cm, H. 61 cm
(Private Collection)
This important monumental frieze provides a glimpse of Kushan dress and religious practice around the time of Kanishka. The dress, jewellery and the naturalistic way in which the figures of this relief are depicted owe much to Greco-Roman art. An interesting feature is the 'Phrygian' cap worn by the obeisant servant – a conical wool or felt headdress that originated in Phrygia in Asia Minor.

much debate over this inscription, not least because year 41 actually falls within the reign dates of the Kushan King Huvishka (r. ca. 126–64 or 146–84 AD), the son of King Kanishka I. The 'Kanishka' referred to in the inscription is therefore unlikely to be the great king himself. He may have been a brother of Huvishka (perhaps serving as co-regent), a usurper or ruler from the period after the death of Vasudeva I when the Kushan Empire was in decline. Whatever the truth of the matter, the inscription is of immense significance to historians, as it encapsulates royal titles from India, Persia, China and Rome. It also indicates that the Kushan kings enjoyed extensive contacts with Rome and regarded themselves as being of equal status.

The Kushan Empire entered a period of slow decline after Vasudeva's death. The Sasanian King Ardashir I (r. ca. 224–40 AD) began a campaign to absorb the area into his empire, a campaign completed by his son Shapur I. From about 230 until 360 AD, the Sasanians ruled this eastern province of their empire through their own princes, governing as Kushan kings. They were permitted to issue their own coinage, comprising gold staters and small bronze coins that combined elements from both empires. The king is usually depicted in Sasanian style on one side, standing at an altar, with what is believed to be the Zoroastrian Wind God Vesho and the bull *Vrsabha* on the reverse. Legends on the coins, in both Sasanian Pahlavi and Greek, read 'Great

Fig. 21 **Red sandstone Bacchanalian relief with Intoxicated Courtesan and Vasantasena**
Kushan period, Mathura; late 2nd century
H. 97 cm, W. 76 cm
(National Museum, New Delhi)
The sculpture is one of the great masterpieces of Indian art, finding its roots in the Bacchanalian scenes of Greece. The obverse side shows a young courtesan who falls to the floor in a state of intoxication. The reverse side is probably a depiction of the early Sanskrit drama 'The Little Clay Cart', which describes the pursuit of a beautiful courtesan by a foolish and cowardly youth. In this relief she removes a garland from above her head, the aroma of which betrays her presence to her suitor as she conceals herself in the darkness and has pushed her jingling anklets up to her knees to silence them as she runs to hide. The delicate and sensitive way in which this relief has been carved can be compared to depictions of scenes from the Buddha's previous lives (jatakas) that were being produced in Gandhara at this time (see fig. 47).

King of the Kushans', reflecting the empire that they had vanquished (fig. 22).

During the rule of the Kushano-Sasanian kings, a small remnant of the Kushan Empire survived in Kashmir and in the Punjab but came under increasing pressure from local tribes and, subsequently, from the Gupta Empire of northern India. The appearance of various groups of Huns, from the mid-fourth century onwards, brought about the final demise of the Kushans and also led to the decline of Sasanian power in the region. The first of these groups was the Kidarites, who began by seizing Balkh from the Kushano-Sasanians and then invaded Gandhara. At around same time, the Hepthalites or Chionites (also known as the White Huns) moved into Bactria from northwest China. Their empire was enlarged throughout the fifth century, until it threatened the Gupta rulers of the Punjab region. The Hepthalites were essentially nomadic and, as a consequence, did not produce sculptural art. They did produce coins and carved gems, however, and it is within this medium that we discover that they, like their predecessors, were influenced by both Persian and Greco-Roman art. Techniques such as cameo and intaglio carving are clear examples of the importation of Western technology via the Silk Road at this time (fig. 23).

A peculiar aspect of Hepthalite custom was a belief that an artificially deformed head was a symbol of high social status. This disfigurement was achieved by binding the head during infancy. As a result, many Hepthalite coins include extraordinary depictions of their kings with dome-shaped skulls. Hepthalite rule lasted until about 560 AD, when an alliance was formed between the Sasanian King Khusrau I (r. ca. 531–79) and the Western Turks of northern China. They succeeded in gaining control of the Kabul region, and of

Gandhara, and ruled the area until the coming of Islam in the late seventh and early eighth centuries. At the time of the monk Xuanzang's visit in 629–30, the empire of the Western Turks extended from the Altai Mountains of Russia to Afghanistan and modern-day Pakistan.

GANDHARA AND MATHURA ART

The migration of the Yuezhi from the western regions of China in about 165 BC, and their establishment of the Kushan Empire have been examined. By the time of Kanishka I (r. ca. 100–26 or 120–46 AD), the Kushan Empire had two capital cities: Mathura (in modern Uttar Pradesh, Northern India) and Peshawar (ancient Puru-shapur, in what is now Northwest Pakistan). Two broad schools of art have been identified: a more Hellenized form in the northwest and a more 'Indianized' style around Mathura. These styles were far from distinct, however, and numerous common elements have been identified.

The Mathura school of art

Mathura

Mathura is located on the right bank of the Yamuna, a tributary of the Ganges some 150 km south of Delhi in Uttar Pradesh. It sits at the junction of India's trade routes and by the first century AD was a thriving religious and commercial centre. Described by Ptolemy as a 'City of Gods', early Indian texts state that the inhabitants lived by trade rather than by agriculture. Hinduism, Buddhism and Jainism all coexisted peacefully, along with the worship of nature-spirits, and traders and acolytes brought religious and cultural influences to the city. Mathura's heyday lasted from the first to the third century AD, until the Sasanian incursions of the mid-third century. Despite a partial revival under the Gupta rulers of the fourth to the seventh century, the city never regained its former glory and eventually lost its position as a commercial and religious centre. Mathura sculpture is typically produced from mottled red sandstone quarried locally. Popular motifs include sensual young women, nature and water spirits (*yakshis and nagas*), architectural elements, flora and fauna, and bacchanalian scenes (see fig. 24). Mathura sculpture is often fleshy and full figured, and its protagonists (both religious and secular) are dressed in diaphanous clothing with multiple folds. While its form is essentially Indian, the influences of Greece and Rome, assimilated via the Silk Road, are also present.

A final example of sculpture from Mathura, discovered in 1871 at Bhutesvar, provides a sense both of the architecture of the time and of the fondness of the inhabitants for mingling the sacred with the sensual (fig. 26).

Fig. 25 **Red sandstone bowl support in the form of a double-sided relief**
Kushan period, Mathura
Ca. 2nd century AD
H. 106 cm
From Palikhera, Uttar Pradesh
(Archeological Museum, Mathura)
Kubera (King of Nature Spirits or *yakshas* and God of Wealth) is proffered wine in Grecian cups by servants in Hellenistic garb. On the reverse he is seen in a state of intoxication, held up by attendants. The function of this sculpture as a bowl support is itself Dionysiac in nature and is a fascinating merge of indigenous beliefs with mythology from lands far to the west. It indicates that the ritual consumption of wine had spread far into India by this time.

Fig. 24 **Red sandstone railing pillar from a stupa (domed structure for Buddhist relics)**
Kushan period, Mathura
2nd century AD
H. 80 cm
(The Cleveland Museum of Art)
The bacchanalian elements of this sculpture are far more extensive than those of the earlier example (fig. 21). Scantily clad maidens dance to the music of imported instruments, a Greek vase and rhyton (a horn-shaped drinking vessel) can be seen on the floor and the spirit of the Roman god Bacchus (Greece's Dionysos) permeates every aspect of the sculpture. With the exception of the red sandstone, which identifies it as a sculpture from Mathura, this could easily be from the Gandhara region and indicates that there were artists who travelled between the two capitals. A celebrated double-sided relief from Palikhera, now in the Mathura museum, takes the theme a stage further (fig. 25).

Fig. 26 **Red sandstone railing from a stupa**
Kushan period, Mathura
2nd century AD
H. 151 cm
From Bhutesvar
(Indian Museum, Calcutta. Photo by Sonya Quintanilla)
This railing consists of five large posts with voluptuous figures of bejewelled *yakshis* (nature or tree spirits). Each figure stands in a relaxed posture while amorous couples carouse on the balconies above. These scenes are essentially secular in nature; only the grotesque dwarf, who symbolizes the forces of evil and is vanquished by the *yakshi*, infuses the scene with any religious significance. In contrast, the reverse side of the railing is decorated with *jataka* stories, tales from the Buddha's previous incarnations. Mathura sculpture of the Kushan period is found throughout the north, east and central parts of India, a notable example being Sanghol, on the Sutlej River in the Punjab. More than one hundred railings and posts carved with female musicians and *yakshis* were discovered at the site, presumably once used to enclose a stupa.

Fig. 27 **Grey schist relief panel with an episode from the Trojan Horse story**
Kushan period, Gandhara, ca. 2nd century AD
H. 16.2 cm, W. 32.3 cm
From Peshawar District, Northwest Pakistan
(British Museum)
This striking frieze shows a horse standing upon a wheeled platform while a figure to the left thrusts a spear into its chest. To his left, with arms raised, stands Cassandra, daughter of Priam, whose warnings against permitting the horse to enter the city were ignored.

Fig. 28 **Bronze figure of a Philosopher**
Roman, ca. 130–40 AD
H. 18.3 cm
Reportedly from Asia Minor
(George Ortiz Collection)

The Gandhara school of art

'In the entrance-hall stood the larger figures of the Greco-Buddhist sculptures done, savants know how long since, by forgotten workmen whose hands were feeling, and not unskilfully, for the mysteriously transmitted Grecian touch.'

(Rudyard Kipling, 'Kim'. Kipling describes the Gandhara sculpture of the Lahore Museum, 'The Wonder House', at which his father, Lockwood, was curator)

The long-destroyed stupa of Kanishka, built at Kanish-kapura, near Peshawar in today's Northwest Pakistan, measured almost one hundred metres across and was dis-cussed by many early travellers, including the monk Xuanzang during the seventh century. Peshawar – or Puru-shapura, as it was called – was the seat of the Kushan Empire, at least during its early period. Other centres were at Taxila, the later capital, the Swat Valley and Hadda and Begram in modern Afghanistan. All of these cities sat astride the ancient routes linking China, Central Asia and the West-ern world, and were part of a region that modern writers have called 'the crossroads of Asia'. The art of Gandhara – almost exclusively Buddhist in nature – draws its influences from Greek, Roman, Persian and local Indian styles. Grey or blue schist seems to have been the preferred medium; stucco and terracotta were used in areas where stone was unob-tainable, and gold and bronze also used, but much more sparingly. The fully developed Gandhara style was extant by the end of the first century AD, epitomized by the *Boddo* coin (shown in fig. 19). It is generally accepted that stucco and terracotta

images are somewhat later than schist sculpture, perhaps because of the depletion of supplies of stone. Early stucco and terracottas have been found, at Taxila for example, but the majority have been attributed to the third to fifth centuries, compared to the first to third for stone.

Classical influences

An extensive repertoire of classical motifs is found in the art of Gandhara: mythological figures such as Eros (or Cupid) and wingless *Puttis* (young boys) with garlands of flowers; figures of Herakles (sometimes transmuted to become the Buddhist deity Vajrapani) and Atlas, centaurs and sea monsters, Corinthian columns and capitals with acanthus leaves and floral scrolls (rinceaux). The British Museum even has a schist frieze that tells the story of the Trojan horse (fig. 27).

Images of the Buddha in Gandhara art are devoid of ornament and are formally posed, adhering closely to the designs of Kanishka-era coins (see fig. 19). Standing Buddha images typically have a high *usnisha* (a raised chignon, indicative of princely origins and superior wisdom), eyes half-closed in meditation and a heavy monastic robe with multiple pleats. Despite the simplicity of style of these Buddha images, Greco-Roman elements are still to be found and, indeed, it has been suggested that they derive from the figure of the Western philosopher or statesman known as *Togatus*, found in the classical world (fig. 28).

Gandhara Buddha images were produced in vast numbers. Free-standing (or sitting) images, usually in stone, were created, as were figures placed in niches against a wall, in common with many stucco or terracotta examples. Very

Fig. 30 **Stucco head of Buddha**
Kushan period, Gandhara
4th or 5th century AD
H. 29.2 cm
Believed to be from Taxila, Northwest Pakistan
(Victoria and Albert Museum)
This head is one of the most celebrated images in all of Gandhara art. It is slightly inclined to one side and possesses a grace and serenity that is without peer. The records of the museum state that the head is from Hadda but most scholars now agree that its style is closer to that of Taxila.

Fig. 29 **Seated stucco Buddhas and tiered stupas with figures in niches**
Kushan period, Gandhara
4th or 5th century
Jaulian Monastery Complex, Taxila

few examples of the latter survive in situ, the Jaulian monastery at Taxila being a rare example. At Jaulian are tiers of niches containing stucco figures of Buddhas, Bodhisattvas and devotees in acts of worship or meditation (fig. 29).

At their best, Gandhara images are sublime, spiritual creations.

Taxila

Bactrian Greeks founded the Gandhara metropolis of Taxila – the likely source of the head illustrated in fig. 30 – during the second century BC, although the Achaemenians and then the Mauryans had occupied the site from the sixth century BC. The Bactrian Greeks were followed, in succession, by Scythians, Parthians, Kushans, Sasanians and finally the Hepthalites (or White Huns), who proved to be the city's nemesis. Greek accounts describe the arrival of Alexander the Great in the spring of 326 BC. Ambhi (Omphis), the king of Taxila, surrendered his kingdom to

Alexander and offered an alliance against the Indian King Porus. Alexander remained at Taxila for a few weeks before marching east to defeat Porus. Following Alexander's premature death in 323 BC, Greek control of the region proved impossible to maintain and the empire fell apart. The Indian empire of the Mauryans under Chandragupta (ca. 311–287 BC) was established, with its capital at Pataliputra (modern Patna in Bihar). Taxila became the regional seat of government, the Mauryans driving out the Greeks from all of Northwest India. Mauryan rule appears to have been despotic and it seems that the embrace of Buddhism by Chandragupta's grandson Ashoka (ca. 269–32 BC) was a reaction to the excesses of the regime. Ashoka carved imperial edicts on rocks and pillars, the latter surmounted by animal capitals, throughout the Mauryan Empire from Afghanistan to Karnataka in southern India* (see also p. 201). The Greeks did not completely disappear from the region during this period, however. Seleucus, one of Alexander's generals, and his successors managed to sustain Greek rule north of the Hindu Kush mountains in Bactria and Sogdiana until about 255 BC, when it became an independent kingdom under the Greek governor Diodotus. During the early second century BC the Greeks of Bactria

* See also the note on India's Grand Trunk Road (p. 66). Ashokan columns are to be found along the road, indicating that it has been used as an arterial highway since the earliest times.

Fig. 31 **Sirkap, Taxila**
Ca. 1st century AD
It is not only the streets of Sirkap
that owe their appearance to
influences from the classical
world. The acanthus-topped
Corinthian columns of the Stupa
of the Double Headed Eagle
reveal that such influences also
extended to the architecture of
some of its buildings (fig. 32).

Fig. 32. **Stupa of the Double-
Headed Eagle**
Sirkap, Taxila, 1st century AD
The double-headed bird is found
in Scythian art and appears to be
a symbol of kingship and power.

extended their influence southwards again, establishing capitals at Taxila and Charsadda. Greek rule was maintained, to some degree, until the first century AD but was gradually eroded by influxes of Scythians, Parthians and Yuezhi. After the Yuezhi's establishment of the Kushan Empire, Taxila became one of its capitals, actually consisting of three separate city sites, these being Bhir Mound (the most ancient), Sirkap and Sirsukh. The capital was moved to Taxila from Peshawar at around the end of the first century AD, first to Sirkap and then, during the second century, to Sirsukh. Sirkap was laid out in a grid pattern, favoured by the city-planners of the Hellenistic world (fig. 31).

Like the eastern Kushan capital of Mathura, Taxila owed its prosperity to the trade routes on which it sat. Sir John Marshall, who excavated Taxila between 1913 and 1934, describes how Taxila was situated at the meeting-point of three great highways linking India with China, Western and Central Asia and Europe. Taxila also benefited from sea trade between Alexandria and Barbaricum at the mouth of the Indus, particularly when periods of hostility between Rome and Parthia closed the east-west land route. A famous visitor to Taxila during the Parthian era was St Thomas who, according to Christian legend, was commissioned by King Gondophares (r. ca. 20–50 AD) to build him a palace. After expending all of the funds provided to him on acts of charity, St Thomas told Gondophares that he had constructed him a palace in heaven. The king's recently deceased brother was miraculously restored to life and confirmed St Thomas's story, leading to the conversion of both men to Christianity. The presence of foreign artisans at Taxila is entirely plausible, given the level of activity along the land and sea routes at this time.

During ancient times, the city would have been dominated by the great Dharmarajika stupa, once over 35 metres in height, though now reduced by centuries of diggings and seismic activity. It was first built by the Mauryan Emperor Ashoka during the third century BC, one of the eight principal stupas built to house relics of the Buddha. It was enlarged during the following centuries (fig. 33).

Marshall unearthed a veritable treasure trove of artefacts at the Taxila sites which, because they date to the earliest period of the Gandhara School, are largely unfettered by indigenous styles and show Greco-Roman influence at its most intense. Buddhist statuary was discovered: in bronze, stone and stucco; pottery; gold and silver jewellery; large numbers of coins and exquisite small items in bone, ivory and shell. Some thirty schist and steatite palette trays were found – possibly used for the application of cosmetics – many with scenes from Greek mythology including bacchanalian themes, amorous couples and figures astride fabulous beasts. Perhaps the most delightful of all the rich finds of Taxila is a single small bronze figure of Harpocrates, now in the site-museum (fig. 34).

Fig. 33 **Remains of the Dharmarajika Stupa**
Taxila
Ca. 1st century AD

Fig. 34 **Bronze figure of Harpocrates**
Probably Roman, first century AD
H. 13 cm
Found at Sirkap, Taxila
(Formerly in the Taxila Museum, now in the Karachi Museum)
Harpocrates, son of Isis, is the Egyptian God of Silence. He enjoins quiet by raising his finger to his lips. A number of scholars have suggested that this figure was made in the west, perhaps at the great trading port of Alexandria in Roman Egypt, and imported to Taxila.

Taxila's heyday was brief. The Hepthalite invasions of the fifth century did not immediately put a stop to the production of Gandhara art but the southern areas were severely affected, with considerable devastation wrought by the Hepthalite King Mihiragula (r. ca. 515–40 AD). When the Chinese pilgrim Xuanzang passed through the region in about 630 AD, Taxila was a deserted ruin. Sir John Marshall found graphic evidence of the mayhem wrought by the Hepthalites during his excavations of the Dharmarajika stupa. He unearthed an open courtyard containing a group of six skeletons, several of which had been decapitated, the charred timbers of the building indicating that it had then been burned to the ground.

Ai Khanum

What is so intriguing about the art of Gandhara is why classical influences should have played such an influential role in the visual expression of a carefully structured eastern religion like Buddhism. It appears that the artists of Gandhara adopted classical prototypes which were already known to them and adapted them to their own purposes.

This view is supported by recent excavations at places such as Ai Khanum, a Greco-Bactrian city on the banks of the Oxus in northern Afghanistan. Ai Khanum occupied a triangular site of about 1800 metres by 1500 metres, completely surrounded by earthen ramparts and flanked on two of its three sides by the rivers Oxus and Kokcha. The city was attacked and destroyed in about 140 BC and subsequently abandoned. The Kushans then occupied the ruins from about the first century BC until around the third century AD but no major repairs were undertaken. It was first excavated by a French academic mission in 1965–68 and may well have been 'Alexandria on the Oxus', one of the cities founded by Alexander the Great. The Hellenistic nature of the city is unmistakable; amphitheatre, gymnasium and courtyard houses are all constructed in Doric, Ionic and Corinthian style. An inscription at the gymnasium invokes the protection of the gods Herakles and Hermes. Other discoveries include a statuette of a young athlete with a wreath, a bronze figure of Herakles and fountain spouts in the form of dolphins and lions. The base of a stele inscribed in Greek at the funerary monument of a man named Kineas

Fig. 35 **A monumental white limestone foot, wearing a sandal decorated with floral motifs**
Greco-Bactrian, ca. 140 BC
L. 28 cm
From Ai Khanum, Northern Afghanistan
(Formerly in the Kabul Museum. Now in a private Japanese museum awaiting future return to Afghanistan)
The temple from which the fragment comes contained a large pedestal for a statue, identified by Bernard as a massive figure of Zeus seated on an ivory throne. Fragments of both hands and this foot were found, all made from imported marble. It seems that the head, hands and feet were of stone and the remaining parts were of unfired clay over a wooden body. Locks of hair made from extensively gilded stucco were also recovered and the complete figure must have closely resembled seated images of Zeus depicted on the coins of Alexander the Great and other Hellenistic rulers. The whole temple complex shows signs of destruction by fire, presumably when the city was attacked in 140 BC. The French discovered exquisite mosaic floors, made from river-pebbles set in red-stucco, but they now exist only in photographs. Ai Khanum is now a moonscape- a mass of craters dug by local treasure-hunters in search of gold artefacts. Local people have also removed its mosaics, columns and bricks for building materials and several columns can now be seen supporting the roof of a nearby chaikana (teahouse).

* Percy Bysshe Shelley, 'Ozymandias'.

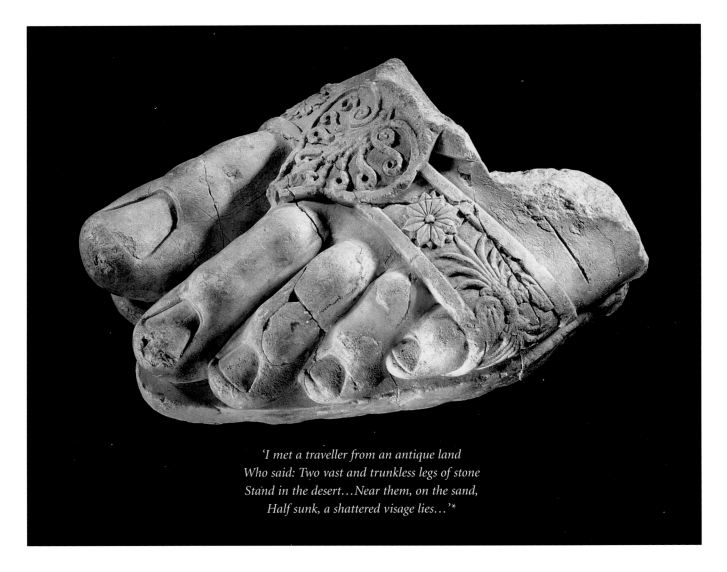

'I met a traveller from an antique land
Who said: Two vast and trunkless legs of stone
Stand in the desert...Near them, on the sand,
Half sunk, a shattered visage lies...'*

Fig. 36 **A gold pendant set with turquoise, lapis lazuli and garnets depicting a king in combat with dragons**
Kushan period, 1st century BC/AD; one of a pair
L. 12.5 cm
From Tillya Tepe, Northern Afghanistan
(Formerly in the Kabul Museum, present whereabouts unknown)
The syncretic style found at Ai Khanum and Tillya Tepe occurs during the period of transition between the end of the Greco-Bactrian kingdom and the establishment of a unified Kushan Empire.

Tillya Tepe

Further evidence of a similar process of Hellenization was discovered by a joint Soviet-Afghan expedition in 1978–79 at Tillya Tepe, near the town of Shibargan in northern Afghanistan. Tillya Tepe was a royal necropolis, built by the Kushans during the first centuries before and after the birth of Christ. Wooden coffins containing four females and one male were discovered, the occupants dressed lavishly and wearing elaborate and extensive gold jewellery. Funerary offerings found at Tillya Tepe included Indian, Roman and Parthian coins, mirrors inscribed in Chinese, an Indian ivory comb reminiscent of carvings from Begram (see below) and cameos in Roman and Greco-Bactrian style. Over 20,000 gold objects were found including jewel-encrusted daggers and a sword, clothing plaques and a vast array of jewellery. What is most fascinating of all, however, is the way in which the early Kushan peoples have merged the artistic heritage of their nomadic roots with the classical forms extant in their new domain. At Tillya Tepe, the 'animal style' of the nomads is combined with Greco-Roman motifs in a startling manner: a dagger hilt with a depiction of a Siberian bear holding a grapevine in its mouth, two buckles showing warriors in Greco-Roman attire with Scythian dragons at their feet and a pair of gold clasps, each showing Dionysos and Ariadne riding a griffin and accompanied by Nike and Silenus. Of particular interest are two gold pendants of kings dressed in Scythian-Achaemenian dress with Indian caste marks on their heads and grappling with Scythian dragons (fig. 36).

Begram

Some 70 km north of Kabul, overlooking the Panjshir River and dwarfed by the peaks of the Hindu Kush, is situated the ancient city of Begram (or Kapisa). The older section of the city dates back to the Bactrian-Greek kings of the second century BC and may have been the site of 'Alexandria under Caucasus', another of Alexander's eastern cities. Kushan kings constructed the area to the south, probably as the summer capital of the great Kanishka (r. ca. 100–126 or 120–46 AD). The city was sacked and burned by the Sasanian King Shapur I in 241, was rebuilt, and then finally abandoned during the Hephthalite invasions of the fifth century. During its years of prosperity, Begram must have been one of the richest of all the cities of the Silk Road.

– perhaps the founder of the city itself – is the earliest structure in the city, possibly dating to as early as 300 BC. The inscription tells us that Clearchos, a student of Aristotle, erected the stele and that he had copied the precepts inscribed upon it at Delphi. The stele itself has disappeared but one of the precepts was inscribed on the base and has survived. Its message, like so many written fragments from the Silk Road, is timeless:

> 'As children, learn good manners
> As young men, learn to control the passions.
> In middle age, be just.
> In old age, give good advice.
> Then die, without regret.'
>
> (Quoted in N. H. Dupree, 1977)

What is particularly significant, however, is that the remains of a monumental sculpture of Zeus, found in an oriental temple with signs of eastern worship, indicate that the assimilation of classical forms that we saw at Taxila was well underway by the era of Ai Khanum and that there are already signs of adaptation of these forms to local custom (fig. 35).

Fig. 37 **Glass goblet or vase with carved and painted relief depiction of the Lighthouse at Alexandria**
Probably Roman and from Alexandria, 1st to 3rd century AD
H. 18 cm
Found at Begram, Afghanistan
(Formerly in the Kabul Museum, present whereabouts unknown. Huntington Archive, photo by John C. Huntington)
This astonishing object appears to have been moulded from molten glass with additional details then attached. A figure of Poseidon stands atop the lighthouse of Pharos and three vessels are carved on the reverse: a war-galley, a merchant ship and a fishing boat.

Excavations were carried out by the French Archeological Mission under J. Hackin and J. Carl between 1939 and 1940, concentrating on the rooms of the palace-complex ascribed to Kanishka. Two chambers were discovered which had been walled up to protect their contents from some approaching invader, perhaps Shapur I. The contents of these rooms are among the greatest treasures in the history of archeology and include objects from the entire length of the Silk Road. The objects have been dated to the first to the third centuries AD, a time of peace and prosperity in Rome, Parthia and China. The land routes between China and the West were open, as were the maritime routes from India to the Mediterranean. Glass vessels from Egypt and Syria, fragments of Han dynasty Chinese lacquer, Greco-Roman bronzes and superb Indian ivories were found in the two chambers. A number of painted glass goblets or vases with classical legends were

Fig. 38 **Bronze bust of Athena, daughter of Zeus, used as an unguent or incense vase and adapted for use as balance-weight**
Probably Roman and from Alexandria, ca. 1st century AD
H. 11 cm
Found at Begram, Afghanistan
(Musée Guimet, Paris. Photo RMN)

Fig. 39 **Ivory plaque with female figures in relief within a gateway**
1st century AD
H. 42.7 cm
From Begram, Afghanistan
(Formerly in the Kabul Museum, present whereabouts unknown)
This plaque was one of a group used to decorate a large throne, some 3 metres in width.

discovered, the most fascinating of which depicts the Lighthouse of Alexandria, complete with buildings, ships and sea creatures (fig. 37).

Among the many bronzes found at Begram are two figures of Harpocrates, similar to the example unearthed at Taxila (see fig. 34 above), and perhaps also from Alexandria. A number of heads or busts of gods from the classical world were found, fitted with rings to attach them to a set of scales as balance-weights. Their hollowed out design suggests that they have been adapted from perfume bottles (fig. 38).

Among other finds at Begram were about fifty plaster plaques of classical subjects, depicted in relief. These casts were almost certainly intended as models for local craftsmen to work from and, it has been suggested, as samples to be shown to clients. All of the objects discovered at Begram

were small and therefore highly portable. The suggestion has been made that they were the stock of some long-forgotten Silk Road trader or perhaps that the chambers were some sort of customs house. What is significant is that the date of the objects is spread over a wide range, from the first century AD to as late as the third. This fact, coupled with the carefully and deliberate manner in which they were secreted away, indicates that they were more likely have been the personal treasures of a Kushan noble.

Although many of these items appear to have come from the Greco-Roman world, indigenous Indian forms are also represented at Begram. A considerable number of delicately carved ivories were found, many retaining traces of coloured pigments. They consist of two broad types: figures and plaques carved in the round and flat panels with incised decoration. The plaques with figures in relief recall *Yakshi* ('nature spirit') images from Mathura (see fig. 24) and the *torana* (gateway) images of the Great Stupa at Sanchi in Madhya Pradesh, dating to the first century AD.

Among a small number of fully three-dimensional sculptures are three large carvings of *Yakshis* or River Goddesses from Begram, each 45 cm or more in height and thought to be the largest of all ancient Indian ivories. Both these figures and the *torana* ladies of Sanchi are strikingly similar to an ivory mirror handle – undoubtedly of Indian origin – discovered in the ruins of Pompeii (fig. 40).

The second category of the Begram ivories – the flat incised panels – includes a casket that can only be described as a masterpiece (figs. 41 and 42).

Fig. 40 Ivory mirror handle with a depiction of a lady with her attendants
Indian, 1st century AD
Discovered at Pompeii
(Museo Nazionale, Naples)
This object must have been made before the destruction of Pompeii in 79 AD, and is further proof of the large amount of traffic in both directions along the Silk Road between India and Rome.

Fig. 41 **Ivory casket with depictions of ladies with their handmaids**
India, 1st century AD
H. 30 cm (approx.)
Found at Begram, Afghanistan
(Formerly in the Kabul Museum, present whereabouts unknown. Huntington Archive, photo by John C. Huntington)

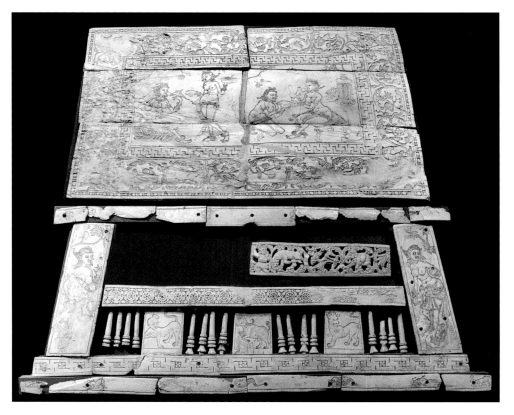

Fig. 42 **Detail of top of fig. 41**
Incised design of ladies with their
maids
India, 1st century AD
Found at Begram, Afghanistan
(Formerly in the Kabul Museum, present
whereabouts unknown. Huntington
Archive, photo by John C. Huntington)
This casket depicts the leisured
existence of court ladies in a
style described by the art
historian Benjamin Rowland as
'gently erotic'. One of the
protagonists plays with a parrot
while another applies her
makeup; each of them assisted by
a maidservant. On the lower
section of the casket is a pair of
Yakshis (nature spirits) and
animals, including a wonderful
monkey wearing a hat. Despite
the undoubtedly local
manufacture of these ivories, they
have not entirely escaped what
Kipling described as the 'Grecian
touch.' The scenes on the top
panel have a Bacchanalian feel to
them and are framed by floral
scrolls (rinceaux).

Fig. 43 **A group of grey schist Bodhisattva figures,
two standing and one bust**
Kushan period, Gandhara, 2nd or 3rd century AD
H: a) 110 cm, b) 137 cm and c) 91 cm
Probably from the vicinity of Takht-I- Bahi near Sahri
Bahlol, Northwest Pakistan
(Spink and Son Ltd)

Images of the Bodhisattva (those destined for Buddhahood), in the guise of a Kushan prince, are among the most elegant of all Gandhara sculptures. Typically, these images wear a turban-diadem that holds in place an elaborate coiffure. The hair is sometimes in the form of a topknot or cockade, sometimes secured by a line of pearls encircling the head. Unrestrained by the austerities associated with the Buddha, these images are adorned with an abundance of jewellery: heavy earrings (often in the form of lions), basubands for the arms and as many as four necklaces are worn, all in a style which evokes the classical world. The robes, too, follow Greco-Roman models and the upper torso is generally bare and muscular. Such Bodhisattva images can be as much as two metres in height but even much smaller images can be magnificent and imposing. A group of three Bodhisattvas – perhaps from the vicinity of the great Gandhara site at Takht-I- Bahi near Sahri Bahlol, 90 km northeast of Peshawar – may well have been carved by the same hand and are breathtaking creations (fig. 43).

Sahri Bahlol and Takht-I- Bahi

Images from the Sahri Bahlol area include a large number of sculptures in both Indo-Scythian and Greco-Roman style. The monastery complex at Takht-i-Bahi (where *Takht* means 'seat' or 'throne' and *Bahi* means 'reservoir') covers an area of about 33 hectares and was first excavated between 1907 and 1909 by D. B. Spooner. It has since been quite extensively restored but remains one of Pakistan's most important Gandhara sites (fig. 44).

One famous example of sculpture from the area is a portrait head of a monk from the Sahri Bahlol area, now in the Peshawar museum (fig. 45). It recalls late Roman portraiture.

A final example, also from the Peshawar Museum, is sculpted from the deep black schist found in the area (fig. 46). As with the jewelled Bodhisattva images in fig. 43, this sculpture is a heroic, princely figure. The recessed *urna* on the forehead may once have contained a jewel.

Sculpture from this middle period of the Gandhara

Fig. 44 **The Monastery Complex at Takht-i-Bahi, Northwest Pakistan**
Kushan period, Gandhara, ca. 2nd century AD

Fig. 45 **A dark grey schist head of a layman or donor**
Kushan period, Gandhara, 2nd or 3rd century AD
H. 29 cm
From Sahri Bahlol, N. W. Pakistan
(Peshawar Museum)

Fig. 46 **A black schist head of a Bodhisattva**
Kushan period, Gandhara, 2nd or 3rd century AD
H. 52 cm
From Sahri Bahlol, N. W. Pakistan
(Peshawar Museum)

Fig. 47 **A grey schist frieze depicting the birth of the Buddha.**
Kushan period, Gandhara, 2nd or 3rd century AD
H. 24 cm, W. 24 cm
(Spink and Son Ltd)

School is not always monumental in style. Scenes from the Buddha's previous incarnations, known as the *jataka* stories, are frequently rendered in the most delicate and sensitive manner (fig. 47).

Queen Maya, wife of King Suddhodana of Kapilavastu (on the borders of Nepal and India), conceives Prince Siddharta, the future Buddha, while dreaming of a white elephant that enters her right side. In this relief she stands holding the branch of a sala tree as the child emerges from her side, a pose that evokes the theme of fertility and is often seen in depictions of yakshis (nature spirits). Supported by her sister Mahaprajapati, Queen Maya is attended by her servants, one of whom holds a palm branch. Similarities between this frieze and the 'intoxicated courtesan' relief from the New Delhi museum (see fig. 21, p. 35) provide clear evidence that the Mathura and Gandhara schools of Kushan sculpture were far from distinct.

Stupas and reliquaries

The domed structure – known as the stupa – has been an important part of Buddhist ritual since the very beginnings of the faith. It appears to have had its origins in the funeral mounds of important rulers and became the symbol of the Buddha's final entry into Nirvana and his attainment of Buddhahood. After the Buddha's cremation his remains were divided into eight equal parts and distributed to each of the neighbouring kingdoms, to be placed in specially constructed stupas. This practice was continued during the Kushan period when stupas were constructed throughout the Gandhara kingdom often, as with the 35-metre-high Dharmarajika stupa at Taxila, on a vast scale. Stupas and reliquary caskets were also produced in miniature to contain the corporeal relics of the Buddha or one of his disciples, such as bone, hair, teeth or ashes; and precious items like jewellery, coins and beads. The stupa in both monumental and miniature form is found throughout the Buddhist kingdoms of the Silk Road and is referred to elsewhere in this book. Two of the most famous of the Kushan reliquaries date to the early period of the Gandhara school of art and have provided a great deal of information about the iconography and the religious practices of the time.

The first of these is the somewhat optimistically named 'Kanishka Reliquary', discovered by D. B. Spooner at the beginning of the last century after some rather adroit detective work. Spooner was searching for the site of the legendary stupa, said by the Chinese pilgrim Xuanzang to have been constructed on the outskirts of Peshawar (ancient Purushapura) to house relics of the Buddha and to have been over two hundred metres high. From 1908 to 1910, Spooner explored two mounds at Shah-ji-ki-Dheri in today's city suburbs as the probable location of the stupa. He

Fig. 49 **Gold relic casket inlaid with garnets**
Kushan period, Gandhara, 1st century AD
H. 6.5 cm
Found at Bimaran, Afghanistan
(British Museum-Heritage Images)

discovered the remains of a large monastery and the base of an immense stupa. The casket was discovered 60 cm below the surface at the exact centre of the stupa mound (fig. 48).

The second Kushan reliquary is somewhat earlier in date and, as a result, is more obviously Greco-Roman in style (fig. 49). It was discovered at Bimaran, west of Jalalabad in eastern Afghanistan and is made of gold set with garnets. The six figures around the side consist of two Buddhas, each flanked by Indra and by a devotee or Bodhisattva. A Corinthian column, each supporting an arch, separates each figure, and between the arches are eagles with outstretched wings, both borrowings from the classical world. There are identifiable links with the classically influenced iconography of Taxila.

Fig. 48 **Bronze relic casket 'The Kanishka Reliquary'**
Kushan period, Gandhara, 2nd century AD
H. 19.3 cm
Discovered at Shah-ji-ki-Dheri, Peshawar, Northwest Pakistan
(Peshawar Museum)
This casket is of great historical importance for a number of reasons. It has an inscription in Kharosthi around the base that contains a reference to Kanishka and a depiction of a Kushan monarch on the exterior, perhaps intended to be the king himself. There is considerable debate about whether this is the personal reliquary of Kanishka or, perhaps, the property of one of the later rulers of the same name. The style of the Buddha on the lid, with its heavy monastic robe and double nimbus are characteristics of early Gandhara images, such as a gold coin from Kanishka's reign (see fig. 19, p. 34). The workmanship of this casket is actually rather ordinary but its significance lies in the effortless fusion of diverse motifs from different countries, all linked by the Silk Road. The Buddha image on the lid, in typically Gandhara dress, is flanked by the two Indian gods Brahma and Indra. On the side, the king wears the topcoat and heavy boots of Kushan royalty and is attended by the two Persian gods of the sun and moon, Miiro and Mao. A line of geese (hamsa) flies above the head of the king, an Indian motif associated with the god Brahma but also a symbol of Kushan nobility. Young boys (putti) supporting a long garland, an emblem encountered in the classical world, link the whole ensemble. All trace of Shah-ji-ki-Dheri has now been obliterated by a huge Muslim cemetery and by housing, although local people still regularly unearth coins and other small objects in the area.

Fig. 50 **Two sections of large stucco bas-reliefs of central Buddhas flanked by disciples**
Kushan period, Gandhara, ca. 3rd/4th century AD
From the monastery at Tapa-i-Shotor, Hadda, Afghanistan. Now destroyed
(Courtesy of Isao Kurita)
The thunderbolt-bearing figure of Vajrapani, protector of the Buddha, sits to the left in the left hand image. He is cast in the guise of Herakles complete with a lion skin draped over his shoulder. These reliefs, and all of Hadda's remaining statuary, were destroyed or looted during the recent fighting in Afghanistan. The mound is still there but, when compared with the photograph above, it presents a pitiful sight (fig. 51).

Jalalabad and Hadda

The area around Jalalabad is rich in both archeological sites and in stories about the life of Buddha Sakyamuni. Xuanzang refers to an immense stupa at Jalalabad, some 90 metres high, and erected by King Ashoka during the third century BC to commemorate the site of the meeting of Sakyamuni with Dipankara. Dipankara, one of Sakyamuni's previous incarnations, informs him of his impending Buddhahood. Also at Jalalabad, in the village of Charar Bagh, was the Shadow Cave where a silhouette of the Lord Buddha was said to appear on one of the walls. Xuanzang visited the cave and saw the Buddha's 'gleaming shadow'. He made a Buddha image from sandalwood to celebrate the event, the first of the seven images taken back to China at the conclusion of his travels.

The technique of working in stucco, a cheap and readily available substitute for the grey schist stone favoured by the sculptors of Gandhara, attained its apogee around the third century at Hadda, near Jalalabad. Hadda's numerous monasteries (*viharas*) were still active at the time of a visit by the Chinese pilgrim Fa Xian in around 400, but the city was ruined and desolate when Xuanzang passed through in 630, wrecked by Hepthalite invaders. Sculpting with stucco, a plaster made from calcium oxide or calcium sulphate, seems to have been invented in or near the Roman port of

Alexandria in Egypt. It is extremely easy to work, with large figures built up around a core of wood or stone. This enables the sculptor to infuse his creations with a greater degree of naturalism and spontaneity. Hadda stuccos still retain the classical elements seen at Taxila and Begram but the city's artists have adapted them to produce a unique style that reveals the full flowering of Gandhara art (fig. 50).

A number of examples of sculpture in 'Hadda style' have recently appeared on the international art market and are likely to cause us to re-evaluate the degree to which the early Christian world directly or indirectly influenced the work of the Gandhara sculptor. Some of these examples are so 'European' in appearance that it seems incredible that they were produced in the East (fig. 52).

A small number of images from Hadda and its environs recall the angels of Western Gothic art (fig. 53).

Hellenistic influence is less evident in the Buddha images from the Hadda area. Red ochre and black pigments were most commonly used and the form is more idealized than the realistic portraits of donors and monks. Jules Barthoux, who excavated the site between 1926 and 1928, believes that some of the Buddhas were 20 metres in height. None has survived but a numinous head of Buddha, immersed in a meditative trance, is still with us and hints at the genius of the sculptors of the Hadda area (fig. 54).

Fig. 51 **The ruined ruins of
Tapa-i-Shotor**
The main courtyard area, Tapa-i-
Shotor, Hadda, Afghanistan
Photographed in August 2000

Fig. 53 **Painted bust of
devata (divine being)**
Kushan period, Gandhara, 3rd to
4th century AD
H. 27 cm
Probably from the vicinity of
Hadda, Afghanistan
(Spink and Son Ltd)
This soaringly beautiful sculpture
still retains it original yellow,
orange, red and black pigments. It
was probably once part of a
Buddhist tableau, perhaps an
attendant figure for a large
Buddha or Bodhisattva. The
remarkable depictions of winged
angels found by Aurel Stein at
Miran in Chinese Central Asia are
from the same genre.

Fig. 52 Two painted terracotta heads of disciples of the Buddha
Kushan period, Gandhara, 3rd to 4th century AD
H. 27 cm and 28 cm
Probably from the vicinity of Hadda, Afghanistan
(Spink and Son Ltd)
These remarkable heads were probably part of large relief, similar to fig. 50 (see p. 50), and appear to represent disciples of the
Buddha. The pigments with which they were decorated have survived virtually intact. Benjamin Rowland is one of a number of
scholars who have compared the images of the Buddha's disciples, found at Hadda, with Gothic portrayals of Christ. His explanation is
that Hellenistic models influenced both Gothic art and images from Gandhara. The legend of St Thomas and his sojourn at the
court of King Gondophares in Taxila (see p. 41) adds a tantalizing dimension to the appearance of these two sculptures.

Fig. 54 **Monumental stucco
head of the Buddha**
Kushan period, Gandhara, 3rd to
4th century AD
H. 66 cm
Probably from the vicinity of
Hadda, Afghanistan
(Private Collection)

Before leaving Hadda it is worth taking a quick at two contrasting examples from the Musée Guimet in Paris, acquired during Jules Barthoux's excavations. The first is a stucco figure of a demon wearing a fur cloak that seems to exude malevolence from every pore (fig. 55).

The second image (fig. 56) is an exquisite head of a Bodhisattva or donor. Its medium – painted limestone – indicates that stucco was not the only material to be used by the sculptors of Hadda.

Fig. 55 A stucco figure of a demon in a fur cloak
Kushan period, Gandhara, ca. 3rd/4th century AD
H. 29 cm
Hadda, Afghanistan
(Musée Guimet, Paris)
The figure of the demon clutches the folds of his cloak about him as he advances. It may represent one of the army of demons summoned by Mara to challenge the fitness of Buddha Sakyamuni to realize Nirvana.

Later Buddhist Art of Gandhara

During the seventh and eighth centuries, before the coming of Islam, the Buddhist art of Gandhara entered its final phase. The paintings and sculpture, discovered in 1937 by the French at the monastery of Fondukistan on the Ghorband River, continue the Indo-Sasanian style that we see in the wall paintings of Bamiyan (figs 57, 58 and 71). Figures in similar style were found at Tepe Sardar (near Ghazni), and at Kakrak. The technique of painting unfired clay, sometimes mixed with horse hair and chopped straw and modelled around a wooden framework, is seen for the first time and replaced the old media of schist, limestone stucco and terracotta. It became the method of choice among the artists of the Silk Road, occurring in Kashmir, in China and parts of Central Asia, and embodied a refined and somewhat feminine style.

The sculptural counterparts of the Fondukistan paintings are equally flamboyant and sensual and may have their roots in the art of the Gupta dynasty of northern India (fig. 58).

Benjamin Rowland describes the face of one of these *devatas* as 'a mask veiled in dreams' and believes that they express 'a sort of world-weary grace.' It is fascinating to speculate about the thoughts that ran through the minds of the creators of these transcendently beautiful images. They must have been aware (from travellers along the great caravan routes that passed through the area), of the destruction wrought by the Hepthalite invaders throughout the region, of the Sasanians and the Western Turks who replaced them and of the advance of Islam. It is reasonable to assume that they worked with a growing sense of unease and yet still were able to create the serene, mysterious countenances of Fondukistan.

The sudden appearance of the marble figures of the Hindu Shahi dynasty, just before the advent of Islam, was a surprising development in the art of the region. The most important finds were at Khair Khaneh 15 km north of Kabul. The Sun God Surya and Vishnu were popular subjects for the Shahi artists and their styles are linked to those of Kashmir. Other sites such as Tagao and Gardez have also

Fig. 56 **Painted limestone head of a donor or Bodhisattva**
Kushan period, Gandhara, ca. 3rd/4th century AD
H. 23 cm
Hadda, Afghanistan
(Musée Guimet, Paris. Photo RMN)

Fig. 57 Wall painting of the Bodhisattva Maitreya, the future Buddha
From Fondukistan, Afghanistan, 7th or 8th century
H. 63 cm
(Formerly in the Kabul Museum, present whereabouts unknown. Huntington Archive, photo by John C. Huntington)
This effulgent, graceful creation – painted on the clay wall of the Fondukistan monastery's main hall – holds a blue lotus in his right hand and a flask in his right, a common attribute of Maitreya. Wall paintings at Penjikent in Tajikistan, Kizil in Chinese Central Asia and Dunhuang in Gansu, reproduced elsewhere in this book, demonstrate the wide distribution of this style of art (figs 165, 199 and 341).

**Fig. 58 Painted clay figure
of a jewelled devata
(a divine being)**
From Fondukistan, Afghanistan,
7th or 8th century
H. 72 cm
(Musée Guimet, Paris. Photo RMN)
This gently smiling figure sits in
the position of royal ease
(*lalitasana*), the rich colours with
which he is decorated almost as
fresh as the day they were
applied.

Fig. 59 **Marble figure of a Bodhisattva contemplating a skull.**
Afghanistan, Shahi period, ca. 5th century
H. 47 cm
(Private Collection)
This previously unrecorded figure of a crowned Bodhisattva, now in a private
collection, sits on a small dais and gazes thoughtfully at a skull lying on the
ground before him. The theme, the evanescence of human existence, is a central
one in Buddhism and occurs many times in the art of the Silk Road (see fig. 198).

* A little known consequence of
the Hindu Shahi dynasty is the
continued existence of a small
community of Hindus in
Afghanistan. In May 2001 they
were ordered to wear symbols to
denote their religious beliefs by
the monotheistic, Taliban rulers
of the country. At that time there
were said to be several thousand
followers of the faith in the
country as a whole, with
800–1000 living in Kabul.
† For more on Al-Biruni please
see section on Khiva (p. 240).

yielded sculptures of Hindu deities, including Siva and
Durga, although a number of Buddhist images have also
been found. When Xuanzang visited the kingdom of Kapisa,
north of Kabul, in 630, he recorded that there were one
hundred monasteries and about 6000 monks in the city but
that there were also ten Hindu temples.* Very little is known
about the Hindu Shahi (after the Persian title, 'Shah' or
'King'). It appears that they emerged as a result of a palace
coup among the Turki Shahi at some point before the ninth
century and established their capital at Udabhandapura
(modern Hund) in Pakistan, to the northwest of Taxila.
Although the Hindu Shahi dynasty was established only
around the ninth cenury, Hindu sculpture was already being
produced in the area and has all been labelled 'Hindu Shahi'
as a matter of convenience. It seems likely that the Western
Turks and the Turki Shahi were one and the same tribe or, at

least, were part of the same confederation but information
about both groups, and particularly the latter, is scarce and
contradictory. The Turki Shahi are not referred to by name
until the eleventh century when they are given mention in
Al-Biruni's work 'The History of India' (*Ta'rikh al-Hind*).†

There is space here for but one example of the marble
sculpture of the Shahis (fig. 59).

The coming of Islam to Central Asia and Afghanistan
during the late seventh to eighth century brought mono-
theism and iconoclasm to the region. Within a hundred
years of its arrival the activities of artists and monks,
Buddhist and Hindu alike, had come to an end and creativity
became the exclusive domain of the new religion.

Fig. 60 **Jaiselmer, Western Rajasthan**

The Old Road through Afghanistan to India

For centuries the wealth of India flowed along a network of highways across the entire sub-continent. Many of the towns along the way and the merchants that controlled the commerce that passed through them became rich. Towns like Jaiselmer in Western Rajasthan (fig. 60) grew out of the desert like mirages. The inhabitants profited from pan-Asian trade and built grand palaces (*havelis*) for themselves from the local sandstone.

The principal trade route from India passed through Taxila, through the Khyber Pass to Bamiyan and across the Hindu Kush to Balkh. From Balkh, the highway led east along the Wakhan Corridor and through the Pamirs to China or north to Termez and onward to Central Asia.

Fig. 61 **The Khyber Pass, Pakistan**

Fig. 62 **Food aid in, scrap metal out**
The Afghanistan-Pakistan border crossing at Torkham, at the western end of the Khyber Pass and the Grand Trunk Road

Fig. 63 **Ruined villages on the road to Kabul**

Bamiyan, itself some 2,500 metres above sea level, was the approximate halfway point of an arduous journey across the country. At the eastern end of this part of the Silk Road is the Khyber Pass, rising through the foothills of the Slueman Range from its starting point, about 16 km west of Peshawar. The 45 km long pass has provided access to India since the beginnings of recorded history (fig. 61).

The pass also contains the western terminus of the Grand Trunk Road, a highway built by the British on the site of an ancient route that traversed the whole Indian sub-continent as far as Calcutta. The modern crossing point into Afghanistan is at Torkham, a bustling frontier post enlivened by characters who seem to come straight from the pages of Kipling (fig. 62).

The road from Torkham into Afghanistan passes through Jalalabad, once the site of innumerable Buddhist shrines and a place for pilgrimage (see the section on Hadda on p. 50). Today, Hadda is wrecked and travelling the old highway – its surface torn up by the tracks of Soviet tanks – is barely less arduous than it was in Xuanzang's day. One of the cruel ironies about today's Afghanistan is that though much of its cultural heritage has been destroyed, entirely new forms of archeological remains have been added within the past twenty years (fig. 63).

Kabul

Kabul has been Afghanistan's capital for little more than 200 years but has been an important Silk Road entrepôt since at least as far back as the Kushan period. The old walls and the

Fig. 64 **Abandoned tanks at Bamiyan**

turning from deep purple to brilliant pink under the rising and setting sun. Two craggy ranges crowned with ancient bastions divide the city and the Kabul River flows through a narrow pass between them to meander through the heart of the city. Travellers have written glowingly of Kabul for centuries and modern visitors continue to be captivated by its lively charm.'

(N. H. Dupree, 1977)

There were periods of intense fighting for control of Kabul between 1992 and 1996 and, at the end of it all, what remains is a travesty of the city she described (fig. 66).

Four years after the fighting ended, large sections of Kabul still lie in ruins and the monuments and grand buildings that once graced its streets are by and large no more. The National Museum, once home to some of the Silk Road's greatest treasures, stands wrecked and roofless, its

Fig. 65 **The Bala Hissar and old walls, Kabul, Afghanistan**
Ca. 5th century but rebuilt during succeeding centuries

citadel (the Bala Hissar) date back to around the fifth century and, although they are much rebuilt and repaired, they still present an impressive sight (fig. 65).

Old guidebooks about Afghanistan are now heart-rending to read. As late as 1977, Nancy Dupree wrote enthusiastically about the very features that drew early travellers to the city:

> *'The city is ringed with mountains, gleaming emerald green in spring; glistening white in winter. Even in summer barrenness they have an ever-changing beauty,*

Fig. 67 **'A ruler from whose brow shone the Light of God...'†**
The tomb of Babur (1483–1530), founder of the Mughal dynasty
The marble is badly damaged by bullets and the roof of the pavilion that covers it seems ready to collapse.

Fig. 66 **Kabul, August 2000**

* The remaining artefacts in the museum's collection are believed to have been destroyed on the instructions of the Taliban government in March 2001, along with the Buddhas of Bamiyan.
†The first words of the inscription on Babur's gravestone.

contents looted or destroyed.* Above it all, on the slopes of a hill called Sher-Darwaza, the great Mughal Emperor Babur lies in eternal repose in the gardens that he loved so much. After Babur's death in 1530 his remains were brought to Kabul from Agra in fulfilment of his instructions, and he was laid to rest in a simple tomb. The fighting did not spare the tomb or the gardens and its appearance today is a metaphor on the impermanence of kingship and power (fig. 67).

Bamiyan

To the west of Kabul is the Valley of Bamiyan, reached by two roads that run through the lower regions of the Hindu Kush, one passing through the Shibar Pass and the other via the Hajigak Pass. The Bamiyan Valley sits on an ancient branch of the Silk Road that linked India with China. It flourished as a centre for trade and religious worship until 1221, when the area was attacked by the armies of Genghis Khan. Genghis' favourite grandson Mütügen was killed during the siege of Shahr-I-Zohak ('The Red City'), a fortress protecting the eastern entrance to the valley. In revenge Genghis ordered the complete destruction of the entire valley and the extirpation of every living creature. What remained was given the name Mobaliq ('accursed city'). Shahr-I-Zohak still lies wrecked and abandoned above the valley, as does the nearby citadel of Shar -I -Gholghola ('The City of Lamentations'), named for the screams of its inhabitants at the hands of the Mongols (fig. 68).

Two immense figures of Buddha, 55 and 38 metres in height, were hewn out of the rock at Bamiyan (fig. 69).

Fig. 68 **Shar -I -Gholghola, 'The City of Lamentations'**
Despite lying in ruins for 700 years, the citadel retains a military role. Until their recent demise, the Taliban used it as an observation post.

Fig. 69 **The Buddhas of Bamiyan**
Photographed in August 2000
Destroyed by the Taliban in March 2001
Modern buildings, damaged during the recent fighting, are visible in the foreground.

Figs. 70 and 70a
The Great Buddha
Bamiyan, Afghanistan, ca. 5th
century
H. 55 metres
Photographed in August 2000
Destroyed by the Taliban in
March 2001
This immense image is probably a
depiction of Vairocana, the
cosmic Buddha. The alcove above
the head was decorated with
murals and small monastic cells,
chapels and assembly halls are
cut into the rock.
(Fig. 70a courtesy of CNN)

The colossal Buddha images at Bamiyan followed closely the Gandhara ideal and were probably carved by the pilgrims who travelled through the region and whose cave-sanctuaries can still be seen cut into the cliffs. The Buddhas were carved into the rock face of the cliff in a somewhat crude fashion and then covered, first with a layer of mud and then with a thinner layer of stucco, moulded to create garment folds. The immense Buddha images at Binglingsi, Longmen and Yungang in China may well have been inspired by the Bamiyan figures, and the monk Xuanzang's description in about 630 captures the sense of awe with which they were regarded:

> 'To the north-east of the royal city there is a mountain, on the declivity of which is placed a stone figure of Buddha, erect, in height 140 or 150 feet. Its golden hues sparkle on every side, and its precious ornaments dazzle the eyes by their brightness…. To the east of the convent there is a standing figure of Sâkya Buddha, made of metallic stone, in height 100 feet.'

(Xuanzang, in Beal 1884)

The entire Bamiyan Valley has been the scene of ferocious fighting over the past few years between the Taliban and opposition groups. The Buddhas were damaged during these years but were not finally destroyed until March 2001, when they were blown up by the Taliban rulers of Afghanistan in one of the most colossal acts of stupidity of recent history. In August 2000, when these photographs were taken, fig. 70 – the larger of the two – had not sustained major structural damage even though the upper part of the head had been blackened by the application of burning tyres. By then, the paintings that graced the caves at Bamiyan had already all but disappeared. Only the large roundels above the head of the large Buddha – neglected and flaking though they were- still remained and gave an idea of how beautiful the site must once have appeared (fig. 71).

The decorative elements and composition of these wall paintings and those that once adorned the walls of the sanctuaries are more Persian than Hellenistic. They reveal the new influences introduced to the area by the Sasanian invasions of the third century. Scholars have termed this new style of art 'Irano-Buddhist' or 'Indo-Sasanian.' It reveals

Fig. 71 **A group of murals located above the head of the Great Buddha**
Bamiyan, Afghanistan, ca. 6th century
Photographed in August 2000
Destroyed by the Taliban in March 2001

Fig. 72 **The Small Buddha**
Bamiyan, Afghanistan, ca. 3rd century AD
H. 38 metres
Photographed in August 2000
Destroyed by the Taliban in March 2001

Fig. 73 **Taliban guard at the feet of the Small Buddha, Bamiyan**

itself in the costumes and the decorative motifs of the Bamiyan paintings: apsarus (celestial nymphs) with flowing ribbons; jewelled diadems containing crescents and spheres, birds with strings of pearls in their beaks and boar's head medallions recall the Sasanian style but the faces of the figures are Indian. The paintings at Bamiyan are the antecedents of a style and technique found all over Central Asia. The pigments used at Bamiyan were mostly produced locally: ochre, sienna and lapis lazuli were the most popular although imported indigo was also widely used. Wall surfaces were treated with a layer of clay mixed with vegetable fibres that was then coated with gypsum or plaster of Paris. Paint was then applied with a binding of animal glue.

The smaller of the two Buddhas, a slightly earlier creation, stood about 400 metres to the east and even by August 2000 had fared much worse than its companion (fig. 72).

The picture is just as bleak in the Kakrak Valley, just to the east. A 6.5 metre high Buddha still stood in a niche on the hillside, even though the paintings that once graced the caves had already gone, but it is safe to presume that this image, too, is now no more.

Through the ages, descriptions of the Buddhas of Bamiyan have ranged from the adulatory to the dismissive. Most, it must be said, are in the same vein as the awe-struck words of Xuanzang, quoted on p. 61. A number of observers were, however, less than impressed by the syncretic style that the Buddhas represented and in the interests of fairness their views should be included here. The indefatigable Robert Byron saw them in the 1930s and his observations are wonderfully vituperative:

> *'Neither has any artistic value. But one could bear that; it is their negation of sense, the lack of any pride in their monstrous flaccid bulk, that sickens…. A lot of monastic navvies were given picks and told to copy some frightful semi-Hellenistic image from India or China. The result has not even the dignity of labour.'*

(Byron, 1937)

But Byron was wrong, of course, and the two old giants of Bamiyan – for the 1,500 years that they survived – ranked among the great artistic creations of the earth.

Beyond Bamiyan there is a road north to Doshi, the point at which it joins the main highway to Balkh. Balkh, the place the Arabs called 'Mother of Cities', was once one of the greatest commercial centres of the entire Silk Road (see p. 204). All roads to Bamiyan and beyond as far as Doshi are still unpaved and are disintegrating from decades of neglect. It is still possible to see caravans of camels struggling along these byways and it is difficult to believe that very much has changed since Xuanzang's day (fig. 74).

There are many trading towns, both large and small, on the main highway from Doshi to Balkh. All have attained

Fig. 74 **A camel caravan on the road to Bamiyan**

differing degrees of importance at various stages in history and many suffered destruction at the hands of the Mongols. The most important of them all is Mazar-e- Sharif, once little more than a village but now capital of Balkh province. The name of the town (meaning 'tomb of the saint') is a reference to the final resting place of Ali (ca. 600–61), son in law of the Prophet and the fourth Caliph of Islam. Ali actually died at Kufa, Iraq in 661, but his followers, fearing that his remains would be desecrated by his enemies, placed them on the back of a white camel that was allowed to wander off into the desert. The camel eventually collapsed from exhaustion and Ali's body was interred at a spot that lay undiscovered until the twelfth century, when its whereabouts were revealed to a mullah in a dream. Sanjar, the greatest of the Seljuk sultans, built a shrine on the spot, in what became the city of Mazar-e-Sharif. The shrine was destroyed by Genghis Khan but was rebuilt by the Timurids in the fifteenth century. Ali's shrine is venerated by Muslims, especially the Shi'ah who regard him as the only true successor to the Prophet. Mazar-e-Sharif is only a short distance from Balkh and, after the identification of Ali's final resting place, it gradually replaced it as the regional capital.

Kazakhstan

Lake Sayram

Jinghe

Usu

Kuytun

Shihezi

Shawan

Changji

Beiting

Zarkent

Korgas

Tachakou

Yining

Huocheng

Urumqi

Jimsar

Mori

Cilik

Turfan

Qijiaojing

Bezeklik

Flaming Mts

Liaod

Tianshan Mountains

Bayanbulak

Jiaohe

Shanshan

China

Balguntay

Toksun

Astana
and Gaochang

Toyok

Przevalsk

**NORTHERN SILK
ROAD**

Subashi

Hejing

Kizil-Qargha

Kirish-
Simsin

Iron Gate Pass

Yanqi

Lake Bosten

Kizil

Shorchuk

**APPROX. COURSE OF
ROUTE OF THE CENT**

Kumtura

Kuqa

Luntai

Korla

Tianshan Mountains

Naryn

Duldur-Aqur

Xinhe

Yuli

Aksu

Karayulgun

Yingpan

Qäwrighul

Kyrgyzstan

Tarim River

Tarim River

Kongqu River

Loulan

Yu

Bedel Pass

Tikanlik

(Ja

Torugart Pass

Lop Nor

Yan

Sanxiandong Caves

Sanchakou

Argan

Uluqqat

Sugun

Wuqi

Tumshuq

Khotan River

Luobuzhuang

Irkeshtam

Kashgar

Ruoqiang

Miran

Hanoi and Mauri Tim Stupa

Taklamakan Desert

Shule

Kara-dong

Waxxari

Yengisar

Mazartagh Fort

Keriya River

Endere

Qiemo

Tajikistan

Niya

Pamirs

Shache

Andirlangar

Tashkurgan

Yecheng

Zhagunluke
Cemetery

Sagan

Dandan-Oilik

Moyu

Rawak Stupa

Domoko

Yotkan

Khotan

Qira

Yutian

Minfeng

Malikawat

**SOUTHERN SILK
ROAD**

Shanpula
Cemetery

THE SILK ROAD
THROUGH CHINA

CHINA

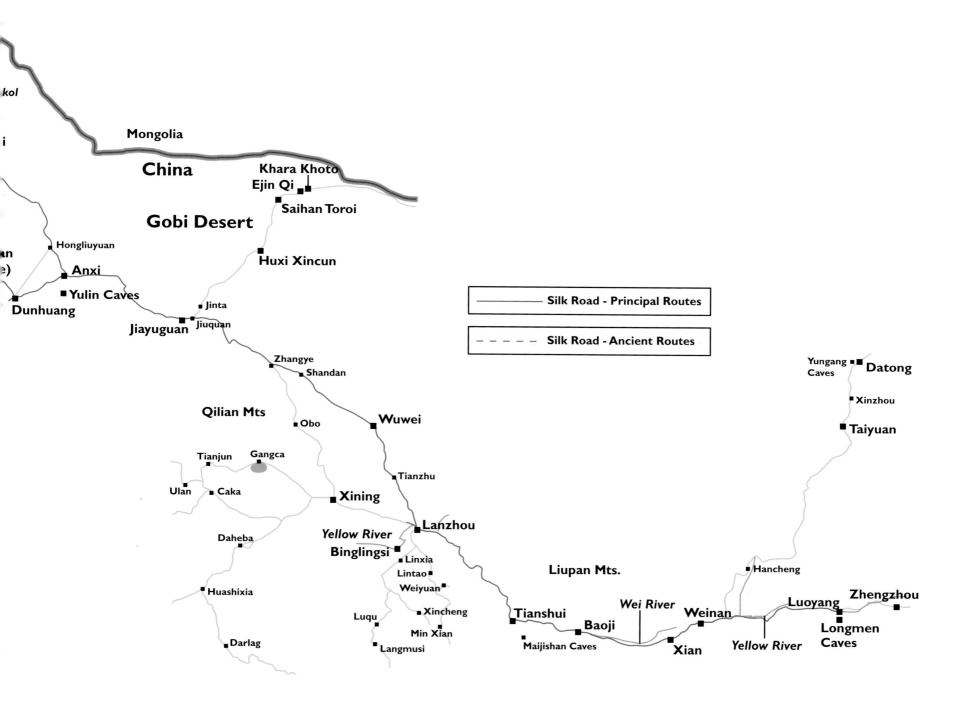

kol

i

Mongolia

China

Khara Khoto

Ejin Qi

Saihan Toroi

Gobi Desert

Hongliuyuan

Huxi Xincun

an

e)

Anxi

Yulin Caves

Dunhuang

Jinta

Jiayuguan Jiuquan

Zhangye

Shandan

Qilian Mts

Obo

Wuwei

Yungang
Caves Datong

Xinzhou

Taiyuan

Tianjun Gangca

Ulan Caka

Tianzhu

Xining

Daheba

Yellow River

Binglingsi

Linxia

Lintao

Liupan Mts.

Hancheng

Huashixia

Weiyuan

Luqu Xincheng

Min Xian

Tianshui

Wei River

Weinan

Luoyang Zhengzhou

Darlag Langmusi

Maijishan Caves

Baoji

Xian

Yellow River

Longmen
Caves

———— Silk Road - Principal Routes

– – – – – Silk Road - Ancient Routes

CHAPTER FOUR

THE INTRODUCTION OF BUDDHISM TO CHINA

'One night in a dream emperor Mingdi saw a deity flying in front of his palace which
had a golden body and emanated sunlight from the neck. The next day he asked his ministers
to explain the identity of this deity. One of them, Fu Yi, replied that he had heard of a sage in India
called 'the Buddha', who had attained salvation, who was able to fly and whose body was of a golden hue.'

(From the *Sutra in Forty-two sections*, probably late Han dynasty [1st–3rd century AD]. Quoted in Paludan, 1998)

A branch of the great Silk Road ran over the Karakorum Range to the Gandhara kingdom of the Kushans and on to India. Along this long and treacherous highway came what Kipling calls a 'river of life',* conveying exotic goods and new ideas about philosophy, literature, science, art and architecture into the Middle Kingdom. The arrival of the Buddhist faith in China is one of many instances of the passage of ideas (one of the Silk Road's most important commodities), along the ancient routes. China's first Buddhists were those of the Mahayana school (the 'Greater Vehicle'), which teaches that all beings can achieve enlightenment and enter nirvana; less emphasis is placed on the renunciation of worldly pleasures and salvation can occur instantaneously. The rival Hinayana school (the 'Lesser Vehicle') is based on the original teachings of the Buddha himself and teaches that man can achieve enlightenment and escape worldly misery only by a long series of births and rebirths and by leading a life of monastic self-denial.

During its early existence, Chinese Buddhism allied itself

Fig. 75 **The White Horse Temple in Luoyang**
Henan province
Ming dynasty (1368–1644) but thought to be built on the site of the original temple

* Kipling's description is of another of Asia's great highways – India's Grand Trunk Road, built by the East India Company and running northwestwards from Calcutta across the entire country as far as the Khyber Pass. The road follows the course of ancient trade routes across the country. The presence of columns, erected by the Mauryan Emperor Ashoka during the 3rd century BC, suggests that the road has been a major route since the earliest times (for more on Ashoka please see p. 201).

with the Daoists. Daoism is believed to have been developed by Laozi during the sixth century BC and is concerned with an individual's relationship to nature and the spirit world. Until the third century AD, Buddhism was little more than a minor sect, regarded by most Chinese as a variety of Daoism. Its early followers were foreigners: merchants from Central Asia and India, hostages of the Chinese and envoys from neighbouring states.

The dream of the Han dynasty Emperor Mingdi (r. 57–75 AD) was a pivotal event in the history of the Silk Road. Mingdi is said to have sent envoys to India to discover more about the teachings of the Buddha. They returned with a group of Indian monks, a number of sacred texts (sutras) and several statues carried, according to legend, on the back of a white horse. These objects were placed in the appositely named White Horse Temple at Luoyang, founded by a Parthian missionary named An Shigao in 148 AD (some sources say 67 AD), and regarded as the earliest Buddhist establishment in China (fig. 75).

After the downfall of the Han dynasty in 220 AD Buddhism spread more rapidly through China. An important figure in the early dissemination of Buddhism was the monk Dao An (ca. 312–85). He worked first in Xianyang and then at the capital, Changan. Dao An attempted to understand Buddhist ideas on their own terms rather than simply equating them to Chinese beliefs and produced an immense catalogue of all Buddhist texts known to exist at the time.

It was not until the Northern Wei dynasty (386–534) that Buddhism was adopted as the state religion, however, and even then it was mainly for reasons of political expediency. The Wei were nomadic peoples of the Toba tribe and preferred the imported ideas of a foreign 'barbarian' god to the Chinese philosophies of Confucianism and Daosim which they neither trusted nor full understood. They may also have felt that a populace devoted to the ideals of peace and humility would be easier to govern. One of the Toba rulers is recorded as saying: 'we were born out of the marches…Buddha being a barbarian god is the one we should worship.' The Northern Wei also encouraged the acquisition and translation of Buddhist texts from India. They brought the celebrated monk Kumarajiva (343–413) to the capital at Datong in Shanxi province. Kumarajiva- son of an Indian father and a princess from Kuqa- translated some 300 Mahayana Buddhist texts from Sanskrit into Chinese and expounded the doctrines of the new faith. Many of the monks who made the hazardous journey to India are unknown to history but two – Fa Xian (337–422) and Xuanzang (600–664) – have left records of their travels.

Fa Xian and Xuanzang

The first of the many Chinese pilgrims to journey to India and return safely to China was Fa Xian (337–422). In 399

Fig. 76 **Rubbing from a 20th-century relief depiction of Xuanzang** Xingjiaosi Temple, Shaanxi province (Xuanzang's burial place)

Fa Xian embarked on a fifteen-year journey, travelling outward through Khotan and across the Himalayas to India. He travelled to at least thirty kingdoms, studying Buddhism under the great Indian teachers of the day at Benares, at the Gandhara capital of Taxila and in Ceylon. He remained in Ceylon for two years before attempting a return to China by sea. During the journey he was shipwrecked on the island of Java and was forced to continue his journey aboard a different vessel. When he returned to China in 414 he devoted himself to translating into Chinese the Buddhist sutras that he had acquired during his journey. The account of his travels, 'A Record of Buddhistic Kingdoms' is an

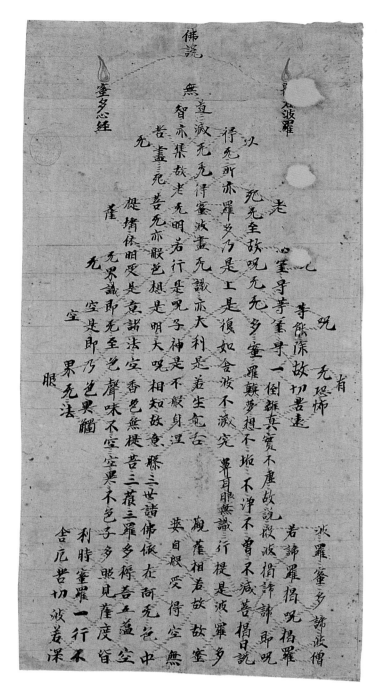

along the Northern Silk Road to Turfan and Kuqa; then across the Tianshan Mountains to Tashkent, Samarkand and Bactria; over the Hindu Kush to the Gandhara kingdom; on a vast circuit of India and finally back to China through the Pamirs and along the Southern Silk Road.

On his return to China, the clandestine nature of his departure was forgotten and both the emperor and the population of Changan fêted him. The Great Goose Pagoda in Xian was built to house the 657 Mahayana and Hinayana texts and the relics that he brought back, and he continued to work for the remainder of his life, translating some 1300 volumes of sutras into Chinese. Seven Buddha images that he carried with him were among the relics and may have provided the inspiration for the Chinese Buddhist sculpture of the age.

The record of his journey, 'Buddhist Records of the Western World (*Si-yu ki*) is, like Fa Xian's volume, an immensely important source of information about the countries of the Silk Road. His exploits were also the inspiration for the renowned sixteenth-century allegorical novel, 'Journey to the West'. There are some surprising, tangible traces of Xuanzang's life still to be found and these simply add further to the colossal reputation of one of history's most remarkable figures (fig. 78).

Fig. 78 **Stone pedestal of the Buddha, inscribed with the name Xuanzang**
Tang dynasty, (618–907)
H. 36 cm
Unearthed in the ruins of the Yuhua Palace, Tongchuan, Shaanxi province in 1977
(National Museum of Chinese History, Beijing)
There is an inscription of twenty characters on the base, which states that Xuanzang, Master of Tripitaka, made the statue of Buddha Sakyamuni in 662. The Yuhua Palace was consecrated as a temple in 651 and Xuanzang resided there from 659 onwards, devoting himself to translating sutras.

Fig. 77 **Scroll containing a copy of the 'Heart of the Perfection of Wisdom Sutra' or 'Heart Sutra', translated by Xuanzang**
9th century
L. 42 cm, W. 22 cm
Found at Dunhuang, Gansu province
(British Library)
Written in the shape of a stupa, Xuanzang's eloquent Sanskrit-Chinese translation opens the mind to enlightenment with the following mantra:
'Gone, gone, gone beyond, gone altogether beyond. Oh, what an Awakening! All hail!'

invaluable source of information about the geography and customs of some of the ancient kingdoms of the Silk Road and is referred to on many occasions in this book. His contribution to the growth of Buddhism in China can also not be overstated.

The celebrated Chinese monk Xuanzang, perhaps the most accomplished of all of the Silk Road's many travellers, set out in 629 from the Tang dynasty capital of Xian. His departure was contrary to the precise instructions of Emperor Taizong (r. 626–49) and his intention, like that of Fa Xian before him, was to obtain Buddhist sutras from India. A number of modern historians have retraced his journey, involving more than 15,000 km and sixteen years of the most arduous travel imaginable. His journey took him

The Northern Wei as patrons of Buddhism

Under Northern Wei patronage many of the greatest Buddhist monuments were constructed – at Yungang and Longmen for example – where immense sculptures of the Buddha and his followers both glorified the new religion and legitimized the rule of the new dynasty.

Yungang Caves

The Yungang ('Cloud Ridge') caves are about 16 km from the first Northern Wei capital of Datong, Shanxi province. They were, for the most part, built between 460 and 494 when the Wei capital moved to Luoyang. There are fifty-three caves, extending about one kilometre along the Wuzhoushan cliffs and containing more than 50,000 Buddhist images. These images represent the middle period of Northern Wei

art when influences from the art of Gandhara and Chinese Central Asia were particularly strong. We know from the accounts of travellers that the immense rock-cut Buddhas of Bamiyan in Afghanistan had an enormous impact on the people who encountered them for the first time (see p. 61). It is therefore easy to understand why they came to serve as models for the early cave-temples constructed in China. These influences are most evident at Yungang in the earlier caves. Five immense Buddhas – including one at Cave 20 which is about 14 metres in height – recall not only the great Buddhas of Bamiyan but also sculpture from the classical world (fig. 79).

The Gandhara style is also apparent in bronze images from the period. A large standing figure of Maitreya (the Buddha of the Future) in the Metropolitan Museum, New York, could easily be mistaken for one of its counterparts in Afghanistan (fig. 80).

The later caves at Yungang, built just before the removal of the capital to Luoyang, are a riot of detail and fuse

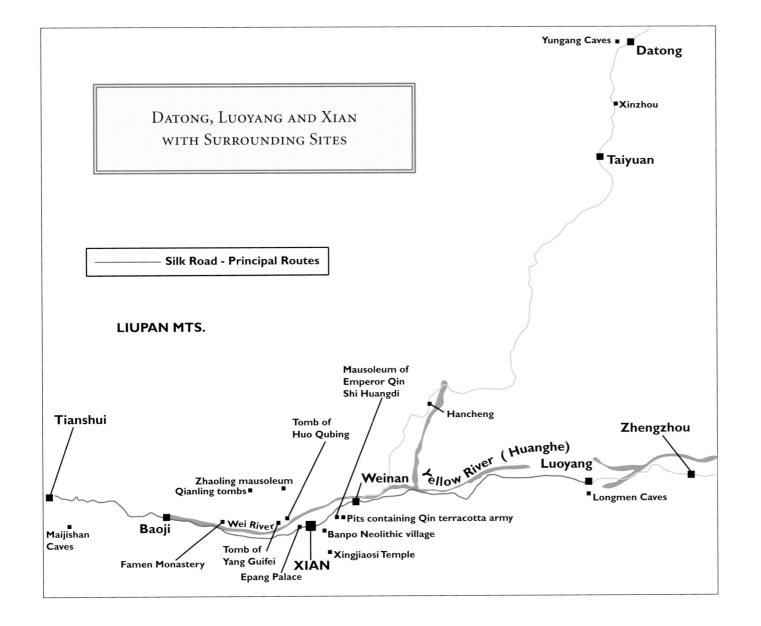

DATONG, LUOYANG AND XIAN
WITH SURROUNDING SITES

Silk Road - Principal Routes

LIUPAN MTS.

Yungang Caves ■ ■ **Datong**

■ **Xinzhou**

■ **Taiyuan**

Mausoleum of
Emperor Qin
Shi Huangdi

Hancheng

Tianshui

Tomb of
Huo Qubing

Zhengzhou

Zhaoling mausoleum
Qianling tombs ■

Yellow River (Huanghe)

Weinan

Luoyang

■ **Longmen Caves**

■ **Wei River**

■ ■ Pits containing Qin terracotta army

Baoji

Banpo Neolithic village

Maijishan
Caves

Tomb of
Yang Guifei

XIAN

Xingjiaosi Temple

Famen Monastery

Epang Palace

Fig. 79 **Rock-cut image of a seated Buddha**
Northern Wei dynasty, erected ca. 460–65
H. 14 metres
Cave 20, Yungang, Shanxi
This colossal image sits with his hands held in the pose of meditation, know as *dhyanamudra*. His thin clinging robe with its sharp creases, the raised cranial protuberance (usnisha) and the overall naturalism of the sculpture recall images from Gandhara. The face has a rather childlike quality, a characteristic trait of Northern Wei sculpture. The ceiling and the front wall of this cave have collapsed, exposing the figures to the outside air.

Fig. 80 **Gilded bronze standing figure of Maitreya, Buddha of the Future**
China, Northern Wei, dated 477
H. 140 cm
(Metropolitan Museum of Art, New York)

elements from the Hellenistic world (such as acanthus leaves and arabesques), with Persian lions, Gandhara draperies, Indian gods (including Siva and Vishnu) and Chinese dragons to create a more indigenous style. At Cave 6 we encounter the fully developed Yungang style at its most superb (fig. 81). The walls are arranged in a series of horizontal tiers with seated or standing images of the Buddha, surrounded by heavenly beings, musicians and flying apsaras. The lower sections contain reliefs depicting episodes from the Buddha's prior lives (known as *jatakas*).

After the relocation of the Wei capital in 494, a number of smaller caves were executed. Figures from this period are more slender and sit in a more relaxed posture reminiscent of Persian sculpture of the Sasanian period. A crowned Bodhisattva in the Metropolitan Museum, New York, recalls the Gandhara murals of Bamiyan and later at Fondukistan (fig. 57), themselves the recipient of motifs from Iran, but the style is essentially Chinese. According to Laurence Sickman, the singular facial expressions of Northern Wei

sculpture are characterized by a 'lingering archaic half-smile' (fig. 82).

During the coming pages we will examine the major sites along the Silk Road as we head west towards the Gandhara region. This was the route along which Buddhism came to China and the artistic styles that we encounter at these places reveal the manner in which Chinese art came to develop its own, unique identity. In 486, the Northern Wei emperor declared that Chinese dress would be worn at court and this had a profound effect on artistic styles. More slender forms with sweeping robes and a greater sense of movement and spirituality replace the heavy stiffness of the Yungang images. Robes that cascade downward to cover the throne characterize seated figures of the period, and standing images are graceful and delicate. When the Northern Wei moved their capital to Luoyang, Henan province, they occupied a city already tied inextricably to the history of the Silk Road from its days as the capital of the Eastern Han dynasty. At the Longmen caves, near Luoyang, we encounter the apogee of the more refined and delicate Wei style.

Fig. 81 **Interior of Cave 6**
Northern Wei dynasty,
late 5th century
Yungang, Shanxi province

Fig. 82 **Stone image of a crowned Bodhisattva.**
Northern Wei dynasty, early 6th century
H.146 cm
From Yungang, Shanxi
(Metropolitan Museum of Art, New York)

Longmen Caves

The Longmen ('Dragon Gate') caves are situated about 13 km south of Luoyang and were constructed by the Northern Wei between 493 and about 535, and by other dynasties at various periods thereafter until around 900. There are more than 2,300 caves and niches at Longmen, containing some 100,000 images of the Buddha and his attendants. The Wei sculptures of the early sixth century and the Tang dynasty creations of the late seventh century represent the main periods of creativity. During this 200-year period twelve principal caves and many smaller ones were constructed. The carvings from the Binyang cave were begun in 505 and include an immense central figure of Amitabha Buddha flanked by his two disciples, Ananda and Kasyapa (fig. 83). Their appearance owes much to the art of Gupta India, probably because of the infusion of ideas from monks journeying to and from the subcontinent.

A Northern Wei relief, also from the Binyang Cave at Longmen, is now in the Nelson-Atkins Gallery, Kansas City (fig. 84). It depicts a procession of imperial donors and demonstrates that the sinification process at the Wei court was well underway by the beginning of the sixth century.

The second high point at Longmen, the latter part of the

Fig. 83 **Amitabha Buddha with his disciples, Ananda and Kasyapa**
Northern Wei dynasty
Built between ca. 505–ca. 523
Cave 140, Middle Binyang Cave, Longmen, Henan province
Amitabha is the Buddha who presides over the Western Paradise. The young Ananda (a childhood friend), and the elder Kasyapa (a former Hindu teacher converted to Buddhism), were his most favoured disciples.

Fig. 84 **Painted grey limestone frieze depicting the empress with attendants, making offerings at a shrine**
Northern Wei dynasty, first quarter of the 6th century
H. 1.93 metres, W. 2.77 metres
From the Binyang cave, Longmen, Henan province
(Nelson-Atkins Museum, Kansas City)
At the Gongxian caves, Henan – northeast of Longmen and of the same period – similar friezes still exist *in situ*.

Fig. 85 **Vairocana Buddha with a Bodhisattva and a disciple**
Tang dynasty, ca. 672–75
H. (Buddha, including pedestal) 17.14 metres
Fengxian temple, Longmen, Henan province

seventh century, is revealed at Longmen's largest structure – the Fengxian temple. The vast sculptures at Fengxian were commissioned by the Tang Emperor Gaozong (r. 649–83) in about 672 and completed around 675. The work was financed by Gaozong's ambitious consort, Wu Zetian, who declared herself ruler of China in 690 and dominated the country for the next fifteen years. An immense statue of Vairocana, the most important of the five cosmic Buddhas, is believed to resemble Wu Zetian herself (fig. 85).

A Bodhisattva and two guardian figures from the Fengxian temple are stupendous manifestations of Tang dynasty art (fig. 86). They illustrate the transition from the linear, heavily robed images of the Northern Wei to the dynamic, fleshy sculptures of the Tang, further evidence of the influence of Gupta India.

Fig. 86 **A Bodhisattva and two guardian figures**
Tang dynasty, ca. 672–75
H. (Bodhisattva on left) 11.54 metres
Fengxian temple, Longmen, Henan province
These three sculptures are to the right of the central cosmic Buddha (fig. 85 above). The left hand figure is a Bodhisattva, the middle one a *lokapala* (a 'heavenly king' who protects one of the four corners of space: in this case Vaisravana, Guardian of the North) and the right-hand figure is a *dvarapala*, heroic guardian of the Buddhist faith. The *lokapala* holds a model stupa (a Buddhist reliquary) in his right hand, his left placed upon his waist in a gesture of triumph and his right foot on the head of a dwarf – representing the powers of evil and ignorance.

CHAPTER FIVE

LUOYANG

Luoyang in Henan province has been a capital of China at various times since the Western Zhou dynasty (1050–771 BC) when it was known as Chengzhou. During the Western Han dynasty (206 BC–9 AD) a new city was established on the Zhou site but with the capital situated at Changan. The Nangong (South Palace) and the Beigong (North Palace) were the most important of the city's buildings during the Western Han dynasty. China's capital was moved to Luoyang in 25 AD, by the first Eastern Han Emperor Guang Wudi (r. 25–57 AD). The reason for the move was that Changan had been destroyed during the bitter two-year civil war that followed the death of the usurper Wang Mang (r. 9–23 AD). Guang Wudi embarked on an ambitious project to construct a new city wall of about 13 km in length. Records from the time reveal that the wall contained twelve city gates, the most important being the Pinchchengmen gate, which faced south and provided access to the South Palace. The North Palace was enlarged by Guang Wudi's successor Mingdi (r. 57–75 AD), whose dream may have led to the introduction of Buddhism to China. Its extent was such that it could accommodate 10,000 people and, it is claimed, could be seen from a distance of 18 km.

The city's commercial activities were centred upon three markets: the Gold Market (Jinshi) within the city walls and the South Market and Horse Market (Nanshi and Mashi), situated outside of the city walls. Within these three markets were said to be 120 different bazaars, each peddling a different type of merchandise, as well as innumerable shops and godowns. There were three Zoroastrian temples in the city, serving the growing number of Persians who had come to reside and conduct business there. A poem, written during the Han dynasty, provides a glimpse of the splendours of Luoyang:

> 'In Lo Town how fine everything is!
> The 'Caps and Belts' go seeking each other out.
> The great boulevards are intersected by lanes,
> Wherein are the town houses of Royal Dukes.
> The two palaces stare at each other from afar,
> The twin gates rise a hundred feet.'

(Translated by Arthur Waley. Quoted in Loewe, 1968.
'Caps and Belts' are high-ranking officials)

Luoyang prospered until the reign of the last Han emperor, Xiandi (r. 189–220 AD). Peasant uprisings in China increased, in protest against the tax burden on smallholders and there was a simultaneous growth in the power of the great landowning families that led to an undermining of government authority. In 190, the rebel Tung Cho of the 'Yellow Turban' sect forced the emperor to abandon Luoyang and seek refuge in Changan. The city was then destroyed in a fire which lasted for more than three days and which reduced palaces, temples and the renowned imperial library to ashes. The poet Ts'ao Chih (Cao Zhi) saw the stricken city about twenty years later and has left an account of what remained:

> 'How desolate is Loyang,
> Its palaces burned down,
> The walls fallen in ruins,
> As brambles climb to the sky…
> There are no paths to walk,
> Unworked fields have to run to waste…
> Lonely is the countryside,
> A thousand li without one smoking hearth.'

(Written in about 211 AD by the poet Ts'ao Chih [Cao Zhi, 192–232]
Quoted in Jenner, 1981)

The Han dynasty finally ended in 220 AD and China slid relentlessly into an abyss. A period of almost 400 years of disunity and suffering followed. Luoyang was rebuilt as the capital under the succeeding Wei dynasty of the Three Kingdoms Period (220–65 AD) on the site of the Han capital, but was destroyed yet again in 311 at the hands of the now heavily sinicized Xiongnu nomads of North China. The period from 304 to 439, known as the Sixteen Kingdoms, consisted of a succession of northern tribal chieftains fighting for dominance. It was not until the late fourth century that the Toba Wei (or Xianbei) managed to unify northern China and establish the Northern Wei dynasty.

When the Northern Wei established their capital at Luoyang in 494, the city finally regained its former glory. The old custom of having two palaces – northern and southern – was abolished and a vast new structure was built on the site of the old Eastern Han North Palace. The building was so

Fig. 87 **Three relief panels from a marble mortuary bed**
China, Northern Qi (550–77) or Northern Zhou (557–81) dynasty
Dimensions: a) H. 60.3 cm, W. 41.6 cm; b) H. 61 cm, W. 54 cm, c) H. 61.5 cm, W. 34.6 cm
(Shumei Culture Foundation, Otsu, Shiga, Japan)

These three carved and painted panels are from a set of eleven, probably parts of a mortuary bed for one of the Turkic nomads who ruled Northern China at this time. A similar bed was found close to Luoyang and is now in the city's museum. Most of the figures depicted are non-Chinese and are shown engaged in various activities. Panel A shows a funeral scene in which a Zoroastrian priest stands before a fire-altar as grieving mourners slash their faces with knives (a custom of the Turkic peoples). In panel B is the four-armed goddess Nana, a deity of the Sogdians of the Samarkand area. Beneath her are musicians from Kuqa, a place famous for its music that gave rise to Japanese Gigaku dance (see section on Kuqa). Panel C comprises a banqueting scene in which further musicians from Kuqa entertain a noble of Sogdian appearance and his Chinese companion.

large that it occupied about one-tenth of the entire city. In the northern part of the metropolis were imperial buildings and parks and, in the southern section, were government offices, temples and the homes of the nobility. The Northern Wei began a concerted program to adopt Chinese customs and dress, progressively relinquishing their nomadic origins. Many of the influential Toba families resisted this process of sinification and attempted to preserve their nomadic way of life, leading to tensions at court. Luoyang's new lease of life under the Northern Wei was extremely brief – the city's great buildings were not completed until 502, in 523 the Wei's northern armies began to rebel and in 529 they attacked the city. By 534 the city had been abandoned once again but, during a brief twenty-year hiatus from 502 until 523, Luoyang flourished as a Silk Road entrepôt and many of its inhabitants became immeasurably rich. Prince Shen of Ho-chien was the richest of them all, it seems. Yang Hsuan-chih's *Record of the Monasteries of Luoyang*, written in 547–50, is the main source of information about this period (see Jenner, 1981). Yang describes how Prince Shen owned 300 dancing girls, a dozen or so Persian horses and a concubine who played the flute so beautifully that she was able to quell rebellions. Prince Shen once laid on a banquet at which guests were served delicacies in vessels of gold, silver, crystal, agate and red jade: 'all exquisitely made in ways not known in the central lands as they all came from the West'. His warehouses, Yang tells us, were 'full of brocade, felt goods, pearls, ice gauze, and mist silk; the quantities of embroidery, coloured silk, and all kinds of silk textile, patterned or plain, as well as money were incalculable'.

The expatriate population of Luoyang lived in the southern suburbs, across the Lo River and there were said to be 10,000 families of foreigners in the city at the beginning of the sixth century:

'From the Ts'ung-ling [Pamir] mountains westwards to Da Qin [Rome] 100 countries and 1,000 cities all gladly attached themselves to us; foreign traders and merchants came hurrying in through the passes every day. This could indeed be called exhausting all the regions of heaven and earth'.

(From *Record of the Monasteries of Luoyang*, by Yang Hsuan-chih, written in 547–50 and quoted in Jenner, 1981)

Foreign merchants congregated at the 'Four Directions Market' – popularly known as the 'Eternal Bridge Market' – south of the Lo River but the main market was located in the western part of the city. The western suburb was home to Luoyang's nobility and to the town's merchants and for this reason the Great Luoyang Market developed here. Yang Hsuan-chih has left a rare portrait of an individual merchant, the commodities trader Liu Bao who was the richest commoner in Luoyang:

'...he traded wherever boat or cart could go or foot could tread. Thus the goods from the whole area within the seas were assembled in his establishments. His property was comparable to a copper-bearing mountain, his wealth to a cave of gold. The scale on which his house was built exceeded the proper limits, and its pavilions and towers

soared up through the clouds. His carriages, horses,
clothes, and ornaments were like those of a prince.'

(ibid.)

The area west of the Great Market was occupied by brewers, men whose grog was so potent that those who consumed it were said to remain inebriated for a month. The best known of Luoyang's brewers was Liu Pai-to. His wine was exported far and wide and once led to the capture of a gang of brigands, rendered powerless to resist the forces of law and order after imbibing quantities of it. The wags of the day composed a ditty to commemorate the event:

'No need to fear the sword or bow
But Pai-to's hooch will lay you low.'

(ibid.)

In the winter of 534 the entire population of Luoyang – as many as two million people – was ordered to move to the new capital of Yeh. In 535 the Northern Wei disintegrated into two rival states, the Eastern and Western Wei, and the two factions fought over the discarded bones of the city. By 538 the palaces and monasteries of Luoyang lay in ruins and only about 15,000 of the city's original population remained. The schism did not prevent the continuing decline of nomadic practices among the Wei and the Toba were eventually absorbed into the general Chinese population, eventually disappearing as a race.

It is not surprising that trade along the Silk Road tended to decline during periods of civil war and political division. It did not cease, however, and China remained cosmopolitan and culturally vibrant. The works of art that have survived from the mid-sixth century, when North China was a battlefield fought over by nomad generals, are small in number but attest to this fact (fig. 87).

By 589, Yang Jian – a man of mixed Chinese and nomad blood who became the first emperor of the Sui dynasty – had forcibly reunified all of China. Ruling as the Emperor Wendi (r. 581–604), he disarmed the private armies of the preceding Period of Disunity, undertook vast public works at his capital of Changan, repaired the Great Wall and became a fervent sponsor of the Buddhist faith. The Sui dynastic annals record that during Wendi's reign there were 230,000 monks, 3,792 temples and shrines and 106,580 new images erected. A determined campaign to redistribute land to the peasants increased the flow of revenue and ushered in a period of great economic prosperity in China. Wendi died in 604, probably murdered by his son Yangdi (r. 604–17). Yangdi embarked on an extravagant scheme to rebuild Luoyang as China's second city. With a display of the profligacy that would eventually lead to his downfall, some two million laborers were employed to construct a vast pleasure park of some 155 square km. When Yangdi visited

the park during the winter months, silk flowers and leaves were attached to the bare branches. His tours, one to the area south of the Yangtze and another to the Western Regions, were acts of magnificent lunacy still marvelled at by the Chinese. During the first, he ordered the construction of canals to link the Yellow River, the Huai and the Yangtze, a vast network approximately 2,000 km long. This network eventually became known as the Grand Canal and extended from Hangzhou in the southeast to Luoyang in the west. A branch also led northwards, almost as far as Beijing. Yangdi sailed southwards from Luoyang to Jiangdu (modern-day Yangzhou) in a four-storey dragon boat accompanied by an entourage of between 100,000 and 200,000 people. Several thousand more vessels followed in his wake, propelled by 80,000 boatmen pulling on ropes of green silk, and the inhabitants living along the canal for a distance of about 250 km were instructed to make piles of expensive delicacies for the party to consume. The historian Witold Rodzinski described them as 'a swarm of imperial locusts'.

During Yangdi's second tour in 609, he travelled to Longxi in Gansu, west to Qinghai and north as far as Zhangye Prefecture in the Hexi Corridor. Yangdi's journey followed the precise route of the Silk Road and, at the time of his visit, Zhangye had already become an important entrepôt for merchants from the Western Lands (see p. 118). At Zhangye Yangdi held an audience for the kings and emissaries of the Western Regions, intended as display of imperial Chinese power. Many of the rulers accompanied him back to Luoyang where a vast reception was arranged outside of the Duanmen Gate. Performers from all over the Western Regions entertained the visitors and the city's merchants were ordered to provide them with as much free food and wine as they could consume.

The excesses of Yangdi's rule weakened China's economy. The situation was made worse by three disastrous attempts to subjugate the Koguryo kingdom of Korea in which as many as 300,000 Chinese soldiers lost their lives. Major flooding of the Yellow River, famine and uprisings among the peasants soon followed and the northern general Li Yuan who, like the Sui emperor Wendi was of mixed Chinese and nomadic origins, seized the opportunity to bid for power. He captured Changan in 617 followed, a year later, by Luoyang. Yangdi sought refuge in Yangzhou where he was eventually strangled with a silken cord and Li Yuan proclaimed himself first emperor of the Tang dynasty. With its capital at Changan, China entered its Golden Age and the Silk Road achieved its apogee.

CHAPTER SIX

CHANGAN (XIAN)

A brief history of the city

Xian is situated in the southern part of Shaanxi province and its temperate climate, abundance of rainfall and soft loess soil have attracted settlements since the Paleolithic age. A fossilized skull unearthed in Dali County to the northeast of Xian has been dated to about 200,000 years ago. Neolithic sites have been discovered all around Xian, most notably at Banpo in the city's eastern suburbs. Banpo, described by archeologists as a Yangshao Culture site, was occupied from about 4500 to about 3750 BC. Banpo's culture was highly sophisticated, producing pottery of red clay decorated in black paint with designs of fish, animals, human faces and geometric patterns. The inhabitants produced stone tools for farming, fishing and hunting, and built grass-roofed roundhouses for their families. Their burial practices, in which husbands and wives were interred separately, indicates that a highly developed society already existed in China even at this early date, and the mysterious symbols and signs engraved on their pottery society suggests that they possessed a primitive form of writing.

The Xian area has been a pivot of Chinese civilisation for much of the past 3,500 years, beginning with the Zhou State during the second millennium BC. The homeland of the Zhou peoples was along the Jinghe River valley in the western part of central Shaanxi province. They lived under constant threat of attack from northern nomads – the Xunyun (later known as the Xiongnu, see p. 24). They were also threatened by the Shang peoples to the east and by other nomadic groups. The Zhou eventually migrated to a more secure area just west of Xian, settling at Zhouyuan between Qishan and Fufeng counties. The city was protected by Mount Qi to the north and the Wei River to the south and remained as the Zhou capital until the final defeat of the Shang in about 1050 BC. A new capital, divided between the twin cities of Feng and Hao to the southwest of modern Xian, was then established by King Wen and King Wu of the Zhou, remaining there for the next 300 years while Zhouyuan was a fortress town and a centre for the performance of dynastic rites. Evidence of the latter function is provided by the large numbers of bronze vessels and inscribed oracle bones discovered there.

Excavations near the village of Zhangjiapo, on the west bank of the Feng River, have revealed what is believed to be the site of the two later capitals of Feng and Hao. These were large well-planned cities with palaces and workshops, underground pipes for water supply and sewage and an agrarian economy supplemented by hunting, fishing and animal husbandry. Slavery was widespread with some unfortunate slaves being compelled to enter the afterlife with their masters: the grave of one Zhou nobleman, excavated at Zhangjiapo, contained two carriages, six horses and a driver!

The Western Zhou fell in about 770 BC after attacks from the north by the Quanrong nomads of northwest China. The capital was destroyed and the Zhou abandoned the Xian area and moved their capital to Luoyang.

The Qin People and the formation of a unified China

The Qin people originated to the West, in the Tianshui area of Gansu province. During the Eastern Zhou period, between 770 and 221 BC, they gradually migrated eastwards, moving their capitals as they went. Xianyang (sometimes spelt Xiangyang), 15km northwest of modern Xian, was selected as the Qin capital in about 350 BC, probably on the council of the influential chief minister of Qin, Shang Yang (d. 338 BC). From their base at Xianyang the Qin systematically defeated the six other rivals of the Warring States Period. By 221 BC, they had unified the country and established the Qin dynasty with its capital at Xianyang. Xianyang was relatively small but was part of a network of palace sites in the area. The early annals record that, by the reign of King Zhuang Xiang (r. ca. 250–47 BC), the network of buildings and roads extended for about 25 km across the city. Each time a rival state was defeated, it is reported that a new palace was built in the style of that territory. More than 120,000 of the country's most powerful families were forcibly relocated to Xianyang and it became an extremely cosmopolitan city. With the establishment of Xianyang as

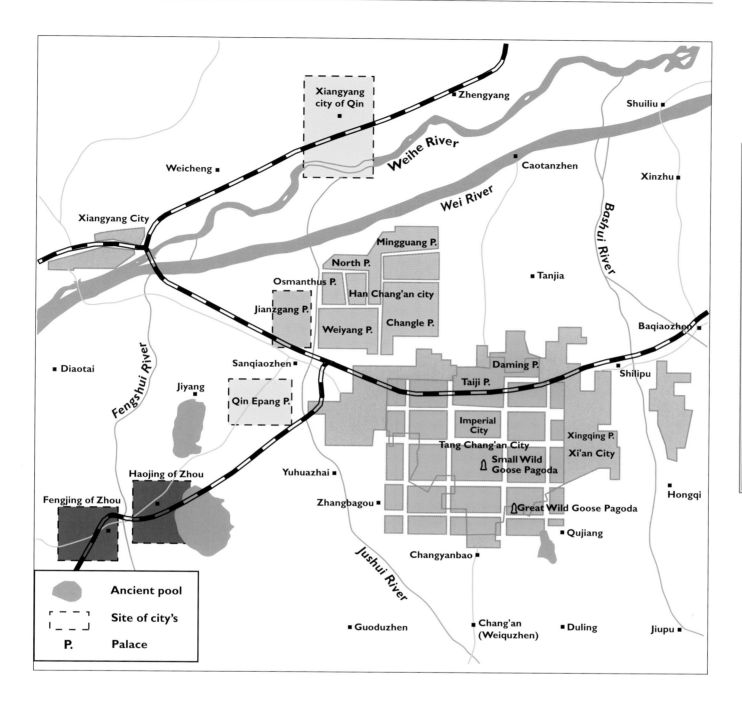

MAP SHOWING
SITES AROUND
XIAN THAT HAVE
SERVED AS
DYNASTIC
CAPITALS IN
CHINESE
HISTORY

(Adapted from 'Xian- Legacies of
an Ancient Chinese Civilization',
1992).

NOTE: The city's ancient
and modern names-
Changan and Xian- will
be used interchangeably
throughout this section.

the dynastic capital in 221 BC, a programme of expansion was undertaken which involved the movement of the city's centre to the south of the Wei River. The Epang Palace, the construction of which started in about 212 BC with a building force of 720,000, was colossal. The dais could accommodate 10,000 people and the entire palace complex – with lesser buildings, parks and gardens – covered an area some 150 km in circumference. Before the front hall of Epang stood twelve colossal statues, each weighing about 120 tons and made from the confiscated and melted-down weapons of the Qin's former enemies. The Epang Palace was destroyed by fire in 206 BC but now rises again in the western suburbs of Xian, recently rebuilt by the Chinese government.

The rule of the Yellow Emperor, Qin Shi Huangdi

(r. 221–10 BC) was autocratic and relatively short but he consolidated Qin control of the country by the introduction of far-reaching reforms that still effect life in China today. Standardization of Chinese scripts, units of measure, dress, calendars, coinage and even the axle-lengths of carts was carried out. The road network was extended by about 7,500 km to the furthest reaches of the Qin Empire, existing sections of rammed earth wall along China's frontier were consolidated and new sections built. The wall was eventually unified as China's first Great Wall, extending some 5,000 km from the Zhili Gulf to the borders of Tibet. A series of forts and watchtowers along the route countered the threat from northern nomads. An army of 300,000 men, led by the Qin general Meng Tian, entered the land of the Xiongnu nomads in Gansu province and secured the area for large numbers of

Fig. 88 **'The Yellow Emperor'**
Qin Shi Huangdi
(r. 221–210 BC)
Modern etching

Fig. 88 **'The Yellow Emperor'**
Qin Shi Huangdi
(r. 221–210 BC)
Modern etching

Fig. 89 **Qin Shi Huangdi's**
tomb
Completed 210 BC
Xian, Shaanxi province

Han Chinese who were forcibly resettled there. By means of large-scale deportations to the remote reaches of the empire, the Qin were able to extend their territory. Even China's name comes from the Chinese pronunciation of *Qin*. Qin Shi Huangdi's achievements were many but they were made at great cost to his people. One of his contemporaries, before fleeing the imperial court, described him as follows: 'The King of Qin is like a bird of prey....There is no beneficence in him, and he has the heart of a tiger or a wolf. When he is in difficulties, he finds it easy to devour human beings....If he realizes his ambitions concerning the empire, all men will be his slaves.' (Wei Liao, adviser to Qin Shi Huangdi).

Qin Shi Huangdi and immortality

'Here at the quiet limit of the world,
A white-haired shadow roaming like a dream
The ever-silent spaces of the East.'

(Alfred, Lord Tennyson (1809–92), 'Tithonus')

Qin Shi Huangdi's love of ceremony and extravagant display is apparent in the vast scale of each of his undertakings. Nowhere is this more apparent than at the site of his own mausoleum, begun soon after he became ruler of Qin in 246 BC (fig. 89). The tomb is one of the largest construction projects ever undertaken by mankind and was the result of Qin Shi Huangdi's desire for immortality. In Sima Qian's 'Records of the Grand Historian', written about one hundred years later, he describes how Qin Shi Huangdi sends the envoy Xu Fu and 3,000 young men and virgins to the Isles of the Immortals, at Penglai in the Eastern Sea. Three spirit mountains, reputed to exist in the Gulf of Bohai (or Chihli), were populated by immortals who possessed the elixir of eternal life. Daoist alchemists are recorded as having prescribed various immortality potions, some containing lethal poisons.

As King of Qin and then as emperor of China, Qin Shi Huangdi ruled for a total of thirty-seven years. The construction of his mausoleum took thirty-six of those years and the entire mausoleum area covers around 56 square km. The actual tomb consists of a tumulus some 50 metres high and 1.5 km in circumference. The tomb has never been excavated because of the scale of archeological work that would be required but descriptions of the construction and contents, by the Han dynasty historian Sima Qian, give some idea of what will be seen when the tomb is finally opened:

'Shortly after he ascended the throne, the First Emperor ordered the Lishan Hills to be prepared for the building of his tomb. When the country was unified, he sent over

Fig. 90 **A group of terracotta warriors**
Qin dynasty, (221–07 BC)
Pit 1 at the tomb complex of the Emperor Qin Shi Huangdi, Xian, Shaanxi province.

700,000 convicts there to build his tomb. Three waterways were dredged and joined together. Coffins were reinforced with copper, and the whole tomb was filled with costly and exotic things. Craftsmen were ordered to make crossbows, which were positioned in such a manner as to shoot down any would-be grave robber. Channels and pools of mercury were installed to represent rivers and seas. The vault and floor of the main coffin chamber were designed to resemble the sky and earth. Candles were made of animal fat, which supposedly could burn forever.'

(Sima Qian, 'Records of the Grand Historian')

The pits to the east *have* been excavated, however, revealing one of the great archeological finds of the twentieth century. Since 1974, when the first discoveries were made by farmers digging a well, an army of eight thousand life-size terracotta soldiers and horses has been unearthed from three immense rectangular pits (figs. 90 and 91). These figures are arranged in offensive battle formation, facing east and standing to attention, awaiting orders from the emperor to attack. Infantrymen, archers and crossbowmen, charioteers and cavalry make up the emperor's army for the afterlife. Figures were made in moulds, using precise mass-production techniques, with individual details added afterwards. This technique was used to produce tomb figures during later dynasties. Their weapons are bronze, many as sharp as the

day they were first made, and treated with a thin layer of chromium to prevent corrosion.

In 1980 two bronze chariots pulled by horses of the same material were unearthed just to the west of the tomb (fig. 92).

Fig. 92 **Bronze chariot with four horses**
Qin dynasty, (221–07 BC)
L. 225 cm, H.152 cm
Tomb of Emperor Qin Shi Huangdi, Xian, Shaanxi province
This carriage, consisting of several thousand components and 1,061 kilograms in weight, is made with astonishing craftsmanship. It is a carriage for an emperor, built to transport him to the next world.

Fig. 91 **Terracotta figure of a general**
Qin dynasty, (221–07 BC)
H. 195 cm
Tomb complex of Emperor Qin Shi Huangdi, Xian, Shaanxi province
This general of the Qin army stands with his hands crossed in front of him as if leaning on a sword. He commands a force of crossbowmen.

The Great Wall of China

'A man'd be better off to die in battle
than eat his heart out building the Long Wall!
The Long Wall-how it winds and winds,
winds and winds three thousand li;
Here on the border, so many strong boys;
In the houses back home, so many widows and wives…'

(Chen Lin [d. 217], 'I Watered My Horse at the Long Wall Caves', translated in
B. Watson, 1984. This song concerns a conscript sent to labour on the Great Wall)

In 214 BC, Qin Shi Huangdi's gifted general Meng Tian led a force of 300,000 men (mostly forced labourers and convicts) to defeat the Xiongnu nomads along the northern frontier. Meng Tian proceeded to join up already extant sections of the wall and built a series of forts and watchtowers. The Qin wall was 10,000 li (about 4,500 km) in length but the cost of its construction in human life was appalling. Sima Qian describes the sufferings of Meng Tian's army, many of whom were interred within the structure as they died:

'the dead reached incalculable numbers, the corpses lay
strewn for a thousand li, *and streams of blood soaked the*
plains. The strength of the common people was exhausted
and five families out of every ten longed for revolt'.

(From Sima Qian, 'Records of the Historian'. Translated by B. Watson, 1993)

The wall's defensive value was incalculable but it also held symbolic significance for the Chinese. It was a dividing line between the agrarian societies of the south and the nomads of the north. From the Qin dynasty onwards, the Great Wall was assiduously maintained as a barrier between civilized China and the barbarian regions beyond. An important point to note about the Qin dynasty wall is that large sections of it were much further north than the present-day wall, completed during the Ming dynasty. The Ming dynasty wall extends from Hebei province in the northeast through Shanxi, Shaanxi and Ningxia provinces to Gansu province in the west. Locally obtainable building methods and materials were used so that different sections of the wall are constructed in different ways. Tamped earth, stone, wood and tiles were used in sections of wall built before the Ming dynasty and rubble faced with stone and paved along the top with bricks, during the Ming. The height of the wall varies, depending on the terrain, but averages about 8 metres with a base width of 6.6 metres and a top width of about 5.8 m; wide enough for five horses or ten soldiers to travel abreast along its ram-parts. The length of the wall was punctuated by more than 2,500 watchtowers with gates set at intervals to permit access to the trade routes and oases of the Silk Road. Contrary to conventional wisdom, the wall is not visible from the moon.

Qin Shi Huangdi died in 210 BC, probably as a result of ingesting the very immortality potions that were supposed to prolong his life. He was interred in his mausoleum with

Fig. 93 **The Great Wall**
This section dates to the Ming
dynasty, (1368–1644)

many of the workers who built it, all of his childless concubines and his eternal terracotta army. He was briefly succeeded by his son Er Shi (r. 210–207 BC), a madman and a puppet of the eunuch Zhao Gao. Er Shi lived a life of idleness as the peasants finally rebelled against the tyranny of the Qin regime and the empire dissolved around him. After Er Shi's death by suicide in 207 BC, the insurgent leader Xiang Yu destroyed Xianyang and slaughtered the entire imperial family. Epang palace is said to have burned for three months. There followed a period of five years of war between the states of Chu (led by Xiang Yu) and of Han (led by the former peasant Liu Bang) and large areas of China were destroyed. Liu Bang was eventually victorious and, in 206 BC, established the Han dynasty – a state of affairs that lasted, with only a brief interruption, for the next 400 years.

Xian during the Han dynasty – China's first 'Golden Age.'

The capital of the Western Han (206 BC–9 AD) is located about 10 km northwest of modern Xian and 2 km south of the Wei River. The Qin capital of Xianyang is just to the north of the river. The plan of the city follows an approximate square and is oriented according to the four directions. Its grid pattern still survives today and can be clearly seen in the satellite photograph above. The city walls were constructed of rammed yellow earth up to 18 metres in height and were about 30 km in length, encompassing an urban area of about 36 square kilometres. During its heyday, in the reign of Wudi (r. 140–87 BC), it was the largest city on earth with a population of over 500,000. The city walls contained a total of twelve gates – three on each axis – and eight major avenues ran through the city in straight lines from east to west or north to south. The centre lane of each avenue was reserved for the emperor, as was the middle arch of each gate. Two immense palaces were built in opposite corners of the city – Weiyang in the southwest and Changle in the southeast, each 5 or 6 square km in area. The Jianzhang Palace was built later, in about 104 BC, just west of the city and within the Shanglin Gardens. The Changle palace was used for administering state affairs during the early part of the Western Han dynasty and later served as a residence for the dowager empress, while the Weiyang palace was the centre of power throughout the Western Han and was also used for great ceremonial occasions. The Shanglin Gardens were built by Wudi at the same time as the Jianzhang Palace and contained 3,000 varieties of flowers and fruit trees; rare animals such as birds from West Asia, Indian rhinoceroses and some of the 'heavenly horses' of Central Asia.

Michael Loewe paints a vivid picture of the affluent lifestyles of the citizens of Changan during its glory days. His account (in Loewe, 1968) is based on a Han document of 81 BC that fulminates against the profligate behaviour of the rich and the well-to-do, in comparison with the wretched conditions endured by the poor. The rich lived in multi-storeyed houses constructed with richly carved crossbeams, their floors covered with embroidered cushions, wool rugs or rush matting, and even the middle classes could afford felts or wild boar hides. The beds of Changan were of fine timber and hung with delicate embroideries and there was so much silk around that even ordinary citizens were said to wear garments fit for queens. The rich wore squirrel and fox furs and wild duck feathers, and the less wealthy wore wool and ferret skins. Their footwear was equally lavish: the rich with shoes of inlaid leather or silk-lined slippers. At weddings the rich flaunted red badger furs and tinkling jades and the well-to-do wore long skirts and jewels. Game was taken out of season, young fish were caught without regard for preserving stocks and it was common to see banquets at which dish after dish was served.

The rich paraded up and down Changan's streets in gold or silver carriages, their horses decked out in breastplates and jewellery and wearing gilt or painted bits and gold or

Fig. 94 **Satellite image of Xian (Changan).**
(TRIC Tokai University/CNES/SPOT)

inlaid bridles. The middle-classes had lacquered equipment, sometimes hung with tassels, for their horses. For entertainment the rich would often keep their own orchestras and choirs and liked to watch tiger-fights and performances by foreign girls. The merely well-off would arrange flute or lute concerts. The extravagance of the age extended to religious practice and the burial of the dead while, the observer notes, the rural poor were treated worse than the animals of the urban rich.

Commerce was conducted at nine markets- referred to collectively as the East and West Markets- and situated in the northwest part of the city on either side of one of the main avenues. Watchtowers were built within each market to maintain law and order and to supervise commerce. During the early part of the dynasty, the markets of Changan were centres for trading in the agricultural produce of the outlying regions. Peasants brought produce to the city and bartered it for farm implements, livestock and household goods. The markets were also used for the practice of divination and for the public execution of criminals and traitors. The nature of commerce in Changan altered during the reign of Wudi (r. 140–87 BC). Under Wudi China expanded her frontiers as far as Korea, Vietnam and Central Asia, secured the rebellious areas in the south and southwest of the country and contained the threat from Xiongnu nomads. After Zhang Qian's journeys from Changan to the Western Regions in 138 and 116 BC (see p. 26), exotic goods began to appear in Changan. Zhang Qian himself is known to have brought back alfalfa (lucerne), grapes and a small number of horses. Trade with the countries to the west began as a process of barter, exchanging silk and weapons for grapes, walnuts, alfalfa and pomegranates and, but above all, for horses. Chinese silks, mirrors, lacquer and weapons from the Han dynasty have been found at archeological sites all over the Western Regions, in Afghanistan and in the graves of nomads in Mongolia (see section on Noin Ula). Wudi's need for horses was acute: during his campaign against the Xiongnu in 119 BC he is said to have lost more than 100,000 of them.

Commerce and Conquest

In 115 BC or 105 BC, Wudi sent the first Chinese embassy to Anxi (Persia), to the court of the Parthian King Mithridates II. The Han historian Sima Qian records that the emissaries were greeted at the Persian border by a force of 20,000 horsemen and escorted to Mithridate's court. They were presented with ostrich eggs and conjurers from Alexandria as gifts for Wudi and were accompanied back to China by a Persian ambassador. The Chinese were already aware of lands to the west of Persia and believed that they might be the place where the sun sets, the domain of the Queen

Mother of the West (*Xi Wang Mu*), a figure in Chinese mythology who was thought to possess the elixir of immortality. Wudi's mission appears to have been the starting point for trade with Persia and culminated in the unfurling of dazzling silk banners at the battle of Carrhae in 53 BC. Marcus Licinius Crassus, Governor of the Roman province of Syria, led an army of infantry against the Parthians near Carrhae. The battle was a disaster for the Romans. They were outmaneuvered and fled in panic when the Parthians unfurled huge silk banners- the first Roman contact with the new material. Within seven years silk had reached Rome, arriving in 46 BC when the silk canopies displayed during a triumphal procession of Julius Caesar are given mention.

In 104, 102 and 42 BC, Chinese armies conducted campaigns across the Pamirs as far west as Sogdiana and Ferghana in Central Asia- opening up the Silk Road even further. During the 42 BC campaign they laid seige to a walled settlement in Sogdiana, probably by the Talas River, an event described in the History of the Former Han (*Han Shu*). The defenders were Xiongnu but the settlement was said to have been protected by a wooden palisade, a structure favoured by the Romans and previously unknown in the East. The Han annals also relate that the defenders adopted a 'fish-scale' formation, perhaps a reference to the Roman *tetsudo* strategy in which legionnaires stood with overlapping shields like the scales of a fish. The sinologist Homer Dubs (Dubs, 1957) postulated that the Xiongnu defenders were assisted by Roman soldiers, probably captives taken at the Battle of Carrhae and sent East as slaves. The Chinese were victorious and captured 145 of the soldiers. Dubs speculated that they were Romans (although the annals are vague), and that they were taken back to China and permitted to settle in one of the frontier towns of the Gansu Corridor. Was this China's first contact with Europeans? The evidence is inconclusive but the story is fascinating, nonetheless.

The growth of commerce with the lands to the west was accompanied by the arrival of small numbers of foreigners at Changan and the beginnings of foreign influence on the art of the period. Many of the early foreigners were entertainers, sent as tribute from far-off lands (fig. 95).

As China expanded her borders into Central Asia merchants and envoys began to arrive in China to swear allegiance to the Han court and to bring exotic goods as tribute. Chinese merchants joined many of the expeditions to the Western Lands and a process of trade and cultural interchange gradually developed. There is abundant evidence of the technical innovations that the Han dynasty acquired from neighbouring countries. These innovations were critical in the development of Chinese civilization and were absorbed via early trade and military contacts on the Silk Road. Gernet (Gernet, 1982) lists a number of them including harnesses, saddles and stirrups (from the steppe nomads), construction methods for bridges and mountain roads, knowledge of medicinal plants and poisons, the cultivation of cotton and seafaring.

The processes of trade and tribute were often difficult to distinguish. Merchants frequently masqueraded as emissaries to the Han court in order to ensure a favourable reception for their goods. During the reign of Chengdi (r. 33–7 BC), it was said that of all the delegations who had come to pay to tribute to the Han, not one of them contained a member of a royal family or even a nobleman. During another, celebrated mission in 166 AD, a merchant passed himself off as an envoy of the Roman emperor Marcus Aurelius and arrived at the Indochinese port of Tonkin to offer elephant tusks, rhinoceros horn and tortoiseshell. The commentator's dismissive description of his merchandise indicates that trade was so highly developed by this point that such hitherto priceless items were no longer regarded as valuable:

'In the beginning of the Yuan-jia period of the emperor Huan the king of Da-Qin, Antun sent envoys who offered ivory, rhinoceros horns, and tortoise shells from the boundary of Annam; this was the first time they communicated with us…Their tribute contained no precious stones whatever, which makes us suspect that the messengers kept them back.'

(From the *Hou Han Shou* ['History of the Later Han'], quoted in Vollmer et al, 1983)

A delicately made bowl, unearthed in Guangdong province in 1954, is the earliest Roman glass vessel to be found in China and is proof that trade with the West was well developed even at this early date (fig. 96).

From 73 AD onwards General Ban Chao (31–103 AD), brother of the great Han historian Ban Ku, began the process of restoring Han rule in Central Asia. By 91 AD the various states of the Tarim Basin had submitted to Han rule – a process achieved by Ban Chao at minimal expense and using local troops. This enabled China to resume its control of the Silk Road. The same year he was appointed 'Protector General of the Western Regions' and, in 97 AD, led an expedition across Central Asia as far as the Caspian Sea – the most distant point yet reached by a Chinese. Also in 97 AD, Ban Chao dispatched an emissary called Gan Ying to Da Qin (Rome). He is believed to have reached the Persian Gulf and, upon arriving, enquired of the Parthians how to proceed further. He was informed that the crossing could take as long as three years and that many who attempted it were afflicted by violent pangs of homesickness that often led to the sufferer's death. Gan Ying was deterred from continuing his journey, thereby preserving the lucrative role of the Parthians as middlemen in the silk trade between China and

Rome. Both countries remained remarkably ignorant of each other – the Romans refer repeatedly to China as the 'land of Seres', a country where silk was produced by combing it from trees, and the Chinese were equally ill informed about the Romans; they believed that the people of Rome were physically similar to the Chinese (they even called the country 'Great Qin' after China), and that they also practised sericulture. The *Hou Han Shou* relates that, 'The people of this land are all inhabitants of great height, with regular features; they are similar to the inhabitants of the Middle Kingdom, and that is why the country is called Da Qin.' The first century A.D. was a period of thriving trade between China and the West when, as the *Hou Han Shou*

Fig. 96 **Moulded blue glass bowl**
Roman manufacture
Western Han dynasty, (206 BC–9 AD)
H. 4.7 cm, D.10.5 cm
Unearthed in 1954 at Hengzhigang, Guangzhou, Guangdong province
(National Museum of Chinese History, Beijing)

Fig. 95 **Bronze figures of storytellers**
Western Han dynasty, 113 BC or earlier
H. 7.7 cm and 7.8 cm
From the tomb of Prince Liu Sheng, Mancheng, Hebei province
(Hebei Provincial Museum -Art Exhibitions, China)
These two figures interact in a delightfully comical manner; the figure on the right appears to cup his hand to hear the words of the figure on the left. Their unusual physiognomy suggests that they may be from one of the countries to the south of China, perhaps representing entertainers sent by a neighbouring state to the Han court as tribute. Prince Liu Sheng, son of the Han Emperor Jingdi (r. 157–140 BC), ruled the prosperous Han territory of Zhongshan, centred around the city of Mancheng in Hebei province. Following his death, Liu Sheng's body was dressed in a suit made from 2,156 jade tablets, sewn together with gold thread, a protection (according to Chinese belief) against decomposition. The figures were probably intended to provide entertainment for Liu Sheng in the afterlife.

Fig. 97 **A group of painted earthenware figures of dancers**
Western Han dynasty,
(206 BC–9 AD)
H. 51.7–59.5 cm
(Eskenazi Ltd)

Fig. 98 **Bronze hanging lamp**
Eastern Han period,
2nd century AD
H. 29 cm, L. 28 cm
(Hunan Provincial Museum, Changsha –
Art Exhibitions, China)
The semi-naked curly haired
lamp bearer is probably a
Southeast Asian. Similar lamps
have been found in the region
now enclosed by the borders of
northern Vietnam – the
celebrated kneeling lamp-bearer
of Lac Truong – and a more
recent discovery (fig. 99) suggest
that during the Chinese
occupation of the area the
process of cultural exchange was
both continuous and widespread.

relates, 'peasant colonies were founded in the fertile lands; inns and posts for changing horses were established along the main routes; messengers and couriers travelled in every season of the year; and the Merchant Strangers knocked daily on our gates to have them opened.'

The Western Han dynasty was an epoch of great affluence and cultural vitality. A number of scholars have remarked that many Western Han works of art are a blend of the mythology and superstitions of the south of China and the rather hard-edged realism of the north. The best of Western Han art is to be found in tombs, as we have already seen in fig. 95 (p. 83). The art of the Western Han has a slightly naïve quality, with the theme of entertainment occurring again and again; in addition to storytellers, musicians and acrobats, figures of dancing women – unearthed in large numbers from Han tombs – are a favourite. Their long, sweeping sleeves convey a tremendous sense of motion (fig. 97).

The art of the Han dynasty does not readily reveal direct influences from the West, despite the fact that trade and contacts with other countries were flourishing. Motifs from steppe art, such as confronting animals or openwork narratives and landscapes, are to be found on Chinese bronze belt plaques and harness fittings. These were probably absorbed via their trade with the Xiongnu and commercial and military contacts (by both land and sea) with the lands to the south of China occurred at least as early as the Western Han dynasty. After the fall of the Qin dynasty in 207 BC, one of the regime's surviving generals named Zhao Tuo fled south and declared an independent kingdom. The kingdom of Nanyue, composed of modern Guangdong, Guanxi and northern Vietnam, lasted until 111 BC, when it was defeated by the armies of the Han Emperor Wudi. The second King of Nanyue – Zhao Mo – died in about 122 BC and the site of what is thought to be his grave was excavated in 1983. He wears the same style of jade suit as Prince Liu Sheng, interred 3,500 km away in metropolitan China (p. 83), and contacts with the southern regions are also revealed by the presence of perfumes and ivory. A silver box and a jade rhyton (drinking horn) found in the tomb reflect contacts with Western and Central Asia. After 111 BC, when the region was absorbed into the Chinese Empire, the new Han rulers of the south introduced Chinese culture and craftsmanship but indigenous styles were not entirely displaced. A number of examples of Han dynasty art reveal contacts with the influences from the southern regions (fig. 98).

Western themes are harder to identify in the early art of metropolitan China. It seems that a sense of cultural superiority amongst the Han meant that their creations were their own or were so heavily sinicized that their origins are rendered unrecognizable. Three rare exceptions are the winged horse – a popular motif in the art of Han China and also passed to its neighbours (see fig. 11), an extraordinary and possibly unique example of a *putto* hunting fish with a trident among vine scrolls, and the motif of the 'goat-man'. The naked, cherub-like *putto* appears on a lacquer plate unearthed at the tomb of General Zhu Ran (d. 249 AD) in Ma'anshan, Anhui province. The plate dates to the Eastern Han dynasty (25–220 AD) and contains an inscription that suggests it was manufactured in Chengdu, Sichuan province. This motif occurs many times in Roman mosaics and on silver vessels and the fact that it has travelled so far, and in a virtually unchanged form, is little short of amazing.* The third example comes from the ancient Near East (fig. 100).

So and Bunker (1995) suggest that such motifs reached China through the intermediary of nomadic art. New metallurgical techniques such as granulation, loop-in-loop chains and an early form of cloisonné were acquired from the West via Chinese contact with the nomads during the Eastern Zhou dynasty and perfected during the Qin and Han dynasties. Bunker describes these new metalsmithing techniques at length in relation to Chinese personal ornament (White and Bunker, 1994).

Fig. 99 **Bronze hanging lamp**
Dong Son Culture, ca. 1st century AD
H. 50 cm, L. 30 cm
Reportedly found in northern Vietnam
(Spink and Son Ltd)

Fig. 100 **Gold inlayed bronze tuning key for a zither (qin)**
North China, 3rd century BC
H. 10.9 cm
(Therese and Erwin Harris Collection)
The recumbent human-headed goat figure† surmounting the key is found in West Asian art of the fourth millennium BC and related, human-headed bull-figures are found on columns at Persepolis.

* For more on this plate, please see *Orientations*, May 2001 issue, pp 52–58.
† Another instance of the goat-man motif has been identified in a fragment of a woollen skirt from the Shanpula area in the Abegg-Stiftung collection (see Keller and Schorta, 2001). For more on Shanpula see p. 183. The goat-man motif is identified and discussed in So and Bunker, 1995.

Fig. 101 **A gold necklace set with gems.**
Sui dynasty, (581–618)
L 43 cm, Wt. 91.25 g
Excavated from the tomb of Li Jingxun in Xian, Shaanxi province in 1957.
(National Museum of Chinese History, Beijing)
This exquisite necklace consists of twenty-eight gold beads each set with ten pearls. In the middle of the clasp is a dark blue pearl incised with a deer and the square ornaments at either end are set with lapis lazuli, a stone found solely in Afghanistan. The two large stones at the bottom are a chicken-blood stone (a type of pyrophyllite), and a large pale blue cabochon, variously described as a sapphire or a lapis bead. The workmanship and design of this necklace recall Persian art and it has also been suggested that such necklaces were the inspiration for the adornments worn by monumental Chinese stone sculptures of Avalokitesvara.

of the Han dynasty it was created to beautify the home and the new qualities of dynamism, naturalism and humour must be due – at least in part – to ideas imported from the classical world.

The financial strain of supporting Wudi's military adventures undermined the economy and after his death in 87 BC the Western Han dynasty was progressively weakened by a succession of ineffectual rulers and by a growing rivalry among the families of imperial consorts. In 9 AD a nephew of the dowager empress, named Wang Mang, declared himself emperor of the short-lived Xin dynasty. Wang Mang's attempts at land reform and curbing the excesses of the rich left him isolated and, in 23 AD, rebellion broke out and Changan was attacked. Wang Mang took refuge in a tower but was sought out and beheaded; seated in full imperial regalia upon his throne.

After Wang Mang's death the Han nobility regained the throne, establishing the Eastern Han dynasty (25–220 AD). The capital was moved from Changan to Luoyang (p. 73), although Changan continued to be an important commercial and political centre. During the chaos of the Period of Disunity, from 221 to 589 AD, the fortunes of the city rose and fell with every change of ruler. It was the capital of, among others: the Western Wei, the Northern Zhou and the early Sui kingdoms. The city was attacked yet again in 316 AD during the Western Jin dynasty when, it was said, 'there were not more than one hundred families. Weeds and thorns grew thickly as if in a forest.'

Changan's fortunes did not fully revive until 581 AD when by Emperor Wendi (r. 581–604) founded the Sui dynasty. Wendi established the Sui capital on a new site, 2 or 3 km to the southeast of the Han city of Changan. The old city was abandoned and turned into an imperial garden and the name Daxing ('Great Resurrection') was given to the new city of Changan. It is on this site that Changan has remained until today.

One of the most tragic of the players on Changan's stage during the Sui dynasty was Princess Li Jingxun, who died on 30 June 608 AD at the age of only eight. Princess Li came from a family that was noble and yet was beset by calamity. Her grandfather died in battle against the nomadic tribes of the north and her father, Li Min, was an official in the government of the Sui dynasty (581–618). Soon after her own early death, Princess Li's father was executed on the orders of the Sui emperor and her mother, too, was poisoned a few months later. At the time of Princess Li's death her family were still affluent and powerful and, perhaps because of regret at her premature death, her funeral was particularly lavish. She was buried just outside one of Xian's gates with an inscription on the sarcophagus that states, 'Open this and you will drop dead.' The curse appears to have been effective since, when the tomb was excavated in 1957, the contents were found to be intact (fig. 101).

Artistic styles such as the carving of narrative scenes on stone and the production of stone sculpture in the round (fig. 15) have no precedent in previous dynasties. Their origins may be traced to the sculpture and carved reliefs of the Greco-Roman world and of Assyria by a process of gradual dissemination along the Silk Road. This is also the case with the more naturalistic style of Han art. During the feudal societies of previous dynasties art was produced almost exclusively for ritual use, but during the affluent years

Xian during China's Second 'Golden Age': The Great Tang dynasty

'A hundred thousand lǐ* of journey, how many dangers?
Desert dragons, when you wag your tongue, will hear
and be humbled.
The day you reach India's five lands, your hair will be white-
The moon sets on Ch'ang-an and its midnight bells.'

(Li Tung, 9th century. 'For the Monk San-tsang on His Return to the Western Regions.' Translated by Burton Watson in Watson, 1984)

By the Tang dynasty (618–907) Buddhism was firmly established in China and, in Changan alone, there were eighty-one monasteries and temples and twenty-eight convents, more than any other city in China. Emperor Taizong (r. 626–49) built the city's most famous landmark, the Dayan ('Great Goose') Pagoda for the monk Xuanzang, to house the scriptures and relics that he had brought from India (fig. 102).

In 648 Taizong's successor Gaozong (r. 649–83) erected the adjacent Daciensi ('Temple of Great Mercy') in memory of his late mother Empress Wende, while he was still crown prince. The Daciensi, more than 24 hectares in extent, has no fewer than eleven courtyards, 1,800 rooms and accom-modation for 300 monks. Other examples of imperially sponsored Buddhist temples in Changan are the Dajianfusi ('Temple of Great Fortune') – comprising the fifteen-storey 'Little Goose' pagoda and covering an area of 10 hectares – and the Zhangjing temple, built outside the East gate by Emperor Daizong and containing forty-eight courtyards and over four thousand cubicles for monks.

The Tang emperors were enthusiastic patrons of Buddhism and members of various sects became involved in court intrigue to advance their own particular cause. A number of monks achieved great wealth and fame at the Tang court and monasteries acquired vast landholdings. Tang dynasty records show that a monk was entitled to five acres of land and a nun to about three, while individual monasteries were allowed an additional holding. This meant that a monastery of one hundred monks would be entitled to as many as 600 acres of land, all tax exempt. By the time of Daizong (r. 762–79), monasteries had acquired most of the cultivable land in the Changan area and people were actually becoming monks to avoid paying tax. This trend generated bitter resentment among the landlord classes and threatened China's economy. The Buddhist church was an economic power in Tang dynasty China. Jacques Gernet describes the contents of a set of monastic accounts from Dunhuang, listing the monastery's various sources of revenue:

Income from lands
Interest on loans [virtually all monasteries derived income

Fig. 102 **The Dayan (Great Goose) Pagoda, Xian**
Tang dynasty, completed 652
H. 64.5 metres

from usury]
Levies on Gardens
Rent from oil presses [oil was used for lamps and for cooking]
Rent from mills [for grinding millet and wheat flour]
Miscellaneous gifts [made on the occasion of festivals]
Fees received for the recitation of sutras, 'spring and autumn Buddha food', and alms given during vegetarian feasts.

)Extracted from Pelliot ms P4081 from Dunhuang. Quoted in Gernet, 1995)

Monks performed services such as the recitation of sutras for the dead, divination, healing and the practice of magic. Charlatanism was rife and many monks paid little more than lip service to Buddhist principles. In 842 an imperial decree, issued by the Daoist Emperor Wuzong (r. 840–46), resulted in the laicizing of more than 3,000 of

*A *lǐ* is equivalent to about 0.45 km. Phrases such as 'a hundred thousand *lǐ*' or 'ten thousand *lǐ*' simply mean a distance beyond imagining.

the most profligate of these 'monk-sorcerers':

'All monks and nuns in the empire who practice alchemy,
sorcery, or incantations; draft evaders; those who bear the
marks of flagellation, tattoos or forced labour [as a result
of previous offences]; who indulge in debauchery,
maintain wives, and disregard the Buddhist precepts; all
these shall be defrocked. All money, provisions, grains,
lands, estates, and gardens owned by these monks and
nuns shall be confiscated by the government.'

(Quoted in Gernet, 1995)

A campaign of persecution of Buddhist orders and other
foreign religions continued until 845 and culminated in the
destruction of temples and monasteries. Buddhist images
were melted down and vast areas of land were expropriated
by the State. These events by no means eradicated Buddhism
in China but it never regained the political and economic
dominance of the country that it had hitherto enjoyed. The
Nestorian, Manichaean and Zoroastrian religions fared far
worse- they all but disappeared from metropolitan China
and were only preserved at all by the presence of adherents
among border peoples such as the Uighurs and Mongols.

The xenophobia of the ninth century marked the
beginning of the end for the Tang dynasty. Intrigue at court
and the behaviour of increasingly exploitative landlords led
to a worsening economic situation and outbreaks of famine
during the second half of the century. Widespread peasant
uprisings followed, the largest led by the rebel leader Huang
Zhao. Huang's army attacked Guangzhou (Canton) in 879
and massacred 120,000 of the town's 200,000 Arab, Indian,
Persian and Southeast Asian residents. In 880 he rode into
Changan in a golden carriage, at the head of an army dressed
in brocade, and proceeded to tear apart the city. By the time
he had finished 'grass grew on the streets and hares and foxes
ran everywhere.' One of the manuscripts discovered at
Dunhuang contains a searing description of the aftermath of
Huang Zhao's attack on Changan (see p. 131). The remnants
of the great Tang dynasty lingered for another twenty-seven
years with power in the hands of warlords.

Xian's streets and walls

'Changan looks like a chessboard-
Won and lost for a hundred years, sad beyond all telling'

(Li Bai [also called Li Po, 701–62], 'Autumn Mediation'.
For a view of Xian's 'chessboard' street pattern, see fig. 94)

Modern Xian is still surrounded by moated walls, 12 metres
high and about 14 km in length. They date to the early Ming
dynasty but were built upon the remains of the original Tang
dynasty walls (fig. 103).

Foreigners in Xian

At its height, during the seventh and eighth centuries up
until the An Lushan rebellion of 755, Changan was the
largest city on earth with almost two million people living
within its walls and suburbs. Foreigners came to the capital
from all over Asia: from the north came Koreans and the
emissaries of various Turkic tribes such as Uighurs and
Tokharians; from the West came Persians, Sogdians and
Khorezmians as well as Arabs, Jews, Indians and Armenoids
(from west of the Caspian); from the lands to the south came
Javanese, Malays, Singhalese and Chams and from further
afield came small numbers of African slaves. The Chinese
attitude to foreigners was contradictory. On one hand they
dismissed all foreigners as barbarians (or *hu*), ridiculing and
caricaturing them at every opportunity. Tomb figures of
foreigners were invariably modelled with humorously
exaggerated features (see section on Tang terracotta
figurines) and written documents from the time almost
always refer to them in a disparaging way. Foreigners were
confined to segregated sections of Changan and were
generally forbidden to intermarry with the Chinese,
although this did not apply to 'strategic' marriages with the
rulers of friendly states.

The Tang government strictly regulated the activities of
merchants. They attempted to control both the sale and
distribution of goods from abroad, particularly when they
were exotic items of interest to the court. Such items were
often regarded as tribute from a submissive nation and a
merchant was expected to present a portion of his wares to
the court or to hand them all in to a government warehouse
at the point of entry. Even the goods that could be sold
without restrictions were confined to specified outlets, such
as Changan's Western Market where merchants were
carefully supervised by government officials. The laws
regulating imports to China were ever changing and often
subject to the whim of a particular customs official: the
sinologist Edward Schafer, in his book *The Golden Peaches of
Samarkand*, refers to the Arab trader Abu Zaid Al-Hasan's
complaint that he was obliged to hand over one third of his
goods to the imperial warehouse upon arrival in the country.

Similar obstacles were placed in the way of merchants as
they sought goods for the return journey to their home
countries. The more desirable and profitable the goods, the
more tightly they were controlled. Schafer describes an edict
of 714 that forbade 'the export or the sale to foreigners of
tapestries, damasks, gauzes, crepes, embroideries, and other
fancy silks, or of yaktails, pearls, gold or iron'. If a foreigner
died in China without a wife or heir immediately to hand his
property was confiscated by the state and, even if he were to
overcome official resistance and take a Chinese spouse, he
could not take her back to his homeland.

Foreign emissaries to the Tang court were treated more
courteously but were also subjected to numerous

Fig. 103 **City walls, Xian**
Early Ming dynasty, 14th century

restrictions. Countries who conducted regular diplomatic relations with the Tang were issued with a number of bronze tokens in the shape of fish. The envoy carried one half and the court retained the other. Upon arrival at Changan the emissary would be received by the *Hung-lu* office, and questioned in great detail about the customs and geography of his homeland. Based on this information, Schafer tells us, the office would create a map of the envoy's country.

The emissary would wait until the day appointed for his audience with the emperor and would prostrate himself before the throne. Extravagant gifts were *de rigueur* and these were handed over to the Officer of Protocol. The envoy seldom received a word from the emperor but was often bestowed with grand titles. Schafer tells us of a typical visit to the court of Xuanzong (r. 712–56) by an envoy from the King of Srivijaya in Sumatra. After presenting his gifts to the emperor the envoy was presented, in the name of his king, with a purple caftan and a gold belt. The title of 'Great Army Leader of the Militant Guards of the Left' was conferred on the king through his envoy and the latter was then ushered out of the imperial presence. A mural in the tomb of Prince Zhanghuai – second son of Emperor Gaozong and Empress Wu Zetian – gives us an idea of the various protocols required of an embassy to the Tang court (see fig.117).

Despite their apparent enmity towards foreigners and the restrictions they placed upon their activities, the Tang Chinese enthusiastically embraced foreign fashions in music,

dress, diet and the arts. There were intermittent persecutions of foreign religions but, particularly during the early part of the Tang dynasty, there was a surprising degree of tolerance. Zoroastrianism reached China from Persia at about the time of the Northern Wei dynasty (386–534) and was flourishing by the Tang dynasty. There were a number of Zoroastrian temples in Changan and another in Luoyang- the religion's spread propagated by refugees from the Sasanian Empire of Persia after the régime had, by 651, been completely overthrown by the Arabs. A tombstone, inscribed in Chinese and the Pahlavi script of Persia and unearthed in Xian in 1955, records the story of the tomb occupants – a man called Su Liang and his wife. They were both Persian Zoroastrians, descended from the rulers of the Sasanian Empire, and had fled to China when the dynasty was brought down.

Manichaeism came to China from Central Asia during the Tang dynasty. It was endorsed by an imperial edict during the reign of Empress Wu Zetian (r. 690–705) and, despite an order in 732 forbidding its practice by Han Chinese, the religion endured among the Uighur communities of Gansu and Xinjiang. In 786 the Manichaeans were permitted to construct the Dayunguangming Temple in Changan. Mani (216 or 217–76), the religion's founder was born in Southern Babylonia. He was probably a Parthian, the dynasty overthrown by the Sasanian King Ardashir I in 224. His father had gone to live in the city of Ctesiphon on the Tigris (south of Baghdad), where he is said to have heard

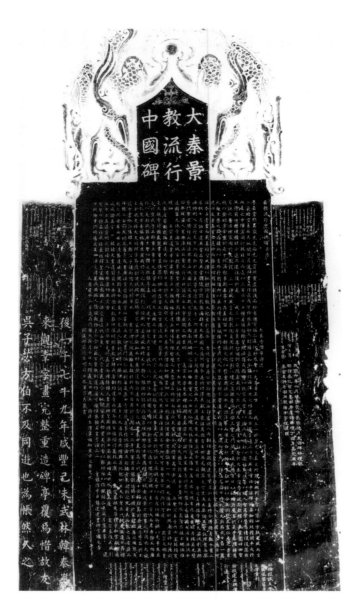

Fig. 104 **Rubbing from a stele inscribed in Syriac and Chinese commemorating the introduction of Nestorianism into China**
Dated 781
H. 2.36 metres
Discovered in 1625 in Zhouzi County, Shaanxi province
(Forest of Stelae Museum, Xian)
The inscription reads: 'At the time when Taizong, the brilliant emperor, was gloriously and splendidly beginning his prosperous reign, governing the people with far-sighted wisdom, there was in the land of Da Qin (Rome) a man of high virtue named Aluoben who, upon the augury of blue clouds, brought hither the true writings. After studying the harmony of the winds, he hastened to confront the dangers and difficulties and arrived in Changan in the ninth year of the Chen-kuan period (e 635 AD). The emperor sent his minister, the Duke Fang Hsüan-ling, with an escort, to receive the visitor in the western suburb of the city and conduct him to the palace. When the books had been transferred to the library and the doctrine examined in his private apartments, the emperor perceived its quality and truth and ordered that it should be preached and spread among the people.' At the bottom of this stele is a list in Syriac of seventy Nestorian priests.

voices ordering him to abstain from meat, sexual activity and the drinking of wine. He joined a group that adhered to these strictures. Mani subsequently journeyed to India where he founded his first Manichaean community, apparently influenced heavily by Buddhist ideas. Upon his return to

Ctesiphon he was permitted to practise his faith but was eventually brought to trial for apostasy at the behest of orthodox Zoroastrian priests at the court Bahram I. He was sentenced to crucifixion and was put to death at Belapat in Susiana in 276. Manichaeism continued to take root however, and soon spread across the Roman Empire to North Africa. One of its most vociferous opponents was the colourfully named Saint Augustine of Hippo (354–430). St Augustine was the son of a pagan who converted to Christianity and eventually became bishop of Hippo in North Africa (now Annaba in Algeria). He wrote a series of polemics, fulminating against Manichaeism and this opposition – coupled with condemnation by the Roman Empire – brought about the decline of Manichaeism in the West. Many of Mani's followers had fled eastwards, however, settling in Central Asia and eventually reaching China and Manichaean communities were set up there during the seventh and eight centuries. Manichaeism is based on two principles: Light (the Spirit) and Darkness (the Flesh). These two principles of darkness and light, representing good and evil, struggle to gain control of the universe. It is man's duty to separate the two forces and render the latter harmless. He must avoid all activities that are detrimental to the light and attempt to free it from the darkness with which it is merged. If the principles are correctly adhered to separation of the two forces will occur immediately after death.

The Nestorians, too, flourished in Changan. The religion's founder Nestorius, Roman Catholic Patriarch of Constantinople, was expelled from the church in 432 as a result of a schism with the Pope in Rome over the nature of the divinity of Christ and the role of the Virgin Mary. Nestorianism spread eastwards along the Silk Road to Central Asia, reaching China in 635. A Nestorian priest from Persia known as Adam, (Aluoben to the Chinese) brought scriptures to Changan and was permitted to construct the Yiningfang temple in the city. By the time of Emperor Xuan-zong's reign (r. 712–56) there were Nestorian temples in Changan, Luoyang and other cities and the Yiningfang temple was renamed *Da Qin* ('Rome'). A stele, discovered near Xian in 1625, commemorates Aluoben's arrival and the introduction of Nestorianism to China (fig. 104). Emperor Taizong (r. 626–49) embraced the new religion with open arms.

Islam made modest inroads into China after the collapse of the Sasanian era, introduced mostly by merchants and former soldiers of the Arab armies. Even after the defeat of a Tang army at the Talas River in 751, Islam remained a religion of foreigners and of a number of the Turkic border tribes. There is some debate over whether the Grand Mosque on Changan's Huajue Lane was established during the Tang dynasty: it has been rebuilt many times and is more often ascribed to the Song dynasty (after 960). Mosques were undoubtedly in existence in Tang China, nevertheless; the Huaisheng Mosque in Canton was established as early as 627

AD, by a relative of the Prophet Mohammed, one of the first Muslim missionaries to the Middle Kingdom.

Finally, there were a number of Jewish traders living in both Changan and Luoyang and they, too, were permitted to practice their religion. Jewish merchants were the most resourceful and adaptable of people and were active the length and breadth of the Silk Road. Jews were especially active in the production, dyeing and trading of silk textiles. Their descendants can be found among the several hundred Chinese Jews still living in Kaifeng, Henan province. The reign of Emperor Wuzong (r. 840–46) – an ardent Daoist – saw a major persecution of foreign religions and the climate of religious tolerance of the early Tang was but a distant memory.

In the open-minded atmosphere of the early Tang period many Chinese developed friendships with foreigners living in China. Abe no Nakamaro, friend of the poet Li Bai, was one such person (see section on Japanese visitors below). Some foreigners attained high positions in the government and acquired great power and fortune. The most infamous of these was the part-Sogdian General An Lushan – a favourite of Emperor Xuanzong – who attempted to usurp the throne in 755 (see p. 97), but many other foreigners gave years of faithful service to the Tang.

Japanese visitors to China

Throughout the Tang dynasty Japanese envoys visited Changan, making the perilous crossing of the East China Sea. Many, such as one Monk Min, lived in the Chinese capital for 26 years to study Buddhist doctrine. Others – like the scholar Takamuko no Kuromaro – who stayed for thirty-four years – learned the processes of government and took his ideas back to Japan where he became involved in the Taika reform movement.*

Abe no Nakamaro (701–70) was a close friend of the well-known Tang poets Li Bai and Wang Wei. He lived in Changan for fifty-four years and was given an official appointment by the Tang court. During the reign of the Tang Emperor Suzong (r. 756–62), he decided to return home to visit his aging parents. The ship carrying Abe almost capsized and drifted as far as the South China coast before he was rescued. Believing him lost, Li Bai wrote the poem 'Mourning Chao', one of the greatest masterpieces of Tang literature:

'Chao left our imperial city for his Japanese homeland,
a lone flake of sail. Now he wanders islands of immortals.
Foundering in emerald seas, a bright moon never to return
Leaves white, grief-tinged clouds crowding our southlands.'

('Mourning Chao' by Li Bai [also called Li Po, 701–62]. In Hinton, 1996)

The ultimate expression of the close cultural links between China and Japan during the Tang dynasty can be seen in the Japanese cities of Kyoto and Nara, both modelled on Changan, and in the contents of the Shosoin repository (see p. 106).

The scholar Kibino Makibi remained in Changan for eighteen years, using the basic structural parts and radicals of Chinese writing to create Japanese Katakana script. His fellow countryman Kukai (Kobo Daishi) studied Esoteric Buddhism at Changan's Qinglong Temple and returned to Japan to found the Shingon sect. Kukai also invented Hiragana script – a simplification of the phonetic Kanji script that revolutionized the writing of literature during Japan's Heian period of 794–1185. It enabled women- who were considered incapable of learning to write complex Chinese characters and were hence not given an education- to express themselves in writing. As a result, women wrote many of the first published works in Japan, the most celebrated being the *Genji monogatari* ('The Tale of Genji') by Murasaki Shikibu.

Persians, Sogdians, and other foreigners

'Where shall we say adieu?
Why not the Ching-I Gate of Changan
Where the Persian waitresses beckon with white hands,
Enticing customers to drink their fill of fine wine?'

(Li Bai [also called Li Po, 701–62]. Quoted in Hayashi, 1975)

The splendours of Tang dynasty Changan captivated the Arab traveller Ibn-Wahad, who visited in about 815:

'The town was very great, and its population extremely numerous. It was divided into two vast halves separated by a long, broad track. The emperor, his ministers, his guard, the supreme judge, the eunuchs, and all those who belonged to the imperial household lived in the eastern part of the city. The ordinary population could not communicate with them and were not admitted to the places there, watered by many canals whose banks were planted with trees and decorated with sumptuous residences. The western part of the town was inhabited by the ordinary people and the merchants. They had great squares there and markets for the necessities of life. At daybreak, officers of the royal household would be seen there, together with purveyors and the servants of the courtiers. They came to this part of town to visit the markets and the merchants' dwellings in order to buy all they wanted, and they did not return until the following morning.'

(Recorded in about 915 by Abu Zaid Al-Hasan and quoted in Drège and Bührer, 1989)

* The Taika Reform Movement sought to change the age-old status of Japan as a nation of loosely affiliated, separate states. Instead, the country would comprise provinces that were governed by a centralized bureaucracy and ruled by the Emperor. The reform edicts required that all government officials submit to a Chinese style civil service examination and drastically curtailed the independence of regional officials- designating the imperial court as a place of appeal and complaint for the people. The overall intention was to bring Japanese society in line with Chinese social practices.

Persians and Sogdians were by far the most active among the merchants. Many Persians were quick to acquire wealth and soon controlled the medicine, spice and jewellery bazaars. The commercial activity of Changan was centred on the East and West markets, each containing innumerable bazaars for many tradesmen including gold and silversmiths, tailors, tanners, herbalists, metalworkers, saddlers and purveyors of food and drink. There were also establishments offering various services: pawnshops, moneylenders, printers and brothels – to name but four – and the Western market, with over 3,000 shops lining its narrow lanes, was the more bustling of the two.

Perhaps the most distinguished among the many thousands of foreigners who made China their permanent home was Peroz (or Firûz), son of Yazdegerd III (r. 632–51 AD), the last of the Sasanian rulers of Persia. Peroz and his son Nyas sought refuge in Changan in about 670 and were appointed 'Generals of the Left and Right' in the Tang army. Peroz was also appointed as ambassador, representing the large Persian community in Changan. One of the sixty-one statues of ambassadors that stand before the tomb of Gaozong and Wu Zetian is believed to be Peroz (see fig. 114).

Musicians, singers and dancers came to Changan to entertain the Tang court and many of them achieved great fame and wealth. Cao Bao, from Kebud in modern Uzbekistan, became a celebrated *pipa* (lute) player – a tradition continued by his son and grandson. During the reign of Xianzong (r. 805–20) a renowned singer from Maimargh (a state in Central Asia) performed at court and, during Xuanzong's reign (r. 712–56), dancing girls from Chach (near modern Tashkent) would dance provocatively until, at the climax, they would pull down their blouses to reveal naked shoulders:

'…*Purple net shirts are set in motion- the Chach*
dancers come!
Girdles droop from gilded thighs, flowered waists are heavy,
Hats revolve with golden bells, snowy faces turn.
I watch- too soon the tune is done, they will not be detained;
Whirling in clouds, escorted by rain, they are off to the
Terrace of the Sun.'

(Bai Juyi [772–846], 'The Geisha of Chach.' Quoted in Schafer, 1963)

The most cherished of all the dancing girls from the Western Lands were the 'Sogdian twirling girls', the best coming from Samarkand. These girls, presented as tribute by rulers of Central Asian states, were all the rage at the beginning of the eighth century. Dressed in crimson robes and green damask pantaloons, they balanced and twirled on the tops of balls that rolled about the stage. Xuanzong was inordinately fond of this dance and his inamorata Yang Guifei is said to have mastered it.

Musicians and dancers also came from southern and eastern Asia. Thus, the Pyu kingdom of Burma sent a thirty-five man orchestra in 802 that played compositions based on the Buddhist scriptures, accompanied by conches and bronzes drums. In 777, eleven Japanese dancing girls were sent to the Tang court and musicians from the kingdom of Funan (in what is now Vietnam) came to live at the Tang capital. Not all of the musicians sent to Tang were allowed to remain, however. Edward Schafer tells the story of the two girls sent to the Tang court by its ally, the Silla kingdom of Korea. They appear to have been chosen as much for their looks as for their musical ability. The Emperor Taizong (626–49) decided that they were to be pitied as he would an exotic parrot and promptly sent them back.

Of all the musical styles to enter China during the Tang dynasty it was the instruments and compositions from the Kingdom of Kucha (Kuqa) that had the most influence. Kuqa musicians introduced the four-stringed lute (*pipa*), a small lacquered drum and a flute. The Gigaku performances of Japan appear to have their origins among the musicians of Kuqa (see sections on Kuqa and the Shosoin). The indefatigable monk Xuanzang visited Kuqa during the seventh century and stated that, 'the musicians of this land outshine those of other kingdoms by their talent on the flute and the guitar.'

The Sogdians, of Eastern Iranian descent and speaking an Indo-European dialect, were consummate merchants whose language became the *lingua franca* of the Silk Road. A Chinese commentary of the time, 'Memoir on the Barbarians of the West', refers admiringly to the traders from Sogdia:

> *They are clever traders. When a boy reaches the age of five years, he is sent to study books. When he begins to understand them, he is sent to study trade. To make profits is regarded by most of the inhabitants as an excellent thing.*'

(Wei Jie, 'Memoir on the Barbarians of the West.' Quoted in Drège and Bührer, 1989)

Caravans from the Sogdian cities of Samarkand, Varakhsha (near Bukhara) and Penjikent (near the Tajik-Uzbek border) brought gemstones, perfumes, silver, wool and cotton textiles and horses across the Gobi via Dunhuang to China. In return the Sogdians purchased raw silk, both as yarn and as woven pieces, and resold it to the Persians, the Byzantines (until the end of the sixth century), the Indians and the nomads of the steppe. A bundle of letters between Sogdian merchants, discovered in a watchtower at the western extremity of the Great Wall by Sir Aurel Stein in 1907, are dated to around 313 and indicate that trade between Sogdiana and China was conducted from an early date. The letters refer to the political instability of the Silk Road at the time and one describes the destruction of the northern capital, Luoyang, by the Xiongnu:

'And, Sir, the last Emperor- so they say- fled from Saragh [Luoyang] because of the famine, and his palace and walled city were set on fire...So Saragh is no more, Ngap [the city of Yeh, to the north] no more!'

(Quoted in Paludan, 1998)

Inscriptions in Sogdian language at Shatial, in Pakistan's upper Indus Valley, demonstrate the extent to which they travelled in search of trade. (For more on this subject see the various sections on Sogdians, Shatial and Chilas elsewhere in this book.)

The Khorezmians were also of Iranian descent and lived south of the Aral Sea between the Oxus and Jaxartes Rivers. They traded textiles and carpets from Bukhara and metalwork from Sogdiana and Khorezmia. There are also records of Khorezmian deerskins, dyed purple or red and sent to the Tang capital to satiate the appetite of court ladies for high boots. Khorezmia also produced furs, although these appear to have reached China in relatively small numbers. The country was also famous for its sugar cakes, known as 'stone honey' and made from a blend of sugar cane and milk. Archeological excavations indicate that the first capital of Khorezm was at Toprak Kala in Uzbekistan but, by the time of the Arab invasions of the early eighth century, the country was fragmented (see section on Khorezm).

Armenians from the northern side of Asia Minor – to the southwest of the Caspian Sea – lived on the main East-West trade routes and took full advantage of their favourable geographical position to conduct trade in both directions. Chinese tomb figures (see below) typically depict Armenoid figures with Caucasian facial features and rather pronounced noses (fig. 108). Some depictions of wine-sellers may be of Armenians but, as with many Chinese ceramic figures, precise identification is difficult.

Tokharians

Over the past twenty-five years a number of mummified corpses have been discovered in the Taklamakan Desert of Xinjiang. Their physiognomy appears to be Caucasian or 'Western' and several are decorated with tattoos and face paintings that resemble the animal style of early nomadic peoples (figs. 105 and 216).

The textiles worn by other Caucasoid mummies – found near Hami on the Northern Silk Road – resemble the 'tartans' worn by both modern-day Scots and by the ancient Celts before them (fig. 106).

All of these factors have given rise to the theory that the mummies are the remains of a lost tribe of European nomads who may have migrated eastwards in very early times and settled in the oasis-cities of Chinese Central Asia.

Fig. 105 **Mummy of 55-year-old male known as 'Cherchen Man'**
Ca. 1000 BC
H. 2 metres
From Tomb 2, Zhagunluke, Cherchen (Qiemo), Xinjiang province
(Photo by J. Newbury)
'Cherchen Man' was interred with three women and an infant. The best-preserved of the women was a veritable Amazon of nearly two metres in height, and the mystery of how they happened to be in such a remote part of China has yet to be unravelled.
Note the orange-yellow face painting on the cheeks.

Fig. 106 **Tartan (plaid) woollen twill**
Ca. 1200–700 BC
From a burial at Qizilchoqa, near Hami, Xinjiang province
(Courtesy of I. Good)
This twill, woven in light brown with light blue and white stripes, resembles some of the cloth fragments discovered in the salt mines of Hallstatt in Austria. The latter were the remains of cloth discarded by ancient Celtic miners and date from about 1300 to about 400 BC. Their approximate dates of manufacture and the colours and designs used correspond closely to the twills found at Hami.

Fig. 107 **Local merchants at the Kashgar Sunday market**

A detail of a cave painting found at Bezeklik shows Tokharian worshippers making donations to the Bodhisattva (see fig 190). Their reddish hair and pale eyes are similar to the mummies discovered around Urumqi, despite the fact that a gap of as much as two thousand years separates them. There is also speculation that the Tokharians were a tribe of the Yuezhi confederation – founders of the Kushan Empire – who were driven out of the Tarm Basin in about 165 BC by the Xiongnu (see section on Kushans). The main evidence for this is that they both spoke dialects of the same Tokharian language found in the Tang dynasty manuscripts of the Tarim Basin- especially those discovered around Kuqa. The Yuezhi left no written texts but etymological links have been established with a number of words that were adopted by the Chinese from the tribe's language long before they were expelled during the second century BC. These include the word *Qilian*, the mountains referred to by the Han historian Sima Qian as the domain of the Yuezhi. The name Qilian apparently derives from the Tokharian word *klyom*, meaning 'heavenly': the Chinese now call this range (on the northern side of the Tarim Basin) the Tianshan, or Heavenly

Mountains while today's Qilian Mountains are to the south. There is an intriguing quote in Pliny's *Natural History*, written around 70–80 AD and containing the Roman view of the world at the time. He refers to the people of China as 'Seres', the name given to the country by the Greeks, but the physiognomy he attributes to them is strange indeed:

'The Seres are of more than average height; they have red hair, blue eyes and harsh voices, and they have no language in which to communicate their thoughts. The merchandise (of the Cingalese) was deposited on the bank on the Seres' side of the river, and they would carry it away and leave the price if they agreed to it...' Admittedly, the information was obtained second-hand from a Sri Lankan ('Cingalese') ambassador to Rome but the possibility that this is an early reference to the Tokharians is a fascinating one.

If the mummies of the Taklamakan were Tokharians, what remains to be answered is where people with such self-evidently Caucasoid features came from. The question is still hotly debated by scholars but what is undeniable is that many of the residents of modern day Xinjiang possess distinctly 'European' features (fig. 107).

The Tokharian traders of the Tang dynasty were to be found at Kizil, Kuqa, and Karashahr on the northern section of the Silk Route and in Kashgar, Yarkand and Khotan on the southern section. They were city dwellers and were therefore important traders with the Chinese and their influences on Chinese culture were extensive. Music and dance from Kuqa were admired and imitated by the Tang Chinese and the Tokharian ladies – renowned for their beauty – introduced new fashions, hairstyles and make up to the Middle Kingdom (see section on Kuqa).

Not all Chinese approved of the infusion of foreign customs. The conservative poet Yuan Zhen (779–831), who eventually served as Prime Minister, was extremely vocal on the subject at the end of the eighth century:

> 'Ever since the Western horsemen began raising smut and dust,
> Fur and fleece, rank and rancid, have filled Hsien and Lo.
> Women make themselves Western matrons by the study of Western makeup;
> Entertainers present Western tunes, in their devotion to Western music.'

(Yuan Zhen [779–831], quoted in Schafer, 1963.
Hsien is Changan and Lo is Luoyang)

Yuan Zhen paints a rich and colourful picture of a typical foreign trader of Tang China, a man who will travel to the ends of the world, who will exploit nature and buy or sell anything to turn a profit:

> 'In search of pearls, he harnesses the glaucous sea-
> He gathers his pearls, and ascends to Ching and Heng.
> In the north, he buys the Tangut horses,
> In the west, he catches Tibetan parrots.
> Fire-washed linen from the Continent of Flames,
> Perfectly woven tapestries from the Land of Shu;
> Slave girls of Yüeh, sleek of buttery flesh;
> Houseboys of Hsi, bright of brow and eye'

(Yuan Zhen [779–831], quoted in Schafer, 1963. Fire-washed linen is asbestos, imported from the Roman Empire and the Continent of Flames is the mythical name for the lands to the south of China. Shu is Sichuan and Hsi was the name given to a tribe from Manchuria).

Tang Terracotta figurines

During the Shang dynasty (c. 1500–1050 BC) and most of the Zhou period (1050–221 BC), members of Chinese nobility were interred with their servants, charioteers and horses in order that they could be served in the afterlife. By the time of the Emperor Qin Shi Huangdi (r. 221–10 BC), real horses were still buried with the emperor but his retinue was represented by vast number of figures in terracotta (see section on Qin Shi Huangdi).

By the early part of the Tang dynasty the practice of burying minqi ('objects or articles of the spirit') was widespread. Foreigners were a great source of fascination to the Tang Chinese and are frequently depicted on tomb figures. Among these voix de silence, representations of Arab and Semite merchants from the lands to the west are common, as are (on rare occasions) pearl divers from the islands of Southeast Asia, Central Asian grooms and acrobats and figures of curly-haired Africans. These figures provide a wealth of information about the society and attitudes of Tang China. They are modelled in a naturalistic and often humorous way and are a reflection of the manner in which the Chinese regarded foreign visitors to the country. By the early part of the eighth century they were being made in vast numbers and tombs of the nobility could contain hundreds of terracotta figures. Prince Li Xian (d. 684), for example, son of the Emperor Gaozong, was interred with no fewer than 777 terracotta figures. The Emperor Ruizong (r. 684–90 and 710–12) decried the growing use of minqi as a means to show off the wealth and social status of the deceased and his or her family, rather than as a genuine expression of grief. Grave goods were carried in processions up to 10 km long and officials competed with each other to see who could produce the most ostentatious display. The problem became so acute that, in 742, sumptuary laws were enacted to specify

Fig. 108 **Terracotta tomb figure of a Central Asian holding a cornucopia (horn of plenty)**
Early Tang dynasty, 7th century
H. 40 cm
(Musée Cernuschi, Paris. PMVP/Cliché)
This humorous and well-modelled figure of a foreigner from the Western Lands is painted in unusual hues of black, pink and green. He kneels as he makes an offering.

the size and quantity of figures permissible for different official ranks: officials above the third rank could have ninety figures, those above the fifth were allowed sixty and those above the ninth, forty. During the early part of the dynasty they were generally unglazed, modelled in a somewhat stiff manner and were generic in style (fig. 108).

From the end of the seventh to the middle of the eighth century pottery figures were modelled in a dynamic and particularized fashion and were expertly glazed. Tri-coloured (or *sancai*) glaze was made by blending copper, iron or cobalt with colourless lead silicate to produce cream, amber, green

Fig. 110 **Terracotta figure, variously described as a pearl diver or a groom**
Tang dynasty, (618–907)
(Shaanxi History Museum, Xian)

and (less frequently) blue. As well as figures of humans, camels, horses, ferocious *lokapalas* (guardians) and creatures from mythology were produced. The best figures from this period are technical *tours de force* (fig. 109).

The peoples of Kunlun (or Kurung), a general term used by the Tang to describe the kingdoms of the South China Sea, were said to have dark skin and curly hair. In fact, the Chinese appear to have been singularly ill informed about the lands to the south of the Kunlun mountain range on the Tibetan Plateau- the source of the name. Some Tang records contemptuously describe all of the peoples of the lands to

Fig. 109 **Tri-colour (*sancai*) glazed figure of a camel carrying a party of musicians**
Tang dynasty, ca. 745
H. (camel) 48.5 cm; (figures) 11–16.1 cm
Unearthed in 1959 from a tomb at Zhongbao Village, Xian
(Shaanxi History Museum, Xian)
This image is a paragon of Chinese ceramic art. The musicians are a mixture of Chinese and Central Asian individuals who play string, wind and percussion instruments including reed pipes, a flute and a type of lute. The central figure dances or perhaps sings to the music as their mount stretches his neck and bellows.

the south as Kunlun peoples, even applying the term to Persians and Indians. The term is most often used, however, to denote the people from the South East Asian archipelago- a source of slaves for the Chinese. The Chinese seem to have admired not only their skill in taming wild animals, such as elephants and rhinoceroses, and also their ability to stay under water for long periods of time. They were sought after and trained as pearl divers (fig. 110).

A small number of Africans reached Changan, probably as slaves aboard Arab ships. Official records from the Tang dynasty indicate that the first African country known to the Chinese was Shunai, located in the southern part of modern-day Somalia. The kingdom is recorded as having sent an ambassador to Tang China in 629. The Chinese sometimes refer to Africans as *Zangi*, apparently after the island of Zanzibar, and also grouped them under the somewhat confusing heading of *Kunlun*. This means that they can be only tentatively identified among the terracotta tomb figures of the Tang (fig. 111).

Terracotta figures of Chinese subjects are a barometer of fashions current among the Tang nobility. The pulchritudinous Yang Guifei, celebrated concubine of the Tang Emperor Xuanzong (r. 712–56), was regarded as the ideal of feminine beauty by the ladies of Tang. Her rubenesque proportions and towering 'cloud-tresses' were widely imitated and are represented in many of the tomb figures of the mid-eighth century (fig. 112).

The renowned Tang dynasty poet Bai Juyi (772–846) captures the moment when Xuanzong is first smitten as he sights Lady Yang emerging from her bath:

> *'Her hair like a cloud,*
> *Her face like a flower,*
> *A gold hair-pin adorning her tresses.*
> *Behind the warm lotus-flower curtain,*
> *They took their pleasure in the spring night.'*

(Bai Juyi [772–846], 'Song of Eternal Sorrow')

Each year the emperor would take her to the hot springs built specially outside Changan so he could watch her bathe. When Xuanzong played board games and was losing, the Lady Yang would set loose her Samarkand lapdog or her pet parakeet to upend the pieces and preserve the emperor's dignity (fig. 112). So besotted was Xuanzong that he neglected his official duties and almost brought the dynasty to an end. An Lushan- an illiterate former slave of Turkish and Sogdian descent- succeeded in gaining the emperor's favour through a combination of intrigue and cunning. In 755 he attempted to seize the throne, marching from Beijing with an army of 150,000. After taking Luoyang he declared himself emperor and Xuanzong fled towards Sichuan. En-route Xuanzong's troops mutinied and he was allowed to escape, only after agreeing that Yang Guifei be strangled. The

rebellion was not quelled until 763, the conflict prolonged by the involvement of Tibetans. Imperial power was eventually restored with the assistance of a large force of Uighurs and an army led by the gifted general Guo Ziyi (697–781). In

Fig. 112 **A terracotta figure of a court lady holding a dog**
Tang dynasty, (618–907)
H. 53 cm
(Eskenazi Ltd)
This figure, and a similar example in the Tokyo National Museum, are a reminder of the fashion of the day for Samarkand lapdogs (see p. 101).

Fig. 111 **Terracotta figure of a dancing black boy**
Tang dynasty, (618–907)
H. 27 cm
(Spink and Son Ltd)

Fig. 113 **Stone portrait of Emperor Taizong's horse Saluzi**
Tang dynasty, ca. 636
L. 206 cm
Formerly at the tomb of Taizong, Zhaoling, Shaanxi province. Now in the University of Pennsylvania Museum, Philadelphia
(University of Pennsylvania Museum)
In this relief Saluzi ('deep brown') is depicted with the famous General Qiu Xinggong, who pulls an arrow out of the horses flanks- a commemoration of a battle in which Qiu saved the Emperor's life.

return for providing assistance the Uighurs demanded the right to sack the city of Luoyang and this they did at the end of 757, and again in 762. A secondary consequence of the An Lushan rebellion was that a marked reduction in the production of ceramic figurines occurred; perhaps because of the destruction of the kilns. Figurines continued to be produced throughout the late Tang era but in smaller numbers and without the exuberant vitality of the middle period.

Tomb sculpture and paintings

Two other aspects of Tang funeral practice provide information about the affluent and cosmopolitan nature of the society of the time: stone sculpture above ground and tomb paintings. Stone sculpture placed above tombs dates back to 117 BC and the mausoleum of General Huo Qubing (see fig. 15). From the first century AD onwards, the Chinese adopted the practice of erecting 'spirit roads' – an avenue of statues and engraved stele lining the approaches to the tomb of an important figure. Statues of men and animals, often mythical beasts, served as a guard of honour for the deceased in the afterlife and a reminder of his or her status. The spirit roads erected at Tang dynasty tombs reflect an empire at the height of its power. The earliest Tang tombs, such as that of

Emperor Taizong (r. 626–49), were erected during a period in which China became the dominant power in Asia; the Ordos region, Inner Mongolia and the Tarim Basin were brought firmly under Chinese control and Taizong's defeat of the Eastern Turks in 630 resulted in some 10,000 Turkish families moving to the capital to live. Contacts with Tibet were enhanced by the marriage, in 641, of the Tang princess Wen Chong to King Songsan Gambo- the country's ruler. Campaigns were also launched against Korea although it was not until 668, long after Taizong's death, that the entire country was finally subjugated as a result of an alliance with Silla, one of its states. Taizong's mausoleum at Zhaoling, northwest of Xian, was built into the side of a mountain and required thirteen years to complete. Fourteen statues of foreign rulers once stood at the northern gate while the east and west galleries contained stone reliefs of his six favourite horses, each of which played a role in one of his military campaigns. The carvings are based on drawings by the court painter Yan Liben (fig.113).

Taizong's eldest son and heir, the hapless Li Cheng Qian, was a Turkophile of absurd proportions. He preferred to speak Turkish rather than Chinese and set up a complete Turkish encampment in the palace grounds where he sat, dressed as a Khan, eating mutton cooked over a camp fire. He was eventually caught plotting and removed from the line of succession.

At the Qianling Mausoleum, northwest of Changan, is the joint burial place for Emperor Gaozong (r. 649–83) and his implacable consort Wu Zetian (r. 690–705), the only woman ever to become emperor of China. The inner wall contains an area of 240 hectares (about 600 acres) and all over the site are reminders of a country enjoying its glory days. A stele at Qianling, erected on Wu Zetian's orders and in memory of her achievements is without an inscription, signifying that her accomplishments were so great that that they could not be expressed by mere words. Statues of winged horses at Qianling recall Assyrian reliefs and a large stone ostrich on Gaozong's tomb is a reminder of the Tang fascination with distant lands. A group of sixty-one stone figures of foreigners stand within the inner enclosure at Qianling, representing the foreign rulers and envoys who were resident in Changan or who came to attend the funeral of Emperor Gaozong (fig. 114).

Of the sixty-one original statues, one has disappeared and the remainder have been damaged at some time in the distant past, perhaps during a period of xenophobia in China. On the back of each statue is an inscription giving the subject's name, title and country of origin. These inscriptions are now illegible but were, according to records from the time, still visible during the Song dynasty (960–1279). Two Persians were identified, including a certain King Balāsh – thought to be King Peroz of Persia – the last ruler of the Sasanian dynasty who sought refuge in Changan from the Arab invasion of his country (see section on Persians in Changan. They now stand in silent serried ranks, paying homage to the late emperor.

Qianling has numerous ancillary tombs containing members of royal relatives – seventeen in the southeast area alone. Some have been excavated in recent years and the murals that line their passageways are a captivating record of court life during the Tang dynasty. Princess Yongtai (684–701), a granddaughter of Gaozong and Wu Zetian, died at the age of seventeen – almost certainly at the hands of the latter. An exquisite mural was found on the eastern wall of the front chamber in Yongtai's tomb, depicting two groups of palace maids who appear to walk in a slow, silent candlelit procession towards her bedchamber (fig. 115).

Fig. 114 **Part of a group of 61 stone statues of foreign dignitaries**
Tang dynasty, ca. 683 AD
Maousoleum of Emperor Gaozong, Qianling, Xian, Shaanxi province

Fig. 115 **Mural depicting a procession of court ladies**
Tang dynasty, 706
Discovered in 1960 at the tomb of Princess Yongtai, Qianling, Xian, Shaanxi province
The ladies in this beautiful painting – some dressed in men's clothes and of differing ages – carry candlestands, horsehair whisks, incense-burners, food-boxes, tall cups, sceptres and fans. Princess Yongtai was not granted a formal burial until after Wu Zetian's death in 705.

Fig. 116 **Mural depicting a game of polo**
Tang dynasty, 706
H.196 cm, W.154
Discovered in 1971 at the tomb of Prince Zhanghuai (Li Xian), Qianling, near Xian, Shaanxi province
The sport of polo was adopted from Persia and soon became the favourite pursuit of Tang nobility, including Emperor Xuanzong (r. 712–56), and was played by both and women. This mural is thought to be the earliest known depiction of the sport.

The murals adorning the walls of Crown Prince Zhanghuai's tomb are quite different. Crown Prince Zhanghuai, born Li Xian, was the second son of Gaozong and Wu Zetian. He was deposed by Empress Wu in 680, banished to Sichuan province and eventually forced to commit suicide in 684. He was not formally buried until after Empress Wu's death and the restoration of Emperor Zhongzong to the throne in 705. The murals of Crown Prince Zhanghuai's tomb are more exuberant than those of Yongtai and are a splendid record of aristocratic pursuits during the Tang dynasty. More than fifty paintings were found in the passageways of the tomb and it is quite clear from their content that Prince Zhanghuai was inordinately fond of hunting and polo (fig. 116).

In the hunting scenes at the tomb, well-dressed Tang nobles hunt with falcons, trained cheetahs and small dogs. Cheetahs and dogs were used for a brief period at the beginning of the eighth century and there are records of both types of animal imported as tribute, particularly from Samarkand (see section on Sogdian murals). Another of the murals from Prince Zhanghuai's tomb depicts a group of foreign emissaries at a time when numerous countries maintained diplomatic relations with the Tang court (fig. 117).

The many images of beautiful women form the last category of murals in Zhanghuai's tomb. Artists began to

depict individual aspects of character and physiognomy and an air of confidence, apparent at the beginning of the 8th century, is reflected in the humour contained in many of the paintings. In one a rather lecherous man with a bulbous nose leers suggestively at a court beauty who holds a rooster. In another, a well-built older lady is accompanied by a female attendant, dressed in the clothing of a Central Asian male and by a female dwarf- all part of the new fondness for exotica (fig. 118).

Other works of art from Tang dynasty Xian

The Daming Palace (the 'Palace of Great Brightness'), in the northwest section of Changan, was the largest of the three palaces built for the Tang rulers- the two others being the Taiji and Xingqing palaces. Built in 662 on the orders of Emperor Gaozong, Daming was situated on high ground and faced south. The remains of the front hall at Daming, the Hanyuan Hall, were excavated between 1956 and 1960 and the dimensions of the building were discovered to be about 67 metres by 29 metres with a floor space of almost 2,000 square metres. It sat above a vast open area of about 600 by about 750 metres. The relics found in the remains of the Daming Palace include large numbers of tiles and bricks with geometric designs, some inscribed with the phrase 'Made by an Official Artisan' to show that they have been

Fig. 117 **Mural depicting a group of foreign envoys to the Tang court**
Tang dynasty, 706 AD
H. 184.5 cm, W. 252.5 cm
Discovered in 1971 at the tomb of Prince Zhanghuai (Li Xian), Qianling, near Xian, Shaanxi province
In this mural, the three Chinese officials on the left greet the three foreign ambassadors on the right as they wait to see the emperor. The envoys have been tentatively identified from their dress and appearance as coming from (left to right): the Eastern Roman Empire, Japan or Korea and one the northeast Chinese minority peoples.

silver objects were discovered, some in Chinese style, and others showing clear foreign influence (fig. 120).

Another of the relics from Hejia Village is a reminder of the intense Chinese affection for horses (fig. 121).

The Tang annals relate that Emperor Xuanzong (r. 712–56) owned 400 horses that were trained to dance. Arthur Waley's account of the sad fate of the horses is the most colourful. Each year, on the emperor's birthday, a group of them would perform a complex dressage to a suite called the 'Tune of the Tilted Cup'. The horses would be either ridden up a steep slope and perform on top of a tall platform, or would dance while held aloft on benches. They would conclude their performance by kneeling before the

Fig. 118 **Mural with three ladies**
Modern copy with enhanced detail. Original Tang dynasty, 706
Discovered in 1971 at the tomb of Prince Zhanghuai (Li Xian), Qianling, near Xian, Shaanxi province.

Fig. 119 **Marble figure of a Bodhisattva with traces of gilding and pigments**
Tang dynasty, ca. mid-8th century
H. 110 cm
Found in 1959 in the precincts of the Daming Palace, Xian, Shaanxi province
(Forest of Stelae Museum, Xian)

inspected and approved by the Ministry of Public Works. A sensual and graceful marble statue of a Bodhisattva found in the ruins of Daming is inspired by the Gupta sculpture of India (fig. 119). The manner of depicting the Bodhisattva revealed in this sculpture became the norm in Chinese art for centuries afterwards. Typically, one hip is thrust out to the side, the arm on the same side is bent at the elbow and held in a raised position and the arm on the opposite side hangs pendant. The robes cling to emphasize the contours of the body and the figure is then adorned with a layer of jewellery. The Daming Bodhisattva is the most supreme example of it type and has been described – with a concession to gender – as the 'Venus of the East'.

During the An Lushan Rebellion of 755, two large terracotta urns were buried for safekeeping in the village of Hejia on the southern outskirts of Changan, on land that had been the residence of Li Shouli, son of Prince Zhanghuai. The pots were discovered in 1970 and found to contain more than 1,000 objects of incalculable value. The treasures include precious medicines and coins from Japan, Sasanian Persia, the Eastern Roman Empire (Byzantium), and a large number from China itself. Some 270 gold and

Fig. 120 **Gilt silver octagonal cup decorated with musicians and dancers**
Tang dynasty, (618–907)
H. 6.4 cm
Unearthed in 1970 at Hejia village, Xian, Shaanxi province
(Shaanxi History Museum, Xian)
One of two octagonal cups excavated at the site, the facets of this vessel are decorated with four musicians and four dancers – all foreign in appearance – and on the handle are two addorsed heads of Central Asian men. The shape of the cup is Near Eastern in origin and may have been made by one of the many Persian or Sogdian silversmiths living in Changan at the time. The popularity of foreign entertainers was at its height during the period before the An Lushan Rebellion and an elaborate musical arrangement called the *Shibu Yue* ('Ten-Part composition') was performed at important banquets and celebrations. Each part was composed in the musical style of a certain country or nationality and the figures on this cup appear to be conducting a performance of this arrangement (see also the section on foreigners in Xian).

Fig. 121 **Gilt silver wine flask with a design of a dancing horse**
Tang dynasty, (618–907)
H. 14.3 cm
Unearthed in 1970 at Hejia village, Xian, Shaanxi province
(Shaanxi History Museum, Xian)
The shape of this wine flask follows the shape of the leather bottles used by the northern nomads.

sovereign with wine cups held in their mouths, as if offering a toast. During the An Lushan Rebellion the horses were dispersed and eventually fell into the hands of a warlord who knew nothing of their imperial pedigree. One day, during a banquet, marching music was played in the camp and the horses began to dance. The grooms believed them to be possessed and, at the instigation of the warlord, they began to beat them with brooms. The horse thought they were being beaten for not keeping proper time to the music and the more they were beaten they harder they danced. Eventually the horses fell dead on the stable floor. (Abridged from Waley, 1952.)

An agate drinking vessel, another of the treasures from the Hejia hoard, is a work of technical genius (fig. 122).

Fig. 122 **Agate drinking horn (rhyton) in the shape of an ox-head with gold spout**
Tang dynasty, (618–907)
L. 15.6 cm
Unearthed in 1970 at Hejia village, Xian, Shaanxi province
(Shaanxi History Museum, Xian)
The medium and style of this *rhyton* suggest that it is Central Asian or Sasanian Persian in origin.

Fig. 123 **The Famen Monastery (Famensi), Fufeng County, Shaanxi province.**
Eastern Han dynasty (25–220 AD)

Famensi

The last of the Tang dynasty sites in the Xian area that we will examine in this book is the Famen monastery in Fufeng County, 120 km west of Xian. Originally founded in the Eastern Han dynasty (25–220 AD) as the Asoka Temple, it was renamed the Famensi during the Tang dynasty. From the Northern Wei (386–534) onwards it was a place of pilgrimage and was said to contain relics of Buddha Sakyamuni himself. The monastery was clearly the recipient of a large amount of largesse, particularly during the Tang

dynasty. There is literary evidence that the relics were carried on a number of occasions in a lavish procession between Famensi and the Tang capital – a distance of over 120 km. In 819, the relics were paraded before a rapturous crowd and put on display in the imperial palace. The Confucianist poet and essayist Han Yu (768–824), a fierce opponent of Buddhism, submitted a blunt memorial to the court in which he criticizes the emperor himself for encouraging the practice of a foreign religion:

> 'You are…putting on for the citizens of the capital this extraordinary spectacle which is nothing more than a sort of theatrical amusement….Now that the Buddha has long been dead, is it fitting that his decayed and rotten bones, his ill-omened and filthy remains, should be allowed to enter in the precincts of the palace?…Without reason you have taken up unclean things and examined them in person.'

(Han Yu, in 819, *Lun fogu biao*, 'Memorial Discussing the Buddha's Bones'. Quoted in Sherman Lee, 1998).

Han Yu's punishment for this outburst was exile to Guangdong but the seeds were sown for Emperor Wuzong's campaign of persecution- launched against the Buddhists from 842–45. About 4,500 temples and monasteries were closed or destroyed and 250,000 monks and nuns were laicized. The treasures of Famensi survived, however. In 1981, part of the pagoda collapsed during a storm and, during a reconstruction project in 1987, a set of three underground chambers was discovered in the foundations. The chambers were excavated and produced four relics, purportedly finger bones of the Buddha, buried in about 874. Only one appears to be of bone, the other three are circular crystal tubes – an acceptable substitute at a time when genuine relics were in both great demand and short supply. One of the relics was intended to be displayed on a tray held by a gilt-silver Bodhisattva, made especially for Emperor Yizong (r. 859–73). Wrapped around the Bodhisattva are more than 200 saltwater pearls – Silk Road imports from the Persian Gulf. A large number of other treasures were also deposited in the foundations- apparently as a commemorative donation for the relics, including 121 gold and silver articles, sixteen porcelain vessels, stone and lacquer objects, 400 pieces of jewellery, imported glass and over 7,000 pieces of silk textile. The porcelains included a number of *mise* ('secret colour') Yue ware vessels, hitherto thought not to have been produced until the Song dynasty. There is room to examine only three of the artefacts from the Famensi here but each has a strong connection with the Silk Road. A complete set of tea-drinking paraphernalia was discovered in the foundations, all in silver and gilded silver (fig. 124). Techniques for working with precious metals were perfected during the Tang dynasty, because of contacts with the craftsmen of Central Asia and Persia, many of whom were resident in Changan. Although tea drinking was known in China from ancient times, by the Tang dynasty it had become an elaborate ritual and was inextricably linked to the practice of Chan (or Zen) Buddhism. Practitioners of this form of Buddhism were expected to meditate for long periods, eschewing both sleep and food, but were permitted to drink tea, the stimulating effects of which kept them awake. The practice eventually spread to the population in general and the intricate form of the Famensi tea implements indicates that, by the late Tang dynasty, it had become an art form:

The second article, a blue glass dish, may be foreign in origin (fig. 125).

Another of the artefacts found at the Famen Pagoda reveals a different type of contact with neighbouring countries. A gilded silver censer (or incense burner) was discovered together with a small figure of the Hindu god Ganesha, the elephant-headed son of Siva (fig. 126). Only a handful of figures of Ganesha have been identified in Chinese art.

Fig. 124 **Set of silver and gilded silver articles for the ritual preparation of tea**
Tang dynasty, ca. 874
Articles are (clockwise from top left): gilt-silver openwork basket for curing newly picked leaves with designs of geese, H. 17.8 cm; gilt-silver container for salt (or possibly a tea caddy) with human figures in landscape, H. 24.7 cm; gilt-silver box for sifting tea with designs of apsaras and cranes, l. 13.4 cm; gilt-silver tortoise-shaped box for storing rolled tea-leaves, L. 28 cm.; gilt-silver device for rolling tea-leaves decorated with clouds and *qilin* (a mythical beast), L. 27.7 cm; (centre) silver salt-holder, H. 17 cm. Found in 1987 at the Famen Temple Pagoda, Fufeng County, Shaanxi province.
(Famen Temple Museum)
The Tang dynasty text, 'The Classic of Tea' by Lu Yu was the first treatise ever written on the drinking of tea. The presence of salt-receptacles at Famensi is a reflection of a fondness among the Tang for taking tea with salt and spice.

Fig. 125 **Blue glass dish decorated with incised and gilded plantain leaves**
Tang dynasty, (618–907)
Probably from Nishapur, Persia or Samarra, Iraq
D. 15.8 cm
Excavated in 1987 at the Famen Temple Pagoda, Fufeng County, Shaanxi province
(Famen Temple Museum)
This dish has an Islamic flavour that suggests it was imported to China, perhaps from Nishapur in Persia or Samarra in Iraq, where similar vessels have been found. The Shosoin repository in Nara, Japan has a number of Persian glass vessels but such items, because of their fragility, are rare.

Fig. 126 **Gilt-Silver Censer with figure of Ganesha**
Tang dynasty, (618–907)
H. (Censer) 41.8 cm
Discovered in 1987 in the foundations of the Famen Temple Pagoda, Fufeng County, Shaanxi province
(Famen Temple Museum)

A rare object, a bronze ewer decorated with human faces (fig. 127), found in the Tang dynasty Qingshan temple close to Qin Shi Huangdi's mausoleum, is not merely influenced by India- it was almost certainly made there.

Other Tang dynasty works from sites other than the Xian area can be found throughout this book. One of the greatest collections of Tang art is not in China but in Japan, at the Shosoin repository in Nara*. Aside from the Shosoin, Tang silk fabrics were also found in large numbers at the Astana cemetery in Turfan, Xinjiang province and are discussed in detail in that section.

Until 1953, when they were moved to a modern concrete structure, Emperor Shomu's possessions were stored in the Todaiji's storehouse, known as the Shosoin. The original wooden structure, 33 metres in length and 14 metres high, is raised above the ground by means of forty pillars. A style of construction known as *azekura-zukuri* was used to minimize the effects of damp; it permits the circulation of air on dry days when the logs contract slightly, and seals the interior on damp days. As a result, the contents have remained in an almost perfect state of preservation for almost thirteen centuries and represent the largest and most important single group of Silk Road artefacts in the world. Chinese envoys to the Tempyo court, Japanese emissaries to the Tang capital and pilgrims, journeying to China in search of Buddhist learning, are all believed to have been the source of the Shosoin's treasures but there are also locally produced items as well.

The Japanese author Ryoichi Hayashi (Hayashi, 1975) has grouped the Shosoin inventory into twelve categories: manuscripts and documents, writing materials, household furnishings, personal attire, table utensils, musical instruments and accessories, games and games pieces, weaponry and armour, medicines and aromatics, 'regalia for annual observances', Buddhist regalia, and craftsmens' tools. Among the 2,794 complete items and the many thousands of fragments are Chinese mirrors, paintings and ceramics; glass and silver vessels from Persia; rugs and silk textiles with Chinese, Persian, nomadic and classical motifs; musical instruments that include the world's only surviving example of an ancient Indian lute (fig. 205), and approximately 170 *Gigaku* dance-masks (see p. 159). Two surprising features of the treasures of the Shosoin repository are the relatively small number of ceramics (the fifty-odd items are mostly functional) and the almost complete absence of gold or silver jewellery. Excavations of Tang sites in China have yielded large numbers of exquisite items of jewellery and the dearth of examples in the Shosoin is mystery.

Many of the Shosoin's treasures exist nowhere else on earth and provide a priceless glimpse of the culture and tastes of the time: little wonder, then, that Ryoichi Hayashi has called the repository 'the final destination of the Silk Road'.

* The Shosoin. The Nara period (710–84) in Japan, also referred to as the Tempyo period, is contemporary with the early Tang dynasty of China and was strongly influenced by it. One of the most devoutly Buddhist emperors of the Nara period was Shomu (r. 724–49), who established monasteries in each province of Japan and made Buddhism the *de facto* state religion. His greatest achievement was the establishment, in 743, of the Todaiji temple in Nara and the construction of its massive, 16 metre bronze image of Vairocana (the cosmic Buddha), known as the Great Buddha (*Daibutsu*). The temple was dedicated in 752 and its Great Buddha Hall (*Daibutsuden*), 88 metres by 51 metres, is the largest wooden building in the world. Shomu abdicated in 749, in favour of his daughter Empress Koken, and died in May 756. At the end of forty-nine days of official mourning his widow, Empress Dowager Komyo (d. 760), dedicated his possessions to the Todaiji temple. Throughout their marriage the emperor and empress remained inseparable and Komyo's dedication, written in her own neat calligraphy, contains a petition to the Great Buddha and concludes with the following remark:

'The list given above contains treasures that have been handled by the late emperor and articles that served him in the palace. These objects remind me of the bygone days, and the sight of them causes me bitter grief'

(Empress Komyo[d. 760], 22 July 756. From the *Kokka Chimpo-cho* ['Catalogue of Rare National Treasures']. Quoted in Hayashi, 1975)

Fig. 127 **Bronze ewer decorated with human faces**
Tang dynasty, (618–907)
Probably from Northern India
H. 29.5 cm
Unearthed in 1985 at the Qingshan Temple, Lintong County, Shaanxi province
(Shaanxi Lintong Museum)
The shape of this ewer resembles traditional Sasanian vessels but the faces are Indian. It may have been carried back to China by one of the many Buddhist monks travelling to India in search of sutras.

The great poets: The intellectual climate of the Tang dynasty

The writing of poetry flourished during the Tang dynasty. One of the main reasons for this was that the civil service examinations, begun by the Sui rulers to select officials from among the scholar class, was expanded by the Tang to include the writing of poetry. Tang emperors actively encouraged the writing of poems:at imperial banquets the emperor would frequently compose a poem and his ministers would then write replies. The cultural influences of the countries to China's west also flowed into the capital and encouraged creativity and, furthermore, the prosperity of the time meant that scholars could travel widely and absorb new ideas. During the reign of Xuanzong (r. 712–56) poets held important posts in the government.

Li Bai (also known as Li Po, 701–62) became a friend of Xuanzong and briefly held a position in the Imperial Academy before becoming disillusioned. He was caught up in the An Lushan rebellion of 755 and joined the staff of Prince Yung, who made an unsuccessful bid for the throne. Li Bai was exiled to the southwest of China but, before reaching it, was pardoned and spent the remainder of his life wandering the country. He loved to frequent the wine shops of Changan and, imbibing freely, would write flamboyant verse about the beauty of the women of the city. When he ran out of money he would exchange the gold tortoise that he carried as proof of his official rank for wine. Li Bai's other favourite themes were friendship, the life of ordinary people, his own hopes and desires and the splendours of the natural world. He wrote almost 900 poems and many of them, like those of his contemporaries, were also set to music. His verse, romantic in the extreme, often possesses a dream-like quality that reflects his boundless imagination:

'I left the rosy clouds of Baidi in the morning.
Covered a thousand li to Jiangling in a day;
While the apes on both banks were still calling.
My boat had sailed ten thousand hills away'
('Leaving Baidi for Jiangling' by Li Bai*)

Li Bai's close friend Du Fu (712–70) lived in Changan for ten years before he was finally appointed to a minor government post. His disillusionment and the poverty he endured are reflected in the subject matter of his poems. Like Li Bai, he was caught up in the An Lushan rebellion and was actually taken prisoner. Many of his greatest poems were written during this period:

'…Having a son's a curse today.
Far better to have daughters, get them married-
A son will lie lost in the grass, unburied.

Why, Sir, on distant Qinghai shore
The bleached ungathered bones lie year on year.
New ghosts complain, and those who died before
Weep in the wet grey sky and haunt the ear'

(Du Fu 'Ballad of the Army Carts', translated by Vikram Seth, 1992. Qinghai Lake -Kokonor or 'The Blue Lake'- was known as the 'Western Sea' during ancient times and is a remote saline lake, situated some 3,200 metres above sea level. Qinghai province has been a place of exile since the Han dynasty. It lies on the main route between China and Tibet and throughout the 740s was the scene of fierce fighting between the armies of the two countries. Tang poets always regarded war as a cause for sadness because it reflected a failure of government.)

Du Fu lived the last decade of his life in exile in Sichuan province where he wrote about half of the 1,400 poems that survive.

Another of the great Tang poets, Wang Wei (701–62) was almost an exact contemporary of Li Bai, although there is no certainty that they ever met. Wang was the child prodigy of a prestigious family. He experienced mixed fortunes as a government official, passing the official examinations and being appointed assistant secretary for music before falling out of favour and spending the remainder of his life in minor posts and enjoying a life of quiet contemplation. During the An Lushan rebellion he sided, albeit reluctantly, with the rebels and was narrowly spared execution when imperial power was restored. Wang Wei's multiple talents included calligraphy and painting and his poems are more reflective than those of Li Bai and Du Fu. His themes are the natural world, solitude and his own faith in Buddhism:

'We send you home to a grave on Stone Tower Mountain;
through the green green of pine and cypress, mourners'
carriages return.
Among white clouds we've laid your bones- it is ended forever;
Only the mindless waters remain, flowing down to the world
of men.'
(Wang Wei, 701–62, 'Weeping for Ying Yao'. Translated by Watson 1984. Ying Yao was a close friend and fellow poet of Wang Wei)

The poet Bai Juyi (772–846) is probably the greatest poet of the later Tang period. He wrote almost 3,000 poems – the most famous of which is 'Song of Eternal Sorrow' – which chronicles the misfortunes of Emperor Xuanzong and the Lady Yang Guifei (see p. 97).

In terms of the sheer number, the quality of its imagery and the diversity of its subject matter, Tang poetry has never been equalled in the history of Chinese literature. During the Qing dynasty (1644–1911) an anthology of Tang poetry was complied, comprising almost 50,000 poems by 2,200 poets – more than the entire repertoire of the previous 2,000 years of Chinese history.

* Other examples of Li Bai's poetry appear elsewhere in this book.

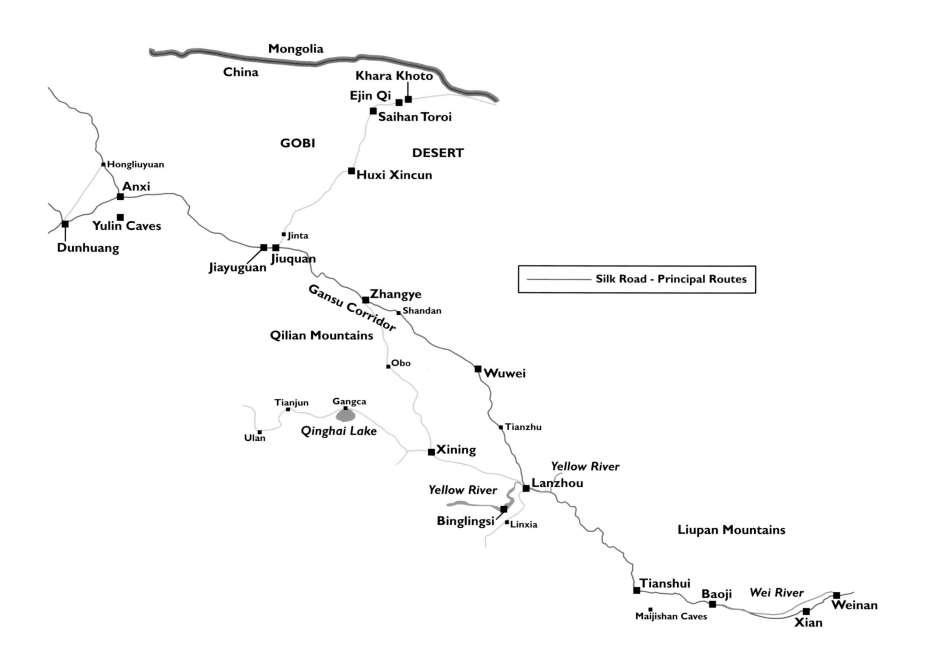

Mongolia

China

Khara Khoto

Ejin Qi

Saihan Toroi

GOBI

DESERT

Hongliuyuan

Anxi

Huxi Xincun

Yulin Caves

Dunhuang

Jinta

Jiuquan

Jiayuguan

Zhangye

Gansu Corridor

Shandan

Qilian Mountains

Obo

Wuwei

Silk Road - Principal Routes

Tianjun

Gangca

Tianzhu

Ulan

Qinghai Lake

Xining

Yellow River

Lanzhou

Yellow River

Liupan Mountains

Binglingsi

Linxia

Tianshui

Baoji

Wei River

Weinan

Maijishan Caves

Xian

THE SILK ROAD
BETWEEN XIAN AND DUNHUANG

THE SILK ROAD BETWEEN XIAN AND DUNHUANG

CHAPTER SEVEN

THE ROUTE WEST FROM XIAN

Xian is regarded as the eastern terminus of the Silk Road although branches continue on to Korea and Japan. We will examine the ancient capitals of these two countries later in the book but, for the sake of brevity, will treat Xian as the starting point for the journey west. Farewell parties were held in the inns along the banks of the Wei River in Xian; willow twigs were broken off, made into a circle and given to the traveller as prayer for his or her safe return:

> *'The travellers' willow tokens are fresh and green*
> *And I offer you a toast*
> *For you are departing towards the setting sun*
> *And soon you will be a part of the past.'*

(Wang Wei [701–62]. For travellers heading east, the starting point would be the Baqiao Bridge on the Ba River, east of Changan, where the same willow branch rituals would occur. For a different translation of this poem see p. 138)

Merchants would leave Xian by the Ximen, or West Gate (fig. 128). They usually travelled in groups in order to reduce the risk of attack (see fig. 157) Dunhuang painting of high-waymen). Horses, mules and the two-humped Bactrian camel – already familiar to the Chinese for a thousand years – were used but, by the end of the eighth century, even a decrepit Ferghana horse cost forty bolts of silk that only the wealthy and officials of high rank could afford. Ordinary travellers used the tough ponies of the steppe: the tarpan (*Equus przewalski*) or the humble donkey.

Fig. 128 **Ximen (West Gate), Xian**

Early Ming dynasty, 14th century
Built on the site of the original
Tang dynasty gate

Camels

'The camel is an unusual domestic animal. He carries a saddle of flesh on his back. He runs rapidly over shifting sands. He shows his worth in dangerous places. He has a secret knowledge of springs. His knowledge is truly subtle!'

(Guo Pu, 3rd century, 'In Praise of the Camel' [*Tuotuo Zan*], quoted in J-P Drège and E.M. Bührer, 1989)

'Exhort all men to make the pilgrimage. They will come to you on foot and on the backs of swift camels from every distant quarter...'

(From the Koran, XXII 27. Translated by N. J. Dawood in Dawood, 1999)

Bronze belt buckles and lamps from China's Warring States Period (475–221 BC) contain depictions of two humped Bactrian camels with riders, suggesting that they had already been in use for some time. At this early date the Chinese appear to have acquired them from the nomadic tribes of the northern frontier, the Xiongnu in particular, evidenced by their frequent appearance on Ordos region belt buckles. By the Han dynasty, camels were bred in large numbers by the Chinese government with large herds in Shaanxi and Gansu provinces. Edward Schafer states that, in 754, the Tang government herds in Gansu alone contained 279,900 cattle, sheep and camels. The animals were kept by wealthy Chinese to be ridden and by merchants as beasts of burden and the fastest were reserved for the 'Bright Camel Envoys' – used to convey messages during times of military emergency. The 'Bright Camel Envoys' were strictly for use in times of national crisis and the Chinese were scandalized when, in 751, the emperor's ill-starred consort Yang Guifei used them to convey a gift of rare Borneo camphor to the Turkic-Sogdian general An Lushan. Based on the records available to us and on depictions of camels and their riders in Chinese art it seems likely that herdsmen and grooms were almost always foreigners: Mongolians, Central Asians and Tibetans. As pack animals, Bactrian camels are without equal: they can survive for seven or eight days without water in high temperatures and for several weeks in cool weather; they store about 35 kg of fat in their humps and can draw on it when food is scarce, shedding as much as twenty to twenty-five per cent of their body weight without ill effect. They can also carry a load of about 150 kg for up to 40 km per day with broad pads on their feet ensuring that they are sure-footed, and have remarkable nostrils that they can close during sandstorms. The camel's hair can be made into cloth and the flesh eaten – especially the hump, which the Chinese regarded as a delicacy:

'Red camel-humps are brought them from jade broilers,
and sweet fish is offered them on crystal trays…'

(Du Fu, 712–70, 'A Song of Fair Women')

Scholars have recently examined the loads carried by pottery camels in tombs of the Northern Wei to Tang Dynasties (fourth to tenth centuries) to obtain an idea of what comprised a typical merchant's cargo. Elfriede Knauer's research in her book *The Camel's Load in Life and Death* reveals that the same type of pack saddle has been used since the Han dynasty or even earlier, consisting of two bamboo poles tied lengthways around the humps and interconnected with ropes. Any type of load can then be securely attached to the resulting framework. An improvement on this is a packboard contraption in which lengths of thick reeds or bamboo are aligned in parallel and connected by two lateral poles. These packboards may also have served as the collapsible lattice walls of the cameleer's *yurt* (nomadic tent). Typical loads, based on what can be ascertained from examining tomb figures, might include skeins and folded lengths of silk fabric, food for the journey (in the shape of a dead rabbit or bird), a pilgrim flask or phoenix-head ewer for water and sometimes a pet monkey or dog perched on top of the saddle (fig. 130). Fanciful loads such as a single musician or even a complete orchestra (figs. 109 and 205) *Shosoin plectrum guard*) are unlikely to have had a counterpart in real life but they do reflect Chinese curiosity about the people living to the west.

Fig. 129 **A Chinese camel caravan, ca. 1925**

(Photo by Alfred Tozer)

Fig. 130 **Glazed earthenware model of a camel**
Tang dynasty, (618–907)
H. 83.3 cm
(Eskenazi Ltd)

This fine example is laden with a pair of saddlebags, modelled as 'monster-masks' and slung between its humps. The animal's load is rendered in accurate detail and includes provisions and equipment for the journey: wooden packboards, a side of meat (with ribs visible), a second haunch of meat, a typical Tang ewer, what appears to be a skein of silk, and a round object resembling a bowl or a loaf of bread. The saddlebags on this example are typical of those carried by real camels at the time, consisting of leather satchels or large canvas bags. The demon mask motif on the bags has been variously described as a stylised depiction of a tiger-pelt or a parody of the facial features of Central Asians. Many pottery camels carry pilgrim flasks decorated with vine-scrolls, palmettes, musicians and dancers in distinctly Hellenistic style. Such flasks imitate metal vessels from West Asia.

The Road West

Near the old caravan route on the Shaanxi-Gansu border are the Lung (Liupan) Mountains. Edward Schafer relates that these mountains were once the source of indigenous green parrots, now hunted to extinction. During the ninth century the men of Lung were obliged to risk their lives to catch parrots to satisfy the insatiable demand for the rare birds at the imperial court in Changan. The highest mountain in the Liupan range – Kongdongshan (2,123 metres) – has been sacred to Daoists for centuries.

The Maijishan Caves

With their animals laden with silk and other goods, merchants would proceed along the Wei River valley. The first important site, as travellers headed west, is the Maijishan caves in Gansu province, 50 km southeast of Tianshui and about 300 km from Xian. Maijishan ('Wheat Stack Mountain') is so named because of its resemblance to a pile of wheat. One hundred and ninety-four caves have been carved from its precipitous granite walls, containing about 7,000 statues in clay and stone and a large number of murals, the latter in poor condition because of the humidity in the region. The site was active as a Buddhist centre from the fifth century to the Song dynasty (960–1279), with restoration work and some additions made as late as the Qing dynasty (1644–1911). Of the 194 caves, seventy-four were carved during the Northern Wei period (386-534) and thirty-nine during the Northern Zhou period (557–81). Along with Dunhuang, Longmen and Yungang – all examined elsewhere in this book – Maijishan is one of China's four most important Buddhist cave sights. Because of their location on the main trade route to the West the sculpture and paintings of Maijishan represent a unique synthesis of artistic styles but the influences of Gandhara and Persia are less apparent. Instead, a number of the sculptures show styles from Southeast Asia and India, perhaps coming up through Sichuan from around the sixth century onwards. The majority of the sculptures at Maijishan are modelled in clay and are warmer and less impassive than the stone statues of Longmen and Yungang.

In an open niche in Cave 9 sits a jewelled figure of

Fig. 131 **The Maijishan Grottoes, Gansu province**

Maitreya, the Buddha of the Future, flanked by two attendant Bodhisattvas and dated to around the sixth century (fig. 132). The influences are those of the Mon (Dvaravati) Buddhas of Thailand, and perhaps of Champa in modern Vietnam.

The largest of the caves is number 4 and is known as the Hall of Scattering Flowers (*San Hua Lou*). There were originally eight stone pillars supporting the roof of Cave 4, recalling Indian rock-cut temples like Ajanta, but this section has now fallen away. An early visitor to the site was enraptured by it:

> 'Up in the blue sky, in the steep rock cliff, the stone is carved to represent Buddha figures. A thousand niches, although fashioned by human effort, are mistakenly thought to be divine workmanship.'

(Written in 949, quoted in Swann, 1963)

On the wall above Cave 4 are paintings of *Apsaras* (celestial beings) that recall those of Dunhuang (fig. 133).

The existence of Maijishan and other Buddhist shrines reflects the fears of travellers along the Silk Road. They were places where the traveller could offer a prayer for perils that were to be faced and to give thanks for dangers that had been safely overcome.

Lanzhou and the Yellow River

After Maijishan, the Silk Road continues west and passes through Lanzhou, the modern provincial capital of Gansu. Lanzhou was an important commercial centre on the Silk Road and sits on the threshold of the Hexi or Gansu Corridor. The government camel and horse-breeding stations situated in the Hexi Corridor meant that, by the Tang dynasty, Lanzhou was a vital way station for the movement of animals that were being escorted to Changan. Lanzhou's position on the banks of the Yellow River (*Huang He*) also meant that it was a transhipment point for goods that were to be sent along the river. Many of these goods were transported on goatskin rafts, some of which are still occasionally to be seen. The river itself is 5,464 km long – second only to the Yangtze – and extends from its source in the Bayankala Mountains on the Qinghai-Tibet Plateau to the Gulf of Bohai. The Yellow River is the most heavily silt – laden river in the world and takes its name from the yellow-ochre colour of its water. The yellow alluvial soils of central China, known as loess, are the source of the silt- blown in over a period of millennia from the Gobi Desert and now found in layers up to 300 metres thick. The Yellow River has carried the loess across about 300,000 square km of the central plain of northern China, creating an immense fertile area from which Chinese civilisation emerged in remotest antiquity. Silting of the river has caused it to breach its banks and change course on innumerable occasions, often with

Fig. 132 **Painted clay figure of the Buddha with an attendant Bodhisattva**
Northern Zhou dynasty (557–81)
Cave 9, Maijishan, Gansu province

Fig. 133 **Wall painting depicting Apsaras**
Northern Zhou dynasty, (557–81)
Cave 4, Maijishan, Gansu province

devastating loss of life, and has caused the river to acquire the sobriquet of 'China's Sorrow.'

The Silk Road heads northwest from Lanzhou along the Gansu (Hexi) Corridor, the route hemmed in by the Gobi Desert to the north and the Qilian Mountains to the South. The corridor is 1,200 km long and between 15 and 200 km wide and links China with Xinjiang and Central Asia. Emperor Wudi (r. 140–87 BC) set up the first of the government horse-breeding stations in the Hexi Corridor. According to one contemporary record, alfalfa was planted for pasturage and thirty-six ranches were established for 300,000 horses, all supervised by a Xiongnu expert named Jinribei. Horses from the Wusun tribe were bred initially but were eventually supplanted by the superior breeds of the Ferghana Valley. The Xiongnu believed that the Qilian Mountains to the south of the corridor were sacred and that

Fig. 134 **Zhang Qian's legacy**
The Shandan Army Horse Ranch
at the foot of Mount Yanzhi,
Gansu province

animals feeding on the vast stretch of pastureland there would thrive and multiply. They also cherished nearby Mount Yanzhi, the occupation of which would, they believed, increase the beauty of their women. Horses are still bred on the pastures of Mount Yanzhi, about 130 km southeast of Zhangye (fig. 134).

Binglingsi

There is some disagreement among historians about the point where the Silk Road crossed the Yellow River. There definitely appears to have been a ferry crossing at the Binglingsi ('Ten Thousand Buddha') Caves, located about 70 km southwest of Lanzhou in Yongjing County, Gansu. The river was quite narrow as it passed through Yongjing County – one place is known to the local people as 'Fox Jump' – and there are stories of a ferry and a bridge that once spanned the mouth of the gorge near Binglingsi. The bridge was said to have been built by a Xianbei tribesman named Qifu around 400 AD. Known as the 'number 1 bridge under heaven', it is now deeply submerged beneath the reservoir created when the Liujiaxia hydroelectric dam was built. The ferry is believed to have crossed to a jetty, situated at the foot of the caves, and the Silk Road continued from the opposite side northwestwards towards Zhangye. Photographs taken before the dam was constructed reveal how the caves dominated the gorge (fig. 136).

When the dam was built the level of the river rose about 20 metres and submerged the majority of the lower caves.

Fig. 135 **General view of the Binglingsi Caves, Gansu province, with a massive figure of the Buddha Maitreya (Buddha of the future)**
The caves were constructed from the 5th–18th century
The 27-metre Buddha dates to the Tang dynasty (618–907)

Many of the sculptures were removed and distributed among the higher caves.

The Northern Liang (421–39), like the Toba Wei (see p. 67), were a non-Chinese people and were fervent sponsors of Buddhism. They controlled an independent state with its capital at Liangzhou (modern Wuwei), dominating a large part of Gansu province. During the early part of the Liang state cave complexes were constructed at the Jinta Temple and at Mt Madi in Minle County, to the south of Liangzhou. The Binglingsi Caves were begun around 420 when the Liang Empire expanded. The Liang also built some of the Mogao caves at Dunhuang at around the same time. Binglingsi comprises some 193 caves and niches (including those now submerged), extending some 200 metres along the western side of the river and built over a period of about 1,500 years from the fifth to the eighteenth centuries. Many early travellers remarked upon the strange rock formations along this stretch of the Yellow River; one seventh-century monk marvelling at 'the magic powers of nature' and comparing their shapes to Buddhist stupas and pagodas.

The sculptures in the early caves, with their clinging robes, evoke the styles of Gandhara and Chinese Central Asia far more than the caves at Maijishan. Among the early grottoes is Cave 169, known as the 'Southern Bridge to Heaven Cave' and built over 60 metres above the original level of the river (before the dam was built). During excavation of the cave in 1963 an inscription was found dating it to 420 AD. Cave 169 contains Binglingsi's finest art and sculptures of the type represented within it typically have large heads and hands with drapery folds created by making deep grooves in the clay (fig. 137).

Fig. 136 **General view of Binglingsi Caves**
(After Zheng, 1953)
Taken prior to construction of the Liujiaxia hydroelectric dam

Fig. 137 **Painted clay figure of a Bodhisattva**
Ca. 420
Cave 169, Binglingsi, Gansu province

Fig. 138 **Wall-Painting of a preaching Buddha with Bodhisattvas and Apsaras**
Ca. 420
East wall of Cave 169, Binglingsi, Gansu province.
Note: the figure kneeling to the Buddha's left is a foreigner.

Fig. 139 **Buddha tableau**
Tang dynasty, (618–907)
Cave 31, Binglingsi, Gansu province

There is a beautiful large painting in Cave 169, of a seated Buddha accompanied by Bodhisattvas and flying apsaras with the name of each deity inscribed to the side (fig. 138). Like the sculptures in the cave, the paintings recall their counterparts in the Gandhara kingdom.

About ten of the caves date to the Northern Wei dynasty (386–534). The thick, enveloping robes and elongated bodies of the Wei sculptures are characteristic of the sixth century. The most notable is Cave 80, dedicated in 520 by its benefactor – a man named Cao Ziyuan – who has left a powerful entreaty written on the cliff face outside of the cave:

'…*may his father and mother and his dependants…be reborn in the Paradise of the West; and may all creatures of every description receive the same blessings.*'

(Quoted in Akiyama, 1969)

There are around one hundred Tang dynasty caves at Binglingsi and sculpture from this period is therefore the most plentiful (fig. 139).

Wuwei

*'With wine of grapes the cups of jade would glow at night
We long to drink but the pipa summons us
If we lie drunk on the battlefield, don't mock us friend;
How many soldiers ever come home?'*

(Wang Han, 687–735?, 'Song of Liangzhou')

In the town of Jiuquan locally mined black, white and green jade is still used to make cups that are said to glow when filled with wine and placed in the moonlight. The strumming of lutes (*pipa*) was used, like a modern bugle, to rally troops for battle.

After crossing the Yellow River, the road heads north-westwards along the Gansu (Hexi) Corridor towards Wuwei (formerly Liangzhou). The Gansu Corridor was the site of numerous battles with the Xiongnu and, during the first century BC, four commanderies were established at Wuwei, Zhangye, Jiuquan and Dunhuang, all linked by a line of defensive watchtowers and armouries. During the Han dynasty the Great Wall extended as far as the Lop Nor region of Xinjiang, protecting trade along the Silk Road. Wuwei was an important garrison town guarding a section of the wall and became the main commercial centre for the region.

An important tomb of the Western Han dynasty was excavated at Leitai, north of the centre of Wuwei, in 1969. Dated to 186–219 AD, the tomb contained bronze models of soldiers, chariots and horses- most notably the celebrated 'flying horse of Gansu' (see fig. 13).

During the Period of Disunity, between the collapse of the Han in 220 AD and the establishment of the Sui dynasty in 581, it was the capital of a number of minor states including the Former Liang and the Southern Liang. Wuwei

was then occupied by the Northern Wei dynasty in 420 and thereafter was an important Buddhist centre. The celebrated monk Kumarajiva (343–413) was a prisoner in Wuwei for over seventeen years and his achievements were commemorated during the Tang dynasty by the construction of a memorial pagoda (fig. 141).

During the Tang period Wuwei continued to be an important Buddhist centre. It was visited by the monk Xuanzang on his way to India and he admired the local wines Xuanzong crossed the border in secret after Emperor

Fig. 141 **The 'Kumarajiva Pagoda'**
Tang dynasty, (618–907)
Wuwei, Gansu province

Fig. 140 **Old city walls (part of a fortress)**
Northern section of Wuwei, Gansu province

Fig. 142 **Bronze bell**
Tang dynasty, (618–907)
H. 2.45 metres
Bell Tower (Dayun Si) at Wuwei,
Gansu province
The sides of the bell are
decorated with designs of flying
apsaras, dragons and tortoises-
reminiscent of the murals of the
Dunhuang Grottoes. At the
beginning of the nineteenth
century an inscribed tablet was
discovered within the temple
precincts where the Bell Tower
stands. The tablet, inscribed in
both Xixia (Tangut) and Chinese
script, has provided the means to
understand a language that had
defied scholars for centuries.

Zhangye was an important trading centre from an early date and local officials regulated the passage of silk (fig. 143).

The excesses of the Sui Emperor Yangdi have already been described (see the section on Luoyang above). However, in preparation for his inspection tour of the Western Regions in 609, he made an important contribution to the development of the Silk Road. Yang Di's trusted official Pei Ju (d. 627) was appointed minister of trade with responsibility for commerce with the states to the west. Pei Ju's report, 'The Illustrated Account of the Western Regions' (*Xiyu Tuzi*) has been lost but sections have been preserved in the 'History of the Sui dynasty' (*Sui Shu*). Pei Ju delineates the geography, customs and habits of forty-four of the states of the Western Lands. Pei organized Yangdi's audience at Zhangye in 609, described by some historians as the first international trade fair on the Silk Road. Emissaries from twenty-seven western states and the entire population of the

Taizong issued an edict forbidding anyone to leave the country without permission. Wuwei was also a checkpoint for travellers entering and leaving China and had a population of about 100,000- many of them merchants from Tibet, India and Central Asia.

In 1036 Wuwei fell to the Xixia (Western Xia or Tanguts), a federation of Tibetan peoples. It continued to be an important trading centre on the Silk Road until the thirteenth century when the Tangut Empire was attacked and its people annihilated by the Mongols. Wuwei remained under the control of the Mongol Yuan dynasty (1279–1368) until Chinese sovereignty was finally restored by the country's Ming rulers during the fourteenth century.

Near the centre of Wuwei is the Bell Tower (*Dayun Si*), built during the Ming dynasty (1368–1644) but containing a massive Tang dynasty bronze bell (fig. 142).

From Wuwei the Silk Road leads in a northwesterly direction across a desolate landscape. To the north is the Badain Jaran Desert of Inner Mongolia and, to the south, the Qilian Mountains. At the approximate halfway point, near the town of Yongchang, are substantial sections of the old Han dynasty wall.

Zhangye

Approximately 300 km northwest of Wuwei the Silk Road passes through Zhangye – formerly known as Ganzhou – another of the four Han dynasty commanderies. The fortified walls of Zhangye were still intact as recently as the turn of the century but have since been demolished.

Fig. 143 **Silk passage certificate issued by the commandant of Zhangye**
Han dynasty, (206 BC–220 AD)
L. 21 cm, W. 16 cm
Unearthed in 1974 at Tiancang, Jinta, Gansu province
(Gansu Provincial Museum)

Fig. 144 **Reclining Buddha**
Xia State (Tangut), ca. 1098
L. 34.5 metres
The Monastery of the Great Buddha (Dafosi), Zhangye, Gansu province

towns of Wuwei and Zhangye lined the roadside to greet the emperor, all dressed in their Sunday best. The Sui annals relate that, 'Horsemen and carts jammed the road while musical performances, singing, dancing and incense-burning created a scene of bustle and excitement.'

There is a large reclining Buddha in Zhangye, the largest in China, at the 'Monastery of the Great Buddha' (*Dafosi*) built in 1098 by the Xixia (Tanguts), who had invaded the area around 1038 and established an independent state (fig. 144).

A famous vistor to Zhangye was Marco Polo, whose great journey from 1271 to 1295 took him through the town. He remained for a year – awaiting permission from Kubilai Khan to continue on to the Mongols' capital – and described the city and its temples in great detail, clearly impressed by what he saw:

'The idolaters have many religious houses, or monasteries and abbeys, built after the manner of the country, and in

these a multitude of idols, some of which are of wood, some of stone, and some of clay, are covered with gilding. They are carved in masterly style.'

(From *The Travels of Marco Polo the Venetian*. Translated by William Marsden in Marsden, 1948)

Marco Polo also describes a journey north of the main Silk Road, from Zhangye to the Tangut city of Edzina or Khara Khoto:

'Leaving this city of Kampion [Zhangye] and travelling for twelve days in a northerly direction, you come to a city named Edzina, at the commencement of the sandy desert, and within the province of Tangut. The inhabitants are idolaters. They have camels, and much cattle of various sorts.... The fruits of the soil and the flesh of the cattle supply the wants of the people, and they do not concern themselves with trade. Travellers passing through this city lay in a store of provisions for forty days, because...that space of time is employed in traversing a desert, where there is not any appearance of dwelling, nor are there any inhabitants...'

(From *The Travels of Marco Polo the Venetian*. Translated by William Marsden in Marsden, 1948)

The Xia (Tanguts)

In the centuries before the Mongol conquest of the region, the Xia State or Xixia (Western Xia) controlled large areas of western Inner Mongolia, Ningxia, Gansu and Qinghai. The old Turkic name for the Xia was Tangut and they were descendants of the Qiang tribal group who occupied Qinghai province and Tibet from around the third millennium BC. The descendants of the Qiang are believed by many scholars to be the peoples of modern-day Tibet and Burma. The Xia also claimed kinship with the Toba (or Xianbei), the founders of China's Northern Wei dynasty (see section on Northern Wei).

The Xia were loyal subjects of the Chinese until the mid-ninth century when internal divisions led to the collapse of the Tibetan Empire and popular dissent weakened the Tang government. After the Tang dynasty collapsed in 907 the Tangut emerged as an independent state. The Tangut Empire (1032–1227) maintained its independence by means of a continuous cycle of alliance and conflict with the Song Chinese and the Liao Khitans. In 1031 a man named Yuan-hao became ruler and achieved recognition of the state by both the Song and the Khitans, expanding Tangut territory to include the whole of Western Gansu including Dunhuang.

Fig. 145 **Gilded and polychromed double headed clay figure of Buddha**
Xia State (Tangut), early 13th century
H. 62 cm
From Khara Khoto, northwestern Inner Mongolia
(State Hermitage Museum, St Petersburg)
This image recalls the story of the two poor men who each dreamed of owning an image of the Buddha. They could afford only one and the Buddha, moved by their piety, caused the image to be divided into two. The method of manufacture of this image (clay modelled around an armature of reed and straw) is used throughout Central Asia.

It was only when, in 1038, he declared himself emperor of the 'Great Xia kingdom' that the Chinese declared him a rebel. A bloody four year war ensued between the Song and the Tangut at the end of which Yuan-hao agreed to refrain from calling himself emperor in his relations with China, in exchange for a generous annual tribute of 255,000 items of silk, silver, tea and cloth.

From the tenth to the thirteenth centuries, the Xia State controlled and levied taxes upon travellers along the caravan routes within the great curve of the Yellow River, a large part of modern Gansu province. From 1020 onwards their capital was Xingzhou (modern Yinchuan) in today's Ningxia-hui Autonomous Region. Their economy was based on agriculture and animal husbandry: they grew millet, wheat, rice, hemp and cotton, and raised horses, camels, cattle, sheep and goats. They were renowned for their fine horses, for the salt they refined from lakes in the Ordos region and for their rhubarb. They also produced their own coinage and excellent iron-work, gold, silver and ceramics. Their creations were heavily influenced by Chinese designs and craftsmen were recruited by the Xia rulers to produce them. The Tangut called themselves 'the White High Great State of Xia', perhaps an allusion to their origins among the snow-capped mountains of Tibet. The population was multi-ethnic, with equal rights afforded to Tangut, Chinese, Tibetan and Uighur alike. The Tangut were originally worshippers of a spirit called *Tengri* but, by the ninth or tenth century, had become Buddhist although their shamanistic beliefs also survived. Tangut Buddhism was heavily influenced by both Chinese and Tibetan teachings and documents relating to both schools have been unearthed at Khara Khoto. Daoism and Confucianism were also well regarded.

Khara Khoto

The city of Khara Khoto (the 'Black Town', Heicheng or Edzina) was situated on the edge of the Gobi Desert at the northern border of the Xia state in northwestern Inner Mongolia and was one of their principal cities. It was first explored by the Russian P. K. Kozlov from 1908–09 and was subsequently visited by both Sir Aurel Stein and Sven Hedin. Sculptures and paintings found at Khara Khoto represent the earliest expression of Sino-Tibetan art; the style and iconography of which reflect the influence of Tantric Buddhism, noted for its extensive pantheon of deities and lengthy rituals that require a large number of images and paintings. The works of art from Khara Khoto's heyday date mainly from the twelfth to fourteenth century, the city's existence continuing long after it was overrun by Genghis Khan's soldiers in 1227. Among the sculptures found at the site is a beautiful double-headed figure of Buddha, the finest among the large number of Khara Khoto artefacts in the Hermitage museum (fig. 145).

There is space here to examine only one of the paintings acquired by Kozlov at Khara Khoto. The cult of Amitabha, Buddha of the Western Paradise, was immensely popular among the Xia. They believed that rebirth in the Pure Land of Amitabha was attainable with prayer and simple faith. Amitabha is frequently shown accompanied and assisted by Avalokitesvara (Guanyin in Chinese), the Bodhisattva of compassion. In the example shown here (fig. 146), he towers above two donors dressed in the robes of the Tangut nobility.

Fig. 146 **Silk scroll painting depicting Amitabha before worshippers**
Xia State (Tangut), 12th century
L. 125 cm, W. 64 cm
From Khara Khoto, northwestern Inner Mongolia
(State Hermitage Museum, St Petersburg)
In this painting the Buddha Amitabha stands upon two lotuses in a robe decorated with a gold dragon, phoenix, clouds and flaming jewels. A cloud-like emanation falls upon two diminutive donor figures at his feet. The man holds a censer (an incense burner) and the woman holds her hands in prayer.

An interesting aside to the paintings unearthed at Khara Khoto is the discovery that a number of the paintings from the site – all produced between the twelfth and fourteenth centuries – are on a plaid (tartan) background. The suggestion has been made that the Tokharians – probably a tribe of the Yuezhi confederation who were driven out of the Tarim Basin in about 165 BC – are descendants of a lost tribe of Celtic peoples. The theory is that they may have migrated eastwards during ancient times and settled in the oasis-cities of Chinese Central Asia (see section on Tokharians). Plaid is not found in Tibet or in China proper, only in the western areas of Gansu, Xinjiang and the Ningxia-hui Autonomous Region. If the resemblance of the plaid of the Khara Khoto paintings to Celtic tartans is not merely the result of chance, these patterns may represent the remains of a Celtic tradition in Asia.

Khara Khoto fell to Genghis Khan in 1227 after its water supply was diverted. A number of legends that surround the city assert that the treasury, comprising some eighty carts of gold, was lowered into a well to keep it from falling into Mongol hands and, to this day, it has never been found. Shards of blue and white porcelain have been unearthed at Khara Khoto, all dating to the Yuan dynasty of the Mongols (1279–1368). This indicates that the town was still an important trading centre during the period of Mongol domination. Another interesting facet to the presence of porcelain at the site is that similar shards have been found at other sites in Inner Mongolia as well as a single shard, decorated with a leaping deer, discovered in Samarkand and now held in its museum (fig. 147).

Fig. 147 **Fragment of blue and white porcelain decorated with a deer**
Chinese, Yuan dynasty
(1279–1368)
Unearthed in Samarkand
(Registan Museum, Samarkand)

The wide dissemination of Yuan dynasty blue and white shards to sites located far inland is at odds with the conventionally held view that Chinese porcelain reached the West exclusively via the sea- routes. It may well be that porcelain was carried on camelback along the entire length of the Silk Road. Recent work by Professor Li Zhiyan of Beijing's National Museum of Chinese History and by John Carswell provides a clue about how it might have been accomplished without the entire shipment being broken en route. According to Professor Li, the porcelain is packed into containers with a mixture of sand, soil, soya bean and wheat- all soaked in water. The concoction then dries to form a solid mass. When a merchant reaches his destination water is again added and the porcelain retrieved intact.

The Mongols put a large part of the Tangut population to death but the city of Khara Khoto appears to have lingered on until about 1372, when it was taken by the Ming Chinese General Feng Sheng. After its capture by the Chinese the city seems to have fallen into decline, perhaps because of the encroaching desert and the development of sea routes in preference to land based trade. The Chinese renamed the bulk of the territory that constituted the Tangut kingdom Ningxia ('Pacified Xia'). It is now known as the Ningxia-hui Autonomous Region of China.

Jiuquan

The province of Gansu takes its name from the first character of the old names for Zhangye and Jiuquan, *Ganzhou* and *Suzhou*. Jiuquan (meaning 'Wine Spring') sits at the western end of the Hexi Corridor and has been a garrison town since 121 BC, together with Wuwei, Zhangye and Dunhuang. Its names comes from a legend surrounding the great Han General Huo Qubing (see section on Xiongnu). Huo was presented with a gift of fine wine by the emperor but chose to share it with his troops by pouring it into a pool.

Foreign merchants lived in the Dongguan section of the city and a wooden drum tower, built during the fourth century and rebuilt many times, points the way to the Western lands (fig. 148).

The city was a capital of the Western Liang state (400–421) of the Sixteen Kingdoms period (304–439) and

was occupied during the eighth and ninth centuries by Tibetans, but its role has always been that of a frontier-town, the first on the Chinese side of the Great Wall. The Mongols ravaged the area during the thirteenth century but as late as the seventeeth century, Jiuquan was still an important place of congregation for foreign merchants. The Portuguese Jesuit Benedict de Goes died of disease in Jiuquan in 1606, after three years of travel-ling the Silk Road, en route to Beijing. His diary describes a thriving city still home to large numbers of foreigners:

'Suzhou City is the place where Western merchants converge.... The city is divided into two sections. Chinese residents live in one section, and in the other are Muslims who hail from the Western Regions. They were traders and most of them married local women and had children. Burdened with family, they settled down here and became local residents. By night the Muslims withdraw into their section of the city and keep to themselves. Otherwise, they are treated just the same as local inhabitants. Their legal disputes are handled by Chinese magistrates...'

(Benedict de Goes, quoted in Che Muqi, 1989)

Fig. 148 **Drum tower**
Built 4th century, rebuilt 19th century
Jiuquan, Gansu province.
Inscriptions over the four gates on each side of the tower declare: 'North is the Gobi Desert, South are the Qilian Mountains, East is the Huashan (a mountain east of Xian) and West is Yiwu (Hami in Xinjiang).' The western side is shown here.

Just to the southwest of Jiuquan are the Wenshushan Caves. The caves have been vandalised over the years and what remains is much restored but the original influences of Tibet are still apparent in the statuary and paintings at the site.

Jiayuguan

De Goes waited twenty-five days for permission to enter China at the Jiayu Pass, about 20 km northwest of Jiuquan. Jiayu Pass (Jiayuguan) has been a frontier post since the Han dynasty when the Great Wall reached as far as the Yumen Pass (the 'Jade Gate'), about 90 km northwest of Dunhuang. It has always been regarded as an important strategic location, set between the Mazong (Horse's Mane) Mountains to the north and the Qilian Mountains to the south. In 1372, the Ming dynasty General Feng Sheng defeated the last of the Mongol armies of the Yuan dynasty that had ruled China since 1279 and built a fortress at Jiayuguan, guarding the entrance to the Hexi (Gansu) Corridor (fig. 149). The Chinese called the fortress 'The Strongest Pass Under Heaven' and built it with walls 11 metres high and 733 metres in circumference. Jiayuguan marked the western terminus of the Ming dynasty Great Wall, built in brick and more durable than the earthen walls of its forebears. From the fourteenth century onwards, Jiayuguan was regarded as the limit of the Chinese Empire.

The territory to the west of Jiayuguan was a place of banishment to the Chinese; only those who were exiled, the courageous monks and merchants who travelled the Silk Road, and invading and defending armies would enter it. As late as 1942, Mildred Cable described the sorrowful aspect of Jiayuguan's west gate and the inscriptions left by the people who passed through it on their way into exile:

'The most important door was on the farther side of the fortress, and it might be called Traveller's Gate, though some spoke of it as the Gate of Sighs. It was a deep archway tunnelled in the thickness of the wall, where footsteps echoed and re-echoed. Every traveller toward the north-west passed through this gate, and it opened out on that great and always mysterious waste called the Desert of Gobi.

The long archway was covered with writings, and anyone with sufficient knowledge to appreciate Chinese penmanship could see at once that these were the work of men of scholarship, who had fallen on an hour of deep distress…

Who then were the writers of this Anthology of Grief? Some were heavy-hearted exiles, others were disgraced officials, and some were criminals no longer tolerated within China's borders. Torn from all they loved on earth and banished with dishonoured name to the dreary regions outside, they stood awhile within the tomb-like vault, to add their moan to the pitiful dirge of the Gate of Sighs.'

(Cable and French, 1942)

An old tradition, still practised in Cable and French's day, was for departing travellers to throw a stone at the fortress wall. If it rebounded they would return safely but, if it did not, they would not see China again.

Fig. 149 **Jiayuguan fortress, Gansu province**
Built in 1372, with later reconstruction

Fig. 150 **Ivory carving of a Bodhisattva riding an elephant**

Probably Indian, ca. 7th century
H. 15.8 cm
From the Yulin Cave, Anxi County, Gansu province
(National Museum of Chinese History, Beijing)

In a closed position, this ivory carving depicts a Bodhisattva riding an elephant and carrying a pagoda. When it is opened, there are no fewer than 50 squares containing some 300 figures depicting stories from the Buddha's previous lives (*jatakas*). It may have been carried to China by one of the many monks who travelled to India during the Tang dynasty to seek Buddhist scriptures. The likelihood that the carving was brought to China by a monk links neatly to the recent discovery of what is believed to be the earliest portrait of the monk Xuanzang, discovered at the Yulin Cave No. 3 in 1980. The image is a wall-painting, dated to the eleventh or twelfth century, and shows a monk accompanied by a monkey and a white horse and standing by a river. A bundle of what appear to be sutras sits atop a lotus flower on the horse's back with rays of light emanating from them in all directions.

Anxi

'Rain falls at dusk on the frontier town
Wild geese fly low.
The new reeds grow,
Rising high and wild.
Countless camel bells ring
Over desolate sands.
Caravans are travelling
To Anxi city with silk rolls.'

(Zhang Ji, 'A Song of Liangzhou.' Tang dynasty)

Continuing on the main artery of the Silk Road, the route passes through the town of Anxi (ancient Guazhou), known to early travellers in equal measure for its delectable melons and its incessant biting winds. Seventy-five kilometres south of

Anxi are the Yulin Caves, also known as Wanfoxia ('The Gorge of Ten Thousand Buddhas'). The forty-two surviving caves cover a period of more than 1500 years from the Northern Wei to the Qing dynasty (1644–1911). Caves 2 and 3 are Tangut (Western Xia) period (1032–1227), the latter with magnificent Chinese style murals. Cave 4 dates to the Yuan period (1279–1368) and its esoteric Tantric iconography reveals the influences from Tibet that we encountered at Khara Khoto. One of the most fascinating of all of the Silk Road artefacts unearthed in China was found at the Yulin Caves (fig. 150).

Anxi is also the point where the Silk Road splits into its Northern and Southern Routes, the former skirting the Tianshan Mountains and the latter running along the edge of the Kunlun range. In fact, a section of the Silk Road loops back from Dunhuang to Hami to rejoin the Northern Route and the point of division can therefore also said to be there.

Fig. 151 **The Mingsha sand dunes**
Dunhuang, Gansu province

Dunhuang and The Caves of the Thousand Buddhas (Qianfodong or Mogao Caves)

It is impossible to overstate the art-historical significance of Dunhuang: 'the art gallery in the desert', 'a cultural treasure house', 'this great museum of the centuries': none of the superlatives that have been applied to the site succeeds in conveying its full importance. The town was established in 111 BC, as one of the four Han commanderies (Wuwei, Zhangye and Jiuquan were the others), and a line of watchtowers still stand to the north and west of Dunhuang. The name itself means 'blazing beacon', a reference to these signal towers- used to warn of approaching danger.

The Caves of the Thousand Buddhas lie in a valley to the southeast of the Dunhuang oasis, at the foot of the Mingsha sand dunes (the 'Dunes of the Singing Sands'). Its name derives from the legend of the monk Luo Zun (or Le Zun) who, in 366, is said to have seen a vision of a thousand Buddhas floating above Mount Sanwei (the 'Mountain of Three Dangers'), on one side of the valley. Another version of the legend relating to Luo Zun concerns his passage through Dunhuang, on his way to India with three disciples. One of them, Zhi Qin, was sent to fetch water from the river that runs along the foot of Mount Sanwei. As Zhi Qin rested and admired the sunset, 'the mountain peaks glistening with the sheen of blue satin in the light of dawn became iridescent. In the centre of the golden rays reposed a giant Maitreya, and emerging out of this radiance were thousands of Buddhas- all at perfect ease, smiling and laughing, sweetly conversing. In the golden light, myriads of fairy maidens flitted among them, making music on various instruments.' (Quoted in Chen Yu, 1989). Zhi Qin was said to have painted a mural on one of the cave walls to record what he had seen and master Luo Zun, upon hearing of his pupil's vision, decided that they would go no further on their journey to India and establish a Buddhist settlement at Dunhuang. A collapse of part of the cliff has destroyed the earliest caves of Luo Zun but his achievements are recorded on a stele, erected at Dunhuang in 698.

Fig. 152 **Exterior of the Dunhuang Caves**

Between the fourth century and the Yuan dynasty (1279–1368) the valley became a centre for Buddhist monks and other travellers along the Silk Road. As merchants and pilgrims passed through they would make a donation to improve the site, as a prayer for protection from the dangers they expected to face on their journey to the West, or as thanks for their safe arrival in China. Documents found at Dunhuang also reveal that the more affluent residents of the town would form clubs to study Buddhism and to sponsor the creation of murals or silk paintings, thereby securing merit for themselves. Cave shrines were carved from the gravel conglomerate of the cliffs and, from the early fifth century of the Northern Liang dynasty (421–39) of the Sixteen Kingdoms, many caves were also decorated with wall paintings. Unlike the rock-cut cave temples and sculptures of Yungang and Longmen (see pp. 69 and 71), the statuary at Dunhuang was made of clay – moulded around wooden armatures and then painted. To date, no fewer than 492 caves have been identified containing 45,000 square metres of murals and over 2,000 sculptures. It is said that if the walls of all of Dunhuang's caves were to be lined up they would form

Fig. 153 **Painted clay figure of the Bodhisattva Maitreya (the Future Buddha), seated with crossed ankles and flanked by lions**
Northern Liang dynasty, early 5th century
Cave 275, Dunhuang, Gansu province
The upper wall behind the figure of Maitreya is filled with seated figures of Bodhisattvas with billowing scarves. Influences from the Greco-Buddhist art of Gandhara are apparent in much of the early sculpture at Dunhuang. The early paintings of Kizil (see p. 154) are similar in style to the paintings of Cave 275 but the latter are less finely drawn and may have been repainted during succeeding dynasties.

a display 50 km in length, the longest art gallery in the world. The paintings and sculpture reveal Chinese, Indian, Greco-Roman, and Iranian influences.

The oldest caves – 268, 272 and 275 – were built during the Northern Dynasties (386-581) and most commonly contain images of the historical Buddha Sakyamuni and Maitreya, the future Buddha. Cave 275 is attributed to the Northern Liang dynasty before 439 (when Dunhuang was conquered and fell under the control of the Northern Wei), and contains the largest of the early images (fig. 153).

S. F Oldenburg of the Russian Academy of Science discovered one of the best of the early paintings from Dunhuang in Cave 263, during his 1914–15 expedition (fig. 154). The mural, commonly known as *Vadya*, was buried under layers of sand and this accounts for its remarkable state of preservation:

The unification of China under the Sui dynasty (581–618) ended almost four centuries of civil war; it also brought greater freedom of travel and an emperor, Wendi (r. 58–604), who actively sponsored the proliferation of Buddhism. The international trade fair at Zhangye, attended by Wendi's son and successor Yangdi in 609 was attended by representatives from twenty-seven nations and augmented the growing tide of foreigners coming to China. Because of Dunhuang's position on the Silk Road, the increasing level of economic activity brought great prosperity to the area and this is reflected in the splendour of the caves established during this

period. A fresh infusion of stylistic influences from India was combined with existing traditions and the result was a fully fledged mature Chinese style. Sui art at Dunhuang coincided with the growing popularity of the Pure Land Buddhist sect. Depictions of the Pure Land of Amitabha Buddha, where the faithful will be reborn, are painted on a grand scale and are filled with metaphors of a blissful afterworld- sumptuous palaces, lotus-ponds and splendid gardens, and heavenly musicians and dancers. Realism and, often, humour replace the somewhat stylized art of the earlier periods (fig. 155).

Although the Sui dynasty lasted for only thirty-seven years, more than one hundred new caves were established. The new interest in Pure Land Buddhism led to the creation of large central images, often of Amitabha Buddha, flanked by attendant Bodhisattvas and realistically portrayed disciples. This style was refined and perfected during the Tang dynasty when Dunhuang, liker the rest of China, enjoyed its 'Golden Age.' Portrayals of foreigners are found increasing numbers during the early part of the Tang dynasty, a consequence of China's extended borders and her increased contacts with neighbouring countries. The Tang annals contain numerous references to paintings of foreigners but there are few extant today (fig. 156).

Fig. 155 **Painted ceiling with a lotus within a square depicting joined rabbits and flying apsaras**
Sui dynasty, (581–618)
Cave 407, Dunhuang, Gansu province
This delightful painting comprises a trio of rabbits, ears joined to form a triangle and running in a circle around the centre of the ceiling. They are surrounded by flying *apsaras* (celestial deities).

Fig. 154 **Mural depicting seven seated Buddhas with six apsaras (celestial beings)**
Northern Wei dynasty, (386–534)
H. 197 cm, W. 69.5 cm
Cave 263, Dunhuang, Gansu province
(State Hermitage Museum, St Petersburg)
The seven Buddhas in this mural, seated in mediation, represent the 'Thousand Buddhas' of the Mogao caves. The graceful movement of the celestial figures recalls the late Gandhara style of Bamiyan (see p. 59) and through it, the art of Chinese Central Asia at sites like Kizil. At the base of the painting (not visible here) are three donor monks.

Fig. 156 **Detail from a painting showing foreigners among the audience of a debate between Vimalikirti and Manjusri**
Early Tang dynasty, 642
Cave 220, Dunhuang,
Gansu province
Note: the north and east walls of Cave 220 are each inscribed with the date 642.

Fig. 157 **Wall painting of merchants confronted by brigands**
Tang dynasty, first half of 8th century
Cave 45, Dunhuang,
Gansu province
In this painting the merchants are Tibetan and Central Asian and stand forlornly in front of a man holding a sword, and beside the goods they have been obliged to unload from their mules. An alternative interpretation, sometimes applied to this painting, is that the merchants are being subjected to extortion by avaricious border-guards. Whichever way it is interpreted the sentiment is the same- the painting is a reference to the Buddhist legend of the rich merchant who remains safe during a long journey by reciting the Lotus Sutra to invoke the protection of the Bodhisattva Avalokitesvara (Guanyin). The sutra is written in a panel above the merchant's heads and reads:

'If you all call upon his name, then from the malicious bandits you shall contrive to be delivered; and the multitude of merchants hearing this, speak these words in unison, saying, 'Namo bodhisattvaya, He who observes the sounds of the world!' Men, by the mere calling upon his name, they shall forthwith gain deliverance.'

('Scripture of the Lotus Blossom of the Fine Dharma', quoted in Knauer, 1998)

The great philosophical debate from the *Vimalakirti-sutra* between the Chinese scholar Vimalikirti and the Bodhisattva of Wisdom, Manjusri is a popular subject in Buddhist art and the presence of foreigners in the audience is a statement that the appeal of the new doctrine is universal. Elsewhere in the audience sits the Emperor of China himself, resplendent in full ceremonial robes and a signal that Buddhism has the imperial seal of approval. Elsewhere in Cave 220, on either side of a composition on the north wall, are paradise scenes in which musicians of various nationalities perform on Western and Chinese instruments. Each group of musicians accompanies a pair of dancers with swirling ribbons, performing one of the new dances from the Western Lands, perhaps the 'Dance of Chach' or the 'Western Prancing Dance' – two of the most popular. A similar scene occurs in Cave 98 at Dunhuang, dating to the mid-tenth century of the Five Dynasties, but by this time there were few foreigners left in China and the participants are Chinese.

Increased levels of commerce along the Silk Road during the Tang dynasty were accompanied by an upsurge in the incidence of highway robbery and a number of murals and inscriptions at Dunhuang reflect the anxieties of merchants (fig. 157).

A key function of the Dunhuang caves was to belay the fears of the faithful. Inscriptions found at the site, on paintings and in block-printed manuscripts, seek protection

Fig. 158 **A group of painted stucco sculptures**
Tang dynasty, 8th century
Cave 45, Dunhuang, Gansu province
In this typical arrangement from the High Tang period, a seated Buddha is flanked by his two most favoured disciples Ananda and Kasyapa, a pair of Bodhisattvas and two *lokapalas* ('Heavenly Kings'). The Buddha and Bodhisattvas still retain a somewhat idealized form while the disciples and lokapala figures display both physical and emotional idiosyncrasies.

for both the sponsor of the item and for the region as whole. The following example, a block-printed inscription dated to 947, is typical and was written at a time when the area was controlled by the Cao clan. The sponsor in this instance was no less a figure than Dunhuang's ruler at the time, Cao Yuanzhong (r. 946-975), a man of evident piety:

> '*The disciple, Military Controller of the Kuei-i Army, Inspector of Guazhou and Shazhou [Anxi and Dunhuang], and other districts, Commissioner for the distribution of military land-allotments within the sphere of his jurisdiction and for the suppression of Tibetan tribes, specially promoted additional Grand Preceptor, inaugural Baron of the prefecture of Qiao, Cao Yuanzhong carved this printing block and offered it on behalf of the municipal shrines of the city, that they may know no troubles; on behalf of the whole prefecture, that they may be intact and peaceful. That the ways leading east and west may remain open and unimpeded. That the barbarians (?) of north and south may submit and obey. May all severe diseases disappear. May the sound of the war-trumpet no longer be heard; may we have the delight of witnessing and hearing good things and all be wetted by (the dew of) fortune and prosperity.*'

(Dated 947. From Waley, 1931)

Cao Yuanzhong's exhortation is hardly surprising when we take into account that, by this date, the Tang dynasty had

collapsed, China was in chaos and the government's proscription of Buddhism between 842 and 845 meant that the religion no longer exercised a major influence on Chinese society. During the High Tang period (705–80) these crises were yet to come and Dunhuang was still enjoying its apogee. Cave 45, where the 'brigands mural' was discovered, contains some of the most beautiful of all of Dunhuang's sculpture. A seated Buddha, his hand raised in *abhayamudra* (the gesture of dispelling fear), is flanked by six attendants who, despite their divine nature, are remarkably human in appearance (fig. 158).

A pair of painted clay leonine figures from Cave 321 are a celebration of the cosmopolitan style of the High Tang. The two sculptures, guardians of the Buddhist faith, once flanked the cave's main shrine and derive their appearance from the griffins of the Near East (fig. 159).

The power and strength of the empire were reflected in the massive images of the High Tang. Two of the largest are the colossal images of the Buddha Maitreya in caves 96 and 130- the 'Northern Great' and 'Southern Great' images respectively. The former is 33 metres in height and is generally ascribed to the reign of Empress Wu Zetian (r. 690–705) and the latter, 26 metres high, to the first half of the 8th century. In Cave 81 is another Buddha of substantial size, this time recumbent as he enters nirvana. Depictions of the moment of the Buddha's final triumph when he finally exits this world and enters nirvana (known as *parinirvana*), are a popular subject for the artists of the High and Middle Tang. A mural in Cave 158 contains a large number of

Fig. 159 **Beast as 'Guard of Laws'**
One of a pair
Tang dynasty, 8th century
H. 90 cm
Cave 321, Dunhuang, Gansu province
(State Hermitage Museum, St Petersburg)
This sculpture is highly unusual in that it does not resemble traditional Chinese *qilin* guardian animals. It has the body of a lion, a dog's face, the tusks of a boar and claw-shaped wings.

foreigners and forms the backdrop for a massive, 15 metre Buddha reclining in nirvana (fig. 160). It is intended, as with other paintings of a multi-ethnic nature, to emphasize the wide appeal of the faith:

Cave 158 was constructed during the Middle Tang when, as a consequence of the turmoil unleashed by the An Lushan rebellion of 755–63, China lost control of many of her western possessions. Between 781 and 848 Dunhuang was controlled by Tibetans, a factor which led to the preservation of the caves in spite of the imperially sanctioned suppression of Buddhism in China from 842–45. During the Tibetan occupation Dunhuang was known as Shazou ('City of the Sands') and this was also the name of the prefecture in which the town was situated. The Chinese warlord General Zhang Yichao (d. 872) and his private army finally drove out the Tibetans in 848, an event commemorated in a spectacular mural in Cave 156. In the painting Zhang Yichao and his wife, the Lady Song each move in a stately procession towards the cave's main Buddha image, accompanied by a retinue of cavalry, servants and musicians. At the rear of the procession are camels carrying the possessions of Zhang and his wife. The mural is a declaration of the power and status of the Zhangs and a number of manuscripts discovered at Dunhuang contain adulatory praise for the great General's accomplishments:

'Our general's triumphant manner embodied grace and martial prowess,
 He so intimidated the barbarian louts that they lost all courage;
 No sooner had the dog barbarians seen that the T'ang armies were victorious,
 Than their retreating troops scattered like stars as they deserted their posts.'

('Chang I-Ch'ao'[Zhang Yichao], Pelliot ms P2962, from Mair, 1983)

From 848 until the Cao family supplanted them in about 920, members of General Zhang's clan governed Dunhuang. By 857, Zhang Yichao had secured all eleven prefectures of the Gansu Corridor and brought them firmly under Tang government control. For the time being at least, the trade routes were secured although, after Zhang's death in 872, much of the territory was lost again. The eminent monk Hong Bian, patriarch of the faith in the area west of the Yellow River, presided over much of Dunhuang's development during this late period of the Tang dynasty and the Zhangs were enthusiastic patrons of the caves. He may, in fact, have been related to the Zhang family through his mother. When Hong Bian died in 862, General Zhang erected a memorial chapel in his honour and a statue of the monk seated in meditation was placed there (fig. 161). Behind him is a mural with two attendants, one a female beneath a tree who recalls the *Yakshi* nature-spirit images of India and the Persian fertility goddess Anahita. In the tree hangs a water bottle and leather satchel- the latter a wonderfully poetic reference to the sutras carried to China by pilgrims travelling the Silk Road.

The French Sinologist Paul Pelliot (1878–1945) arrived a year later and purchased a further group of 6,000 manuscripts for about 90 British pounds. They were sent to the Bibliothèque Nationale de France and the Musée Guimet. He was followed in 1911 by the Japanese Zuicho Tachibana – emissary of Count Kozui Otani, Abbot of the Honganji Temple in Kyoto. Stein returned in 1913, acquiring more treasures and, as late as 1914, Sergei Oldenberg obtained 600 scrolls and a number of fragments from the site for the St Petersburg's Institute for Oriental Studies. By the time Langdon Warner of Harvard's Fogg Art Museum arrived in 1923, many of the caves had been ransacked or vandalized by White Russians fleeing the revolution in Russia. The sheer quantity of material acquired at Dunhuang, especially from Cave 17, means that much of it has yet to be studied. There is also the possibility that some of the later finds are forgeries: Islam Akhun, the catering agent for Macartney (the British Consul in Kashgar) was discovered by Stein to have faked manuscripts from the Khotan region as early as 1899, and much work remains to be done.

The treasures of Dunhuang, and especially of Cave 17, are of incalculable value as a source of information about life

Fig. 160 **Mural showing a group of foreign mourners from a *parinirvana* scene**
Mid-Tang dynasty, late 8th or early 9th century
Cave 158, Dunhuang, Gansu province
This painting reveals the funeral customs of various nationalities, or at least the Chinese perception of those customs. One of the mourners cuts off his ear, another falls on his sword while another slashes his chest with knives- the latter a custom followed by Turkic peoples (see fig. 87).

Fig. 161 Painted stucco statue of Hong Bian
Late Tang dynasty, ca. 862
Cave 17, Dunhuang, Gansu province
The statue of Hong Bian was originally in what is now known as Cave 17 but was removed sometime during the eleventh century, and placed higher up the cliff - it was returned to the cave during this century. Cave 17 was then filled with thousands of manuscripts, paintings on silk, textiles and other objects and the entrance sealed. It was originally thought that these items were concealed to prevent them from falling into the hands of the Tanguts (Western Xia), who invaded the area in about 1038. However, the careful manner in which the objects were sealed into the cave has led scholars to suggest that the contents may actually represent a ritual deposit of sacred objects. Whatever the reason for their disposal, the contents remained hidden until 1907 when the British-Hungarian explorer Sir Marc Aurel Stein (1862-1943) visited the site. Stein had heard rumours that the custodian of the caves, a Daoist priest called Wang Yuanlu, had discovered a number of manuscripts during restoration work. Stein was refused permission to examine the manuscripts until he and Wang discovered a common interest in the seventh century monk Xuanzang. After protracted negotiations and a contribution to the upkeep of the caves, Stein acquired about 10,000 manuscripts and paintings from Cave 17- written mostly in Chinese and Tibetan but with other texts in Khotanese, Tangut, Uyghur, Kok Turkic, and even Hebrew. His finds were sent to the British Museum in London and were subsequently divided into three groups: for the British Museum, the India Office and the Archeological Survey in New Delhi.

and religious practice along this section of the Silk Road. There is time for no more than a glimpse of the contents of the manuscripts found in Cave 17 in this book but even the briefest survey provides a cascade of information about the glory days of the Silk Road. Pre-eminent among them is the

'Diamond Sutra', the world's oldest complete printed book (fig. 162).

A concise summary by Lionel Giles (Giles, 1944) provides a wealth of detail about many of the other documents. In a paper roll, referred to as S.3935, the prayers of a Military Superintendent are articulated. He vows to read sections of sutras in honour of his deceased parents. He prays that their spirits will travel to the Pure Land, that 'blessings of all kinds may daily descend' upon all of the members of his family and 'that the King's highway may be free and open, and that robbers and thieves may be driven away'.

Narrative ballads figure prominently among the manuscripts. One of the most poignant is 'The Lament of the Lady of Qin', one of several versions in the British Library. It recounts the sack of Changan in 880, by the rebel leader Huang Zhao (see p. 88). The ballad concludes with a haunting description of a great city laid waste during the twilight years of the Tang dynasty:

'Ch'ang-an lies in mournful stillness: what does it now contain?
Ruined markets and desolate streets, in which ears of corn are sprouting.
Fuel-gatherers have hacked down every flowering plant in the Apricot Gardens;
Builders of barricades have destroyed the willows along the Imperial Canal…
All the pomp and magnificence of the olden days are buried and passed away;
Only a dreary waste meets the eye: the old familiar objects are no more.

Fig. 162 **The Diamond Sutra (Detail from the Frontispiece, showing the Buddha preaching to his disciple Subhuti)**
Chinese translation of the *Vajracchedikaprajnaparamitasutra* by Kumarajiva (see p. 57)
Tang dynasty, dated 868
H. 26.5 cm, L. 533 cm
Discovered by Sir Aurel Stein in Cave 17, Dunhuang, Gansu province
(British Library)
The document is a woodblock-printed book in the form of a scroll with an illustrated frontispiece (shown here). The scene depicts the Buddha preaching to Subhuti, one of his ten chief disciples. The colophon at the end of text reads: 'reverently [caused to be] made for universal free distribution by Wang Jie on behalf of his two parents on the thirteenth day of the fourth moon of the ninth year of Xiantong [11th May 868]'. Block-printing techniques had already been in existence for more than 100 years by 868, and the quality of the work suggests that the printer was already an adept craftsman. The document may have been produced in Sichuan, a known centre of printing at this time. The principal idea in the Diamond Sutra is the realisation of the illusory nature of all phenomena.

The Inner Treasury is burnt down, its tapestries and embroideries a heap of ashes;
All along the Street of Heaven one treads on the bones of State officials.'

(Attributed to Wei Chuang, ca. 880. Quoted in Giles, 1944)

One of the versions of the same text in the British Library (S. 692), ends with a wistful verse added by the young novice monk who transcribed it:

'*Now I have made this copy fair,*
Five pints of good wheat should be mine;
But wheat's so dear that in despair
I must my secret hopes resign.'

(Quoted in and translated by Giles, 1944)

The material aspirations of another young man are revealed in one more of the manuscripts from Cave 17:

'*Chinese slaves to take charge of treasury and barn,*
Foreign slaves to take care of my cattle and sheep.
Strong-legged slaves to run by saddle and stirrup when I ride,
Powerful slaves to till the fields with might and main,
Handsome slaves to play the harp and hand the wine;
Slim-waisted slaves to sing me songs, and dance;

Fig. 163 **Silk embroidery on silk backed with hemp cloth depicting Buddha Sakyamuni Preaching on the Vulture Peak**

Tang dynasty, 8th century
H. 241 cm, W. 159.5 cm
Discovered by Sir Aurel Stein in Cave 17, Dunhuang, Gansu province
(British Museum-Heritage Images)
This outstanding embroidery is on a scale comparable to the majestic cave murals of Dunhuang. Its theme is Buddha Sakyamuni's preaching of the Lotus Sutra at Rajagriha on Mount Grdhrakuta (the Vulture Peak). His posture – with the right arm extended straight down – is emblematic of the great event.

Dwarfs to hold the candle by my dining couch.'

(Translated by Arthur Waley. Quoted in Schafer, 1963)

This traditional prayer, recited by a young bridegroom, indicates that the practice of slavery was still widespread during the Tang dynasty. During the early part of the dynasty most slaves were foreigners: prisoners taken during China's territorial expansion, those given as tribute to the court or simply kidnapped and sold like any other Silk Road commodity. During the latter part of the dynasty, as the economy collapsed and famine threatened, many starving or heavily indebted Chinese sold themselves into slavery.

Among the other documents from Cave 17 are examples of great humour and charm. 'A Debate Between Tea and Wine' (S. 406) includes the respective claims of Tea, 'flower of the myriad trees' and Wine, 'drunk by the sovereigns of the Earth', that each is superior to the other. The debate passes back and forth until Water intervenes and tells them they are both depend for their existence on him! A letter admonishing a man for his state of inebriation recalls the sort of understated, polite criticism to be found in correspondence between Victorian gentlemen:

'*Yesterday, Sir, while in your cups, you so far overstepped the observances of polite society as to forfeit the name of gentleman, and made me wish to have nothing more to do with you. But since you now express your shame and regret for what has occurred, I would suggest that we meet again for a friendly talk. Respectfully yours...'*

(From ms S. 5636 and quoted by Giles, 1944)

A final summary might include a request for the return of a donkey (S. 5864), a question about rights of irrigation from a canal (S. 2103), many notices summoning members of various clubs to attend meetings and a long treatise on the intricacies of Chinese chequers (S5574). A project is currently underway to collate all of the Stein manuscripts in the British Library and, as the work continues, more and more fascinating stories of the Silk Road will undoubtedly emerge.

There is room to examine only three of the priceless objects from the hidden library of Cave 17 – two silk embroideries and a painting, each a paragon of Silk Road art. The first, an emroidery on a silk and hemp cloth backing, is one of the largest and finest Chinese examples in existence (fig. 163).

A second embroidery is secular in style and, when it was found, was folded over and sewn into a bag. It is one of the most perfect examples of Tang Dynasty silk embroidery (fig. 164).

As we saw in the documents from Cave 17, the political and religious uncertainties of late Tang dynasty gave rise to a

Fig. 164 **Silk embroidery with flowers and ducks**
Tang dynasty, 8th century
H. 92 cm, W 24 cm
Discovered by Sir Aurel Stein in Cave 17, Dunhuang, Gansu province
(British Museum-Heritage Images)

sense of anxiety among the populace. This is reflected in a greater sense of piety among the town's residents and an increased desire for personal salvation. Depictions of the 'Bodhisattva Avalokitesvara (*Guanyin*) as Guide of Souls' are found in paintings from the late Tang to the early Song. In an example from Cave 17 the Bodhisattva leads a finely dressed lady to a paradise in the clouds (fig. 165).

The collapse of the Tang dynasty in 907 brought China's 'Golden Age' to an abrupt end. There followed fifty years of black chaos, known as the period of 'Five Dynasties and Ten Kingdoms', when local military governors declared themselves ruler or even 'emperor' of whatever slice of territory they happened to hold. Dunhuang fell under the control of the Cao family in about 920 and remained so for the next hundred years. The new ruler of Dunhuang, Cao Yijin (d. 936) sought to consolidate his grip on power by the arrangement of strategic marriages with the neighbouring rulers of the Uighur kingdom of the north and east, and of Khotan to the west. In Cave 98, referred to in an inscription as the 'Cave of the Great King', Cao Yijin and the King of Khotan are shown leading retinues of family members, the two families meshed together by marriage (fig. 166).

The Song Emperor Taizu reunified China in 960 and the country then enjoyed three centuries of relative peace. While trade along the Silk Road never regained the levels it enjoyed during the Tang dynasty, it did not cease and envoys and merchants from other countries still came to the Middle Kingdom. The Northern Song imperial tombs at Gongxian in Henan province demonstrate that China was far from insular during this period. The spirit roads leading to the tombs of the Song emperors are lined with immense figures of foreign ambassadors- including Arabs, Khotanese, Southeast Asians, Uighurs and Koreans. The Song were militarily weak and peace with rival states such as the Khitan and Jurchen in the north and the Western Xia in the west was maintained by diplomacy and the payment of tribute rather than by force. The Song were primarily concerned with retaining the territory they held within metropolitan China and were less preoccupied with places such as Dunhuang,

situated beyond its borders. As result of this policy the Liao dynasty of the Khitans (907–1125) was able to flourish and to retain control of a vast area of northern China, including Manchuria and most of modern-day Mongolia. The Western Xia (Tangut) Kingdom (1032–1227) ruled a similarly large area of Ningxia, Gansu and Inner Mongolia centred around the cities of Xingzhou (modern Yinchuan) and Khara Khoto (see p. 120).

The Cao rulers of Dunhuang succeeded in retaining their independence by perpetuating Cao Yijin's strategy of forging

Fig. 165 **Ink and polychrome painting on silk, showing the Bodhisattva as Guide of Souls**
Tang dynasty
Late 9th century
H. 80.5 cm, W 53.8 cm
Discovered by Sir Aurel Stein in Cave 17, Dunhuang, Gansu province
(British Museum)
The Bodhisattva depicted, despite the absence of an Amitabha Buddha in his headdress, is almost certainly Avalokitesvara. The elegant lady with her elaborate coiffure and rich clothes is doubtless a princess or aristocrat and is led towards the celestial palace at the top left of the painting.

Xia. Motifs from Esoteric Buddhism began to appear in the eighty caves built during the Western Xia period and a number of earlier caves were redecorated. One of the best known images from the Western Xia period is a portrait of the Western Xia emperor, his young son and a retinue of servants on the east wall of Cave 409 (fig. 167).

The Western Xia's control of Dunhuang was short lived. In 1227 the armies of Genghis Khan laid waste to the Western Regions, annihilated the populace and began a gradual process of subjugation that would culminate in the establishment of the Yuan dynasty in 1279. Genghis Khan's grandson Khubilai Khan (r. 1279–1294) permitted religion freedom in China, probably as a result of a tolerance for other faiths, learned during childhood from his mother, the redoubtable Sorghagtani Beki. He was also influenced by his

Fig. 166 **Wall-painting depicting the King of Khotan and his consort**
Five Dynasties, ca. 920
Cave 98, Dunhuang, Gansu province
Behind the King of Khotan stands his Queen, a daughter of Cao Yijin, wearing a necklace and crown of green Khotan jade and carrying a censer (an incense-burner). The King himself wears a splendid robe, decorated with sun and moon emblems and embroidered with dragons. Elsewhere in the cave is a mural with leaders of various neighbouring states listening to a sermon by the scholar Vimalikirti.

matrimonial alliances with the Uighur Khans and with the neighbouring King of Khotan. They also sent generous tribute to the Song court. These strategies were successful until about 997 when the Cao clan fractured. Cao Yanlu and Cau Ruibing, two grandsons of Cao Yijin, were murdered by a relative, Cao Zhongshou. By about 1019 Dunhuang had fallen under the control of the Uighurs although the Cao family continued to rule with Uighur consent. Cao loyalties shifted back and forth between the Liao and Song courts and, in 1036, the self-styled 'Prince of Dunhuang' Cao Xianshun (son of Cao Zhongshou) also swore allegiance to the Western Xia. It appears that Dunhuang remained at least nominally independent and under Cao-Uighur control until about 1072, when it fell firmly under the sway of the Western

Fig. 167 **Mural depicting the Western Xia emperor**
Xia State (Tangut), (1032–1227)
Cave 409, Dunhuang, Gansu province
This scene is a fascinating window on a brief phase of the Silk Road's history. The emperor wears the white felt crown and boots of a nomad prince yet his robe carries the coiled dragons of Chinese imperial mythology. His servants stand behind, diminutive and insignificant, stretching upwards to cover the great man with a broad parasol and wielding fans decorated with more dragons. His bow, sword and shield are carried in state to the rear of the painting and he stands on a lavish carpet. The line of seated Buddhas along the top edge of the mural are a reminder that the portraits are of the cave's sponsor, a fervent Buddhist.

'Head of the Office of Buddhist Affairs', a Tibetan lama named Phags-Pa (or Baisiba in Chinese). Under Phags-pa's guidance, Khubilai and the Mongol population as a whole – hitherto believers in shamanism – were drawn to the sorcery and necromancy of Tibetan Lamaistic Buddhism. Lama temples were built all over China and the survival of Dunhuang was assured. Many of Dunhuang's caves were restored during the Yuan dynasty and the murals are replete with *mandalas* (cosmic diagrams) and deities from esoteric Buddhism.

The Yuan dynasty proved to be Dunhuang's swansong, however. In 1368 the restoration of Chinese sovereignty occurred and the Ming dynasty was established. China became more inward looking and the fortunes of the Silk Road and many of its caravan cities fell into decline. When trade revived – as a result of the great European explorations of the fifteenth century onwards – it was via the sea routes and not by land. The cities of the Silk Road receded from history and were by and large forgotten until the beginning of this century, when the activities of Stein, Pelliot, von Le Coq and others revived the public's interest.

Jingh

Zarkent ■Korgas
Huocheng ■ **Yining**
Cilik

Tianshan Moun

Przevalsk **China**

Su
Kizil-Qargha
Kizil
Kumtura ■
Duldur-Aqur Xinhe
Tiar Shan Mountains ■ Naryn **Aksu** Karayulgun

Kazakhstan *Tarim River*

Bedel Pass

Sanxiandong Caves Sanchakou
Uluggat Wuqi Sugun ■ Tumshuq
Irkeshtam **Kashgar**
Hanoi and Mauri Tim Stupa *Khotan River*
Shule
■Yengisar **Taklamakan Desert**
Mazartagh Fort ■
Kara-dong
Tajikistan ■ Shache
Keriya Ri
Pamirs ■ Tashkurgan **Yecheng** ■ Niy
Andi
Sagan Dandan-Oilik
Moyu ■Rawak Stupa
Yotkan **Khotan**■Domeko
Malikawat ■ ■Qira Yutian M
Shanpula
Cemetery

THE SILK ROAD THROUGH CHINA BEYOND DUNHUANG

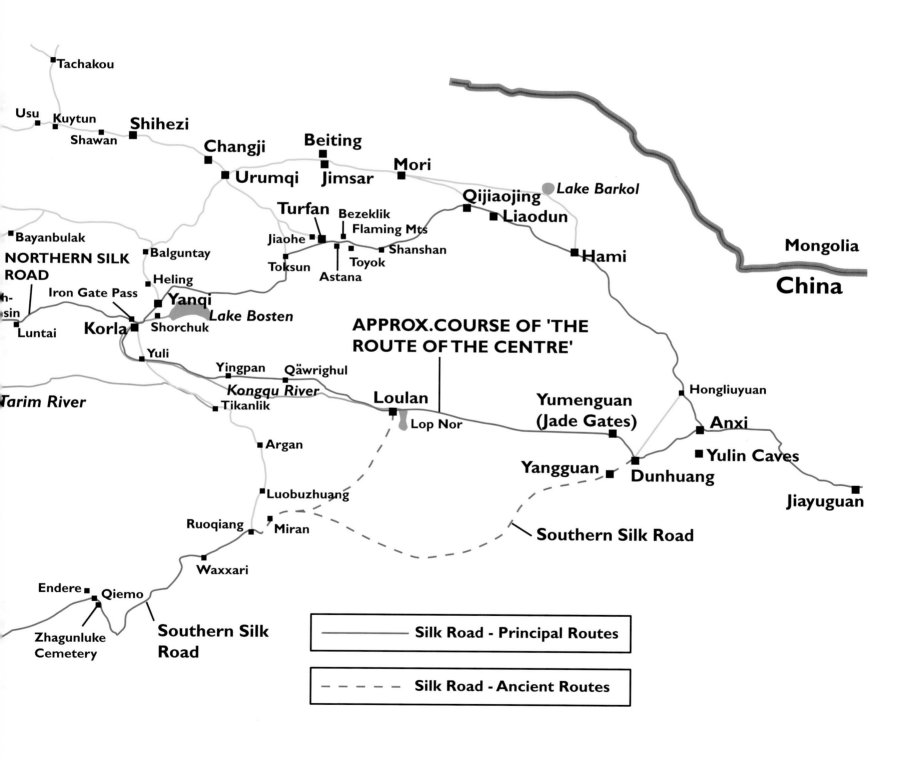

Tachakou

Usu
Kuytun
Shawan
Shihezi

Changji

Beiting

Urumqi
Jimsar
Mori

Qijiaojing
Lake Barkol

Bayanbulak

**NORTHERN SILK
ROAD**
Balguntay

Heling

Iron Gate Pass

Yanqi
Lake Bosten
Shorchuk

Korla

Luntai

Yuli

Turfan
Bezeklik
Flaming Mts
Jiaohe

Toksun
Toyok
Astana
Shanshan

Liaodun

Hami

Mongolia

China

Yingpan
Qäwrighul

Kongqu River
Tikanlik

Tarim River

**APPROX.COURSE OF 'THE
ROUTE OF THE CENTRE'**

Loulan
Lop Nor

**Yumenguan
(Jade Gates)**

Hongliuyuan

Anxi

Argan

Yulin Caves

Luobuzhuang

Yangguan
Dunhuang

Ruoqiang
Miran

Southern Silk Road

Jiayuguan

Waxxari

Endere
Qiemo

**Southern Silk
Road**

Zhagunluke
Cemetery

Silk Road - Principal Routes

- - - - - Silk Road - Ancient Routes

A section of the Silk Road winds out of Dunhuang, following the course of the Shule River. On the southwestern outskirts stand the ruins of a nine-storey structure, the White Horse Pagoda, built during the fourth century by the monk Kumarajiva to memorialize his favourite steed. To the northwest and southwest of Dunhuang and 86 km apart are two strategic passes, the Yumenguan and the Yangguan, both located in what used to be Han dynasty sections of the Great Wall.

The Yumenguan (Jade Gate Pass) is situated in the Gobi Desert, 90 km northwest of Dunhuang and is the gateway to the Northern Silk Road. A spur leads from Dunhuang to the main route at Hami. In later years caravans carrying jade would pass through the Yumenguan on their way from Khotan and it became known as the Jade Gate. It came to be regarded by generations of Chinese as the end of the civilised world:

'For years, to guard the Jade Pass and the River of Gold,
With our hands on our horse-whips and our sword-hilts,
We have watched the green graves change to snow
And the Yellow Stream ring the Black Mountain forever.'

(Liu Zhongyong, 8th century, 'A Trooper's Burden')

'The bright moon lifts from the Mountain of Heaven
In an infinite haze of cloud and sea,
And the wind, that has come a thousand miles,
Beats at the Jade Pass battlements…'

(Li Po [Li Bai] 701–62, 'The Moon at the Fortified Pass')

The remains of this small fort with two portals known, on account of its shape, as the 'Square City' or 'Lesser Fangpan' is all that remains of Yumenguan. The site is one of the most desolate and remote places on earth and its position was not finally ascertained until 1907, when Aurel Stein discovered inscribed wooden slips on which the site is named. He also explored a network of ancient forts to the north of Dunhuang, built during the Han dynasty along the westernmost extension of the Great Wall. This section of the wall extends westwards along the course of the Shule River to the dried up salt lake of Lop Nor, situated less than 300 km from Yumenguan. A line of about sixty beacon towers, each within site of the other, enabled the garrisons to warn of the approach of invading Xiongnu. Stein found bundles of tamarisk, ready to be set alight, still scattered near the towers and legend has it that wolf-dung was also burned because it emitted dark, easily visible smoke. One of the many stories associated with the beacon towers, compared by Stein to the Roman defence roads known as *limites* (singular *limes*), is the sad tale of the Lady Baosi. Baosi was the favourite consort of King You of the Zhou dynasty and, during an attack of ennui, she persuaded the king to light the beacon signals. The rulers of neighbouring kingdoms rushed to the king's assistance but found the couple enjoying a feast on a local mountainside. When Zhou territory was actually invaded some time later the king's allies ignored the beacon fires: he was killed and Baosi was captured.

The road to the southeast from Yumenguan to Dunhuang is equally desolate. Early travellers must have gazed at a road that stretched endlessly before them and been overwhelmed by a sense of hopelessness (fig. 169).

The gateway to the Southern Silk Road is Yangguan, built during the Han dynasty and situated about 70 km southwest of Dunhuang (fig. 170). Yangguan, or the 'Gate of Yang', is said to derive its name from Yang Ming, an official of ancient times who fled through the gate to evade a warrant for his arrest. The remains of a citadel can still be seen at the site and so many artefacts are strewn around the area – coins, arrowheads, pottery shards and even gold jewellery – that the local people call it 'Curio Depot' or 'Relic Bank'. To the Chinese it was a remote, forbidding spot – a place for farewells:

'A morning rain has settled the dust in Wei Town,
Willows are green again in the tavern dooryard
Wait till we empty one more cup-
West of Yang Gate there'll be no old friends.'

(Wang Wei [701–62], 'A Song at Wei Town'. Willows are symbols of farewell for the Chinese: for a different version of this poem and more about willows, see p. 110)

By the end of the Tang dynasty the incursion of sand and flood had led to the abandonment of the area and Yangguan was forgotten. Yumenguan and Yangguan were gateways to the Western Regions and Chinese beliefs in the evils that awaited travellers to these areas go right back into antiquity. To the Chinese, the lands to the west were *terra incognita* and were inhabited by monsters:

Fig. 168 **Remains of the fort at Yumenguan (Jade Gate Pass)**
Han dynasty, (206 BC–220 AD)
D. 28 × 28 m

'O Soul, go not to the West
Where level wastes of sand stretch on and on;
And demons rage, swine-headed, hairy-skinned,
With bulging eyes;
Who in wild laughter gnash projecting fangs.
O Soul, go not the West
Where many perils wait!'

(Attributed to Qu Yuan, '*Ta Chao*' 'The Great Summons', third century BC. Translated by Arthur Waley in Waley, 1941)

Another version runs:

'O soul, come back! For the west holds many perils:
The Moving Sands stretch on for a hundred leagues.
You will be swept into the Thunder's Chasm, and dashed in
pieces, unable to help yourself;
And even should you chance to escape from that, beyond is
the empty desert,
And red ants as huge as elephants, and wasps as big as gourds.
The five grains do not grow there; dry stalks are the only food;
And the earth there scorches men up; there is nowhere
to look for water.
And you will drift there for ever, with nowhere to go
in that vastness.'

(Attributed to Qu Yuan,* 'Chao Hun' 'The Great Summons', 3rd century BC)

The northern and southern routes of the Silk Road skirt the rim of the Tarim Basin. The Tarim Basin extends over an area of 530,000 square km (about fifteen times the size of Taiwan), across Xinjiang, China's largest and westernmost province. The basin is almost completely enclosed by mountains: the Tianshan to the north, the Kunlun to the south and the Pamirs to the west. Within the Tarim Basin is the Taklamakan, China's largest desert and some 337,000 square km in extent. In Turkic, Taklamakan means 'the place from which no living thing returns' or 'the desert of certain death.' The Chinese called it 'Liu Sha' or 'Shifting Sands' because of the constant movement of its dunes. A modern-day traveller, Sir Clarmont Skrine, British consul-general at Kashgar in the 1920s, has captured the overwhelming desolation of the place:

'To the north in the clear dawn the view is inexpressively
awe-inspiring and sinister. The yellow dunes of the
Taklamakan, like the giant waves of a petrified ocean,
extend in countless myriads to a far horizon with here
and there an extra large sand-hill, a king dune as it were,
towering above his fellows. They seem to clamour silently,
those dunes, for travellers to engulf, for whole caravans
to swallow up as they have swallowed up so many in
the past.'

(Skrine, 1926)

Fig. 169 **'A thousand miles of moonlight': The Silk Road between Yumenguan and Dunhuang**

Fig. 170 **The remains of a citadel at Yangguan**
Han dynasty, (206 BC–220 AD)

The cities of the oases along the fringes of the Tarim Basin were sometimes abandoned because of invasion or because of the drying up of glacier-fed streams. If a proportion of the population left the town, there was frequently not enough manpower to maintain the *kariz*, the system of irrigation canals and wells. The amount of cultivable land would soon become insufficient to support the remaining population and the town would eventually be left for the desert to reclaim.

* Qu Yuan, (340?–278 BC) was a member of the ruling house, a statesman and diplomat. He was eventually banished by the court as result of slanders by rivals and, in despair, he drowned himself in the Mi-lo – a tributary of the Yangtze. The traditional date of his death is the fifth day of the fifth moon (month) and annual commemoration of the event is said to be the origin of China's Dragon Boat Festival.

CHAPTER EIGHT

THE NORTHERN SILK ROAD

'The desert which lies between Ansi [Anxi] and Hami is a howling wilderness, and the first thing which strikes the wayfarer is the dismalness of its uniform, black, pebble-strewn surface…. The twelve hard stages between Ansi and Hami offered many new varieties of objectionable water. Sometimes it ran from beneath boulders in a limpid stream, sometimes it lay in a sluggish pool, its surface covered with a repulsive scum; at other times it burst through the soil, and sometimes it was drawn from a well with bucket and rope; but whatever its immediate source, it was always brackish and thirst-creating.'

(Cable and French, 1942)

This description of the Northern Silk Road between Anxi and Hami is not the complaint of some ancient traveller. It was written in 1942 when the journey from Kashgar to the old Chinese capital of Luoyang – today, a four- or five-day train ride – took five months. The Anxi-Hami section has few wells and what little water there was to be found was often brackish or contaminated with sulphur. The journey took about two weeks and crossed a section of desert known as the 'Black Gobi'. This area was where the monk Xuanzang became lost during the seventh century after straying from the main route. One of the frequent sandstorms, known as *karaburans*, obliterated Xunazang's path and he faced disaster when he dropped his water bag. He was saved by his skinny roan horse, which carried him to a small oasis.

Hami

Hami (ancient Yiwu or Kamul) is the first of a series of oasis towns along the foot of the Tianshan or Celestial Mountains. The mountains act as a barrier between the Dzungarian Plain of Southern Mongolia and the Taklamakan Desert of Xinjiang that extends for 2,000 km from east to west and 400 km from north to south. The melt water from the Tianshan is collected in wells linked by underground canals known as *kariz* or *kyariz*. Some are 40 km in length and the network of *kariz* accounts for the fertility of the soil in the Turfan region, an area with negligible rainfall. The *kariz* were invented in ancient Persia and are still used in many parts of Central Asia.

Hami is renowned for its melons although 'Hami' melons are actually grown throughout Xinjiang. There are more than thirty varieties produced around Hami. They have been a delicacy for centuries and Hami honeydew melons were sent as tribute to the Chinese court from ancient times right up until the Qing dynasty. Preserved remains of Hami melons, found in the Astana necropolis at Turfan, indicate that they have been cultivated for at least 1,300 years.

The residents of Hami were hospitable to outsiders to an extraordinary degree: Marco Polo describes how the man of the house would share all of his possessions, including his wife, with a guest:

'When strangers arrive, and desire to have lodging and accommodation at their houses, it affords them the highest gratification. They give positive orders to their wives, daughters, sisters, and other female relations, to indulge their guests in every wish, whilst they themselves leave their homes, and retire in the city, and the stranger lives in the house with the females as if they were his own wives….The women are in truth very handsome, very sensual, and fully disposed to conform in this respect to the injunction of their husbands.'

(From *The Travels of Marco Polo the Venetian*. Translated by William Marsden in Marsden, 1948)

A spur of the Silk Road runs northwest from Hami through the Tianshan Mountains to the ancient trade post at Lake Barkol. Barkol was known as the State of Pulei during ancient times and was populated by nomads who raised fine horses, cattle and camels. Lake Barkol (once known as the Pulei Sea) is west of the town of the same name and was the site of numerous battles with the Xiongnu. In 73 and 74 AD, the Han Emperor Mingdi sent large expeditions against the ruling Xiongnu clan, the Huyan, and the area was secured. A memorial tablet, 1.4 metres high, once stood on the shores of Lake Barkol but has now been removed to a museum. It commemorates the achievements of Pei Cen, Prefect of Dunhuang during the Eastern Han dynasty (25–220 AD). The inscription is dated 137 AD and celebrates Pei Cen's rout of the Xiongnu that was said to have brought peace to the border regions. There are still signal towers lining the route

Fig. 171 **The old city Gaochang**
Near Turfan, Xinjiang province

westwards from Lake Barkol and this strand of the Northern Silk Road is said to have run along the northern foothills of the Tianshan, to the kingdom of Jushi during the Han dynasty and to Beiting during the Tang dynasty. The Jushi were the original nomadic peoples of the area but were progressively displaced, from about 60 BC, by successive waves of Chinese settlers. By the sixth century AD, when the Gaochang Kingdom was established in the area, there were few indigenous Jushi left.

TURFAN

'...lonely, silent old Kaochang [Gaochang], crumbling back to dust and wholly undisturbed by the hand of any restorer.'

(Cable and French, 1942)

The main Northern Silk Road runs directly from Hami to Turfan, across the southern foothills of the Tianshan Mountains. A route also existed to the north, between Turfan and Jimusa (Beshbalik or Beiting) where it joined the northern Tianshan route. Turfan is situated some 150 metres

below sea level, the lowest elevation on earth after the Dead Sea. Its old name, 'Land of Fire' or 'Oasis of Fire', is a reference to its searing heat: summer temperatures can reach 45 degrees celsius and annual rainfall is seldom more than 16 mm. Because of the aridity of the area an astonishing array of artefacts have survived in near pristine condition. The early inhabitants of the Turfan oasis were the Jushi nomadic peoples, their capital at Jiaohe (Yarkhoto) just to the west of the modern city. The Chinese and Xiongnu fought each other for possession of the Turfan oasis throughout the Han dynasty but the Chinese eventually prevailed. Large numbers of Chinese settlers arrived during the period of turmoil that followed the collapse of the Han dynasty and, by the end of the fifth century, Turfan was a thriving centre on the Silk Road with a well-integrated community of Chinese and Central Asians. In 499 the Qu family – with the joint support of the Han, the remaining Jushi nomads and other nationalities – established the independent kingdom of Gaochang. The capital of Gaochang state was at the city of Gaochang (Khocho or Karakhoja), about 45 km south-east of modern Turfan. The rulers of the Gaochang state survived

Fig. 172 Silk fragment with hunting motif.

Tang dynasty, (618–907)
L. 44 cm, W. 29 cm
From Tomb 191, Astana cemetery, Turfan, Xinjiang province
(Xinjiang Uighur Autonomous Regional Museum)

Note the use of the 'Parthian Shot' motif on this textile in which a hunter shoots backwards from a galloping horse. The 'Parthian Shot' is said to have been one the strategies used to defeat the Roman armies of Crassus at the battle of Carrhae (see p. 283).

for nine generations by simultaneously ingratiating themselves with the northern nomads and paying tribute to the Chinese court. The men of Gaochang wore local attire but the women adopted Chinese dress and hairstyles. After the Sui dynasty reunified China in 589 the Qu rulers maintained good relations with the new government. The ruler at the time, Qu Boya, attended the Sui Emperor Yangdi's grand Silk Road 'summit' at Zhangye in 609 (see pp. 75 and 118). He joined the party of rulers who escorted the emperor back to Changan and later married a princess from the Sui royal house.

Qu Boya's son, Qu Wendai, was a somewhat Machiavellian individual who is remembered for his desire to appoint Xuanzang as Buddhist patriarch of the kingdom, when the venerable monk passed through in 630. Xuanzang refused and was forced to go on a hunger strike before Qu Wendai would release him and permit him to continue his journey. Qu inadvertently brought about the demise of the Gaochang kingdom when he attempted to exploit its status as a Silk Road entrepôt. He attempted to levy exorbitant taxes on passing merchants and frequently detained the caravans who carried goods to Changan. The Tang government was enraged by Qu's behaviour and Emeror Taizong sent troops to attack Gaochang in 640. As the army approached, Qu Wendai is said to have died of fright and his son quickly submitted to the control of the central government. The Tang renamed the area Xizhou (Western Prefecture) and the Qu clan were exiled to Luoyang. For the following one and a half centuries the area enjoyed a period of peace and prosperity when the production of, and trade in silk flourished. Central Asian merchants, particularly Sogdians, set up trading centres along this section of the Silk Road and their artisans worked side-by-side with Chinese craftsmen. Artistic motifs from the empires of Persia and Gandhara flowed freely into the region (fig. 172).

A population census was conducted in 640 when Tang China regained control of Turfan: officials recorded a population of 37,000 in 8,000 households. The Tang were great administrators and record keepers and a large quantity of documents of various types have been unearthed in the Turfan region. Inscribed wooden slips and documents on bone, terracotta and paper in Chinese, Kharosthi, Kuchean, Sogdian, Tibetan, Uighur and Kharakhanid have been found

Fig.173 Epitaph of Liang Yanhui

Tang dynasty, dated 664
H. 34 cm, W. 34 cm
Found at Tomb 183, Astana cemetery, Turfan, Xinjiang province
(Archeology Institute of Xinjiang province)

This terracotta epitaph concerns Liang Yanhui, the occupant of Tomb 183. Liang was a resident of Gaochang and served as treasurer to the Qu family, rulers of the Gaochang Kingdom. After Tang China regained control of Turfan in 640, Liang served as cavalry commander of the garrison and then worked for the governor's office in Xizhou Prefecture, the new name for Gaochang. His tenure therefore covers the periods of both Qu family and Tang rule.

Fig. 174 **Deed in Sogdian concerning the purchase of a slave girl**
Gaochang Kingdom period, dated 639
L. 28.3 cm, W. 46.3 cm
Found at Tomb 135, Astana cemetery, Turfan, Xinjiang province
(Xinjiang Uighur Autonomous Regional Museum)
This ink on paper document, written with exquisite neatness, is dated 639, just before the end of the Gaochang Kingdom. It states that Yanasena, the son of Uta of the State of Shi, is paying 120 'drachmas of the Sasanian King Peroz' (r. 459–84) in Gaochang market to a man with the name of Uhusufert, for the purchase of a slave girl born in the region of the Turks.

Fig. 175 **Female Mummy**
Tang dynasty, 713–41
From the Astana cemetery
Turfan, Xinjiang province
(Turfan Museum)

and testify to the cosmopolitan nature of the region at that time. These documents also provide fascinating glimpses into the everyday life and economic conditions of the Silk Road (fig. 173).

A second document, also discovered at the Astana cemetery, illustrates both the economic conditions and the diverse nationalities around at the time (fig. 174).

The Astana cemetery

The Astana cemetery, 40 km southeast of Turfan, has already been mentioned several times in this book. It contains over 400 tombs, built in the Chinese style and accessed by walkways. The cemetery contains the dead of Gaochang, both Han Chinese and other ethnic groups, and documents found at the site indicate that it was in use at least as early as the late third century but had ceased to be used by the end of the eighth century. The arid climate has preserved both the bodies and many of the artefacts interred there and the contents of the graves provide a fascinating window on the

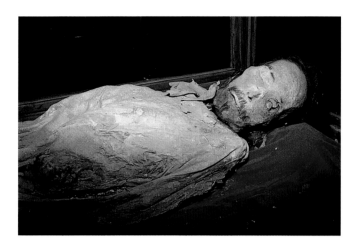

Fig. 176 **Male Mummy**
Tang dynasty, 713–41
From the Astana cemetery, Turfan, Xinjiang province
(Turfan Museum)

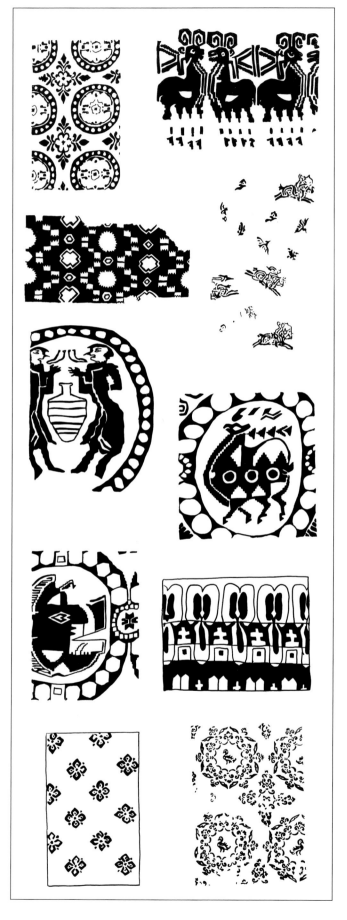

Fig. 178 **A schematic diagram of different motifs found in Turfan silks**
(Drawing by Antonia Tozer)

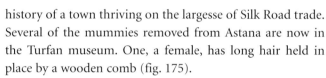

Fig. 177 **Tomb figure of wood, paper and silk, seventh century**
Tang dynasty (618–907)
H. 30 cm
Tomb 206, Astana cemetery, Turfan, Xinjiang province
(Xinjiang Uighur Autonomous Regional Museum)
This beautifully made figure wears an elaborate suit of clothes made from silk. The motifs on the upper part of her dress are typical Persian pearl roundels and the details of her face are superbly rendered. The rolled up pawnshop tickets that make up her arms indicate that she was manufactured in Changan (Xian).

history of a town thriving on the largesse of Silk Road trade. Several of the mummies removed from Astana are now in the Turfan museum. One, a female, has long hair held in place by a wooden comb (fig. 175).

A second mummy, that of a young non-Chinese man, has long brown hair (fig. 176).

Expeditions by the Japanese explorer Count Kozui Otani in 1902 and 1910, by Aurel Stein in 1914 and by Chinese archeologists from 1959 onwards, have unearthed more than 10,000 objects. A number of silk funeral banners from Astana contain the figures of Fu Xi and Nu Wa, ancestors of mankind in Chinese mythology. Such banners were typically hung on the ceiling or back wall of a tomb and prove that the residents of this remote outpost of the Chinese empire still clung to the legends of the Central Plains. The scarcity of paper in the Western Regions meant that documents were often recycled for other purposes when they were no longer required. The residents of Turfan also followed the practice of burying their dead with paper hats, belts and shoes, reusing this scarce commodity, and many of the documents discovered from this period have thus been found in graves. A beautiful female tomb figure from Astana has arms made from recycled pawnshop tickets! (fig. 177).

Motifs on Turfan silks

Many of the surviving early Chinese silks have been found in the arid western regions of Gansu and Xinjiang and large numbers were recovered from the Astana necropolis. During the Tang dynasty woven brocades and embroideries as well as simple printed silks were produced. Among the many motifs found on silk textiles excavated at Turfan sites are

Fig.179 **Posy of artificial flowers made from silk gauze**
Tang dynasty, seventh or eighth century
L. 32 cm
Unearthed at the Astana cemetery, Turfan, Xinjiang province
(Xinjiang Uighur Autonomous Regional Museum)

'tree-leaf' and 'chessboard' patterns; hexagons; leaf-like hearts; diamonds composed of dots; winged horses and sacred birds (fig. 178).

Many of these motifs have filtered through from India and Persia and the medium through which they came is known to us. During the sixth century, increasing numbers of Central Asian settlers arrived in the Turfan area and by the seventh century they had established a community at the Turfan oasis, in the village of Chonghua. The most populous were the Sogdians and documents found at Turfan indicate that Sogdian and Chinese weavers worked together and exchanged ideas. The security and stability of traffic along the Silk Road also facilitated the importation of silk textiles from elsewhere in China. Patterned Sichuan silks have been found at Turfan, for example, and are generally finer than locally produced fabrics.

One of the most marvellous silk artefacts found at Astana was not a piece of fabric at all but a posy of artificial flowers that are exquisite (fig. 179).

Sogdian merchants introduced two important religions from Persia to the Turfan area, namely Zoroastrianism and Manichaeism (for more on these religions see p. 89). Manichaeism did not flourish in China until after the An Lushan rebellion of 755–63. The Uighurs, a tribe related to the Eastern Turks, were asked to assist the Tang to put down the rebellion and in 762 their ruler Bogu Khagan converted

to Manichaeism and declared it to be the Uighur state religion. The Tibetans took advantage of the weakened state of the Tang to seize control of the Kuqa and Turfan regions. From about 790 until about 840 Turfan remained in Tibetan hands, a situation that persisted until control of the whole area was wrested by the Uighurs. During the ninth and tenth centuries, while much of Chinese Central Asia was under Uighur control, Buddhism, Nestorian Christianity, Zoroastrianism and Manichaeism all appear to have flourished to differing extents. Turfan retained its religious diversity until the tenth century when the Uighur ruler of Kashgar converted to Islam. This conversion began an irreversible process of submission to Islam that would eventually encompass the whole of Central Asia and would endure until the present day.

The Turfan area remained under Uighur domination until 1283, when the Mongols arrived, and did not return to full Chinese control until the Qing dynasty campaigns of the mid-eighteenth century. During the earliest period of Uighur control the Turfan area enjoyed its greatest cultural and religious diversity and many of it most fascinating works

Fig. 180 **Painted leaf from a Manichaean book (both sides shown)**
Tang dynasty, 8th or 9th century
H. 12.4 cm, L. 25.5 cm
Found in the city walls of Gaochang (Khocho), near Turfan, Xinjiang province
(Museum für Indische Kunst, Berlin)
This large fragment depicts a church ceremony on one side with a priest ministering to a Uighur noble with his attendants. In the foreground are two Persian-Manichaean gods facing a group consisting of Hindu deities: Ganesha and three others who appear to be Vishnu (as the boar incarnation, Varaha), Brahma and Shiva. On the reverse (pictured below) is a depiction of the feast of Bema, held each spring to commemorate the death of Mani.

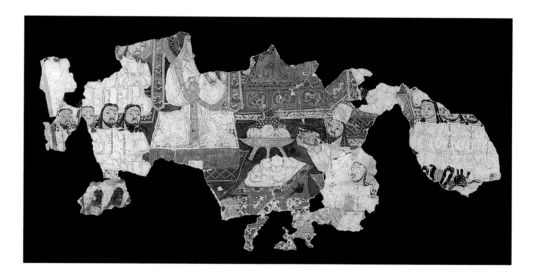

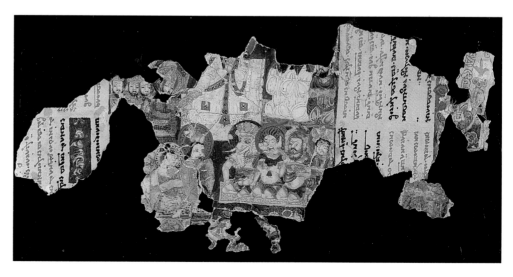

Fig. 181 **Wall painting depicting a contemplative figure**
Gaochang Kingdom period or early Tang dynasty, 602–54 (established by radiocarbon dating)
H. 44.5 cm, W. 22.4 cm
Gaochang (Khocho), Nestorian Temple, near Turfan, Xinjiang province
(Museum für Indische Kunst, Berlin)

Fig. 182 **Wall painting depicting Palm Sunday**
Tang dynasty, 683–770 (established by radiocarbon dating)
Gaochang (Khocho), Nestorian Temple, near Turfan, Xinjiang province
H. 61 cm, W. 67 cm
(Museum für Indische Kunst, Berlin)
In this painting a Nestorian priest sprinkles consecrated water over his congregation, who stand before him with heads bowed. Above them a horse's leg can be seen and has been interpreted as a reference to Christ's entry into Jerusalem.

of art were produced. An example are the Manichaean paintings – discovered in the city walls of Gaochang by Albert von Le Coq – concealed behind later Buddhist paintings. Until they were discovered it was thought that all of the sacred texts of the Manichaeans had been lost (fig. 180).

Little trace of the Zoroastrian religion has been found at Gaochang except for few documents relating to animal sacrifice. Nestorianism, which arrived in China around the seventh century, is better represented at Gaochang. The Nestorian temple at Gaochang, discovered and excavated by von Le Coq from 1904 to 1905, was situated north-east of the city walls. A wall painting, removed from the temple by Le Coq and now in the Berlin Museum, shows a figure in long robes and turned up shoes, perhaps part of a solemn procession (fig. 181).

One of the most astonishing finds from Gaochang's Nestorian temple is a wall-painting thought to be a depiction of Palm Sunday (fig. 182).

Among the many Buddhist sculptures discovered at Gaochang by Albert Grünwedel are serene Buddha images, smiling *devatas* and grotesque demon heads in both Chinese and Indo-Persian styles. A large three-tiered structure at Gaochang – the Buddhist Gamma Temple – resembles the stupas of the Gandhara kingdom to the west. Each of its tiers would have contained sculptures, a technique found in Gandhara temples and also at Jiaohe (see below).

Jiaohe (Yarkhoto)

> 'One can wander from end to end of these lonely, melancholy, derelict cities, where on stormy nights the howling winds make play, and the swirls of sand spin down the forgotten avenues like Dancing Dervishes; and nothing can be too weird or too fantastic for the imagination to devise after lingering, even only for a few hours, in such surroundings.'

(Cable and French, 1927)

As has already been mentioned, Jiaohe was the capital of the Jushi people as early as the Han dynasty. The Chinese moved the capital to Gaochang after seizing control of the area but the administrative capital of the Turfan oasis alternated back and forth a number of times. The name Yarkhoto means 'cliff town', a reference to its strategic location on a plateau surrounded by two deep valleys. The ruined city of Jiaohe (Yarkhoto), 8 km west of Turfan, dates back to the Han dynasty and was a fortress intended to protect against raids by the Xiongnu. The ruins are about 1,600 metres by 300 metres and date mostly to the Tang dynasty, a period when the city's population numbered in excess of 5,000 and when it was an important trading and Buddhist centre. Among the ruins of Jiaohe are the remains of a large Buddhist stupa (fig. 184).

Headless stucco figures set in niches adorn the central part of the 5,100 square metre main temple (fig. 185). They are now worn and damaged but are still strongly reminiscent of Gandhara sculptures such as those in Taxila's Jaulian monastery (see fig. 29).

'The History of the Tang' (*Tangshu*), provides us with a brief description of the kingdom of Gaochang in general and of Jiaohe in particular:

'It numbers in all twenty-one towns. The king has his capital in the town of Jiaohe which is none other than the former royal court (of the country) of Jushi at the time of the Han dynasty . . . The kingdom has two thousand crack soldiers. The ground is fertile. Corn and crops produce two harvests a year. There is a plant there called baidie (almost certainly cotton). It flower is picked so that it can be woven to make cloth. The custom (of the inhabitants) is to plait their hair into a coil, which hangs behind the head.'

(*Tangshu*, 'History of the Tang', quoted in Drège and Bührer, 1989)

Fig. 183 **Overall view of Jiaohe (Yarkhoto)**
Near Turfan, Xinjiang province

Fig. 184 **Remains of a Buddhist Stupa**
4th century (radiocarbon dated)
Jiaohe (Yarkhoto), near Turfan, Xinjiang province
This structure consists of a large central stupa with four groups of twenty-five small stupas, one group set at each corner, making a total of 101.

Fig. 185 **Remains of stucco seated Buddhas**
Main Temple, Jiaohe (Yarkhoto), near Turfan, Xinjiang province

A large amount of information about the changing economic conditions of the Turfan oasis at the time of the Silk Road has been obtained from recent studies of coins found in the area. One such examination, of silver Sasanian coins found at Turfan, collates the reign dates of more than 150 silver Sasanian and Arab-Sasanian coins. The coin dates peak during two periods: the late fourth century and the late sixth and seventh centuries. Corresponding documents found in Turfan suggest that during the first period coins were not used as currency: cloth was the principal medium of exchange. During the second period coins were circulated and most often used in commerce involving expensive goods. The Qu rulers of Gaochang appear to have encouraged the circulation of such coins because of their role in taxation and in payments by the government. One such coin was found in the mouth of a corpse at the Astana necropolis.

To the east of Gaochang, carved into the sides of the Flaming Mountains, is Toyok (fig. 186). Toyok contains a large number of caves honeycombed into the rock and was first explored by Stein and later by von Le Coq. In one cave – known as the Manuscript Room – von Le Coq found large numbers of manuscripts, many showing signs of fire damage as if some unknown ancient had tried to destroy them.

Turfan abounds with grapes. There are several varieties but the best are the famous 'mare's teat', grapes that are made into wine. Zhang Qian, emissary of the Han dynasty Emperor Wudi, brought grapes to China from the Ferghana region of Central Asia. They were originally planted in the capital at Changan but were eaten rather than used for making wine. As late as the Tang dynasty wine was still an exotic drink and did not become widely popular until the Chinese conquest of Gaochang in 640. 'Mare's teat' grapes were subsequently taken to Changan where vineyards were established. Poems by Li Po and others celebrating the virtues of imbibing wine appear more frequently after this event.

The Flaming Mountains

> *'Fire clouds over the mountain never dispel;*
> *Birds dare not approach within a thousand* li.'

(Cen Shen [715–70], who served for many years as an official on the western frontier)

The Flaming Mountains comprise a line of crenellated red sandstone hills, rising to as much as 850 metres above sea level, and extending for 100 km to the north of Gaochang. In

Fig. 186 **The Toyok Caves**
Near Turfan, Xinjiang province

Fig. 187 **The Flaming Mountains**
Near Turfan, Xinjiang province

the midday sun the hills shimmer and exude a hot vapour that makes them appear as if they are on fire. Surface temperatures have reached 80°C and legends about the mountains are legion. The sixteenth-century allegorical novel *Journey to the West* concerns the adventures of the monk Xuanzang (p. 67). Xuanzang was a historical figure but the adventures described in *Journey to the West* are apocryphal. When Xuanzang passes the mountains he is prevented from proceeding further by a 'mountain of flame'. His companion Monkey borrows a palm-leaf fan from Princess Iron Fan and uses it to extinguish the flames. The Uighurs say that the mountains take their colour from the blood of a dragon that once ravaged the area and was eventually slain by a young hero.

Bezeklik

At the western end of the Flaming Mountains, about 55 km northeast of Turfan, are the caves of Bezeklik (in Turkic, 'the place where there are paintings and ornaments'). More than eighty caves have survived, about forty of which are decorated with paintings. They extend for about one

Fig. 188 **Wall paintings depicting Uighur royalty making offerings to the Buddha**
Uighur period, 8th/9th century
From Cave 9, Bezeklik, Xinjiang province
D. (left) H. 62.4 cm, W. 59.5 cm; (right) H. 66 cm, W. 57 cm
(Museum für Indische Kunst, Berlin)
The two murals show Uighur royalty carrying flower offerings in a solemn procession. Each party stands upon a beautifully decorated carpet and is dressed in lavish clothes. The men wear high crowns, tied under the chin with ribbons, tall nomads' boots and belts from which daggers, flint-pouches, awls and knotted kerchiefs are suspended. The ladies wear sandy coloured robes with wide collars decorated with spirals. Their coiffures are broad and secured with pins and they wear elaborate crowns- the left hand one compared by one scholar to 'a goldfish rising'. To the right is an inscription that reads: 'This is the picture of Her Highness Princess Joy'.

kilometre along the Murtuk River gorge and were protected from unwelcome visitors by a long winding ascent to the cliff top. They were first explored by von Le Coq in 1905, by representatives of Baron Otani in 1908–9 and, finally, by

Aurel Stein at the end of 1914. The best paintings date to the period of Uighur domination (ninth to thirteenth centuries). The paintings are in both Indo-Persian and Chinese styles and represent the Uighur Empire at its height. By the tenth century the Uighurs controlled an area from the Gansu (Hexi) Corridor to Khotan. The Silk Road brought great wealth to its rulers and Bezeklik flourished as a centre for Buddhist learning. The murals of Cave 9 and Cave 20 were painted around the time the imperial family of the Uighur Gaochang Kingdom converted from Manichaeism to Buddhism and celebrate the cultural and economic riches of the epoch (figs. 188, 189 and 190).

Depictions of the *parinirvana*, when the Buddha finally exits this world and enters nirvana, are usually scenes of grief. Scenes of grieving mourners do exist at Bezeklik but there are also clusters of figures who, though they too are onlookers at the *parinirvana*, are full of joy and life (fig. 189).

A final fragment of painting from Bezeklik may represent a rare depiction of the mysterious Tokharians, a race of Indo-European origin who once populated the oasis towns of the Northern and Southern sections of the Silk Road. Many of them had pale eyes and reddish-brown hair (fig. 190).

Fig. 189 **Fragment from a mural depicting musicians from a *Parinirvana* scene**
Uighur period, 9th century
H. 106.5 cm, W. 106.5 cm
From Cave 20, Bezeklik, Xinjiang province
(Tokyo National Museum)
The musicians in this lively painting are of various nationalities and reflect the ethnic diversity of this part of the Silk Road. The instruments they play include two kinds of flute, a lute (*pipa*), a tambourine and a hand-drum. The Kingdom of Kuqa (or Qiuci) was renowned for its musicians and it may well be that Kucheans figure among members of this orchestra (see p. 159).

Many of the larger paintings from Bezeklik were taken by von Le Coq to Berlin and installed in the Ethnological Museum. During the Second World War the museum was struck several times by Allied bombs and many of the wall paintings were damaged or destroyed. Others disappeared at the end of the war, perhaps to the Soviet Union, leaving us with only a photographic record. Bezeklik itself is in a rather forlorn state today. The walkways have been restored but the remaining paintings are damaged and faded.

The main Northern Silk Road continues west from Turfan and heads through the towns of Toksun, Yanqi (Karashahr) and on to Korla. To the northwest, the road branches off towards Urumqi, across the Dzungarian Plateau and then onwards over the Tianshan Mountains to Lake Issyk Kul. Many travellers used this route to avoid the perilous crossing of the Taklamakan Desert and the Pamir Mountains. The route also joined up with other tracks including the spur that originated in Hami. This route was called the 'Tianshan Bei Lu' ('Road North of the Celestial Mountains') by the Chinese and followed the foothills of the Tianshan and then the Pamirs. The topography of this route made for easier travel than the main Northern Silk Road, the flatter terrain accessible in many parts to the use of carts with their increased load capacity. The whole area had been a battleground for centuries, however, and most travellers preferred to take their chances crossing the Tarim Basin and the high passes through the Pamirs. Only during the peaceful period of the eighth- and ninth-century High Tang and the *Pax Mongolica* of the late thirteenth and fourteenth centuries did the road achieve great popularity. The Venetian explorer Marco Polo traversed the entire region during the latter period. The main Northern and Southern routes of the Silk Road combined at Kashgar. From Kashgar one of the routes led westwards over the Pamirs, passed through the city of Balkh in Afghanistan and then continued on to Merv (see p. 229).

Urumqi, the first stop on the modern road that follows the ancient Tianshan route, is now the capital of the Xinjiang province. It was not established as a city until the eighteenth century and thus played no role in the early history of the Silk Road. The Protector General's Office for the region north of the Tianshan Mountains was instead at Beiting, or Beshbaliq in Jimsar County.

Beiting is situated about 150 km northeast of Urumqi and was a walled garrison town during the Tang dynasty (618–907), protecting the trade caravans on this section of the Northern Silk Road. In 840 Beiting was taken by the Uighurs, former allies of the Tang. The Uighur capital was at Gaochang, renamed Qoco or Khocho, with Beiting as a subsidiary capital. The two cities remained Uighur strongholds until the arrival of the Mongols during the thirteenth century. From 1979 onwards Chinese archeologists excavated a large ritual mound, some 250 metres in

circumference. Wall paintings similar to those at Bezeklik were discovered there, as well as altars for Buddhist images that recall the art of the Gandhara kingdom. A Uighur prince dressed in gold appears in one of the paintings and it has been suggested that the complex is his tomb.

The Ili River rises in the western Tianshan and flows westward across the frontier region into Lake Balkash in Kazakhstan. The Ili Valley is relatively flat and fertile and is home to thirteen or fourteen different ethnic groups, including Kazakhs, Mongolians and Khirgiz. The Kazakhs, reputed to be descendants of the Wusun nomads, are the most numerous. The lush pasturelands of the Ili River Valley were the source of the 'Heavenly Horses' of the Wusun and large numbers of horses are still bred there.

West of Urumqi is a stretch of the 'Tianshan Bei Lu' ('Road North of the Celestial Mountains') that early travellers would have described as a 'blank on the map'. The

Fig. 190 **Detail of a mural depicting Tokharian donors offering bags of money**
Uighur period, 9th century
From Cave 20, Bezeklik, Xinjiang province
(Formerly in the Museum für Indische Kunst, Berlin. Disappeared after 1945)

700 km between Urumqi and Yining contained no settlements of any significance apart from the occasional fortification until the Tang dynasty. The ruins of Yanggabaxun City – west of Shihezi on the banks of the Manas River – are a possible exception, although little now remains of the town except its earthen walls. During the Tang dynasty there was an important transit station at Gongyue ('Crescent') City, about 25 km from Yining in the Ili River Valley (see map). Written records and Arab coins found in the area indicate that Gongyue was a centre for the region's silk trade. A branch of the Silk Road appears to have run between Gongyue and Kuqa, connecting the 'Tianshan Bei Lu' ('Road North of the Celestial Mountains') with the main Northern Route.

Close to the China-Kazakhstan border is Lake Sayram (Sailimu Hu or 'Best Wishes Lake'), situated about 2,000 metres above sea level. Sayram is the largest mountain-lake in Xinjiang, covering an area of about 450 square km. Its waters contain a large quantity of calcium carbonate that turn them to a deep azure blue. In ancient times nomadic herders inhabited the shores of the lake and little has changed since then: today Kazakhs and Mongols predominate. The annual Nadam fair is held every July by the lake and its horseracing, sheep-tossing and wrestling events honour traditions that have existed since the days when the Silk Road passed through the area. There was once a shrine at Sayram – built in a pine grove on the western shore – though nothing of it now remains. It was called Jinghai temple and was a place where travellers would invoke the protection of the gods to ensure a safe journey.

Beyond Sayram this section of the Northern Silk Road crosses the border with modern-day Kazakhstan near the town of Korgas. The route continues onward, passing both north and south of Lake Issykul towards Tokmak (p. 279).

****

Returning to the main Northern Silk Road, travellers heading west from Turfan passed through the small oasis town of Toksun. From Toksun there was a choice of two routes to the town of Karashahr (modern Yanqi). The first involved an ascent westward through the Tianshan Mountains along the course of the Ala (Algu) River. This route rises to more than 3,000 metres above sea level and then turns south along the Ulastay River to Karashahr. The route is marked by an ancient beacon tower at the Algu Mountain Pass. This route is thought to have been preferred by camel and horse caravans because of its abundant water and grazing. The other route is more direct but requires a harrowing journey through a 100 km gorge known, for good reason, as Dry Gully (*Gan Gou*). Throughout this stretch of the journey not a blade of grass can be seen and the only water comes from the occasional flash flood.

Karashahr is about 300 km from Turfan and is situated close to Lake Bosten (Bagrash), the largest lake in Xinjiang. The lake is fed by the Kaidu River, known as the 'River of Flowing Sand' on account of the 100-metre thick layer of loose sediment that forms it bed. Lake Bosten is the source of the Kongqu (Peacock) River, named for the intense blue of its waters. The Kongqu, along with the River Tarim, once flowed right across the northern Taklamakan to Lake Lop Nor but their waters now dissipate long before they reach it. During the Wang Mang interregnum of 9–23 AD, the Chinese were unable to maintain control of the kingdoms of the Western Regions. Even after the establishment of the Eastern Han dynasty in 25 AD, the states of the Northern and Southern Silk Road continued to vie for dominance. In 41 AD, the kingdom of Yarkand subjugated the neighbouring states of Khotan, Shanshan (Loulan) and Kuqa (Qiuci) and became the dominant force on the Southern Silk Road. In 60 AD the kingdom of Khotan rebelled against Yarkand control and the domination of the southern route became split between two kingdoms, the area between Kashgar and Niya remaining under Khotanese control and the area around Lop Nor as far as Cherchen falling under Shanshan control. On the Northern Route, Karashahr was the dominant kingdom. During much of the first century AD the kingdoms of the northern and southern routes were threatened by Xiongnu attacks and by Chinese attempts to re-establish central control. The formidable General Ban Chao (31–103 AD) began to restore Han rule in the Tarim Basin area from 73 AD onwards and had succeeded in doing so by 91 AD.

By the time Xuanzang passed through in 630 AD, Karashahr (ancient Agni) was a prosperous kingdom, raising revenues by levying taxes upon passing merchants. Vines and millet grew in the area and local people traded fish, presumably from Lake Bosten just to the east, as well as salt, The residents, according to Xuanzang, wore woollen clothing and kept their hair cut short.

Karashahr ('Black Town')

Sites at Karashahr (modern day Yanqi), Khora and Shorchuk were excavated by Aurel Stein during his 1906–08 expedition. The site at Shorchuk was visited briefly by Alfred Grünwedel and Albert von Le Coq in 1906, and then by Sergei Oldenburg of the Russian Academy of Science in 1909–10. Stein called Shorchuk 'Ming-oi' ('Thousand Dwellings'), a name also applied to other sites in the region. Shorchuk is situated about 60 km south of Karashahr. A series of free-standing shrines along a ridge at the site were all destroyed by fire in antiquity. Fragments of clay figures survived the fires, albeit in a damaged state, but the nearby caves have yielded clay statues, intended to be set in niches, wall paintings of great beauty and a number of important manuscripts. The sculpture and paintings found in the cave shrines date mostly to the seventh to ninth century. A transition occurs during the later part of the eighth century from a 'Western' Indo-Persian style to a more 'Eastern' Chinese style. Stein recovered fragments of a wall painting from a temple, damaged but not destroyed by some ancient conflagration, in the north-western part of Shorchuk. They depict monks transcribing sutras, receiving instruction from older monks and kneeling in prayer as *apsaras* (celestial figures) descend from the heavens. These fragments, though beautiful, are not the principal murals of the shrine. Stein appears to have missed two large and sumptuously decorated sections, perhaps from the doorway to the main sanctuary of the temple. Both were recovered by Sergei Oldenburg during his 1909–10 expedition and are now in the State Hermitage Museum in St Petersburg. The larger of the two sections shows a pair of Bodhisattvas and a group of monks, probably a depiction of the Buddha's First Sermon, in the Deer Park at Sarnath (Benares). The figures are superbly and colourfully drawn with many of the details picked out in gold (fig. 191).

The ferocious depiction of Vajrapani reflects an interest in physiognomy among the artists of Shorchuk. This interest is also revealed among the many hundreds of clay sculptures found at the site. As with the sculpture of Gandhara, they must have been set in niches within the monastery walls and were manufactured by building up layers of clay over a reed-bundle core. The final section was moulded and fitted as the final layer and finer details such as jewellery and scarves were also moulded and added at the end. The finished sculpture was then painted. Stein recovered several hundred clay figures from the sanctuary of one of the ruined shrines at Shorchuk but the statues acquired by von Le Coq at the better preserved cave temples still retain their vibrant colours. They are sculpted with great humour and vitality and tell us a great deal about the attitude of the local residents to foreigners and to those who eschewed the Buddhist faith (fig. 192).

Fig. 191 **A mural depicting Bodhisattvas and monks, apparently listening to a sermon**
8th to 9th century
H. 101 cm, W. 108 cm
Temple K 9 E, Shorchuk (Ming-oi), Karashahr (Yanqi), Xinjiang province
(State Hermitage Museum, St Petersburg)
The group of monks is flanked, on the left of the mural, by Avalokitesvara wearing his characteristic deerskin robe and by Maitreya, Buddha of the Future. The bearded figure behind them with bulging eyes is Vajrapani, the thunderbolt bearing Bodhisattva.

Fig. 192 **Two clay figures of seated Brahmins (Hindu priests)**
7th to 8th century
H. (left) 42.4 cm; (right) 45.8 cm
Shorchuk, Kirin cave, Karashahr (Yanqi), Xinjiang province
(Museum für Indische Kunst, Berlin)
These two ill-tempered and rather comical figures are Hindu priests. They sit in their knee-length stockings, the figure on the left resplendent in a panther skin, and engage in noisy debate over the merits of Buddhism. They are characters from *jataka* stories about the Buddha's prior lives but such individuals may well have passed through the oasis towns of the Silk Road from time to time.

The shrines at Shorchuk – like most of the Buddhist remains along the northern route – are Hinayana ('Lesser Vehicle'), while those of the southern route are mainly Mahayana ('Greater Vehicle'). Scenes of preaching, a characteristically Hinayana theme, are found in many of the paintings around Karashahr. Among the small number of objects found by Stein at Khora, close to Karashahr, was just such a scene, painted on wood and showing the Buddha preaching to disciples. The style is similar to that of the sites around Kuqa, in particularly Kizil, which will be examined later.

The route westward from Karashahr runs along the foot of the Tianshan Mountains to Korla. There is little trace of the Silk Road around Korla except for the Iron Gate Pass just north of the town. The Northern Silk Road once passed through the Iron Gate Pass, a steep ferrous-coloured ravine at the entrance to a 14 km gorge in the upper reaches of the Kongqu River. The Tang dynasty poet Cen Shen (715–70), who spent years as an official on the western frontiers, wrote evocatively of Iron Gate Pass:

'An Iron Pass commands the western border of the sky,
Where scarcely any travellers pass by…
A bridge spans the gorge thousands of feet deep.
Hemmed in between cliffs winds a narrow path.
I climb up the western tower for the view.
Just one glance, and my face turns grey.'

(*Iron Gate Pass* by Cen Shen [715–70]. There is another Iron Gate Pass on the Silk Road, near Derbent in Uzbekistan. It was also named for the colour of its rock, although the Kushans may have installed an actual gate there of colossal size. Xuanzang passed through it on his way to Balkh)

The route from Korla to Kuqa continues for about 300 km along the southern foothills of the Tianshan Mountains. To the south is the Tarim River and beyond it the vast wasteland of the Taklamakan.

KUQA (Kucha or Qiuci)

'This country was above 1,000 li from east to west and 600 li from north to south; its capital being 17-18 li in circuit…This country yielded millet, wheat, rice, grapes, pomegranates, and plenty of pears, plums, peaches and apricots. It produced also gold, copper, iron, lead, and tin: its climate was temperate and the people had honest ways; their writing was taken from that of India, but has been much altered; they had great skill with wind and stringed instruments.'

(Xuanzang, quoted in Wriggins, 1996)

In addition to the economic conditions described by Xuanzang silver and sal ammoniac, used in the tanning of leather, were mined in the nearby mountains. He also

Fig. 193 **A mural depicting the King and Queen of Kuqa**
600–50
Kizil, Maya Cave (Site III), Xinjiang province
(L'Imprimerie Nationale, Paris)
These portraits were destroyed during the Allied bombing of Berlin during World War Two but photographs have survived. They reveal a king with pale skin and reddish brown hair and a finely featured queen dressed elegantly in a wide skirt decorated with brown and blue flowers.

describes a strange custom among the Kucheans, the habit of flattening the backs of the skulls of their offspring with a wooden board. His observations have been born out by recent excavations of tombs in the area and such practices may be compared to those of the Hepthalites (see p. 36). There is still a market in Kuqa town each Friday, occupying the bed and banks of a dried up river. It is smaller than the great Kashgar market but is boisterous enough, a reminder that the lifeblood of these oasis towns was derived from Silk Road trade.

At the time of Xuanzang's visit in 630 a Buddhist king of Indo-European appearance ruled Kuqa. Xuanzang was unimpressed with the king, saying that he had 'little prudence or ability, and allows himself to be dominated by powerful ministers'.

Kizil

In the middle part of the seventh century, not long after Xuanzang's visit, large numbers of Persian emigrés sought, and were granted sanctuary in Kuqa as the Sasanian Empire collapsed about them. At about the same time, in 658, the town was brought under Chinese control and became the headquarters for the entire Tarim Basin. Kuchean art from the period has therefore absorbed influences from Persia and China but it retains a character of its own. Kuchean wall paintings have a strong affinity with the 'Indo-Persian' style of Bamiyan in Afghanistan (p. 61). The two sites are both centres for Hinayana Buddhism and visiting pilgrims from the former may well have brought Persian influences to Kuqa long before the arrival of Sasanian refugees. The oldest of Kuqa's paintings date to around 500 and have been designated as the first Indo-Persian style. They are characterized by somewhat muted colours – red, browns and yellows – but with bright green (made from powdered malachite) used to highlight drapery, jewellery and other fine detail. The later phase, called the second Indo-Persian style and dating from about 600–750, can be recognized by the presence of bright (malachite) green and vivid (lapis lazuli) blue and by the appearance of complex jewellery and headdresses. These two styles are both apparent in the paintings of Kizil*, a large number of which were acquired

during the third and fourth expeditions of von Le Coq, in 1906 and 1913 respectively, and transported to the Berlin Museum. The Kizil site is about 70 km north-west of Kuqa on the upper part of the Muzart River. It consists of about 235 cave temples cut into the hillside, many barrel-vaulted and with a pedestal or pillar for a devotional image. The most common type has narrow passageways on either side of the main chamber to enable worshippers to circumambulate around the central image (fig. 194).

Kizil's paintings are joyously beautiful and, with the exception of Dunhuang, are without equal in Central Asia. Their subject matter includes scenes of the Buddha preaching, flying *devatas*, scenes from the Buddha's life and previous lives (*jatakas*), and depictions of the heroic exploits of Bodhisattvas (*avadana* tales). The paintings are religious but the participants are often involved in secular activities, as the examples below will reveal. Kuchean music and dance were renowned throughout the kingdoms of the Silk Road and it therefore not surprising that both activities occur with great frequency in the painting of Kizil (fig. 195).

Another mural from the same cave shows Nanda, half-

* The practice of dividing Kizil's paintings (and therefore the paintings of the Kuqa area as a whole) into first and second Indo-Persian styles has been thrown into question by recent research by Professor Marianne Yaldiz at the Berlin Museum. Samples of straw taken from the back of a number of the museum's wall paintings have been subjected to radiocarbon testing and the preliminary results indicate that the dates are spread far more widely than was previously thought, ranging from 237 to 650. The two styles also appear to be mixed, not distinct from each other. The dates given in the descriptions above are the radiocarbon age, where this is known, and the generally accepted date where it is not.

Fig. 194 **The Kizil Grottoes**
Xinjiang province

Fig. 195 **A mural depicting celestial musicians**
Early 5th century
H. 159 cm
Cave of the Statues, Kizil, Xinjiang province
(Museum für Indische Kunst, Berlin)
This painting is executed in the earlier Indo-Persian style, before the introduction of lapis lazuli blue, and comes from the Cave of the Statues, named for the large quantity of clay sculptures found there by von Le Coq.

Fig. 196 **A mural depicting the cowherd Nanda listening to the Buddha preaching**
406–25 (established by radiocarbon dating)
H. 60 cm, W. 33 cm
Cave of the Statues, Kizil, Xinjiang province
(Museum für Indische Kunst, Berlin)
In this scene Nanda, surrounded by his cattle, leans upon a gnarled club and listens intently as the Buddha preaches to his left. He is so absorbed in the Buddha's words that he is oblivious to the frog that he crushes with his club. The story relates that the frog declines the opportunity to escape so as not to distract Nanda and is rewarded with reincarnation as a god.

Fig. 197 **A mural depicting swimmers**
6th/7th century
H. 37.8 cm, W. 39.5 cm
Cave of the Seafarers, Kizil, Xinjiang province
(Museum für Indische Kunst, Berlin)
The man on the right, clearly the principal protagonist, is larger and swims more confidently than his companions. The style, like the last two, is of the first Indo-Persian type and the influences of Gandhara are particularly strong (see fig. 43). The Maitrakanyaka story concerns a rich merchant from Benares in India who drowns at sea. His son Maitrakanyaka grows up unaware of his father's fate and, ignoring the pleas of his mother, decides to follow the same profession. He is soon caught in a storm and shipwrecked. He spends years as the captive of a succession of beautiful sirens until he finally escapes and reaches a city of iron. There, he meets a man condemned to eternal torment for insulting his mother. Maitrakanyaka realizes that he is guilty of the same misdeed and agrees to take on the man's punishment as penance. He immediately ascends to heaven as a Bodhisattva. The whole of the Maitrakanyaka legend once adorned the main wall of the cave, a remarkable subject for a place so far from the sea.

Fig. 198 **A mural of a monk meditating before a skull**
Cave of the Seafarers, Kizil, Xinjiang province
341–417 (established by radiocarbon dating)
H. 56.6 cm, W. 27.2 cm
(Museum für Indische Kunst, Berlin)

The notion that human existence is ephemeral is a fundamental tenet of Buddhism. It is one that we encounter repeatedly, both in the perpetual rising and falling of the civilisations of the Silk Road and throughout all of history:

'The boast of heraldry, the pomp of pow'r,
And all that beauty, all that wealth e'er gave,
Awaits alike th'inevitable hour:
The paths of glory lead but to the grave.'

(Thomas Gray [1716–71], 'Elegy Written in a Country Churchyard')

Mention should also be made of one other example of the early style, still to be seen on the ceiling of Cave 17. The entire ceiling is covered in depictions of *jataka* tales from the Buddha's previous incarnations. One scene is of great interest to historians of the Silk Road and is said to show a Bodhisattva guiding a caravan of merchants through the darkness. His hands are raised aloft and turn into torches to light the way while two of the merchants stand next to him and raise their own hands in gratitude.

The second Indo-Persian style*, with its greater use of colour, was seen in the portrait of the Kuchean King and Queen (fig. 193) at the beginning of this section on Kuqa. There is space only for only one other example here and it is one of Kizil's most effulgent paintings (fig. 199).

brother and disciple of the Buddha, in his guise as a cowherd (fig. 196).

The Cave of the Seafarers, sometimes called the Cave of the Navigator, contained a small fragment of a painting that was discovered among the rubble. It shows three men swimming among water lilies – perhaps a scene from the Maitrakanyaka *avadana* legend – and is one of Kizil's splendid paintings (fig. 197).

The last example of the first Indo-Persian style is also from the Cave of the Seafarers and shows a monk meditating before a *memento mori* (fig. 198). The subject matter is truly astonishing and one that we are more accustomed to seeing in the paintings of European artists like Holbein (see also fig. 59).

The sentiment of the mural in fig. 198 is best summarized by a line from a manuscript found in Cave 17 at Dunhuang (quoted in Giles, 1944):

'You may pile up a mountain of riches, but you will only have a coffin when you die.'

Fig. 199 **A mural depicting a goddess with a celestial musician**
Previously dated to around 600–650 but recent radiocarbon dating has established a date of 410–435
H. 209 cm, W. 134 cm
Cave of the painted floor (Cave 171), Kizil, Xinjiang province
(Museum für Indische Kunst, Berlin)
The female figures, both of them voluptuous and heavily jewelled, stand beneath a tree in blossom as flowers rain down around them. They are each enveloped by wide, sweeping necklaces and trailing drapery and a sense of great intimacy exists between them. There is a virtual mirror image of this painting, damaged and faded but surely by the same hand, on the end wall of Cave 163 at Kizil. Both paintings may tell the story of the Buddha and the Goddess of Music. The Buddha – who disguises himself as a musician – challenges a woman, proud of her musical skills, to a lute-playing contest. She is shamed by the Buddha's superior playing and becomes his devotee.

* See note on p. 155.

Fig. 200 **The Caves at Kumtura, Xinjiang province**

Fig. 201 **Painted clay figure of a Bodhisattva**
7th/8th century
H. 62.5 cm
Kumtura, Main Area, near Kuqa, Xinjiang province
(Museum of Museum für Indische Kunst, Berlin)

Sites around Kuqa

Note: for a detailed map of sites around Kuqa please see page 164 (the Kashgar section)

Kumtura

An ancient trail led along the Muzart River to the important Buddhist site at Kumtura. Pack animals are unable to negotiate the route today and Kumtura has been left largely to its own devices, seldom visited and with many of its caves covered in soot from the campfires of hunters and shepherds (fig. 200).

Kumtura's aspect, like that of so many such places, is startlingly beautiful. The site is situated 28 km north-west of Kuqa beside the Muzart River and comprises 112 rock-cut temples and shrines as well as free-standing buildings. The work at Kumtura appears to have been started in the fifth century but the majority of the paintings date to the eighth to tenth centuries of the Tang dynasty. Most therefore encompass the second Indo-Persian style but a third style is also apparent at Kumtura, one not found at Kizil. Many of the paintings show a marked Buddhist Chinese influence-evident in facial characteristics, jewellery and costume that we encountered in the art of Shorchuk and at the Turfan oasis. It is remarkable that Kumtura and Kizil, situated in such close proximity, have developed such disparate styles of art. The explanation is most likely to be found in the great

Fig. 202 **Painted ceiling containing Bodhisattva figures**
5th to 6th century
From New Cave 2, Kumtura, Xinjiang province
Discovered in 1977

political upheavals of the eighth century when Chinese power in the Tarim Basin ebbed and flowed with each passing year.

There is room here for two examples of Kumtura's art. The first, a richly painted clay figure of a Bodhisattva in Indo-Persian style, is strongly reminiscent of sculpture from Fondukistan (fig. 201).

A new cave, discovered in 1977, has a domed ceiling decorated with a roundel containing a series of Bodhisattva figures standing in various poses around a central lotus (fig. 202).

Subashi

Xuanzang, delayed for two months in Kuqa because of severe winter weather, visited the monasteries of Subashi, which he called *Zhaohuli*. The ruins are about 20 km north of Kuqa and are divided in two by the Kuqa River. They were identified as the ancient city of Subashi by the French Sinologist Paul Pelliot during his 1907 visit. They are the largest group of ruins in the Western Lands with 100 temples that were, according to Xuanzang, 'so beautiful that they seemed to belong to another world.'

Pelliot reached Subashi in June 1907 and began to excavate the site. He found relatively little except for coins, graffiti in Brahmi and Chinese script, and about fifteen funerary urns made of a clay and wood, cylindrical in shape and with conical lids. The best of the group now resides in

the Musée Guimet and is covered with cherub-like figures (or puttis) dancing and playing musical instruments. The first Otani mission had visited the site four years before and discovered a casket of the same type. The Otani casket, now in the Tokyo National Museum, has similar cherubic figures on the lid and a complete orchestra of Kuchean musicians in mid-performance (fig. 204).

Kuqa's music was the best in the world, according to Xuanzang. Around the outside of the Otani casket figures wearing masks of animals and bearded Persian kings and dance to the music of flutes, drums and harps. This form of dance is believed to have originated in the Western Regions and was extremely popular in the Kuqa area. It entered Japan from China during the 7th century and came to be known as *Gigaku* dancing (also called *kure-uta* or 'Wu singing'). At the eye-opening ceremony for the Great Buddha at Nara's Todaiji temple in 752 there were reported to have been sixty Gigaku performers and musicians and in the city's Shosoin repository there are no fewer than 170 Gigaku masks (see section on Shosoin). The most famous poet of the Middle Tang period, Bai Juyi, provides a vivid description of a Gigaku performance at the Tang court:

> 'Skilled dancers from Hsi-liang,
> Persian masks and lion masks.
> The heads are carved of wood,
> The tails are woven with thread.
> Pupils are flecked with gold

Fig. 203 **Ruined stupa and temples**
West bank, Subashi, Kuqa, Xinjiang province
5th to 6th century

Fig. 204 **Painted wood funerary casket with depictions of an orchestra**
6th to 7th century
H. 32.3 cm
Subashi, Kuqa, Xinjiang province
(Tokyo National Museum)

And teeth capped with silver.
They wave fur costumes
And flap their ears
As if from across the drifting sands
Ten thousand miles away.'

(Bai Juyi [772–846], quoted in Hayashi, 1975)

The Shosoin repository also contains five, perfectly preserved four-stringed lutes of Persian origin and the world's only surviving example of an ancient five-stringed

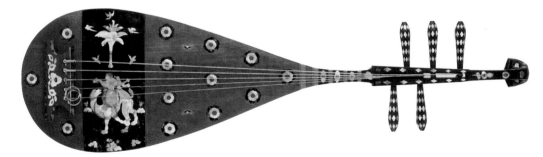

Fig. 205 **Plectrum guard, part of an Indian five-stringed lute (biwa), decorated with a palm tree and a musician on camel-back**
8th century
L. (plectrum guard only) 30.9 cm;
L. (instrument) 108.1 cm
From the Shosoin repository, Nara, Japan
(Shosoin repository, Nara, Japan)
This plectrum guard, part of a complete sandalwood and chestnut lute, is inlaid with a mother-of-pearl depiction of a musician on camelback. The figure may be a Persian.

And fragrant orchids smile,
Even the cold glare of light
Before Ch'ang-an's twelve gates
Is softened,
And the sound of twenty-three strings
Moves the heart of His Celestial Majesty.'

(Li Ho [791–c. 819], quoted in Hayashi, 1975)

Duldur-Aqur is a monastic complex to the west of Kuqa. Its buildings were freestanding and have yielded far fewer wall paintings than the more durable cave-structures of Kizil and Kumtura. Adding further to the site's decay are the traces of a great fire that seems to have engulfed the complex during the ninth century. The damage to the monastery at Duldur-Aqur is reminiscent of the conflagration at Shorchuk and was so severe that Pelliot was able to find only fragments of mural and a small number of wooden statues. The wooden figures, together with two life-sized painted clay Bodhisattva heads, are strongly reminiscent of the art of Gandhara. The paintings date from about 500 to the ninth century: many are in the first Indo-Persian style of the sixth century; with a solitary *devata* head surviving from the second period and many more from the period of Tang Chinese influence during the eighth century. Among the wrecked murals of Duldur-Aqur are glimpses of a wonderful legacy: a pair of Kuchean princes, perhaps portraits of two of the kingdom's rulers but now portrayed as actors in a scene from the Buddha's life, and a large and realistic depiction of a Brahmin (fig. 206).

Kizil-Qargha, about 15 km north of Kuqa, was successively investigated by Otani's representative, Stein, Pelliot and von Le Coq between 1903 and 1913 but the paintings discovered there were both few in number and fragmentary. The same was true of the fifty-two caves at

lute (*biwa*), variously attributed to India, Western Asia or Persia (fig. 205).

The most famous lute player of the day, Po Ming-ta, was a Kuchean. His composition 'Trill of the Spring Warbler' or 'The Spring Nightingale Sings' is still performed in Japan. Another of the musicians plays the harp- the Tang court adored music and was spellbound by the playing skills of the great harpist Li Ping, said to have been a Persian:

'Li Ping strums his harp
In the Middle Kingdom.
As jade crumbles on Mount K'un-lin
And the phoenixes cry,
As the lotus weeps dew

Fig. 206 **Mural fragment depicting the head of a Brahmin**
Early 6th century
H. 17 cm, W. 24 cm
Duldur-Aqur, Kuqa, Xinjiang province
(Musée Guimet, Paris)

Kirish-Simsin, about 40 km northeast of Kuqa where the murals were, for the most part, heavily coated in soot and defaced by iconoclasts.

One of Kuqa's most famous sons was the monk Kumarajiva (343–413), son of an Indian father and a Kuchean princess. Kumarajiva translated some 300 Mahayana Buddhist texts from Sanskrit into Chinese and expounded the doctrines of the new faith for the Northern Wei rulers of China (see also p. 67).

The road from Kuqa to Aksu

The route from Kuqa to Aksu is about 260 km in length and continues to follow the foothills of the Tianshan. Along the route are the remains of beacon towers built during the Han dynasty. To the northwest of Kuqa the ancient route crossed the Yanshui Gorge (the Gorge of Salt Waters) and followed the course of the dry riverbed. Only during the summer months, when melt water flows down from the Tianshan, does the river come to life. At other times it is a bleak moonscape, salt encrusted and flanked by strange rocks whittled by the wind (fig. 207).

The oasis town of Aksu was the centre of the ancient kingdom of Baluka, although there is some dispute over whether the capital was there or at Karayulgun just to the northeast. Baluka was one of the kingdoms of the Western Regions.

A branch of the Northern Silk Road veers northwest from Aksu to cross the Tianshan Mountains through the 4,284-metre Bedel Pass to Lake Issyk-kul and on to Samarkand. Another strand of this route originated in Turfan and passed north of the Tianshan, linking up with the other route near Bishkek (formerly Frunze) in Kyrgyzstan. A number of passes linked the two branches-either between Lake Barkol and Hami or between Turfan and Jimusa (formerly Beshbalik, the Uighur capital, called Beiting by the Chinese). The route from Aksu was followed by Xuanzang in 630 and required an ascent through the Bedel Pass, passing around the 6,995 metre peak of Khan-Tengri, (the 'Prince of Spirits'). At the end of a calamitous week long crossing, during which about one third of the men in his party and many of the pack animals were killed, he reached Issyk-kul (the 'Warm Lake'), kept from freezing year round by volcanic activity beneath its surface. Xuanzang's stark description of the glaciers on the slopes of Mount Khan-Tengri provides a succinct reminder that travellers on the Silk Road were sometimes required, quite literally, to take their life in their hands:

Fig. 207 **Yanshui Gorge in snow**

'This mountain is steep and dangerous, and reaches to the clouds…hard-frozen and cold sheets of water rise mingling with the clouds; looking at them the eye is blinded with the glare, so that it cannot long gaze at them. The icy peaks fall down sometimes and lie athwart the road, some of them a hundred feet high, and others several tens of feet wide.'

(Xuanzang, in Beal, 1911)

Fig. 208 **Stone Balbals or
tomb markers.**
Western Turk, 6th to
8th century
Balasagun, Kyrgyzstan.
The Balbals at Balasagun have
been collected from sites all over
Kyrgyzstan (for more on
Balasagun, see p. 279).

The original route of the Silk Road is now partly beneath the
surface of Issyk-kul, probably as a result of volcanic activity,
and the southern shore contains the remains of a large
number of settlements. Throughout the region are 'Balbals',
anthropomorphic grave markers erected by the Western
Turks around the sixth to eighth century to celebrate the
men they had slaughtered in battle. Their victims were
presumably the Hepthalites, defeated in about 560 AD by an
alliance of Western Turks and Sasanians. Piles of stones on
Western Turk graves are said to represent the number of
enemies killed by the warrior lying within – one stone for
each man killed – and the fact that some contain a thousand
stones indicates that Xuanzang was living in dangerous times
(fig. 208).

West of Issyk-kul near Tokmak – the ancient domain of
the Wusun nomads – Xuanzang met the Khan of the
Western Turks ensconced in his winter capital at *Suye* (see Ak
Beshim on p. 279). At this time, during the early Tang
dynasty, the Western Turks were at the height of their power:
their domain extended from China to the borders of Persia
and from the Altai Mountains in the north to Kashmir in the

south. The Turki Shahi, who achieved dominance in
Afghanistan around this time, may have been the same
people although the historical records of the latter are scant
(see p. 53). The summer capital of the Khan of the Western
Turks was at Tashkent (Chach) and his winter headquarters
were here, in the lush pastures around Issyk-kul. During the
winter months the Khan moved his court – including his
soldiers and his herds of cattle, sheep and horses – to the
shores of the lake. Xuanzang gives an amusingly haughty
description of the splendours of the Khan's residence:

*'The Khan lived in a great tent which was decorated with
golden flowers, whose brilliance dazzled the eyes. The
official ushers had spread long mats at the entrance, and
they sat on these in two rows. They were all wearing
bright costumes of silk brocade. The Khan's personal guard
stood behind them. Although he was a barbarian prince,
living in a felt tent, you couldn't help looking at him (and)
experiencing a feeling of admiration and respect.'*

(Xuanzang in Beal, 1911)

Buddhism had already made modest inroads to the area by the time of Xuanzang's visit and the religion became more popular during the ensuing years. At Ak-Beshim in the Chu Valley near Bishkek, identified with the Turk's winter capital of Suye or Suyab, two Buddhist temples have been discovered, dating to the seventh or eighth century. A Nestorian Christian church was discovered nearby in 1954, also dating to around the eighth century. The co-existence of these two faiths indicates that a strong spirit of religious tolerance existed. Further south, at Kuva in the eastern Ferghana Valley are the ruins of a Buddhist shrine, excavated in 1957–58 and found to contain a massive image of Buddha, more than twice life-size. At Adjina-Tepe, in Tajikistan, the remains of a Buddhist monastery bear testament to the wide reach of this religion.

West of Tokmak, the Silk Road traverses the verdant plain to the north of the Alexandrian Mountains, watered by nineteen rivers and known as the 'Land of a Thousand Springs' (*Bing Yul*). Travellers heading west would eventually reach Tashkent, now modern capital of Uzbekistan but once one of the most important caravan cities on the Silk Road.

The Aksu-Kashgar route on the Northern Silk Road

For a detailed map of sites around Aksu please see page 164

Tumshuq (Toqquz Sarai) is located on a mountain-ridge near Maralbashi on the Northern Silk Road, about 300 km before Kashgar. Both Pelliot and Von Le Coq investigated the site and mural fragments and sculpture were found, the latter in both wood and painted clay. Evidence of a devastating fire was found among the ruins, just as at Toyok, Shorchuk and Duldur-Aqur, part of an apparent sequence of destruction along the oases of the Tarim Basin. A surprising number of wooden sculptures have survived, by the grace of the region's arid climate. Von Le Coq recovered a gilded Buddha head and a complete seated Buddha, both dated to around the fifth century and in distinctly North Indian style. Among Pelliot's finds are three relief panels containing clay figures that participate in episodes from the Buddha's present and past lives. The *Sanjali-avadana* (or *Sankhacarya-avadana*) relief is especially engaging (fig. 209).

Kashgar

Kashgar (Kashi) is 3,700 km from Changan – a year's journey. It stands at the eastern foot of the Pamirs, at the junction of the Northern and Southern Silk Roads, and is a quintessential caravan city. Travellers heading for China would pause at Kashgar after descending from the Pamir or

Karakorum ranges. They would exchange their yaks and mules for camels in preparation for the perilous traversal of the Taklamakan. Westward bound travellers would have reached Kashgar, exhausted but relieved, and rested before exchanging their own beasts in preparation for the ascent of the mountain passes at the fringes of Chinese territory. The Silk Road went westwards over the Terek and Torugart Passes in the Tianshan (Heavenly) Mountains and on to the kingdoms of Ferghana and Sogdiana, through Tashkent and Samarkand, and across the Oxus River to Merv (present-day Mary in Turkmenistan). At Merv the Silk Road joined the more southerly route that had passed through the Wakhan Corridor to Balkh in Afghanistan.

Kashgar was known from the earliest times as a fertile and thriving commercial centre and, from the Han to Tang dynasties, it was called Shu-le. It fell under Chinese control during the first century BC and became a protectorate of the Middle Kingdom, although the Yarkand and Khotan states

Fig. 209 **Clay relief depicting a scene from the *Sanjali-avadana***
6th to 7th century
H. 75 cm, W. 76 cm
Tumshuq (Toqquz-Sarai), Great Temple B
(Musée Guimet, Paris. Photo RMN)
This is one of the most delightful of all the Buddhist tales. The historical Buddha, during a past life, was an ascetic by the name of Sankhacarya. One day, as he sat meditating on the stump of a tree, his stance and breathing were so perfect that a bird laid its eggs on top of his head. In order to avoid frightening the mother, Sankhacarya remained motionless until the eggs had hatched. In this relief a pair of celestial *apsaras* peer down approvingly at the bird seated on his head. The style is that of the late Gandhara sculpture of Fondukistan.

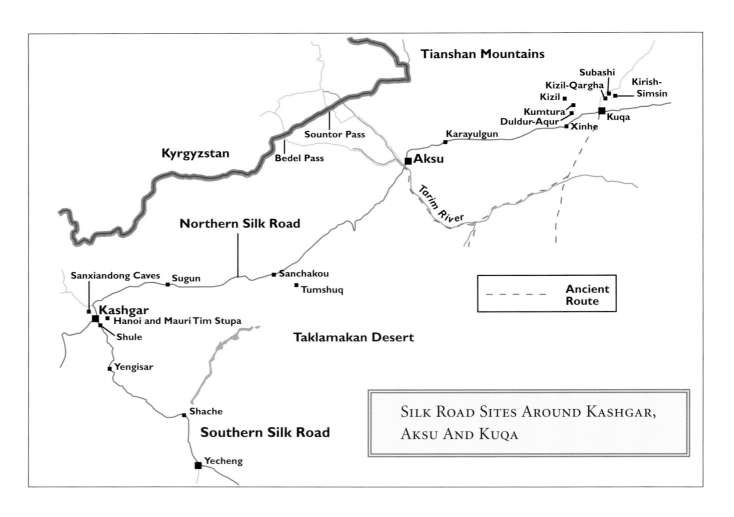

Map: **SILK ROAD SITES AROUND KASHGAR, AKSU AND KUQA**

also exercised control during periods of Han political instability. It was not until 74 AD that the Chinese general Ban Chao brought Kashgar and Khotan firmly under Chinese control. Chinese dominance of the area was intermittent at best, however, and the city appears to have been invaded by Kushans from the Gandhara kingdom around 107 AD. The

Fig. 210 **The livestock section of the Kashgar Sunday Market, Xinjiang province**

Kushan occupation of the city led to the introduction of Buddhism and the remains found around the city are China's oldest and most westerly traces of the new faith. There is evidence that both Mahayana and Hinayana Buddhism were practised in Kashgar; the monk Kumarajiva spent a year in the city during the fourth century and was converted to the former, and Xuanzang passed through in 644 to find more than 1,000 monks of the latter school. At the time of Xuanzang's visit Kashgar had accepted the sovereignty of Tang China but in 670 Tibet undertook a campaign of expansion throughout the southern Tarim Basin and captured Kuqa, Khotan, Kashgar and Karashahr.

Old Kashgar can still be found in the bazaar that surrounds the fifteenth-century Id Kah Mosque, China's largest. The Sunday Market takes place on the eastern edge of town, just beyond the Tuman River. The market has been at the centre of Kashgar's commercial life since at least the Tang dynasty:

'*extending over ten* li, *with goods stacked high to the heavens, and visitors like swarms of bees. Precious and rare treasures can easily be found, and there are numerous varieties of fruit and animals...*'

(From *An Eyewitness Account of the Western Lands*, Tang dynasty. Quoted in Yung, 1997)

Today, a hundred thousand people converge on the town each Sunday. The ethnic diversity of the visitors matches the range of goods on sale: Uighurs, Tajiks, Kyrgyz and Han Chinese predominate. The livestock area is the most vigorous section of the market and gives the best sense of how industrious Kashgar must have been during the Silk Road's heyday. Xuanzang mentioned that the local inhabitants made fine woollen carpets and these are still to be found at the market but the dazzling lustrous silks of old are almost gone. Khotan and Yarkand (Shache) are still silk-producing centres. In Khotan, the tie-dye method is used with symmetrical patterns and black and white as the main colours; supplemented by reds, yellows and blues. Yarkand silks are brightly coloured: emerald and jade green, magenta and apricot are favourites. Khotan and Yarkand silks can still be found but imported synthetic textiles are now as likely to be seen in the market place.

Kashgar's later history was a direct consequence of the disintegration of the Uighur State after the death of Kutluk Bilge Khan in 805. War erupted between the Uighurs and their Kyrgyz neighbours and in 840, after a bitter famished winter, the Uighur capital at Karabalghasun on the Orkhon River (in present-day Mongolia) was captured and their ruler, or Kaghan, was assassinated. The Uighurs fled south and the kingdom fragmented into three groups, centred around the west side of the Yellow River in Gansu and the northern and southern parts of the Tianshan Mountains. The largest group went to the northern Tianshan region, establishing their capital at Karakhoja, modern Turfan (see p. 141), and its descendants still form the most populous Uighur community in China. The southern Tianshan Uighurs allied themselves with other Turkic clans like the Karluks, Turgish and Basmils and established the Kharakhanid Kingdom – its capital at Kashgar. In 934 the Kharakhanid ruler of Kashgar, Satuk Bughra Khan embraced Islam – the first state of the Western Regions to do so. The Kharakhanids waged war against the Buddhist Uighurs of the northern Tianshan and most of the stupas and monasteries around Kashgar were destroyed. Some remains survive, however, most to the north of the city. A number of Buddhist stupas were found near the village of Hanoi (Hanoyi or Khan-ui) about 30 km east of Kashgar. The oldest appears to have been the Topa Tim stupa, first explored by Stein in 1900. It was still 100 metres around at the base and may date to as early as the first century AD, contemporary with and similar in form to the great Dharmajika stupa at Taxila (fig. 33). A stupa at Kurghan Tim, northwest of Kashgar, is the largest mound in the area and was still 25 metres high when Stein first saw it in 1900. Kurghan Tim was built on a square base like many large structures and small reliquary stupas found in Gandhara. One of the best preserved and most important of Kashgar's stupas is at Mauri Tim, just north of Hanoi (fig. 211).

Hanoi itself is the site of a Tang dynasty walled city and may well have been the original site of the capital of the Kashgar city-state, (or Shu-le as it was then called). The remains of city walls and streets, about 75 metres by 95 metres, have been identified. Hanoi appears to have been abandoned around the eleventh century and traces of fire damage at the site indicate that it was at least partially destroyed in antiquity.

The second-or third-century AD Sanxiandong ('Three Immortals Caves'), about 20 km northwest of Kashgar, are believed to be the oldest Buddhist caves in China. They are cut into the southern cliff beside the Qiakmakh River but

Fig. 211 **The Mauri-Tim Stupa, near Kashgar, Xinjiang province**
Built and enlarged between the 5th and 10th centuries and earlier
Mauri-Tim is built on a square base in the manner of the Gandhara stupas and sits on a high mound, seeming much taller than its height of 11.5 metres.

Fig. 212 **The ruins of Hanoi, near Kashgar, Xinjiang province**

Fig. 213 **Sanxiandong,
('Three Immortals Caves')**
2nd to 3rd century AD
Near Kashgar, Xinjiang province

of Uighur society but it is Yusuf's remarks about merchants that is of the greatest interest to historians of the Silk Road:

'Deal with them, hold open your gates for them.
Treat them well
so that your good name will spread.
It is these who will carry your name through the world,
who will spread your reputation, good or bad....
If you want to be sure to become famous,
let the merchant have just pay for his goods.
If you want to create a good name for yourself, O Lord,
Treat well the caravan people.'

(Yusuf Has Hajip, *Kutatku Bilik,* ca. 1070. Quoted in Lattimore, 1950)

By the time of Marco Polo's visit to Kashgar during the thirteenth century, the city state was firmly under the control of the Mongols, as was the rest of the region. Commerce along the Silk Road flourished during the period of the Mongol Empire when travellers could journey unimpeded along its entire length. Kashgar's inhabitants were Muslim although a small community of Nestorian Christians was also tolerated. Marco was impressed with the beauty of the city but was less enthusiastic about the behaviour of its inhabitants:

'They have handsome gardens, orchards, and vineyards.
[An] abundance of cotton is produced there, as well as flax
and hemp. Merchants from this country travel to all parts
of the world; but in truth they are a covetous sordid race,
eating badly and drinking worse.'

(From *The Travels of Marco Polo the Venetian.* Translated by William Marsden in Marsden, 1948)

After the collapse of the Yuan dynasty in 1368, the Tarim Basin descended into chaos with only a brief period of stability when Timur took control of the region at the end of the fourteenth century. By this time the Silk Road was already in decline and its cities fading into obscurity.

have suffered from a thousand years of iconoclasm and are in a poor state. Of the three surviving caves, only one has traces of wall paintings and these are no match for the glories of Dunhuang or Kizil. In the middle cave is a headless stone statue of a seated Buddha and the site itself occupies a beautiful spot above the river (fig. 213).

The Uighur rulers of Kashgar were fully aware of the importance of merchants to the continued prosperity of the state. The Uighur scholar Yusuf Has Hajip was a chancellor to the Khan during the eleventh century. His book *Kutatku Bilik* ('The Knowledge Befitting a Ruler') was written around 1070 and describes the social, political and cultural life of the Uighurs. It provides guidance to rulers in order that their reign might be a just one. His advice covers the various strata

CHAPTER NINE

THE SOUTHERN SILK ROAD

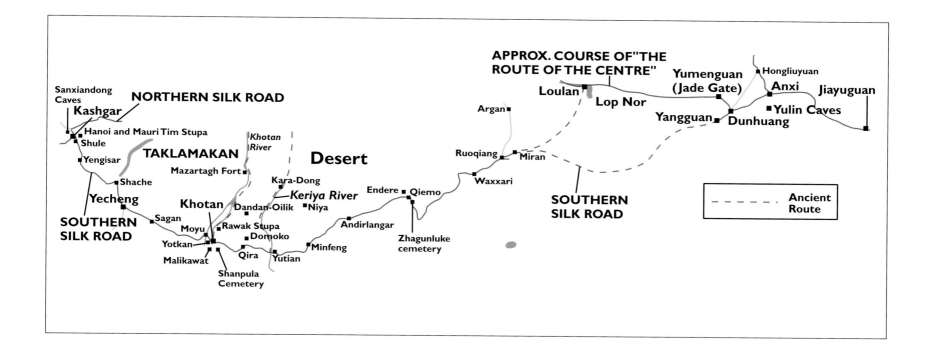

MAIN SITES ALONG THE
SOUTHERN SILK ROAD

The Chinese called this route 'Nan Shan Bei Lu' ('The Road North of the Southern Mountains'). It travels in a south-westerly direction from Anxi, via Dunhuang and Yangguan, or the 'Gate of Yang'(see p. 139), following the northern foothills of the Kunlun Mountains and skirting the southern edge of the Taklamakan to Loulan, Khotan, Yarkand and Kashgar. At Kashgar the Northern and Southern Silk Roads merge. The southern route was more strenuous because the oases along the route were more widely spaced, but it was more direct and travellers often preferred it because its remoteness meant that there was less likelihood of attack from brigands. Between Dunhuang and Cherchen there were few places to obtain provisions and travellers had to carry their water and food with them. The crossing of the Taklamakan Desert was one of the most dangerous stretches of the Southern Silk Road (see Niya below).

The lake at Lop Nor, once fed by the Tarim and Kongqu (Peacock) rivers, has a mysterious past. Sven Hedin, Stein

Fig. 214 **The dried up lake bed at Lop Nor**
(Photo by: Christoph Baumer)

and others charted the location of the lake at the beginning of the century and concluded that it was a 'wandering' body of water. More recent Chinese research contradicts this view: the most likely explanation is that the Tarim River has periodically altered its course and forms a new lake. As late as the 1950s Chinese scientists visited the present site and saw a colossal expanse of water from which they were able to catch large fish. By 1973 it was a desiccated salt basin surrounded by marshes, a consequence of the Tarim River changing its course in its lower reaches and thereby depriving Lop Nor of its water supply. Lop Nor has always enjoyed a fearsome reputation, a reputation sustained by its current status as China's centre for nuclear testing. West of the Lop Nor lake is Loulan, (the Chinese transliteration of 'Kroraina') – a garrison town of the Loulan or Shanshan kingdom, first seen by Sven Hedin in 1900. A shortage of water meant that Hedin was able to make only a cursory examination of the site but one of his men returned on the following day to retrieve a spade and realized its full extent. Hedin returned in 1901 and spent a week exploring but it was not until Aurel Stein's visits in 1906 and 1914 that it was examined fully.

Loulan
Loulan marks the eastern edge of the Shanshan Kingdom, its capital probably at Miran or possibly Charkhlik (Ruoqiang),

although this is still a matter of debate. The kingdom itself was originally called Loulan and was mentioned in the reports of Emperor Wudi's envoy Zhang Qian. It was awkwardly placed, trapped between the Xiongnu and the Han, and was subject to a number of bitter power struggles. In 77 BC, a Chinese official assassinated the Loulan king, an appointee of the Xiongnu, during a banquet in his own capital and the kingdom was renamed 'Shanshan'. The king's replacement had been residing as a hostage in the Chinese capital and was sent home to assume the crown. He appears to have been in no doubt about the precariousness of his position:

'For a long time I have been in Han. Now I am returning home deserted and weak at a time when sons of the former king are alive, and I fear that I may be killed by them. There is a town [called] I-hsün ch'eng in the state, whose land is fertile. I would be grateful if Han could send one leader (chiang) to set up an agricultural colony there and accumulate a store of field-crops, so that I would be able to rely on the support of Han prestige.'

(*Han Shu*, History of the Former Han. Quoted in Rhie, 1999)

The Chinese responded to this request by establishing a post in the Shanshan kingdom, the precise location of which

Fig. 215 **The stupa and ruins at Loulan, Xinjiang province**

(Photo by Christoph Baumer)

remains unclear. During the Eastern Han dynasty (25–220 AD), the Chinese consolidated their control of the region through the efforts of General Ban Chao. After the death of Ban Chao in 103 AD the threat to the region from raids by Xiongnu nomads again increased. Ban Chao's son Ban Yung, the last of the Han generals in Central Asia, responded to the renewed threat by establishing a military post at Loulan in about 124 AD. The post marked the starting point for a third route of the Silk Road. The route was known as the 'Tianshan Nan Lu' ('Road South of the Celestial Mountains'), or the 'Route of the Centre', and ran from Loulan along the course of the Kongqu River through Korla and past Lake Bosten to Yanqi (Karashahr) where it rejoined the Northern Silk Road. The route traverses the desolate wastes of the northern Taklamakan and there is little sign today that there was anywhere en route for travellers to obtain victuals. It appears to have fallen into disuse after Loulan was abandoned, sometime during the fourth century, probably because of a dwindling of water resources.

Stein set off towards Loulan in December 1906, departing from Charkhlik (Ruoqiang) and heading in a north-easterly direction to Loulan. He followed approximately the same route as that followed by Marco Polo during a harrowing month-long crossing some 650

years before. Marco called this part of the eastern Taklamakan the 'Desert of Lop' and describes the phantoms who lured men off the paths to their deaths:

'…this desert is the abode of many evil spirits, which amuse travellers to their destruction with most extraordinary illusions. If, during the daytime, any persons remain behind on the road…they unexpectedly hear themselves called to by their names, and in a tone of voice to which they are accustomed. Supposing the call to proceed from their companions, they are led away by it from the direct road, and not knowing in what direction to advance, are left to perish…Marvellous indeed and almost passing belief are the stories related of these spirits of the desert, which are said at times to fill the air with the sounds of all kinds of musical instruments, and also of drums and the clash of arms; obliging the travellers to close their line of march and to proceed in more compact order.'

(From *The Travels of Marco Polo the Venetian.* Translated by William Marsden in Marsden, 1948)

The monk Xuanzang describes hearing similar voices during his crossing of the Khotan-Niya section of the Taklamakan (see p. 179). Stein's journey was barely less arduous: he carried his water supplies in the form of frozen blocks of ice and was forced to sew pieces of oxhide directly onto the lacerated pads of his camels' feet. Along the route Stein picked up large numbers of Chinese coins, arrowheads and other small objects- the detritus of centuries of travellers. In one such find he discovered a neat line of over 200 Han dynasty copper coins, extending for about 30 metres along the road. Some hapless ancient wayfarer had trudged along Stein's route, centuries before, and had lost them when the string of his purse had come untied.

One of the most important of Stein's discoveries at Loulan was a single bale of yellow silk, 48 cm wide. The discovery of wooden measuring devices and an inscribed fragment of the fabric led Stein to conclude that 48 cm was the standard size for the bales of silk that were traded by merchants along the Silk Road. He made further discoveries in an enormous rubbish-tip about 30 metres across, including wedge-shaped and rectangular documents written on wood, and others on paper and silk in Chinese and in the Kharosthi script of northwest India. A single torn fragment of paper contained writing in Sogdian, the *lingua franca* of Silk Road trade. The documents date from about 260 to 330 AD when both Loulan and the entire 'Route of the Centre' appear to have been abandoned. The documents provide an insight into the administration of the Chinese garrison at Loulan and the problems of sustaining it. A number of the documents instruct that food rations to the men of the garrison be reduced. Some reveal the anxieties of men sent to this remote outpost. One letter, presumably never sent, was written by a man named Chao Chi and captures the mood of the place:

> 'I am living in a far off region and my brothers, sisters and children are all at home. I am afraid the children might not be getting enough to eat.'

Among the larger objects found by Stein at Loulan are wooden architectural fragments, superbly preserved and decorated with Western classical motifs. A Corinthian capital and an Ionic double-bracket capital are among them. Similar fragments were found at Niya and their existence proves that even remote sections of the Silk Road were susceptible to outside influences. Figural sculpture was also found in and around Loulan, dated to around the third century and comprising Buddha, Bodhisattva and guardian figures. They draw on elements from both Gandhara and Chinese art to create a uniquely Central Asian style.

Fig. 216 **'The Beauty of Loulan': Mummy of young woman**
Ca. 2000–1800 BC (Radiocarbon date)
H. 152 cm
From the necropolis at Qäwrighul (Gumugou), Xinjiang province
(Photo by J. Newbury)
The woman wore clothes of wool and fur, a hat with a goose feather and fur moccasins. Found with her in the grave were a simple comb, a winnowing tray and a basket containing wheat. Her hair is auburn, parted at the centre and frames a face that still retains an expression of grace and serenity. She was about forty-five when she died.

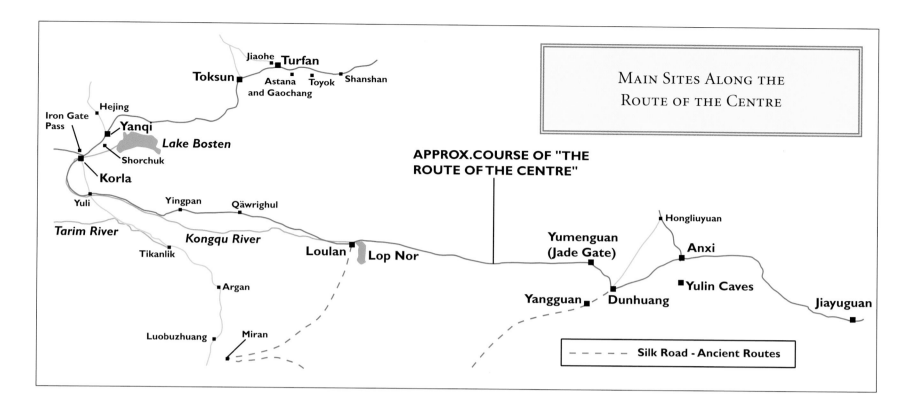

MAIN SITES ALONG THE
ROUTE OF THE CENTRE

APPROX.COURSE OF "THE
ROUTE OF THE CENTRE"

- - - - - Silk Road - Ancient Routes

Other sites on the 'Tianshan Nan Lu' or the 'Route of the Centre'

As we have seen, the 'Route of the Centre' followed the course of the course of the Kongqu River through Korla to Yanqi. At Qäwrighul (Gumugou), about 70 km northwest of Loulan, are the remains of an ancient settlement located on the north bank of the river. An ancient necropolis at Qäwrighul was excavated by Chinese archeologists in 1979 and was found to contain several graves enclosed by tight concentric rows of wooden stakes. Excavations of the site have yielded extraordinary human remains, preserved by the regions arid climate. The mummified bodies found at the site are Caucasian in appearance and pose fascinating and as yet unanswered questions as to how they got there. The most famous of all the mummies of Qäwrighul is the 'Beauty of Loulan', buried in simple clothes of wool and fur (fig. 216).

Radiocarbon dating of the Qäwrighul graves produced the astoundingly early date of around 2000 BC for some artefacts and an even earlier date for others. If 2000 BC is accepted as the date for the Qäwrighul mummies it means that they pre-date the similarly Caucasoid, Cherchen mummies of the Southern Tarim Basin by about one thousand years (see p. 175), and also precede the arrival of Han Chinese in the region. The second issue is an incredibly important and politically sensitive one. Who these people were and how they came to be living in a remote part of Xinjiang so long before the known beginnings of inter-national travel along the Silk Road has yet be established. The Beauty of Loulan has become an icon for the Uighur population of Xinjiang, many calling her 'the mother of the nation', and a local artist has produced a remarkable and credible impression of how she may have appeared (fig. 217).

Continuing westward along the course of the Kongqu River, the 'Route of the Centre' can be made out, even today, by beacon towers that still mark the way. Near the town of

Fig. 217 **Artist's impression of the 'Beauty of Loulan'**

Fig. 218 **Woollen robe with yellow designs of paired warriors, animals and trees on a red ground**
Han /Jin Dynasties (3rd century BC to 5th century AD)
L. 110 cm
Unearthed at tomb 15, Yingpan, Yuli County, Xinjiang in 1995
(Archeology Institute of the Xinjiang Uighur Autonomous Region)
A trumpet-shaped Sasanian cup of moulded white glass testifies to Yingpan's role as a Silk Road entrepôt. Beyond Yingpan, however, there are few remains except for the occasional beacon tower until the Northern Route is rejoined beyond Korla and Lake Bosten.

From Loulan a spur led in a southwesterly direction across the western part of the salt marshes that surround Lop Nor. After about 150 km travellers rejoined the Southern Silk Road at Miran, a small remote settlement and one of the jewels of the Silk Road.

Miran

Stein's 1906 discovery of Miran was serendipitous. He had learned of the ruins from his local guide Tokhta Akhun and had decided to inspect them en route to his principal objective, the city of Loulan. Stein left Charkhlik (Ruoqiang) in December 1906 en route for Loulan and came upon the ruins about 80 km to the northeast. There was time for no more than a cursory inspection and Stein left the site without realising that he had discovered the most important early Buddhist site in China. He returned the following year and made incredible finds at a site whose art is awash with foreign influences from the Greco-Roman world, Gandhara and India. Mario Bussagli (Bussagli, 1963) calls Miran 'an outpost of Gandharan art' and fugitives from the Sasanian invasion of the Kushan Empire during the third century may indeed have populated it. Miran was a fortified town of the Shanshan kingdom – the capital according to some scholars – from the Han dynasty until the fourth century when it was abandoned. The town's fortunes revived briefly when Tibetans reoccupied it from the eighth to ninth centuries. During the Tibetan occupation a circular fort, still in existence today, was built at Miran, apparently after the rest of the town had been deserted. Stein found mountains of refuse within the fort, much of it of interest only to a scatologist! More than one thousand documents in Tibetan were also recovered, however, and the dates that they carry suggest that the fort was occupied from about 775 to 860. Pieces of lacquered leather armour from the Tibetan period are a reminder that the martial function of Miran continued long after its stupas and monasteries had fallen into disuse. During the Tibetan occupation they effectively controlled all traffic along the Southern Silk Road, but by this date, the 'Route of the Centre' had already ceased to be used when its water sources dried up and the small settlements along the way were progressively abandoned. The Northern Route was not safe either- its oasis towns were under constant threat at from Uighurs and Tibetans- and for a long period China was deprived of a key source of revenue. When the Tibetans were finally expelled from Miran around 860, the desert quickly reclaimed the town's irrigation system and then devoured the town itself. It remained one of the Taklamakan's 'lost cities' until Stein's arrival in 1906.

Miran's apogee occurred around the third to fourth century when the town was a flourishing Buddhist and commercial centre. Stein identified fifteen buildings including three stupa shrines (M III, M V and M XIV); at least two and possibly three stupas with square bases; several

Tikanlik are the ruins of Yingpan, a Buddhist settlement of considerable size with the remains of a pagoda still discernible on a northern slope. Yingpan is about 200 km west of Loulan in Yuli County and very recent excavations of the town's burial grounds have revealed some incredible artefacts. Since 1995, Chinese archeologists have been investigating the tombs and what they have unearthed indicates that Western classical motifs were flowing into the area from the very beginnings of the Silk Road's history. Most of the artefacts date to the Han dynasty (206 BC–220 AD) and the Western and Eastern Jin dynasties (265–420 AD). The occupant of Tomb 15 was a fine-looking man of about thirty years of age, 1.8 metres tall and dressed in sumptuous silk and woollen garments. A gold-leaf mask covers his face. The robe he wears is covered with pairs of human figures, animals and trees in unmistakably Hellenistic style (fig. 218).

****

towers and smaller structures, and the Tibetan Fort*. In Shrines M III and M V, remarkable paintings were discovered that bear witness to the penetration of classical art in a virtually unadulterated form to the remotest regions of Central Asia. The two examples shown below have not survived. When Stein returned to Miran in 1914 with hopes of removing them he discovered that a clumsy attempt by a representative of Baron Otani had destroyed them. We have only Stein's photographs to show how splendid they must have been (fig. 219). Smaller fragments have survived, however, and all but two are now in the National Museum in New Delhi. All of Miran's murals are so similar in style that they must have been painted, if not by the same hand, at least by the same group of artists. A clue is provided by the presence of two Kharosthi inscriptions on the paintings of Shrine M V.

Stein postulated that *Tita* was a form of Titus, a Roman name used throughout the Near East. *Tita*, or Titus was exceedingly familiar with Western classical motifs and was also skilled in the technique of *chiaroscuro* (treatment of light and shade), used widely in Hellenistic painting and mosaic. Stein has left us a remarkable description of what kind of person he may have been:

> '...a sort of Roman Eurasian by blood, brought up in the Hellenistic tradition...whom his calling had carried no doubt through the regions of eastern Iran, impregnated with Buddhism, to the confines of China'.

(Stein, 'Serindia', 1921)

Benjamin Rowland (Rowland, 1938), compares the Miran paintings with the celebrated Romano-Egyptian mummy paintings of Fayum and the possibility that Tita had been active in both places is an intriguing one (fig. 220).

When Shrine M III was explored by Stein it was found to comprise the remains of a stupa about 2.75 metres across and with about 4 metres of its original height still remaining. The stupa had been erected within the walls of a rotunda and the surviving wall paintings come mostly from a lower frieze within that part of the structure. A beautiful painting of Buddha and six disciples passing through a forest was removed from M III and now resides in the New Delhi Museum. Both M III and M V had figures of winged male figures akin to Western angels. The 'angels of Miran' are nothing short of amazing and no one was more surprised at their discovery than Stein himself:

> 'How could I have expected by the desolate shores of Lop-nor, in the very heart of innermost Asia, to come upon such classical representations of cherubim?'

(Stein, 1964)

In the outer passage of Shrine M V one of the angels, large eyed and with a mop of dark curly hair, peers out from

Fig. 219 **Mural (no longer extant) depicting two episodes from the Visvantara-Jataka**
3rd century
Shrine M V, Miran, Xinjiang province
(After Stein, 1912)
Shrine M V at Miran consisted of a hall and a stupa built of sun dried bricks. The remains of murals were found on the side of the passageway outside of the structure's main walls and on the circular passage that surrounded the Stupa. The Visvantara-Jataka scene shown here was found on the circular wall and depicts the last of Buddha Sakyamuni's previous incarnations as Prince Visvantara. He is shown (top) giving away a royal white elephant to a group of Brahmins. A short Kharosthi inscription on the elephant's right thigh reads: 'This fresco is [the work] of Tita, who has received 3,000 Bhammakas [for it]'. The scene below shows him leaving the palace with his wife and children. In the lower sections of each scene are garland-bearing figures of the most exquisite beauty, in rich colours that can only be imagined from the descriptions left to us by Stein. In one, a procession of pensive young men carry a long garland: some dressed in smart tunics and others wearing the Phrygian caps of Asia Minor – motifs found in both classical art and in the art of Gandhara (see fig. 20). In the other (left to right): a young woman, her hair decorated with white flowers and a crimson cloak trailing across her shoulders, plays a four-stringed lute; a bearded man (perhaps a Parthian) with thick curly hair holds a glass goblet and a young man, perhaps a Kushan prince, wears a conical cap lined with red and holds and object resembling a pomegranate.

* There was also an important Tibetan fort, the ruins of which still exist, at Mazartagh, beside the Khotan River on the ancient route that leads north from Khotan.

Fig. 220 **Encaustic on wood funeral portrait of a young man**
Romano-Egyptian, ca. 160 AD
From Fayum, Egypt
(Altes Museum, Berlin)

beneath a scene of a youth fighting with a lion. The youth's predicament recalls the tribulations of Herakles (or Hercules) and the Nemean Lion. Stein photographed the painting in 1907 but the original was destroyed during the misguided attempts of Otani's emissary to remove it (fig. 221).

The ruins of a shrine or *vihara* (a chapel for a sacred image) were excavated in 1907 and again in 1914. Stein designated the site M II and discovered a rectangular platform, measuring 14 metres by 11 metres and with the possible remains of a stupa upon it. The sides of the platform were badly damaged by wind erosion but on two were a series of niches containing the remains of colossal stucco sculptures. Five large seated figures of Buddha in the style of Gandhara images of the 4th or 5th century were among them. A head from the third of the five Buddhas, a full 54 cm in height, was removed by Stein and is now in the British Museum. Other large stucco sculptures, also in Gandhara style, were found when Stein returned to Miran in 1914, at a shrine designated M XV.

This entire section of the Southern Road was brutally difficult for travellers. The route crossed deserts of shifting sands that often obscured the trail and there was little sustenance to be found. A branch of the road out from Miran turned southwards, over the Kunlun Mountains, to Tibet but the main Southern Route continued westwards along the foothills of the Altun Mountains to the small town of Charkhlik (Ruoqiang), another caravan centre of the Shanshan Kingdom. Chinese historical documents are ambiguous about the location and site of the capital of the Loulan Kingdom (i.e. before 77 BC when it was renamed the Shanshan Kingdom). The name given in Chinese historical documents was *Wu-ni* or *Chü-mi* and has been pinpointed as either Loulan or Charkhlik. It is therefore possible that Charkhlik was the capital of both the Loulan and, subsequently, the Shanshan kingdom but the subject is still a matter of dispute. Little else is know about Charkhlik- even the usually reliable observer Xuanzang had little to say when he passed through the town in 644.

The next oasis town, Qiemo (Cherchen) is 340 km to the southwest and sits on the river of the same name. The *Han Shu* ('History of the Former Han') tells us a little about Qiemo:

> '*Shanshan is situated on the Han communication route; to the west it is connected with Qiemo at a distance of 720 li [about 360 km]…From Qiemo onwards the states all sow the five crops [rice, two types of millet, wheat and beans].*'

(*Han Shu* ['History of the Former Han'], quoted in Che Muqi, 1989)

Until the 1950s – when the road was built – Qiemo's sole means of contact with the outside world was on camels or donkeys. The journey to Korla, a distance of about 800 km, took forty days. The area is lacerated by sandstorms, known as *karaburans,* sometimes for days at a time. During ancient times Qiemo was a headquarters for the Chinese Protector General of the Western Regions but was subsequently absorbed into the Shanshan Kingdom. In Kharosthi documents found along the Southern Silk Road it is referred to as *Calmadana* but few remains have been found other than an ancient stupa.

Marco Polo provides a lucid picture of the knife-edge existence endured by the people of the 'province of Charchan'. He relates that the chief city of the province is 'likewise named Charchan' and passed through a region whose inhabitants were so accustomed to raids by marauding nomads that:

> '*…when they are aware of the approach of any body of troops, they flee, with their families and cattle, into the sandy desert, to the distance of two days' journey, towards some spot where they can find fresh water, and are by that means enabled to subsist.*'

(From *The Travels of Marco Polo the Venetian.* Translated by William Marsden in Marsden, 1948)

Fig. 221 **Mural (no longer extant) depicting a youth in combat with a griffin above a winged angel, 3rd century**
From the inner wall of the south passage, Stupa Shrine M V, Miran, Xinjiang province
(After Stein, 1921)

Fig. 222 **Structure N.3. The remains of a large timber framed building.**
Ca. 4th century
Niya, north of Minfeng, Xinjiang province.
This building, thought to have contained government offices, is the largest such structure at Niya. The walls are shattered by wind and time but the wooden frame still stands and the remains of wattle walls can still be seen. It was from this structure that Stein unearthed a wooden altar or table that now graces the collections of the British Museum (fig. 227). It was also here that, during his last visit in 1914, Stein recovered manuscripts of the type described below.

The recent discovery of 3,000-year-old mummified remains at the Zhagunluke cemetery near Qiemo has caused great excitement. The mummies, like those of Qäwrighul, appear to be Caucasoid in appearance (see figs. 105 and 216) and suggest that tribal groups were migrating over vast distances from a very early date.

A six-day journey westward from Qiemo, through a region described by Stein as a 'silent uninhabited waste' brought travellers to the town of Endere. This section of the road, Stein observes, is most notable for its infrequent brackish wells, broiling heat and voracious mosquitoes but there are also patches of vegetation where water from the Kunlun Mountains moistens the parched land. Stein excavated Endere in 1901 and 1906 and discovered a settlement and a large stupa from around the third century and a fort dating to the late seventh or early eighth century. The fort showed signs, first of Chinese occupation and then of Tibetan usage, perhaps the result of changing military fortunes. Stein found a small number of Kharosthi documents on wood and leather at Endere, some referring to a place called *Saca*, which may be the town's ancient name. One of the documents, written in both Kharosthi and

Brahmi script, dates to around 230 AD and is addressed to Vijida Simha, King of Khotan. The use of Brahmi script is fascinating because it gives credence to early accounts that there was a substantial Indian community in Khotan (see section on Khotan) and that Indian cultural influence was strong. Stein also found a wooden votive plaque at Endere, painted with a seated figure of the Hindu god Ganesha – additional proof that the area was a willing recipient of motifs from the great country to the south. In the letter to the King of Khotan, the king is referred to as *hinajha*, an Iranian title meaning 'generalissimo' and this suggests that there were also Iranians living in the region.

Niya

> 'And, little town, thy streets forevermore
> Will silent be; and not a soul to tell
> Why thou art desolate, can e'er return.'

(John Keats, 'Ode on a Grecian Urn')

Niya (referred to as *Cadota* in a number of documents found at Loulan) is a four-day journey from Endere. It occupies a

Fig. 223 **Remains of a
Buddhist stupa**
Ca. 3rd century AD
H.6 metres (approx.)
Niya, north of Minfeng,
Xinjiang province

indicating that it was once a major commercial centre on the
Southern Silk Road. The town was situated at the western
extremity of the Shanshan Kingdom and may even have
been one of its capitals. It appears to have been abandoned
around 350, perhaps when the Niya River changed course or
dried up and deprived the town of its water supply. In
contrast to the monasteries and shrines of Miran, most of
the buildings are residential. Stein discovered about forty
different buildings at Niya, most built with a strong wooden
framework and, in many cases, with adjacent stalls for
livestock. The timber frames of many houses are still
standing and the withered stumps of ancient orchards still
protrude from the sand. Stein's description captures the
desolate appearance of the site:

> *'Like the open sea the expanse of yellow dunes lay
> before me, with nothing to break their wavy monotony
> but the bleached trunks of trees or the rows of splintered
> posts marking houses which rose here and there above
> the sand crests.'*
>
> (Stein, 1912)

A single ruined stupa of modest size stands at the centre of
the site, to the north of building N.3 (fig. 223). It was built of
mud-brick before 300 AD and consists of a cylindrical dome
on a square base. The style is similar to many other stupas of
the Shanshan Kingdom – Endere and Loulan in particular –
and also resembles early Gandhara examples. This is not
surprising when the large numbers of documents discovered
at Niya are examined. They reveal that the majority of
foreign travellers passing through Niya, up until the time of
its abandonment around 350, were Kushans (Yuezhi) from
Gandhara and there appears to have been a community of
them residing in the town.

vast area beside the dried up bed of the Niya River- as much
as 30 km north to south and 5 km east to west. To reach it
requires a journey by jeep and camel, north from the town of
Minfeng (New Niya) across 100 km of lifeless, post-
apocalyptic wilderness. During visits in 1901, 1906, 1914 and
1931, Stein unearthed extensive remains at the site,

The remains of a Buddhist temple were excavated by a
Chinese expedition in 1995 (fig. 224). The main hall of the
temple is about 25 square metres and a number of
fragmentary wall paintings were recovered.

All over the site there is a pervasive sense, similar to the
atmosphere at Pompeii, of time being frozen. An old pond,
extinct for almost two millennia, is still hemmed by the dead
stumps of fruit trees, planted for shade by the town's
occupants (fig. 225).

Fig. 224 **Buddhist Temple
93A35**
Ca. 4th century
Niya, north of Minfeng,
Xinjiang province

The dwellings at Niya almost all contain the remains of
large red terracotta pots and it may be that the inhabitants
were forced to use them to store water as the river receded.
Fruit stones, wooden implements such as bobbins and the
occasional manuscript still lie scattered about the ruins and
archeologists have quite literally only scratched Niya's
surface. The buildings visible above the constantly moving
sands are widely spaced, sometimes kilometres apart, and
there can be little doubt that there are dozens or even
hundreds of structures still to be unearthed.

Large numbers of documents were discovered at Niya. During his first visit in 1901, Stein unearthed more than 250 from a rubbish tip attached to dwelling N.5, situated about 3 km north of the stupa. The documents are on sheepskin and wood and are written mainly in Chinese and Kharosthi. The wooden examples are of two types: large rectangular documents that tended to involve official and legal issues and wedge-shaped tablets that were generally concerned with day-to-day matters. The ingenious construction of the square type ensured that an unauthorized person could not read the contents without either breaking the seal or cutting the strings. Stein found no paper documents at Niya although Chinese researchers discovered a few fragments in 1959. This is significant, given that the site was not abandoned until around the mid-fourth century and paper is thought to have been invented by the court eunuch Cai Lun in 105 AD, more than two hundred years earlier. It seems that the new technology was slow to reach these remote parts of Central Asia. Clay seals on the Stein documents show Persian, Indian and classical motifs- themes that are repeated on the wooden architecture of the site. Figures of Athena, Herakles, Zeus, helmeted busts and winged horses are common. The contents of these documents have provided a wealth of information about the social, economic and military life of the Silk Road during the third and fourth centuries. A large number of the Chinese documents are concerned with customs ontrol and with regulating the passage of foreigners (especially Kushans) through Shanshan State. There are also numerous references to other cities in the region: Dunhuang is mentioned frequently and was quite clearly a city of great importance at this time.

Samplings from the Kharosthi documents of Niya and Loulan are a window on the vanished life of the Shanshan Kingdom. The following are all from Stein's excavations and are, to borrow a phrase from the American poet Archibald MacLeish, 'shard of broken memories':

'…At present there are no merchants from China, so that the debt of silk is not to be investigated now. As regards the matter of the camel Tamcina is to be pestered. When the merchants arrive from China, the debt of silk is to be investigated. If there is a dispute, there will be a decision in our presence in the royal court.' (no. 35)

'His majesty the king writes, he instructs the cozbo [functionary]… as follows:..Li?ipeya reports that they took out three witch-women. They killed only the woman belonging to him, the remaining women they released. About this matter you received a command from Apgeya that recompense was to be made to Li?ipeya for this woman…' (no. 63)

Fig. 225 **Old pond with the remains of an arbour** Niya, north of Minfeng, Xinjiang province

'His majesty, etc … L?imsu informs us that that a female camel belongs to them and Simasriae in common. A man called Sugika and her daughter Smagasae rode off on this camel from Simasriae's farm and fled away. He and his father went after them with the frontier guards and brought this camel back. (As a result) two parts of this camel belonged to these two, the father and son, and two parts to the guards (for their services)…' (no. 71)

'His majesty, etc…Li?ipeya informs us that he has a slave called Kacana. Sagana beat him. As a result of that beating the man Kacana died on the eighth day. Here you, the cozbo Somjaka received an oral command that the witnesses had to swear an oath and if Kacana had died as a result of Sagana's beating, a man was to be awarded as recompense…' (no. 144)

'Concerning the son of Tsina, a novice, and an adopted child, to be carefully preserved by Simema….In the 7th year of his majesty Citughi Mahiriya, the son of heaven, in the 3rd month, 5th day, at this date. When the Khotanese plundered the kingdom of Cadota [Niya], at that time three young men of Khotan carried off the woman Tsinae. They came and gave her as a present to the mother of cozbo [functionary] Somjaka in the house of the kitsayitsa Luthu. They gave that woman Tsinae along with her sons and daughters…That woman Tsina[e] gave her son, a novice, five distis high, as an adopted child to the man Kacana. As milk-payment a

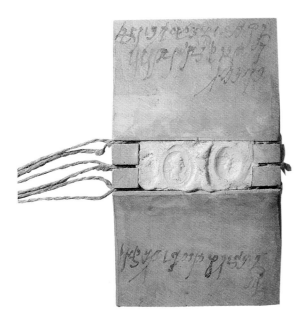
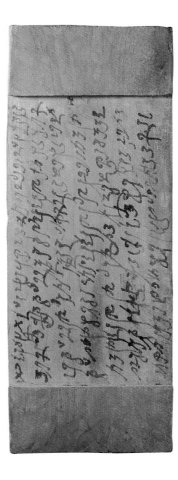

Fig. 226 **Wooden tablet written in Kharosthi**
3rd to 4th century
L. 26.7 cm, W. 10.2 cm
Probably from the vicinity of Niya, Xinjiang province
(Spink and Son Ltd)
Two clays seals on the upper section are both in classical style, the left one
depicting a king and the right a winged horse. As far as the content is concerned,
the upper section (the cover tablet) is addressed to a monk called Sronasena
and states that the document concerns a woman named Ramasria from the
Catisa Devi estate. The inscription below the seals on the cover identifies them
as the seals of the ogu (administrative officer) Pideyalya and the cozbo
(functionary) Punasena. The main inscription on the inside is dated as year two
of King Vasmana (around 315) and concerns a woman named Sacgia, the slave of
Ramasria who is the sister of the monk Sronasena. The document requests that
Sacgia be sent to work on the Catisa estate and that payment for her services
will be a four-year old camel, given by Ramasria to Sronasena. The last two lines
record the name and titles of the witness and the scribe, Nandasena. Some of
the names contained in this document also occur in the Stein documents
translated by Burrow (see Burrow, 1940).

*front of the order of monks… Whichever monk does not
partake in the activities of the community of monks shall
pay a fine of one roll of silk…. Whichever monk strikes
another monk, (in the case of) a light (blow the fine is)
five rolls of silk, (in the case of) a moderate (blow) ten
rolls of silk, (in the case of) an excessive (blow) fifteen rolls
of silk…'* (no. 489)

*'His majesty, etc … Sagamovi complains to this effect. He
is a native of Yave Avana. There is a potter (kulala) called
Camca and this Sagamovi is his son. A member of the
kilme [district] of the ogu [administrative officer] Asoka,
he used to dwell when young next door to Cato. At that
time Cato took to wife the daughter of the sramana
Sundara, called Supriya. After that this Sagamovi and
Supriya[e] fled from the house of Cato to the kingdom of
Kuci [presumably Kuqa]. They stayed a long time in the
kingdom of Kuci. Then they came back to their own
country through the influence of me the great king […].
Whatever this Sagamovi had in the way of wives, sons,
daughters, and slaves, this Sagamovi abandoned all claim
to them. Now the sramana Sundara and L?ipana are
causing trouble in Yave Avana about the woman
Supriya[e]. They are demanding a ransom (lode). When
this sealed wedge-tablet reaches you, forthwith careful
inquiry is to be made, whether it is true that the sramana
Sundara and L?ipana are causing trouble to this
Sagamovi about a ransom for Supriya[e]. They are to be
stopped. They are not to make claims to Supriya[e]
against Sagamovi.'* (no. 621)

(All abridged from Burrow, 1940)

Such documents continue to be found in the area. One
example, written in Kharosthi and unearthed in 1981,
provides a clue to the reasons for Niya's abandonment. It is
dated to around the middle of the 4th century, a time when
the town's water supply was apparently becoming erratic:

*'At the time when the river water dried up, Kampila
abandoned his wife Ui…'*

(Quoted in Rhie, 1999)

Another recently discovered document from the area refers
to a transaction involving a slave. The currency involved,
namely a camel, appears to have been one of the units of
choice at the time: camels, bolts of silk and lengths of carpet
are mentioned again and again (fig. 226).

A group of forty documents were discovered about 2 km
north of old Niya in 1959, as well as two grave sites. One of
the tombs contained the remains of a man and woman and
yielded a beautiful group of textiles, including a brocade in
the shape of a rooster and what is thought to be one of the

*vito horse was given. This transaction was made in the
presence of the cozbo Somjaka…'* (no. 415).

*'In the 10th year of his majesty the great king, Jitugha
Mahagiri, son of heaven, in the 12th month, 10th day…
the community of monks in the capital laid down
regulations for the community of monks in Cadota
[Niya]. It is heard that the novices do not pay attention to
an elder, they disobey the old monks. Concerning this
these regulations have been laid down by his majesty in*

earliest examples of Batik. The Batik – a wax-resist dyed cotton – is in dark indigo blue and contains designs of a goddess holding a cornucopia ('horn of plenty') and the remains of what appears to have been a Herakles figure with a lion. The richness of the textiles found at Niya demonstrate that the town was a flourishing centre for trade and also show, once again, that motifs from the classical world penetrated to the furthest extremities of Chinese Central Asia.

As we have mentioned, the classical themes of the clay document seals are repeated on Niya's wooden architecture. The absence of moisture in the region has meant that many wooden objects have survived and they bear a strong resemblance to the architecture of Loulan. Pillars with acanthus decoration, Corinthian capitals, amazing griffin-like creatures and the *purnaghata* ('vase of plenty') are all found. Most splendid of all is a table or altar, found by Stein during his 1901 visit and originally identified by him as a chair (fig. 227).

Beginning in 1988, a series of Sino-Japanese expeditions have visited Niya and made new discoveries about the town and its inhabitants. The culmination of this work was the discovery, in 1995, of a necropolis serving the town's rulers. Artefacts found in the graves included shells, coral and glass from the countries to the west and fine silks imported from metropolitan China. One silk fragment, unearthed from Tomb 3 and dating to the second or third century AD, is inscribed with the phrase 'marriage of the families of the King and Marquis' (*wang hou he hun*). The inscription suggests that strategic marriages were commonplace between the rulers of the Silk Road city states of the Western Regions at this time, and recalls the alliances between the Han and the Xiongnu (see fig. 7).

The Chinese monk Fa Xian, who visited India between 399 and 414, visited Shanshan in 399, travelling for seventeen days across the desert from Dunhuang. The journey was not a pleasant one:

> 'In the river of sand, there are evil demons in great
> number and winds so scorching that, when you meet
> them, all die and not one escapes. Above, no bird flies;
> below, no beast walks. In whatever direction you look, and
> as far as you can see, when you seek to know where you
> must go, you are unable to decide. There are only the relics
> of the dead to serve as guide.'

(Fa Xian, quoted in Drège and Bührer, 1989)

If the evidence of documents is anything to go by both Niya and Loulan were already abandoned by the time of Fa Xian's visit. It is therefore unclear as to which towns he is referring to when he describes a kingdom, ardently Buddhist and containing more than 4,000 monks following the Hinayana doctrine and using Indian texts.

Fig. 227 **Carved poplar wood table or altar**
1st to 4th century
H. 60 cm, L. 67.8 cm, D. 45 cm
Unearthed in1901 from Structure N.3, Niya, Xinjiang province
(British Museum)
Items of furniture of such an early date are extraordinarily rare. The use of lotus flower motifs suggests that it had some sort of ritual function in Buddhism.

The Niya-Khotan section

The road between Niya and Khotan was no more merciful to travellers. Xuanzang travelled the road in the opposite direction in 644 and describes a particularly treacherous expanse of the Taklamakan in which the drifting sands and sandstorms, known as *karaburans*, claimed the lives of innumerable travellers and sirens lured men to their doom:

> 'There is neither water nor herbage to be found, and hot
> winds frequently blow. When these winds rise, then both
> men and beasts become confused and forgetful…At times
> sad and plaintive notes are heard and piteous cries, so that
> between the sights and sounds of this desert men get
> confused and know not whither they go. Hence there are
> so many who perish in the journey. But it is all the work
> of demons and evil spirits.'

(Xuanzang, in Beal, 1884)

Four days west of Niya, on the Khotan road is Keriya (Yutian), once an important oasis town on the Southern Silk Road and surrounded by the semi-obliterated remains of shrines and settlements. Site around Keriya, all explored by Stein, include Khadalik, Farhad-beg-yailaki and Darabzandong, all apparently abandoned around the end of the eighth century, presumably when water supplies were exhausted. Indian influence was also active here: at Khadalik Stein found the remains of wall paintings from about the sixth century containing images of Buddha and of Ganesha (the elephant-headed son of the Hindu god Siva) holding a basket of his favourite sweatmeats. The area is still yielding its secrets and it seems that many more towns along the old Silk Road are still buried beneath the sands of the Taklamakan. One such place is Kara-dong, about 190 km north of Keriya and visited by both Hedin and Stein. Stein believed Kara-dong to be a stopping place on an ancient communication route that once followed the course of the Keriya River in a north-south direction. The Keriya appears to have once flowed as far as the Tarim River, and the old trail appears to have followed its course until it joined up with the 'Tianshan Nan Lu' or the 'Route of the Centre', thereby creating a more direct route between Khotan and Kuqa. In 1993 a Sino-French expedition found the remains of a large temple and what appears to be a stupa mound. The site appears to have been occupied from about the second to the fourth century and the delicate paintings of Buddhas discovered on the temple walls are therefore, along with those of Miran, among the earliest in Central Asia.

Stein explored the oasis town of Domoko, just to the northwest of Keriya (Yutian), during his first expedition (1900–1901) and attempted to identify the location of the town of 'Pi-mo'. Pi-mo is described at length by Xuanzang and was the site of miraculous events. In Xuanzang's day a sandalwood figure of the Buddha stood in the city, some 6 metres high and said to date back to the time of Sakyamuni himself. It emitted a constant bright light and possessed the ability to cure diseases and grant wishes. After the Buddha's departure from the world the statue was said to have ascended into the skies and flown north where it alighted in the town of Ho-lo-lo-kia. The residents of the town were atheistic and paid no respect to the statue. An arhat (a monk who has attained enlightenment) arrived in the town and warned the residents that, seven days hence, the city would be destroyed by a deluge of sand and earth. The Arhat's warnings were ignored and, on the evening of the seventh day, the city was obliterated. The only survivor was the Arhat, who escaped through a tunnel. Xuanzang relates that the town of Ho-lo-lo-kia is now no more than a great sand-mound and Stein set out to find it. About 50 km west of Keriya Stein came across a ruined town to which the locals had attached a legend, almost identical to the one attributed to Ho-lo-lo-kia. Further research at the site convinced Stein that he had discovered not Ho-lo-lo-kia but Pi-mo, the earlier home of the statue and the place where Xuanzang had heard the legend. Pi-mo was still occupied when Marco Polo- who called the town 'Pein'- passed through during the thirteenth century.

Khotan

The Khotan-Kashgar section of the Southern Silk Road skirts the lower margins of the Taklamakan. Khotan (known as Yutian or Hetian in Chinese and Kustana in Sanskrit) was perhaps the greatest of the kingdoms of the Southern Silk Road. The town of Khotan, and the kingdom of the same name, were famous for nephrite jade and have supplied China for at least two thousand years. The town is situated between two rivers – the Karakash (Black Jade River) and the Kurungkash (White Jade River) – and boulders are washed down from the Kunlun Mountains to the south and are harvested from the riverbeds. Khotan was once a source of both dark green and white jade but only a relatively small amount of the latter is still obtained from the bed of the Kurungkash River. The travels of the legendary Emperor Mu during the third century BC took him as far as the Kunlun Mountains and, as early as the Western Han dynasty, there are references to Khotan as a source of jade. Sima Qian's annals, 'Records of the Grand Historian' (*Shi Ji*) relate that:

'The emperor [Wudi] also sent envoys to trace the Yellow River to its source. They found that it rises in the land of Yutian among mountains rich in precious stones, many of which they brought back with them. The emperor studied the old maps and books and decided to name these mountains, where the Yellow River has its source, the Kunlun Mountains.'

The Tang Annals (*Xin Tang Shu*) refer to the ease with which precious jade could be gathered during ancient times:

'There is a jade river in Yutian State. People find exquisite jade in the river whenever the moon shines the brightest.'

Legends about the founding of Khotan, in both Tibetan sources and in the accounts of Chinese pilgrims, relate that the city was founded by a group of Indian nobles from Taxila – banished from the court of Ashoka during the third century BC for blinding Kunala, the great king's son. Ashoka was known to have been an ardent Buddhist, suggesting that Khotan may have been one of the first kingdoms of the Tarim Basin to adopt the new religion. The kingdom fell to the Chinese around the first century BC and was the head-quarters of General Ban Chao between 77 and 91 AD but it continued to prosper as a centre for trade and for the study and practice of Hinayana, and later Mahayana Buddhism.

Yotkan, situated about 10 km west of Khotan, is thought to have been the ancient capital of the Khotan Kingdom. Aurel Stein explored many sites – too many to mention here – in and around Khotan during all three of his expeditions. His discoveries at Yotkan concur with early Chinese records, which state that the town was a thriving commercial and religious centre. There were no surviving structures at

Yotkan – it has been submerged beneath paddy fields – but local treasure seekers have dug down to a depth of about 5 metres, revealing strata containing pottery fragments, terracotta figures, jade, seals, coins and manuscripts. The coins found by Stein at Yotkan fall into two broad types: copper examples from the first or second century AD and square-holed examples from the Tang dynasty (618–907). The earlier coins bear legends in both Chinese and Kharosthi, evidence that there was already a substantial Indian community in Khotan during the Han dynasty and that it coexisted with the Chinese settlers in the area. He also found extensive traces of gold leaf, suggesting that the faithful applied the precious material to buildings and images during worship. This is born out by the observations of the monk Fa Xian, a visitor to the kingdom in 401:

> 'Seven or eight le (li) to the west of the city there is what is called the King's New Monastery, the building of which took eighty years, and extended over three reigns. It may be 250 cubits in height, rich in elegant carving and inlaid work, covered with gold and silver, and finished throughout with a combination of all the precious substances.'
>
> (Fa Xian, in Legge, 1886)

By the time of Fa Xian's visit, the kingdom was firmly dominated by the Mahayanists. He tells us that the kingdom had four great monasteries (or fourteen, depending on the translation) and many smaller ones. The greatest of them was the Gomati Monastery – its patron the king himself – and Fa Xian describes a procession in which a large image of the Buddha flanked by two Bodhisattvas is carried on an immense four-wheeled carriage from the monastery to the city gates. Upon arriving at the gates the King of Khotan and his entourage would dress in simple clothes to greet the procession and pay homage by scattering flowers and burning incense.

Khotan's prosperity also depended on sericulture and on the production of fine carpets. Khotan carpets are referred to in many of the Kharosthi documents unearthed by Stein at Loulan and Niya and appear to have been a popular barter-

commodity. According to the Tibetan annals, sericulture reached Khotan around the second century AD, during the reign of King Vijaya Jaya. The Chinese jealously guarded the secret of silk production and it was not until King Vijaya Jaya married a Chinese princess that the Khotanese acquired the technology to produce it (fig. 228).

Dandan-Oilik

The Silk Princess panel (fig. 228) was recovered by Stein at the monastery complex of Dandan-Oilik, on the eastern edge of the Khotan oasis. Dandan-Oilik (in Uighur, 'the place of houses with ivory') is located to the north of the Southern Silk Road and, based on information gleaned from coins and documents, the town appears to have flourished from the fourth to the eighth century. It was abandoned towards the end of the eighth century – a consequence of invasions by Tibetans – and was quickly inundated by the sands of the Taklamakan. On this panel, an attendant on the left points to the cocoons concealed in the princess's headdress and on the far right a lady holds a beating comb and sits before a loom. To her right sits a four-armed deity, perhaps the god of silk weaving. Xuanzang recounts the legend, current at the time of his visit in 644, about the Silk Princess and her role in the introduction of sericulture* to Khotan:

> 'In old time this country knew nothing about mulberry trees or silkworms. Hearing that the eastern country [i.e. China] had them, they sent an embassy to seek for them. At this time the prince of the eastern kingdom kept the secret and would not give the possession of it to any. He kept guard over his territory and would not permit either the seeds of the mulberry or the silkworms' eggs to be carried off.
>
> The king of Kustana [Khotan] sent off to seek a marriage union with a princess of the eastern kingdom [China], in token of his allegiance and submission. The king being well affected to the neighbouring states acceded to his wish. Then the king of Kustana dispatched a messenger to escort the royal princess and gave the following direction:

Fig. 228 **A painted wood panel depicting the story of the Silk Princess**
Ca. 6th century
H. 12 cm, W. 46 cm
From Dandan-Oilik, Xinjiang province
(British Museum-Heritage Images)

Fig. 229 **The D 8 Monastery at Dandan-Oilik, Xinjiang province**
(Photo by Christoph Baumer)

'Speak thus to the eastern princess. Our country has neither silk or silken stuffs. You had better bring with you some mulberry seeds and silkworms, then you can make robes for yourself.'

The princess, hearing these words, secretly procured the seed of the mulberry and silkworms' eggs and concealed them in her head-dress. Having arrived at the barrier, the guard searched everywhere, but he did not dare to remove the princess's headdress. Arriving then in the kingdom of Kustana…they conducted her in great pomp to the royal palace. Here then they left the silkworms and the mulberry seeds. In the spring-time they set the seeds, and when the time for the silkworms had come they gathered leaves for their food; but from their first arrival it was necessary to feed them on different kinds of leaves, but afterwards the mulberry trees began to flourish. Then the queen wrote on a stone the following decree, 'It is not permitted to kill the silkworm! After the butterfly [silk-moth] has gone then the silk may be twined off (the cocoon). Whoever offends against this rule may he be deprived of divine protection.'

(Xuanzang, in Beal, 1884)

This story has an interesting and important counterpart in the annals of the Eastern Roman Empire. In around 550, a group of monks arrived in the capital, Constantinople and presented themselves at the court of the Emperor Justinian. They claimed to know the secret of sericulture and offered to bring silkworm eggs to Constantinople. According to one version, that of Procopius, the monks came from 'Serindia' – they may have been Nestorians from Khotan – and Justinian offered to reward them if they could supply the eggs. The monks returned two years later with eggs concealed in their staffs and Byzantium thus acquired the process of silk production.

Other painted wood panels from Dandan-Oilik contain

* One of the cruel ironies of Khotan's sericulture industry is that it flourished right up until the modern age and, only in recent years, has fallen into decline. As recently as 1959 there were seven million mulberry trees in Khotan Prefecture and the annual output of silkworm cocoons reached a peak of 1,200 tons. During the 1960's China suffered the excesses of the Cultural Revolution during which widespread and arbitrary deforestation occurred. By 1979 there were only two million mulberry trees in Khotan and annual cocoon output had fallen to 400 tons [Figures from Che Muqi, 1989]. The Chinese government is now making a concerted effort to revive the industry and production is again rising.

Fig. 230 **A painted wood votive panel depicting the God of Silk**
Ca. 6th century
H. 33 cm, W. 20.2 cm
From Dandan-Oilik, Xinjiang province
(British Museum)
The bearded figure on this panel wears a gold crown and is dressed in princely robes. He holds the same objects as the four-armed figure in the 'Silk Princess' panel, namely a goblet, a weaver's comb and a shuttle for a loom.

Fig. 231 **Painted wood votive plaque with an image of a rat-headed deity**
Ca. 6th century
H. 10.6 cm; W. 44.8 cm
From Dandan-Oilik,
Xinjiang province
(British Museum)

depictions of the Hindu gods Indra and Brahma and a pair of aristocratic figures of Turkish appearance on camel and horseback, carrying libation cups. A further panel contains a beautiful image of Siva seated above two white Nandi bulls on one side and, on the reverse, a bearded figure of Iranian appearance, identified as the God of Silk (fig. 230).

Khotan is awash with legends like these and one of the most interesting is the story of the rat-king, represented in another of the painted panels from Dandan-Oilik (fig. 231).

Xuanzang described a number of small hills to the west of Khotan, which the local people believed were built by a tribe of sacred rats. The legend relates that the King of Khotan was able to fight off an attack by the Xiongnu when the rats consumed the invaders' bowstrings and harnesses. A shrine was erected by the Khotanese to the west of the capital and the rats were worshipped as saviours of the kingdom.

The excellence of Dandan-Oilik's paintings reflects the great skill of the artists of Khotan. A number of Khotanese painters were active in China during the Sui and early Tang dynasties and two of the most distinguished were Weichi Boqina and his son, Weichi Yiseng – members of the Khotan royal family. They specialized in a 'relief' style of painting in which layers of paint were built up on silk until the portrait or subject emerged. Khotanese artists are also recorded as having worked at the Tibetan court during the ninth century and strongly influenced the development of Tibetan art.

Stein discovered large numbers of stucco images at Dandan-Oilik; seated and standing Buddhas as well as *Gandharvas* (celestial deities, sometimes known as musicians of the gods). These images were produced in moulds and were then fastened to the walls of approximately ten shrines or monasteries identified at the site. They are closely linked to the Greco-Buddhist art of Gandhara, a consequence of the spread of Buddhism along the Silk Road. A pair of large bronze Buddha heads, as well as two moulded clay figures of Harpocrates (the Egyptian god of silence) and a chubby baby Herakles (Hercules), all found at Yotkan by the Otani Mission of 1910, are further proof that East-West trade was thriving. The two Buddha heads date to around the third century and may well be the oldest Buddhist sculptures in eastern Central Asia.

Other motifs from the classical world are found on the remains of a pair of trousers from the Shanpula cemetery in Luopu County, about 20 km southeast of Khotan. Shanpula occupies an area of about 20 hectares and contains hundreds

Fig. 232 **The Shanpula cemetery, Luopu County, near Khotan, Xinjiang province**

Fig. 233 **Remains of a pair of trousers with designs of a centaur and a warrior**
Han dynasty, ca. 1st century AD
L. 116 cm
Unearthed from Tomb 1 at Shanpula, Luopu County, Xinjiang province in 1984
(Xinjiang Uighur Autonomous Regional Museum)

This textile fragment is unique among all of the archeological finds of China. The upper section depicts a centaur blowing a long horn as his cape billows behind him. The lower part shows a warrior of distinctly non-Chinese appearance wearing a colourful tunic and carrying a spear. Its singular design raises intriguing questions about how it arrived at the site. Luopu was a prosperous centre for iron smelting during the Han dynasty and would therefore have attracted foreign visitors in large numbers. The fragment may therefore have been imported from Parthian Iran or Western Central Asia or may have belonged to some Indo-European migrant who settled in the area during ancient times. We already have evidence that there were Iranians in the Tarim Basin area from the contents of the letter to the King of Khotan found at Endere (see p. 175). The motifs on this textile fragment are therefore not entirely surprising but they are a further sign of the high level of commercial and religious activity that was occurring along this section of the Silk Road.

of graves dating from the Han dynasty onwards (fig. 232).

Cultural relics recovered from the site have revealed much about the cultural and commercial activity of the Silk Road (fig. 233).

Among the many cultural relics recovered from Shanpula is an embroidered design of a stag, strongly influenced by the nomads to the north (fig. 234).

Chinese authority was reasserted over the whole of the Tarim Basin during the seventh century and Khotan became one of the key garrisons of the Western Regions. Even after Chinese power declined during the eighth century the kingdom continued to be an important commercial centre. A celebrated portrait of the King of Khotan in Cave 98 at Dunhuang, painted around 920, reveals something of the enduring prosperity of the kingdom. His bride, a daughter of the Cao rulers of Dunhuang, wears a crown and necklace of Khotan jade (see fig. 166). As late as the thirteenth century, when Marco Polo visited, the inhabitants of Khotan had converted to Islam but trade continued to flourish and the state was still sending embassies to China during the Ming dynasty (1368–1644).

Rawak

Rawak ('High Mansion'), north-east of Khotan, is believed to be one of the largest and most important sites in Central Asia, despite the fact that only the stupa is visible above the sands of the Taklamakan. The stupa at Rawak, about 9.5 metres in extant height, is the largest on the Southern Silk Road. Stein discovered the site in April 1901 and worked for eight days in scorching heat and raking sandstorms. He uncovered about ninety sculptures adorning both sides of the walls of the stupa court: the site and its statuary dating to around the fourth to sixth centuries. The base of the stupa consists of a cross-shaped platform with a staircase at each end, a more refined version of the type found in the Gandhara region. The sculptures unearthed by Stein – and those discovered by later Japanese and German expeditions

Fig. 234 **Embroidered design of a stag**
Han dynasty, (206 BC–220 AD)
H. 7 cm (approx.)
From the Shanpula cemetery, Luopu County, Xinjiang province
(Kashgar Museum)

– were mostly life-sized painted stucco images of standing Buddhas, carved in relief, but four guardian figures (*lokapalas*) and a number of exquisitely jewelled Bodhisattvas were also found. The earliest are strongly reminiscent of Gandhara sculptures, most notably those of the Jaulian Monastery at Taxila (see p. 39). They date to around the fourth century or even possibly a little earlier. Later images, perhaps fifth century in date, are smaller in size and are more closely related to the styles of early Chinese Buddhist art- at Binglingsi, for example (see p. 115). Whether Rawak served as a prototype for the early Buddhist art of China or whether it acquired the styles developed there is unclear. The relief sculptures of Rawak were too brittle for Stein to recover intact and were therefore measured, photographed and then covered again with sand. Most examples of Rawak sculpture in western museums are therefore little more than fragments and Stein's photographs of the sculptures, still in situ, are far more impressive (fig. 236).

Most of the ruins around Khotan are in poor condition. This is most likely a consequence of the fact that the area fell to the Muslim Karakhanid Turks during the tenth century and the destruction of Buddhist sites that we saw at Kashgar occurred here as well. Given the turbulent history of the region it is miraculous that any artefacts have survived at all.

In early Chinese records, Karghalik (Yecheng) is referred to, first as *Tzu-ho* and, subsequently, as *Chu-chü-po*. The town sits on a fertile oasis between Khotan and Yarkand.

The area west of Khotan is now a fertile and populous hinterland, thanks to modern irrigation methods, but during the heyday of the Silk Road it was a different and far more hostile environment. The city of Yarkand (Shache) sits on the Yarkand River and was capital of the kingdom of the same name. By 100 BC it was firmly under Chinese control and became one of the 36 states of the Western Regions. Yarkand flourished as result of its position at a junction of the caravan-routes that led west to Central Asia and south over the Pamirs to Ladakh and on to India. During the Wang Mang interregnum (9–23 AD) China lost control of many of these states and Yarkand seized the opportunity to increase its power. For a brief period, from about 33–61 AD, it was the most powerful kingdom of the Western Regions, dominating Khotan, Shanshan and Kuqa. Its power did not last, however, and Khotan soon reasserted control over the area. For a brief period, from about 63 to 73 AD, the Southern Silk Road was dominated by the kingdoms of Khotan and Shanshan. By 94 AD, the redoubtable General Ban Chao had seized control of the entire Tarim Basin, defeated the Xiongnu and placed the region firmly under Chinese suzerainty. Yarkand continued to prosper, however. From about the sixth century AD the kingdom became a centre for silk production to rival Khotan and the town became as rich as Kashgar.

Fig. 235 **The Rawak Stupa**
Ca. 4th century

Fig. 236 **Photograph of painted stucco sculptures of standing and seated Buddhas**
Ca. 4th century
On the inner south-west wall of the Rawak Stupa Court, Xinjiang province
Photograph by Aurel Stein
(After Stein, 1907)
Visible above and to the right of the seated Buddha are several rare examples of standing Buddhas. The sculptures shown in this photograph have fared badly since Stein's visit. Local authorities removed the sand covering them and they were left exposed for a time. They were then subjected to vandalism and what remained was eventually reburied.

Silk Road - Principal Routes

Irkeshtam

Kashgar

Yengisar

Ghez Canyon

SOUTHERN SILK ROAD

▲ Mt Kongur

Yarkand (Shache)

▲ Muztagh Ata

Tajikistan

Tashkurgan

Yecheng

PAMIRS

Tajikistan

Afghanistan
Wakhan Corridor

Khunjerab Pass

■ Taloqan

Khudabad ■

Pakistan

Batura Glacier ■
Passu Glacier ■   ■ Shishkot

China

Hunza River   Karimabad

Nomal ■

Kargah ■   ■ Gilgit
Danyor

■ Chitral

Indus River

Jaglot ■

Thor
Shatial   ■   ■

Indus River

Chilas ■

Pakistan

Dasu ■
Jalkot ■

▲ Nanga Parbat

India

Charikar
■ Shotorak
■ Begram

Besham ■
Mingora ■   Thakot

Kabul   Jalalabad

Mt Pirsar

Mansehra ■

Hadda ■

Sahri Bahlol ■

Charsadda ■   **Mardan**

Peshawar

Khost ■

Shah-ji-ki-Dheri   **Attock**   **Taxila**

Indus River

THE SILK ROAD
BETWEEN CHINA AND INDIA

SECTION V

The Silk Road Between China and India

Fig. 237 **The plain at the top of the Ghez Defile, Xinjiang province**

Beyond Yarkand the Southern Silk Road runs northwest along the southern fringes of the Taklamakan, through Yengisar to Kashgar. At Kashgar, the circle is completed and the Northern and Southern Roads merge. From Kashgar begins the long road to India, the ancient route of devotees, traders and conquerors. The modern road – retracing the old highway – rises from the Kashgar plain towards the Pakistani border. It passes through the eastern Pamirs, soon joining and following the course of the Ghez River. At the top of the Ghez Canyon, the landscape opens out into a vast plain surrounded by sand dunes. The landscape is bleak and forbidding, a foretaste of what awaited travellers through the high passes to India (fig. 237).

Marco Polo journeyed through the high plains of the Pamirs during the thirteenth century and describes a barren landscape, devoid of pasturage and food supplies and occupied by 'a tribe of savage, ill-disposed, and idolatrous people' who lived by hunting. Towering above the road are the massive peaks of the Pamirs – Mt Kongur and Muztagh Ata, both exceeding 7,500 metres. The lake at Kara Kul, surrounded by verdant pasturelands, offers a brief respite but its elevation is so great – around 3,800 metres – that it has been known to freeze even in mid-summer. Further on the road comes to the small town of Tashkurgan, 3,600 metres above sea level and almost 300 km from Kashgar.

Tashkurgan

Tashkurgan ('Stone Tower') was the capital of the Pamir kingdom of Sarikol. The 'Stone Tower' is mentioned in many early chronicles, in particular those of the Alexandrian geographer Ptolemy. Writing in about 140 AD, Ptolemy obtained his information from the reports of a Macedonian Greek merchant named Maes Titianus, active about 50 years before. Maes did not make the journey himself but employed a network of agents to reconnoitre a new route between the Mediterranean and China. The intention was to bypass the Parthian merchants of Persia, intermediaries in the lucrative early trade of the Silk Road. Ptolemy utilized the information contained in Maes Titianus' reports as well as from contemporary travellers and estimated that the distance between Hierapolis (Membij) in Syria and *Sera Metropolis*, (presumably Xian and referred to as the place where foreign merchants obtained their silk), was about 11,000 km. He records that the halfway point on the journey, and therefore the point midway between China and the West, was the 'Stone Tower'. In fact a number of Central Asian cities – Tashkent for example – have names which approximate to the 'tower of stone' or 'stone castle' but the most likely location was Tashkurgan on the eastern edge of the Pamirs. Ptolemy also tells us that the journey from the 'Stone Tower' to *Sera Metropolis* took seven months.

At the time of Xuanzang's visit in 644 AD, the town and state were called 'Qiepantuo' (Persian for 'Mountain Road') and the region was populated by followers of the Buddha. The kingdom seems to have flourished between the fifth and eighth centuries when it submitted to Tibetan control and, during the latter part of the Tang dynasty, the town was a Chinese military outpost. Xuanzang was impressed with the king, a man he describes as 'upright and honest…his external manner is quiet and unassuming; he is of a vigorous mind and loves learning'. He was less impressed with the populace. He describes them as 'without any rules or propriety…Their appearance is common and revolting'. The rulers of the Qiepantuo kingdom believed themselves to be descended maternally from the Han Chinese and paternally from the Sun God. Xuanzang records a local legend from the time before the founding of the kingdom, when Tashkurgan was a desert valley in the Pamirs. A king of Persia had taken a Han Chinese princess as his bride and had sent an escort to accompany her to his domain. When the party reached Tashkurgan they were prevented from proceeding further by the presence of brigands in the area. The princess was placed on an isolated mountain peak and guarded day and night. When order was restored to the area the party was about to proceed when they discovered that the princess was with child. The officials escorting her to Persia, fearing the wrath of the king, were panic stricken but were told by her servant that she had been visited by a god of the sun each day at noon and it was he who was father of the child she carried. Afraid to return to Persia, the party built a palace on top of a nearby mountain from which the princess ruled the area. At length, she bore a son 'of extraordinary beauty and perfect parts…able to fly through the air and control the winds and snow'. He came to rule the entire region and, even after his death, he continued to perform miraculous deeds. He died at a great age and was interred in a great mountain cave about 45 km southeast of Tashkurgan. His remains were seen by Xuanzang and had not decomposed, giving the impression that he was asleep. From time to time the people of the kingdom would change his clothes and place incense and flowers at his side. There is still a citadel at Tashkurgan, built of rammed earth and, according to local legend, the old abode of the Han Princess. The deserted, silent 'Princess' Castle' is saturated with atmosphere and mystery and there are traces of more ancient remains at the site, but archeological evidence suggests that the date of the present structure is no earlier than the Yuan dynasty (1279–1368) (fig. 238).

On the Kashgar side of Tashkurgan is the Tangitar Gorge, identified by Aurel Stein as the place where Xuanzang was set upon by bandits. In the ensuing mêlée Xuanzang's magnificent white elephant, presented by the Indian King Harsha to carry him and his precious Buddhist relics back to China, was drowned.

Fig. 238 **The Princess Castle, Tashkurgan, Xinjiang province**

To the south of Tashkurgan the modern road follows the approximate course of the old Silk Road. After about 30 km the road divides into two, one route passing into Pakistan between the Pamirs and the Karakorums through the 4,730 metre Khunjerab Pass, and the other following the Wakhan Corridor to Afghanistan. The first route is known today as the Karakorum Highway and is the highest public road in the world. It first follows the course of the Khunjerab and Hunza Rivers and finally, south of Gilgit, the great Indus – the 'Father of Rivers'. The highway, known by its familiar title 'the KKH', sticks to the Indus Valley right down as far as Thakot, south of Besham, and then makes a gentle descent to

Fig. 239 **The Khunjerab Pass at the borders of China and Pakistan**

Fig. 240. Xuanzang's crossing point on the Indus River
Attock Fort and the Indus River beside the Grand Trunk Road, Northwest Pakistan
The remains of a Mughal era bridge and the old highway are visible.

the upland plateau of modern day Islamabad. A short distance to the west of Islamabad is the ancient Kushan capital of Taxila (see p. 39), the point from which Buddhism began its spread into China. The route of the KKH therefore approximates to one of the two principal 'pilgrim roads' between India and China, although there were many other subsidiary paths across the mountains. The second route, also terminating in Taxila, passed along the Wakhan Corridor to Balkh in the ancient Greek kingdom of Bactria, and then turned south to cross the Hindu Kush. It then passed through Bamiyan and then continued down through the Khyber Pass into what is now modern Pakistan.

The journeys of two of history's most celebrated Buddhist monks – Fa Xian in about 400 and Sung Yun around 520 – approximately followed the first route. Sung Yun was a monk from Dunhuang who was sent by the Northern Wei rulers of China as an ambassador to the King of the Hepthalites- rulers of Northwest India at that time- to obtain Buddhist sutras. The indomitable Xuanzang favoured the second route, when he made his way back to China from India in 644. All three record that mischievous dragons and evil spirits populated the mountains between China and India: it seems that the fears of travellers who attempted to cross the mountains engendered these stories. Xuanzang has left us with a particularly colourful description of such

creatures. As he headed from Peshawar towards Taxila on his way to India, instead of keeping to the course of today's Grand Trunk Road – the most direct route, even in antiquity – he veered off north to explore the Buner and Swat Valleys (the latter known by its ancient name, *Uddiyana*). At Attock, south of Hund, he crossed the Indus to rejoin the old highway:

> *'Its waters are pure and clear as a mirror as they roll along with impetuous flow. Poisonous* Nâgas *[water spirits] and hurtful beasts occupy the caverns and clefts along its sides. If a man tries to cross the river carrying with him valuable goods or gems or rare kinds of flowers or fruits, or especially relics of the Buddha, the boat is frequently engulphed by the waves.'*

(Xuanzang, from Beal, 1884)

The Karakorum ('Black Mountain') route, as we have seen, passes through the Khunjerab Pass. The Tajik name Khunjerab means 'Blood Valley', perhaps a reference to the bandits from Hunza and Wakhi who continued to prey on caravans heading to and from Kashgar right up until the end of the nineteenth century. The vistas of the route through the Karakorums must have terrified early travellers. The road passes through a treeless alpine wilderness with little shelter from the brutal weather and few opportunities for travellers

Fig. 241 **The Passu Glacier, Northern Pakistan**

to obtain supplies. The only sign of life is the occasional wild yak and the odd glimpse of the rare, elusive Marco Polo sheep. During its passage along the course of the Hunza River the road passes through the Gojal Region, a high plateau ravaged by floods, rock and mudslides. Near Passu the majestic Batura Glacier, 60 km in length, nudges the edge of the highway. The glacier is in a constant state of advance and retreat and, as recently as 1976, it devoured both the road and the bridge that carried the road over the river. Further on is the white expanse of the Passu Glacier, gigantic and awe inspiring, an utter contrast to the grey ice of the Batura (fig. 241).

All along the Karakorum Highway are inscriptions pecked or chiselled onto the rocks by the side of the road and along the riverbanks. To date, around 30,000 petroglyphs and 5,000 inscriptions in more than ten different languages or writing systems have been identified. The earliest, usually depicting animals and hunting scenes, date back to prehistoric times and the latest date to around the fifteenth century. These inscriptions record the passage of generation after generation of travellers and their distribution has enabled scholars to confirm that today's KKH follows the approximate course of the ancient road. They were also left by local inhabitants, however, and their contents tells us who ruled the area at that time, what the prevailing religious beliefs were and what type of culture existed. From the first to around the ninth century AD, the dominant religion in the area was unquestionably Buddhism. Dedicatory inscriptions and drawings of Buddhas, stupas and Buddhist symbols occur with great frequency.

The Hunza Valley

The first of the major sites containing petroglyphs is situated near Karimabad, a modern town set high above the junction of the Hunza and Nagar Rivers, 50 km from Passu. The historic capital of Hunza was Baltit and Karimabad has developed as an offshoot of the old town. The medieval forts at Baltit, and the even older one at Altit – each around 2,800 metres above sea level – are remarkable examples of early wooden architecture. Baltit Fort was the seat of the Hunzakut royal family until the 1950s and was then abandoned. It was restored between 1992 and 1996 and is now a museum. The earliest parts of the building, according to radiocarbon tests conducted during the restoration work, date back to the first half of the thirteenth century and it is clear that the structure has presided over the old road for centuries. Its wooden construction, distinctly Tibetan in appearance, has allowed the structure to survive the region's frequent earthquakes and to facilitate the rapid repair of damage inflicted by successive waves of invaders (fig. 242).

Fig. 242 **Baltit Fort, Hunza Valley, Northern Pakistan**
In the foreground are the lush orchards of the old town of Baltit and beyond, to the north, are the Karakorums with the peak of Ultar II visible.

Fig. 243 **The Sacred Rock of Hunza, beside the KKH near Karimabad, Northern Pakistan**
Altit Fort is just visible on the cliff in the distance.

Two kilometres below Karimabad is the old village of Ganesh and 2 km beyond that is the Sacred Rock of Hunza, on the banks of the Hunza River (fig. 243). The Sacred Rock of Hunza is known to local people as Haldeikish ('the place of the male ibexes'), a frequent theme of its many petroglyphs. Though much damaged by centuries of rock falls and by the hammers of men searching for rubies, the Sacred Rock survives as nothing less than a visitors' book of the centuries. The old road appears to have run right past it to Ganesh. One of the earliest inscriptions at the site, on a second slightly smaller rock, is a Kharosthi reference to the first Kushan emperor: 'the most devout, the great king, steadfast, [Kujula] Kadphises'. This suggests that by the reign of Kujula Kadphises (ca. 30–80 AD), the Kushans were already in firm control of the area (fig. 244).

There are inscriptions in Sogdian, the Silk Road's *lingua franca*, and a remarkable Chinese inscription on the second, smaller boulder at the site (fig. 245), referring to the passage of an ambassador from the court of the Northern Wei (386–534).

The inscription in fig. 245 refers to the passage of an

Fig. 244 **Kharosthi inscription referring to Kujula Kadphises
(ca. 30–80 AD)**
The Sacred Rock of Hunza
Near Karimabad, Northern Pakistan

Fig. 245 **Chinese inscription referring to the embassy of Gu Wei-long**
Ca. 6th century
The Sacred Rock of Hunza
Near Karimabad, Northern Pakistan
'Gu Wei-Long, envoy of the Great Wei is despatched to Mi-mi'.*
The monk Sung Yun was dispatched by the Wei on a diplomatic mission to the
Hepthalite rulers of Gandhara in about 520, and it may well be that Gu Wei-
Long was his contemporary.

ambassador from the court of the Northern Wei (386–534)
and translates as follows (see opposite):

There are also Tibetan words among the inscriptions at
the site and these may well date to the eighth century when
Tibetans dominated the area.

The Hunza Valley is lush and fertile – a stark contrast to
the arid wilderness of much of the trail from China. Stone
irrigation channels have created a verdant landscape of pop-
lars, apricot and walnut trees, and fields of maize and wheat.
Early travellers must have experienced a palpable sense of
relief as the valley opened up before them. The longevity of
the inhabitants of Hunza is renowned and the existence of a
green valley high among the Karakorums has led to its
identification with the legends of Shangri La. The truth is
more prosaic but the utter isolation of the place, until the
opening of the KKH, has ensured that these legends have
endured. The Hunza people of today belong predominantly
to the Ishmaili sect of Islam – their spiritual leader the Aga
Khan – but their physiognomy speaks of blood infused from
many countries of the Silk Road (fig. 247).

Many Hunzakuts claim descent from soldiers left behind
during Alexander's campaigns through the Swat Valley in
327 BC. This belief occurs elsewhere in the Northwest
Frontier areas, most notably the Kalash people of the Hindu
Kush valleys southwest of Chitral. The Kalash worship a

Fig. 247 **A man of Hunza**

Fig. 246 **'Shangri La'**
The Hunza Valley, facing south
from Baltit Fort along the Hunza
River. The peak of Rakaposhi
in the Karakorums is visible in
the distance.

* The inscription is discussed at
length by Ma Yong in Jettmar,
1989. He identifies Mi-mi as the
region known to Arab
geographers as 'Maymurgh',
situated to the southeast of
Samarkand although Jettmar
disagrees and suggests that the
place was an as yet, unidentified
town in the Gandhara region.

pantheon of gods, drink wine and sacrifice animals. The evidence is sparse but blue eyes and fair hair are not uncommon among both Hunzakut and Kalash alike. What is undeniable is that Northwest Pakistan's position on an ancient trade route has attracted visitors – and surely settlers, too – from many of the countries of the Silk Road.

The road continues southwards along the Hunza River for 105 km from Karimabad towards Gilgit in sight of the great peaks of the Karakorum Range- Rakaposhi, Diran and Malubiting are all over 7,000 metres and dominate the landscape. About 10 km east of Gilgit the Hunza River joins the Gilgit River, just to the west of the town of Danyor. An ancient trade route leads west up the Gilgit River into the Hindu Kush, through the region known today as the Northern Areas, but the main KKH continues southwards. Danyor is an important site on the pilgrims' road to India. In later centuries the riverbank was used as a place for cremation by Hindus (known as a burning *ghat*) but the

Fig. 248 **Inscribed rock at Danyor, near Gilgit, Northern Pakistan.**
Ca. 8th century

Fig. 249 **The Kargah Buddha**
Ca. 7th or 8th century
The entire aspect and location of this Buddha are quite magical. The spot has clearly been chosen with care: beneath him is a quiet glade with a stream running through it and he faces the setting sun so that only when the last rays fall upon him, does the entire figure become illuminated.

Fig. 250 **The Meeting Point of Three Ranges**
South of Gilgit, Northern Pakistan
Facing north, the Hindu Kush and the old road (now followed by the KKH) are to the left, the Himalayas to the right and the Karakorums in front. The Gilgit River forks to the left and the Indus to the right in this photo.

large number of inscribed boulders in the area indicate that it was a meeting place for the faithful during the seventh and eighth centuries. Among incised drawings of hunters and animals is a large and clear depiction of a cross, left there by Nestorian Christians. In Danyor town, in the garden of a local man named Yurmaz Khan, is a massive rock about 4 metres in length. The rock was inscribed in Sanskrit in about the eighth century and sets out the names of a line of local rulers, perhaps men of Tibetan descent who came to dominate the area (fig. 248).

Ten kilometres from Gilgit, at Kargah, a massive figure of the Buddha has been carved on the cliff face. He has presided over the area since the seventh or eighth century, standing with his right hand raised in *abhayamudra* – the gesture of dispelling fear (fig. 249).

Nearby are the masonry remains of four stupas and a Buddhist monastery. During the 1930s, a large number of birch-bark manuscripts were found within the largest of the stupas. Dating to around the fifth century the 'Gilgit Manuscripts' contain the original Sanskrit canon of Buddhism.

Between 730 and 783 Gilgit and its surrounding area were the scene of sporadic warfare between Tibet and China. The local rulers of the kingdom of Little Balur, transferred their loyalties from one side to another with increasing desperation and were attacked by both sides for their pains.

Forty kilometres south of Gilgit is the confluence of the Gilgit and Indus Rivers. The point where the rivers meet also marks the point of convergence of three great mountain ranges: the Himalayas, the Karakorums and the Hindu Kush (fig. 250).

Fig. 251 **Nanga Parbat, 'The Naked Mountain', Western Himalayas**

From the meeting point of the three ranges the Silk Road follows the course of the Indus as it heads southwestwards and then south towards Taxila. In the opposite direction a section of road leads east and southeast along the Indus Gorge to Skardu, headquarters of the Baltistan area. The Baltis' ancestry is a strange mix of Mongol and Tibetan (the latter still spoken there), a legacy of centuries of conquest. The Indus rises in Tibet and flows through a deep cleft towards Gilgit, dividing the Karakorum from the Himalayas. Dominating the entire area is the eighth highest mountain in the world: Nanga Parbat ('The Naked Mountain') at the western limit of the Himalayas, is a colossus of over 8,000 metres (fig. 251).

Shatial and Chilas

The biggest concentration of petroglyphs and inscriptions is to be found on the rocks beside the Indus at Shatial and Chilas. There is a very logical reason for this: Chilas has been the principal crossing-point of the Indus since time immemorial and is also the junction of routes leading north and south. There are ancient routes leading from Chilas to the Babusar Pass and across the Kaghan Valley to Mansehra. Another route leads across the Indus, traversing the Khinnar Valley to Gilgit – a distance of about 150 km.

In the Chilas area, gold has been washed from the sand of the Indus River for centuries. During the summer, meltwater from the mountains causes the Indus to flood and gold dust is washed downstream where villagers collect it. Commentators from the Classical world, including Herodotus, Strabo and Megasthenes, describe a large tribe of mountain-dwelling Indians who collected gold dust from giant anthills. The ants, said to be as big as foxes, threw gold-laced sand in the air as they burrowed. A possible

explanation for this legend is that the men who conducted the lucrative trade in the gold wished to conceal its origin.

Ancient records reveal that Chilas was the name given to the entire district – not just the city. Early travellers called it 'Vira Somonagara' or 'The Heroic City of the Moon' and have inscribed the name at Thalpan Bridge just east of Chilas. There are petroglyphs on both sides of the river at Chilas. The earliest date to the first or second century BC and were left by nomads from the northern steppes who travelled the grand old road. The drawings are in 'animal style' with hunting and battle motifs most frequently depicted. Scythians, Parthians and Yuezhi – the last migrating into the area from China's Gansu province and eventually founding the Kushan Empire – all appear to have left some of these early petroglyphs. At the Chilas I site a modern bridge marks the site of what must have been the ancient crossing place. Chilas I, like its ancient name, really does resemble a barren rock-strewn moonscape. As the visitor wanders around he can easily imagine himself as a voyager to some long

Fig. 253 **Petroglyph depicting the Buddha seated beneath the Bodhi tree and a stupa**
Ca. 8th century
Chilas I site, Northern Pakistan
This Kashmir Style image, with its beautiful devata (celestial or divine being) depicts the period before the Buddha's enlightenment, as he meditates beneath the Bodhi tree at Bodghaya.

Fig. 252 **Modern day traders on the 'long old road to China'**
Pakistani lorry drivers with their elaborately decorated vehicles near Shatial, Northern Pakistan

deserted other world in which, here and there, ancient travellers have left their mark.

By the first century AD the Silk Road was fully established and passing merchants and Buddhist pilgrims began to leave their marks on the rocks. There are inscriptions in Brahmi, Sogdian, Iranian, Kharosthi and Sanskrit; and drawings containing motifs from Buddhism, Hinduism and Nestorian Christianity. The fifth to eighth centuries saw the domination of the area by Buddhists and the petroglyphs reflect this. Buddhist pictographs in late Gandhara style are to be found in abundance at Chilas but there are also influences from China, Kashmir and Tibet. The most popular motifs from this period are seated images of Buddha, standing Bodhisattva figures and stupas- the last often drawn with flying prayer banners. Inscriptions, usually in Brahmi, have been left by generations of passing travellers. They frequently invoke the protection of the Buddha or Avalokitesvara – 'Salutation to the Buddha' and 'Salutation to Lokesvara-The work of Shimadeva, along with his wife' are typical inscriptions. The pilgrim Shimadeva seems to have been especially pious: he has left his name on a number of drawings at Chilas (fig. 253).

A second example, also in Kashmir style and also from the Chilas I site, shows a man with Central Asian features genuflecting beside a stupa (fig. 254).

These images are not safe from the attentions of modern-

Fig. 254 **Petroglyph depicting a stupa with attendant**
Ca. 8th century
Chilas I site, Northern Pakistan

day iconoclasts. A number of the petroglyphs show signs of recent defacement: a beautiful drawing of a seated Buddha with three smaller attendants, all bearing injuries inflicted during a recent attack with a sharp tool, is but one example.

After the eighth century a strange group of people appeared in the locality. Described by Ahmad Dani as the

Fig. 255 **The Indus and high desert at Thor, Northern Pakistan**

Fig. 256 **Petroglyphs at Shatial, Northern Pakistan, an ancient crossing point on the Indus**

Fig. 257 **Petroglyph depicting an ithyphallic figure assaulting a second figure**
Ca. 5th century(?)
Thor, Northern Pakistan
(After Jettmar, K. et al., 1989–1994)
The later edition, of the second figure with the dog or goat, is visible to the right.

people of the 'Battle-Axe Culture' they rode and danced on horseback, worshipped Vishnu and Shiva and wielded large fan-shaped axes. Their language was Brahmi and their art is littered with wheel symbols, horses and axe motifs. They disappeared from history as mysteriously as they emerged.

Just outside Chilas are more large boulders, one with a Kharoshthi inscription referring to the great Parthian King Gondophares (r. ca. 20–50 AD), for whom St Thomas the Apostle was asked to construct a palace in Taxila:

'Vitaspa priyati Guduvharasa raja'

('Beloved of Vitaspa, King Gondophares')

It is unsurprising that there should be invocations to the Buddha throughout this region. The landscape is a harsh, treeless wilderness with few places to find food (fig. 255).

Inscriptions in Sogdian language have been found in large numbers at Shatial Bridge, 30 km from Chilas which, like its neighbour, is an important crossing point on the Indus. Iranian inscriptions (at the western end of the site), and Brahmi (at the eastern end), have also been identified and it appears that Shatial was some sort of ancient entrepôt where Sogdian traders exchanged their goods for merchandise brought up from India and Gandhara. Research by Karl Jettmar and others indicates that this was indeed the case. Sogdian merchants may have been prevented from continuing further and Shatial therefore

Fig. 258 **'Fa Xian's Crossing'**
On the Indus near Besham, Swat District, Northern Pakistan
The KKH is visible above the far bank of the river.

seems to have marked an international boundary between two worlds (fig. 256).

There seems to have been little love lost between the Sogdian fire Zoroastrians of the north and the Brahmi speaking Buddhists of the south. Graffiti and sexually explicit drawings on the rocks at Shatial and at the mouth of the Thor Valley, 33 km to the east, contain taunts from both sides. In a number of the drawings are monkeys with upper bodies in the shape of phalli and, at Thor (also known as Sthavira – 'the most venerable'), an androgynous figure with long Buddha-like earlobes clutches a monk's begging bowl as he is violated by a figure with a large phallus. The second figure seems to have a cranial bump (*usnisha*), usually associated with the Buddha. Karl Jettmar (Jettmar, 1989) proposes that the drawing was left by a Sogdian merchant: a lewd imputation to a supposed predilection for homosexuality among the Buddhists of the lands to the south. To the right is a further drawing of a man in a Persian coat – the dress favoured by Sogdian merchants – sodomizing what appears to be a dog or a goat. The latter appears to have been added later, perhaps in retaliation to the initial taunt (fig. 257).

The road from Shatial to Besham, a distance of 140 km, passes through a region known as Indus Kohistan. The Indus cuts a deep narrow gorge flanked by vertical cliffs devoid of vegetation. Pakistani and Chinese engineers dynamited the modern route through the rock within the past thirty years, at considerable cost in human life. The area is barren and harsh, deprived of sunlight by the high cliffs in places and prone to rock falls and flash floods. It is not surprising that travellers on the old route avoided it, preferring instead to head over to Jalkot across the Sapat plateau towards the Harban Valley or via the Babusar Pass (see map).

Besham

Just to the south of the town of Besham, the Indus plunges through a steep sided gorge. Aurel Stein believed that this was the site of a harrowing crossing made by the monk Fa Xian. The monk describes a point on the Indus where men had bored through the rock and suspended ladders. After descending the ladders, Fa Xian crossed by a hanging rope-bridge (fig. 258).

Fig. 259 **Mount Pirsar (Aornos)**
West of Thakot, Northern Pakistan
The far bank, including Pirsar itself, are in the Swat Region whereas the near bank, including the town of Thakot, are in Hazara. The Pirsar heights, and the ruins of an ancient fort upon it, were fully explored by Aurel Stein in 1904. He identified the peak as the likely site of the 'Rock of Aornos'; a fortress stormed by Alexander the Great during his winter campaigns of 328–327 BC. By the spring of 327 BC Alexander and his army had crossed the Indus and accepted the surrender of Taxila (see p. 39).

Fig. 260 **Edicts of the Emperor Ashoka (ca. 269–232 BC)**
Mansehra, Northwest Pakistan

Fig. 261 **The Taxila Valley with the old road to Mansehra (now the KKH) rising to the right**

Thakot

'…He wandered on
Till vast Aornos seen from Petra's steep
Hung o'er the low horizon like a cloud;
Through Balk, and where the desolated tombs
Of Parthian kings scatter to every wind
Their wasting dust, wildly he wandered on…'

(Percy Bysshe Shelley, 'Alastor, or the Spirit of Solitude')

Shelley's geography is fanciful but the places are real. About 10 km west of Thakot and the Indus is the 2,160 metre peak of Pirsar (fig. 259).

Just beyond Thakot the road veers away from the Indus and, after a brief climb, begins its slow descent through the Hazara region towards the Peshawar Plain. The road passes through the village of Batagram with its Kushan-era Buddhist remains and then continues on south through pine forests, eventually flattening into the Pakhli Plain that surrounds the city of Mansehra.

Mansehra is situated 90 km from Thakot, at the junction of the main road leading north and a second route leading across to Kashmir. It has evidently been an important city for centuries. The great Mauryan Emperor Ashoka (r. ca. 269–232 BC) left fourteen inscriptions on three large rocks at Mansehra during the third century BC (fig. 260). Ashoka was a conqueror who came to regret the suffering caused by his military campaigns. He embraced the concept of non-violence espoused in Buddhism and his edicts, found in all parts of India except for the extreme south, urge tolerance and restraint. The edicts, now faded almost to the point of illegibility, are written in Prakrit in the local Kharosthi script and reveal a remarkably compassionate side to a man who lived in a time of conflict and invasion:

'That person who does reverence to his own sect and disparages other sects- does all this only out of attachment to his own sect. That person…by acting thus injures very greatly his own sect.'

(Rock Edict no. XII, Mansehra. Abridged from Dani, 1983)

After Mansehra the journey nears its end. Ninety-five kilometres from Mansehra, after passing through the city of Abbottabad – built by the British as a hill-station during the nineteenth century – the road descends to the Peshawar Plain and arrives at Taxila, among the greatest of all the cities of the Silk Road (fig. 261; see also p. 39).

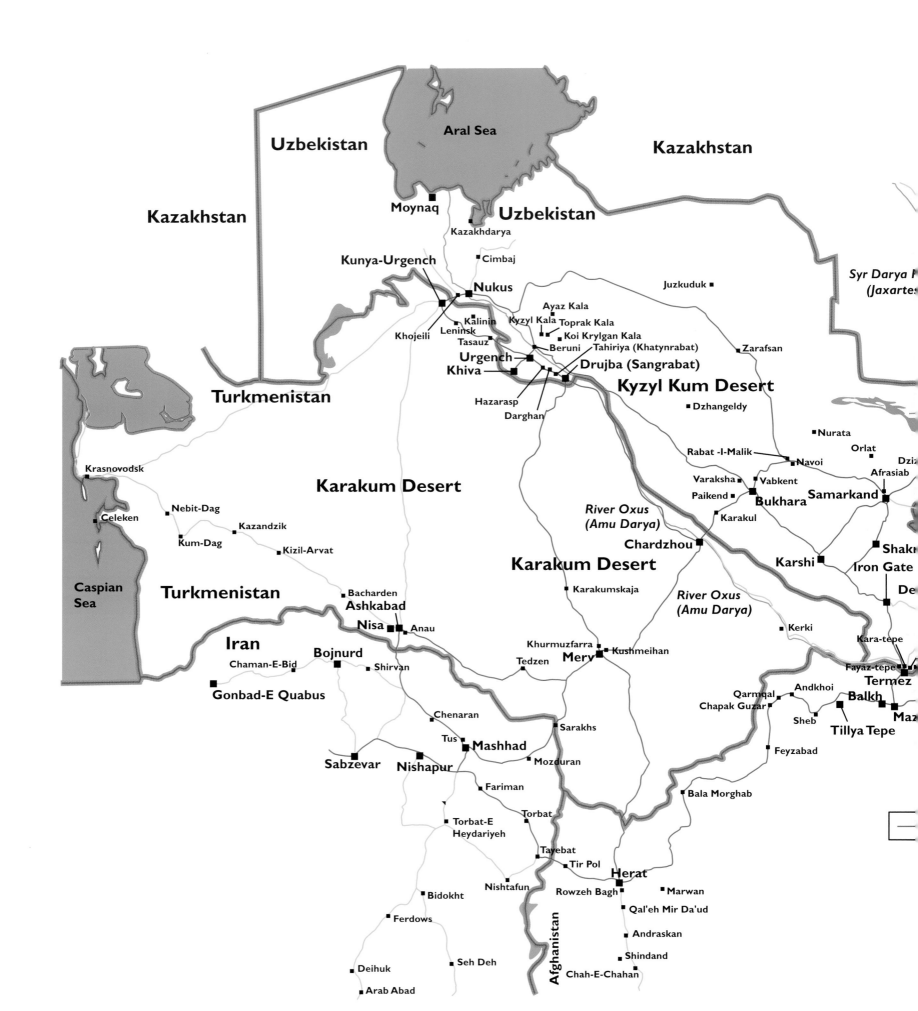

Uzbekistan

Kazakhstan

Aral Sea

Kazakhstan

Uzbekistan

Moynaq ■

Kazakhdarya ■

■ Cimbaj

Syr Darya
(Jaxartes

Juzkuduk ■

Kunya-Urgench

Nukus ■

Ayaz Kala ■
Kyzyl Kala ■ Toprak Kala ■
■ Kalinin
Leninsk ■ Koi Krylgan Kala ■
Khojeili ■ Tasauz ■ ■ Beruni Tahiriya (Khatynrabat) ■ Zarafsan ■

Urgench ■
Khiva ■ **Drujba (Sangrabat)** ■

Hazarasp ■ **Kyzyl Kum Desert**
Darghan ■

■ Dzhangeldy

■ Nurata
Orlat ■
Rabat -I-Malik ■ Navoi ■ Dziz

Varaksha ■ ■ Vabkent Afrasiab ■
Paikend ■ **Bukhara** **Samarkand** ■

Krasnovodsk ■

Karakul ■

Karakum Desert

River Oxus
(Amu Darya)

Nebit-Dag ■

Celeken ■

Kazandzik ■

Kum-Dag ■

Kizil-Arvat ■

Chardzhou ■ **Shakr** ■
Karshi ■ **Iron Gate**
De ■

Karakum Desert

■ Karakumskaja

River Oxus
(Amu Darya)

Kerki ■

Kara-tepe ■

**Caspian
Sea**

Turkmenistan

Bacharden ■
Ashkabad

Nisa ■ ■ Anau

Iran

Bojnurd ■

Chaman-E-Bid ■ ■ Shirvan

Khurmuzfarra ■ ■ Kushmeihan
Tedzen ■ **Mery** ■

Fayaz-tepe ■
Termez ■

Qarmqal ■ Andkhoi ■
Chapak Guzar ■ **Balkh** ■
Sheb ■ **Maz** ■
Tillya Tepe

Gonbad-E Quabus ■

Chenaran ■

Sarakhs ■

Feyzabad ■

Tus ■ **Mashhad** ■

Sabzevar ■ **Nishapur** ■

Mozduran ■

Bala Morghab ■

Fariman ■

Torbat-E ■
Heydariyeh

Torbat ■

Tayebat ■
Tir Pol ■ **Herat** ■

Bidokht ■

Nishtafun ■

Rowzeh Bagh ■ ■ Marwan

Qal'eh Mir Da'ud ■

Ferdows ■

Andraskan ■

Shindand ■

Afghanistan

Deihuk ■

Seh Deh ■

Chah-E-Chahan ■

Arab Abad ■

THE SILK ROAD THROUGH CENTRAL ASIA

Kazathstan

Zarkent • Korgas
Huocheng •

Kalcagaj •

Cu • Cilik •

Kaskelen • **Alma-Ata**

Kulan • **Bishkek** **Tokmak** **China**

entau

kestan Karabulak • Talas • Balasagun •

rar Arys • Issyk-Kul **Przevalsk**
Cimkent • Isfijab *Lake Issyk-Kul* Barskoon
• Lenger Pokrovka •

shkent • Kara-K'ul **Kyrgyzstan**

Namangan **Tianshan** Naryn • **Aksu**
Akhsiket **Mountains**
Pap • **Andijan**
Kokand Kuva • Uzgen • Tash Rabat
Margilan • • **Osh** caravanserai
Khujand **Ferghana** Torugart pass Bedel Pass
Kanibadan • Aravan
• Kyzyl-Kija
Isfara •
Turkistan Mountains Ulugqat • Sanxiandong Caves Sanchakou •
Sugun
Mount Mugh Irkeshtam • **Kashgar**
Yagnob Valley Hanoi and Mauri Tim Stupa
Zerafshan Mountains Shule

Dushanbe Ghez Canyon •
Tajikistan ▲ **Mt Kongur**
ayan • Dangara ▲ **Muztagh Ata**
in-tepe •
• **Kurgan-T'ube** **Pamirs** • Tashkurgan
• Kolkhozabad
• Parchar
Ai Khanum Chorog •
Feyzabad •
Kunduz Wakhan Corridor **Khunjerab Pass**
f • **Taloqan** Khudabad •
Pakistan Batura Glacier •
Afghanistan Passu Glacier • Shishkot
Hunza River Karimabad
• Nomal

TRADE ROUTES AND PRINCIPAL
SITES OF CENTRAL ASIA

CHAPTER TEN

SILK ROAD SITES IN SOUTHERN CENTRAL ASIA

Merchants did not favour the branch of the Silk Road that led westwards from Kashgar, through the Wakhan Corridor and over the Pamirs to Afghanistan. Marco Polo followed the route during the thirteenth century but travellers found little in the way of food or water in the high mountain passes and were vulnerable to attacks by bandits. Those that did brave the journey arrived at length in the old kingdom of Bactria with its capital at Balkh (Bactra).

Balkh

'After Akcha, the colour of the landscape changed from lead to aluminium, pallid and deathly, as if the sun had been sucking away its gaiety for thousands and thousands of years; for this now was the plain of Balkh, and Balkh they say is the oldest city in the world.'

(Robert Byron, 1937)

Balkh was already a thousand years old when it fell to the armies of Alexander the Great in June of 329 BC. He married a local beauty, the legendary Roxane, daughter of a Sogdian ruler named Oxyartes. It was the capital of the ancient kingdom of Bactria, comprising the land to the north of the Hindu Kush and south of the Hissar Mountains. The entire area, known to the Greeks as the 'land of a thousand cities', is littered with archeological remains and was once home to a powerful empire. The city itself sits on a fertile plain, nourished by the waters of the Amu Darya (Oxus). It owed its prosperity to the fact that it straddled a lattice of trade routes and also due to the rich mineral resources of the surrounding area. Gold, silver and rubies were mined in the area and, in the hills of the Badakshan to the east, was the only source of lapis lazuli known to the ancient world. One of the Silk Road's many strands led southwestwards from Balkh to Herat and on to Persia while another route crossed the Amu Darya (Oxus) to the north to reach Termez. There were several routes from Termez: one headed west across the Karakum ('Black Sands') Desert to Merv, where it bifurcated, reaching the Parthian capital of Nisa via Ashkabad or passing through Sarakhs (Saraghs) to arrive at Masshad in Iran. There was also a road to the northeast from Termez to Tashkent (Chach) passing through Dushanbe, a Soviet-era

town built on the site of an ancient settlement. The third route passed north through Iron Gate Pass (fig. 276) and then either continued northwest through Karshi to Bukhara or veered off to the northeast to Samarkand and on to Tashkent. The choice of routes depended, of course, on an individual traveller's final destination but it was also influenced by the seasons and by whether there were brigands or civil disorder along the way.

There was also a great road to the south and southeast from Balkh, passing over the Hindu Kush through Bamiyan to the Khyber Pass. From the Khyber Pass ran what came to be known as the Grand Trunk Road, a long arterial highway that linked to a vast network of trade routes across the entire sub-continent (for more on this route see p. 66).

Inspired by the teachings of Buddhism, the Kushans built great temples around Balkh and the remains of two Buddhist structures still stand to the south of the walls: Top-I-Rustam, the site of a large stupa containing a Buddha-relic and Takht-I-Rustam, atop of which once stood a large monastery that counted the Buddha's washing-basin among its possessions. Later structures, like the fifth-century Dilberjin Kazan in the northwest of the site, reveal that some of the inhabitants were also followers of Hinduism. A splendid painting discovered at Dilberjin depicts Shiva and Parvati with the bull Nandi. Balkh is one of the proposed birthplaces of Zoroaster and the city was a centre for Zoroastrianism during the Achaemenid and Greco-Bactrian periods. The religion seems to have been followed by some of Balkh's populace right up until the Arab conquest of the area at the end of the seventh century. During the fourth century Balkh was looted by a Sasanian army and the northern part of the city fell into disuse and became a burial ground. The city did not perish, however; it was still a thriving commercial and religious centre when Xuanzang visited in 630, a hundred Buddhist monasteries and about 3,000 monks still to be found in the area.

Balkh was again wrecked during the Arab conquests of the late seventh century, not long after Xuanzang's visit, but its fortunes had revived by the tenth, a pattern of death and rebirth that was to be repeated throughout the city's history. According to Arab accounts of the medieval period Balkh had been destroyed and rebuilt more than twenty times by

Fig. 262 **The mud walls of the Bala Hissar (Fort) at Balkh, Northern Afghanistan.**
Mostly Timurid period (1370–1506) but built on early, partly Kushan-era foundations. The Timurids extended the walls to a circumference of about 10 km and, in places, they still stand 20 metres high.

Fig. 263 **Masjed-I-Hajji Piyada (Masjed-I-No Gumbad – 'the mosque with nine domes')**
Balkh, Northern Afghanistan, mid-9th century
This mosque, built of baked brick, is said to be the oldest in Afghanistan. The intricate stucco decoration on the arches resembles that of Samarra, 125 km north of Baghdad on the Tigris, the capital of the Abbasid Caliphate during the second half of the ninth century. The columns have their antecedents in the Zoroastrian temples of Sasanian times (see also fig. 319). Balkh has so far escaped the ravages of Afghanistan's civil war but the Masjed-I-No Gumbad is in desperate need of shoring up to prevent it from collapse.

the sixteenth century. By the tenth century it was enjoying a period of renewed prosperity thanks to continuing trade with India and onward commerce with cities to the east and west. Balkh became a centre for Islamic scholarship and was revered by Arab geographers who called it 'mother of cities', 'the dome of Islam' and 'paradise on earth.' By the ninth century there were said to be forty mosques in the city although, today, only one has survived from that time (fig. 263).

One of Balkh's most celebrated sons was the great Sufi poet Mawlana Jalaluddin Balkhi (1207–73), known by the familiar name of Rumi. Rumi was born in Balkh but left the city in about 1218 with his parents, ahead of the Mongol advance. After a decade or so of wandering he finally settled in the Turkish city of Konya in Anatolia, then the capital of the Seljuk sultanate of Rum (from where he derives his name). Rumi's 26,000-verse epic 'Mathnavi' is considered by many scholars to be the greatest of all Persian poems. After his death Rumi's devotees formed a sect called *Mawlawiyah*, better known in the West as the Whirling Dervishes.

Balkh continued to thrive until 1221 when it was comprehensively flattened by the armies of Genghis Khan. A

contemporary account describes what happened after the city fell to the Mongols:

> '[Genghis Khan] commanded that the population of Balkh, great and small, few and many, both men and women should be driven out onto the plain and divided up according to their usual custom into hundreds and thousands to be put to the sword; and that not a trace should be left of fresh or dry…. And they cast fire into the garden of the city and devoted their whole attention to the destruction of the outworks and walls, and mansions and palaces.'
> (Ata-Malik Juvaini, *The History of the World Conqueror*. Quoted in Mukhtarov, 1993)

Marco Polo visited Balkh later in the thirteenth century and has left a vivid description of a once great city, laid waste by Genghis:

> '… we shall now speak of another named Balach; a large and magnificent city. It was formerly still more considerable, but has sustained much injury from the

Tartars, who in their frequent attacks have partly demolished its buildings. It contained many palaces constructed of marble, and spacious squares, still visible, although in a ruinous state.'
> (From *The Travels of Marco Polo the Venetian*. Translated by William Marsden in Marsden, 1948)

When the Arab traveller Ibn Battuta (1304–77) passed through Balkh during the first half of the 14th century it was still a desolate ruin:

> 'We crossed the river Oxus into the land of Khurasan and after a day and a half's march through a sandy uninhabited waste reached Balkh. It is an utter ruin and uninhabited, but anyone seeing it would think it inhabited on account of the solidity of its construction. The accursed Tinkiz [Genghis] destroyed this city and demolished about a third of its mosque on account of a treasure which he was told lay under one of its columns.'
> (Ibn Battuta. Translated by H. A. R. Gibb in Gibb, 1929)

Fig. 264 **The Buddhist complex at Fayaz-tepe**
Bactria, Kushan period, 1st to 2nd century AD
Termez, Southern Uzbekistan

Under the Timurids the city rose, once again, from its ashes. It was rebuilt during the 1360s by Amir Husayn, a companion of Timur, the city walls extended to a circumference of 10 km and the citadel reconstructed. By this time the Silk Road was in decline and the city's fortunes came to depend on whichever invader currently held sway. A cycle of destruction and rejuvenation continued until the nineteenth century, when the city's role as a regional capital was usurped by the town of Mazar-i Sharif. In 1852–53 Balkh was abandoned and became a deserted ruin, inhabited by ghosts.

The settlements constructed at Balkh, Termez, Dalverzin-tepe and elsewhere by the Kushans were on old Greco-Bactrian foundations. These sites were generally laid out in a rectangular form, enclosed by walls of sun-dried brick or earth up to 20 metres in height and surrounded by a moat. At each corner were towers from which the town's defenders could launch arrows.

Termez and its associated sites

The plain façade of the Kushans' cities were a contrast to their interiors. Interior walls were decorated with murals of court life, religious scenes and fabulous animals. Old Termez was built on a natural rise on the right bank of the Amu Darya (Oxus) River, occupying a site of more than 400 hectares to the southwest of today's city. Although there are remains dating back to the first millennium BC, Termez enjoyed its heyday during the Greco-Bactrian and Kushan periods. The ruins of a customs house and a guesthouse suggest that trade was already being conducted by the beginning of the Christian era. The Kushans called Termez 'Tarmita' and, when the Buddhist faith came to dominate the region during the first and second centuries AD, they erected a large number of monasteries and stupas in and around the city. The greatest of these were the large complex of caves at Kara-tepe just to the northwest of old Termez and the monastery of Fayaz-tepe to the north. Kara-tepe ('Black Hill') now sits in the sensitive border zone between Uzbekistan and Afghanistan but in its day, particularly the second and third centuries, it flourished as a centre for Buddhist learning. More than twenty-five caves were cut into the sides of three hills at the site and free-standing, mud-brick structures were also erected. Generations of travellers have left graffiti on the cave-walls with inscriptions in many of the languages of the Silk Road.

Fayaz-tepe occupies an equally colourful location beneath a military radar installation. The complex comprises a Buddhist temple and monastery, built around the time of Christ, and a small stupa of mud-brick (fig. 264).

A limestone relief of a Buddha seated beneath a bodhi tree is the most celebrated of Fayaz-tepe's many treasures (fig. 265).

A larger stupa, built of mud and terracotta bricks and

Fig. 265 **Limestone relief depicting Buddha Sakyamuni seated beneath the Bodhi tree, flanked by two attendant monks**
Bactria, Kushan period, 1st to 2nd century AD
H. 75 cm, W. 62.5 cm
From Fayaz-tepe, Southern Uzbekistan
(Museum of the History of the People of Uzbekistan, Tashkent)
This relief, in a style strongly reminiscent of Gandhara, depicts the Buddha shortly before the moment of his enlightenment as he meditates beneath the bodhi tree at Bodghaya, Bihar State, India. The Corinthian columns at each side are a flourish from the Classical world.

known as the 'Bastion of Zurmal' still stands to the east of old Termez. The ancient structure is fragile and near to collapse but it still dominates the surrounding area (fig. 266).

Airtam

Airtam comprises a group of Buddhist monuments, situated about 18 km east of Termez on the bank of the Amu Darya. This religious centre was constructed during the Kushan period and extended for almost 3 km along the riverbank.

Fig. 266 **Buddhist Stupa, known as the 'Bastion of Zurmal'**
Bactria, Kushan period, 1st to 2nd century AD
H. 16 metres (approx.)
Termez, Southern Uzbekistan

Fig. 267 **Limestone frieze
with three female musicians
separated by acanthus
leaves**
Bactria, Kushan period, ca. 1st
century AD
Airtam, near Termez, Southern
Uzbekistan
(State Hermitage Museum, St Petersburg)
Several more fragments of the
same frieze were found a year
later in the remains of a Buddhist
sanctuary on the nearby
riverbank. The middle figure plays
a type of lute, one of the earliest
known depictions of a stringed
instrument.

The lower half of a large limestone relief from Airtam consists of the legs of a pair of male and female rulers or deities, with a dedicatory inscription on the base. Fragments of another celebrated frieze were found in the Amu Darya in 1932 and now reside in the Hermitage in St Petersburg. They show half-figures of three celestial female figures holding musical instruments (fig. 267). The figures are executed in a Hellenistic style but their physiognomy is Asiatic, not unlike the sculpture of Palmyra (see fig. 411).

About 175 km northeast of Termez is the city of Denau. The road to Denau follows the course of the Surkhan Darya River, a tributary of the Amu Darya (Oxus), and then veers east towards the modern Tajik capital of Dushanbe. North and south of Denau are the Kushan cities of Khalchayan – where a palace containing polychromed sculpted clay friezes was discovered – and Dalverzin-tepe. Both were extensively excavated by Soviet archeologists during the 1960s and 1970s.

Khalchayan and Dalverzin-tepe

Khalchayan, on the right bank of the Surkhan Darya River, is thought to be one of the earliest Kushan settlements, although its moated fortress dates backs even further – to the Greco-Bactrian era of the second or third century BC. Soviet archeologists discovered the remains of a palace at Khalchayan, thought to have been built around the first century BC by the Gerai clan. The Gerai are believed to have been one of the Yuezhi tribes who laid the foundations of the Kushan Empire that emerged during the reign of Kujula Kadphises (ca. 30–80 AD). The clan appear to have come to use the palace as their dynastic temple. It was in ruins by the end of the third century AD but fragments of the murals and clay reliefs that adorned its walls still exist. The clay sculptures are of gods and princes: heroic, life-sized portraits of men in three-quarters or half relief. The central relief contains a king and queen seated upon a throne while to one side a battle rages with archers on horseback firing

backwards – a motif found all along the Silk Road (see fig. 172). Another frieze contains children with garlands, a borrowing from the Hellenistic world seen on 'The Kanishka Reliquary' (fig. 48). There is an overwhelming sense of deep inner spirituality to the sculptures and, sometimes, an air of suffering too (figs. 268 and 269).

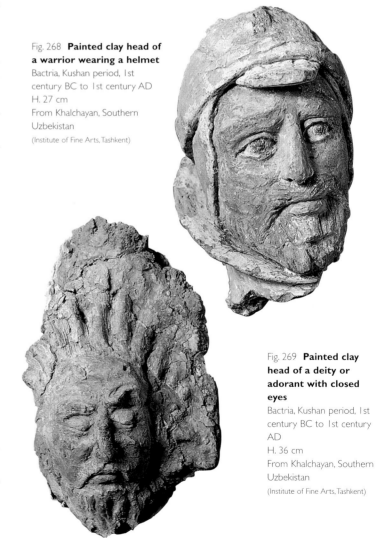

Fig. 268 **Painted clay head of
a warrior wearing a helmet**
Bactria, Kushan period, 1st
century BC to 1st century AD
H. 27 cm
From Khalchayan, Southern
Uzbekistan
(Institute of Fine Arts, Tashkent)

Fig. 269 **Painted clay
head of a deity or
adorant with closed
eyes**
Bactria, Kushan period, 1st
century BC to 1st century
AD
H. 36 cm
From Khalchayan, Southern
Uzbekistan
(Institute of Fine Arts, Tashkent)

Fig. 270 **Painted clay head of a princely donor wearing a conical hat**
Bactria, Kushan period, 1st to 2nd century AD
H. 49.5 cm
Unearthed from the 'King's Hall', Temple 1, Dalverzin-tepe, Southern Uzbekistan
(Institute of Fine Arts, Tashkent)

The second major settlement in the Denau area, Dalverzin-tepe was also built during the Greco-Bactrian period but enjoyed its heyday during the first to third centuries of the Kushan era. Dalverzin-tepe was a large fortified city – almost certainly a northern capital of the Kushans – and was found to contain mansions for the rich and temples for Buddhists, Zoroastrians and local deities. A 36 kg hoard of gold unearthed in 1972 included beautifully inlaid necklaces, bracelets, earrings and buckles. The hoard also contained small unworked ingots stamped with their weights in Kharosthi script and some with dedicatory references to their intended recipients. The gold was hurriedly forced into a crudely made vessel with a narrow neck, causing many of the pieces to be damaged. Like so many of the Silk Road's cities, Dalverzin-tepe's glory-days were soon at an end. The Sasanians swept through sometime during the latter half of the third century AD and flattened the town. The ruins were patched up and inhabited until about the seventh century with the unused parts utilised, as at Balkh, for a necropolis.

Fig. 271 **Painted clay figure of a donor**
Bactria, Kushan period, 1st to 2nd century AD
H. 73 cm
From Temple 1, Dalverzin-tepe, Southern Uzbekistan
(Institute of Fine Arts, Tashkent)

Hundreds of Kushan era clay sculptures were found in two Buddhist temples at Dalverzin-tepe and some are truly spectacular. At Temple 1 painted clay figures of what appear to be royal donors were found. They are stylistically related to Gandhara sculptures from further south but are uniquely Central Asian in style (fig. 270).

A beautifully modelled figure of a Buddhist donor, painted in black and red pigments, was also recovered from Temple 1 (fig. 271).

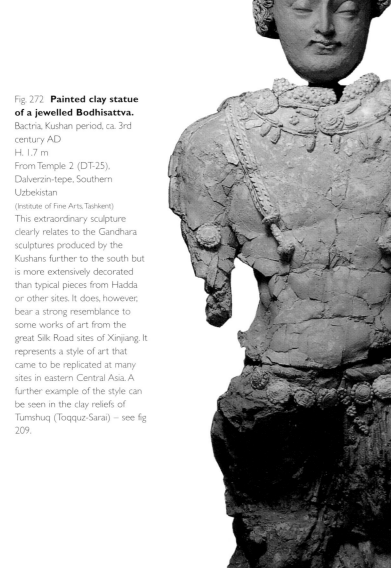

Fig. 272 **Painted clay statue of a jewelled Bodhisattva.**
Bactria, Kushan period, ca. 3rd century AD
H. 1.7 m
From Temple 2 (DT-25), Dalverzin-tepe, Southern Uzbekistan
(Institute of Fine Arts, Tashkent)
This extraordinary sculpture clearly relates to the Gandhara sculptures produced by the Kushans further to the south but is more extensively decorated than typical pieces from Hadda or other sites. It does, however, bear a strong resemblance to some works of art from the great Silk Road sites of Xinjiang. It represents a style of art that came to be replicated at many sites in eastern Central Asia. A further example of the style can be seen in the clay reliefs of Tumshuq (Toqquz-Sarai) – see fig 209.

Fig. 273 **Painted clay statue of a jewelled Bodhisattva**
Bactria, Kushan period, ca. 3rd century AD
H. 1 metre
From Temple 2 (DT-25), Dalverzin-tepe, Southern Uzbekistan
(Institute of Fine Arts, Tashkent)
The recessed urna on the forehead of this sculpture was found to contain fruit stones and a gold button, all sealed in place with gypsum.

One of the great finds in Temple 2 (DT-25) at Dalverzin-tepe was a massive figure of a jewelled Bodhisattva. Sans feet, the sculpture still reaches a height of 1.7 metres (fig. 272).

From the same temple comes a heroic figure of a Bodhisattva, also strongly reminiscent of Gandhara sculpture (fig. 273).

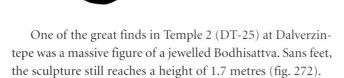

Fig. 274 **Fragment of a mural depicting a priest holding aloft a child**
Bactria, Kushan period, ca. 1st century AD
H. 27 cm, W. 26 cm
From Dalverzin-tepe, Southern Uzbekistan
(Institute of Fine Arts, Tashkent)

Dalverzin-tepe's murals, painted on clay, are more friable and have therefore survived only as fragments. The most striking is a mysterious image of an, as yet, unexplained temple ritual – perhaps a baptismal or fertility rite (fig. 274).

Among the small objects found at Dalverzin-tepe (see p. 207) are the gold hoard described above and an ivory comb, unquestionably of Indian origin and a testament to a high level of Silk Road trade between the Kushans and their southern neighbours (fig. 275).

Successive empires fought to keep the north-south trade routes open. The road north from Bactria led over the Hissar Mountains of Tajikistan through Iron Gate Pass into the land of the Sogdians (fig. 276). Iron Gate Pass is situated 3 km west of Derbent in modern Uzbekistan and was described by the monk Xuanzang. There may well have been a colossal gate there, perhaps erected by the Kushans to protect their empire from invasion, though nothing remains of it today.

The routes north from the Iron Gate Pass are discussed in detail in later pages.

Fig. 275 **Ivory comb with a depiction of ladies at their toilet**
India, 2nd to 3rd century AD
H. 9.2 cm, W. 7.8 cm (maximum)
Dalverzintepe, Southern Uzbekistan.
(Institute of Fine Arts, Tashkent)
This comb, though not as finely made as the ivory casket discovered at Begram, has a similar theme (see fig. 42). The reverse of the comb shows figures on an elephant.

Fig. 276 **The Gateway to Sogdiana Iron Gate Pass**
The Buzgala Defile, near Derbent, Uzbekistan

CHAPTER ELEVEN

THE COMING OF ISLAM TO CENTRAL ASIA

After the Muslim defeat of the Sasanian Empire in 651, Arab armies sought to bring Islam to the land beyond the Oxus, Transoxiana, known to them as Mawana 'an nahr ('what is beyond the river'). That same year, an Arab army from Basra (in Mesopotamia in today's Iraq), succeeded in taking the great oasis city of Merv (Mary in modern Turkmenistan, see p. 229). During the early years the Arabs lacked a power base and were compelled to rule through the nobles and administrators of the former, Sasanian regime but by the end of the century some 50,000 families from Kufa and Basra are said to have joined their soldier husbands in Merv and the city became the base for the Muslim conquest of Central Asia. During the Umayyad Caliphate (661–750) and the

early part of the Abbasid Caliphate (749–1258), Merv was the capital of the eastern Islamic territories. This state of affairs prevailed until the transfer of the capital to Nishapur during the Tahirid dynasty (821–73).

The garrison at Merv was strengthened in 676 by the arrival of an additional 4,000 men from Basra, among them Qutham ibn al-Abbas, a cousin of the Prophet. The men of Basra and Kufa rarely collaborated and the conquest of Central Asia progressed slowly as a result. The first military forays across the Oxus began in 673, led by Ubaidallah ibn Ziyad, governor of Khurasan – the eastern part of the former Sasanian Empire. Termez was taken in 676 and attacks were launched against the great caravan cities of Bukhara and

Fig. 277 **Women at prayer, Shiraz, Iran**

Samarkand, ruled by the Khorezm dynasty. General Qutaiba ibn Muslim, appointed governor of Khurasan in 704, consolidated Arab control of the region. Bukhara fell to the Arabs in 709, followed by Samarkand in 712. Qutaiba is said to have systematically killed off all of the scholars of Khorezm in an attempt to erase the country's culture. He established a large Arab garrison at Samarkand and, during 713-714, rampaged through Chach (Tashkent), Khujand (Khodjent) and Ferghana. Qutaiba swept all before him, brushing aside all opposition including attempts by surviving relatives of the last Sasanian ruler, Yazdegerd III to raise an army against him and to elicit Chinese support. Qutaiba's advance was finally checked when news reached him in 714 that his patron Hajjaj ibn Yusuf, governor of Iraq and the eastern provinces, had died. He campaigned through Ferghana for a further year until, in 715, the Caliph Walid died and Qutaiba was recalled to Merv. He was then killed; probably on the orders of the new caliph, Sulaiman- Qutaiba's bitter enemy- and the momentum of the Arab's advance was quickly lost. In the years after Qutaiba's death the Arab tribes of Khurasan were riven by internal disputes and few territorial gains were made. Agents of the Abbasids worked tirelessly to achieve the overthrow of the Umayyad Caliphate and, north of the Syr Darya (Jaxartes) River, the Türgesh Turks rallied to the cause of the beleaguered Sogdian armies who had fled to the Ferghana Valley in 721. In 724 the Türgesh Turks heavily defeated a Muslim expeditionary force sent into the Ferghana Valley. Between 728 and 738 the Turks controlled almost all of the territory north of the Amu Darya (Oxus) and at times it appeared that the Arabs might be completely ousted from Transoxiana. A cache of documents found by Soviet archeologists at Mount Mugh, northern Tajikistan, in 1933 provide a remarkable record of the tumultuous years that followed the death of Qutaiba. The Sogdian chieftain Divastich, the last ruler of Penjikent, fled to the mountain citadel of Mugh after the fall of Penjikent to the Arabs. He was captured at Mugh in 722 and executed but his archive survived and provides an invaluable source of information about the economic and social conditions of Sogdiana (see p. 268).

The death of the Türgesh Khagan Su-lu brought about the disintegration of the Turks' state. With the threat to their rule removed, the Arabs were able to introduce a process of reconciliation and pacification to Central Asia. The last Umayyad governor, Nasr ibn Sayyar, succeeded in 737 and pursued a strategy of amnesty and tax reform among his subjects (mawali) and among the Sogdian landowners. Many people voluntarily converted to Islam and Sogdian merchants financed many of the Arabs' expeditions.

The rise of Islam had a profound effect on trade along the Silk Road. By 751, its followers had conquered Byzantine Syria, the whole of North Africa, Sasanian Persia and much of Central Asia. The power of Islam held sway from Spain to

the Ferghana Valley, Arab traders controlled both maritime and land-routes and Muslim Persia developed a domestic silk industry that rivalled China's. Foltz (Foltz, 1999) outlines three levels at which Islam spread throughout Central Asia: at the political level (as an instrument of foreign-policy); at the commercial level (followers and converts enjoyed greater opportunities for trade), and at the level of assimilation (successive generations would forget the ways of the past).

During the first half of the eighth century, the Tang government of China attempted to regain control of the lucrative trade routes across Central Asia. Arab and Chinese armies finally clashed in July 751, at the River Talas in modern Kazakhstan. The Tang army, led by the gifted Korean general Gao Xianzhi, fought for five days but was eventually defeated by the Arab troops of Ziyad ibn-Salih. Many Chinese were captured and sent to work in Samarkand and Damascus where they taught skills to the native craftsmen, including the techniques of paper and silk manufacture. Few of them ever made it back to China although a man named Du Huan is said to have done so in 762 and wrote an account of his adventures. A more enduring consequence of the battle was that Chinese control of Central Asia was lost for the next thousand years. Although the Arabs did not pursue the fleeing Chinese troops and the battle marked the limit of their territorial expansion, they remained the dominant force in Silk Road trade until the coming of the Mongols in the early thirteenth century.

The arrival in Khurasan of the Abbasid missionary Abu Muslim in 748 was the catalyst for a revolt against Umayyad rule. In 750 the Umayyad dynasty came to an end and the capital of the caliphate was moved from Damascus to Baghdad. The demise of the Umayyad Caliphate was coupled with the ascent of Persian culture and language in Central Asia. The old languages and cultures of Bactria, Khorezm and Sogdiana* disappeared from the pages of history and were replaced by all things Persian – a revival of traditions from the pre-Islamic era. The reasons for the 'Persianization' of Central Asia are complex but include the fact that the merchants of Central Asia were prepared to embrace Islam and accept foreign rule so long as the trade routes and the commerce they conducted along them were safeguarded. Persian quickly became the language of choice among the Arab soldiers and Sogdian traders of Central Asia. The large number of slaves, sent west to work across the Abbasid Empire, brought Persian ideas with them if they managed to return home and refugees from the old Sasanian regime also encouraged the spread of the language in Central Asia.

This period of the Abbasid Caliphate (749–1258) gave rise to many technological and cultural developments, many of which reached the West via the Silk Road. One process, learned from captured Chinese craftsmen at the Battle of

* The continued existence of a small pocket of Sogdian speakers in the Yagnob Valley of modern Tajikistan is one of the twentieth century's most exciting discoveries (for more on this see p. 269).

Talas in 751, was that of papermaking (see above) though other innovations were made by local men. One of the most celebrated of these men was Mohammed ibn Musa al Khorezmi (d. ca. 845), a gifted mathematician whose name gave us the word 'algorithm'. His treatise on so-called 'Arabic' numerals led to the spread of the system of numbers we use today. The word 'algebra' is derived from the title of another of al-Khorezmi's works: al-gabr or al-gebr originally meant 'to reset' bones but was subsequently adapted to mean the 'setting' of a mathematical equation.

The Arabs saw no contradiction between the process of trade and the ideal of a restrained lifestyle encouraged by Islam. Muhammad himself was a merchant in the city of Mecca, a town through which caravans had passed and conducted trade for centuries. There are a number of remarks ascribed to the Prophet (known as hadiths), which place merchants at the very highest rung of society:

'The honest, truthful Muslim merchant will stand with the martyrs on the Day of Judgement.'

'I commend the merchants to you, for they are couriers of the horizons and God's trusted servants on earth.'

(Quoted in Liu, 1996)

If the merchants of all types were highly regarded in the Islamic world, those who traded in textiles – especially silk – were the most esteemed of all. In the Koran there are several references to silk, equating the wearing of the precious material with entry into Paradise:

'As for those that have faith and do good works, God will admit them to gardens watered by running streams. They shall be decked with bracelets of gold and of pearls, and arrayed in garments of silk.'

(From the Koran, XXII 22-4. Translated by N. J. Dawood, in Dawood, 1999)

The Abbasid caliphs of Baghdad presided over a thriving metropolis, visited by traders from the remotest corners of the world. Palace and government workshops produced textiles known as tiraz, a Persian word meaning 'embroidery'. Tiraz textiles were embroidered with an inscription in silk thread, usually a laudatory message referring to the name, accomplishments and regnal dates of the caliph. The tiraz system spread throughout the Islamic world, including Sicily and Spain, and ensured that large quantities of high quality textiles were produced. The tiraz system continued well into the thirteenth century but, after the central control of the caliphate began to weaken, local rulers took over the tiraz workshops and produced textiles that celebrated their own achievements rather than those of the caliphs (see fig. 280).

In addition to tiraz textiles, the ruling classes of the Abbasid Empire especially prized silk robes and carpets, both locally made and imported. A Byzantine ambassador to

Baghdad in 917 described the palace of the caliph, al-Muktadir, as containing 38,000 curtains – including 12,000 of gold brocade – and 22,000 carpets. A forebear of al-Muktadir, the mighty Harun Al Rashid (r. 786–809) left behind an enormous treasury, the contents of which were recorded at the time of his death. The contents, like the treasures contained in the Shoso-in repository of the Japanese Emperor Shomu (p. 106), are a cornucopia of goods from the countries of the Silk Road (fig. 205). Harun Al Rashid was a man who loved silk.

4,000 embroidered robes
4,000 silk cloaks, lined with sable, mink and other furs
10,000 shirts and shifts
10,000 caftans
2,000 drawers of various kinds
4,000 turbans
1,000 hoods
1,000 capes of various kinds
5,000 kerchiefs of different kinds
500 (pieces of) velvet
100,000 mithqals of musk*
100,000 mithqals of ambergris†
1,000 baskets of Indian aloes
1,000 precious china vessels
Many kinds of perfume
Jewels valued by the jewellers at 4 million dinars
500,000 dinars
1,000 jewelled rings
1,000 Armenian carpets
4,000 curtains
5,000 cushions
5,000 pillows (mikhadda)
1,500 silk carpets
100 silk rugs
1,000 silk cushions and pillows
300 Maysani carpets
1,000 Darabjirdi carpets
1,000 cushions with silk brocade
1,000 inscribed silk cushions
1,000 silk curtains
300 silk brocade curtains
500 Tabari carpets
1,000 Tabari cushions
1,000 pillows (mirfade)
1,000 pillows (mikhadda)
1,000 washbasins
1,000 ewers
300 stoves
1,000 candlesticks
2,000 brass objects of various kinds
1,000 belts
10,000 decorated swords

* Musk is an aromatic substance used in the production of perfumes. It is secreted by an abdominal gland in the male musk deer.
† Ambergris is a grey secretion obtained from the intestines of the sperm whale. It was also used in the production of perfumes-giving permanence to fragrances obtained from flowers. As well as being extracted from the bodies of captured whales the substance is washed ashore, especially on the islands of the South Seas and on the coast of Africa, or is found floating in the ocean. Arab traders peddled the substance along the Silk Road and appear to have disguised its origins-Persian scholars believed that it came from a spring beneath the ocean and the Chinese thought it was the spittle of dragons. Perfumes and other aromatics were an important part of religious ritual and were also an aphrodisiac for the well-to-do gentlemen and ladies of the countries along the Silk Road. There are so many tales of the role of perfumes in courtship and lovemaking that one (related in Schafer, 1963) will have to suffice here. A beautiful Chinese courtesan in eighth-century Changan (Xian), who went by the name of 'Lotus Fragrance', is said to have worn a perfume of such delightful aroma that when she promenaded about the town besotted bees and butterflies followed her about.

50,000 swords for the guards and pages (ghulam)
150,000 lances
100,000 bows
1,000 special suits of armour
50,000 common suits of armour
10,000 helmets
20,000 breast plates
150,000 shields
4,000 special saddles
30,000 common saddles
4,000 pairs of half-boots, most of them lined with sable,
mink and other kinds of fur, with a knife and a kerchief in
each half-boot
4,000 pairs of socks
4,000 small tents with their appurtenances
150 marquees

(Ibn al Zubayr, quoted in Liu, 1996)

The *hadiths* criticize the wearing of silk but the Koran does not and both Harun Al Rashid and his wife Zubaida were inordinately fond of the precious material. She is said to have worn a robes made from a multi-coloured silk called *washi*, a single length of which cost 50,000 dinars, and appears to have been a veritable fashion icon to the ladies of the court.

The ebb and flow of the Islamic states of Central Asia

'Worlds on Worlds are rolling ever
From creation to decay,
Like the bubbles on a river
Sparkling, bursting, borne away.'

(Percy Bysshe Shelley, *Worlds on Worlds* – Chorus from *Hellas*)

During the ninth century a number of semi-autonomous Islamic states began to emerge in Central Asia. The Tahirids (821–73) and Saffarids (867–908) were quickly followed by the empire of the Samanids (875–999), a dynasty founded by an Iranian noble, Saman, from northern Afghanistan. A convert to Islam, Saman and his son Asad were able to achieve little more than local prominence during their lifetimes but around 820 Saman's four grandsons became governors of Herat, Samarkand, Ferghana and Tashkent. Nasr ibn Ahmad (r. 864–92), son of the Ferghana governor, eventually assumed control of all Transoxiana and, by 892, Nasr's brother Ismail (r. 892–907) was in control of the entire eastern region of the Abbasid Caliphate, headquartered in the town of Bukhara.

The Samanids ruled with the consent of the Abbasid caliphs in Baghdad but enjoyed a large degree of autonomy.

Samanid territory reached its greatest extant during the reign of Nasr II ibn Ahmad (r. 914–43), from Tashkent (Chach) in the north and Ferghana in the northeast to Ray (south of Tehran) in the southwest. Under Samanid rule the trade routes, both east and west, became safe again and commerce flourished. Midway between Samarkand and Bukhara, the massive brick-built caravanserai at Rabat-I Malik (built before 1078) attests to the high level of commercial activity along the Silk Road during the tenth and eleventh centuries (see fig. 323). In Kalter (Kalter, 1983) a list of trade goods compiled by the tenth-century Arab geographer Mukadasi is provided. Rugs and prayer mats from Bukhara and Samarkand; woollen cloth and fine weavings; cotton, silk, soap, cosmetics; bows and other weapons; armour, horse-fittings, tents, foodstuffs (including raisins, nuts, sesame and honey); livestock (including horses, sheep and cattle); hawks for hunting; gold, silver, sulphur and iron- all were exported to China and the West. Kalter also mentions the tens of thousands of Samanid coins found in Scandinavia and lesser numbers of the same that were unearthed in Central Europe, a testament to the commercial reach of the Silk Road traders of Central Asia.

Surviving works of art from the Samanid period are scarce. Earthenware pottery is an exception and was produced in large quantities at Nishapur and Samarkand (Afrasiab) from the ninth to the eleventh century. Several types of pottery were produced, the most distinctive being a red or buff body with polychrome designs beneath a colourless glaze, apparently made only at Nishapur. The typical vessel was a thinly potted bowl with flaring sides but ewers were also made. Colours typically included black, red, yellow and green and the popularity of huntsmen and cavaliers as subject matter suggests that Sasanian influence was still strong. Ceramics with designs in black or brown on a smooth cream or white ground were made at both centres although at Nishapur the designs tended to be stylized and stark in appearance. Black on white 'Samarkand ware' (actually made at several centres) was painted in a less austere manner than its Nishapur counterpart. Pithy decorative inscriptions in neat, geometric Kufic script were the order of the day – typically blessings, poems and quotations from famous people (fig. 278).

Ceramics with a red or pink slip and covered with underglaze painting in shades of yellow, white and manganese brown are found only at Samarkand. Typical motifs are stylized birds or animals within roundels and bold Kufic inscriptions. The fourth type is known as splash ware and was made at both centres. Bowls and plates with green, yellow and purplish manganese brown running glazes were made, reminiscent of but not necessarily derived from Tang sancai ceramics (see p. 96). Examples from Samarkand are undoubtedly finer, many covered with a fine sgrafitto* design resembling a spiderweb (fig. 279).

* *Sgrafitto* decoration was applied by first covering the body of the vessel with a white slip and then creating the design by scratching through it with a sharp point to create a line drawing.

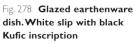

Fig. 278 **Glazed earthenware dish. White slip with black Kufic inscription**
Eastern Iran or Transoxiana, probably Samarkand, 9th to 10th century
D. 30 cm
(Private Collection)
The inscription reads: 'He who is afflicted by greed, his nightmares are of poverty.'

Fig. 279 **Shallow dish in glazed earthenware with underglaze painting in green, manganese-brown and yellow. Decorated in *sgrafitto* technique with Kufic script in the centre.**
Samanid period, 10th century
D. 41 cm
(Registan Museum, Samarkand)
There is considerable debate over whether splash-wares were inspired by Tang *sancai* ceramics. There is no doubt that Chinese merchants were active in Afrasiab at this time and the possibility cannot be excluded.

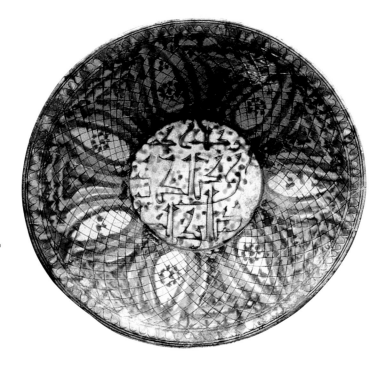

Ceramics wares of the Samanid period were utilitarian objects. They could rarely be described as being great art. This was not the case with the mere handful of textiles to have survived from this period. Silk cloth was the Silk Road's staple currency and patterned silks (known as zandaniji) were more valuable than almost any other commodity. The 'St Josse silk', produced in Khurasan around 960 for the Samanid amir (governor) Abu Mansur Bukhtegin, was formerly in the church of St Josse sur Mer in the Pas de Calais. Its motifs are an extraordinary mix of styles from the countries of the Silk Road (fig. 280).

Glasswork of the Samanid era was exceptionally fine and, like many other art forms from the period, it draws inspiration from Sasanian prototypes. Vessels were blown and sometimes decorated with a molten thread laid upon the surface in a spiral or a swirl (fig. 281).

Of the great buildings that once stood in the Samanid's capital city, Bukhara, almost nothing of the period remains. The mausoleum of Ismail Samanid, dating to the beginning of the tenth century, is the only Samanid structure still extant in the city (see p. 248). There is no doubt, however, that many of the Islamic world's greatest minds were nourished by the Samanids. The greatest of them all was Ibn Sina, or Avicenna (980–1037), known for centuries as 'the prince of all learning' and the fruits of his intellect are one of the Silk Road's most precious commodities. His medical encyclopaedia, known simply as 'The Canon' (*Qanun*), found its way to Europe via the Silk Road and was the standard reference on the subject for five hundred years. Ibn Sina, though born in Balkh, was educated in Bukhara and received encouragement and financial support from enlightened Samanid rulers, under whom Persian language and culture enjoyed a renaissance (for more on Ibn Sina, see p. 249).

Another beneficiary of Samanid patronage was Al-Biruni (973–1048), one of the most remarkable scholars and scientists of the ancient Islamic world. Al-Biruni was a son of Khiva and was educated under the Samanids but his career after about 1017 was spent far from home, in the service of Sultan Mahmud of Ghazni. The multilingual Al-Biruni accompanied Mahmud on his campaigns across India and has left a treasure-store of information about the subcontinent during the medieval period (for more on Al-Biruni, see p. 240).

Despite their Persian ancestry the Samanids were ardent Sunni Muslims and they embarked upon a concerted campaign to first convert, and then provide military training to the region's Turkish tribesmen. These Turkish military slaves embraced Islam but retained their own traditions, language and culture. By the latter part of the tenth century those Turks who had embraced Islam were welcomed into the very heart of the Samanid government. In 961 a Turkish slave-soldier named Alptigin, who had already become commander in chief of the army, successfully engineered his own appointment as governor of Khurasan. He was quickly divested of his post, however, and sought refuge in the town of Ghazni in modern Afghanistan. After his death in about 963 he was succeeded by another ex-slave named Sebuktigin (r. 977–97), founder of the Ghaznavid Empire, who seems to have regarded himself as a loyal vassal of the Samanids. To the north another Turkish dynasty, the Kharakhanids displaced the Karluks of the region east of Ferghana and established themselves at the town of Uzgen on the banks of a tributary of the Jaxartes (Syr Darya) in modern

Fig. 280 **Woven silk on cotton textile decorated with elephants, camels and dragons. The 'St Josse silk'**
Samanid period, Khurasan, ca. 960
H. 51 cm, W. 61.5 cm.
Formerly in the church of St Josse sur Mer, Pas de Calais
(Musée du Louvre – Photo RMN)
The Kufic inscription on this textile reads: 'Glory and happiness to *amir* Abu Mansur Bukhtegin, may God prolong (His favours to him?)'. The St Josse silk is a product of Central Asia yet the dragons at the elephants' feet recall those of China, the camels along the border wear ribbons in Sasanian style and the textile itself, though it possesses 'a barbaric boldness and ostentation that are of the very heart of Asia',* came thousands of miles along the Silk Road to wrap a Christian relic in a French church. Another interesting point is that this textile is a representational art form, seemingly at odds with the belief in Islam that depictions of humans and animals are wrong. In fact the Koran does not proscribe such images; objections occur only in the *hadiths*, the traditional sayings ascribed to the Prophet.

Kyrgyzstan. The Kharakhanids, the first Turkish tribe to adopt Islam, appear to have emerged in the area around Balasagun on the Cu (Chu) River (see p. 279). During the middle part of the tenth century their territories were extended eastwards as far as Kashgar where they established their capital under Satuk Bughra Khan (d. ca. 955). Under Bughra Khan Harun the Kharakhanids took advantage of confusion among the Samanids, caused by internal dissent and by pressure applied by the new Buyid rulers of Persia. In 992 Harun entered Bukhara virtually unopposed and it was only his sudden illness and premature death that prevented the town from being immediately incorporated into the Kharakhanid Empire. The Samanids appealed for help to the Ghaznavid Turks under Sebuktigin. In return for his assistance Sebuktigin was given control of Khurasan, leaving only Transoxiana (the lands between the Oxus and the Jaxartes), under Samanid control. During their final years the Samanids were sandwiched precariously between the Ghaznavids – who controlled Khurasan and Afghanistan to the south and southwest – and the Kharakhanids, who held the steppes around the Cu (Chu) and Ili Rivers and Kasgharia to the northeast. The end was not long in coming. In 999 fighting erupted between the last Samanid ruler, Abd al-Malik II and the illustrious Mahmud of Ghazni (r. 998–1032), son of Sebuktigin. Abd al-Malik was defeated by Mahmud close to the city of Merv and the Samanids abandoned Khurasan to the victors. The Kharakhanid ruler Arslan Ilek Nasr grasped

Fig. 281 **Small blue glass ewer**
Samanid period, ca. 10th century
H. 10 cm
From Afrasiab, Samarkand
(Registan Museum, Samarkand)

* (Phyllis Ackerman, quoted in Liu, 1996).

the opportunity later that year and seized Bukhara, took Abd al-Malik prisoner and annexed the whole of Transoxiana. The fall of the Samanid dynasty marked the end of Persian domination of Central Asia. From 999 onwards the area was divided between the Ghaznavids and the Kharakhanids, both Turkish dynasties. The area became 'Turkicized' and has remained so to the present day.

A brief accord was reached between Ghaznavids and the Kharakhanids, with Mahmud taking Arslan's daughter in marriage, but the alliance soon fell apart. By 1005, Mahmud had conquered the Punjab and now controlled north-western India, Afghanistan and Khurasan. In 1006, while Mahmud was campaigning in India, Arslan invaded Khurasan and seized Balkh and Nishapur. Mahmud drove them out of Khurasan in 1008 and the Ghaznavids progressively enlarged their empire until, by 1025, it extended as far west as Iraq and as far south as the Ganges. The same year Mahmud attacked the Kharakhanid ruler Alitigin and advanced briefly as far as Samarkand. He did not hold the city for long however, and retired to Khurasan. Transoxiana remained under Kharakhanid control but, in 1040, the Ghaznavids were defeated close to Merv by the Seljuks- another Turkish tribe who appear to have lived around the mouth of the Syr Darya (Jaxartes) River. After their defeat by the Seljuks the Ghaznavids were expelled from Khurasan and confined to their domains in northern India and Afghanistan. The Seljuks quickly seized more territory and, in 1055, entered Baghdad where the Abbasid caliph effectively handed over control of all of Central Asia to them. The Seljuk Empire was expanded east and west until it extended from the Mediterranean to the Oxus. In 1071, the Byzantine Emperor Romanus Diogenes was taken captive by the then sultan Alp Arslan (r. 1063–72). After Diogenes's defeat the Seljuks established the Sultanate of 'Rum' (ie 'eastern Rome') in present-day Turkey, thereby laying the foundations for the emergence of the Ottoman Empire some two centuries later. In 1072, Alp Arslan attacked the territory of the Kharakhanids. Balkh, Bukhara and Samarkand changed hands, once again, and the Kharakhanids were reduced to little more than vassals of the Seljuks although another branch of the tribe still retained control of the lands around the Ili River and Kashgaria.

Alp Arslan's son Malikshah (r. 1072–92) allowed the Persian vizier Nizam-al-Mulk to administer the Seljuk's empire for twenty years. Nizam al-Mulk was one of the most enlightened statesmen of his day. He helped to establish a system of madrassahs or theological seminaries (known as *nizamiyah* after the first part of his name). The madrassahs provided students with free instruction in religious science. His work 'The Book of Government', written around 1090, influenced much of the political thought of the time. Nizam al-Mulk was a devout Sunni Muslim who fomented against the Ismaili sect of the Shi'ites who were terrorizing the

region at that time. Known as the Assassins, they were an offshoot of the Sevener Shi'ites and used murder to further their political ends. Nizam al-Mulk himself fell victim to the sect in 1092.

The period of peace and intellectual enlightenment ushered in by the Seljuks was short-lived, however. After the Kharakhanid ruler Arslan Khan Muhammad's death in 1129, the Seljuk Empire fractured as a result of nepotism and feuds among the ruling clans. The eastern part of the Seljuk Empire was sustained for a while by Sultan Sanjar (r. ca. 1118 to1157), Malikshah's youngest son and the last of great Seljuk rulers. Sanjar was given the governorship of Khurasan when he was little more than ten years old with his headquarters at Merv. He survived attempts by Kharakhanid khans to break free of Seljuk control and, by 1118, was ruler of both Ghaznavid Afghanistan and Transoxiana with his capital at Merv. The Seljuk domains in the east held together until 1141 when a new threat emerged in the shape of the Kharakhitai, the first of many waves of Mongols who would decimate the countries of the Silk Road over the following centuries.

The Prester John Legend and Islam at a hiatus

The Kharakhitai were a non-Muslim tribe of Mongolian descent, said to be descendants of the Liao dynasty Khitans of China.* In about 1128 they entered Kashgaria with an army and attacked the Kharakhanids from the rear. As the Kharakhitai moved westwards they wrested town after town from the Muslims, a campaign that culminated in 1141 with the defeat of the Seljuk Sultan Sanjar and the seizure of the great Silk Road cities of Samarkand and Bukhara. In the same year the Kharakhitai invaded Khorezm and before long were presiding over an empire that extended from Hami in China's Xinjiang province to the Aral Sea. The religious beliefs of the Kharakhitai were mixed and included Buddhism, Manichaeism and Nestorian Christianity. The mosques of conquered towns were sometimes converted into Buddhist temples or Nestorian churches. For two centuries, first under the Kharakhitai and, subsequently, under the armies of Genghis Khan and his clansmen, the Islamic supremacy of the central section of the Silk Road was severely challenged. It did not recover until the fourteenth century when Mongol rule began to decline. The beleaguered Frankish Knights of the Crusades heard stories of a Christian king in the East who was beating back the forces of Islam and the legend of 'Prester John' was born. In fact the Kharakhitai were driven by Mammon, not God, a

* The word 'Cathay', long used by Europeans as a term for China, derives from the tribe's name.

fact that failed to dispel a belief in Europe that a second front was about to be opened in the battle against the forces of Islam.

The legend gained greater currency during the second half of the twelfth century when at least one forged letter, purportedly from Prester John himself, was sent to Manuel I Comnenus, Emperor of Byzantium (r. 1143–80):

'...I, Prester John, who reign supreme, surpass in virtue, riches and power all creatures under heaven. Seventy kings are our tributaries. I am a zealous Christian and universally protect the Christians of our empire, supporting them by our alms. We have determined to visit the sepulchre of our Lord with a very large army, in accordance with the glory of our majesty to humble and chastise the enemies of the cross of Christ and to exalt his blessed name… For gold, silver, precious stones, animals of every kind and the number of our people, we believe there is not our equal under heaven.'

(An extract from a forged letter, purportedly from Prester John to Manuel I Comnenus, Emperor of Byzantium, ca. 1165)

The letter created a sensation in Europe and men set out, both *officio* and *ex-officio*, to search for him, many no doubt enticed by the 'gold, silver [and] precious stones' referred to in the letter. Marco Polo himself mentions Prester John in his *Travels* and the quest continued well into the fourteenth century but no trace of the great man was ever found. Europeans eventually turned their attention to Africa, in particular to the kingdom of Ethiopia, which had a long tradition of Christian belief. The search for Prester John undoubtedly led to greater contacts between Europe and China, however, and was a factor in a brief but significant revival of commercial activity along the Silk Road before the highway entered a period of terminal decline during the fourteenth century.

A short period of relative calm before a raging storm: The Khorezmshahs

After the death of the Seljuk Sultan Sanjar in 1157 his former vassals, the shahs of Khorezm (the area east and south of the Aral Sea), quickly moved into the former Seljuk territories. Like the Seljuks the Khorezmshahs were Muslim Turks who saw themselves as defenders of the faith against the pagan Kharakhitai. In spite of this they sought help from the Kharakhitai when it suited them and remained their nominal vassals. In 1172, the Kharakhitai intervened in a dispute between two brothers, Takash and Sultan-shah who

fought for the throne of Khorezm. They first supported Takash but, when he refused to pay them tribute, they switched sides and began to support his brother. Assistance from the Kharakhitai enabled Sultan-shah to retain control of the Khurasan region until his death in 1193, while Takash remained firmly in control of Khorezm. After Sultan-shah's death, Takash became master of both domains and wasted no time in invading Iraq. During the reign of his son Muhammad (r. 1200–1220), the Khorezmian territories were expanded to include the Ghurid lands in Afghanistan. The Ghurids, a clan confederation of Iranian origin, were former vassals of the Ghaznavids and in 1151 replaced them as rulers of Afghanistan, forcing the latter to flee to the Punjab region. During the long reign of their ruler Muhammad of Ghur (1163–1206) the Ghurids expanded eastwards, first seizing the Punjab from the Ghaznavids and then, by 1203, defeating the Hindu rulers of the Ganges Basin. The Ghurids were Sunni Muslims and were great builders, counting two of Islam's finest buildings: the Qutb Minar in Delhi and the 65 metre high Jam Minaret at the site of their former capital of Firuzukh in Afghanistan among their achievements.

It was inevitable that Shah Muhammad of Khorezm and Muhammad of Ghur would come to blows. The first battle occurred in 1204 and the Khorezmian ruler lost it. The Ghurids then proceeded to attack Khorezm itself but were driven back by a combined force of Khorezmians, Kharakhitai and soldiers sent by their vassal, the Kharakhanid ruler of Samarkand. Now at the height of his powers, Shah Muhammad of Khorezm rebelled against Kharakhitai rule and, with the consent of the Kharakhanid ruler of Samarkand, marched on both that city and on Bukhara. The Kharakhitai made a vain attempt to regain sovereignty of the region but were defeated and, by 1210, had ceased to play a major role in Transoxiana. The Kharakhanid prince of Samarkand – the last of the line – soon rebelled against Muhammad but was executed, leaving the Khorezmian in sole charge of a vast, though loosely connected empire extending from the Pamirs in the east to Azerbaijan in the west. All Central Asia and almost all of Afghanistan and Persia were his and in 1217, he threatened even Baghdad. Muhammad ruled from a series of fortified towns across Central Asia with his capital at Kunya Urgench (Gurganj). During the brief, twilight years of the Khorezmian Empire, he postured and preened himself as the Mongol storm gathered in the east. René Grousset provides a succinct summation of the differences between the doomed Khorezmian Muhammad and the 'World Conqueror', Genghis Khan: 'Of the two, the nomad barbarian was the ruler, while the Iranized Turk, an emperor of Islam and a king of the sedentary states, was nothing but a knight errant' (Grousset, 1970).

CHAPTER TWELVE

THE MONGOLS

Fig. 282 **'The World Conqueror' Temuchin, known as Genghis Khan (ca. 1165–1227)**

(National Palace Museum, Taiwan, Republic of China)

In 1218, with the Mongol conquest of North China complete, Genghis Khan sent his most trusted general Jebe Noyen to campaign against the remnants of the Kharakhitai in East Turkestan, its people already weakened by seven years of depredations at the hands of Küchlüg, leader of the Turko-Mongol Naiman tribe. A Nestorian Christian, Küchlüg had terrorised the region between Tashkent and Kashgar and forcibly converted many of its Muslim inhabitants. By 1218 he had more or less assumed control of the Kharakhitai domains and was deemed by the Mongols to represent a genuine threat to their territory. There may also have been an element of revenge to the decision to attack Küchlüg: he is said to have killed a son-in-law of Genghis Khan's son Jochi. In any event, 20,000 Mongols with Jebe at their head were soon sweeping down to Kashgar. Küchlüg fled towards the Pamirs but was captured and killed, thereby

removing the last barrier between the Mongols and the Khorezmshahs. Genghis Khan, at least initially, sought to open trading relations with the Khorezmshahs. The same year three envoys were sent to Muhammad in his capital at Kunya Urgench (Gurganj) with, (in the words of the Persian chronicler Juzjani) the following message:

'I am master of the lands of the rising sun while you rule those of the setting sun. Let us conclude a firm treaty of friendship and peace. Merchants and their caravans should come and go in both directions, carrying the valuable products and ordinary goods from my land to yours, just as they do from your land to mine.'

(Juzjani, 'Tabaqat-I-Nasiri'. Quoted in Ratchnevsky, 1991)

The same year, a trade caravan of 450 Muslim merchants on their way from Mongolia and accompanied by a Mongol envoy stopped in the Khorezmian frontier town of Otrar (on the Oxus in modern Kazakhstan). The city's governor, Inal-khan – a relative of Shah Muhammad's mother – decided that the merchants were spies and ordered that they be killed and their goods seized. Genghis Khan was said to have been incandescent with rage and sent envoys to Muhammad demanding that Inal-Khan be handed over for punishment. Muhammad refused and had one, or possibly all of the envoys murdered as well. These actions by Muhammad and Inal-Khan were to propel the world into an abyss, setting in motion a chain of events that would lead to the deaths of millions of people from the Danube to the Sea of Japan.

Muhammad's fragile and newly fledged empire, riven by hatred between its Iranian and Turkish peoples, was no match for the well-organized legions of Genghis. Genghis is said to have launched his campaign against Khorezm with a force of 150,000 to 200,000 men. Otrar was the first to fall, taken in February 1220 after a five-month siege. The hapless Governor Inal-Khan, who had ordered the killing of the merchants, was captured and tortured to death, one chronicler reporting that molten silver was poured into his eyes and ears.

The city of Bukhara was next to be besieged, also in February 1220, this time by a force led by Genghis himself. Most of the populace fled the city and were spared but the

500 or so Turkish soldiers who attempted to defend the city were annihilated. One of the chroniclers, Juvaini, reported that Genghis entered the city's great mosque, declared himself 'the scourge of God' and yelled abuse at the worshippers there but this tale is apocryphal in the extreme. What is not in dispute, however, is that the Mongols plundered Bukhara and as they did so a fire broke out which reduced the city to ashes. A graphic account from an eyewitness to the destruction of Bukhara contains a terse summation of what awaited those unfortunate enough to find themselves in the path of the Mongol advance:

'Amadand, u kandang, u sukhtand, u kushtand, u burdand, u raftand.'

(They came, they uprooted, they burned, they slew, they despoiled, they departed)

(Quoted in Lawton, 1991)

Samarkand was attacked in March 1220, again by an army led by the World Conqueror himself. The inhabitants resisted for only five days before surrendering. About 30,000 Turkish defenders were slaughtered but most of the citizenry were spared- many of the towns' best craftsmen sent back to Mongolia to work for their new masters. The Mongols destroyed the aqueduct in Afrasiab, the oldest section of the

city, an act that led to its abandonment. Most of the town seems to have escaped, however – a view supported by a description by Marco Polo, who passed through the city only about sixty years later:

'Samarcan is a noble city, adorned with beautiful gardens, and surrounded by a plain, in which are produced all the fruits that man can desire.'

(From *The Travels of Marco Polo the Venetian*. Translated by William Marsden in Marsden, 1948)

The Khorezmian capital, Kunya Urgench (Gurganj) held out until April 1221 (or even later, according to some commentators). The siege was so protracted that no fewer than three of Genghis Khan's elder sons, including Ögödei became involved. As the city fell, the last of the defenders are said to have huddled on a low mound known as Forty Mullahs Hill and were slaughtered. Their contorted remains are still visible at the base of the mound (fig. 284).

The inhabitants of cities who resisted the Mongols were usually massacred and such was the case with the citizens of Kunya Urgench: twenty-four were killed by each Mongol soldier. The Mongols then breached a nearby dam and the city was quickly submerged by the waters of the Oxus (Amu Darya). As his kingdom was demolished around him, Shah Muhammed fled westwards with the Mongols in pursuit. He

Fig. 283 **Ruins of the Mongol capital at Karakorum, Upper Orkhon River, Mongolia**
Founded ca. 1220 by Ögödei, son of Genghis Khan

died of pneumonia on a small island in the Caspian in December 1220; spared, at least, the spectacle of seeing his capital destroyed. (For more on Kunya Urgench, see p. 239).

During the early part of 1221, Genghis Khan continued his campaigns across the Oxus. Balkh, Merv and Nishapur were taken in rapid succession and all flattened. At Merv, Genghis's son Tolui is said to have sat on a golden chair and watched as the population was massacred, the mausoleum of the great Seljuk Sultan Sanjar put to the torch and his body removed. The town of Herat resisted and was destroyed, although its civilian populace were uncharacteristically spared, followed in short order by Thaleqan and Bamiyan. During the siege of Bamiyan, Genghis' favourite grandson Mütügen was killed and he ordered every living thing in the city to be extirpated. Ghazni was next to be taken and Prince Jalal ad-Din, son of Muhammad and last scion of the Khmorezmshahs, was almost captured. In the event he escaped across a river and found refuge in Delhi at the court of the sultan. He campaigned against the Mongols for another ten years, partially restoring the Khorezmian Empire in the process and forcing Ögödei to launch a new invasion of Persia to restore order. He was finally killed in 1231, by a Kurdish assassin in the mountains of Azerbaijan.

Genghis Khan died in August 1227 at the age of about sixty, probably as a result of injuries sustained in a fall from a horse. His grandson Batu (son of Jochi who had predeceased him) inherited the western part of the empire. This region – the steppes to the north of the Aral Sea and west of the Irtysh River – later became the realm of the Golden Horde. Genghis' second son, Chagatai, inherited the lands extending from Bukhara and the Oxus in the West to the Tarim Basin in the east and his third son, Ögödei, received the area to the east of Lake Balkash, southern Siberia and the western part of Mongolia. His youngest son Tolui was bequeathed the Mongol heartlands between the Tula, upper Onon and upper Kerulen rivers.

Ögödei was elected Great Khan in 1229. With his capital at Karakorum on the banks of the Upper Orkhon River, Ögödei presided over a second conquest. By 1231 the Mongols had taken control of Persia and by 1241 they had seized the southern area of Russia and advanced as far as Hungary, Poland and Romania. A sense of how terrifying the Mongols must have seemed can be gleaned from contemporary accounts. A description by a Persian observer is one of the most vivid:

> *'Their stench was more horrible than their colour. Their heads were set on their bodies as if they had no necks, and their cheeks resembled leather bottles full of wrinkles and knots. Their noses extended from cheekbone to cheekbone. Their nostrils resembled rotting graves… Their chests, in colour half-black, half-white, were covered with lice which looked like sesame growing on bad soil. Their bodies, indeed, were covered with these insects, and their skins were as rough-grained as shagreen leather, fit only to be converted into shoes…'*

By July 1241, Mongols troops under an army led by Batu were at the gates of Vienna and the whole of Western Europe lay supine before them. Then, in December 1241, Ögödei died and the Mongols withdrew, returning to Karakorum to participate in proceedings to appoint a new Great Khan (known as a *khuriltay*). The respite was brief, however, and by 1256 the Mongols were again rampaging through Persia. Hulägu, brother of the Khan Mangu and first of the Il-Khans, began his campaign by putting down the sect of the Assassins at Alamut in the mountains in the north of the country (see p. 297). Baghdad was attacked and destroyed in 1258 and the last Abbasid caliph sewn into a sack and trampled to death by horses. Syria was next and many of its cities, including Aleppo and Damascus, were sacked. Very little representational art survives from the Mongol period-nomadic peoples are not generally known for the fineness of their artistic creations. Furthermore, the Mongols did not generally interfere with the religious beliefs of their subject-peoples and Islam (with its dislike of images of humans or animals) still held sway in Central Asia and the Middle East. Persian paintings and manuscripts of the early fourteenth century provide a rare glimpse, however, of what the Mongols raids must have been like for those unfortunate enough to be on the receiving end (fig. 285).

The limits of the Mongols' westward expansion were reached in 1260 when they attacked Egypt. The Mamluks – mercenaries of Turkish origin who had first supported and then overthrown the Ayyubid sultans of Egypt – realized that Hulägu's army of only 20,000 men was insufficient to sustain an assault. The Mongols were pushed out of Egypt and Syria, too, was soon reconquered.

Fig. 284
**'Golden lads and girls all must,
As chimney-sweepers come to dust.'***
Victim of the Mongols 'Forty Mullahs Hill', Kunya Urgench, Turkmenistan

* William Shakespeare, 'Cymbeline', Act IV, scene 2.

Fig. 285 **Painting on paper depicting the capture of Baghdad by Mongol troops**
Illustration from *The Universal History of Rashid al-Din*
Early 14th century
D. 37.2 cm × 29 cm
(Staatsbibliothek, Berlin)

To the east, the Mongol advance continued. In 1259, Khubilai brother of Nagu became the Great Khan and during his long rule (from 1259–94), the Song rulers of China were defeated and the entire country fell under Mongol control. Khubilai and his descendants, with their capital at Beijing, ruled China as the Yuan dynasty until 1368. The Mongols also advanced into Burma, Indo-China and Java but failed in two attempts to reach Japan; the second foiled by a typhoon, was described by the grateful Japanese as a *kamikaze* or divine wind.

The Mongols and the Silk Road

There is little doubt that the Mongols were one of the most bellicose and pitiless nations ever to have stalked the earth. Genghis Khan himself, in a much-quoted remark, describes his own vision of supreme bliss:

'Man's greatest good fortune is to chase and defeat his enemy, seize his total possessions, leave his married women weeping and wailing, ride his gelding, use the bodies of his women as a nightshirt and support, gazing upon and kissing their rosy breasts, sucking their lips which are as sweet as the berries of their breasts.'

But his legacy, and that of his successors, was far more than one of despoilment and death. The linguistic make-up of Central Asia was permanently altered by Mongol rule. The Persian language was supplanted by Turkic dialects although the urban dwellers of Central Asia still use the former even today. Religious changes also occurred. The more mystic forms of Islam, such as Sufism or Dervishism, became popular as a result of the cataclysmic events experienced on a virtual daily basis by the populace. Crime – especially theft – was ruthlessly stamped out and, for a fleeting moment, centuries of anarchy and strife among the countries along the Silk Road came to an end. With their safety guaranteed, merchants practised their craft as never before:

'Under the reign of Jenghiz [Genghis] Khan, all the country between Iran and Turan [the lands of the Turks] enjoyed such peace that a man might have journeyed from the land of sunrise to the land of sunset with a golden platter upon his head without suffering the least violence from anyone.'

(Abu'l Ghazi Bahadur, Khan of Khiva [r. 1643–65] in his treatise 'Shajare-I Turk', a work containing a wealth of detail about the Mongols. Quoted in Grousset, 1970)

While the resurgence of trade benefited mainly the rich, the century and more of the *pax Mongolica* can have been little worse, to the beleaguered citizenry of Central Asia, than the endless cycle of warfare and revolt described in the preceding pages. An interesting innovation of the Mongols was the use, for the first time, of the passport, known as a *paizi* or *gerege* (fig. 286). The *paizi* consisted of a bronze or iron plate, inscribed or inlaid in silver with *Phags-Pa* script, named after and devised by a Tibetan monk in the service of Khubilai to enable the Mongols to accurately transcribe Chinese names. Two types of plaque were issued: one to officials as a badge of office and the other to important guests or persons on state business. Post stations were set up at intervals of about 40–50 km and travellers carrying *paizi* were able to traverse

the empire unimpeded, a system which greatly facilitated trade and diplomatic contacts (fig. 286).

Among the many Europeans to travel the Silk Road at this time were Marco Polo (whose contentious exploits are mentioned throughout this book), Johannes di Plano Carpini – sent to Karakorum in 1246 by Pope Innocent IV – and William of Rubric, an emissary of Louis IX of France. Both Carpini and Rubric mentioned that westerners were already at Karakorum. One, a Frenchwoman named Paquette, had accompanied her Russian husband who served the Khan as an architect. A Parisian goldsmith named Guillaume Boucher is said to have lived with the Mongols from about 1246 to about 1259, serving first Guyuk and then Mangu. He designed a golden tree, beneath which sat four golden lions with wine and *kumiss* flowing from their mouths.

By the first half of the fourteenth century, trade was so well developed that European merchants began to compile guides for travellers. The most famous of these was *La Practica della Mercatura* ('The Practice of Trade'), compiled in 1340 by Francesco Balducci Pegolotti (fl. 1315–40). There is no evidence that Pegolotti, a mercantile agent in the employ of the powerful Bardi family of Florence, ever travelled to China. He was more of a latter-day Herodotus, a gatherer of information and stories from travellers. Nevertheless, his book is a mine of information about trade routes, taxes payable on merchandise, the location of the principal markets and the comparative values of moneys, weights, and measures. He talks at length about the cost of such journeys:

'You may calculate that a merchant with a dragoman, and with two men servants, and with goods to the value of twenty-five thousand golden florins, should spend on his way to Cathay from sixty to eighty sommi of silver, and not more if he manage well; and for all the road back again from Cathay to Tana*, including the expenses of living and the pay of servants, and all other charges, the cost will be about five sommi per head of pack animals, or something less. And you may reckon the sommo to be worth five golden florins. You may reckon also that each ox-waggon will require one ox, and will carry ten cantars Genoese weight; and the camel-waggon will require three camels, and will carry thirty cantars Genoese weight; and the horse-waggon will require one horse, and will commonly carry six and a half cantars of silk, at 250 Genoese pounds to the cantar. And a bale of silk may be reckoned at between 110 and 115 Genoese pounds.'

(Francesco Balducci Pegolotti in 1340, translated by Yule, 1914. * Tana is Azov, a town just east of the Black Sea)

The astute observations of another traveler, Ibn Battuta of Tangiers (1304–77), have also survived. Ibn Battuta set out in

Fig. 286 **A Paizi or Gerege (Passport Medallion) inlaid in silver with Phags-pa (*Baisiba*) script**
Mongolia or China
Yuan dynasty (1279–1368)
D.11 cm
(Vahid Kooros Collection)
Most *paizi* have a lobed handle with a *kirttimukha* (demon) mask to facilitate attachment to a belt or strap. After the Ming expelled the Mongols from China in 1368, the new regime appears to have tried to erase all trace of them. The Mongol capital at Karakorum was destroyed in 1388 and the accoutrements of Mongol rule, including *paizi*, were done away with. As a result there are only about twelve *paizi* in existence today. The inscription on this example is typical and reads:
'By the strength of Eternal Heaven, an edict of the Emperor [Khan]. He who has no respect shall be guilty.'

1325 on a twenty-four year journey through Egypt, Iran, Central Asia and northern India. After residing in Delhi for eight years he took a ship to China, stopping off in Java and Sumatra on the way. His descriptions are far more precise than those of Marco Polo's, raising the oft-asked question of whether the latter ever actually made the journey. Ibn Battuta is regarded by many, both within and without the Islamic world, as one of the greatest travellers in history. One seventeenth-century admirer summarised his accomplishments thus:

> *'He it was who hung the world,*
> *that turning wheel of diverse parts,*
> *upon the axis of a book.'*

A contemporary of Ibn Battuta was an English knight called Sir John Mandeville who wrote an account of the thirty four years he spent travelling the world and of the cultures and customs of the places he visited. His work is commonly known as *The Travels of Sir John Mandeville* and first appeared in French in about 1356, followed by an English edition around 1375. Until the nineteenth century, Mandeville was celebrated as one of the greatest travellers of the Middle Ages but when the intrepid explorers of the Victorian era arrived on the scene it became clear, not only that he had not actually been to the places he describes, but that in all probability he did not even exist. It has been suggested that the true author was a French physician named Jean de Bourgogne but whatever the truth of the matter, *The Travels of Sir John Mandeville* is still one of the most colourful and interesting of the many accounts of the countries of the Silk Road.

Much has been written about the many Europeans who travelled to the Orient during the years of the *pax Mongolica*. A little know fact is that a number of Chinese travellers journeyed west during the same period. What the stolid citizens of Europe's cities thought of them is unknown but a few made the journey and lived to tell the tale. Perhaps the most celebrated was the Chinese Nestorian Monk Rabban Bar Sauma (d. 1294). In about 1275 Sauma and his disciple Mark set off from Peking to visit the Holy Land. They passed through Tabriz – then under the control of the Mongol Khan Arghun (r. 1284–91) – and visited the city's Nestorian prelate. Arghun sent Sauma as an envoy to Rome. From Rome he continued on to Gascony where he met the king of England and thence to Paris where he met Philip, the French king.

Before Karakorum was destroyed in 1388, merchandise from all the Mongol domains flowed into the city. Excavations of graves in and around the site have unearthed large numbers of coins from the Arab world and China, while Rubric tells us of rich fabrics from China and Persia, furs from Russia and Eastern Europe and slaves from every province of the Mongol Empire. Perhaps the strangest relic from Karakorum is an Egyptian pharaoh mask of about 20 cm in height, discovered in the grave of a Mongol woman and now displayed in the Ulaan Bator Museum. It was, perhaps, booty from their campaigns in Egypt in 1260.

In the arts, the forcible movement of peoples to serve the Mongols resulted in a wide dissemination of new styles and ideas. Islamic art, particularly, was revitalized by influences from China that travelled westwards during the years of the *pax Mongolica*. The emergence of Persian miniature painting during the fourteenth century was undoubtedly a result of patronage by the Il-Khans, who also encouraged the writing of poetry and historical literature. An intriguing conundrum, still to be satisfactorily unravelled by scholars, is the existence of the Hazara peoples of Afghanistan. The origin of the Hazaras is hotly debated but some claim that they are descendants of the invading armies of Genghis and his successors, perhaps of the 'thousands' left behind in each conquered city to propagate the race and to maintain control of the populace. Others claim that the Hazaras migrated to Afghanistan long before Islam and others still, that they are the heirs to Timur. A recent study (Mousavi, 1998) suggests that they have existed in Afghanistan since the pre-Christian era but that their blood and language has mingled with those of other groups, the men of Genghis and Timur among them. Whatever the truth of the matter, they are a strikingly handsome race: a living demonstration of the extent to which trade and conquest led to the movement of peoples over vast distances along the old trade routes (fig. 287).

Fig. 287 **A Hazara man on the road to Bamiyan**

One of the consequences of the resurgence of Silk Road trade during the period of Mongol domination turned out to be an utter catastrophe for the West. Bubonic plague, contracted from fleas feeding on infected rats, had begun in a famine-affected area of northern China. It afflicted a Kipchak army laying siege to the Genoese port of Caffa in the Crimea and subsequently spread to the cities along the Mediterranean shoreline. Constantinople was stricken in 1347 and, within twenty years, Europe was decimated. In the five year period between 1347 and 1352, about 25 million people died – a third of Europe's population. In *The Decameron*, the Italian writer and eyewitness Giovanni Boccaccio writes:

> *'How many noble men, how many beautiful ladies,*
> *how many light-hearted youths, who were such that*
> *Galen, Hippocrates, or Asclepius would declare them*
> *the healthiest of all humans, had breakfast in the*
> *morning with their relatives, companions, or friends,*
> *and had dinner that evening in another world with*
> *their ancestors!'*

****

CHAPTER THIRTEEN

TAMERLAINE (TIMUR) AND THE TIMURIDS

'The world's great age begins anew,
The golden years return,
The earth doth like a snake renew
Her winter weeds outworn:
Heaven smiles, and faiths and empires gleam,
Like wrecks of a dissolving dream.'

(Percy Bysshe Shelley, ,'The World's Great Age', from *Hellas*)

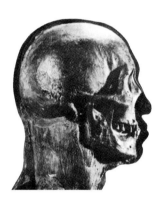

Fig. 288 **The skull and reconstructed face of Timur (1336–1405)**
The former exhumed and photographed by Mikhail Mikhailovich Gerasimov in 1941, at the Gur-e Mir mausoleum, Samarkand
(After Gerasimov, 1971)

The last of the great nomad emperors was born in 1336 in the town of Kesh (modern Shakhrisabz, or 'The Green City'), in the Kashka Darya valley to the south of Samarkand. His father was a chief of the Barlas clan, Turkicized Mongols who had entered Transoxiana with Chagatai. His skills as a warrior are said to have been honed during his early career as a sheep rustler and raider of caravans and he soon attracted a band of followers, not only from the Barlas but also from many of the other tribes marauding across Transoxiana at the time. After the death of Khan Tarmarshin in 1334 there followed thirty years of warfare between the Mongol Khans and the Turkish emirs. At the time of Timur's birth the Chagatai *ulus* (territorial apanage) was divided in two – the area around the Talas and Ili rivers (known as Semirechiye or Moghulistan), and Transoxiana itself. The rulers of Semirechiye regarded themselves as the rightful heirs to the Chagatai *ulus* and launched repeated attacks on Transoxiana with the intention of reintegrating the domains. Timur and his one-time ally and friend Husayn fought off the attacks and sought to restore the *ulus* and make Transoxiana the centre of a vast empire. Their collaboration was short lived, however, and Husayn was defeated at Balkh in 1370. Husayn relinquished control of his armies and was permitted to depart Balkh and go on pilgrimage to Mecca but was killed (with or without Timur's assent) soon afterwards. At Balkh, Timur declared himself ruler of the Chagatai *ulus* and extravagantly claimed that he was a descendent of Genghis Khan. To legitimize his position a series of khans of the Chinggisid line were appointed, each as powerless as their predecessor.

As *de facto* ruler of the Chagatai *ulus* Timur embarked on a thirty-year period of military campaigns. The earliest were against Moghulistan (the region around the Talas and Ili Rivers) and Khorezm, followed by Khurasan and Persia. In

1386 he launched a three-year campaign to consolidate his dependencies in Iran and the Caucasus and to protect the western part of his empire from Tokhtamish, a former ally who had seized control of the Golden Horde territory in the Volga region. Tokhtamish was contained by a series of campaigns and at one point Timur's army reached the outskirts of Moscow. By attacking the Golden Horde Timur briefly succeeded in shifting the focus of trade from the Volga region back to the Central Asian Silk Road. Timur was more than simply a destroyer- he was also a great patron of the arts and a devout Muslim. Samarkand, Timur's capital, regained its status as a great commercial centre and artisans from all over the conquered territories were forcibly relocated to work on its glorious new buildings. The capture of Baghdad in 1393 and Delhi in 1398 brought about an even greater cultural influx to the Timurid capital and augmented Pan-Asian trade further still.

In 1399, Timur went westwards again, his longest campaign yet, taking Baghdad (once again) and attacking the Mamluks in Syria and the Ottomans in Anatolia. In Syria Aleppo, Hims and Damascus were taken and the Ottomans were defeated near Ankara in 1402- their Sultan Bayazid taken hostage. In the spring of 1404 Timur withdrew from his newly captured territories and returned to Samarkand. Timur was nearing seventy but this did not prevent him from making plans for his most ambitious campaign yet- against the Ming emperor of China. While back in Samarkand, Timur convened a *khuriltay*, a Grand Assembly to celebrate his military victories. Ambassadors from the furthest reaches of the Silk Road came to pay homage: emissaries from the Byzantine Empire – already in its twilight years – and from the Chinese Emperor Yung Lo, his country faced with the threat of imminent invasion. One of the most distinguished observers at the *khuriltay* was Ruy Gonzalez de Clavijo, representative of King Henry III of Castile. Clavijo was an astute observer and has left a record of a great city enjoying its golden age:

> 'Every year to the city of Samarqand much merchandise of all kinds came from Cathay, India, Tartary, and from many other quarters besides, for in the countries round the Samarqand territory commerce is very flourishing…'

(Ruy Gonzalez de Clavijo. Translated by Guy Le Strange in Le Strange, 1928)

It is clear from Clavijo's observations of commerce at Samarkand that Chinese merchants were still risking the perils of the road to trade with the cities of Central Asia. Their faith in providence was sometimes misplaced, however:

> 'During the month of June of this year, immediately before the date of our coming to Samarqand, there had arrived a caravan of eight hundred camels bringing merchandise

> from China. Then it was that Timur having come home from his western campaigns had received that Chinese Embassy bearing the message sent him by the Emperor of China: and he forthwith had ordered the whole of this caravan, men and goods, to be taken into custody and that none should return to China.'

(*ibid.*)

By the autumn of 1404, Timur had assembled a huge army and set off on his greatest campaign: the conquest of China and the forcible conversion of its people to Islam. In Otrar, north of Tashkent, he paused for the winter but in February of 1405 he fell ill and died. Timur's death at Otrar spared China from invasion and was also a neat piece of historical symmetry – the beginning of the Mongols' westward expansion was sparked by the murder of the members of a trade caravan by the city's governor in 1218 (see p. 277). After Timur's death his empire rapidly disintegrated amid internecine battles between members of his family. By 1407, the empire had shrunk to include only Khurasan, Afghanistan and Transoxiana. Despite this, the long reign of Timur's fourth and youngest son Sharukh (r. 1405–47) and the brief rule of Sharukh's son Ulugh Beg (r. 1447–49) brought a measure of stability and ensured the continuation of trade. Sharukh ruled Khurasan from Herat in modern Afghanistan while Ulugh Beg governed Transoxiana from Samarkand. Both were enlightened men of letters who oversaw a renaissance in literature, art, science and architecture. Islamic art flourished, delicately illustrated manuscripts were produced and the great poets of the day extolled the achievements of the Timurids, not only in Persian but in Arabic and Chagatai (Eastern Turkish), too.

Ulugh Beg was a scholar of great eminence. As a mathematician and astronomer he knew no equal and the massive sextant from the observatory he constructed on a hill overlooking Samarkand can still be seen today (fig. 337). Ulugh Beg also built huge madrassahs in Samarkand and Bukhara; theological colleges where the pious might advance their knowledge of Islam. But it was not too last and, in the end, the Timurids proved to be as ephemeral as their predecessors. In 1449, Ulugh Beg was assassinated on the orders of one of his sons; his fascination with science deemed a heresy. There followed a bleak period of decline for the remainder of the fifteenth century as the Timurids were relentlessly supplanted by the Uzbeks. The last Timurid was Babur (1483–1530), a man who suffered ignominious defeat at the hands of the Uzbek Khan Ubaydullah in 1512 and yet went on to found the Mughal Empire of India – a dynasty that was to last for three hundred years.

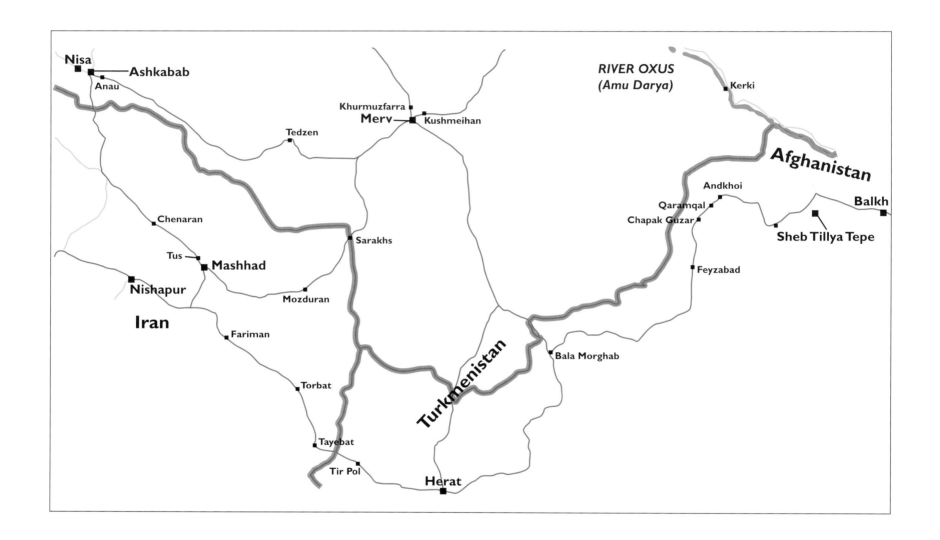

Nisa
Ashkabab
Anau

Khurmuzfarra
Tedzen
Merv Kushmeihan

RIVER OXUS
(Amu Darya)
Kerki

Afghanistan

Andkhoi
Qaramqal
Chapak Guzar
Balkh

Sheb Tillya Tepe

Chenaran
Tus Mashhad
Nishapur
Sarakhs
Feyzabad

Iran
Mozduran

Fariman

Turkmenistan
Bala Morghab

Torbat

Tayebat
Tir Pol
Herat

THE SILK ROAD SITES
BETWEEN BALKH AND NISA

CHAPTER FOURTEEN

SILK ROAD SITES BETWEEN BALKH AND NISA

But what of the caravan towns of the Silk Road before the coming of the Mongols? They had, after all, already been commercial entrepôts for centuries, and sometimes millennia before the arrival of Genghis Khan. In fact, Genghis' armies arrived during the twilight years of the Silk Road when trade was already faltering and alternatives to the land routes were being explored. Arabs had been consummate seafarers for centuries and the merchants of Song dynasty China (960–1279), cut off from the traditional land routes through Central Asia by the tumultuous events described above, became accomplished sailors. They competed head to head with the Arabs and built great six-masted ships of four storeys and 40 metres in length. Song dynasty porcelain and copper coins have been found in Sri Lanka, the Persian Gulf and the east coast of Africa.

It is often said that little or nothing remains of the Silk Road in Central Asia but this is far from the truth of the matter. If one looks a little way beneath its 'Sovietized', industrialized, urbanized surface one can still find the footprints of the giants who strode across the pages of its history. The rapid development and (sometimes) careless restoration of the great caravan-cities of Central Asia has, for the most part, been a feature only of the past fifty years. There are people alive today – as old photographs can attest – who have seen the cities of the Silk Road (albeit in a reduced and ruinous state), as they would have appeared to Avicenna, to Genghis Khan or to Timur. Even today, nearly 600 years after Timur's death, traces of the halcyon days of the Silk Road can still be found. At Merv, next stop on the road west from Balkh and Termez, the old city crumbles back to dust but its tumultuous past is plain for all to see.

Merv

With the possible exception of Kunya Urgench (Gurganj) in northern Turkmenistan, there are few Silk Road cities whose aspect today reveals their history as visibly as Merv. As we have seen, Merv was the capital of the eastern Islamic territories and a centre for trade during the Umayyad and early Abbasid periods. By the time the capital was moved to Nishapur during the short-lived Tahirid dynasty (821–73), Merv had already been a major settlement for more than one thousand years. The routes from Merv went in a number of

direction: north to Khorezm (either directly crossing the Karakum or northeast to Chardzhou on the Bukhara road and then veering off to follow the Amu Darya), east to Balkh and Termez, southwest to Sarakhs and Nishapur, and west to Nisa. The Murgh (Murghab) River Oasis was occupied at least as far back as the beginning of the first millennium BC although the earliest structures at Merv date to the early Achaemenid period (sixth to fifth century BC). They include the massive oval ramparts of the Erk Kala citadel, residential buildings and a system of irrigation canals. From the end of the fourth century BC the region became known as Margiana and was ruled by the Seleucids. A detachment of Alexander's army arrived in 328 BC though not, it seems, the great man himself. The town was shifted to a site further south and renamed Alexandria. The Seleucid ruler Antiochos I (r. ca. 281–261 BC) renamed the area to the south of the Erk Kala as Gyaur-kala (*Antiochia Margiana*) and surrounded it with a massive square wall and moat. At the beginning of the second century BC, Margiana fell under Parthian control and Merv was greatly expanded (fig. 289).

Under Parthian rule Merv was a thriving commercial centre with a mint operating – if evidence from coin finds

Fig. 289 **The Erk Kala ('The Oval Citadel') at Merv, Turkmenistan**
Early Achaemenid period, 6th to 5th century BC
H. 50 metres (approx.)
To the south of the citadel are the square walls of Gyaur-kala, built around the third century BC.

Fig. 290 **The Kys Kala fortress at Merv, Turkmenistan**
Sasanian period, ca. 6th century

can be relied on – from the reign of King Phraates II (r. ca. 138–128 BC). The Erk Kala fortress was rebuilt during the later Parthian period, possibly by Roman prisoners taken at the battle of Carrhae in 53 BC (see p. 283). By this time the city was the most important in Central Asia and is mentioned in the *Geographica* of the renowned Greek scholar Strabo (ca. 63 BC – ca. 21 AD) and in the *Natural History* of Pliny the Elder (23–79 AD). Both men, perhaps obtaining their information from a common source, describe the rich soil and the city's vineyards. During the first century AD the northern areas of the oasis were settled, a process that continued when Merv fell under Sasanian rule during the third century. The Sasanians refortified the walls and, built the two hauntingly beautiful fortress palaces of Kys Kala ('Maiden's Castle') to the west of the Gyaur Kala (fig. 290).

The Sasanians were extremely tolerant of other religions, despite their own adherence to the Zoroastrian faith. A Buddhist stupa was built in the southeast corner of the Gyaur Kala during the fourth century and was probably still in existence when Merv was lost to the Arabs in 651. There was also a vibrant Christian community in the town. During the fourth century Merv, both as an outpost of the Persian Empire and as a commercial centre, was the most important city in Central Asia. Constant nomadic incursions during

the fifth century threatened the city's prosperity but both trade and the construction of new buildings appears to have continued.

The Buddhist remains at Merv mark the westernmost penetration of the religion. Buddhist sculpture found at Merv was strongly influenced by that of Gandhara. A massive head of Buddha is typical: some 75 cm in height, it is made of from the preferred materials of Buddhist artisans the length and breadth of the Silk Road- a mixture of clay and straw which is then painted. The head was found at the site of the stupa in the southeast corner of the Gyaur Kala and concealed nearby was an outstanding vessel shaped like an amphora (fig. 291). The vessel is painted in black, red and blue with four scenes: a man of noble appearance shown hunting, then feasting, then upon his death-bed and finally, being mourned as he is carried to a burial mound. The ephemerality of human existence is a popular theme during this period of the Silk Road's history, hardly surprising when one considers the tumultuous events taking place at the time (see also figs. 59 and 198). The vessel may have started life as an ossuary though it had been adopted for use as a container for Buddhist manuscripts, now sadly reduced almost to dust. The painting bears a strong resemblance to Sogdian murals at Afrasiab, Penjikent and Varaksha, shown elsewhere in this book.

Beside the stupa are the remains of a monastery (*sangharama*) of about 140 square metres with some thirty-two rooms arranged around a central courtyard. The large size of the Buddha head found at the Gyaur Kala would suggest that it was made locally but a number of small, highly portable images of Buddhas and Bodhisattvas may well be imports from Gandhara (fig. 292).

The city was captured by the Arabs in 651 and became the capital of Khurasan, the easternmost province of Islam. Under Arab patronage the city was expanded to the west of the Erk Kala, in an area now known as Sultan Kala, and new structures were erected along the Majan canal. Abu Muslim, the missionary who brought the Abbasids to power during the eighth century, was chiefly responsible for the development of the Majan suburb around the canal. The mosque, government buildings and a jail were all erected at this time and the town's bazaars were also expanded as commerce flourished.

As Sultan Kala expanded Gyaur Kala was progressively abandoned. During the eleventh century, the Seljuk Sultan Malikshah (r. 1072–92) erected a protective wall around Sultan Kala, enclosing an area of about 400 hectares. During the eleventh and twelfth centuries under Seljuk domination Merv enjoyed its greatest period of prosperity as capital of an empire that extended from the Amu Darya to the Mediterranean. It became the greatest city of the Muslim world after Baghdad and its merchants roamed far and wide. It was famous for the production of a silk and cotton blankets; fruits (especially pears, grapes and melons); cheese, oil, hay, ceramics and metalwares (especially steel and

copper). The pinnacle of the town's prosperity was attained during the long and illustrious reign of the great Seljuk Sultan Sanjar (r. 1118–57). During Sanjar's reign the whole area became more fertile after a dam was erected on the Murghab. At its peak, Merv occupied an area of 1,800 hectares and contained a population of about 150,000. Sanjar's own mausoleum: its great dome, visible a day's march away, still ranks among the greatest structures of the Islamic world and was the centre of the medieval city (fig. 293).

The great scholars of the day flocked to Merv during this period. Among them were the renowned poet and mathematician Hakim Omar Khayyam (c. 1048–c. 1125), who is said to have assembled his astronomical tables at the Merv observatory, and the celebrated geographer Yaqut al-Hamavi (d. ca. 1229). Yaqut complied a geographical dictionary from information contained in Merv's libraries and from his own travels in Khorezm. His dictionary lists

Fig. 292 **A grey schist figure of the Buddha seated on a pedestal with a second Buddha and worshippers**
Gandhara, ca. 3rd century
H. 21 cm
Unearthed at the Buddhist Stupa, Merv, Turkmenistan
(Turkmenistan National Museum, Ashkabad)

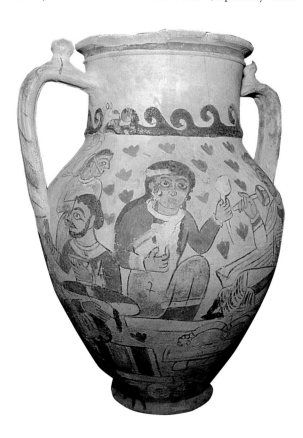

Fig. 291 **A painted clay vessel painted with episodes of life and death**
Sasanian period, ca. fifth century
H. 46 cm
Unearthed at the Buddhist Stupa, Merv, Turkmenistan
(Turkmenistan National Museum, Ashkabad)

Fig. 293 **Mausoleum of Sultan Sanjar**
Seljuk, mid-12th century
The massive square structure measures 27 metres on each side and the top of its double dome is 36 metres above the ground. The building's beautiful, ornate brickwork is typical of the Seljuks (see figs 368, 373, 386 and 388). The interior was once decorated with stucco mouldings and fragments still remain.

Fig. 294 **Remains of Old Nisa, Turkmenistan**
Parthian, ca. 2nd century BC to 3rd century AD

almost every town and village of the Islamic world, including many long-vanished Silk Road towns.

Sultan Sanjar's death in 1157 marked the beginning of the end for the Seljuks. By the end of the twelfth century, Merv and all of Khurasan were under the control of the Khorezmshahs. The city's prosperity was little affected by the change but in 1221 the city faced its nemesis in the shape of the Mongols. On 25 February of that year the city fell to Genghis's youngest son Tolui. The entire population, except for about 400 artisans, was massacred and a pitiful band of survivors were also slaughtered when they attempted to return to their homes a few days later.

The city did revive: during the reign of Timur's son Shahruk (r. 1405–47) a new, albeit smaller city was established to the south of the Sultan Kala. Known today as Abdullah Khan Kala, it was a shadow of medieval Merv and the focus of Timurid power and splendour shifted to Samarkand, Shakrisabz and Herat. The town sputtered through periods of Uzbek Shaybanid and Persian Safavid domination during the sixteenth and seventeenth centuries but by then, the merchants of the Silk Road had dwindled away.

As mentioned earlier one of the many strands of the Silk Road to emanate from Merv led in a southwesterly direction to the frontier town of Sarakhs on the Turkmenistan-Iran border. Sarakhs has been occupied since the Achaemenid period and the remains of fortifications from both this and the Bactrian era have been found. Sarakhs became an important stopping place on the Nishapur-Merv road, about half way on an arduous twelve-day journey across hills and desert. The route was punctuated by a series of castles and caravanserais but centuries of invasions have ensured that few buildings remain today. A massive earthen mound just to the south of modern Sarakhs marks the site of a Seljuk-era fortress and beside it is the mausoleum of the religious leader Abu Fazl (d. 1024). The latter is a rare survivor from the heyday of the Silk Road and one of the few examples of Seljuk architecture still standing in Turkmenistan. Immediately across the border from Sarakhs is the town's Iranian namesake.

The second road from Merv to Persia went west across the Karakum ('Black Sands') Desert to the Turkmen capital of Ashkabad. Ashkabad is a modern city – it was demolished by a massive earthquake in 1948 – but the town and its environs have played an important role in Silk Road commerce for at least two millenia. The most important of the many sites around Ashkabad is Nisa, situated about 15 km to the west of the modern city and once the capital of the Parthians.

Nisa

Located near the village of Bagir beside the foothills of the Kopet Dagh Mountains, the site consists of two parts: the fortified palace and temple complex of Old Nisa and the town of New Nisa, standing closeby. Parthian Nisa, known as Parthaunisa, was first mentioned in the journals of the eminent geographer Isidore of Charax* during the first century AD. Archeological evidence indicates that the site is much older, however. Old Nisa (Mithradatkirt), was probably founded during the second century BC by the eponymous Mithradates I (r. 171–138 BC). New Nisa is just as old; it takes its name from the fact that it survived until about the seventeenth century, whereas Old Nisa was abandoned around the third century AD when the Parthian Empire collapsed.

Old Nisa covered an area of about 14 hectares on a hilltop about 10 metres above the valley. The site's defensive walls were in a five-sided configuration, punctuated by forty-three rectangular towers, and were 9 metres thick in places – rendering the entire fortress virtually impregnable. In the centre and southern part were religious and royal buildings with thick mud-brick walls. The South Complex contained a large square audience hall of about 20 metres by 20 metres, two storeys high with colossal fluted columns. In the same complex stood a round hall about 17 metres across, set within a square perimeter of corridors, and a tower temple enclosed by vaulted corridors. The remains of massive clay statues of women in heavy clothing and men in armour, brightly painted and realistically modelled, were

* *The Parthian Stations*, written by Isidore of Charax during the first century AD, is believed to have been commissioned by the Roman Emperor Augustus. The work lists places and distances along the trade routes from Mesopotamia to Central Asia.

Fig. 295 **A painted clay head of a princely warrior**
Parthian, 2nd century BC
H. 46 cm (approx.)
From the square hall, South Complex, Old Nisa, Turkmenistan.
(Turkmenistan National Museum, Ashkabad)

Fig. 296 **White marble statue of 'The Goddess of Nisa'**
Parthian, 2nd century BC
H. 48 cm (approx.)
From the Square House treasury,
North Complex, Old Nisa,
Turkmenistan
(Turkmenistan National Museum,
Ashkabad)

Fig. 297 **White and grey marble statue of Rodoguna**
Parthian, 2nd century BC
H. 59 cm (approx.)
From the Square House treasury,
North Complex, Old Nisa,
Turkmenistan
(Courtesy of the Turkmenistan National
Museum, Ashkabad)
The first of these, an almost
complete figure of a goddess,
stands regally in long robes with
a scarf draped across her
shoulder. The second, made from
two types of marble, is one of
the greatest treasures of the
entire Silk Road. The subject is
Aphrodite Anadyomene –
'Aphrodite Rising from the Foam'
– better known as 'The Birth of
Venus' and a subject handled
most famously by Botticelli. She
stands with her head tilted
slightly forward and her arms,
now missing, are raised to her
hair. The tenderness of an
Aphrodite is absent here,
however- the face of this figure is
animated and flushed with
determination. According to
legend, Rodoguna – daughter of
the Parthian ruler Mithridates I –
was washing her hair when
news came that the enemy
was preparing to attack.
She immediately abandoned
her toilette, donned her armour
and led the Parthian troops
into battle.

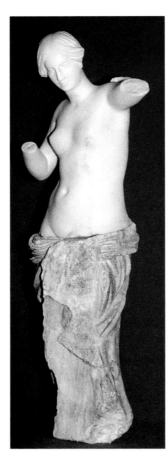

found in the square hall (fig. 295). They probably stood within niches in the upper tiers and represent deified members of the Arsacids, the ancient Iranian dynasty that founded and ruled the Parthian Empire.

The northern part of Old Nisa – the North Complex – contained the 60 metre by 60 metre treasury (known as the Square House), consisting of a courtyard surrounded by six long rectangular rooms. The Square House was the important building of the site and, during excavations from 1948–52, extraordinary treasures were unearthed from its different chambers. Its rooms had been piled with treasures and then each chamber was bricked up and sealed with an official clay stamp. Although the rooms had been entered and plundered, probably when the dynasty fell to the Sasanians in the third century AD, many of the treasures have survived. One of the rooms contained marble statues, strongly Hellenistic in style and the oldest such sculpture in Central Asia. It may provide the antecedents for the classically influenced sculpture of sites like Ai Khanum (see p. 42). Both complete and fragmentary marble stautues were

Fig. 298 **A miniature silver-gilt figure of a cherub**
Parthian, 2nd century BC
From the Square House treasury, North Complex, Old Nisa, Turkmenistan
(Turkmenistan National Museum, Ashkabad)

found including a head of Aphrodite that copies the celebrated *Aphrodite of Knidos* by the Greek master, Praxiteles (ca. 400–330 BC). The two finest complete sculptures are an exquisite standing figure, known as 'The Goddess of Nisa' (fig. 296) and a representation of Rodoguna, daughter of Mithridates I in a combination of white and grey marble (fig. 297).

A group of miniature silver-gilt figures of exceptional quality, also recovered from one of the chambers of the Square House treasury, reveals both Hellenistic and nomadic traditions (fig. 298).

One of the most important finds ever made at a Silk Road site occurred at the North Complex treasury in September 1948, only a month before Ashkabad was devastated by a massive earthquake. What at first appeared to be a pile of disintegrating ivory fragments soon turned out to be a group of more than forty *rhyta* or *rhytons* (horn-shaped vessels for libations; fig. 299). The rhytons were carefully excavated and then expertly restored and are now on display in both the Hermitage Museum and in Ashkabad. The ivory rhytons of Nisa are without peer in the ancient world. Their subject matter is the mythology of the Hellenistic realms: the gods of Olympus, centaurs, griffins and other fabulous beasts. Their surface was embellished with gold, silver, gilt-bronze and set with semi-precious stones and coloured glass. Much of the decoration and parts of the rhytons themselves are now lost but what remains is incomparably beautiful.

Among the more prosaic items recovered from the treasury complex were large numbers of coins bearing the town's mint mark, and a storeroom containing huge wine jars. Some 2500 *ostraka* (inscribed tile fragments) provide a wealth of information about both Parthian housekeeping (including the distribution of the wine), and also about the chronology of dynastic rulers.

Old Nisa was a Parthian city and did not survive the end of the empire. It became a burial ground but New Nisa continued to be an important caravan city well into the medieval period. Mukadisi intoned on the town's beauty during the tenth century and it is reasonable to assume that its fortunes were tied to that of Merv.

Just east of Ashkabad, about 15 km along the road to Merv, is the town of Anau. Isidore of Charax mentions it as an important Parthian caravan town and it was known during the medieval period as Bagabad. Anau's most famous landmark was the Dar-ul-Jemala, or Sheikh Jamaliddin Mosque, built in about 1450 and in terms of its size and beauty a rival to the great buildings of Samarkand and Bukhara. It was one of Central Asia's most cherished monuments until 1948, when the great earthquake of that year reduced it to a pile of rubble.

No one knows how long the Tolkuchka Bazaar has operated on Ashkabad's northern outskirts. The traditional age-old commodities of livestock, carpets and silk are still to be found alongside the factory produce of the region. Old photographs of the bazaar are a reminder that today's market is simply a continuation of an ancient tradition (fig. 300).

Ashkabad and its sites are the last Central Asian towns before the Iranian border. The historical and modern borders are not the same, of course, but the Kopet Dagh Mountains that run along today's frontier have always created a natural barrier between the two worlds. The road south from Nisa ran through these mountains and headed for Masshad and Nishapur (see pp. 287 and 288).

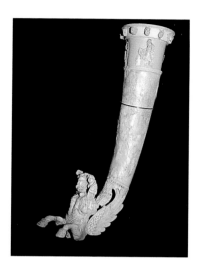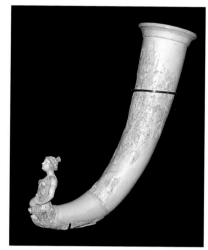

Fig. 299 **Ivory rhytons**
Parthian, 2nd century BC
From the Square House treasury,
North Complex, Old Nisa,
Turkmenistan
(Turkmenistan National Museum,
Ashkabad)

Fig. 300 **Old photograph of a Turkmen Bazaar**
Believed to be the Tolkuchka
Bazaar, Ashkabad
Early 19th century

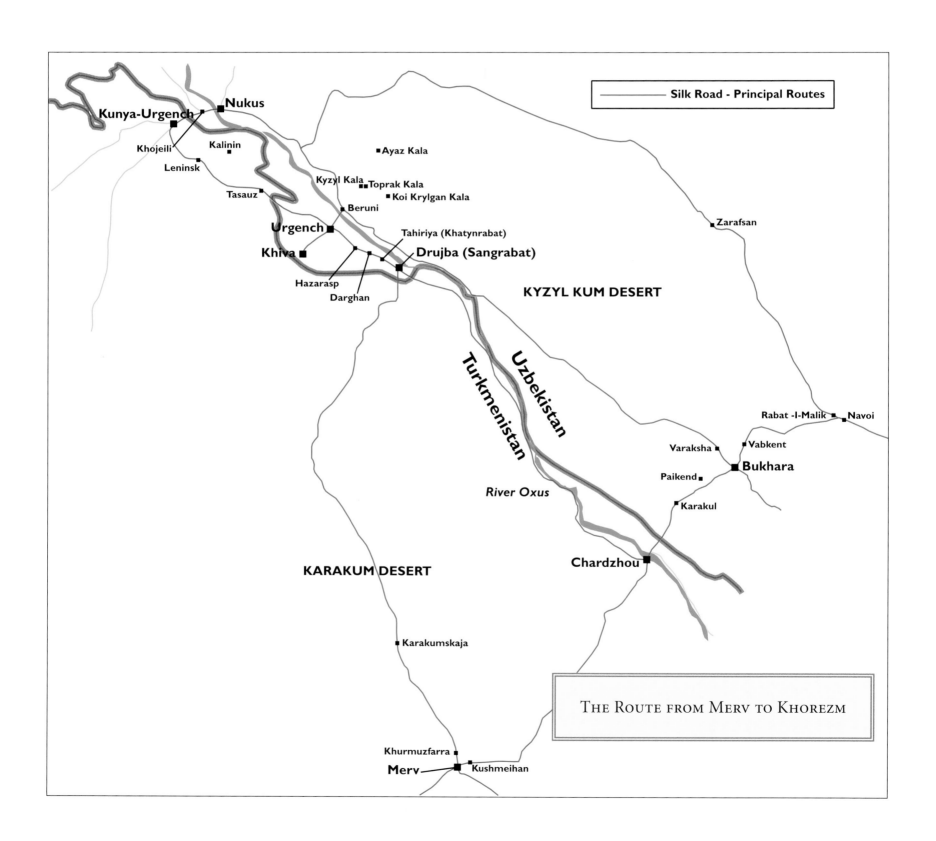

THE ROUTE FROM MERV TO KHOREZM

Silk Road - Principal Routes

Kunya-Urgench
Nukus
Khojeili
Kalinin
Leninsk
Tasauz
Kyzyl Kala
Toprak Kala
Koi Krylgan Kala
Ayaz Kala
Beruni
Urgench
Tahiriya (Khatynrabat)
Khiva
Drujba (Sangrabat)
Hazarasp
Darghan
Zarafsan

KYZYL KUM DESERT

Uzbekistan
Turkmenistan

Rabat -I-Malik
Navoi
Varaksha
Vabkent
Paikend
Bukhara
Karakul

River Oxus

Chardzhou

KARAKUM DESERT

Karakumskaja

Khurmuzfarra
Merv
Kushmeihan

CHAPTER FIFTEEN

THE ROUTE NORTH FROM MERV TO KHOREZM

The last of the routes emanating from Merv is the one that leads north to Khorezm, the ancient domain of the Massagetae Scythians. The most direct, but most dangerous route led directly across the Karakum via a series of isolated caravanserais, infrequent brackish wells and the occasional nomad settlement whose inhabitants either offered shelter to travellers or robbed them, depending on their inclination at the time. One of the few large towns along this route was Khurmuzfarra, a little way north of Merv and the last place to obtain victuals before crossing the Karakum. The town flourished until the time of the Mongols, when it was surrendered to the advancing sands. This route joined the Oxus close to the town of Sangrabat (modern Drujba) and then followed the river to Khiva and Kunya Urgench (Gurganj)- great cities in the land of Khorezm.

The other way, slower but less perilous, was to follow the main road from Merv to Bukhara in a northeasterly direction for about 250 km, a journey of about six days. This route passed through the fortified town of Kushmeihan with its Parthian-era citadel, noted for its excellent raisins but lost to the desert sands by the end of the twelfth century. The route joined the Oxus at Amul (modern Chardzhou), and then turned to follow the river as far as Khorezm. Lack of water and fodder for animals were perennial problems and a series of fortified caravanserais built along the way provided only a partial solution. Some researchers report that it is still possible to pick out the old caravan trails from lines of greenery, stretching out across the desert where pack animals have left their droppings and fertilised the parched soil.

The road beside the Oxus followed the river's lower bank because a system of irrigation channels had created a narrow tract of cultivable land extending for hundreds of kilometres to the north and south of Amul, located precariously between the Kyzyl Kum (Red Sands) Desert to the north and the Kara Kum (Black Sands) Desert to the south. Amul, or Chardzhou (meaning 'crossroads') is just that: an ancient river crossing and a place where two important strands of the Silk Road intersected. The road through this tract was served by a series of evenly spaced *rabats* (caravanserais) – some fortified and some not – many of which eventually grew into towns. At Sangrabat, the road joins the other route to Khorezm and at Tahiriya (Khatynrabat), its caravanserai

thought to have been erected by the Tahirids during the time that ninth-century travellers entered the land of Khorezm.

The towns of Khorezm

Two days beyond Khatynrabat was Darghan, during the tenth century the second largest town in Khorezm after Kunya Urgench. Darghan was famous for its gilded and jewel-encrusted mosque and its 500 vineyards that extended for more than 10 km along the riverbank. Raisins produced in these vineyards were exported along the Silk Road. Three or four days beyond Darghan, after passing through the town of Hazarasp, travellers arrived at Khiva. Before we examine Khiva, brief mention should be made of the town of Kath, located a day away on the right bank of the Oxus and once the capital of Khorezm. Al-Biruni described the town in the late tenth century, referring to the palace of the Khorezmshahs – visible from a distance of 15 km – and a clay and brick-built citadel with triple walls called al-Fir. Not long afterwards the citadel collapsed into the river and the old part of the town was abandoned. Mukadisi visited the town at about the same time and relates that, 'the town is constantly flooded by the river, and the inhabitants are moving (farther and farther) away from the bank'. He also describes the piles of refuse in the streets. Al-Biruni describes the capture and death of the last ruler of the Afrighid dynasty of Khorezm in 995. The new rulers of Khorezm established their capital at Gurganj and Kath faded into obscurity.

On the opposite bank of the river to Kath the town of Khiva, 30 km southwest of Urgench*, was undergoing a metamorphosis from pleasant provincial town to major Silk Road city.

Khiva

Despite its undeniable beauty and its deserved status as a UNESCO World Heritage Site, all but a handful of the city's buildings date to the eighteenth and nineteenth centuries, long after the Silk Road had ceased to play an important role in global commerce. Archeological excavations during the 1970s and 1980s suggest that the town is 2,500 years old but

* Urgench in Uzbekistan is of relatively recent vintage, only fully coming into its own when the population of Kunya ('Old') Urgench was displaced by water shortages in the late sixteenth and early seventeenth centuries. Kunya Urgench is located 200 km to the northwest, in modern Turkmenistan.

Fig. 301 **The East walls of the Ichan Kala, Khiva, Uzbekistan**

19th century and earlier

Fig. 302 **The Mausoleum of Sayid Allauddin**

Khiva, Uzbekistan, 14th century

for much of its early history it was little more than a small settlement on the caravan routes from Persia, a tiny oasis flanked by the limitless wastes of the Karakum and Kyzyl Kum deserts. Merchants would stop to drink at the Kheiwak Well, still in existence in the northwestern corner of the Ichan Kala – the old inner town or *shahristan*.

After the death of the last Afrighid ruler in 995, Khorezm was forcibly unified by the Khorezmshah Mam'un. When Mam'un died in 1017 control of Khorezm fell to the Ghaznavids, masters of Transoxiana until their defeat by the Seljuks in 1040. During this brief period, from 995 to 1040,

Khiva flourished as never before. The town's ceramics, glass and metalwares were second to none and a network of irrigation canals, or *ariks*, kept the desert at bay.

Under the Khorezmshah Takash (r. 1172–1200) and his son Muhammad (r. 1200–1220), Khorezmian territory was expanded to include Khurasan and the former Ghurid domains in Afghanistan. The Khorezmian capital during these years was at Gurganj but Khiva also benefited from Silk Road trade and the city expanded beyond the walls of the Ichan Kala. The Mongols arrived in 1220 and Khiva did not escape. The walls of the Ichan Kala appear to have been torn down and the area within became a burial ground. It did not revive until the fourteenth century, when the Ichan Kala's necropolis was filled in and the city's potters began to produce again. Under the Timurids Khiva revived further and the walls of the Ichan Kala were rebuilt. By the sixteenth century, the old capitals of Kath and Gurganj had dwindled away as a result of devastation by both the Mongols and by the armies of Timur. The population of Khorezm, reduced and weakened by these attacks, were unable to maintain the network of irrigation canals and the region suffered from alternate floods and drought. The population shifted eastwards and, by the seventh century, Khiva emerged as the principal town of Khorezm, capital of the newly named Khivan Khanate of the Uzbeks. By this time, however, the Silk Road was little more than a memory and Khiva became a rather sinister provincial town, lost among the desert wastes – a refuge for slavers and brigands.

The remarkable buildings we see in today's Khiva were built mainly during the eighteenth and nineteenth centuries and are therefore well beyond the scope of this book. Among the few structures to survive from the pre-Mongol and Mongol eras are fragments of the city walls, the Tomb of Sayid Allauddin and some of the wooden pillars of the Jame (Friday) Mosque.

Khiva's suburbs, the Dishan Kala, were enclosed by walls of about 10 km in length. The shahristan or inner town, the Ichan Kala, was also enclosed by walls although these were thicker and up to 8 metres in height. Most of the Ichan Kala's walls still stand, 2.1 km in extent and punctuated every 30 metres or so by colossal round towers. On each side, at the points of the compass, are huge gates. The walls of both the Dishan Kala and Ichan Kala have been rebuilt many times but they still provide a sense of how the ancient town may have appeared (fig. 301).

The Tomb of Sayid Allauddin, in the central part of the Ichan Kala, is the oldest surviving original building in Khiva. It was built as two chambers – a mausoleum and an attached mosque – and is renowned for its beautiful majolica decoration (fig. 302). Sayid Allauddin was a Sufic master who died in 1302 and, according to an inscription, his mausoleum was erected by his pupil and successor Emir Kulyal (d. 1370).

Fig. 303 **Wooden columns in the main hall, Jame (Friday) Mosque, Khiva**
H. 3.15 metres
10th to 18th century
The columns of the Jame Mosque are carved with great skill. The motifs that cover them are floral and geometric and the many Koranic references are in Kufic, on the early pillars and Arabic on the later ones. At least four of the columns date to the tenth century, probably salvaged from the city of Kath after it was inundated by the Oxus. Many other date from the twelfth to fourteenth centuries and may have come from Gurganj.

The Jame (Friday) Mosque, at the dead centre of the Ichan Kala, was erected between 1788 and 1799 on top of earlier ruins. The roof of the mosque's main hall has openings to let in light and air and the 213 wooden pillars that support it are frequently bathed in sunlight (fig. 303).

Gurganj

'Seven times destroyed and seven time rebuilt' is the legend attached to Gurganj, successor to Kath as the capital of Khorezm. Gurganj is the name given to the town by the Mongols but the Arabs called it Jurjaniya and, after 1646, it was known as Kunya Urgench ('Old Urgench').

There is archeological evidence that the site has been occupied since about the sixth century BC. Topographical research at the site indicates that during its heyday – from the tenth to fourteenth centuries – it covered an area as large as 1,000 hectares, making it one of largest cities in Asia. The late tenth to the early eleventh century was, after Khorezm had been unified by the Khorezmshah Mam'un, a time of wealth and splendour for the inhabitants of Gurganj. Under royal patronage the great scholars of the day formed the 'Court Academy' located, it is believed, atop the Kyrk Molla ('Forty Mullahs Hill') in the northeast part of the town. The hill is is now a cemetery and has never been fully excavated but we know something of the men who frequented the

academy. The peerless astronomer and philosopher Avicenna (980–1037) was one of them (see p. 249). Another was Avicenna's contemporary Al-Biruni (973–1048), one of the most remarkable scholars and scientists of the ancient Islamic world.

Fig. 304 **Overall view of the ruins of Gurganj (Kunya Urgench), former capital of Khorezm**

Al-Biruni

Abu Raihan Al-Biruni was born in Khiva, present-day Uzbekistan but moved to what is now Afghanistan in about 1017. He accompanied his patron, King Mahumd of Ghazni on his military campaigns around India, travelling for a period of twenty years. During his journeys he mastered Hindu philosophy and religion, mathematics and geography and was conversant in Arabic, Persian, Sanskrit, Turkish and Hebrew. Al-Biruni's magnum opus, *The History of India (Ta'rikh al-Hind)* was the principal source of information about the country for the following 600 years. His accomplishments include theories about the earth's rotation on its axis, hydrostatic laws of physics and the notion that the Indus valley had once be a sea basin. He also examined the phenomena of creation and of what happens to the soul after death.

Al-Biruni is known to have corresponded with the great philosopher Ibn Sina (Avicenna). Al-Biruni was renowned for his pithy remarks. When he was asked, for example, why scholars always flock to the doors of the rich whilst the rich are not inclined to call at the doors of scholars he retorted that, 'The scholars are well aware of the use of money, but the rich are ignorant of the nobility of science.' (Quoted in A. L. Mackay, *Dictionary of Scientific Quotations*, London, 1994)

It was Mahmud of Ghazni who caused the demise of the Gurganj academy. In 1017 he demanded that it be transferred to his capital at Ghazni in Afghanistan. Al-Biruni complied and followed Mahmud for the next two decades but Avicenna fled to Persia, eventually settling in Hamadan.

Much of the Khorezmians' economic prosperity appears to have been built upon trade with nomadic Turks but the Baghdad caliphate and the Chinese court were also recipients of the region's products. There was also a thriving trade with the territory to the north and west of the Caspian known as Khazaria (see p. 243). The tenth century geographer Mukadasi has left a detailed list of the commodities traded by the merchants of Khorezm. He mentions trade with the kingdom of *Bulghar*, or Bulgaria, on the Volga – the source of many of the Khorezmian's most valuable commodities, which they subsequently sold on at a profit:

'… *sables, miniver, ermines, and the fur of steppe foxes, martens, foxes, beavers, spotted hares, and goats; also wax, arrows, birch bark, high fur caps, fish glue, fish teeth [probably walrus tusks], castoreum [a musky secretion from the scent glands of a beaver, used as a fixative in perfume and incense], amber, prepared horse hides, honey, hazel nuts, falcons, swords, armour, khalanj wood, Slavonic slaves, sheep, and cattle. All these came from Bulghar.*'

Locally produced commodities included:
'*grapes, many raisins, almond pastry, sesame, fabrics of*

striped cloth, carpets, blanket cloth, satin for royal gifts, coverings of mulham *fabric, locks, Aranj fabrics [a type of cotton], bows which only the strongest could bend, rakhbin [a kind of cheese], yeast, fish, boats (the latter also exported from Tirmidh) [Termez].*'

(Mukadasi, ca. 985. Quoted in Barthold, 1981)

One other commodity is mentioned from the century preceding Mukadasi – watermelons so succulent that they were packed into lead containers lined with snow and conveyed to the caliphs of Baghdad. If it survived the journey intact, a single melon was worth 700 dirhams – equivalent to more than 2 kg of silver!

The Ghaznavids' domination of Transoxiana was brief. The Seljuks defeated them in 1040 and for the next 150 years Gurganj languished as something of a backwater. Under the Khorezmshah Takash (r. 1172–1200) and his son Muhammad (r. 1200–1220), the city was, for a fleeting moment, once again capital of a great empire. The renowned geographer Yaqut al-Hamavi (d. ca. 1229) lived in Gurganj from 1219–20 and thought it one of the most beautiful cities of the Islamic world:

'*There is hardly a town in the world comparable to the capital of Khorezm for its riches and metropolitan grandeur, its number of inhabitants, and its proximity to wealth and fulfilment of religious aspirations and regulations.*'

(Yaqut al-Hamavi. Quoted in Knobloch, 1972)

But Muhammad, 'the knight errant', was undone by hubris. When his relative the governor of Otrar ordered the slaughter of a trade mission sent by Genghis Khan, the Mongol demanded that he be handed over for retribution. Muhammad refused and Gurganj was doomed. The Mongols arrived at the end of the year 1220 with a force exceeding 100,000 men. The siege began with a small force appearing before the city gates and driving off the Khorezmians' cattle. The defenders gave chase but were lured into an ambush near the city, losing a thousand men before sunset. The noose around Gurganj was quickly tightened. Before long the Mongols were using their catapults to fire sections from the trunks of mulberry trees, hardened by soaking in water, into the town. Their choice of projectile soon changed to baskets of burning naptha and the town began to burn. One commenator reported that the Oxus was diverted away from the town in order to accelerate the conflagration but the Mongols also suffered setbacks. An attempt to build a bridge across the Oxus ended with the Khorezmians surrounding a force of 3,000 Mongols and killing them all. Rashid al-Din reported that the bones of slaughtered Mongols formed hillocks around the city and other commentators reported arguments between Jochi and

Chagatai. The former promised mercy to the defenders if they surrendered but in the end it was the more bellicose views of Chagatai that prevailed. Ata-Malik Juvaini says that 100,000 artisans were spared and carried off to work in the Mongols' eastern domains. Young women and infants were also spared but the rest were divided up into groups of twenty-four and put to the sword, each group dispatched by one Mongol. If Rashid al-Din's report that there were 50,000 Mongols present at the conclusion of the siege is accurate, 120,000 Khorezmians were massacred in one day. Forty Mullahs Hill (*Kyrk Molla*), once the site of the great court academy of the Khorezmshah Mam'un, was the highest point of refuge in the stricken city. The bones of the defenders still lie scattered about the base of the hill (see fig. 284). The Mongols' final act was to destroy the dam that protected the town from the Oxus. What remained of old Gurganj was submerged by the waters of the river. Juvaini wrote that, 'Khorezm became the abode of the jackal and the haunt of the owl and the kite'.

Despite its utter destruction, within a hundred years Gurganj had risen from the ashes and the catalyst was Silk Road trade. By the early fourteenth century, Gurganj had been rebuilt to serve the caravans travelling to the Golden Horde territory in the Volga region. Ibn Battuta described newly revived Gurganj as a vigorous commercial centre, 'the largest, greatest, most beautiful and most important city of the Turks, shaking under the weight of its populations, with bazaars so crowded that it was difficult to pass'. The handful of buildings that still stand in Gurganj date mostly to this period – the Sultan Takash Mausoleum (fig. 305) and the Fakhr-ad-din Razi, (or Il Arslan) Mausoleum – both date to the late twelfth or early thirteenth century and are the only structures at Gurganj to survive relatively intact from the pre-Mongol, Khorezmshah era.

There are a number of buildings from the immediate post-Mongol period. The Turabeg Khanum Mausoleum is located in the northern part of the town and is thought to have been built around 1370 for the Sufi dynasty, rulers of Khorezm until 1388. The building is also said to be connected with Turabeg, the wife of Kutlug Timur, Mongol governor of Khorezm. The structure is one of Central Asia's most perfect architectural masterpieces (fig. 306).

The tottering Kutlug Timur Minaret (visible in fig. 304) was erected around 1320 and, at 64 metres, is the tallest such minaret in Central Asia. Age and seismic activity have left it in a precarious state. Aside from the minaret and the other buildings described above, there is a shattered fortress (the Ak Kala), the portal of a caravanserai and a few rebuilt mausolea.

Continuing caravan trade during the second half of the fourteenth century ensured that Gurganj remained prosperous but the growing political and economic power of the Sufi Khorezmshahs attracted the attention of Emperor

Fig. 305 **Sultan Takash Mausoleum**
Gurganj (Kunya Urgench), Turkmenistan, completed ca. 1200
H. 18 metres, W. 11.45 metres
Sultan Takash (r. 1172–1200) was one of the greatest of the Khorezmshah rulers. His blue domed mausoleum is said to mirror the shape of nomadic tents.

Fig. 306 **Turabeg Khanum Mausoleum**
Gurganj (Kunya Urgench), Turkmenistan, ca. 1370
The entrance portal is 25 metres high and leads to an inner chamber topped by a dome, the underside of which is decorated in tilework with 365 geometric designs, each representing a day of the week.

Fig. 307 **The inner dome of the Turabeg Khanum Mausoleum**
Gurganj (Kunya Urgench), Turkmenistan, ca. 1370
The designs resemble stars and the calendar theme is continued with the twenty-four windows beneath the dome, representing the hours in a day, four small windows lower down for the weeks in a month and four further windows for the seasons.

Fig. 309 **Painted clay portrait of Khorezmian King**
Toprak Kala, Western Uzbekistan, ca. 3rd century AD
(State Hermitage Museum, St. Petersburg)

Timur. In 1372, in 1379 and again in 1388, Timur campaigned against the Sufi rulers of Khorezm. Gurganj was besieged in 1379 and was sacked after the Sufi khan tossed a gift of melons presented by Timur into the moat. In 1388 the Sufi khan rebelled again and this time Timur left nothing to chance. The city was levelled and barley sown on the site. Gurganj's fortunes never fully revived and it was reduced to little more than a rest stop on the caravan trails. A fifteenth-century visitor, Ibn Arabshah (d.1450) lamented the decline of the Silk Road in Khorezm:

'There used to advance convoys of travellers from Khorezm, making the journey in wagons as far as the Crimea, securely and without fear, a journey of about three months…But now through these places from Khorezm to the Crimea nothing moves or rests and nothing ranges there, but the antelopes and the camels…'

(Ibn Arabshah [d.1450]. Quoted in Knobloch, 1972)

The Elizabethan merchant Anthony Jenkinson saw the town in 1558 and described its buildings as, 'ruined and out of good order' and, when the Oxus changed its course during the seventeenth century, the town was finally abandoned and the capital transferred to Khiva. Today, the site is a vast necropolis. From the day that the city was finally abandoned, local people have followed time-honoured practice and gradually taken over the ruins for use as a graveyard. There can be no more fitting an end for a city afflicted, over so long a period, with so much death and devastation.

The Castles of Khorezm

A network of *kala* (fortified settlements) is strung out across the Kyzyl Kum desert. They were all built to a similar plan-enclosed by a double set of defensive walls with lookout towers and firing points for archers. The largest and best known is Toprak Kala, about 45 km northeast of Urgench across the Amu Darya.

Toprak Kala
Toprak Kala is believed to have served as Khorezm's capital from about the second to sixth or seventh century, during which it appears to have part of the Kushan Empire. The site was first excavated in 1938 but has been examined many times since and the richness of the artefacts found at the site suggests that it was an important and prosperous town, deriving its wealth from Silk Road commerce. A Zoroastrian temple and a palace have been identified, both on raised platforms. The palace contained a series of great halls containing murals and large clay sculptures. The Hall of Kings, some 280 square metres in area, contained over life-size clay statues of the Khorezmian kings and their consorts. These sculptures are in typically Kushan style and are strongly influenced by the Hellenistic world (fig. 309).

A smaller fortress, Kyzyl Kala, stands just to the west of Toprak Kala (fig. 310).

Among the other fortified remains of Khorezm are Ayaz Kala, about 60 km northeast of Toprak Kala and Koi Krylgan Kala, 30 km to the southeast. Koi Krylgan Kala ('The Fort of the Dead Rams') comprises a temple and mausoleum dating back to the third or fourth century BC. The central structure is a two storey round tower, about 10 metres high and 45 metres in diameter and is thought to have served as a mausoleum for one of the Khorezmian kings. The tower is also thought to have been used to store funerary objects, for

Fig. 308 **Overall view of Toprak Kala, Western Uzbekistan**
Ca. 3rd century AD
The fortifications are visible to the rear and the remains of the royal palace can be seen in the foreground.

Fig. 310 **Overall view of Kyzyl Kala, Western Uzbekistan**
Ca. 3rd century AD

the performance of dynastic rites and as an observatory. It is surrounded at a distance of 15 metres by a concentric, circular fortress wall. In the second century BC the settlement was looted and burned but the ruins were subsequently reinhabited and the town lingered on until the second or third century AD.

By the seventh century, the Kushan Empire had fallen to the Hepthalites and, when the security of merchants could no longer be guaranteed, the Khorezmian trade routes withered away. Beginning at the end of the seventh century the Arab general Qutaiba systematically reduced the towns of Khorezm and many of its intelligentsia fled to the region north and west of the Caspian controlled by the Khazars. The Khazars were a Turkic people who originated in Central Asia. They originally held shamanistic beliefs but later adopted Judaism, Islam and Christianity, learned Hebrew and Slavic, and settled in the cities and towns of the northern Caucasus and Ukraine. The Khazar Empire attained its apogee during the ninth and tenth centuries when it was one of the most important trading powers of the Silk Road. The Khazars were the founders of the Ukrainian city of Kiev and Khazaria controlled much of the trade between China, Central Asia, and Europe. The Khazars traded silks, furs, candle wax, honey, jewellery, silverware, coins, and spices, engaging in direct commerce with Khorezm, (by now firmly under the control of the Arabs), Volga Bulgharia and with port cities in Azerbaijan and Persia. Khazaria was overthrown in the tenth century by the Rus' khaganate and control of Silk Road commerce in the Caucasus fell to the new power.

The Oxus and the Aral Sea

'At length upon the lone Chorasmian shore
He paused, a wide and melancholy waste
Of putrid marshes.'

(Percy Bysshe Shelley, 'Alastor', or the 'Spirit of Solitude')

The Elizabethan merchant Anthony Jenkinson passed through Khorezm in 1558–59. His remarks about the region's fragile water supply now seem especially prescient:

'The water that serueth all that Countrey is drawen by diches out of the riuer Oxus, vnto the great destruction of the said riuer, for which cause it falleth not into the Caspian sea as it hath done in times past, and in short time all that lande is like to be destroyed, and to become a wilderness for want of water, when the riuer of Oxus shall faile.'

(Anthony Jenkinson in 1558. Quoted in Knobloch, 1972)

According to the observations of early geographers, the Aral Sea was on the periphery of the area traversed by the Khorezmian section of the Silk Road and marked the limit of

Fig. 311 **The Oxus (Amu Darya), near Urgench, Uzbekistan**
The depleted dregs of a once great river falter near Urgench

Fig. 312 **The Ships' Graveyard. Beached trawlers at Moynaq, formerly on the Aral Sea**

point at which the Oxus flowed into the sea. Fish caught from the Aral's slightly brackish waters were a Silk Road commodity and were exported far and wide. The Aral's waters were a rich source of fish until the 1960s when the great inland ocean – once the fourth largest in the world – fell victim to the worst environmental catastrophe of the twentieth century. Overuse of the waters of the Oxus (Amu Darya) and Jaxartes (Syr Darya) Rivers for irrigating the vast cotton fields of the former Soviet Union reduced the flow into the Aral Sea to such an extent that it began to dry up. Between 1960 and 1992 the Aral Sea lost half of its area and three quarters of its volume. Its water levels continue to fall by a metre a year and as the waters recede chemicals that have accumulated from years of pesticide use are blowing into the atmosphere, causing horrific levels of cancer, respiratory diseases and birth defects among the local populace. The town of Moynaq, once the largest fishing port on the Aral, is now 100 km from the shore and has become a cruel travesty of itself (fig. 312).

All of the fish and most of the animals that were sustained by the Aral have disappeared. A rare and bizarre exception are the domestic cattle that graze on the contaminated remains of its dried up bed (fig. 313).

expansion for many of the empires that held sway in Central Asia. There was a route skirting north of the Caspian Sea to Khazaria but most merchants headed southwest to Persia or crossed the Caspian by boat. The only settlement of note on the southern shore was Khalijan, a collection of huts at the

The plans to save the Aral – diverting Siberian rivers, building a canal or pipeline from the Caspian to name but three – have all come to nothing and the great sea is almost certainly doomed.

Fig. 313 **Surreal World: A herd of cattle return from a peaceful day's grazing on the bed of the Aral Sea**

Fig. 314 **The ruins of Mizdarkhan, near Khodzeili, Uzbekistan**

The end of Khorezm as a trading power

By the first half of the fourteenth century all of Khorezm lay in ruins. Ibn Battuta remarked that the whole way from Gurganj to Bukhara, there was but one populated spot – Kath, the much-depleted former capital. This was far from the end of its misery, however. During Timur's three campaigns against the recalcitrant Sufi rulers of Khorezm, he tore a swathe through the region and what remained resembled the trail of a tornado. Ruined cities still dot the banks of the Oxus, many fit only for use as graveyards. The towns of Mizdarkhan and Yusup Ishan near Khojeili are a testament to the destructive power of Timur's armies. Mizdarkhan was once almost as large as Gurganj and was renowned for its decorative tilework. Timur reduced it to rubble (fig. 314).

In the centuries after Timur Khorezm continued, periodically, to play a role in trade (particularly trans-Caspian commerce), first with the Golden Horde and in later years with the Russians. It was never again to play a role in international dealings between China and the West. The years immediately after Timur's death were a time of decline and introspection for the once great trading powers of the Silk Road. The Byzantine Empire fell to the Ottoman Turks in 1453 and China, its sovereignty newly restored by the Ming, effectively closed its borders to the outside world. Khorezm became a backwater and so it remained until the late nineteenth century when Czarist Russia and Britain began to contest the Great Game and attention was again focused on the region.

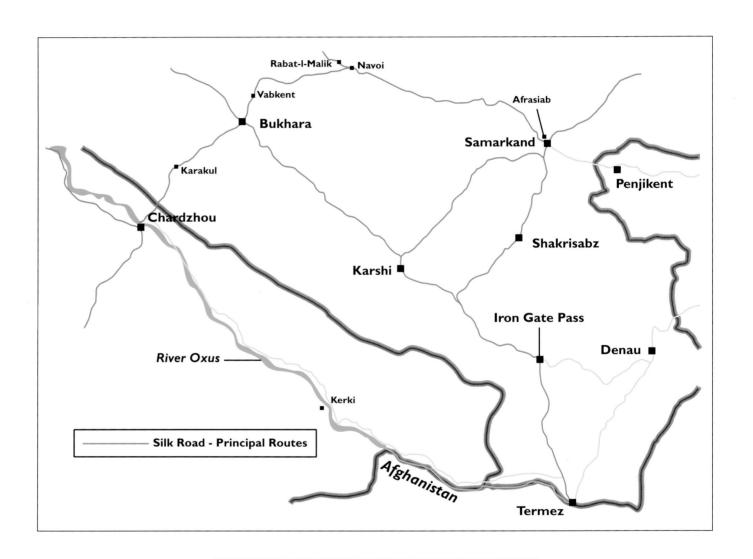

Rabat-I-Malik ■ ■ Navoi

■ Vabkent

■ Bukhara

Afrasiab

■ Karakul

Samarkand

■ Penjikent

Chardzhou

■ Shakrisabz

Karshi ■

Iron Gate Pass

River Oxus

Denau ■

Silk Road - Principal Routes

Kerki ■

Afghanistan

Termez ■

THE ROUTES NORTH
FROM THE IRON GATE PASS

CHAPTER SIXTEEN

THE ROUTES NORTH FROM THE IRON GATE PASS

The three principal routes beyond the Iron Gates all originate in the town of Karshi, the ancient Sogdian city of Nakhsheb (called Nesef by the Arabs). The northwestwardly route was the main ten- or eleven-day Balkh-Bukhara road and Karshi was an important oasis-town upon it. There were also two roads to the northeast; the first a direct but steeper route along the lower bank of the Kashka Darya River, across the Zerafshan mountains through Shakhrisabz (Kesh) and via the Takhtakaracha Pass to Samarkand. The other route from Karshi led through the Jam Pass and along foothills straight to Samarkand. The second was longer but was less precipitous and therefore easier for caravans to follow.

Karshi's position on the main Balkh-Bukhara road made certain that it experienced periods of both prosperity and perdition. Arab geographers of the medieval period describe it as a large urban centre on the Kashka Darya. The oldest part of the town was at Yorkurgan, about 10 km to the west of modern Karshi and occupied from at least the sixth century BC. By the third century AD Yorkurgan was one of the largest cities in the region, its centre dominated by massive twin temples. It was destroyed during the Sasanian conquests of the third to fourth century but was resurrected during the seventh to eighth as the Arab city of Naksheb. During this period Karshi was said to have had a citadel of more than 30 metres in height. Karshi's heyday was during the ninth to thirteenth century when it became one of the most important towns on this part of the Silk Road, famed for its vineyards. The whole area fell under Mongol control in 1220 and the valley in which Karshi sits was designated as pastureland for the nomads' horses. The modern town emerged during the early fourteenth century and took the name of Karshi ('Palace') when the Mongol Kabak Khan built a luxurious residence there. Even during the Timurid era Karshi remained an important caravan city on the road south to Balkh and India.

At the end of the road to the northwest of Karshi was Bukhara, one of the legendary cities of the Silk Road.

Bukhara

Irrigation of the lower Zerafshan Valley during the first millennium BC resulted in the rapid growth of population centres. Bukhara, sitting as it does at the crossroads of east-west and north-south trade routes, was an immediate beneficiary of this growth. By about 500 BC it was already an important centre, defended by a citadel that has stood in one form or other ever since. Today it is the site of the Ark Fortress, residence of the former emirs of Bukhara and the old *shahristan* (the inner town around it) occupied an area of about 13 hectares to the east. During the seventh century AD the city fell under the control of the Bukhar-Khudats and the Ark was expanded and the city walls extended to enclose the main residential area. In the early eighth century the city covered a square of as much as 55 hectares containing bazaars, workshops and places of worship for Nestorians, Buddhists, Manichaeans and Zoroastrians.

In 673 the Arab armies crossed the Oxus and threatened the city. They were successfully bought off with the payment of tribute and the town did not fall under full Arab control until 709 when it was taken by the great General Qutaiba (see p. 213). During the next century and a half the city was the scene of frequent revolts by the Sogdians and local Turks against the forces of Islam but it continued to expand. By the middle of the ninth century a double ring of walls encircled the city and most of its inhabitants had embraced the new religion, aided in part by the offering of financial incentives to attend the city's mosques.

In 892 the city was selected as the capital of the semi-autonomous Samanid dynasty by its founder, Ismail ibn Ahmed (r. 892–907). Under the Samanids the city flourished as a centre of learning. Scientists and craftsmen flocked to the city, drawn by the promise of Samanid patronage. The Ark was completely enclosed by high walls and a palace, said to be the most beautiful in the Islamic world, was built near the Registan Square. Workshops were established to manufacture commodities for export along the Silk Road. A contemporary visitor, the geographer Mukadasi who saw the town during the late tenth century, lists the town's merchandise:

> '... *soft fabrics, prayers carpets, woven fabrics for covering the floors of inns, copper lamps, Tabari tissues, horse girths (which are woven in places of detention), Ushmuni [Egyptian] fabrics, grease, sheepskins, oil for anointing the head.*'

(Mukadasi, ca. 985. Quoted in Barthold, 1981)

Fig. 315 **Mausoleum of Ismail Samanid (r. 892–907)**
Bukhara, Uzbekistan

The mausoleum of Ismail Samanid, the founder of the dynasty, dates to the beginning of the tenth century and is the only Samanid structure still extant in Bukhara and is one of the earliest examples of Islamic architecture in all of Central Asia (fig. 315). That it exists at all, given the depredations the city suffered at the hands of the Kharakhanids, the Mongols and many other invaders, is little short of miraculous.

This mausoleum, one of the most celebrated buildings in the whole of the Islamic world, is traditionally thought to have been constructed by Ismail Samani for his father but Ismail himself, and his grandson Nasr II were also interred there. Its ornamental brickwork resembles basketry and owes many of its features to the pre-Islamic architecture of the Sogdians. The dome, 9.25 metres in diameter, is supported by squinches, arches that span each corner of a square building. The squinch was probably invented by the Sasanians and, in later centuries, made possible the construction of great buildings like Istanbul's Blue Mosque and St Paul's Cathedral in London.

Among the scholars to profit from the beneficence of the Samanids were the poets, who wrote their verse in both Arabic and Persian. The best of the former was Ismail Bukhari (810–70), a native of the town who compiled a volume of some 600,000 sayings of the Prophet Muhammad (*hadiths*). He also wrote verse:

'As Samarkand is called the Beauty of the Earth,
So Bukhara is the pillar of Islam and the Muslim hearth.'

(Ismail Bukhari. Quoted in Kirichenko, 1997)

Among the poets who wrote in Persian, Abu Abdullah Rudaki (c. 859–941) stands supreme. His poetry has a wistful quality that seems to make the centuries fall away:

'The Ju-yi Mulian we call to mind,
We long for those dear friends long left behind.
The sands of Oxus, toilsome though they be,
Beneath my feet were soft as silk to me.
Glad at the friend's return, the Oxus deep
Up to our girths in laughing waves shall leap.
Long live Bukhara! Be thou of good cheer!
Joyous towards thee hasteth our Amir!
The moon's the prince, Bukhara is the sky;

Among the celebrated viziers of Samanid Bukhara were the tenth-century historian Nukh Ibn Mansur and a colossus of world history, the great Avicenna.

Ibn Sina or Avicenna

Abu Ali al-Hussain Ibn Abdallah Ibn Sina was born in 980 in Afshona, 25 km from Bukhara. Ibn Sina, known in the West as Avicenna, was the most famous physician, philosopher, encyclopaedist, mathematician and astronomer of his time. His early education took place in Bukhara and, by the age of ten, he was already said to be conversant with the entire contents of the Koran and with a number of sciences. He became interested in Greek and Islamic philosophy under the guidance of his teacher, Abu Abdallah Natili, and quickly established a reputation as a gifted physician. During the early period of Ibn Sina's study he developed dual convictions – the first that even the best teaching provides only a hint of the problems one must face when dealing with a subject and the second, that solving the remaining problems depends on the intelligence of the individual. Ibn Sina summarizes this notion with the remark that: "the heart of learning is a direct insight into the rational principles on which the world is constructed." At the age of seventeen Ibn Sina successfully cured the Samanid Prince Nooh Ibn Mansoor of Bukhara of a life-threatening illness when all of the court physicians had given up hope. Declining the Prince's offer of a reward, he requested only that he be granted access to the court library. The opportunities for the peoples of the Silk Road to access the wisdom of other nations was, without doubt, one of its most important characteristics. Ibn Sina's first sight of the royal library was both a defining moment in his life and his first opportunity to partake of that wisdom:

'I found there many rooms filled with books which were arranged in cases, row upon row. One room was allotted to works of Arabic philology and poetry, another to jurisprudence and so forth, the books of each particular science having a room to themselves. I inspected the catalogue of ancient Greek authors; I saw in this collection books of which few people have heard even the names, and which I myself have never seen either before or since.'

(Ibn Sina. Quoted in Lawton, 1991)

Fig. 316 **Bust of Avicenna (Ibn Sina, 980–1037)**
(Avicenna Museum, Afshona, Uzbekistan) This image of Avicenna is a reconstruction of the great man's face, made from his skull after it was disinterred from his tomb in Hamadan, Iran.

The culmination of his early education came at the age of twenty when Ibn Sina produced a twenty-volume appraisal of the philosophical sciences as a whole, under the title *Sum and Substance*. After his father's death in 1012 Ibn Sina left Bukhara with Abu Sahl, a friend and fellow scholar, in the direction of Jurjan, a kingdom on the southeast coast of the Caspian Sea and the latter's homeland. En route, Abu Sahl died in a desert sandstorm but Ibn Sina survived and was eventually welcomed at Gurganj (Kunya Urgench) by Prince Qabus ibn Vush-magir, an ally of the Khorezmshah and a supporter of the Samanids. At Gurganj he is also believed to have met the celebrated mathematician and geographer Abu Raihan Al-Biruni (973–1048) – see p. 240.

Ibn Sina subsequently moved to Hamadan in Persia where he wrote his greatest work *Al-Qanun fi al-Tibb*, known simply as the 'Canon' in the West and the most important medical reference ever written. The 'Qanun' extends to over a million words and is a survey of the entire extent of medical knowledge during the eleventh century, drawing from both ancient and Islamic sources. The text also includes Ibn Sina's original ideas on such diverse subjects as the contagious nature of tuberculosis, the spread of diseases by water and soil, and the interaction between psychology and health. He describes the therapeutic effects of no fewer than 760 drugs, discusses anatomy, gynaecology and child health and was the first to detail the intricate workings of the human eye and of the function of the aorta to control the flow of blood to and from the heart. The

'Qanun' was translated into Latin by Gerard of Cremona during the twelfth century and became the standard textbook for European medical schools for the next 500 years. Both Latin and Hebrew editions were printed in large numbers and, even as late as the sixteenth century, it was re-issued more than twenty times.

Ibn Sina's second great work, also completed during his sojourn in Hamadan, was his philosophical treatise *Kitab al-Shifa* ('The Book of Healing'). The book is a vast undertaking, covering a wide spectrum of knowledge from philosophy to science and his contributions to the fields of mathematics, geology, metaphysics, ethics, economics and politics were centuries ahead of their time and are virtually unparalleled in history. His philosophy is a synthesis of Aristotelian tradition, Neoplatonic* influences and Muslim theology.

In 'Kitab al-Shifa' Ibn Sina also contributed to the fields of physics, astronomy and music. In physics he studied the phenomena of heat and light, including the observation that the speed of light must be finite, and also investigated specific gravity and the thermometer. In the field of music he studied harmonies and the ear's detection of sounds.

From Hamadan, Ibn Sina journeyed to Isfahan and it was here that he spent his final years as scientific adviser and physician to the ruler. The exertions of constant travel and the political upheavals in the region during this period

Fig. 317 **The tomb of Avicenna (Ibn Sina)**
Hamadan, Iran

Fig. 318 **The Kalan Complex, Bukhara**
The minaret dates to ca. 1127

* Neoplatonism was developed in the third century AD by Plotinus, who saw reality as one vast hierarchical order containing all the various levels and kinds of existence.

Fig. 319 **Southern Portal, The Magok-I-Attari ('Tomb of Attari') Mosque, Bukhara**
12th century

damaged his health and he died during a military campaign in 1037 AD, apparently from colic (fig. 317).

Like his contemporary Al-Biruni, Ibn Sina was a master of the pithy remark:

'The world is divided into men who have wit and no religion and men who have religion and no wit.'

His ideas are among the most precious of all of the Silk Road's commodities.

Many of Bukhara's greatest monuments were constructed during the Kharakhanid era (992–1211). The walls of the inner residential area were rebuilt and the Ark was strengthened with terracotta bricks. The Kalan Mosque and Minaret and the main portal of the Magok-I-Attari ('Tomb of Attari') Mosque were all built during the first half of the twelfth century (fig. 318).

The Kalan ('large' or 'high') Minaret and mosque were originally constructed in 1121–22, during the reign of the Kharakhanid ruler Arslan Khan Muhammad (r. 1102–29). The minaret collapsed soon after it was built, destroying a large section of the mosque as it fell. Both structures were

rebuilt during Arslan Khan Muhammad's lifetime and the minaret has survived until today. It stands almost 50 metres in height, built of baked bricks upon an octagonal base, and so impressed was Genghis Khan with the tower that he is said to have ordered that it be spared when the city was pillaged in 1220. The Kalan Mosque was also rebuilt but it did not survive the fires that swept through the city when it was taken by the Mongols. The mosque that now stands on the spot where Genghis is said to have berated the city's faithful was completed during the sixteenth century.

The Magok-I-Attari ('the recessed mosque of the perfumers') is one of the city's most ancient and fascinating buildings. Its foundations stand below the level of the surrounding land in the centre of Bukhara on a spot that excavations suggest has been used as a place of worship for as much as 2000 years. During the tenth century a building known as the Mokh Mosque was erected on the site of a Zoroastrian fire temple, itself raised over an earlier Buddhist temple. It was not long before the Mokh Mosque was destroyed by fire and, during the twelfth century, a new mosque was erected in its place of which the southern portal still survives (fig. 319). The eastern entrance and dome were added

Fig. 320 **The Karakul Gate and the remains of the city walls, Bukhara**
Ca. 16th century

during the sixteenth century but the southern portal contains a mixture of quarter columns (a style inherited from the pre-Islamic Sogdian era), patterned brick decoration and glazed and unglazed tiles.

In 1141, Bukhara fell to the Kharakhitai although the members of the city's ruling clan – the Sadrs or Burkhanids – were permitted to retain power. The city enjoyed a brief spell of independence and prosperity despite continuing raids by Turkish nomads. In 1207 Shah Muhammad of Khorezm, the new ruler of Transoxiana, seized the town. Shah Muhammad reinforced the citadel and began civic works but they were no more than castles built on sand. In 1220 the whole of Central Asia was convulsed by the Mongol invasions and the city was sacked and virtually destroyed by a fire that broke out as it was pillaged. Those citizens not massacred by the Mongols were taken into slavery and when Ibn Battuta saw the town a century later he remarked that, 'all but a few of its mosques, academies and bazaars are now lying in ruins'.

Bukhara was rebuilt under the Timurids but it was never again a match for the effulgence of Samarkand. The buildings erected during the following centuries were more often reiligous than commercial and the city's role changed progressively from Silk Road entrepôt to spiritual centre. The city's covered bazaars and many of its great mosques and madrassahs were built during the sixteenth century, when it

became the capital of the Uzbek Shaybanid Khanate. At the time it was said that there were as many places of worship as there were days of the year. The old city walls were also rebuilt and gates erected – a few still stand. In fact, most of Bukhara's 13 km long walls were still standing until 1920, when they were destroyed by Bolshevik shellfire (fig. 320).

Bukhara has remained an important religious centre right up to the present day but its commercial significance has declined: with the opening up of the sea lanes to Europe and the closure of China's borders under the Ming dynasty (1368–1644), the East-West trade routes and the towns that sat on those routes withered away.

Silk Road sites around Bukhara

Paikend

About 60 km and a day's journey southwest of Bukhara is the old transit-station of Paikend. Called the 'copper city' or the 'city of the merchants', Paikend is even older than Bukhara and sat on the main Silk Road between Samarkand and Merv. Each village in the region owned an individual caravanserai near the town from which they conducted trade with China. There was even maritime, trans-Caspian commerce with the lands to the west. Until the mid-ninth century there were more than a thousand such caravanserais, many garrisoned with men to prevent attacks by marauding Turks. When the region fell to the Samanids the threat was removed and the *rabats* fell into disuse. During the eleventh century the Zerafshan River appears to have changed it course and Paikend's inhabitants began to abandon the town.

Early in the twelfth century the Kharakhanid ruler Arslan Khan Muhammad (r. 1102–29) attempted to restore Paikend to its former glory but his plans to cut a water channel through the hill on which the town was built came to nothing and the town faded slowly into obscurity.

Varaksha

Excavations at Varaksha in the Bukhara oasis have revealed the remains of a Sogdian city dating to about the fifth to eighth century. The remains of the one-time residence of the Bhukar-Khudats are situated in the Kyzyl Kum (Red Sands) Desert, about 40 km northwest of Bukhara on the old road to Khorezm. The ruins occupy a triangular site of about 9 hectares and appear to have flourished from the fifth to the tenth centuries, although other remains dating back to the first century BC have also been found. An area around Varakhsa of about 12 square km shows signs of widespread cultivation- including a network of irrigation canals. Varaksha was the last stop on the caravan route before merchants embarked on the seven- or eight-day crossing of the Kyzyl Kum to Khorezm and was a major economic centre. During the fifth and sixth centuries the site was occupied by the Hepthalites and a citadel constructed from rammed earth. Beside the citadel was the palace of the Bhukar-Khudats, built in the architectural style of the Sogdians at Afrasiab (Samarkand) and Penjikent. Within the palace Soviet archeologists discovered three large rooms –

Fig. 321 **The remains of Varaksha, near Bukhara**
8th century

the Red Room, the East Room and the West Room – all decorated with wall-paintings in Sogdian style but with recognizable influences from India. Winged griffins and leopards are shown in combat with splendidly dressed, princely figures on elephant-back. The richness of the murals suggests that the inhabitants of Varaksha were enjoying a period of great economic prosperity (fig. 322).

Like many of the great cities of the Silk Road, Varaksha's glory days were brief. In about 784 the Bukhar-Khudat ruler Buniat was beheaded in the Royal Palace for fomenting dissent against the Arabs. The town did not die with Buniat and was still an important commercial centre in the twelfth century but by then the focus of trade had shifted to Bukhara and the area had reverted to desert by the time of the Mongol conquests. Today, the ruins lie forlorn and forgotten, strewn with pottery shards and partly submerged by the sands of the Kyzyl Kum.

Fig. 322 **Wall painting depicting a warrior on elephant back attacked by leopards**
From the central hall, Royal Palace at Varaksha, Uzbekistan, ca. 8th century
(State Hermitage Museum, St Petersburg)

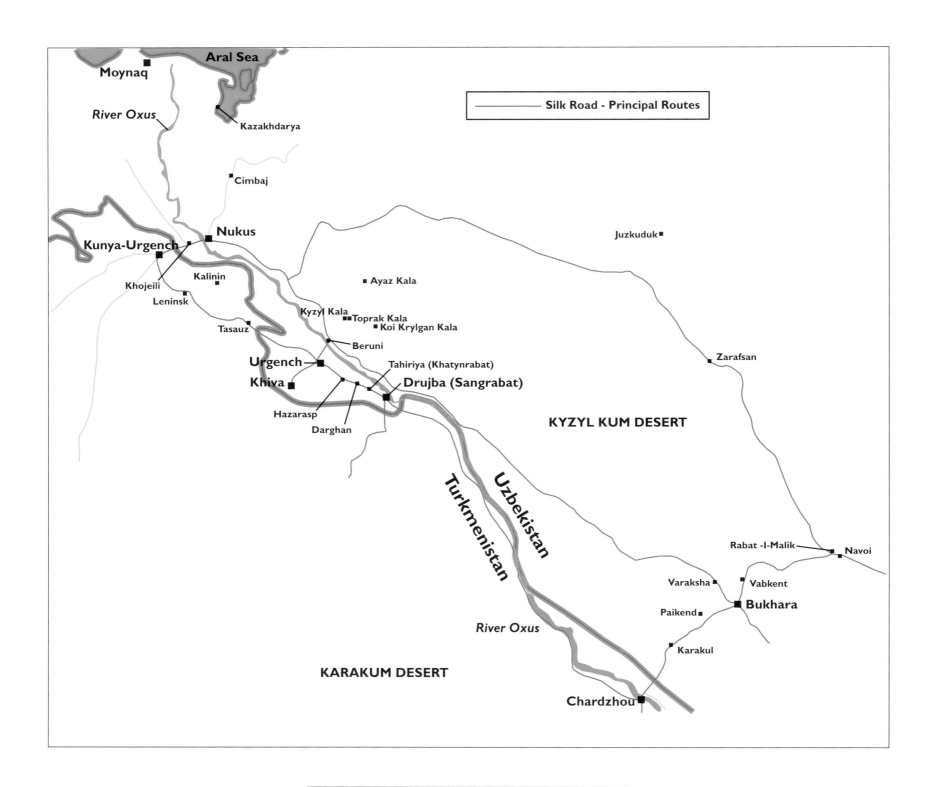

Moynaq

Aral Sea

River Oxus

Kazakhdarya

Cimbaj

Nukus

Kunya-Urgench

Khojeili

Kalinin

Leninsk

Tasauz

Ayaz Kala

Kyzyl Kala

Toprak Kala

Koi Krylgan Kala

Beruni

Urgench

Tahiriya (Khatynrabat)

Khiva

Drujba (Sangrabat)

Hazarasp

Darghan

Juzkuduk

Zarafsan

KYZYL KUM DESERT

Uzbekistan

Turkmenistan

Rabat -I-Malik

Navoi

Varaksha

Vabkent

Paikend

Bukhara

River Oxus

KARAKUM DESERT

Karakul

Chardzhou

Silk Road - Principal Routes

THE ROUTES TO THE NORTHWEST
FROM BUKHARA TO KHOREZM

CHAPTER SEVENTEEN

THE ROUTES TO THE NORTHWEST FROM BUKHARA AND SAMARKAND TO KHOREZM

There were three principal routes from Bukhara to Khorezm. The longest, but probably the safest, was to head southwest through Paikend to the town of Amul (modern Chardzhou) on the Amu Darya. The route then followed the lower (west) bank of the river through a narrow of strip of irrigated, and therefore relatively fertile land between two deserts (for more on this route see p. 237). There were two principal northerly routes (and probably some minor trails as well), both more direct but with a perilous crossing of the Kyzyl Kum Desert with no assured supply of water or food. Both routes ran north of the Amu Darya, a journey of at least eight days through a series of widely spaced caravanserais. Some of the caravan stops were so far apart that travellers were forced to journey for a day and a night to reach the next stop on the route.

The Royal Road from Bukhara to Samarkand

The journey from Bukhara to Samarkand took six or seven days and, at least as early as the Kharakhanid era (992–1211), the highway between the two cities came to be called the Royal Road (the *Shah Rah*). This road followed the course of the Zerafshan River for almost 300 km and is part of the main East-West section of the Silk Road from China. The Kharakhanids built a network of caravanserais along the road and the towns between Bukhara and Samarkand flourished. A tall, slender minaret still stands at Vabkent, 25 km from Bukhara on the Royal Road. It was built in 1196–97, only seventy years after the Kalan Minaret and, at almost 39 metres, is almost as impressive. Further out across the arid steppe that divides the two cities, about 70 km east of Bukhara, is Rabat-I –Malik, one of the most massive and imposing of all of the Silk Road's myriad caravanserais:

> *'Think, in this battered Caravanserai*
> *Whose Portals are alternate Night and Day,*
> *How Sultan after Sultan with his Pomp*
> *Abode his destined Hour, and went his way.*
>
> *They say the Lion and the Lizard keep*
> *The Courts where Jamshyd gloried and drank deep:*
> *And Bahrám, that great Hunter- the Wild Ass*
> *Stamps o'er his Head, but cannot break his Sleep.'*

(Edward Fitzgerald [1809–83], *The Rubaiyat of Omar Khayyam of Nishapur*)

Fig. 323 **The Rabat-I -Malik Caravanserai, near Navoi**
Kharakhanid era, 10th or 11th century
The Rabat-I-Malik Caravanserai (The Prince's Caravanserai), near Navoi and the old Silk Road town of Karmana (ancient Karminia), was built before 1078 by the Kharakhanids. Old photographs of Rabat-I-Malik show large sections of wall and half-columns still intact but after years of 'brick-mining' by locals only the massive front portal remains. Work is currently underway to expose the foundations of the old walls.

The Sogdians

The men who trudged along the Royal Road during the Kharakhanid period were continuing a tradition established by those most consummate of Silk Road traders, a people of Persian stock known collectively as the Sogdians. Little is known about them; they could never have been said to constitute a nation or empire, they were more of a loosely affiliated group of city-states. What is not in doubt, however, is that they possessed great commercial prowess: evidence of the activities of Sogdian merchants have been found at many places and over a wide area of the Silk Road. They seemed to have travelled anywhere and everywhere in search of profit and traces of them are still to be found- in the documents and murals of Xinjiang, in the petroglyphs at Chilas in Northern Pakistan and in the poems and stories of Tang dynasty Xian. By the second century they played a key role in

Fig. 324 **Silk child's coat**
Sogdiana, 8th century
L. 48 cm, W. 82.5 cm
(The Cleveland Museum of Art)

Silk Road trade in both directions- the Chinese bought jade, precious stones, exotic animals and slaves from Sogdian merchants and the countries to the West purchased the silks, mirrors and weapons that they acquired in China. There were colonies of Sogdian merchants in many Chinese towns and they carried their religion and customs with them as they travelled. The Sogdian language became the Silk Road's *lingua franca* and, from the second century until they were invested by the Arabs during the eighth century, Sogdian cities were centres of cultural excellence. Every work of art that the Sogdians produced – their paintings, their metalwork, their textiles, their sculpture and even their grave

artefacts – are flamboyant expressions of wealth and power, acquired from Silk Road trade. The great Sogdian cities of Varaksha, Afrasiab (Samarkand) and Penjikent are all examined in this book and all reveal astonishing levels of artistic skill.

Excavation of the Sogdian burial grounds at Orlat, situated on dry sections of the Saghanaq river bed to the northwest of Samarkand, have revealed much about their burial practices and their fondness for hunting and jousting. The Sogdian dead were either exposed on towers – their flesh stripped by vultures or dogs before the bones were placed in ossuary caskets – or they were interred in pits or catacombs. At Orlat they were interred and despite the fact that many graves were looted in antiquity, many artefacts remain. Weapons, ceramics and bone belt buckles were found in a total of ten burial mounds and some, like a jade scabbard slide from China, were of foreign manufacture. The bone belt plaques are all superbly worked with themes that are strangely reminiscent of the European knights of medieval times (fig. 325).

By the early eighth century the Sogdians were finished as an economic and political force in Central Asia. They and Divastich, the last ruler of Penjikent, fled the city with the Arabs in pursuit. They sought refuge at Mount Mugh in modern Tajikistan but were eventually overrun and slaughtered in 722 (see p. 268). This was not the end of the Sogdians, however. During the 1930s, Soviet researchers discovered that the inhabitants of several villages in the

Fig. 325 **Polished and engraved bone plaque for a belt buckle depicting a hunting scene**
Sogdian, 1st to 2nd century AD
L. 13.5 cm
Orlat Burial Grounds, Koshrabad district, Samarkand region, Uzbekistan
(Institute of Fine Arts, Tashkent)
On this plaque, men on horseback hunt deer, wild horses and goats.

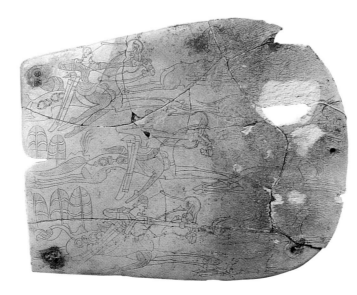

remote Yagnob Valley of Northern Tajikistan still spoke the ancient language of the Sogdians. More than one thousand years after they disappeared from the Central Asian stage, these precious few descendants of the men who helped to sustain the Silk Road during its most vibrant years are still to be found in the mountains of Tajikistan (see p. 269). The modern descendants of the Sogdians, it is said, are the Tajiks but, as with so much of Central Asia history, the subject is a matter of fierce debate.

Samarkand

> '...Sweet to ride forth at evening from the wells
> When shadows pass gigantic on the sand,
> And softly through the silence beat the bells
> Along the golden road to Samarkand.
>
> We travel not for the trafficking alone;
> By hotter winds our fiery hearts are fanned
> We make the golden journey to Samarkand.'

(James Elroy Flecker [1884–1915], 'The Golden Journey to Samarkand')

Of all the cities that make up the long journey to the West, few possess as much magic and mystique as Samarkand. A turn of the century visitor, Michael Shoemaker, said that it was 'the home of all the romance and poetry in the East' and for 2,500 years it successfully maintained its position as the richest and most populous metropolis on the Central Asian Silk Road.

Samarkand sits on the southern bank of the Zerafshan River and to the northeast of the modern town is Afrasiab, a hilly area covering about 220 hectares and the site of the most ancient parts of the city. Samarkand is believed to have been an outpost of the Persian Achaemenid Empire and was already a large fortified city when the armies of Alexander the Great arrived in 329 BC. It was here, at Maracanda as it was known to the Greeks, that Alexander ran through his boyhood friend Cleitus with a spear. Both men had engaged in a drunken argument and Cleitus had claimed that Alexander's accomplishments palled against those of his father, Philip of Macedonia. Under Greek rule the city's fortifications were strengthened and the city developed around the Afrasiab site. At Afrasiab the Greeks built great palaces, markets and a network of irrigation canals. The water-supply system was further improved during the Kushan era (first century BC to fourth century AD) by the construction of a lead aqueduct. Under Kushan rule the city's Sogdian inhabitants began to explore trading possibilities with the lands to the east and west. By the third century there were communities of Sogdian merchants along the entire eastern section of the Silk Road and Samarkand, as Sogdiana's capital, became a rich, cosmopolitan city. The arrival of Hepthalite (Hunnic) invaders

during the fourth and fifth centuries caused trade to falter and the city to contract but by the sixth century, the former Hepthalite domains were ruled by an alliance of Turks and Sasanians and it flourished once again. The Sogdians produced great works of art, influenced to some degree by all of the countries with whom they traded. The artists of Byzantium, China, India and Persia have all left their mark on Sogdian art, by direct involvement or by the diffusion of motifs and methods along the Silk Road (fig. 326).

Vargoman can be seen on the west wall receiving ambassadors from China and Korea, as well as a party of mountain-dwellers, each envoy carrying gifts for the great man. On the eastern wall is the most delightful scene of all: a Chinese princess makes her way across a river aboard a large red boat, accompanied by her servants and a group of musicians who serenade her as she journeys to the Sogdian court (fig. 327).

Like so many of the great civilisations of the Silk Road, Sogdiana seems to have withered almost as soon as it bloomed. When the Chinese monk Xuanzang passed through in 630 the town was thriving, 'the merchandise of many countries was found and the craftsmanship of artisans appeared superior to that of other countries', he observed. But in 712, Samarkand fell to the Arab armies of General Qutaiba ibn Muslim. The main Zoroastrian temple of the Sogdians was immediately replaced by a mosque and a section of the city's protective wall was taken down. At the Battle of the Talas River in 751 the victorious Arabs brought captured Chinese papermakers, and possibly silkweavers too, to Samarkand and a local industry became established. Within a short space of time Samarkand paper was renowned throughout the Islamic world but the upheavals occurring throughout Central Asia during the eighth

Fig. 326 **Mural depicting visiting ambassadors at the royal court at Samarkand**
Sogdian, 7th century
From the south wall of Room 1, Afrasiab, Samarkand, Uzbekistan
(Museum of Afrasiab)
This and the other murals at Afrasiab adorned the walls of the ruler's palace and the houses his nobles. They were installed in the museum in the exact arrangement in which they were discovered. In this celebrated and richly painted mural, members of the Chaghanian mission are seen visiting the court of the Sogdian ruler Vargoman. An inscription on the painting refers to the visit of ambassadors from Chaghanian (the area around the Surkhan Darya Valley near modern Denau) and Chach (modern Tashkent). Leading the procession is a princess seated beneath a canopy upon a white elephant, the accompanying inscription suggesting that she is destined to marry the Sogdian ruler. Her entourage, on camelback and on horseback, brings gifts for the ruler including a flock of sacred swans. The Chaghanian ambassador himself, lavishly dressed, holds aloft his official mace as he approaches on horseback.

Fig. 327. Mural depicting a Chinese princess aboard a boat with servants and musicians
Sogdian, 7th century
From the east of Room 1, Afrasiab, Samarkand, Uzbekistan
(Museum of Afrasiab, Samarkand)

century and the campaigns against the Sogdians adversely affected trade. The fortunes of Samarkand and its merchants did not fully revive until the ninth century when it became part of the Samanid domains. A new citadel was constructed and the city walls were rebuilt with a gate at each of the four points of the compass. A large commercial district also de-veloped to the south and west of Afrasiab and the merchant classes, many as converts-of-convenience to the new religion, began to grow rich once again. The tenth century geographer Mukadasi listed Samarkand's export goods during the Samanid era as 'silver-coloured fabrics (*simgun*), large copper vessels, artistic goblets, tents, stirrups, bridle-heads, and straps' (quoted in Barthold, 1981).

Over the next three hundred years control of the city changed hands a number of times but it continued to thrive as a commercial centre. Under the Kharakhanids (992–1211), Afrasiab was rebuilt as an administrative and military base and its main mosque enlarged, but the city was doomed. In 1220 it was attacked by the Mongols, its defenders cornered in Afrasiab's mosque and slaughtered. The Mongols then proceeded to tear down the city's aqueduct and Afrasiab was abandoned for all time. Samarkand's population fell to less than a quarter of its original number and, at the time of Ibn Battuta's visit during the first half of the fourteenth century, the city had still not been fully rebuilt:

> '…I journeyed to Samarqand, which is one of the largest and most perfectly beautiful cities in the world. It is built on the bank of a river where the inhabitants promenade after the afternoon prayer. There were formerly great palaces along the bank, but most of them are in ruins, as also is much of the city itself, and it has no walls or gates.'

(Ibn Battuta. Translated by H. A. R. Gibb in Gibb, 1929)

Ironically, the city's glittering age occurred during the final years of the Silk Road. The Samarkand of the Timurids was capital of a vast empire and a series of grandiose construction projects caused the city to take on a form that can still be seen today. Walls 7 km in length were built around the town, now positioned to the south of old Afrasiab, and a citadel built in the western part of the city to contain Timur's residence and treasury – the Kok-Saray, or 'Blue Palace'. During the late fourteenth and the first few years of the fifteenth century, Timur embarked on a veritable orgy of construction in Samarkand with the help of craftsmen brought from the conquered territories. Within the newly rebuilt walls he installed six gates with roads leading from each to the Registan Square, in Timur's day the city's central point, covered by a domed bazaar. Samarkand's population was large – about 150,000, according to Ruy Gonzalez de Clavijo, representative of King Henry III of Castile – and included Turks, Arabs, Moors, Greeks and Armenians and Indians. There was a strong contingent of Christians, too- Catholics and Nestorians among them- and the Registan Square and the surrounding markets were filled with goods from the countries of the Silk Road:

> 'The markets of Samarqand further are amply stored with merchandise imported from distant and foreign countries. From Russia and Tartary come leathers and linens, from Cathay come silk stuffs that are the finest in the whole world, and of these the best are those that are plain without embroideries. Thence too is brought musk which is found in no other land but Cathay, with balas rubies and diamonds which are more frequently to be met with in those parts than elsewhere, also pearls, lastly rhubarb with many other spiceries. The goods that are imported to Samarqand from Cathay indeed are of the richest and most precious of all those brought thither from foreign parts, for the craftsmen of Cathay are reputed to be the most skilful by far beyond those of any other nation… From India there are brought to Samarqand the lesser spiceries, which indeed are the most costly of the kind, such as nutmegs and cloves and mace with cinnamon both in the flower and as bark, with ginger and manna: all these with many other kinds that are never to be found in the markets of Alexandria.'

(Ruy Gonzalez de Clavijo. Translated by Guy Le Strange in Le Strange, 1928)

During the rule of Timur's grandson Ulugh Beg, the Registan Square began to be transformed from a commercial to a place of worship and for the study of Islam. The three madrassahs (seminary colleges) that make up the Registan ensemble together constitute one of the wonders of the Islamic world and became the model for the civic projects of the Safavids of Persia and the Mughals of India. The British MP and future Viceroy of India George Curzon saw

Fig. 328 **The Registan Square, Samarkand**
15th to 17th century
The oldest of the three structures (visible to the left) is the Ulugh Beg
Madrassah, built around 1420. The massive front portal is flanked by a pair of
minarets and is decorated with marble panels around the base and blue, green,
turquoise and yellow tiles and mosaic-work above. Across the square is the Shir
Dar ('lion bearing') Madrassah, built by the city's Uzbek Governor Yalangtush
Bakhadur between 1619 and 1636. It is a perfect mirror in style and composition
of the Ulugh Beg Madrassah but is embellished with even more startling
decoration of brick and tile mosaic work. At the top of the front portal, in each
corner, are the creatures from which the building takes its name – large felines,
more like tigers than lions, hunting white deer and on the backs of each of them
a rising sun with a human face. These motifs, extraordinary given the tradional
Muslim dislike for figurative art, have been the subject of much debate and may
be a manifestation of the power of the rulers of the day. The third of the
Registan's structures is the Tela Kari ('Gold Work') Madrassah, built just after the
Shir Dar Madrassah, between 1646 and 1660. The Tela Kari Madrassah is the
largest of the three and was built to replace the structurally flawed Bibi Khanum
Mosque (see below). The interior of its azure coloured dome is decorated with
richly painted and gilded papier-mâché.

the Registan during the 1880s and called it 'the noblest
public square in the world'. It still presents a dazzling sight
(fig. 328).

Today's visitors to Samarkand are still awed by the
Registan but amidst all of the tour groups and the noise of
the modern city it is easy to forget that the square was, until
very recently, an important place of worship (fig. 329).

Fig. 329 **Photograph of the Registan Square, Samarkand**
Ca. 1890

Fig. 330 **Photograph of a barber at work in the Registan Square, Samarkand**
Ca. 1900

commissioned the building for a favourite – his grandson and heir Muhammad Sultan – who died campaigning in 1404. A year later, Muhammad was joined by the great man himself and during the following years other princes were placed there too, the assassinated Ulugh Beg among them. Timur's progeny are reposed around him beneath marble tombstones and his own cenotaph, a massive 1.8 metre slab of dark green jade, is said to be the largest piece of the material in the world (fig. 332). The jade slab over Timur's grave was damaged in 1740 during an attempt by the Persian invader Nadir Shah to steal it. The actual tombs are in a crypt beneath the chamber, positioned exactly beneath the cenotaphs above. The building is topped by an ovoid ribbed dome, more than 30 metres in height and covered with radiant blue tiles.

Old photographs of the Registan also reveal that the religious function of the square did not entirely displace its ancient purpose as a place of commerce (fig. 330).

One of the few surviving early Timurid structures is the Gur-e Mir ('The Grave of the Prince'; fig. 331). Timur

Another of Samarkand's earliest and most important monuments has a funerary role. The Shah-I Zindah necropolis was built on the southern slopes of Afrasiab Hill over almost nine hundred years, from the eleventh to the nineteenth centuries. It developed around the tomb of Kusam ibn Abbas, a cousin and companion of the Prophet

Fig. 331 **The Gur-e Mir, Samarkand**
Timurid, completed in 1404

Fig. 332 **The sarcophagi of Timur, Ulugh Beg and Mir Sayid Barakah**
The Gur-e Mir, Samarkand
Timur lies at the feet of his religious mentor Mir Sayid Barakah and at his feet lies Ulugh Beg.

who was with the first Arab armies in Transoxiana and died at Samarkand in about 677. The legend is that Kusam ibn Abbas (in Persian, Shah-I Zindah or the 'living king') was decapitated by the city's Sogdian defenders and jumped with his head into a nearby well. There he is said to remain until his services are required and he will re-emerge, as the defender of Islam. The necropolis was abandoned after the Mongol conquest of 1220 but was subsequently rebuilt during the fourteenth century by Timur. A series of sixteen small mosques and domed mausolea were built along a narrow lane of about 70 metres in length as a burial place for the clergy of Samarkand and for Timur's family and friends. The mausolea in the lower section were, for the most part, built by Ulugh Beg and the buildings as a whole reveal the evolution of architecture and glazed tile decoration during the Timurid era (fig. 333).

The Bibi Khanum Mosque is one of the most majestic edifices to have survived from Timur's reign. Its construction was begun in 1399 when Timur returned to Samarkand, fresh from his triumphs in India. The mosque was built as the city's main place of worship and was dedicated to Timur's favourite wife, Sarai Mulk ('Bibi') Khanum, a Mongolian princess of surpassing beauty. A Timurid manuscript, the 'Zafarnama' of Sharaf al-Din, describes the construction of the building. Five hundred stonemasons

Fig. 333 **The Shah-I Zindah Necropolis, Samarkand**
11th to 19th century (mostly 14th to 19th century)

Fig. 334 **Bibi Khanum Mosque, Samarkand**
Completed in 1404–05
Photographed in 1929

Fig. 335 **Bibi Khanum Mosque, Samarkand**
After restoration

from Azerbaijan, Persia, Syria and India laboured on the massive structure, creating a building 130 metres by 100 metres. Ninety-five elephants were brought from India to Samarkand to convey building materials and its dome, according to Sharaf al-Din, 'would rank supreme were it not for the sky itself'. Timur personally supervised, and often meddled in the construction of the mosque. According to Ruy Gonzalez de Clavijo, the ailing Timur was carried each day to the site and threw the workers coins and gobbets of meat to urge them on. The result was stupendous but it was built too quickly and began, almost immediately, to shed large chunks of masonry, often during worship. The passing years reduced the building to a virtual ruin and in 1897 an earthquake left only a tottering wreck of a building, the courtyard around it and a massive marble Koran-lectern. The courtyard became a cotton market and so it remained until an ambitious Soviet restoration project resurrected the building during the 1960s and 1970s. Today, some of its former glory is restored and the contrast with its former state could not be more marked (figs. 334 and 335).

Beside the Bibi Khanum Mosque is Samarkand's bazaar, a focus for the city's commerce for aeons. There is a degree of post-Soviet drabness about the bazaar today but the spice-sellers, so admired by Clavijo, are still to be found (fig. 336).

Fig. 336 **Spice merchant, Samarkand bazaar**

There is space to look at only one other of the city's architectural treasures from the Silk Road era. Timur's grandson and heir Ulugh Beg was renowned more for his erudition than for his military exploits. As governor of Samarkand he invited the most eminent scholars of the day to the city, including the renowned Turkish astronomer Qazi Zadeh Rumi. Under Qazi Zadeh Rumi's tutelage astronomy became Ulugh Beg's greatest passion and in 1420 he ordered the construction of an observatory on top of a hill in the northeast corner of the city. He and his fellow astronomers identified the coordinates of 1,018 stars and calculated the length of a calendar year to within a minute of today's measurement. Ulugh Beg's calculations travelled east and west along the Silk Road and were used by Chinese, Arab and European scholars at least until the seventeenth century. In 1447 he became ruler of all Transoxiana, ruling from Samarkand, but his interest in science was regarded as heretical in some quarters and in 1449 he was assassinated. The observatory was demolished after Ulugh Beg's death and its whereabouts remained unknown until 1908 when the foundations of the building and an 11-metre section of a marble sextant were discovered by the Russian archeologist Vladamir Vyatkin. The sextant is in near perfect condition with marks showing the degrees and minutes still visible

Fig. 337 **The remains of a giant sextant, Ulugh Beg Observatory, Samarkand**
Ca. 1420
L. 11 metres (approx.)

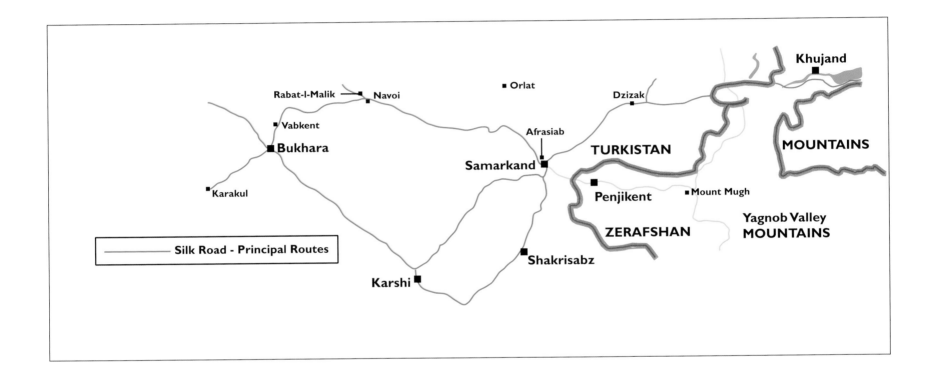

Silk Road - Principal Routes

Khujand

Rabat-I-Malik — Navoi   Orlat   Dzizak

Vabkent   Afrasiab

Bukhara   Samarkand   TURKISTAN   MOUNTAINS

Karakul   Mount Mugh

                                                        Penjikent

                                                                      Yagnob Valley
                                    ZERAFSHAN   MOUNTAINS

                                                  Shakrisabz

                        Karshi

SILK ROAD SITES
AROUND SAMARKAND

CHAPTER EIGHTEEN

SILK ROAD SITES AROUND SAMARKAND

Aside from Samarkand, some of Timur's mightiest structures were erected in the city of his birth- Shakhrisabz, 90 km to the south on the Termez-Samarkand section of the Silk Road. This route led across the Zerafshan mountains and passed through the Takhtakaracha Pass and though steep and somewhat difficult for caravans, it was the most direct route between the two cities.

Shakhrisabz

Shakhrisabz, known as the 'Green City', was called Kesh during the Sogdian era and was renowned for the fertility of its soil and for its mild climate. Until Timur was born there in 1336 the city was a small and unassuming place, known chiefly for the quality of its fruit. Under Timur's administration the city was transformed, however, and though much of what he built was demolished during the sixteenth century by the Shaibanid emir of Bukhara, there is enough remaining to reveal its former grandeur. Timur's palace, the Ak Serai ('White Palace'), was begun in 1379 and was still being worked on when Clavijo saw it in 1404 (fig. 338). The entrance was 22 metres wide and between 40 and 50 metres in height. Beyond this massive portal was Timur's great reception hall, covered in gold and blue tiles so beautiful, according to Ambassador Clavijo that 'even the craftsmen of Paris, who are so noted for their skill, would hold that which is done here to be of very fine workmanship." Babur, the last scion of the Timurids and the first emperor of the Mughal dynasty, was equally impressed. In his memoirs (the *Baburnama*) he wrote that 'Few arches so fine can be shown in the world'. The whole structure was built of fired brick and decorated with polychrome tiles and mosaic-work. Only the two towers of the main portal (*pishtaq*) still stand today, each with huge Kufic inscriptions proclaiming the might of Timur: 'The Sultan is the shadow of God'. At the top of the portal, incomplete but still decipherable, is a mantra for the Timurid age that reads, 'Let he who doubts our power and munificence, look upon our buildings'.

A short distance to the south of the Ak Serai is the Dar as-Siyadat ('Palace of Power'), the mausoleum of the Barlas clan of which Timur and his descendants were members. Only the northern part survives today but the complex once

Fig. 338 **The entrance towers of the Ak Serai ('White Palace'), Shakhrisabz, Uzbekistan**
Timurid period, completed 1396

comprised a mosque, a madrassah (theological college) and dynastic tombs. One of them was built for Timur himself but in the event he was interred in Samarkand and the marble sarcophagus that had been prepared for him remained empty. The sole surviving a tomb above ground is that of Jehangir – Timur's oldest son – who died in 1376 at the age of only twenty-two, after falling from a horse.

Just to the west of the Dar as-Siyadat is the beautiful Kok Gumbaz mosque, named for its blue dome and built in 1435 by Ulugh Beg as the town's main place of worship (fig. 339).

Across a small square from the mosque is a burial complex – the Dar as-Tilovat ('Palace of Respect and Consideration') – begun by Timur and expanded by Ulugh Beg as another place of final repose for members of the family.

Fig. 339 **The Kok Gumbaz mosque, Shakhrisabz, Uzbekistan**
Timurid period, ca. 1435

Penjikent (Bunjikath)

Another of the Silk Road cities within striking distance of Samarkand is Penjikent (Bunjikath), about 65 km to the east along the Zerafshan River in modern Tajikistan. Penjikent developed on a plateau above the river and flourished from the fifth to eighth century as the most eastern city of Sogdiana, although the town dates back much further. The site has been thoroughly investigated since 1946 and was found to cover a total area of 13.5 hectares, about 8 hectares of which were already in existence by the fifth century. It consisted of a fortified city (*shahristan*), a citadel and a necropolis. Most of the inhabitants were Zoroastrians but Buddhist and Nestorian Christian remains have also been discovered. The city received a large influx of Sogdian aristocracy around 712 when Samarkand fell to the Arab armies of General Qutaiba, and this may explain why there is an abundance of wall paintings and wooden sculpture of such true brilliance. Excavations at Penjikent have exposed a residential area of streets crammed with several hundred, two and three storey clay and mud-brick houses (each with numerous rooms), as well as shops and workshops. A third of the houses were found to contain rich murals and exquisite woodcarvings in large numbers, making Penjikent one of the most important sites of the entire Silk Road. In 722 Penjikent's ruler Divastich revolted against the growing power of the Arabs in Central Asia. The city was attacked and burned and Divastich was pursued to Mount Mugh, about 130 km to the east, where he was eventually captured

Fig. 340 **The remains of the city of Penjikent, Tajikistan**
Sogdian, abandoned ca. 780

and put to death. As a result the Sogdian inhabitants of Penjikent abandoned the city until about 740, when a peace treaty enticed them to return and begin to rebuild it. The charred remains of Divastich's palace were replaced by barracks, presumably for the Arab conquerors, but the city's renewed period of vigour was a brief one; it was abandoned in about 780.

The murals adorning the clay walls of Penjikent's aristocracy date mostly to the first half of the eighth century. The subject matter is truly remarkable and reveals influences from both Iran and India. Episodes from the Persian epic of *Rustam*, lavish banquets, scenes from an Indian epic in which a Brahmin (a Hindu priest) plays dice with a ruler, and some of Aesop's *Fables* are a few examples of the subject-matter of these paintings. The so-called 'Blue Hall', named for the blue lapis background of its murals, contained some of the best examples and most are now in the State Hermitage Museum in St. Petersburg. The links to the paintings of Varaksha and Afrasiab are numerous and immediately apparent but there are connections, too, with the murals of Fondukistan and Kizil (pp. 53 and 154). One of the most engaging is from a Zoroastrian temple of seventh century date and shows a group of female Fravashis, protector spirits somewhat akin to the Western notion of 'guardian angels' (fig. 341).

In contrast to the monumental bas-reliefs of the Sasanian rulers of Persia, Sogdian aristocrats portrayed themselves neither as gods nor as giants among ordinary men. In their paintings they surround themselves with the heroes of mythology- the intention, it seems, was for the owner of the house to assimilate the qualities of these men and to acquire merit by association with them. The mural depicting the valorous Rustam from Penjikent's Blue Hall was originally 12 metres long and shows the hero of medieval Persian liter-ature in combat with demons (fig. 342). The origins of the Rustam epic are lost in antiquity but many of the events are set out in the great Persian text, the 'Epic of Kings', the *Shanama* by the tenth century poet Ferdosi. Penjikent's murals mirror the exploits set out in Ferdosi's literary cycle; the hero gallops about on a chestnut horse, 'his skin…bright and dappled as though flecked with petals of red roses on saffron',* slaying demons and fighting dragons. In one much-quoted passage from the *Shanama*, Ferdosi describes the decoration of a mythical palace in the illustrious city of Siyavush gird. The words were written almost three hundred years after the last of Penjikent's murals were created but the description is an apt one:

> *'A city famous for its rosaries,*
> *Its lofty palaces, and orchard-grounds.*
> *He limned [painted] within the hall full many a picture.'*
> *Of kings, of battle, and of banqueting'*

(Ferdosi, 'The Epic of Kings, the *Shanama*', quoted in Yarshater, 1983)

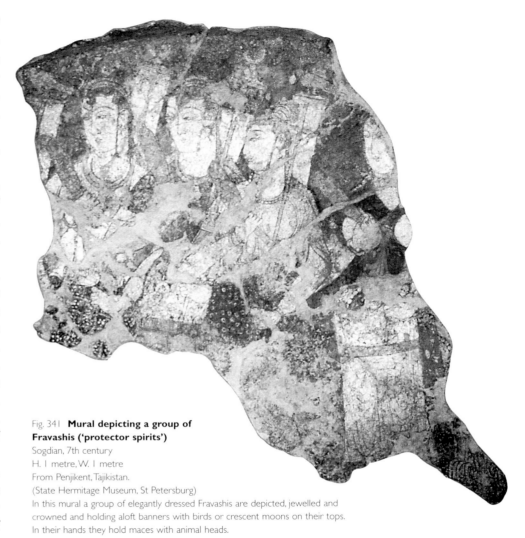

Fig. 341 **Mural depicting a group of Fravashis ('protector spirits')**
Sogdian, 7th century
H. 1 metre, W. 1 metre
From Penjikent, Tajikistan.
(State Hermitage Museum, St Petersburg)
In this mural a group of elegantly dressed Fravashis are depicted, jewelled and crowned and holding aloft banners with birds or crescent moons on their tops. In their hands they hold maces with animal heads.

Fig. 342 **Mural containing a scene from the *Rustam* epic**
Sogdian, first half of the 8th century
H. 1 metre
From 'The Blue Hall', Sector VI, Room 41, Penjikent, Tajikistan.
(State Hermitage Museum, St Petersburg)

* From Ferdowsi (Ferdosi), 'The Epic of Kings, the *Shanama*'. Translated by Reuben Levy in Ferdowsi, 1967.

Fig. 343 **Fragment of a mural with a depiction of a siege engine (manjaniq)**
Sogdian, first half of the 8th century
From the east wall of the main hall of Devastich's palace, Penjikent, Tajikistan
(State Hermitage Museum, St Petersburg)
The main hall of Devastich's palace was 18 metres by 12 metres and the murals that once covered its walls appear to be records of contemporary events. The siege engine shown here is probably a representation of one used during the Arab siege of Samarkand in 712 and, no doubt, used to good effect at Mount Mugh in 722. In this respect these scenes are a portent of Divastich's own death. Some of the other fragments do indeed depict Arabs and a coronation scene may show Devastich himself, initially courted by the new rulers of the region as rightful ruler of Samarkand.

The wooden sculptures and murals from Penjikent show evidence of the conflagration that engulfed the city in 722: the former are badly charred and the latter are in pieces. The destruction of Divastich's palace was so thorough that only small fragments of murals survive but among them are some quite beautiful examples of Sogdian art (fig. 343).

The examples we have seen so far have been concerned with religion, heroism and war but the last we have space for here is a detail from a genre scene (fig. 344).

The slender, elegant figures depicted in Penjikent's murals and wood sculpture are also found on Sogdian silver vessels. The Sogdians were particularly gifted silversmiths and their creations were exported along the Silk Road (fig. 345).

When the inhabitants of Penjikent fled the town in 722 they sought refuge at Mount Mugh, about 130 km east of Penjikent in the upper reaches of the Zerafshan River. During the 1930s Soviet archeologists excavated the remains of a Sogdian castle at Mugh after a local shepherd discovered documents from the personal archive of Divastich, last of the Sogdian rulers. These and further discoveries included paper, leather and wood documents written in Sogdian, Arabic, Turkish and Chinese and dealing mostly with administrative and legal matters. One fragment contains what appears to be a legal decision regarding an application for a divorce:

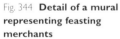

Fig. 344 **Detail of a mural representing feasting merchants**
Sogdian, first half of the 8th century
From Sector XVI, Room10, Penjikent, Tajikistan
(State Hermitage Museum, St Petersburg)
The richly dressed bon-viveurs depicted in these murals perhaps represent the ideal of the urbane, sophisticated Penjikent merchant enjoying the fruits of Silk Road commerce. The attention to detail is quite remarkable: here a cherubic figure is just visible on the gold or silver cup in the merchant's hand; a distant reference, perhaps, to the bacchanals of Ancient Greece.

Fig. 345 **A gilt silver plate with a depiction of a battle scene**
Sogdian, 7th century
Found in 1893 at Perm oblast, selo Kulagysh in the Ural foothills
D. 21.8 cm
(State Hermitage Museum, St Petersburg)
On this wonderfully compact plate two Sogdian warriors, probably heroes from
a literary epic, participate in a duel. One is armed with a bow and the other a
lance, while broken and discarded weapons lie all about them.

*'If Catta decides that she will not remain as a wife with
Ut-tegin, but will part (?) with him, she shall leave him.'*

(Document No. 3 from Mount Mugh. Quoted in Azarpay, 1981)

Also found at Mugh was a fragmentary description of the
heroic Rustam's struggle with the demons, an episode related
in the Persian epic, the *Shanama*, by Ferdosi. Other episodes
from the this epic have been successfully matched with
scenes in the wall paintings of Penjikent (see p. 266). The
castle at Mugh was comprehensively flattened by the Arabs
and, as a result, few substantial artefacts have survived. A rare
exception is a fragment from a beautifully painted wooden
shield, covered in leather and painted with a depiction of the
valiant Rustam, now in the Hermitage Museum. It still shows
the marks of the arrows that struck it.

Little is known of the Sogdians after the ninth century.
During the late eighth and early ninth centuries many
Sogdians left Transoxiana and took up residence at Nishapur
in Persia, and Baghdad and Samarra in modern Iraq. The
Sogdians were never a unified political power nor, by this
period, were they an economic power. They were gradually
absorbed into local populations until they became
indistinguishable, both culturally and linguistically, from
other communities. The coup de grâce was delivered during
the thirteenth century by the armies of Genghis Khan and
there the story ended – or so it was believed – until the early
part of the last century.

The Yagnob Valley

In the villages of the Yagnob River Valley in the Zerafshan
mountains of Tajikistan, about 80 km north of Dushanbe,
around 2000 local people still speak a dialect descended from
Sogdian. The Sogdian language was usurped by Persian from
the ninth century onwards and was believed to have been
extinct until Soviet researchers made one of the great
philological discoveries of the twentieth century. Yagnobi is a
spoken language, however- written Sogdian exists only in
ancient manuscripts like those of Mount Mugh and the
letters discovered by Stein near the Great Wall (see p. 92).
Yagnobi is spoken, it seems, by fewer people than any other
language in the world and the inhabitants of the villages are
slowly moving away from the valley in search of improved
economic conditions. The prospects for this, the last
remnant of Sogdian civilisation are bleak.

There is a caravan road south from Mount Mugh,
through the mountains to the modern Tajik capital of
Dushanbe. Dushanbe is a new city that did not even emerge
as an urban centre until the rail-link with Termez was
established in the 1920s. There was a settlement at
Dushanbe, however, at least as far back as the Bactrian-Greek
period of the third century BC. A small ivory head of
Alexander found at Dushanbe attests to its role as a
stopping-place on the road south to India. This was a
subsidiary part of the Silk Road, nonetheless. For a large part
of the Silk Road's history, Sogdian Samarkand and China
were the focus of much of its trade and this is reflected in the
importance of the great east-west caravan trails.

Fig. 346 **Heir to the Silk Road**
Villager of the Yagnob Valley, Tajikistan

THE SILK ROAD
BETWEEN SAMARKAND AND CHINA

CHAPTER NINETEEN

SILK ROAD SITES BETWEEN SAMARKAND AND CHINA

*'I shall be telling this with a sigh
Somewhere ages and ages hence:
Two roads diverged in a wood, And I-
I took the one less travelled by…'*

(From Robert Frost [1874–1963], *The Road Not Taken*)

There were two principal routes leading from Samarkand to China with many side routes and tracks linking them. The point of divergence for the two routes was the town of Dzizak, renowned for its wool (see map). From Dzizak the more southerly route passed through the Tajik town of Khujand and along the Ferghana Valley via Margilan, Kuva, Andijan and Osh. Beyond Osh the route veered south across the Pamirs, through Gulcha and Sary Tash before turning east again through Irkeshtam and on to Kashgar. An alternative route from Osh passed through Uzgen and then led southeastwards through Kök-Art and the Kögart Pass to Kashgar (see map). The passes through the Pamirs and Tianshan ranges varied according to the seasons but the two

key ones on this route seem to have been at Kögart and Irkeshtam. The better known Torugart Pass – 3,752 metres high and about 90 km northeast of Kök-Art – is now the main crossing point between Kyrgyzstan and China but this was not always the case. The Tash Rabat caravanserai, located 90 km north of the Torugart Pass in the At Bashi range, is of relatively recent vintage, probably the work of a fifteenth-century Mongol ruler named Muhammad Khan. Tash Rabat is a massive structure, 35 by 32 metres, and the fact that it has been heavily restored in recent years does not detract from its status as one of the most important stone buildings in Central Asia. It sits on a caravan route that heads north to Lake Issyk-kul (fig. 347).

Fig. 347 **The Tash Rabat caravanserai, Kyrgyzstan**
Ca. 15th century
(Photo by William Mackesy)

All of the early written sources indicate that the more southerly route, from Dzizak through Ferghana to Osh, is the more ancient of the two. One reason may have been that the terrain between Dzizak and Tashkent was arid steppe, devoid of nourishment for travellers. Only within the past hundred years has irrigation produced a fertile plain and the landscape transformed from that encountered by early wayfarers. The main northerly route from Samarkand gained favour over the shorter and more direct Ferghana Valley route during the sixth to seventh century, when civil war became a threat to travellers and when the Western Turks held sway. With their winter capital to the west of Lake Issyk-kul and their summer capital in Tashkent (formerly Chach), the western Turks became conspicuous consumers of imported goods and merchants were not slow to accommodate their needs (see p. 162). This was the route followed, in the reverse direction, by the Chinese monk Xuanzang and his detailed observations have meant that our knowledge of the towns along the way is quite extensive. After Dzizak, the northerly route traversed the steppe to Tashkent, continued onwards to Chimkent and Otrar in Southern Kazakhstan and then turned east. The eastward road passed through the Karatau hills, crossed the Talas River at the oasis town of Taraz (Dzhambul) and then passed through desert to the town of Kulan. After Kulan, the road continues east into modern Kyrgyzstan, past the modern capital of Bishkek (a mere staging-post until the nineteenth century) and along the Cu (Chu) River Valley through the fertile plain known as the 'Land of a Thousand Springs'. The road went via Tokmak, near the former Kharakhanid capital of Balasagun, and through the Boom Gorge to arrive at the 'Warm Lake', Issyk-kul. There are the remains of settlements on both the northern and southern shores of the lake but the main route to China seems to have passed to the south. On the southern shore of Lake Issyk-kul, at Barskoon, the main northern route turns southward and ascends through the Barskoon Gorge in the Tianshan Mountains to the 4,284 metre Bedel Pass. The Bedel Pass is an ancient crossing point into China and is only about 200 km northwest of the important Chinese Silk Road town of Aksu (see p. 161).

THE TOWNS ALONG THE SILK ROAD BETWEEN SAMARKAND AND CHINA

The Southern Route

Khujand

Khujand (formerly Khodjent), the second largest city of Tajikistan, sits on the Syr Darya (Jaxartes) River at the entrance to the Ferghana Valley and was the site of Alexander the Great's easternmost city- Alexandria Eskhate ('Alexandria the Furthest'). For a city of such prodigious antiquity there is disappointingly little remaining. In common with many other Central Asian cities, Khujand was subjected during the Soviet period to a rapid and indiscriminate process of modernisation that erased much of its history. Indeed, the only structure dating back to the Silk Road era is a mud fortress in the centre of the town, close to the riverbank.

The region between Samarkand and Khujand was known as Ushrusana and, until the arrival of the Arabs, was a Sogdian province. During his campaigns of 713–14, Khujand was captured by General Qutaiba ibn Muslim and the damage wrought by both his forces and also by the Mongol armies of the thirteenth century, are further reasons as to why so little of the city's history remains. Khujand was nevertheless an important stopping-place on the route through the Ferghana Valley and was renowned for its vineyards and gardens.

The Ferghana Valley played an important role in the history of the Silk Road from the very beginning. The waters of the Syr Darya produced a rich, fertile plain more than 250 km in length, still home to about one third of Uzbekistan's population. The first foreign visitor to describe the valley was the Chinese envoy Zhang Qian, who saw it during the second century BC (see p. 26). The abundance of blood-sweating 'heavenly' horses, superior in every respect to Chinese mounts, ensured that Ferghana would remain one of the principal destinations for merchants from the Middle Kingdom until medieval times. There is eyewitness evidence that magnificent horses could still be found in the vicinity of Bukhara as late as 1825. The renowned explorer and veterinarian William Moorcroft (1767–1825), was in Bukhara that year to procure thoroughbred mounts for the British Raj. His efforts were thwarted by the emir, who needed every horse he could find for his campaign against the Kitay-Kipchak rebels, but Moorcroft tells us that only five years earlier the territory along the Oxus was 'a great mine of horses'. The intervening years, a time of rebellion, had led to the breaking up of what Moorcroft called 'the

Fig. 348 **Photograph of the street in front of the Kok Mazar cemetery, Margilan, Uzbekistan**
Taken around 1905

finest horse markets in the world' but there were still a few fine animals to be seen including a splendid black stallion that he attempted to purchase and dispatch to England (Alder, 1985). The question of whether such horses were indigenous to the Ferghana valley or whether Ferghana was simply a place of congregation for horse-traders has never been satifactorily resolved, however.

There were numerous caravanserais and small settlements on the southern route through the valley and Margilan, just north of the modern town of Ferghana, is one of the most important.

Margilan

In the *Baburnama*, the memoirs of the founder of the Mughal dynasty Babur (1483–1530), he describes Margilan as 'a fine township full of good things. Its apricots and pomegranates are most excellent'. He is less charitable about its people: 'Its people are Sarts, boxers, [who are] noisy and turbulent. Most of the noted bullies of Samarkand and Bukhara are Marghinanis'. (From Beveridge, 1969)

The town dates back to around the second century BC, the very beginnings of the Silk Road, and was originally known as Marginan. Like Khujand, however, it has little to show for its long history. Only in a rare, old photograph can one glimpse the appearance of the town before the Soviet era (fig. 348).

Margilan's heritage is now more intellectual than architectural: it has been known for the quality of its silks for centuries and is now the centre of silk production for the whole of Uzbekistan. Many local people are involved in the rearing of silk cocoons and the town's factories employ many others. There are two types of silk production in Margilan: a pair of vast Soviet-style factories, each with more than 10,000 workers and a smaller concern known as the Yodgorlik plant that still produces the precious material in the traditional way (fig. 349).

The Ferghana Valley was a centre for Buddhism right up until the advent of Islam. At Kuva, 35 km northeast of Ferghana town on the Andijan-Margilan road are the remains of a town occupying some 12 hectares. Evidence of glassmaking, pottery manufacture and metalworking indicate that Kuva was an important commercial centre. A Buddhist temple of the seventh or eighth century was found to contain life-sized clay statues of deities. One of the most striking is a massive bust, complete with a large central *urna* (third eye), variously decribed as depicting the Buddha or the Hindu god Siva (fig. 350).

The Mongols did not spare the town during their campaigns of the thirteenth century and it was subsequently abandoned.

The next key stop on the southern route was the town of Andijan, located on the Andijan-Say River in the eastern

Fig. 349 **Silk production by hand at the Yodgorlik factory, Margilan, Uzbekistan**

Ferghana Valley. Andijan is now an important industrial centre, criss-crossed by irrigation channels and engaged in the production of cotton, silk and different kinds of fruit. The old part of the town was all but obliterated in 1902 by a massive earthquake but in its day Andijan was a major stopping place on the caravan route to China. Its most famous resident was Babur, descendant of Timur and founder of the Mughal dynasty of India, born in the town in 1483.

The route continues eastwards from Andijan for a further 35 km, crossing into Kyrgyzstan and arriving at Osh, the country's second city. Extravagant claims are made about Osh – that its history dates back 2,500 or even 3,000 years but it has little to show for it. Osh is now a somewhat grim provincial town without a single monument from its early history. The town attained its apogee in the medieval period, particularly during the ninth to twelfth centuries, when it grew fat on Silk Road commerce. For at least a thousand years Osh has been an important place of pilgrimage for Muslims because of a legend that the Prophet Muhammad once prayed atop Takhti Suleyman (Solomon's throne), a massive 500-metre high rock that towers above the town. Babur built a shrine there in 1497 and the structure is now the oldest building in Osh, dating to a time when the Silk Road had already become part of the past. The only real reminder of Osh's status as a Silk Road town is the bazaar that still straggles for about a kilometre along both banks of the Ak-Buura River. Kyrgyz, Tajik and Uzbek merchants still profit from trade with China but today it is synthetic clothing, plastic toys and kitchenware that clutter the stalls. Felt hats and knives are the only local products that attest to the rich heritage of Ferghana's craftsmen.

The disappointing dearth of history in the modern town of Osh is more than made up for by two heavily defaced rock carvings, high on a rock in the small town of Aravan, 25 km to the west (fig. 351).

Fig. 350 **Painted clay bust, possibly depicting Shiva**
Kuva, Ferghana Valley, Uzbekistan,
7th to 8th century
H. 64 cm
(State Fine Arts Museum of Uzbekistan)

Fig. 351 **Rock engravings depicting 'heavenly horses'**
Aravan, near Osh, Kyrgyzstan, probably late first millennium BC
The heavenly horses of Ferghana disappeared long ago but in the Valley there are still a few reminders of the 'blood-sweating dragon-steeds', so coveted by China's Emperor Wudi. Soviet archeologists discovered more than 100,000 petroglyphs at Saimaly-Tash in the Ferghana Range near Kök-Art, and others at Aravan and Airymach-Tau near Osh. Among them are a number of depictions of horses whose resemblance to those found in early Chinese art is quite remarkable. Who left these images and why they did so will probably never be known but one can speculate that some wandering Chinese horse trader of the Han dynasty may have placed them there.

The last big town before the mountain passes to China is Uzgen, northeast of Osh on the banks of the Kara Darya River, a tributary of the Jaxartes (Syr Darya). Like Osh the town has an ancient history and some of its buildings still survive. Uzgen flourished during the eleventh and twelfth centuries as a capital of the Kharakhanids and once occupied a much larger site between the Kara Darya and Jassy Rivers. The narrowness of the Kara Darya Valley at Uzgen perhaps meant that tolls could be levied on passing caravans, a source of revenue for the town that contributed to its rapid growth. The Mongols emasculated Uzgen but a few precious monuments have survived – a minaret and three joined mausolea, reminders of Uzgen's heyday and rare examples of pre-Timurid architecture. The minaret has been rebuilt in recent years by a joint German-Kyrgyz project and now stands about 27 metres in height. The Kharakhanids probably erected it during the eleventh century, and its

Fig. 353 **Old photograph of the minaret at Uzgen before restoration**
Taken around 1905

Fig. 352 **The minaret at Uzgen, Kyrgyzstan**
Kharakhanid period, ca. 11th century

design and its decorative brickwork of rhombuses and rosettes provided a model for the great minarets of Vabkent and Bukhara, built during the twelfth century by the same regime. The original structure stood much higher, perhaps over 40 metres, and a rare old photograph makes for an interesting comparison with its appearance today (figs. 352 and 353).

The three mausolea are situated to the south of the minaret, a group of three joined structures, each with a

Fig. 354 **The three mausolea at Uzgen, Kyrgyzstan**
Kharakhanid period
Constructed (left to right)
ca. 1152, 1013 and 1186

single chamber and a domed roof (fig. 354). The oldest of the three is in the centre and was built for the first Kharakhanid ruler Nasr ibn Ali (Arslan Ilek) who died around 1013. On its heavily restored façade, traces of *girikh* (geometrical arabesque) decoration are still discernible. The northernmost (left hand) mausoleum was built in 1152 for Jalal ad-Din Husayn and is decorated with flowing Naskhi calligraphy on the arch and inside with incised terracotta ornamentation. The third, southernmost mausoleum was completed in about 1186 and is the most ornate of the three-richly decorated throughout its external and internal surfaces with geometric, floral and calligraphic motifs that occur subsequently at the Shah-I Zinda necropolis in Samarkand (see p. 261)

There were many other routes criss-crossing the Ferghana Valley, including a more northerly trail from Khujand along the Syra Darya River through the towns of Pap, Akhsiket and Namangan. Of the three, Akhsiket is the most important and was the capital of the Ferghana Valley under the Samanids. Under the Kharakhanids the focus of power shifted to Uzgen but the town continued to draw revenue from trade. Its metalworkers were noted for the excellence of their steel and weapons and armour were exported to many of the countries of the Silk Road. Akhsiket steel was as nothing against the Mongol holocaust, however, and the town was destroyed and abandoned.

The Northern Route

Travellers who braved the crossing of the sterile region to the northeast of Dzizak would eventually come to the Tashkent oasis- the old principality of Chach. The oasis is watered by the Chirchik River and was inhabited as early as the sixth century BC, sitting as it does at a crossroads of old trade routes. During the early period of the Arab campaigns the capital of Chach was located in what is now the centre of modern Tashkent. Known simply as Chach Madina ('capital of Chach'), the town comprised a rectangular citadel, a palace and a Zoroastrian fire-temple. Merchants and nobles occupied large houses and sometimes castles, prospering from trade with both Turkish nomads and with China. During the eighth century Chach was attacked by both Chinese and Arab armies. The Chinese arrived in 749, capturing and executing the ruler, according to Arab accounts, 'for the non-fulfilment of his duties as vassal'. The man's son appealed to the Arabs for help and the result was the Battle of Talas River, fought in July 751, at which the Chinese were defeated and divested of all influence in Central Asia for the remainder of the Silk Road's history (see p. 213).

Sometime during the Chinese or Arab campaigns in Chach, Chach Madina was destroyed by fire and the capital was moved to a new site about 5 km to the northwest. The new town was named Binkath and quickly became the largest city in Transoxiana. Arab geographers have left a detailed description of the appearance of the town:

'The town of Binkath was surrounded by two lines of walls, of which the outer line had seven gates and the interior line ten gates. The shahristan *[inner town around the citadel] had three gates, the citadel two…The palace and prison were in the citadel, the cathedral mosque outside but close to it, the bazaars partly in the* shahristan, *but chiefly in the* rabad *[suburbs]. The length and breadth of the town from side to side of the outer walls was approximately one* farsakh *. In the town and its neighbourhood there were many gardens and vineyards.'*

(Quoted in Barthold, 1981)

Under Samanid rule during the ninth and tenth centuries Binkath was a thriving commercial centre. The Arab geographer Mukadasi outlined the town's trade goods during the tenth century. They included: 'high saddles of horse hide, quivers, tents, hides (imported from the Turks and tanned), cloaks, praying carpets, leather capes, linseed, fine bows, needles of poor quality, cotton for export to the Turks, and scissors'. (Quoted in Barthold, 1981.) He also mentions that the town produced porcelain of matchless quality.

From the eleventh century onwards the town became known as Tashkent ('city of stone') and was controlled by the Kharakhanids, then by the Kharakhitai and finally by the Khorezmshahs. At the beginning of the thirteenth century the Khorezmshahs were under threat from the Turko-Mongol Naiman tribe and a decision was taken to evacuate Tashkent and then destroy the town. Whether or not the town was actually destroyed is unclear, but the fact that the chroniclers of the Mongol campaigns of only a few years later do not mention it would indicate that it probably was.

The town enjoyed a brief revival of its fortunes under Timur and his descendants when a series of mausolea were built. The three fifteenth-century mausolea north of the Navoi Literary Museum are the oldest surviving buildings in Tashkent. They were built for Yunus Khan (grandfather of the Mughal Emperor Babur), for the Kazakh Prince Kaldirgach Bey and for Sheikh Khavendi Takhur (known as Sheikhantaur).

Soon after the Ming rulers of China restored sovereignty to their country in 1368, the doors to land-based international trade slammed shut and, as with many other places in Central Asia, Tashkent's importance as a caravan city declined. During the sixteenth century it fell to the Uzbek Shaybanid Khanate and settled into a role of provincial trading centre. So it remained until 1865 when it fell to the Russians and became a key participant in the 'Great Game', as a base for that country's conquest of Central Asia. On 26 April 1966 an earthquake devastated Tashkent and much of its remaining architectural heritage was lost. The city's past survives only in a few, heavily restored Timurid buildings like the Sheikhantaur complex described above, and in early photographs (figs. 355 and 356).

The town of Isfijab in Southern Kazakhstan is two or three day's journey through the mountains that lie to the north of Tashkent. Isfijab, known as 'the town on the White River', was also called Sayram and the modern town – 10 km east of Chimkent – still carries this name. Isfijab was one of the largest towns on this section of the Silk Road with a poulation of about 40,000 and was home to merchants from Samarkand, Bukhara, Nakhsheb (Karshi) and Balkh, as well as to local traders. The merchants of Isfijab roamed far and wide, trading cotton, glassware, ceramics, weapons, copper, iron and slaves. It was well known as a centre for the slave trade- captives from the region's endless cycle of war. According to the tenth-century geographer Mukadasi, the town contained no fewer than 1,700 caravanserais for merchants. The Mongols brought Isfijab's prosperity to an end and, when trade revived under the Timurids, it was the adjacent town of Chimkent that came to dominate this part of Southern Kazakhstan.

Close to the point where the Arys River flows into the Syr Darya (Jaxartes), about 130 km northwest of Chimkent, is the town of Otrar. Otrar is now a dead city, ruined and

abandoned, but it was not always so. It once sat at the intersection of a number of caravan routes: west across the Kyzyl Kum to Khorezm, south along the Syr Darya to Chach and east along the Arys River to Taraz and Balasagun. The Soviet archeologist A. N. Bernshtam remarked that 'it is really hard to find a more advantageous and more perilous site in the whole of Central Asia than that of Otrar'. The central ruins are situated in an area of about 20 hectares on top of a pentagonal hill, and the site was occupied as far back as the first century AD. The town used to be known as *Kangu-Turban* or *Turarband* and, during the eighth and ninth centuries, it was the capital of the Kangar Turks. The local rulers minted their own coins, suggesting that the oasis enjoyed a high degree of autonomy.

Figs. 355 and 356 **Haji Akhror Madrassah (Islamic seminary) and the Ankhor Chaikana (teahouse)**
Both still extant but heavily restored
Tashkent, Uzbekistan
Both photographed around 1909

* The distance that a laden mule will walk in an hour, varying from about 5 to 6 km.

Fig. 357 **The Burana minaret**
Balasagun, Kyrgyzstan,
Kharakhanid period, 11th century
H. 24.6 metres
The minaret once stood about
45 metres in height but lost its
top section during an
earthquake. The stone circles in
the foreground of this
photograph are millstones,
gathered from other parts of the
country and brought to the site
for safekeeping. Also deposited at
the site and visible to the left are
Balbal grave-markers, once
erected by nomadic Turks above
the graves of their companions
to designate how many of the
enemy the occupant had slain
(see fig. 208).

Khorezmshahs. The men of the caravan were all Muslims, with the possible exception of a single Hindu, and the merchandise carried included gold and silver, Chinese silk and furs. Inal-khan ordered them to be detained as spies, probably because of a desire to acquire their goods, although one version has it that the Hindu member of the caravan spoke to him with undue familiarity. Whatever the reason, and whether or not Shah Muhammad was a party to the governor's action, the caravaneers were massacred to a man and their goods sold off to the merchants of Samarkand and Bukhara. A solitary survivor – a camel driver – managed to escape and carried the news to Genghis Khan. Genghis at first exercised restraint, sending an envoy named Ibn Kafraj Bughra and two Mongol escorts to Shah Muhammad's capital at Kunya Urgench. They carried Genghis's protest with them and demaded that Governor Inal-khan be submitted to justice. Muhammad's response was to order the death of Ibn Kafraj Bughra and to shave off the beards of the two Mongols. From this point conflict between the Mongols and the Khorezmshahs became inevitable and the events at Otrar and Kunya Urgench ignited an inferno that burned as far as the gates of Vienna and consumed the lives of millions of people- most of them innocents.

Otrar fell to the Mongols after a five-month siege in February 1220. At the end, Inal-khan barricaded himself inside the citadel with 20,000 of his troops. When they ran out of arrows, they were forced to bombard the Mongols with roof tiles but it was all to no end. Inal-khan was captured and, according to the contemporary historian Nasawi, was killed by molten silver being poured into his eyes and ears.

Many of the towns obliterated by the Mongols were not rebuilt for decades or centuries, and some were never rebuilt. Otrar, however, rose quickly from its ashes and by the middle of the thirteenth century was once again a major commercial centre. During the thirteenth and fourteenth centuries Otrar became known for the minting of coins and a number of large civic buildings were erected, including a madrassah and a mosque.

By the second half of the fourteenth century the town was part of Timur's empire and it was here, in February 1405, that the great man died, in the midst of preparing an invasion of China. During Timur's reign a mausoleum was erected above the grave of the twelfth-century Sufi and poet Akhmed Yasavi in the town of Turkistan, 40 km north of Otrar. Akhmed Yasavi's teacher and mentor Arslan-Baba was interred in Otrar and Timur erected a mausoleum above his grave as well. Two fretwork columns are all that remains of the original structure.

The sixteenth and seventeenth centuries were a period of decline for Otrar: a time of struggle between Uzbeks and Kazakhs. The Kazakhs were firmly in control of the town by 1510 but were then afflicted with raids from Dzungarian

By the tenth century the town had adopted its modern name of Otrar and had expanded to occupy an area of 200 hectares. As Islam took root in Southern Kazakhstan, the urban centres enjoyed a period of unparalleled prosperity. With commercial activity came a rise in cultural activity and the emergence of men of letters. One of them was the brilliant scientist Abu Nasr al-Farabi (870–950), born at Vasij in the Otrar oasis.

At the beginning of the thirteenth century Otrar submitted to the Khorezmshahs but the decision to do so proved to be a fateful one. On a single day in 1218, Otrar's governor made one of those decisions on which the fate of worlds revolves: the decision of Gavrilo Princip to assassinate Archduke Franz Ferdinand in 1914, and the decision of Hitler to invade Poland in 1939 were no more disastrous for mankind; and the consequences of his actions still reverberate down through the centuries. The governor of Otrar, a man named Inal-khan (or Inalchik), was a relative of Shah Muhammad of Khorezm but whether or not he was acting under the latter's orders remains unclear. A caravan of 450 merchants and about 500 camels arrived in Otrar in 1118, dispatched by the Mongols to initiate trade with the nomads. Many of the southern Kazakh towns – Sayram and Turkistan among them – were destroyed and what remained of Silk Road trade collapsed. By the mid-seventeenth century the town had been abandoned for good.

To give an idea of the exigencies endured by travellers along the northerly route, the Florentine mercantile agent Francesco Balducci Pegolotti (fl. 1315–40) reported that the journey from Otrar to Yining in China's Ili Valley took forty-five days using pack-mules. From Yining another seventy days were required to reach the garrison town of Jiuquan in Gansu (see p. 122). The road from Otrar led southeast along the Arys River and then east as far as the Talas River. The main crossing point of the Talas is at Taraz (Dzhambul), once one of the largest towns in the region, and nearby is the site of the Battle of the Talas River, fought between Arabs and Chinese in 751 (see p. 213). Mukadasi described Taraz during the 10th century and mentions that it was famous for its goatskins. He also tells us that it was a large fortified city with a moat and four gates and that the main mosque was situated between its markets.

The road east from Taraz follows the route of the modern M39 highway and crosses desert to the town of Kulan, near to the modern city of Lugovoy. According to Mukadisi's description, Kulan had already been abandoned by the tenth century and the castle and vineyards that graced the town during the seventh and eighth centuries were already long gone. Beyond Kulan, the road continued in an easterly direction into today's Kyrgyzstan. Bishkek (Frunze), the Kyrgyz capital, was no more than a stop on a caravan trail during the Silk Road era.

The town of Balasagun, 60 km to the east of Bishkek and about 10 km south of the modern town of Tokmak, was far more important. Balasagun was once a regional capital of the Kharakhanid Empire and from the tenth to twelfth centuries, was pre-eminent among some eighty caravan towns along the Cu (Chu) River valley. The large number of Chinese coins found at the site attest to the commercial importance of the town. In 1128 the Kharakhanid rulers of Balasagun found themselves under threat from another Turkish tribe, the Karluks of the lower Ili Valley, whom they themselves had displaced during the tenth century. They sought help from the Kharakhitai, the 'Black Khitans' who had ruled China as the Liao dynasty. The Kharakhitai obliged by seizing control of Balasagun and establishing their capital there, although their treasury appears to have been at Uzgen. When the Mongol armies arrived the city surrendered without a fight and was spared but from the thirteenth until the fifteenth century the town entered a period of slow decline and was eventually abandoned altogether.

The heavily restored Burana minaret, the remnants of two mausolea and a mound of earth, 100 metres by 100 metres, are all that remains of the once prosperous Silk Road town of Balasagun (fig. 357).

Fig. 358 **Lake Issyk-kul with the Tian Shan Range to the south**
Taken at Balykchy, Kyrgyzstan

About 8 km southwest of Tokmak, just to the northwest of Balasagun, are the remains of the important settlement of Ak-Beshim. Ak Beshim is believed to be the site of the town known, in Xuanzang's day, by the Chinese name of *Suye* or *Suyab*. Suye was the winter capital of the Western Turks (see also p. 162). During excavations from 1953–54 and 1955–58, Soviet archeologists uncovered two Buddhist temples and the vestiges of a Nestorian Christian church. In the first of the two temples the remains of four large Buddhas were discovered seated on high thrones and in the second, a large image within a niche was found. More artefacts were reported to have been discovered during 1998 excavations.

The road from Balasagun follows the Cu (Chu) River eastwards for a further 140 km and then enters the Boom Gorge before it reaches the shores of the 'Warm Lake', Lake Issyk-kul (fig. 358).

One hundred and seventy kilometres long by 70 km wide, Issyk-kul is the world's second largest alpine lake and the volcanic activity beneath its surface means that it never freezes despite being 1,600 metres above sea level (see also p. 161). At least part of the old road is now submerged beneath the lake, courtesy of the same volcanic activity, but it appears that the main highway to China originated at Barskoon on the southern shore. From Barskoon the road ascends through the Barskoon Pass and across the Central Tianshan. Xuanzang came this way in 630 and almost died in the process (see p. 161). The whole area abounds with peaks of over 5,000 metres: the 7,439 metre Pik Pobeda ('Victory Peak') and the 6,995 metre Khan-Tengri (the 'Prince of Spirits') are the two highest.

Once over the Tianshan and through the Bedel Pass, travellers found themselves on the home stretch to China, the Celestial Kingdom.

PERSIA AND BEYOND

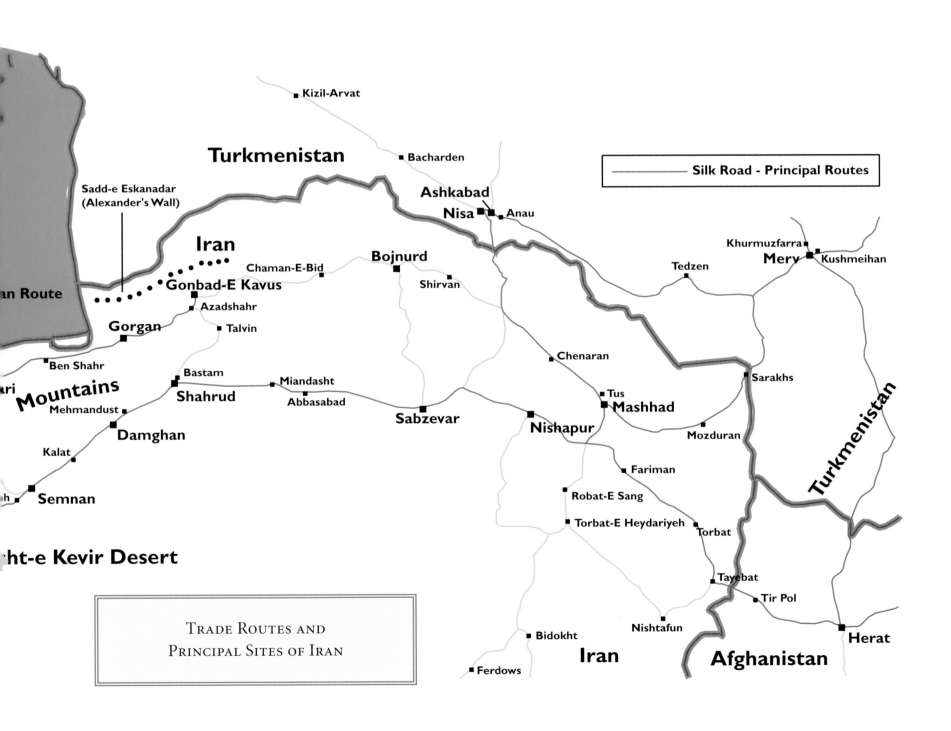

Kizil-Arvat

Turkmenistan

Bacharden

Sadd-e Eskanadar
(Alexander's Wall)

Ashkabad

Nisa ■ Anau

Silk Road - Principal Routes

Iran

Chaman-E-Bid

Bojnurd

Khurmuzfarra

Mery Kushmeihan

an Route

Gonbad-E Kavus

Shirvan

Tedzen

Azadshahr

■ Talvin

Gorgan

Chenaran

Ben Shahr

Bastam

Miandasht

Sarakhs

ari

Mountains

Shahrud

Abbasabad

■ Tus

Mashhad

Turkmenistan

Mehmandust

Sabzevar

Nishapur

Damghan

Mozduran

Kalat

Fariman

Semnan

Robat-E Sang

■ Torbat-E Heydariyeh

Torbat

ht-e Kevir Desert

Tayebat

■ Tir Pol

TRADE ROUTES AND
PRINCIPAL SITES OF IRAN

■ Bidokht

Nishtafun

Iran

Afghanistan

Herat

■ Ferdows

'And strange at Ecbatan the trees
Take leaf by leaf the evening strange
The flooding dark about their knees
The mountains over Persia change

And now at Kermanshah the gate
Dark empty and the withered grass
And through the twilight now the late
Few travelers in the westward pass

And Baghdad darken and the bridge
Across the silent river gone
And through Arabia the edge
Of evening widen and steal on

And deepen on Palmyra's street
The wheel rut in the ruined stone
And Lebanon fade out and Crete
High through the clouds and overblown'

('YOU, ANDREW MARVELL', by Archibald MacLeish, 1892–1982)

We have already examined the two great westward branches of the Silk Road that originated at Merv. The first led through the Parthian capital of Nisa and then crossed the Kopet Dagh Mountains into modern Iran and the second headed southwest through Sarakhs (Saraghs). The two routes converged at Masshad in Iran, capital of Khurasan* province and a Silk Road city of incalculable religious and commercial significance. The passage of the Silk Road through Iran and beyond followed a clearly identified and well-documented route. The modern highway that runs across the north of the country follows the ancient way, originating in Masshad, passing through Nishapur and then skirting the northern edge of the 200,000 square km Dasht-e Kevir (the Great Salt Desert), along the southern foothills of the Alborz Mountains. At Tehran (ancient Ray) the route divides. The northerly route passes through Gazvin and Tabriz before entering Turkey and continuing onward to Istanbul (Byzantium). The more southerly route leads to Hamadan and Kermanshah and then on through Baghdad and Palmyra to the Mediterranean ports and beyond.

There were subsidiary routes that originated in Ray and led south through Kashan, Isfahan, Yazd, Kerman, Bam and onwards to India. There was also a route to India from Masshad, down through the eastern part of the country and a route east from Masshad through Herat to Balkh. The southern routes were vital arterial thoroughfares for early trade but lack of space places them beyond the scope of this book and we must limit ourselves to the main east-west highway.

* Khurasan ('land of the rising sun') is now Iran's largest province although it used to comprise a much greater area. It included Afghanistan and Central Asia as far as the Oxus River and was the eastern part of the former Sasanian Empire.

CHAPTER TWENTY

PARTHIANS AND SASANIANS

Before examining the Silk Road cities that lie along the route through Iran, we will look briefly at the two great eras of Persian history that dominated much of its trade.

Parthians

By 331 BC, Alexander the Great had completed his conquest of Persia. The Achaemenian Empire was brought to an end after defeats at Granica in 334 BC, Issus in 333 BC and Gaugamela in 331 BC. Susa was looted and Persepolis put to the torch and the last Achaemenian king, Darius III Codomannus, fled to Bactria where he was assassinated by his cousin Bessus. Alexander continued eastwards and conquered Afghanistan and northern India before dying in Babylon in 323 BC at the age of only thirty-two. After Alexander's death his empire was divided and the eastern part – Iran, Mesopotamia and Northern Syria – fell to one of his generals, Seleucus I Nicator (r. 312–281 BC). Seleucus founded the Hellenistic Seleucid dynasty and established or expanded cities at Damghan (Hecatompylos), Ray and Susa; populating them with Greek migrants who intermarried with, and absorbed the traditions of the local Iranian population. By the time of his death the Seleucid Empire controlled Iran, Iraq, Afghanistan, Syria and Turkey. The western part of the empire was controlled from Antioch in ancient Syria (modern southeast Turkey), and the eastern dominions from Seleucia (near Ctesiphon), on the Tigris but the dynasty was short-lived. By 238 BC, the Parthians – a nomadic Iranian tribe from Central Asia – had seized control of the area between the Caspian and Aral seas. Their founder, Arsaces I (c. 250–c. 211 BC), and his successors gradually seized the Seleucids' lands, establishing capitals at Nisa, Damghan (Hecatompylos), Ray and Ecbatan. During the reigns of Mithradates I (r.171–138 BC), and Artabanus I (r. 127–124 BC), the Iranian Plateau and the Tigris-Euphrates valley fell under Parthian control with a new capital established at Ctesiphon (see p. 313). By 113 BC, Mithradates II (r. 123–88 BC) had defeated the Scythian tribes threatening the north and in 92 BC, the first contacts with the Roman Empire to the west were made. No treaties were concluded and the seeds for future conflict between the two powers were sown. Under Mithradates II, the Parthians occupied northern Mesopotamia and the great caravan city

of Dura Europos in modern Syria, near the border with Iraq (see p. 325). Because of their position on the trade routes between Asia and Rome the Parthians amassed great wealth, both by commerce and from the customs duties levied on goods travelling through their territories. Many merchants attempted to circumvent Parthian-controlled territories to avoid these taxes and a secondary route developed through the Caucasus. In 115 BC or 105 BC, the Chinese emperor Wudi and the Parthian king Mithradates II exchanged ambassadors – the Chinese sent gifts of silk and the Parthians sent acrobats and ostrich eggs to the imperial court – and both countries appear to have enjoyed cordial relations (see p. 82).

By 64 BC the last vestige of the Seleucids had been defeated by the Roman proconsul Pompey (106–48 BC). Syria was absorbed into the Roman Empire and an uneasy standoff with the Parthians ensued, with their common frontier close to Dura Europos. The truce came to an abrupt end in 53 BC when Marcus Licinius Crassus, Governor of the Roman province of Syria, led an army of infantry against the Parthians near Carrhae. The battle was a disaster for the Romans. They were outmanoeuvred by Parthian cavalry who fired backwards as they galloped away from the enemy in a manoeuvre known as the 'Parthian Shot' (see fig. 172). The sight of huge silk banners, unfurled by the Parthians, also terrified the Romans. This is thought to have been the Roman's first contact with the precious material that, within seven years, had reached the markets of Rome.

Over the next 200 years the Romans launched a succession of invasions but none of them achieved more than limited success. Between 113 and 117 AD the Roman emperor Trajan (r. 98–117 AD) made considerable inroads into the Parthians' domains, capturing Ctesiphon and reaching the shores of the Persian Gulf before dying of disease. His successor, Hadrian elected to make peace rather than capitalise on the gains the Romans had made but the dynasty had become weakened by internal feuds and external pressure. The Romans to the west, the Kushans in the east and nomadic tribes to the north all served to undermine Parthian rule. In 164–65 AD the Roman general Gaius Avidius Cassius captured the cities of Ctesiphon and Seleucia, but his army was assailed by an epidemic of what

Fig. 359 **A bronze statue of a Parthian prince**
Parthian, 2nd to 1st century BC
H. 1.9 metres
Discovered in 1934 among the ruins of a temple at Shami, Khuzestan province
(National Museum, Tehran)

emperor Septimius Severus attacked Parthia again in 197–98. Ctesiphon was sacked but, because of a lack of provisions for his troops, the Romans were forced to retreat. Septimius Severus laid siege to Hatra in 199 but failed to take it. Conflict quickly ensued between two claimants to the Parthian throne, Vologeses IV or V and Artabanus IV. They were finally overthrown in about 224 by Ardashir I (r. 224–41), the founder of the Sasanian Empire. Ardashir was the son of Babak, a descendant of *Sasan* (from whom the dynasty takes its name) and a vassal king of Persis- modern Fars in southwestern Iran.

The Parthians utilised the proceeds of commerce to build cities and pursue the arts. The artistic excellence of the Parthians was evident in the last section, in the finds at their early capital of Nisa in modern Turkmenistan. A Parthian innovation, first appearing on coins struck in the first century BC was the use of 'frontality', the use of the frontal pose in place of the profile. They were also consummate sculptors and the massive bronze portrait of a Parthian prince or military commander from Shami, in the mountains around Malamir in southwestern Iran, is probably the greatest of their statuary (fig. 359). This figure, like much of their early sculpture, is characterised by influences from the Greek world.

Another work of art from Shami, this time from a tomb, is further evidence that the Parthians could produce objects of great delicacy (fig. 360).

Parthian merchants travelled to China from an early period. Jacques Gernet (Gernet, 1995) relates the story of the Parthian trader who conducted his business in the early sixth century, along the Yangtze between Sichuan and the East China Sea. Within a short period he had accumulated

appears to have been smallpox. They retreated from the Parthians' territories, spreading the disease as they went, but despite these setbacks Silk Road commerce still managed to continue. Throughout the second century AD, cities like Palmyra and Hatra flourished. The former was under Roman control but was culturally Parthian and both cities contained influences from both worlds. The Roman

Fig. 360 **A mother of pearl plaque of two horsemen, perhaps from a casket**
Parthian, 2nd to 1st century BC
H. 4 cm (approx.)
From a tomb at Shami, Khuzestan province
(National Museum, Tehran)

enough material wealth to fill two junks but was still greedy for more. When he reached Mount Niu-t'ou in the Xincheng commandery he encountered a Buddhist monk and was converted to the faith. He decided to divest himself of his material possessions and proceeded to sink one of his junks. Just as the second junk was about to be sunk a group of monks arrived and implored him to use what remained of his wealth to carry out pious works.

(From Hsü kao-seng chuan by the monk Ta-hsüan [596–667]. Related in Gernet, 1995)

Sasanians

From the foundation of the dynasty in 224 AD, until its destruction by the Arabs in 637–51, the Sasanians ranged far and wide in search of territory and profit. As they fought for control of Silk Road traffic the Sasanians exerted pressure on the Roman (Byzantine) Empire to the west and the Kushans, and their successors the Hepthalites, in the East. By the time of Shapur I (r. 241–71 AD) the empire extended from Sogdiana and Iberia (Georgia) in the north to the Mazun region of Arabia in the south; and from the upper Tigris and Euphrates valleys in the west as far as the Indus River in the east. Shapur I launched campaigns against the Roman Empire- invading Syria, Anatolia and Armenia and laying siege to Antioch. In 260 he defeated the Roman Emperor Valerian at Edessa (modern Urfa in Turkey) and took him prisoner- an event celebrated in one of the great Sasanian rock reliefs at Naqsh-e Rustam, just to the north of Persepolis. The centres of the empire were Ctesiphon on the Tigris and Bishapur and Firuzabad in Fars province. Bishapur was built with the help of Roman slaves captured with Valerian, who may have installed its mosaic floors.

Under the Sasanians a new wave of Persian nationalism enveloped the country and new styles in art and architecture developed. The state religion was Zoroastrianism although Jews, Christians, Manichaeans and Buddhists were tolerated to varying degrees by different kings. The Sasanians' language was Pahlavi and they excelled in the arts: their architecture, sculpture, textiles and metalwork were renowned throughout the world. The squinch – an arch that spans each corner of a square building – was a Sasanian innovation that allowed the addition of a dome. Sasanian metalwork was exported the length of the Silk Road and influenced the work of Sogdian and Chinese craftsmen. Their techniques originated with the Achaemenians but the Sasanians perfected them. Their skills in casting, chasing and embossing were second to none and Persian silver became one of the most prized commodities of the Silk Road. It is therefore entirely fitting that one of the finest of the Sasanians' creations was found not in Persia but in a remote area of China (fig. 361).

Sasanian silversmiths attained their highest standard during the long reign of Shapur II (r. 309–79), possibly

Fig. 361 **A gilded silver flask**
Sasanian, 5th century
H. 37.5 cm
Unearthed in 1983 from the tomb of General Li Xian at Guyuan, Ningxia province,China.
(Guyuan Museum, Ningxia province, China)
This flask is decorated with three couples and appears to represent soldiers taking leave of their loved ones as they depart for war. On the handle is a helmeted figure of a Westerner and the style is unmistakably Persian. General Li was governor of the town of Guyuan (ancient Yuanzhou) and assigned to protect the Silk Road. He probably obtained the flask from a passing merchant.

because craftsmen were brought to Persia from other parts of the empire. The most common vessel was the shallow plate, typically decorated with scenes of royal heroism, hunting or mythology. They were produced long after the death of the ruler they depict and are therefore difficult to date. There are examples in most museums around the world – the Hermitage has one of the largest collections – and many have been preserved in Iranian institutions (fig. 362).

The Sasanians also perfected the technique of glass production. Like the silversmiths, they built upon the skills of their predecessors and produced bowls and vases of exceptional quality, often blown into a mould to produce dimpling or geometric patterns. Examples have been found all along the Silk Road – the Famensi Pagoda near Xian and the Shosoin repository in Nara, to name but two (see pp. 104 and 106).

Sasanian Iran was a major producer of silk and was also a broker for Chinese silk that it sold on to the west. Silk weaving appears to have developed in Iran as a result of the captives brought back to the country by Shapur I (r. 241–71 AD), during his campaigns against the Roman Empire. In 260 Shapur captured the Roman Emperor Valerian and more than 70,000 captives were taken to Iran. The expertise they brought with them led to the development of silk manufacturing, centred in Shapur's capital at Bishapur. The Sasanians soon achieved renown in both the east and west for their polychrome fabrics, some woven with golden thread or trimmed with precious stones. It appears that they imported silk yarn from China, perhaps buying it through intermediaries in India, and dominated trade in the precious fabric until Byzantium managed to develop its own sericulture around the sixth century.

The fifth century was a time of tribulation and decline for the Sasanian kings. Nomadic groups, especially the Hepthalites, attacked them from the north and east and their dominions were beset by famine and drought. In 484 the Hepthalites captured and killed the Sasanian king Peroz (r. 459–84) and for twenty years Persia became a tributary state. The dynasty revived under Khusrau I (r. 532–79) and Khusrau II 'the Victorious' (r. 591–628). They formed alliances with a new power in the East- the Turks- and the Hepthalites were defeated. Khusrau II also launched military campaigns against the West, capturing Antioch in 611, Jerusalem in 614 and Alexandria in 619. They built grand palaces at their capital, Ctesiphon and at Bishapur and Firuzabad, consisting of massive rectangular buildings with an entrance arch and *iwans* (covered or vaulted halls) that became the model for the mosques of the Islamic era. The great reception *iwan* and half of the façade of Khusrau I's palace at Ctesiphon still survives (fig. 400).

It was not to last, however. In 623, the Byzantine emperor Heraclius attacked from Armenia, seizing Ganzak (probably the site now called Takht-e Suleiman in the northwest Iranian province of West Azerbaijan) and destroyed its fire-altar. The Sasanians retaliated, forming an alliance with the Avars and besieging Constantinople but the city held and Khusrau II's reign ended with his execution in 628. The last scion of the Sasanians was Yazdegerd III (r. 632–51), Khusrau's grandson. The new force in the region, the Arabs, took advantage of the weakened state of both Byzantium and Persia and attacked. The decisive battle occurred in 636 at al-Qadisiyya, on one of the Euphrates canals, not far from al-Hirah. The Sasanian general Rustam was killed during the battle and Ctesiphon, the capital, was seized. Yazdegerd III fled east and although his armies rallied they were decisively beaten at Nehavand, south of Hamadan in 642. Yazdegerd spent his remaining years as a fugitive in the eastern territories of Khurasan until 651, when he was assassinated at Merv. With the death of Yazdegerd the Sasanian dynasty came to an end although several of the king's relatives sought refuge in China, at the Tang court (see p. 92).

Fig. 362 **A gilded silver plate with Ardashir I (r. 224–41) slaying Ardavan V (r. 216–24 AD)**
Sasanian, 3d century
D. 24 cm (approx.)
Reportedly found in the Gorgan area
(Tabriz Museum)
This large and superbly executed plate shows Ardashir I, founder of the Sasanian dynasty, slaying the last king of the Parthians, Ardavan V.

CHAPTER TWENTY ONE

THE MAIN EAST-WEST SILK ROAD ACROSS IRAN

Masshad

Masshad, located 875 km northeast of Tehran, is Iran's holiest city. The town used to be called Sanabad and did not become a place of mass pilgrimage until the sixteenth century. Imam Reza, Eighth Imam of the Shi'ite tradition and heir to the Abbasid Caliphate, passed through Sanabad in 817 en route between Baghdad and Merv. He died after eating grapes, possibly poisoned on the orders of the Caliph Ma'mun. Ma'mun instructed that Imam Reza be interred in Sanabad, beside the tomb of his own father, the celebrated Caliph Harun Al Rashid (r. 786–809) and thereafter the town became a place of pilgrimage for the Shi'ite faithful. The town became known as Masshad ('the place of martyrdom') but it did not attain international status as a pilgrimage site until many centuries later. Masshad's geographical location placed it firmly in the path of every invading army

to march the old trade routes and the city endured an all too familiar cycle of destruction and reconstruction. The original shrine was destroyed in the tenth century by Sebuktigin (r. 977–97), founder of the Ghaznavid Empire and was then rebuilt in 1009 by his son, the formidable Mahmud of Ghazni (r. 998–1032). When the Mongols attacked and destroyed the nearby town of Tus in 1220, Masshad received much of its populace and began a period of expansion that culminated in the fifteenth century when it became capital of Khurasan. Sharukh (r. 1405–47), the son of Timur, expanded Imam Reza's mausoleum and his wife, the devout and gifted Gohar Shad, built a mosque on the site that still bears her name. These structures, built during the period of 1405–18, still stand although successive Iranian rulers down to the present have embellished them (fig. 363).

Fig. 363 **The Holy Shrine of Imam Reza, Masshad**
15th century and later

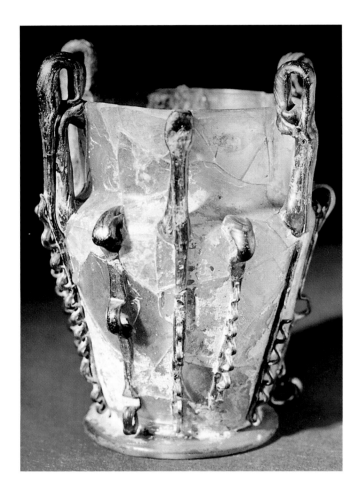

Fig. 364 **Glass mosque lamp, free-blown with applied decoration**
11th century
From Nishapur,
Khurasan province
(National Museum, Tehran)

Fig. 365 **The tombstone of Omar Khayyam of Nishapur**
20th century
Imamzadeh Mohammad
Mahrugh shrine, Nishapur,
Khurasan province

for its spices, dyes, carpets and silks; and religious patronage by Shah Abbas I in the seventeenth century, and by successive rulers thereafter ensured that the city's fortunes did not decline with those of the Silk Road. Millions of pilgrims still visit Masshad today and Sir Roger Stevens describes the city as containing, 'probably the greatest concentration of religious buildings in the world' (Stevens, 1962).

Before the Mongols obliterated the town of Tus, 22 km northwest of Masshad, it was the provincial capital and an important commercial centre. Little remains of pre-Mongol Tus, except for part of the clay ramparts, and the town is now best known as the birthplace of the poet Ferdosi (c. 935–1020). Ferdosi is most famous for his epic work the *Shanama* ('The Epic of Kings') written over a period of thirty years, but he is also remembered for his meticulous recording of Persian culture and history and for helping to preserve the Persian language, Farsi, at a time when the remaining (mainly rural) parts of Iran were converting to Islam and there was a genuine concern that the old traditions, language and culture would be subsumed by those of the Arabs. Some of the heroes of Ferdosi's *Shanama* appear in works of art along the Silk Road, most notably the episodes from the Rustam cycle discernible in the wall paintings of Penjikent, Tajikistan (fig. 342). Ferdosi was inadequately recompensed for his masterpiece by Sultan Mahmud of Ghazni (r. 998–1032) and responded with a withering satire on the king's character and forbears.

Tus sits just east of a road that ran, and still runs to the north of the main east-west Silk Road (see map). The Masshad-Gorgan road runs parallel with the better-known route and continues right along the Caspian coast to Astara, on the Iran-Azerbaijan border. This route was never a match for the main east-west route but it did pass through a number of important commercial and cultural centres and these are examined later in this book.

Nishapur

The main highway from Masshad to Tehran crosses a stretch of barren red waste for 115 km before reaching the town of Nishapur (Neyshabur). Nishapur is now a small, somewhat somnolent place with few old buildings but it was once Khurasan's capital and a flourishing artistic and commercial centre. The town was found during the rule of the Sasanian King Shapur I (r. 241–71) but attained its heyday during the ninth and tenth centuries. Along with Samarkand and Ray it was an important producer of fine ceramics, as well as locally mined turquoise and glass (fig. 364). Excavations at Nishapur reveal that exceptionally fine glassware was produced under the Samanids (875–999) and the Seljuks (1037–1194).

Nishapur's most celebrated luminary was the poet, Hakim Omar Khayyam (c. 1048–c. 1125). Omar Khayyam's

Despite its precarious strategic position and despite frequent raids from Central Asia by Turkish nomads, Masshad continued to prosper both as a religious and commercial centre. Both pilgrims and merchants followed the same east-west highway and both activities – worship and commerce – became inseparable. The town is still noted

poetry gained widespread popularity in the West during the Victorian era when it was translated, and sometimes embellished, by Edward Fitzgerald. He is best known for his rhyming quatrains (*rubaiyat*), much altered and adapted by Fitzgerald but inexpressibly beautiful, nonetheless:

> *'We are no other than a moving row*
> *Of Magic Shadow-shapes that come and go*
> *Round with the Sun-illumined Lantern held*
> *In Midnight by the Master of the Show;*
>
> *But helpless Pieces of the Game He plays*
> *Upon his Checkerboard of Nights and Days;*
> *Hither and thither moves, and checks, and slays,*
> *And one by one back in the Closet lays.'*

(Edward Fitzgerald [1809–83], 'The Rubaiyat of Omar Khayyam of Nishapur')

In Iran he is better known as a mathematician and astronomer; his poems are too fatalistic and include too much imbibing of alcohol for some. He is buried in the grounds of the sixteenth-century shrine of Imamzadeh Mohammad Mahrugh (fig. 365).

Nishapur's glory days were brief. During the mid-twelfth century it was attacked by Turkish nomads and damaged by an earthquake and, in the thirteenth century, it suffered two Mongol attacks and a further earthquake. The city was rebuilt each time but was eventually superseded by Masshad.

The road west from Nishapur is no less desolate than the previous stretch. After a further 115 km, in an open field just west of the small town of Sabzevar, stands one of Iran's finest and best-preserved Seljuk era minarets (fig. 366). Bereft of its balcony, it still reaches to almost 30 metres in height and is all that remains of the Silk Road town of Khosrogerd, obliterated by the Mongols in 1220.

The road west from Sabzevar enters Semnan province and crosses a flat expanse of walnut coloured desert as it skirts the Dasht-e Kevir. All along the east-west highway are the scattered ruins of caravanserais, built to provide sanctuary for the merchants and pilgrims who were making their way to or from Masshad. One of the oldest and best know is Ribat I Sharif, northeast of Masshad on the Merv road. Another Seljuk creation, it was built around 1114–15 on an immense double courtyard plan. Many were built later, most notably during the long reign of the Safavid ruler Shah Abbas I (1571–1629). A large and impressive example of a Safavid period (1502–1722) caravanserai stands beside the Tehran road, about 110 km east of Shahrud (fig. 367). This massive stone and brick structure has a four-iwan* courtyard arrangement that is also utilised in other large Islamic buildings such as mosques, madrassahs and palaces.

Shahrud is 250 km from Sabzevar and marks the approximate halfway point between Masshad and Tehran. Shahrud is a modern town but its older counterpart, Bastam,

Fig. 366 **The Khosrogerd minaret, near Sabzevar**
Seljuk period, 1111–12
H. 28.5 metres

Fig. 367 **Miyan Dasht caravanserai**
Safavid period (1502–1722)
East of Shahrud, Semnan province

is a few kilometres to the north. Part of Bastam's mud-brick defensive walls still stand but the true source of the town's fame is that it was the birthplace of the Sufi Bayazid-e Bastami (d. 874). The shrine complex of Bayazid is grouped around a courtyard on the southern outskirts of the town

* A covered or vaulted hall open at one end.

Fig. 368 **Shrine complex of the Sufi Bayazid-e Bastami**
Seljuk period, 1120–211 (minaret) and Il-Khanid (Mongol period), 14th century (other buildings)
Bastam, Semnan province

and it buildings all date to many centuries after his death. The complex comprises a brick Seljuk period minaret with fine decorative geometric bands, and a pair of conical tomb towers and a mosque built during by the Mongol rulers of Persia, the Il-Khans, during the fourteenth century. One of the conical roofed buildings with its turquoise-blue tiles is said to mark the location of Bayazid's shrine (fig. 368).

One of the many connecting routes between the main east-west Silk Road and the secondary route along the Caspian runs north from Bastam to Azad Shahr in Golestan province (the eastern half of the former Mazandaran province). The road to Azad Shahr ascends from flat lowland desert through fertile valleys and vast forests and crosses the eastern end of the Alborz Mountains. Just beyond Azad Shahr is the town of Gonbad-e Kavus – home to a structure that, in Robert Byron's view, 'ranks with the great buildings of the world'.

Gonbad-e Kavus

Gonbad-e Kavus, known previously as Jurjan, was once the capital of the Ziyarid dynasty and sat on a trade route leading from the Caspian provinces – north to Khorezm and east to Masshad. The funeral tower that gives the town its name was built in 1006 by Kavus ibn-e Vashmgir (r. ca.

976–1012), one of the Ziyarid rulers of Tabarestan, a region now comprising the provinces of Mazandaran and Golestan. Kavus was well known as a soldier, poet, philosopher, calligrapher and patron of such scholars as Al-Biruni (see p. 240). He was also notorious for his cruelty and, in 1012, he was slain by a member of the Assassins. He is said to have been sealed inside a glass coffin that was then suspended from the room of the enormous 55-metre tower (fig. 369). During the 1890's, Russian archaeologists sank a 12 metre shaft in the foundations but found not trace of Kavus's tomb, lending credence to the legend of the suspended coffin. The brick tower with its grey-green conical roof stands atop a 15-metre high mound and can be seen from 30 km away. The interior contains one of the earliest examples of stalactite decoration in an Islamic building.

Kavus (or Qabus) also gave his name to a remarkable text written by his grandson Kai Ka'us Ibn Iskandar, one of the Ziyarid line. Kai Ka'us wrote *Qabus Nama* ('A Mirror for Princes') in 1082 when he was sixty-three years old, as a guide to correct behaviour for his young son Gilanshah. The book contains advice on such diverse subjects as eating, playing backgammon and chess, romantic passion, playing polo and (most importantly for this book), on the pursuit of commerce. In his preface to the work Kai Ka'us reveals that he does not expect his son to heed the advice contained in the work but hopes that others will. The Ziyarids faced uncertain times; as vassals of the Seljuks they were forced to pay large sums as tribute and were under constant threat from Turcoman invasion. Gilanshah proved to be the last of the line. After a reign of only seven years he was overthrown in 1090 but the book remains as a testament to paternal love and integrity. The Ziyarids benefited from Silk Road commerce and, although Kai Ka'us possessed a somewhat disdainful attitude to the merchant class, he recognized their importance to society:

'My son, although commerce is not an occupation which can with complete accuracy be called a skilled craft…as the Arabs express it, 'Were it not for venturesome men, mankind would perish'. What is meant by these words is that merchants, in their eagerness for gain, bring goods from the east to the west, exposing their lives to peril on mountains and seas, careless of robbers and highwaymen and without fear of living the life of brutal people or of the insecurity of the roads. To benefit the inhabitants of the west they import the wealth of the east and for those of the east the wealth of the west, and by doing so become the instrument of the world's civilization.'

(Kai Ka'us Ibn Iskandar, from 'A Mirror for Princes' [*Qabus Nama*]. Translated by Reuben Levy in Iskandar, 1951)

This historical realm of the Ziyarids abuts the modern border with Turkmenistan and its inhabitants speak Turkmen as readily as Farsi. About 30 km to the north of Gonbad-e Kavus, and close to that border, are the remains of an ancient defensive wall known as Sadd-e Eskanadar ('Alexander's Wall', fig. 370). The wall has nothing to do with Alexander: it is likely that it was built during the sixth century by the Sasanians to protect the Gorgan Plain from nomadic attack. The wall has crumbled or been plundered for building materials but is still a remarkable feat of engineering.

The highway west from Gonbad-e Kavus leads along the Caspian coast to the town of Gorgan, formerly known as Astarabad ('City of Mules') and capital of the newly created Golestan province. Gorgan is thought to have been established by the Arabs during the eighth century and was once an important caravan town and a place for commerce between Turcoman* nomads and Iranians from the plains. The town's proximity to the steppe left it vulnerable to raids by nomads and it has been destroyed and rebuilt a number of times.

In the borderlands of Iran and Turkmenistan the nomads still hold impromptu horse fairs where they buy and sell the spirited Turcoman and Caspian breeds. Recent genetic research in the US (summarised in Firouz, 1995), suggests that Turcoman and Caspian horses share common

Fig. 369 **The Gonbad-e Kavus**
Built 1006
Gonbad-e Kavus, Golestan province.

* The Turcomans are thought to be descended from the nomads of the Mongol Altai region. There are several million in the region, most residing in Turkmenistan but more than one million live in Iran, mainly in the northeastern part of the country.

Fig. 370 **Sadd-e Eskanadar ('Alexander's Wall')**
Ca. 6th century
The horse is a Scythian, an ancient breed now being revived by one of the local ranchers, Louise Firouz.

Fig. 371 **The Tarik Khana Mosque**
Built ca. 775
Damghan, Semnan province

gene markers with around 90 per cent of modern breeds. This means that Turcoman and Caspian horses are the ancestors of both oriental horses and of Europe's best breeds. There is, in addition, considerable DNA evidence that these two breeds are also the ancestors of Arab horses. If this is true, the heavenly horses of Ferghana, so beloved of the Chinese Emperor Wudi, are descendants of the Turcoman and Caspian and not the Arab, as is usually written.

The road west from Gorgan follows the Caspian coast through Sari, capital of Mazandaran province, and Rasht, the capital of Guilan. Both Sari and Rasht are linked by road with the main Silk Road to the south. Sari was capital of Tabarestan (now comprising Mazandaran and Golestan provinces), during the Sasanian era but its surviving buildings date to the latter part of the Islamic era, mostly to the fifteenth century. Rasht is one of the wettest places in Iran and is famous for its tea and silk. It has few buildings of architectural interest and did not become a proper town until the fourteenth century, when the Silk Road was already entering its twilight years. Russian armies have occupied the town on a number of occasions, most recently in 1920 when

it was severely damaged by the Bolsheviks. Despite the high level of precipitation in the coastal region, the Alborz Mountains to the south ensure that very little moisture penetrates to the central plateau. The coastal plain contains fertile agricultural land and fish and game are abundant, but until as late as the nineteenth century, the region was so densely forested and so covered by malarial swamp that it was unable to support a large population. The mountains have also left the area somewhat cut off from the rest of Iran and this may explain why the inhabitants were never entirely subjugated by the armies of Islam. For all these reasons the coastal route never offered serious competition to the main Silk Road to the south.

To return to the main Silk Road at Shahrud, the highway continues to skirt the northern edge of the Dasht-e Kevir desert. Confirming that the modern highway follows the course of the old road is not difficult: there are the remains of earthen ramparts, broken down fortresses and abandoned caravanserais on both sides of the road for kilometre after kilometre. The desert here is more fertile than the part further east towards Masshad. In the summer there are patches of green but in winter there is an endless expanse of verdure, as far as the eye can see. Fifty-five kilometres west of Shahrud is Damghan – the site of Hecatompylos – one of the Greek cities founded by Alexander the Great* and home to Iran's oldest mosque.

Damghan

Discoveries made at Tepe Hissar, southeast of Damghan, indicate that the area has been settled since the third millennium BC. Hecatompylos is on the southern outskirts of the town and is thought to have been one of the settlements founded by Alexander. Alexander's empire quickly disintegrated after his death in 323 BC and by around 312 BC Persia had fallen to one of his generals, Seleucus Nicator (r. 312–281 BC). Hecatompylos flourished under the Seleucids and became a capital during the Parthian era (256 BC–226 AD). Parthian rule was more or less contemporary with the Han dynasty of China and the development of global Silk Road during this period meant that the town's prosperity was assured. When Islam came to Iran in the middle of the seventh century, Damghan was still an important city and the country's Abbasid rulers erected a mosque that has survived to the present day. The Tarik Khana ('God's House') Mosque, built around 775, is Iran's oldest and recalls the buildings of the pre-Islamic era (fig. 371). Its simple design consists of an almost square courtyard surrounded by single arcades on three sides and, on the Mecca-facing (qebla) side, a prayer hall with triple colonnades. The massive brick columns and high arches are reminiscent of Sasanian buildings.

The remains of a square minaret of the same date, which probably collapsed during an earthquake, can still be seen beside the mosque. It was replaced just before the Seljuk era by a 25 metre high, round minaret that still stands. Judging by the extent of building activity in Damghan just prior to, and during the Seljuk period, the town seems to have prospered throughout the life of the Silk Road. Despite the depredations of the Mongols, of Timur, of the Afghans during the eighteenth century, and of innumerable earthquakes, several other pre-Seljuk and Seljuk buildings have survived. The Pir-I Alamdar mausoleum was built around 1026 just before the Seljuk conquest of Iran, when the area was still controlled by the Ghaznavids. Its use of decorative brickwork subsequently acted as a model for Seljuk architecture throughout their domains (fig. 372).

By the time that Damghan's other tomb tower was built thirty years later, the Seljuks were firmly in control of the former Ghaznavid dominions. The 15 metre high Chihil Dukhtaran ('Forty Daughters') tomb tower, built in 1054–55, continues the use of geometric and calligraphic motifs in brick that was to be the hallmark of Seljuk architecture for the next century and a half.

To the west of Damghan the Silk Road continues for 110

km along the edge of the Dashte-Kevir to the town of Semnan, capital of the province and once a major caravan city. It was probably founded during the Sasanian period and still has a thriving bazaar. The Masjed-e Jame (Friday Mosque) is in the heart of the bazaar – further evidence of the way in which, for the people of the Silk Road, faith and commerce were frequently intertwined. Timur's son Sharukh built the mosque in 1425 but its minaret is much older (fig. 373).

The landscape between Semnan and Tehran, a distance of 228 km, was no more hospitable to ancient travellers and still requires a monotonous journey across scrubby desert. About 50 km southeast of Tehran is the town of Eivanakei (ancient Charax*). Near Eivanakei is the Girduni Sudurrah

* Not to be confused with the ancient trading port of *Charax Spasini*, at the head of the Persian Gulf, just south of Basra.

Fig. 372 **The Pir-I Alamdar tomb-tower**
Constructed 1026–27
Damghan, Semnan province

Fig. 373 **Masjed-e Jame minaret**
Seljuk period, first half of
11th century
Semnan, Semnan province
The decorative brickwork of
this minaret continues the
tradition of Damghan's Pir-I
Alamdar tomb tower.

Fig. 374 **Double-wefted (two-sided) silk representing the tree of life flanked by winged lions**
Early Islamic period, 7th or
8th century
From Ray, Tehran province
(Islamic Museum, Tehran)

* 'The Parthian Stations',
probably written just before the
birth of Christ, is a rare account
of the post-stations on the
ancient caravan trail from
Antioch to the borders of India.
Little is known about its author,
Isidore of Charax. It appears that
he was born in *Charax Spasini*,
just south of Basra in modern
Iraq, and may have been
commissioned by the Roman
Emperor Augustus to produce
the work. Only fragments of the
work have survived but the
names of the post-stations along
the route and the distances
between them have enabled
historians to make inferences
about the relations between the
Parthians and their neighbours.

Pass in the Alborz Mountains, at or close to the ancient site of the Caspian Gates. The Gates were one of the most important strategic points of classical times and were a thoroughfare for merchants and conquerors for centuries. The modern road probably runs a few kilometres south of the ancient highway, and therefore the pass as well.

Modern Tehran is a polluted, cacophonous, slightly deranged place but it was not always thus. The ancient capital of Iran was at Ray, 7 km southeast of Tehran and now absorbed by the suburbs of it newer neighbour. Until 1220, when the Mongols destroyed Ray, Tehran was little more

than a village on its outskirts. Many of the displaced citizens of Ray fled to Tehran and it began to grow, although it did not finally achieve prominence until 1795, when the first Qajar ruler Agha Mohammad Khan selected it as the national capital in place of Shiraz. Tehran, like Ray, sits in the southern foothills of the Alborz and on the northern edge of the Dasht-e Kevir desert. Travellers on the east-west trade routes would have been obliged to pass through the town and this helps to explain why both cities endured in the face of endless invasion and destruction. Most of Tehran's buildings were built during the Qajar period (1779–1924) or later, and are therefore beyond the scope of this book.

Ray (or Shahr-e Ray)

The former capital of the Persian Empire is now all but lost among the suburbs of Tehran. Under the Achaemenians it was known as Rhaga or Rhagae and Alexander rested in the city for five days during his pursuit of their last great king, Darius III. It was expanded during the rule of Seleucus Nicator (r. 312–281 BC), founder of the Seleucid dynasty, and renamed Europos. By the second century BC it had become the spring capital of the country's Parthian rulers and renamed Arsacia and, according to Isidore of Charax,* it was 'the greatest of the cities in Media'.

Ray continued to flourish under the Sasanians and the remains of a citadel can still be seen on a hillside above the

Fig. 375 **Shallow bowl decorated with a falconer on horseback**
Ca. 12th century
Ray, Tehran province
(Islamic Museum, Tehran)
This overglaze painted, enamelled and gilded *Minai* bowl has an inscription around the rim in angular (Kufic) and cursive (*naskhi*) script.

town. When the Arabs arrived in the seventh century it became the Abbasid city of Mohamadiyeh, birthplace of great Abbasid Caliph Harun Al Rashid in 763. Under the Arabs the city's artisans continued the tradition of manufacturing exquisite silk textiles begun during the Sasanian era (fig. 374).

By the tenth century Ray was known by its current name and survived capture by Mahmud of Ghazni in 1029 to become a capital of the Seljuks. Ray's ceramics were admired, (and exported) far and wide, especially during the Seljuk period when lustre wares and polychrome painted wares (known as *Minai*), were produced in large numbers (fig. 375).

In 1220 the Mongols eviscerated Ray and its inhabitants fled to Tehran, Savé and Varamin. They spared only one building – an immense 20-metre brick funeral tower, said to be the mausoleum of the Seljuk ruler Toghrol I. The building, now bereft of its conical dome, was once decorated with typical Seljuk carved brick and Kufic inscriptions but these are lost, probably as a result of somewhat reckless repair work conducted during the 1880s. The tower recalls the celebrated mausoleum at Gonbad-e Kavus but, though still beautiful, it is now a shell (fig. 376).

Fig. 376 **The Toghrol Tower**
Seljuk period, built in 1139
Ray, Tehran province

Varamin

About 40 km south of Tehran on the road from Ray, Varamin sits on a flat, fertile plain. It became the regional capital after the Mongol's destruction of Ray and remained so until it was superseded by Tehran during the sixteenth century. Its important buildings therefore date to the period between the thirteenth and sixteenth centuries. They include the Masjed-e Jame (Friday Mosque), built by the Mongol Il-Khans between 1322 and 1326 and the only such mosque to have been erected by them in one continuous operation. Sir Roger Stevens (Stevens, 1962), saw the building in its unrestored state and described it as 'unquestionably the most interesting building south of the Elburz [Alborz] between Sultaniyeh and Damghan.' It is built in the four-*iwan* style and decorated with brick and glazed tilework. For eighty years, from 1220 to about 1300, the essentially nomadic Mongols built little in Iran but when activity resumed at the beginning of the fourteenth century, it was characterised by a greater use of colour. Glazed tiles and gloriously painted stucco decoration were a feature of the mosques, tombs and palaces of the Il-Khans. The Varamin mosque is dominated by its massive dome and its *mehrab* (the niche in the Mecca-

Fig. 378 **The Tomb Tower of Ala ad-Din**
Mongol period, completed 1289
Varamin, Tehran province

Fig. 377 **The Masjed-e Jame (Friday Mosque)**
Mongol period, 1322–26
Varamin, Tehran province

facing wall) is so richly decorated, according to Arthur Pope, 'that it defies pictorial representation' (fig. 377).

A rare structure from the second half of the thirteenth century stands in the centre of the town. The Tomb Tower of Ala ad-Din was completed in 1289 and is decorated in a more restrained manner than the Masjed-e Jame, with a Kufic inscription just below the conical roof and blue faience tilework. The exterior consists of thirty-two right-angled flanges (fig. 378).

There were two principal directions for the Silk Road beyond Tehran and Ray. The first led northwest through Ghazvin to Tabriz and the second headed in a southwesterly direction to Hamadan. There were actually two routes to Hamadan: the first via Savé and the other leading up to Ghazvin and then veering off to climb the Amirabad Pass and passing through Darjazin (or Darazin). The road south from Ray passes through Qom, Kashan, Isfahan and beyond, leading eventually to India.

CHAPTER TWENTY TWO

THE RAY-TABRIZ ROAD

One hundred and thirty kilometres northwest of Tehran in Zanjan province is Ghazvin, a Silk Road city with a past. It lies 1800 metres above sea level, at the northwest corner of the Iranian Plateau. This is where the Alborz and Zagros mountains meet and Ghazvin sits on an ancient crossroads, with routes to Tehran, Tabriz, Hamadan and Rasht all radiating from the town. The main Tehran-Baghdad highway, now of course impassable, ran through Ghazvin, part of a network of roads built by the Achaemenians to link the furthest extremities of their empire.*

The city is believed to have been founded by the Sasanian King Shapur I (r. 241–71) and named Shad-I Shapur ('Shapur's Joy'). During the early Islamic period it was repeatedly attacked by a tribe of mountain dwellers from the Alborz known as the Dailamites. After the Arabs captured the town in 644 it became a garrison town from which raids were launched against the Dailamites. After they were subjugated the town enjoyed a brief period of peace before enduring new predations at the hands of the Assassins (see the section on Alamut below). The town was sacked by the Mongols in 1220 and 1256, flourished briefly as the Safavid capital under Shah Tahmasp in the sixteenth century and was then attacked, yet again by an Afghan army in the eighteenth century. Adding the fact that the region is also prone to earthquakes, it seems remarkable that anything of old Ghazvin survives at all, but it does.

Two Seljuk era monuments have survived the city's turbulent past. The Madrassah Heidariyeh stands behind high walls in the eastern part of town. It follows the plan of a Sasanian fire-temple, comprising a square hall covered by a dome but is properly oriented towards Mecca. It walls are inscribed in stucco relief with Kufic calligraphy and the carved decoration of its *mehrab*, also in stucco, has been described as being the richest and loveliest in Iran (fig. 379).

Ghazvin's other Seljuk monument is the four *iwan* Masjed-e Jame (Friday Mosque). The mosque occupies an area of 4,000 metres and was probably built on the site of a pre-Islamic, Zoroastrian fire-temple. Much of the building was built during the Safavid and Qajar periods, well outside the scope of this book, but the prayer hall and sanctuary behind the south iwan – covered by a dome 15 metres across – date to the Seljuk era. The dome, along with one of similar diameter in Isfahan, is the largest Seljuk period dome in Iran (fig. 380).

The Castles of the Assassins

'Where they smile in secret, looking over wasted lands,
Blight and famine, plague and earthquake, roaring deeps and
fiery sands,
Clanging fights, and flaming towns, and sinking ships, and
praying hands.'

(Alfred, Lord Tennyson, 'The Lotos-Eaters')

Fig. 379 **Stucco relief of the Madrassah Heidariyeh, Ghazvin**
Seljuk period, 12th century

* The Royal Road: The Achaemenian King Darius the Great (522–486 BC) constructed The Royal Road from Susa, the ancient capital of Persia, to Sardis (east of modern Izmir in Turkey). The road extended over a distance of more than 2,400 km with post stations along the way. The Greek historian Herodotus wrote admiringly of the king's messengers who covered the entire distance in nine days and who were delayed by 'neither snow, nor rain, nor heat, nor gloom of night.' Alexander the Great followed parts of the Royal Road during his campaigns against the Persian Empire and a large section of the Silk Road through Turkey, though it did not come into existence until the dawn of the Christian era, corresponds to the ancient route.

Fig. 380 **The Masjed-e Jame (Friday Mosque), Ghazvin**
Seljuk period, 1113–15
The tiles were added later.

Fig. 381 **Alamut, Castle of the Assassins**
Northeast of Ghazvin,
Zanjan province

The Frankish knights who returned to Europe from the Crusades during the eleventh and twelfth centuries carried tales of 'The Old Man of the Mountain', the leader of a religious sect known as the Assassins, ensconced at a series of mountain fortresses near the source of the Alamut river, deep in the Alborz mountains of northern Iran to the northeast of Ghazvin. The most famous of the castles is Alamut, built around 860 on a rocky outcrop above the village of Gazur Khan, about 80 km northeast of Ghazvin. The name of the sect may derive from the word *hashishiyun* (hashish), the taking of which is said to have enabled the sect's members to carry out the political murders of prominent Muslim figures. The Assassins were an offshoot of the Sevener Shi'ites (followers of the seventh Imam, Ismail), and were considered a threat by the Sunnis. Sevener members were widely persecuted and murders committed by the Assassins were a response to this persecution. The group considered themselves to be guardians of their faith and conducted a campaign of terror for 120 years. In 1092 they murdered Nizam al-Mulk, the prime minister of the Seljuk Turks, a Sunni and a Persian (see pp. 218 and 317).

The killing was ordered by the Old Man of the Mountain himself, Hasan-I Sabah (ca. 1040–1124), and the leader of the sect. They resisted numerous attempts to dislodge them and continued to operate from Alamut right up until 1256, when they were slaughtered by the Mongols. Marco Polo has left a vivid description of the Old Man's acolytes, left insensate by opiates and by the carnal pleasures of the sect's handmaidens and sent out to kill his enemies:

'...when any of the neighbouring princes, or others, gave umbrage to this chief, they were put to death by these his disciplined assassins; none of whom felt terror at the risk of losing their own lives, which they held in little estimation, provided they could execute their master's will'.

(From *The Travels of Marco Polo the Venetian.* Translated by William Marsden in Marsden, 1948.9)

Sultanieh

The road from Ghazvin heads northwest across mostly flat terrain to the town of Zanjan. What earthquakes and Mongol armies have left of Zanjan is of scant appeal to historians but 40 km southeast of the town, just off the main route to Tabriz, is one of Iran's most spectacular monuments. At Sultanieh, the mausoleum of the Il-Khan Sultan Uljaitu (r. 1304–17) dominates the plain and announces the power of the Mongols to all who look upon it (fig. 382). The building is over 50 metres high and consists of a pointed egg-shaped dome atop a massive octagon with a minaret at each corner – a new development over the customary, square gallery hitherto seen in structures of this type. It is incredible to think that the entire building, including the dome, is made of brick. A number of commentators have remarked on the manner in which the deep, pierced niches of the supporting walls suffuse the building, despite its massive size, with a sense of lightness:

'The lower courses merge with the neutral tones of the ground and mountains, but above these the blue dome, vivid and gleaming with its brilliant crown of minarets, seems to float in the sky.'

(André Godard in Pope and Ackerman, 1964–65)

The dome has lost most of its turquoise blue tiles but still presents an impressive sight. This is precisely what Uljaitu intended. His mother was a Christian who had Uljaitu baptized with the name Nicholas. He later became a Sunni Muslim and then, probably in 1309, was converted to Shi'ism. His original intention was to transfer the remains of Ali (son-in-law of the Prophet) and Hossein – the first and third Imams revered by Shi'ites – from their resting places in Iraq to the Sultanieh mausoleum. But the citizens of Nejef and Karbala, where the remains were enshrined, refused to

Fig. 382 **Mausoleum of Sultan Uljaitu, Sultanieh** Completed in 1313

part with them and the plan came to nothing. Uljaitu returned to Sunnism before his death and was buried in the great mausoleum.

Sultanieh has withstood time, earthquakes and the depredations of the Timurids, who sacked the town in 1384. Arthur Pope described it as 'one of Persia's supreme architectural achievements' and the great buildings that were to come – the Taj Mahal among them – owe an immense debt to Uljaitu and his architects.

Beyond Sultanieh the flat plain of the desert is left behind, the landscape becomes rich and green and the road becomes more undulating as it enters the provinces of

Azerbaijan. Iranian Azerbaijan (now further divided into East and West provinces) occupies the northwestern corner of Iran, an area of about 100,000 square km. It is bordered to the north by the Aras River, which divides Iranian Azerbaijan from the independent, former Soviet republic. Azerbaijan has long been a centre of civilization. It formed part of Urartu and later of Media and, in the fourth century BC, was conquered by Alexander the Great. Alexander renamed the region Atropatene after one of his generals, Atropates, who established a satrapy. During the third century AD it fell under Sasanian rule and was then under Arab control from the seventh to the eleventh century. In the eleventh century it fell to Turkish nomads and, ever since, has been a predominantly Turkish-speaking area. When the Mongols arrived in 1220, Azerbaijan became part of their empire. Under Hulägu, brother of the Khan Mangu and first of the Il-Khans, Azerbaijan was situated at the core of a Mongol khanate extending from Syria to the Oxus. The capital of the khanate was, for a long period, at Tabriz – a Silk Road city with a long and illustrious history.

Tabriz

The town, now capital of East Azerbaijan province (*Azerbaijan-e Sharqi*), is 280 km northwest of Zanjan and 625 km from Tehran. It sits at 1,300 metres within a fertile valley to the north of Mount Sahand (3,707 metres) and enjoys mild summers but exceptionally harsh winters. The volcanic soils of Mount Sahand have made its water brackish and generations of the town's inhabitants have had to bring water from a long distance away by aqueducts (*qanats*). The town has also endured earthquakes throughout its history, most notably in 858 and 1041 – when the town was all but destroyed – and there are few surviving monuments as a result. The traditional founders of Tabriz were the Sasanians but it seems more likely that the Arabs were the first to develop the town. It flourished under the Seljuks and under the Mongol Il-Khans (1256–1335) it was, for a time, capital not only of Azerbaijan but also of the entire khanate. During the *pax Mongolica* of the Il-Khans, Silk Road trade boomed and the few early buildings that survive date to this era. The Blue Mosque (Masjed-e Kabud) was completed in 1465 and

Fig. 383 **The Arg-e Tabriz (or Arg-e Alishah)**
Tabriz, East Azerbaijan province
Completed in 1310

is justly famous for its beautiful faience tilework, but it has been virtually destroyed by earthquakes and what one sees today is the result of recent renovation. The massive, tottering bulk of the Arg-e Tabriz (or Arg-e Alishah) is all that remains of the Masjed-e Ali Shah, built in 1310 by Uljaitu's vizier and once one of the largest mosques ever constructed (fig. 383). Within a few years most of the structure fell victim to an earthquake and all that can be seen today is a single wall of the citadel, 35 metres in height. It stands somewhat forlornly in a car park in the centre of the town.

Under the Il-Khans, Tabriz was a vibrant, cosmopolitan place and most commercial activity was focussed on the bazaar. The narrow, bustling passageways through the old bazaar extend for 3 km. It has existed for at least a thousand years but the present structure, with its high domes and arches, dates mostly to the fifteenth century. Two guests of the Il-Khans, Marco Polo in about 1294 and Ibn Battuta in 1334, have left descriptions of the town during its heyday. Marco Polo called Tabriz 'Tauris' and his description suggest that the town's raison d'être was trade:

'The inhabitants support themselves principally by commerce and manufactures, which latter consist of various kinds of silk, some of them interwoven with gold, and of high price. It is so advantageously situated for trade, that merchants from India, from Baldach [Baghdad], Mosul [also in Iraq], Cremessor [presumably Kermanshah], as well as from different parts of Europe, resort thither to purchase and to sell a number of articles. Precious stones and pearls in abundance may be procured at this place. The merchants concerned in foreign commerce acquire considerable wealth, but the inhabitants in general are poor.'

(From *The Travels of Marco Polo the Venetian.* Translated by William Marsden in Marsden, 1948)

The peripatetic Ibn Battuta (1304–77), an Arab from Tangier, visited Tabriz's bazaar in 1334 and seems to have been somewhat overwhelmed by what he saw:

'I passed through the jeweller's bazaar, and my eyes were dazzled by the varieties of precious stones that I beheld. They were displayed by beautiful slaves wearing rich garments with a waist-sash of silk, who stood in front of the merchants, exhibiting the jewels to the Turks' wives, who bought them in large quantities to outdo each other. A riot broke out among them- may Allah preserve us from such a din! We went on to the ambergris market, and witnessed the same rowdiness, if anything even worse.'

(Ibn Battuta. Translated by H. A. R. Gibb in Gibb, 1929)

The bazaar has since been rebuilt but is still one of the finest markets of the entire Silk Road (fig. 384).

Fig. 384 **The jewellers' section of the Tabriz Bazaar**
Mainly 15th century
Tabriz, East Azerbaijan province

Marco Polo refers to the existence of a Christian monastery, 'Saint Barsamo', near Tabriz although its identity is unclear. There are, however, six churches still in existence in the town – nineteenth – or twentieth-century structures but at least one of them, St Mary (Kelisa-ye Maryam-e Moghaddas), is built on the site of a much older church.

Three Poets: Nizami, Saadi and Hafiz

The Seljuk and Mongol eras were a time of unprecedented contact with neighbouring countries. People were forcibly relocated from one city to another but there was also a large amount of pan-Asian trade conducted at times when the routes were safe for merchants to travel. A number of the Persian world's greatest poets flourished during this period and the content of their work reveals the cosmopolitan nature of life in the Silk Road towns of the twelfth to fourteenth centuries, much as we saw in the poetry of Tang dynasty Changan (Xian). Arguably the three best poets of the age were Nizami, Saadi and Hafiz and a brief sampling of their work will demonstrate that, despite a constant cycle of invasion and political intrigue, there existed a spirit of internationalism and a profound awareness of the customs and traditions of other lands.

Nizami

The romance of the *Haft Paykar* ('The Seven Beauties') is one of the most beautifully descriptive epic poems in all of Persian literature. It was completed in 1197 by the poet Nizami of the Azerbaijani town of Ganja (now Gyandzha), and its principal theme is the idea that self-knowledge can place one on the path to wisdom and perfection. The poem tells the story of Bahram V (r. 420–38), the Sasanian king, who was born to Yazdegerd I after years of childlessness. Bahram is sent to be educated in Yemen and there, within a locked room in a castle, he discovers seven portraits of the most beautiful women he has ever seen. The portrayals are of princesses from every corner of the Silk Road: Furak, the daughter of the Rajah of India; Yaghma Naz, daughter of the Khagan of the Turks; Naz Pari, daughter of the king of Khworezm; Nasrin Nush, daughter of the king of the Slavs; Azar-Gun, daughter of the king of Morocco; Humay, the daughter of the Roman Caesar, and Dursiti, a beautiful Iranian princess from the House of Kai Ka'us. He falls in love with them all and when he ascends the throne contrives to marry them. Each lady is installed in a pavilion and the poem describes his visits to them, each on a particular day of the week, when they entertain him with stories in the manner of Sheherazade of 'The Thousand and One Nights'.

Nizami did not travel to the places he describes but his creations are an imaginative *tour de force*. Princess Yaghma Naz tells Bahram the story of a king in Iraq whom the astrologers have warned of the dire consequences that would follow, should he ever decide to take a wife. Instead he tries to content himself with a succession of slave-girls purchased from all corners of the globe. None prove to be suitable, due largely to the machinations of an old woman who panders to the girls' vanity to create turmoil at court. In the following extract a slave trader arrives with a thousand slaves-girls

from Chinese Central Asia, among them a young woman of exquisite beauty who will eventually become consort to the king:

> 'Until one day a man who dealt in slaves brought information
> to a royal slave
> That from the picture-house of China's realm* a merchant
> had with thousand huris come.
> Virgin slave-girls of countries different: some of Khallukh,**
> some also of Cathay.
> Each one, in face, a world-illuming sun; a love-compeller,
> one who lovers burnt.
> Among them a young slave-girl like a fay, who from the
> morning star had borne off light.
> An ear-bored (slave-girl), (but) an unbored pearl; appraised
> by the pearl-seller at a life.
> Her lips like coral- (coral) clasped with pearls; bitter in
> answer she, but sweet in smile.
> One who bestowing sugar-sprinkling smiles, makes all eat
> (only) sugar many years.'

(From *Haft Paykar* ['The Seven Beauties'], by Nizami Ganjavi [c.1140–1209]
Translated by C. E. Wilson in Nizami, 1924)

Saadi

A near contemporary of Nizami, the author Saadi (1207–91), though little known in the West, is one of Iran's most treasured writers and is still widely quoted in everyday conversation. He wrote two of the world's greatest masterpieces – *Golestan* ('The Garden of Roses'), a mixture of prose and verse, and *Bustan* ('The Orchard'), a *masnavi* or continuous narrative poem. His writings are suffused with wit and insight into the vanity and foibles of man. Unlike Nizami he was a traveller, studying for a number of years in Baghdad and living out his last years in his birthplace, Shiraz. His wry observations of the greed and hyperbole of merchants during the boom years of the pax *Mongolica* are a delight. He recounts the tale of the merchant he meets on the Persian Gulf island of Kish, who boasts of his plans to make a business trip, so lucrative that its proceeds will enable him to retire:

> 'I want to carry Persian brimstone to China, where I have
> heard it bears a very high price; from thence I will
> transport China ware to Greece, and take the brocades of
> Greece to India, and Indian steel to Aleppo. The glassware
> of Aleppo I will convey to Yemen, and from thence go with
> striped cloths to Persia; after which I will leave off trade
> and sit down in my shop.'... I replied: "Have you not heard
> that once upon a time a merchant, as he was travel-ling in
> the desert, fell from his camel? " He said that the covetous
> eye of the worldly man is either satisfied through
> contentment or will be filled with the earth of the grave.'

(Saadi [1207–91]. Translated by Reuben Levy in Kritzeck, 1964)

* 'China's realm' means Chinese Central Asia or Chinese Turkestan. ** Khallukh (presumably as in 'Karluk' Turk) was a town in the Central Asian steppe famous for the beauty of its women).

Hafiz

'Sweet maid, if thou would'st charm my sight,
And bid these arms thy neck infold;
That rosy cheek, that lily hand,
Would give thy poet more delight
Than all Bokhara's vaunted gold,
Than all the gems of Samarkand.

Boy, let yon liquid ruby flow,
And bid thy pensive heart be glad,
Whate'er the frowning zealots say:
Tell them, their Eden cannot show
A stream so clear at Rocnabad,
A bower so sweet as Mosellay.'

(From 'Oh Turkish Maid', an ode from *Divan* [Poetic Works] by Hafiz [1320–89 or 1390]. Translated by Sir William Jones in Arberry, 1954)

Like Saadi, Hafiz was born and died in Shiraz. He is revered as Iran's greatest lyric poet and perfected the form of verse known as the *ghazal*. One critic summarises his appeal thus, 'His poems project at once the sweetness of the joys of this world and its inadequacies'. During his lifetime he was known and admired throughout the Islamic world but he does not appear to have travelled and remained, like Nizami, a voyager of the mind. In contrast to the breeziness of the last quotation, some of Hafiz's poetry has an intensity that is almost unbearable:

'Not all the changes that thy days unfold
Shall rouse thy wonder; Time's revolving sphere
Over a thousand lives like thine has rolled.
That cup within thy fingers, dost not hear
The voices of dead kings speak through the clay?
Kobad, Bahman, Djemshid, their dust is here.
'Gently upon me set thy lips!' they say.

What man can tell where Káus and Kai have gone?
Who knows where even now the restless wind
Scatters the dust of Djem's imperial throne?
And where the tulip, followed close behind
The feet of Spring, her scarlet chalice rears,
There Ferhad for the love of Shirin pined,
Dyeing the desert red with his heart's tears.'

('Comfort' by Hafiz [1320–89 or 1390]. Translated by Gertrude Bell in Arberry, 1954)

The way south from Tabriz

Tabriz was not the Il-Khanid capital for the whole Mongol era. The first capital of the Il-Khans was at Marageh, 130 km south of Tabriz and close to Lake Orumieh, the largest lake in Iran. The first of the Il-Khans, Hulagu (r. 1256-1265), built an observatory at Marageh known as the Rasat-Khaneh or 'Star House'. The remains are still visible on a hill to the

Fig. 385 **The Rasat-Khaneh ('Star House') Observatory with the remains of a sextant**
Constructed between 1260 and 1272
Marageh, East Azerbaijan

west of the town and predate Ulugh Beg's observatory in Samarkand by 200 years (fig. 385).

The Mongols pastured their ponies around Marageh and this is probably where the town gets its name, ('the village of pasturage'). Strangely enough, given the destructive tendencies of the Mongols, all the surviving monuments but one are Seljuk. The town's pride and joy are four tomb towers; there was once a fifth, which collapsed in 1938. The oldest is the Gonbad-e Sorkh ('Red Tower'), built in 1148 and noted for the brilliance of its decorative brickwork (fig. 386). André Godard believes that its glazed external ornament is the first occurrence of such decoration in northern Iran. The Gonbad-e Sorkh was built on the orders of Sa'd Badim, ruler of Azerbaijan at the time.

The Borj-e Khohar-I (or Madar-I, 'Cylindrical Tower') is Marageh's second oldest; a Kufic inscription above the entrance dating it to 1167–68. The tower is a simple cylinder but is embellished with turquoise tiles (fig. 387).

Beside it is the Gonbad-e Kabud ('Blue Tower'), dating to 1196–97. It is traditionally believed to be the tomb of Hulagu's mother but this is impossible, given its early date. The Gonbad-e Kabud is decorated over almost its entire surface with ornamental brickwork and its designs are highlighted with tile mosaic (fig. 388).

The fourth and final tower, the Gonbad-e Ghaffarieh, stands beside the Safi Chai River and dates to the Il-Khanid period. It was completed around 1328 and is richly decorated with black, white and blue glazed bricks set in plaster. The Gonbad-e Ghaffarieh is though to have been constructed for Shams od-din Karasunkur al-Mansouri, viceroy of Syria, who sought refuge in Iran in 1311.

Fig. 386 **The Gonbad-e Sorkh ('Red Tower')**
Completed in 1148
Marageh, East Azerbaijan

Fig. 387 **The Borj-e Khohar-I (or Madar-I, 'Cylindrical Tower')**
Constructed from 1167–68
Marageh, East Azerbaijan

Fig. 388 **The Gonbad-e Kabud ('Blue Tower')**
Constructed from 1196–97
Marageh, East Azerbaijan

There are two principal routes to the south from Marageh. One leads through the Kurdish town of Sanandaj (formerly Sehna) to Kermanshah and the second passes through the town of Takab to Hamadan. Sanandaj was the capital of Kurdistan during the medieval period but there is little remaining of the old town. Takab, too, has little to offer by way of ancient remains but 40 km north of the town is remote, mysterious Takht-e Suleiman, one of Iran's most important ancient sites.

Takht-e Suleiman ('Throne of Solomon')

The fortified settlement of Takht-e Suleiman in West Azerbaijan province (*Azerbaijan-e Gharbi*) occupies an area of 12 hectares and comprises remains from the Parthian, Sasanian and Mongol periods (fig. 389). The site is at an altitude of 2,400 metres in an area dominated by a remarkable conical hill known as Zendan-e Suleiman (Solomon's Prison'). Takht-e Suleiman contains a Sasanian palace and Zoroastrian fire temple as well as Il-Khanid buildings, all clustered around a glistening blue lake, about 100 metres across.

The inner, mud-brick fortifications date to the Parthian era but were enclosed by a Sasanian era stone wall with thirty-eight towers, the remains of which still stand. Pottery shards found at the site indicate that it was occupied much earlier- around the sixth century BC and scholars believe that Takht-e Suleiman may be the Parthian city of Praaspa. Mark Anthony attacked, but failed to subjugate Praaspa in 36 BC. Throughout its history it has been an important religious centre and pilgrimage site. The Sasanian kings, with their court at Ctesiphon near modern Baghdad, would come to pay homage at Takht-e Suleiman, reputedly the site of both the Atur-Gushnasp ('King of the Warriors') fire-altar and of Zoroaster's birthplace. The remains of the fire temple sit on the northern shore of the lake and have walls almost 4 metres thick.

The main entrance gate to Takht-e Suleiman was built during the Sasanian era (when it was known as Ganzak or Shiz). The Mongols, who called the town Saturiq, reinforced the walls, strengthened the gate and added a Kufic inscription.

Returning to Tabriz, this branch of the Silk Road continues on northwestwards through Maku to the Turkish frontier. Around Maku are several, centuries-old Armenian churches. The most important is the St Thaddeus Church and Monastery, known locally as Kara Kelisa (the 'Black Church') and situated about 18 km south of Maku. The church has been rebuilt many times but part of it dates to the tenth century. Armenian legend relates that the Apostle Thaddeus journeyed here in 66 AD and built what is claimed to be the world's first Christian church.

The modern frontier with Turkey is at Bazargan, in the shadow of the 5,137 metre high Mount Ararat. We will examine the Silk Road through Turkey in a later section but first, we will return to the other main route from Ray.

Fig. 389 **Takht-e Suleiman ('Throne of Solomon')**
The remains are Parthian, Sasanian and Il-Khanid but the site may date to the Achaemenian period (550–330 BC)
North of Takab, West Azerbaijan province

CHAPTER TWENTY THREE

THE RAY-HAMADAN ROAD

As we have seen, the road from Ray to Hamadan followed two routes – the first via Savé and the other heading to Ghazvin and then turning south through the Amirabad Pass and passing through Darjazin (or Darazin). Both routes cross arid plain but there are also green oases fed by water from underground irrigation channels known in Xinjiang as *kariz* and in Iran as *qanats*. Savé is a quiet town but, at the end of the twelfth century, it was the winter capital of the Seljuks during their twilight years. The town was an important caravan city on the road from to Baghdad and was renowned for its pottery. There was also a road from Savé to Isfahan. Two Seljuk minarets survive in Savé: one on the outskirts is attached to the Masjed-e Jame (Friday Mosque) and dated 1110–11; and the second is in the centre at the Masjed-e Maidan. The first is said by a number of commentators to be Iran's finest and the second was built in 1061, the oldest dated Seljuk minaret in the country.

The town was destroyed by the Mongols but was rebuilt by them by the time Marco Polo passed through later in the thirteenth century. He called the town 'Saba' and relates that the Magi, the Three Wise Men of the New Testament, set out from there with gifts for the infant Christ. The same claim has been made about Kashan in Isfahan province. Polo goes on to relate a local legend that the Three Wise Men were buried in Savé but no evidence of this has been produced.

The second route passes through Darjazin (Darazin); a small town about 65 km from Hamadan noted for its two Mongol tomb structures – the *Hud* Tower and the *Azhar* Tower – both dating to the fourteenth century. The two routes from Ray combine at the town of Rowan. The 3,570 metre Mt Alvand dominates the approach across cultivated plains to Hamadan, arguably the most important and ancient of all of Iran's Silk Road cities.

Hamadan (Ecbatan)

Hamadan has one of the highest elevations and, therefore one of the mildest summer climates, of any Iranian town: this has ensured its survival as a major metropolis for two and a half millennia. The founding of Hamadan is attributed to a king of the Median Empire. The Median Empire, occupying western Iran and southern Azerbaijan province, emerged in about 800 BC and, around the seventh century

BC, the Medes established their capital at Ecbatan (a Greek word meaning 'The Place of Assembly'), now submerged beneath the modern city of Hamadan. Little is known about the Medes – they left no written records – but they are believed to have been an Indo-European people who spoke an Iranian language related to Old Persian. During the seventh century BC they extended their rule over Persia and in 612 BC, captured the Assyrian capital of Nineveh and put an end to their empire. In 550 BC, the Medes were overthrown by Cyrus the Great and became part of the Achaemenian Empire and during the second century BC, Media became part of the Parthian kingdom.

Both the Achaemenians and Parthians developed Hamadan, both of whom adopted the city as their summer capital. What remains of Median and Achaemenian Ecbatan is to be found on Hegmatana Hill (*Tappe- ye Hekmatane*), a mound in the centre of the city. The royal citadel of ancient Ectaban was said to have been surrounded by seven defensive walls, with the innermost two being coated with gold and silver. At Hegmatana Hill only earthen walls remain and even these are rapidly disappearing under layers of new mud, applied by gangs of labourers. The old walls are still visible but are slowly being 'conserved' by the application of this new layer so that they are beginning to resemble a half-eaten cake that has been re-iced (fig. 390).

The discovery of foundation tablets, gold and silver drinking vessels, and jewellery – all from the Achaemenian era – suggests that the great kings kept their treasury at Ecbatan. At Ganjnameh, 5 km from Hamadan on the slopes of Mount Alvand, are two Achaemenian era inscriptions that refer to Darius the Great and to Xerxes but these, and the depleted remnants of Hegmatana Hill, are all that is left of the city's illustrious past.

Just to the southeast of Hegmatana Hill is Mosalla Hill (*Tappe-ye Mosalla*), thought to have been the site of a Parthian period temple, dedicated to Anahita (or Anaitis, the Zoroastrian goddess of the waters, procreation and fertility). The only ancient relic of substantial size is the massive *Sang-e Shir*, or Stone Lion, that sits in a square in the southeastern part of the city, a stone's throw from Mosalla Hill. Variously ascribed to Alexander the Great or the Parthians, it is still recognisable despite many centuries of rubbing by wistful

Fig. 390 **The Last of Ecbatan.**
Hegmatana Hill, Hamadan, August 2000

Hamadanis. According to the Arab commentator Masudi (d. 956), the lion used to stand beside the 'Lion Gate' (Bib al-Asad) on a low hill overlooking the road to Ray and Khorasan (fig. 391).

There has been a Jewish community in Hamadan as least as far back as the Sasanian era and a small number still remain, many engaged in the manufacture and sale of jewellery in the bazaar. The Mausoleum of Esther and Mordecai, just west of the central square, is built in Islamic style but is actually the most important Jewish shrine in Iran and was once a place of international pilgrimage (fig. 392). The occupants of the tomb are traditionally believed to be Esther, Jewish Queen of the Achaemenian ruler Xerxes (486–65 BC) and her uncle Mordecai, both of whom secured protection for the Jews of the Persian Empire. Most scholars now agree that Esther was in fact interred in Susa and that the crypt contains the remains of Shushan Dokht, the Jewish wife of the Sasanian ruler Yazdegerd I (r. 399–420).

One of history's most sublime geniuses, Ibn Sina, or Avicenna (980–1037) lived in Hamadan for several years. His greatest work, *Al-Qanun fi al-Tibb*, known in the West as the 'Canon', was written during his residence in Hamadan and he is buried there, in a simple tomb covered by an elaborate modern structure.

Under the Seljuks, Hamadan was the capital for fifty years but the depredations of the Mongols in the thirteenth century, the Timurids in the fourteenth, the Turks in the eighteenth and of earthquakes throughout its history have meant that little trace of that era remains. A rare and beautiful exception is the Gunbad-i Alaviyan, a four-sided

Fig. 391 **The Sang-e Shir, or Stone Lion**
Parthian period (256 BC–226 AD), or earlier
L. 3.51 metres
Hamadan, Iran

Fig. 392 **The Mausoleum of Esther and Mordecai**
Constructed in the thirteenth century, probably on the site of a 5th century tomb

tomb built on the site of a Dervish monastery to house the mortal remains of generations of the Alavi clan, rulers of Hamadan for 200 years (fig. 393). The stucco ornamentation of the mehrab and the intricate geometric and floral decoration of the exterior are among the most beautiful in Iran. There is some dispute over the building's age: dates from the twelfth to the fourteenth century have been ascribed to it.

Beyond Hamadan the Silk Road ascends the Abbassabad Pass and passes through Kangavar, now a small town with a large Kurdish population but once the site of a Parthian era temple dedicated to Anahita (goddess of the waters,

Fig. 393 **Gunbad-i Alaviyan**
12th to14th century

procreation and fertility). After Kangavar the road continues through Kermanshah province and 30 km before Kermanshah town, it passes the huge, vertical sand-coloured cliffs at Bisotun. The cliffs at Bisotun, the *Baghistanon Oros* or 'Mountain of the Gods', overlook the Royal Road to

Fig. 394 **The exposed foundation stones of the Royal Road at Bisotun, Kermanshah province**
A colossal blank relief, attributed to Khusrau II (r. 591–628), is visible beyond the road.

Fig. 395 **Old stone bridge at Bisotun, Kermanshah province**
Safavid period (1502–1722) but on Sasanian supports

Ctesiphon. During recent work to improve the modern road surface the foundations of the ancient highway were briefly exposed – an extraordinary and possibly unique glimpse of the Silk Road as it once looked (fig. 394).

High above the road, Darius the Great has left inscriptions in Babylonian, Elamite and Old Persian. They commemorate Darius's defeat of the usurper Gaumata in 522 and list the names of the former's ancestors. A bas-relief shows Darius towering above the prostrated body of Gaumata while the nine governors who had contested the great king's right to the throne are chained before him. In part of one inscription, Darius declares:

'Eight of my family were kings before me. I am the ninth. We inherit kingship on both sides.'

A smaller Parthian relief with three figures and a large, Seleucid period reclining Hercules are lower down the cliff and there are also Sasanian remains. The Sasanian king, Khusrau II (r. 591–628) seems to have been the architect for a vast blank panel, 220 metres by 55 metres, carved onto the cliff-face at Bisotun. It was never completed, perhaps because of Khusrau's death.

Beside the old road to Kermanshah in the southern part of the site, is an intact seventeenth-century caravanserai built beside the remains of a much older one. The Mongols also erected a stopping place for caravan traffic and the remains are still discernible. The beautiful Safavid bridge spanning the river to the north of the caravanserai is built on Sasanian period foundations and reveals the original course of the old Royal Road that runs along the cliff base (fig. 395).

Kermanshah (Bakhtaran)

Kermanshah is now a city of 600,000 mainly Kurdish inhabitants. The town's occupation of a strategic position on the old caravan road to Baghdad has brought it great prosperity but has also left it vulnerable to attack. The Arabs sacked Kermanshah in 649, the Buyids attacked it in the tenth century, the Seljuks in the eleventh and the Mongols in the thirteenth. It was also pulverized by Iraqi missile and bomb attacks during the Iran-Iraq War and, as a result, nothing remains of the old town. There is an important archaeological site just outside the town, however- the monumental Sasanian rock reliefs at Taq-e Bostan, ('The Arch of the Garden'), 5 km to the northeast.

Taq-e Bostan

With one other exception, Taq-e Bostan's reliefs are the only Sasanian rock carvings outside the Fars province. They decorate two grottoes cut into a cliff beside a large pool and are a continuation of a tradition begun by the Achaemenians, in which monumental reliefs are utilised to proclaim the power of the throne and the divine right of its occupant to rule (fig. 396).

The garden at Taq-e Bostan contains fragments of Sasanian capitals and broken statuary, probably from Bisotun and other nearby sites, but the most interesting part of the site are the bas-reliefs carved within the two grottoes and on the exterior wall just to their right. The influences are Byzantine, Roman and possibly Greek as well. The exterior relief represents the investiture of Ardashir II (r. 379–83), the

brother* of one of the greatest of all the Sasanian kings, Shapur II. Ardashir II came to the throne at an advanced age and was quickly deposed and the rather triumphalist tone of this relief was perhaps an attempt to bolster his position as ruler (fig. 397).

The cave to the left of the Ardashir relief is the smaller and later of the two grottoes. On the back wall of the right hand cave are two figures leaning on their swords – Shapur II ('The Great', r. 309–79) and his son* Shapur III (r. 383–88). An inscription in Pahlavi, identifying the two rulers, accompanies this relief.

The largest cave was the last to be carved and was almost certainly intended to occupy the centre part of a triptych, the left-hand part of which was never completed. In this cave, the back wall is carved with a king on horseback; probably Khusrau II (r. 591–628) surnamed Parviz ('the Victorious'), the last great Sasanian ruler before the advent of Islam. Khusrau conducted a war against Byzantium, during which his armies reached Chalcedon (modern Kadikoy, opposite

Fig. 396 **Bas-relief showing Darius the Great with a Median official**
Achaemenian, 6th century BC
From the Treasury at Persepolis
(National Museum, Tehran)
In this remarkable relief, Darius sits on his throne while his son, Crown Prince Xerxes stands behind him. Before them are two incense burners and a Median official, believed to be the 'Chiliarch' who commands both the Treasury and the Army. He holds his hand before his mouth as a mark of respect.

Fig. 397 **Bas-relief depicting the investiture of Ardashir II**
Sasanian, late 4th century
H. 3 m. W. 5.5 metres
Taq-e Bostan, Kermanshah province
The Zoroastrian deity Ahura Mazda stands to the right and presents the crown to Ardashir while, to the left, Mithra stands holding a sacred bunch of twigs, known as the *barsom*. Beneath their feet is a prostrated figure, perhaps a defeated Roman soldier.

* Other authorities say Shapur III was Ardashir II's son and Shapur II's grandson.

Constantinople), and captured Antioch, Damascus and Jerusalem. In the lower section of the Taq-e Bostan relief Khusrau sits in full armour astride his favourite horse, Shabdiz, a lance in his hands while above him the same ruler is invested with his crown by Ahura Mazda and Anahita, goddess of the waters (fig. 398).

The entrance to the cave is decorated with 'Tree of Life' motifs with acanthus leaves that we have seen in a number of works of art in this book. Above them are two cornucopia and at the apex of the arch is a royal crescent flanked by two winged figures bearing diadems and cups. The motifs on the both the façade and interior of this cave resemble Roman (Byzantine) art so strongly that it seems highly likely that artists from Constantinople were responsible. One source, the poet and traveller Al-Hamadhani (968–1008), reported that the sculptor was one Fatus (or Katus) ibn Sinimmar Rumi (i.e. a man of Byzantine Rome).

On the left wall of the cave is a scene of Khusrau II hunting wild boar in a swamp and on the right the same ruler appears in pursuit of deer. The reliefs show various stages of the royal hunt: in one the king stands in a boat firing an arrow at wild boar while musicians perform an accompaniment. Elephants and camels are used extensively and can be seen participating in the hunt and carrying off the spoils and boatloads of women who appear to perform a 'cheerleading' function (fig. 399).

On the left hand wall towards the rear is a much later relief that still retains its original colours. It was added to by the Qajars during the nineteenth century and is perhaps an attempt to bask in some of the reflected glory of the Sasanians.

The westward road from Kermanshah departs the borders of modern Iran and leads through the Zagros Mountains to the Mesopotamian plateau and Baghdad. The Zagros Mountains are a series of parallel ranges, extending for 900 km across southwestern Iran. They rise to about 3,900 metres and have acted as a natural barrier for millennia. The lands beyond the Zagros, in modern Iraq and Syria, will be examined in the next section.

Fig. 398 **Bas-relief depicting a ruler, probably Khusrau II, on horseback and at his investiture**
Sasanian
Probably late 6th or early 7th century
Taq-e Bostan, Kermanshah province

Fig. 399 **Bas-relief depicting Khusrau II hunting wild boar**
Sasanian, probably late 6th or early 7th century
Taq-e Bostan, Kermanshah province

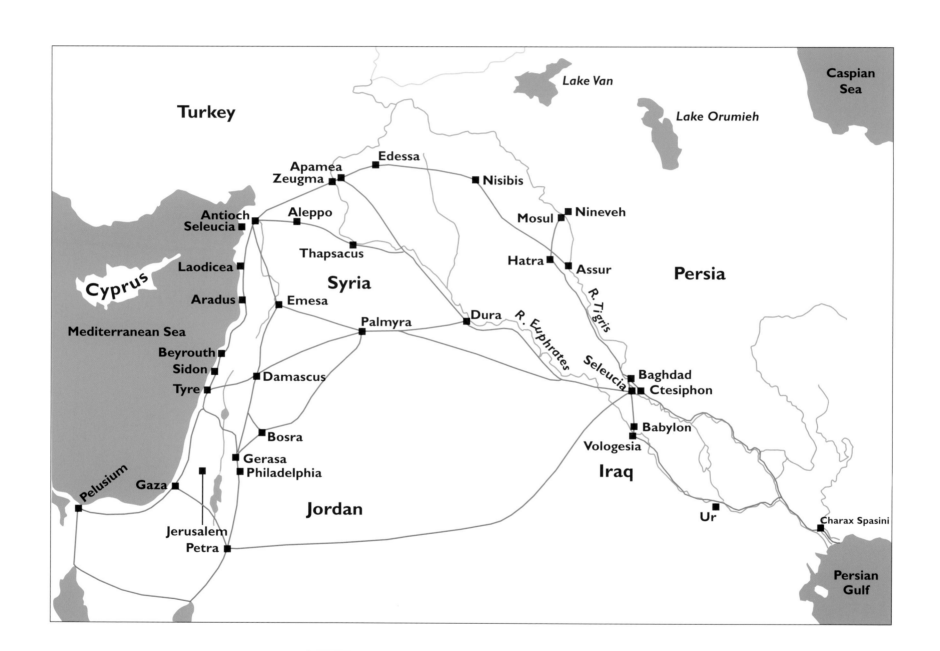

TRADE ROUTES OF THE NEAR EAST
(Adapted from Rostovtzeff, 1932)

NOTE: for a detailed map of the Silk Road through Iraq see page 324

CHAPTER TWENTY FOUR

THE SILK ROAD THROUGH IRAQ

Babylonia

> '10: … Alas, alas, that great city Babylon, that mighty
> city! for in one hour is thy judgment come.
> 11: And the merchants of the earth shall weep and mourn
> over her; for no man buyeth their merchandise any more:
> 12: The merchandise of gold, and silver, and precious
> stones, and of pearls, and fine linen, and purple, and silk
> and scarlet, and all thyine [scented] wood, and all
> manner vessels of ivory, and all manner vessels of most
> precious wood, and of brass, and iron, and marble,
> 13: And cinnamon, and odours, and ointments, and
> frankincense, and wine, and oil, and fine flour, and
> wheat, and beasts, and sheep, and horses, and chariots,
> and slaves, and souls of men.
> 14: And the fruits that thy soul lusted after are departed
> from thee, and all things which were dainty and goodly
> are departed from thee, and thou shalt find them no more
> at all.
> 15: The merchants of these things, which were made rich
> by her, shall stand afar off for the fear of her torment,
> weeping and wailing,'
> (King James Bible: Revelation, chapter 18, v.10–15)

Ancient Babylonia occupied southeastern Mesopotamia,
between the Tigris and Euphrates Rivers from Baghdad
down to the Persian Gulf. It takes it name from the capital,
Babylon, established after the military successes of the
Akkadians against the Sumerians around 2300 BC. Babylon
sits beside the Euphrates, just west of the Iraqi town of Kish
to the south of modern Baghdad, and for 2000 years – until
it fell to Alexander the Great in 331 BC – it was the most
magnificent city in the Middle East. The Assyrians destroyed
Babylon in about 689 BC but its grandeur was restored by
Nebuchad-nezzar II (r. 604–562 BC), conqueror of the
kingdom of Judah and destroyer of Jerusalem. Nebuchadnezzar II is credited for the construction of the Hanging
Gardens of Babylon- one of the Seven Wonders of the
World- built for a wife who missed the mountains of her
home in Media.

In 539 BC, after Nebuchadnezzar's death, Babylonia fell
to the Persian armies of Cyrus the Great (r. 559–529 BC).

Babylonia and its capital remained under Achaemenian
control for the next 200 years but the application of heavy
taxation and demands for the payment of tribute enraged
the populace. When Alexander defeated the Achaemenian
forces in Babylon in 331 BC he was hailed as a saviour.
Alexander had extravagant plans for Babylon – he planned
to make it one of his capitals and to deepen the Euphrates for
shipping as far as the Persian Gulf but his plans did not
survive his death in the city in 323 BC. Alexander's
successors, the Seleucids, abandoned the city, preferring to
build their own capital of Seleucia on the Tigris. In 50 BC the
Sicilian historian Diodorus observed that of the once great
metropolis of Babylon, 'only a small part of the city is now
inhabited and most of the area within its walls is given over
to agriculture'.

In 126 BC the Parthians, already in control of Iran,
conquered the lands once occupied by the old kingdom of
Babylonia. Except for three brief spells of Roman occupation
– by Trajan in 114 AD, Avidius Cassius in 165 AD, and
Septimius Severus in 198 AD – the Parthians remained in
firm control of the Tigris-Euphrates Valley for the next 350
years. They were able to control all commerce between Asia
and the Roman world until the Sasanians finally defeated
them in 226 AD. Seleucia, Ctesiphon, Hatra and Dura
Europos all grew into major caravan cities under Parthian
rule and smaller towns and villages – ruined and abandoned
since Assyrian times or even earlier – were rebuilt with the
proceeds of Silk Road commerce.

Ctesiphon

The twin towns of Seleucia and Ctesiphon sit on opposite
banks of the Tigris, about 35 km south of Baghdad. Ctesiphon was founded by the Parthians around 140 BC and
occupies the east (left) bank and, while Seleucia fell into
decline during the second century AD, its neighbour continued to flourish right up until the early years of Islam. When
the armies of Avidius Cassius entered Ctesiphon in 165 AD
they were struck down by an epidemic, probably smallpox.
Very little is known about Parthian Ctesiphon but Italian
excavations between 1964 and 1976 have revealed a
considerable amount of information about the town during
the Sasanian era when it was the capital of the empire. The

Fig. 400 **The Taq-i Kisra ('Hall of Khusrau'), Ctesiphon, Iraq**
Sasanian, 6th century
Photographed before 1888 when the right section collapsed
(After Dieulafoy, 1884)

Italians succeeded in identifying the 700-hectare circular city known as *Veh Ardashir* (in Persian: 'the beautiful city of Ardashir') constructed by the first Sasanian king, Ardashir I (r. 224–41). The city was expanded by many of Ardashir's successors- most notably Khusrau I (r. 532–79), who built a new residential district to house captives from Antioch known as *Veh Az Antiok Khusrau* (in Persian: 'better than Antioch [has] Khusrau [built this]'). Part of Khusrau's palace, the Taq-i Kisra ('Hall of Khusrau') still stands and hints at the splendour of what Arab geographers described during the ninth century as the most beautiful citadel in the world. *Taq-i Kisra's* complete façade survived until 1888 when the right half collapsed during a flood. Its colossal *iwan* (open reception hall) is 50 metres by 25 metres and its 35 metre high arch is the tallest of its type in the world (fig. 400)

The Sasanians were followers of Zoroaster but Ctesiphon also became a centre of Nestorian Christianity and it remained the overall capital of the empire- even during the reign of kings who used it only as their winter residence. Ctesiphon was called Al-Madain ('the cities') in Arab sources and it was attacked and plundered by them in 637. It was subsequently abandoned.

When the last Umayyad caliph, Marwan II, was defeated in 750, Abdul Abbas ('The Blood Shedder') put to death all but one of the male members of the dynasty and established

the Abbasid Caliphate. The capital of the Umayyads, Damascus, was abandoned and the power-base of the new regime shifted east. Abdul Abbas built himself a palace at Anbar on the left bank of the Euphrates but his death in 754 brought to an end any plans to develop the site further.

Baghdad

The second Abbasid Caliph was Al Mansur (r. 754–75), a brother of Abdul Abbas, and he established his capital in 762 near the site of what was then a Sasanian village on the banks of the Tigris. His reasons for doing so are laid out succinctly in an account by the tenth-century Arab geographer Mukadasi. Mukadasi ascribes the following words to Al Mansur's counsellors:

'We are of [the] opinion that thou shouldst found the city here between the four districts of Bûk and Kâlwadhâ on the eastern bank, and of Katrabbul and Bâdurâyâ, on the western bank: thereby shalt thou live among palms and near water, so that if one district fail thee in its crops or be late in its harvest in another will the remedy be found. Also thy city being on the Sarât Canal, provisions will be brought thither by the boats of the Euphrates, and by the caravans through the plains, even from Egypt and Syria. Hither, up from the sea, will come the wares of China,

while down the Tigris from Mosul will be brought goods from the Byzantine lands. Thus shall thy city be safe standing between all these streams, and thine enemy shall not reach thee, except it be by a boat or by a bridge, and across the Tigris or the Euphrates.'

(Mukadasi. Quoted in G. Le Strange, 1924)

As capital of an empire that extended from North Africa to the western borders of China, Baghdad (variously, 'Founded by God' or 'The City of Peace') grew, in little more than fifty years, to a size that rivalled Constantinople. Under Al Mansur's grandson Harun Al Rashid (786–809), its resident population is said to have reached two million, supplemented by innumerable transient visitors including merchants on the long-distance trade routes and *hajji* on the pilgrims' road to Mecca. There is no stone available within 100 km of Baghdad and the city was therefore built of brick. The first major structure was the *Madinat al-Salam*, the Round City. Three concentric, circular walls were erected by workers brought in from Syria, Persia and Babylonia and four gates were raised around the perimeter, spaced equally at the northeast, southeast, southwest and northwest quadrants. During the early stages of the city's construction, Al Mansur attempted to remove building materials from Khusrau's palace at Ctesiphon but the plan was soon abandoned on the grounds of cost. The caliph's palace stood at the centre of the inner circle and was known as the 'Golden Gate', the 'Palace of the Green Dome' or the 'Golden Palace'. It covered an area of 33,000 square metres and was capped by a massive green dome some 36 metres in height. A figure of a horseman wielding a lance was said to have stood atop the dome and is supposed to have rotated in the direction of trouble when the capital was threatened. The dome itself endured until 941 when it collapsed during a storm.

Beside the Golden Gate was the Great Mosque, its prayer hall connected directly with the palace. Nothing whatsoever survives of Al Mansur's Round City except, perhaps, the marble *mehrab* of Baghdad's Khasaki Mosque (built in 1658), which some scholars believe came from the Great Mosque. In fact the only palace to have survived relatively intact from the early Abbasid period is at Ukhaidir, almost 200 km to the south of Baghdad. During the reign of Al Mansur's son Mahdi the city grew beyond its circular walls and spread across to al-Rusafa on the opposite (east) bank of the river, and southwards to the suburb of Kharkh. Kharkh quickly became the commercial hub of Baghdad - each street offering a particular type of merchandise- while the seat of government became centred on the east bank. A network of canals surrounded the city, providing water for irrigation and a means to transport goods. Canals dug during the pre-Islamic era already linked the Tigris with the Euphrates and the complete network would facilitate the movement of

goods almost to the front gates of Kharkh's bazaars. Many of the various markets in the Kharkh suburb have been identified in contemporary accounts: the Market of the Clothes-Merchants, the Market of the Butchers, the Poulterers' Section, the Oil-Merchants' Quadrangle, the Street of the Pitch-Workers and the Market of the Sellers of Cooked Meats are all named (Le Strange, 1924). The markets were once situated within the Round City but Al Mansur had them removed on the advice of a Greek envoy, who observed that the markets enabled spies and enemies of the Abbasids to infiltrate the very heart of the capital.

The Four Markets, west of the Round City near the Garden of Kass, flourished throughout the Abbasid period and contained the shops and godowns of both local and foreign merchants. To the north of the Four Markets was the Attabiyin Quarter, home to the *Dar-al-Kazz* (the Silk House), where Attabi textiles (half silk, half cotton) were woven in various colours and exported throughout the Islamic world. The chief market of east Baghdad was along the Khurasan Road and the two halves of the city, on either side of the Tigris, were linked by bridges of boats. The extent to which Baghdad became a centre for global trade is apparent from numerous and detailed accounts by visitors during the Abbasid period. What they observed is beautifully summarised by the nineteenth century Islamicist, August Muller:

'We know that hither came all the products of the world in constant stream. Spices of all kinds, aloes and sandalwood for fumigation, teak for ship building, ebony for artistic work, jewels, metals, dyes and minerals of all kinds from India and the Malay archipelago; porcelains and – what is indispensable to the oriental- musk from China; pearls and white-skinned slaves from the lands of the Turk and the Russian; ivory and Negro slaves from East Africa; – all were brought here by traders and navigators after long and arduous journeys by land and sea. At the same time the city merchants carried on a profitable trade with China in the products of the Caliphate: dates, sugar, glassware, cotton and iron. Even more brisk was the internal trade between the various provinces of the empire, all of which trade flowed through Baghdad. Egypt's rice, grain, linen and paper; Syria's glass and metal ware, Arabia's spices, pearls and weapons; Persia's silks, perfumes and garden produce, all found their way here.'

(August Müller. Quoted in Levy, 1929)

Under Harun Al Rashid (786–809) and his son Al Mamun (813–33), Baghdad was at its most splendid. Scores of Chinese junks, towed up the Tigris from Basra, tied up along a vast network of jetties to offload their cargo and the city's streets teemed with merchants from every corner of the empire. Large Jewish and Christian communities existed in Baghdad and were, generally speaking, well assimilated and prosperous. Harun's fondness for amorous adventures and for music is legendary. *The Tales of the Thousand and One Nights*, or *The Arabian Nights Entertainments* are fairytales and many derive from beyond the Abbasids' realms- from Turkey, India and Greece for example- but they paint pictures of Baghdad, Damascus and Cairo during the Abbasids' Golden Age. Most scholars agree that the stories are an accumulation of several centuries of tales told by travellers on the Silk Road- at least as far back as the Sasanian era- and were perhaps told to while away long evenings at remote caravanserais. The stories of lavish ceremonies conducted in Harun's audience chamber are probably true: one account describes the reception given to envoys of Emperor Charlemagne who were presented with elephants and a bronze water clock. The stories are full of references to commerce with the neighbouring countries of the Silk Road and also to journeys made for no other reason than the sheer joy of travelling:

'I was born, Commander of the Faithful, in Baghdad, and was left an orphan while I was yet a very young man, for my parents died within a few days of each other. I had inherited from them a small fortune, which I worked hard night and day to increase, till at last I found myself the owner of eighty camels. These I hired out to travelling merchants, whom I frequently accompanied on their various journeys, and always returned with large profits. One day I was coming back from Balsora [Basra], whither I had taken a supply of goods, intended for India, and halted at noon in a lonely place, which promised rich pasture for my camels…'

('The Story of the Blind Baba-Abdalla' from *The Arabian Nights Entertainments*. Selected and Edited by Andrew Lang, Longmans, Green and Co, 1898)

'In the reign of Harun Al Rashid, there lived in Baghdad a merchant named Ali Cogia, who, having neither wife nor child, contented himself with the modest profits produced by his trade…. He packed up his wares, and …joined a caravan that was going to Cairo. The results of the journey gladdened his heart. He sold off everything almost directly, and bought a stock of Egyptian curiosities, which he intended selling at Damascus; but as the caravan with which he would have to travel would not be starting for another six weeks, he took advantage of the delay to visit the Pyramids, and some of the cities along the banks of the Nile.

Now the attractions of Damascus so fascinated the worthy Ali, that he could hardly tear himself away, but at length he remembered that he had a home in Baghdad, meaning to return by way of Aleppo, and after he had crossed the Euphrates, to follow the course of the Tigris. But when he reached Mosul, Ali had made such friends

with some Persian merchants, that they persuaded him to accompany them to their native land, and even as far as India, and so it came to pass that seven years had slipped by since he had left Baghdad…'

('Story of Ali Colia, Merchant of Baghdad', *ibid.*)

At the time of Harun's death in 809, a bitter power struggle erupted between his sons Amin and Mamun. Amin was installed as caliph and Mamun appointed governor of Khurasan but civil war quickly ensued. Armies sent by Amin against Mamun were crushed and, in September 812, a siege of Baghdad commenced. It lasted a year and at the end of it Amin was dead and half the city lay ruined. Mamun initially tried to remain loyal to his Persian roots (his mother was a Persian concubine), and run the empire from Khurasan but in 819 he succumbed to the inevitable and entered the city to take up the reins of power. His trusted general Tahir al-Husain was rewarded with the governorship of Khurasan, soon establishing the more or less autonomous though somewhat short-lived, Tahirid dynasty, (821–73).

Mamun's rule was a time of cultural excellence. His most enduring achievement was his establishment of the House Of Wisdom, an institute for the acquisition of foreign works of literature and for their translation into Arabic and Syriac. The philosophy of Aristotle and Plato was translated from the Greek and the medical works of Hippocrates and Galen, almost forgotten in Europe, were also translated and reintroduced to the West via Sicily and Spain. Hunain ibn Ishaq (809–77), a Christian doctor, ran the House of Wisdom but his patron, though culturally enlightened, was politically inept. Khurasan was lost to Tahir al-Husain in 821 and Mamun's successor, Al Muhtasim (833-842), was unable to stop the process of decay. Al Muhtasim was the son of a Turkish mother and retained an abiding hatred for both Persians and Arabs. His palace guard comprised mercenaries and slaves from Turkestan and North Africa who displayed nothing but contempt for the citizenry of Baghdad: a favourite pastime was to ride pell-mell through the streets, trampling with their horses anyone unfortunate enough to get in their way. Resentment against both Al Muhtasim and his guards developed to such a pitch that he decided, in 836, to relocate the Abbasid capital further up the Tigris to Samarra, 100 km north of Baghdad, and there it remained until 893. When Baghdad resumed its role as capital there was one important change- the new caliph declined to live in the Round City and elected, instead to live on the east bank of the river. This tradition continued with his successors who either rebuilt the palaces of their predecessors or constructed new ones.

Continuing conflict with the Byzantines weakened the Abbasids still further, as did the Zanj (or Zindj) slave revolt, erupting in 869 and not extinguished until 883. Independent states began to emerge in Egypt, Persia and other parts of the caliphate. In 867 came the Saffarids of eastern Persia and, in Central Asia at about the same time, appeared the Samanids. The Fatimids appeared around 900 in North Africa and the Buyids of northwest Persia were strong enough, by 945, to seize Baghdad. The Ismaili founders of the Fatimid dynasty (909–1171) were a force to be reckoned with. Their core beliefs were the acceptance of Ismail (the seventh descendant of the Prophet Muhammad's son-in-law Ali), as his spiritual successor, or imam, and the claim that they were descendants of the Prophet's daughter, Fatimah. From humble beginnings in eastern Algeria the Ismailis had, by 909, installed their own ruler in Tunisia, thereby founding the Fatimid dynasty. In 969 they conquered Egypt and founded its capital, al-Qahira ('the victorious'), known today as Cairo.

The Abbasid practise of hiring Turkish slaves (known as Mamluks) to safeguard their rule, begun by the Caliph Al Muhtasim during the ninth century, had continued to the extent that they became de facto rulers of the empire, wielding the strings of a succession of puppet rulers. The last effectual Abbasid caliph and the last to be permitted to deliver Friday prayers at the city's mosque was Al-Rahdi (r. 934–40). Five years after Al-Rahdi's death the Buyids, Shias from northwest Persia, seized the city without a fight. The following year, 946, the Buyids unseated the caliph, put out his eyes and replaced him with the first of a line of lackeys. The Buyids retained their hold on the Abbasids until 1055, when they were ousted by the Seljuks, a Turkic tribe from the region to the north of the Oxus. The Seljuks, like the Abbasids, were Sunnis and they sought to expunge the Shi'ite influence that had prevailed in the religious and political life of the city under the Buyids. The practice of installing a succession of malleable Abbasid caliphs continued under the Seljuks but their vassals were, at least, accorded more respect.

The early years of Seljuk rule in Baghdad was marked by a succession of catastrophes. In 1055, a famine occurred of such severity that the inhabitants are said to have resorted to cannibalism. The famine was followed by outbreaks of pestilence and then by a series of fires, which destroyed the markets on the left bank of the river and severely damaged the Kharkh district. In 1062 there was a disastrous flood that damaged the palace-buildings of the caliph and in 1065 and 1066 there were pitched battles between Shi'ites and Sunnis and further fires. To cap it all, there were more floods between 1069 and 1075, the worst of which occurred in 1074 when the water levels reach a height of almost ten metres.

Despite these problems the Seljuks revived commercial activity on both land and sea. Cotton cloth, silk fabrics, glass, dyes, ointments, slaves and arms were sent out from Baghdad in all directions. Single ships and sometimes convoys, set out from Basra for India, China and Java and the land routes were also active and relatively safe. The Seljuks

were just as interested in conquest, however, and trade did not attain the levels enjoyed during the golden age of the Abbasids in the ninth and tenth centuries. The second Seljuk Sultan, Alp Arslan (r. 1063–72) launched attacks against the Byzantine Empire and, in 1071, defeated their armies at Manzikert (modern Malazkirt in Anatolia) and captured Emperor Romanus Diogenes. Romanus was released after prostrating himself before the victorious Seljuks and in exchange for a large ransom, but was blinded and overthrown when he returned to Constantinople. Alp Arslan himself died the following year and was succeeded by his son Malikshah (r. 1072–92). Under Malikshah, ably assisted by his gifted administrator Nizam-al-Mulk, the Seljuk Empire experienced a cultural renaissance. Malikshah ordered the construction of a new commercial quarter on the east bank – the Suk al-Madina (Tughril City), comprising shops houses and a mint. He also began the construction of the Jami al-Sultan (Sultan's Mosque), finally completed in 1130 and utterly destroyed during the Mongol conquest. Malikshah's vizier Nizam-al-Mulk was murdered by the Assassins in 1092 but his great Nizamiya College, constructed between 1064–66 within or close to the Tuesday Market at the southern end of the east bank, was his most enduring legacy. Many of the finest scholars of the day taught at the Nizamiya, including the theologian Abu Hamid al Ghazali (known as Algazel in the West), the mystic Abd al-Qadir Jilani (whose mausoleum still stands in Baghdad), and Baha al-din, biographer of Saladin.

Malikshah's death in 1092 was followed by a protracted struggle between rival claimants to the throne. By the early part of the twelfth century Baghdad was capital only of Iraq and the city endured a further round of floods, fires, a major earthquake and religious insurrection. The launching of the First Crusade in 1095 produced a rallying cry that rang throughout the Muslim world but the now decadent Seljuks paid little heed. Even when Jerusalem fell to the Christian armies and a delegation arrived in Baghdad to beg for assistance, their pleas were ignored. Similar deputations came from Tripoli in 1108 and Aleppo in 1110, but the response was the same.

The last great Seljuk ruler was Sanjar (ca. 1118–57) but his power base was at Merv in modern Turkmenistan and Baghdad was no more than a provincial capital. After Sanjar's death in 1157, the Seljuk Empire continued to disintegrate. The Abbasid Caliph al Nazir (r. 1180–1225) enjoyed the longest reign of the entire line and succeeded in restoring some of the power and prestige of the *ancien regime*. The Seljuk's dominance of Iraq came to an end in 1194 when their last sultan, Tughril II (1177–94), was killed at Ray by the leader of the Khorezmshahs, another Turkish dynasty from the area south of the Aral Sea.*

The Khorezmshahs then threatened to march on Baghdad, demanding that they be granted the sultanate in

* A branch of the Seljuks survived after 1194, establishing a state in Anatolia (the sultanate of Rum, i.e. the land of the Romans, or Byzantines). With its capital at Konya, the Seljuk state continued to exist until the Mongols conquered it in 1243.

place of the Seljuks. Al Nazir refused and a standoff between the Abbasids and Khorezmshahs ensued that would last for the next twenty years. During this period Baghdad was again beset by natural calamities and large sections of the city were left depopulated. Wild animals are said to have roamed in parts of the town and a number of accounts refer to lions being killed in the city's streets. The Khorezmshah Muhammad (r. 1200–20) consolidated the dynasty's control of Persia and Central Asia and resolved to march on Baghdad but his advance was delayed by the onset of winter and by disaffection among his troops. Just as he was ready to proceed towards Baghdad, Governor Inal-khan of the frontier town of Otrar in Central Asia reaped the whirlwind with his disastrous decision to arrest and execute a party of merchants from Mongolia (see p. 277). This colossal act of folly would have grave consequences for Baghdad. It led to the unleashing of the Mongol firestorm on half the civilized world and although the city escaped its flames for some forty years, it too was eventually consumed by the conflagration.

The first mention of the arrival of the Mongols within sight of Baghdad was in 1243 but it proved to be a false alarm. Mongol envoys did arrive at the city in 1246 during their invasion of Mesopotamia but it was not until 1257 that Hulagu's armies finally approached. The rather indolent caliph Mustasim was given an ultimatum to come to Hamadan to pay homage to Hulagu but he refused to do so. Any attempts to make preparations to defend the city were also undermined by long-standing and bitter divisions between the town's Shia and Sunni communities. The city was finally sacked on 11 January 1258, beginning with a bombardment from all sides with rocks and burning naphtha from the Mongols' siege engines. Hulagu's army included a corps of Chinese firework makers who kept his mangonels supplied with projectiles and the city was soon in flames. Baghdad's irrigation dykes were then breached and the city inundated with water.* The Caliph Mustasim was executed on 10 February, his death bringing the Abbasid dynasty to an end. The Mongols were superstitious about shedding royal blood and the caliph was therefore rolled in a carpet (others say a sack), and trampled to death by horses. The city's population, perhaps as many as 800,000 people, was then assembled outside the walls and put to death. The Muslim world was convulsed by the news that Baghdad, 'the mother of the world and the mistress of cities' had fallen while some Christians celebrated, comparing it to the description in the New Testament of the destruction of Babylon (see p. 313). Furthermore, Hulagu's men spared a number of Nestorian Christians and the khan himself is said to have had a Christian wife. The Mongol onslaught continued through the Middle East: Aleppo fell in 1260, soon followed by Damascus. Egypt was the next target but events far to the east in China brought the terrible Mongol juggernaut to a halt. In 1260 Hulagu received news that his

brother Mangu, the Great Khan, had died. A dispute over succession erupted with Hulagu favouring another brother, Kubilai, and others (most notably his cousin Berke, khan of the Golden Horde), preferring another. Hulagu shifted his army to the Caucasus, leaving no more than a weak force in Syria, and the country's Mamluk rulers saw an opportunity to turn the tide. The Mamluk ruler Baybars (r. 1260–77) raised an army and, in September 1260, defeated a force of Mongols led by Kitbuga at Ain Jalut ('Goliath's Spring'), near the town of Nazareth in today's Israel. Kitbuga was killed and, though the Mongols conquest of the East continued unabated, their power in the West was broken forever.

As for Baghdad, Hulagu had ordered the rebuilding of mosques and tombs venerated by local people but the city's light was never again to burn as brightly. Visitors like Ibn Battuta, who passed through some seventy-five years later, describe a city whose madrassahs and libraries had been rebuilt but which no longer attracted the great minds of the day and others described great swathes of the city as being ruined and abandoned. Baghdad was no longer the first city of the Islamic world: it was now merely a provincial capital and the trade routes across the north via Tabriz and Turkey henceforth assumed a greater prominence.

There were two principal routes leading in a westerly direction from Baghdad towards Syria and the Mediterranean coast. These routes were in use long before Baghdad even existed and, although they fell in and out of favour as a result of changes in the fortunes of the towns along the way, they continued to be used right up until the modern era. The development of both routes was influenced by the vital need for water and fodder on the journey and the most direct route was not therefore necessarily the best. The longer, but better provisioned route followed the Tigris in a northerly direction through Samarra to Mosul, and then turned west to cross the Jazirah Plain to cross the Euphrates at Karkemish (Jarablus), just to the south of Zeugma. West of the Euphrates this route continued through Aleppo and then either branched northwestwards via Antioch in the Orontes Valley and across Anatolia to Constantinople, or it turned south towards the Mediterranean ports and Damascus.

The second route was more direct but necessitated a crossing of about 500 km of desert and exposure to possible attacks by nomads. This route began at Baghdad or one of the earlier capitals of southern Mesopotamia and followed the Euphrates as far as Abu Kamal on the modern Syria-Iraq border. Here, or just beyond at Dura Europos, the route turned westwards and headed straight across the rock-strewn Syrian Desert (Badiat ash-Sham) for about 210 km to Palmyra. West of Palmyra the road continued through Homs (Emesa) and then divided into a number of branches that led, like the Tigris route, to Damascus and the Mediterranean. There was a direct caravan trail from Palmyra to Damascus and a number of subsidiary ways,

* For a painting of the Mongols' siege of Baghdad see fig. 285.

leading south to the Nabataean city of Petra and onwards to the Red Sea. These routes all involved crossing desert and could be extremely dangerous for travellers- camels require water every four to five days and wells were therefore dug at intervals of 100 km or so. If the members of a caravan missed a well they would almost inevitably perish.

Samarra

The first major town on the Tigris route was at Samarra, about 100 km north of Baghdad on the east bank of the river. As we have seen, the town superseded Baghdad as the Abbasid capital between 836 and 893. Before it became capital Samarra was a small, fortified settlement on the post road leading north, known only as the place where the Roman Emperor Julian the Apostate was killed in 364. The Sasanians built a 300 km long irrigation canal, the Nahrawan, which supplied the plains beyond the Tigris to the east of Baghdad. There were inlets on the canal to the north and south of where Samarra now stands, and the Abbasid Caliph Harun Al Rashid (r. 786–809) selected the more southerly spot as the site for a palace called al-Mubarak. He never completed it – it was abandoned in 796 – but Caliph Al Muhtasim (r. 833–42) chose a site between the two inlets and began to construct his new capital. The Arabs called the place *Surra man ra'a* ('He who sees it, rejoices'), although it is unclear whether their appellation is a pun on an ancient word, 'Samarra', or whether it was subsequently shortened to produce the town's final name. What is clear is that Al Muhtasim and his successors built a vast city, extending some 50 km along the Tigris and covering an area of 150 square km. The city was excavated from 1911–13 by the German archaeologist Ernst Herzfeld and the remains of palaces and gardens were uncovered on both sides of the river. About 5,700 Abbasid buildings have been identified as well as three equestrian racecourses, discovered to the east of the city. Samarra was built of brick (both fired and unfired), and rammed earth with wide avenues and palaces for the princes of the royal house. His Turkish guards were billeted in houses well away from the town and were supplied with Turkish slave girls to marry, in order that they did not mingle with the Arab citizenry. Al Muhtasim's own palace complex was known as the Dar al-Khilafa ('House of the Caliphate') and occupied an area of 125 hectares. His main residence was the Jausaq al- Khagani, with a triple arched façade known as the Bab-al-'Amma that still stands. Fragments of wall paintings were recovered from the Jausaq al- Khagani's harem (fig. 401). The themes are hunting, dancing, banqueting and the like, and the participants are depicted with scalloped fringes, oval eyes with large pupils, and small feet. According to Grube (Grube, 1966), they find their origins in the classically influenced paintings of the East such as those of Miran in Chinese Central Asia (see figs. 219 and 221).

Samarra's most prolific builder was Al Mutawakkil (847–61), the next but one caliph after Al Muhtasim. Al Mutawakkil doubled the city's size and built around nineteen palaces. His congregational mosque, built between 848 and 852, measures 239 metres by 156 metres and was the largest such building in the world right up until the modern era. Its 52 metre high minaret has an extraordinary spiral ramp on the exterior which rises ever more steeply as it ascends, in order to preserve its symmetry (fig. 402).

The interior walls of Samarra's palaces and houses were decorated with carved or moulded polychrome stucco panels. These panels incorporate three basic styles that may have developed one from another or have occurred simultaneously: vine leaves and scrolls within cartouches, vegetal motifs with a more abstract or geometric form, and complex moulded spirals and lobes. The last had a profound effect on the art of Byzantium.

Al Mutawakkil was murdered in 861 and was followed by a succession of weak rulers, appointed amidst interference from the Turkish guards. The city quickly fell into decline and was attacked and looted by Bedouins. Its chief function, from the tenth century onwards, was as a pilgrimage centre: the town contains the tombs of the tenth and eleventh Shi'ite

Fig. 401 **Wall painting from the Jausaq al- Khagani, Samarra**
Abassid period, ca. 836–39
H. 50 cm, W. 50 cm
This painting is a reconstruction by Ernst Herzfeld of fragments found at the palace harem and now held in the Museum of Turkish and Islamic Art, Istanbul.
(Staatliche Museen zu Berlin- Preußicher Kulturbesitz Museum für Islamische Kunst)

Fig. 402 **The Great Mosque of Al Mutawakkil at Samarra**
Abbasid era, built 848–52
The unusual design of the minaret was replicated in 861 at the Abu Dhulaf Mosque just to the north of Samarra, as well as at Ibn Tulun's (ca. 868) mosque in Cairo. Its shape is said to derive from that of ancient Babylonian ziggurats and was also the inspiration for depictions of 'The Tower of Babel' by European artists like Pieter Breughel the Elder.

Imams and is also the place where the twelfth Imam is reputed to have disappeared into a fissure in the ground. Samarra's hopes of remaining a viable commercial centre were delivered a final *coup de grace* in the thirteenth century. To the south of Samarra the Tigris changed its course, shifting eastwards and forcing the transfer of the main Baghdad-Mosul highway to the west bank.

The Samarra-Mosul route along the Tigris passed close to Hatra (modern Al-Hadhr), one of the Silk Road's most important caravan cities. Hatra is located about 100 km southwest of Mosul, just west of the ancient Assyrian city of Assur, in a semi-desert region between the Tigris and Euphrates known as Al-Jazirah. It was first settled around the second century BC by Aramaic tribes of Adiabene, a semi-vassal state in upper Mesopotamia allied with the Parthians. By the first century BC it had become a fortified city, used as a buffer against Roman attack, with close political and commercial links to the Parthian capital at Ctesiphon. What little is known about Hatra has been gleaned from classical sources, local legends and almost 400 Aramaic inscriptions from the city's buildings and from the pedestals of its statues. From these various sources it seems that by the second century AD the city was ruled by a dynasty of Arab princes:

the inscriptions frequently refer to their rulers as 'kings of the Arabs'. They remained loyal to the Parthians and withstood attacks by the Roman armies of Trajan, in 116–17 AD, and Septimius Severus in 198–99 AD. The city finally fell to the Sasanian King Shapur I in 240 – betrayed, the legend has it, by al-Nadira, daughter of the Hatran king. It gains mention again in 363 when a Roman army passed through the town and found it ruined and deserted. The city was then more or less forgotten until European travellers wrote admiringly about its grand monuments in the nineteenth century. German archaeologists led by Walter Andrae first explored the site in the 1900s but it was not properly excavated until an Iraqi team arrived in 1951.

The city covers an area of about 320 hectares and is surrounded by two circular earthen walls, an outer and an inner, with the former some 3 km in diameter. The inner wall is of double thickness and is built on stone foundations within a moat. This wall contains some 160 defensive towers with a gate at each of the four cardinal points to allow access. Anyone entering through these gates was forced to make an immediate ninety degree turn, a device intended to slow any invading army and leave it vulnerable to counter-attack. The centre of the city contains a large complex known as the

Fig. 403 **Overall view of the Palace, Hatra, Iraq**
Parthian period, 1st to 2nd century AD
The vaulted *iwans* of Hatra's palace may have served as a prototype for later Islamic buildings

Great Temple, 400 by 300 metres in area and built from a rubble and mortar core with a facing of stone. The complex consists of two parts – a sanctuary and a courtyard – and contains a number of temples and shrines dedicated to Hatran deities. The principal temple was the one dedicated to the Mesopotamian sun god Shamash but in keeping with its role as a Silk Road city, Hatra also honoured gods from almost the entire pantheon of near-eastern deities: the Greek gods Hermes and Hercules, the Arabic gods Allat and Shamiyah, and the Aramaic deity Atargatis.

Hatra is the best-preserved example of a Parthian city and its art and architecture are a mix of Iranian, Hellenistic and Roman elements. Many of its great structures were built during the first to second centuries AD when the merchants of the Silk Road brought untold riches to the town (fig. 403).

The numerous limestone and marble sculptures of Hatra wear lavish clothes and jewellery and reveal contacts, not only with neighbouring cities like Ctesiphon and Palmyra but also with distant states in India and Central Asia. The similarities between Hatran and Kushan sculpture have been remarked upon many times and it may be that the former was the intermediary through which the art of Gandhara acquired its Hellenistic flavour. Hatra's sculptures are depictions of its deities, its rulers, its military commanders and its merchants. The Aramaic inscriptions on the bases of the statues are fragmentary and often difficult to decipher but pioneering work by F. Safar (Safar, 1951–54), has produced a wealth of information about the individuals depicted and about life in the city during its brief period of

Fig. 404 **Grey marble statue of King Atlw (Uthal)**
Parthian period, 1st century AD
H. 2.24 m
Found in the Third Temple, Hatra, Iraq
(Mosul Museum, Iraq)
The inscription on the pedestal reads, 'Atlw, the king of Natounashri, worshipper of God, blessed by God'.

opulence. A typical inscription is on a statue of King Atlw (fl. ca. first century AD) found in the Third Temple, his right hand raised in the characteristic gesture of prayer (fig. 404).

Smaller sculptures from Hatra are typically in both bronze and marble. The scale is reduced but they are, in general, more finely wrought. Bronze images of Greek deities, including Heracles and Bacchus were discovered at the site, as was a group of exceptionally beautiful marble images (fig. 405).

The old highway beside the Tigris continues in a northerly direction to the town of Mosul, now a settlement

Fig. 406 **The Friday Mosque of Nur al-Din Mosque, Mosul, Iraq**
Completed in 1172
H. (of minaret) 52 metres
The mosque is named after its builder, Nur al-Din Zangi.
(Photo by Geoffrey King)

Fig. 405 **A white marble figure of a female deity, probably Aphrodite**
Parthian period,
ca. 2nd century AD
H. 33.4 cm
Discovered south of the Great Temple, Hatra, Iraq
(Baghdad Museum)
This exquisitely modelled figure wears a necklace, bracelets and anklets and holds a laurel wreath and what appears to be a ball in her left hand. The figure is probably a representation of Aphrodite, the Greek goddess of love and fertility.

of more than half a million people on the west bank of the river. The city is located on the old caravan routes to Europe and close to the Assyrian ruins at Nineveh. Its population is principally Kurdish although there are still Christian Arabs and a small number of Turcomans residing in the town. Its greatest period of prosperity was from the eighth century under the Abbasids, when it was the most important city in northwestern Iraq, until the arrival of Hulagu's Mongols in 1258.

Two of the town's old mosques still stand and are both of exceptional historical interest. The Mosque of Nebi Yunus is said to be located at the burial place of the Old Testament's Jonah. The mosque is built on a mound above part of the old city of Nineveh and has never been excavated. The other, the great Friday Mosque of Nur al-Din, completed in 1172 during the Turkish Zangid dynasty, is famous for its elaborate brickwork and crooked minaret (fig. 406).

Part of Mosul's city walls still stand despite the ministrations of Hulagu's army in 1258, and Marco Polo found that the town still prospered at the time of his visit. For centuries, Mosul has been known both for its carpets and for muslin, the fine gauze cotton cloth that takes its name from the town. Marco Polo was an admirer of both the cloth and of the entrepreneurial skills of the town's inhabitants.

'All those cloths of gold and silk which we call muslins are of the manufacture of Mosul, and all the great merchants termed Mossulini, who convey spices and drugs, in large quantities, from one country to another, are from this province.'

(From *The Travels of Marco Polo the Venetian*. Translated by William Marsden in Marsden, 1948)

The arrival of the Mongols disrupted two industries at which the craftsmen of Mosul excelled. During the first half of the thirteenth century, the metalworkers of Mosul produced dishes, candlesticks, ewers and vases inlaid with copper, silver and gold. Such vessels were prized throughout the Islamic world and were an important export. The second was the art of book illustration, the centres of which were at Mosul and Baghdad, and which reached its apogee during the thirteenth century. The very small number of surviving manuscripts reveals both Western (Byzantine) and Eastern influences and concern themselves primarily with botanical and medical (especially pharmaceutical) matters (fig. 407).

After the Mongol conquest of Iraq there occurred a further diaspora of craftsmen and artists, with centres such as Cairo and Damascus the beneficiaries of their talents.

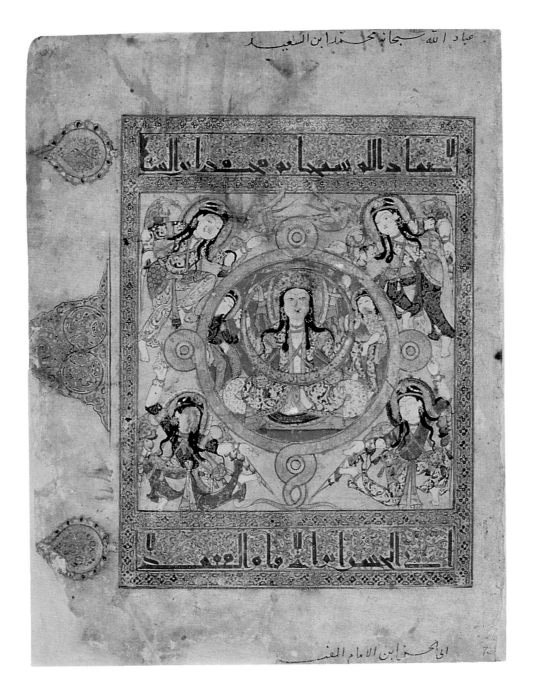

Fig. 407 **Frontispiece to the *Kitab al-diriyak* 'The Treatise on Snakebite'**
Probably from Mosul, Iraq
Dated 1199
H. 21 cm, W. 14 cm
(Bibliothèque Nationale de France)
Seljuk craftsmen fleeing the Mongol advances in Khurasan are thought to have been responsible for the sudden appearance of these painted manuscripts. They recall the painted *Minai* pottery of Seljuk Iran (see fig. 375), as well as much earlier Buddhist imagery.

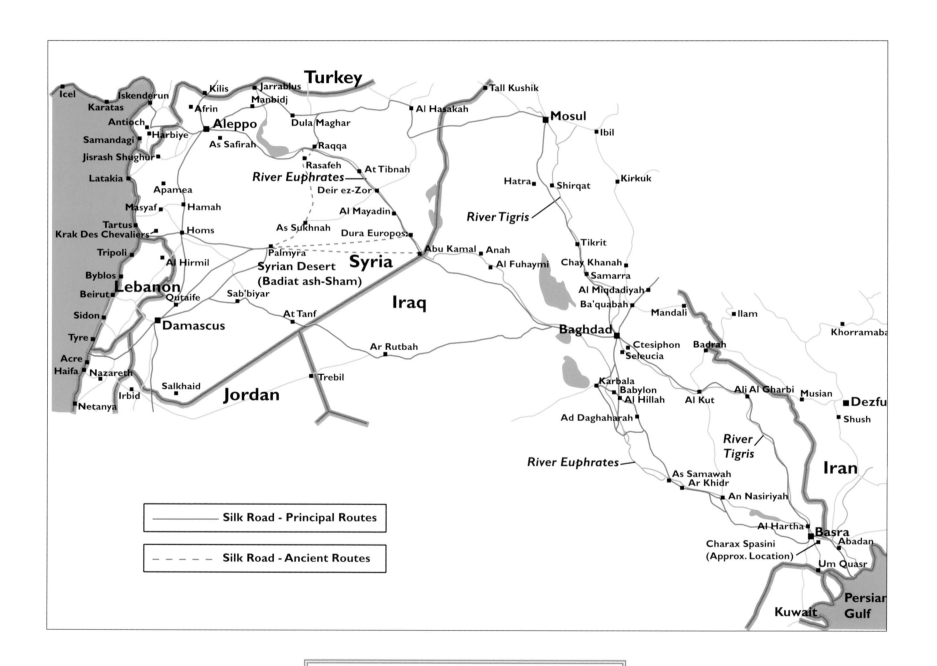

TRADE ROUTES AND PRINCIPAL SITES
OF SYRIA AND LEBANON

CHAPTER TWENTY FIVE

SILK ROAD SITES OF SYRIA AND LEBANON

The route beside the Euphrates crosses into modern Syria near Abu Kamal the approximate midpoint between the western Seleucid capital of Antioch and the eastern capital at Seleucia on the Tigris, to the south of Baghdad. A continuous line of steep cliffs delineates the boundary between the great Syrian Desert plateau and the Euphrates Plain. Seleucus I Nicator (r. 312–281 BC), founder of the Seleucids, established a fortified settlement around 300 BC a little further up the Euphrates; about 90 km southeast of Deir ez-Zor on a natural plateau overlooking the river, and named it *Europos* after his home town in Macedonia. The geographer Isidore of Charax, writing at about the beginning of the Christian era, states that the town was founded by Nikanor, one of Seleucus's generals. The prefix *Dura-* meaning 'fort' or 'city'- was added and Dura Europos grew to become one of the greatest caravan cities of the entire Silk Road. Dura Europos fell to the Parthians in 113 BC and remained a semi-independent city-state (apart from a brief occupation by the Roman Emperor Trajan from 116–17 AD), until 168 AD when the whole area was brought firmly under Roman control. Dura flourished as an entrepôt for the transshipment of goods arriving from the Gulf and from Seleucia (and later Ctesiphon), to Palmyra – some 210 km away across the desert. The flourishing trade between Palmyra and Dura lasted for little more than four centuries: Dura fell to the Sasanian King Shapur I in 256 AD and was torn down, and in 273 the Romans attacked and partially destroyed Palmyra. The site was ignored for the next 1,600 years despite its colossal size and prominent position. During the nineteenth century a number of travellers noticed the ruins and a brief survey was conducted in 1898. It was not until 1920 that it became internationally known, however, when a British army detachment was camped at the site and stumbled upon a number of beautifully preserved wall paintings in what came to be called the Temple of the Palmyrene Gods (also called the Temple of Bel). James Henry Breasted of the University of Chicago's Oriental Institute was in Iraq at the time and was able to make a brief visit before local civil unrest forced him to leave. Dura was more thoroughly investigated by the French in 1922 and 1923 and by a series of U.S.-French expeditions from 1928–37. The French were led by Franz Cumont of the

French Academy and the Americans by Michael Rostovtzeff of Yale University, who called Dura 'the Pompeii of the desert'.

Their findings revealed that there are no significant traces of occupation prior to the Seleucid period. The city was built on an easily defensible promontory with the river one side, deep ravines on two others and the desert on the fourth (fig. 408). It was laid out on a typically Hellenistic grid pattern, much as we saw at Sirkap, Taxila (see fig. 31). The city is built around a central marketplace (*agora*) and completely surrounded by a defensive wall with guard-towers. Its main gate – called the Palmyra Gate – faced west towards that city.

The early colonists at Dura were Macedonian or Greek war veterans (*cleruchs*) who were granted landholdings against a promise of future military service against the Parthians. The Seleucid and early Parthian city was built around the central area. The Seleucids worshipped mainly Greek gods – in particular Artemis, Apollo and Zeus – but Artemis was subsequently fused with the Babylonian fertility goddess Nanaia, probably as a result of the influence of the town's local Semitic inhabitants who served and often intermarried with the Macedonians.

Dura fell to the Parthians in 113 BC, apparently without a fight. The Parthians were broad-minded masters and Greek continued to be used as the official language. The language of Jesus- the Semitic tongue, Aramaic- was used in the western part of the empire and became the *lingua franca* of the merchants of this part of the Silk Road. The Parthians also tolerated the entire pantheon of deities- Greek, Babylonian, Aramaic, Arabic and Phoenician are all represented in Dura's temples, as are local gods who could ensure a good harvest and abundant rainfall. The Parthians rebuilt the city's largest temple – dedicated to Artemis-Nanaia – and erected new ones dedicated, among others, to Zeus and also to the Semitic god Bel. The Seleucid habit of decorating temples with free standing sculptures was discontinued and replaced with wall paintings, and occasionally limestone reliefs, that displayed strong Persian influences in both style and content. The city enjoyed its greatest period of affluence under Parthian rule. The Greek marketplace (*agora*), originally built to an open plan, was

Fig. 408 **Overall view of Dura Europos, Syria**
(Photo by Geoffrey King)

Fig. 409 **Fresco depicting the Ark of the Covenant in the Temple of Dagon, God of the Philistines (1 Samuel, v-vi)**
Ca. 245 AD
H. 150 cm
Reconstruction of the Synagogue from Dura Europos, Syria
(Damascus Museum. Photo by Edward Gibbs)

converted to a vast covered bazaar and the merchants who frequented it built luxurious houses with inner courtyards.

A major earthquake struck Dura in 160 AD, followed by a final period of construction, beginning around 168 AD when the Roman armies of Emperor Lucius Verus captured the city and ejected the Parthians. Dura remained under Roman control for the remainder of its existence and a pronounced tailing off of Silk Road commerce appears to have occurred. The Roman garrison was established in the northwestern part of the city and this section was walled off and many of its dwellings demolished. New civic buildings were erected in this section of the town, including baths and an amphitheatre and new temples erected for the gods Mithra and Jupiter Dolichenus, both beloved of the large number of Syrians who made up the Roman garrison at Dura.

A vast amount of information about garrison-life in Dura during the period of Roman occupation has been obtained from inscriptions at the site and from some 200 parchments and papyri. The documents record troop-strengths, duty-rosters and routine matters but say little about the campaigns in which the men engaged. There was also a sizeable Jewish community in the city and a synagogue was built during the second half of the second century AD near the west wall. It was progressively enlarged and its walls covered with murals – many showing scenes from the Old Testament – so that, by about 245 AD, it appears to have been one of the city's most splendid buildings (fig. 409).

Evidence of early Christian worship was also discovered at Dura, within what is possibly the earliest church of the entire Roman world. The Christian Baptistery appears to have begun life as a private home, just south of the Synagogue, in about 230 AD. Early Christians were still subject to persecution and therefore worshipped in secret but at Dura their confidence appears to have grown to the point where, by about 240, the Baptistery had been enlarged and richly decorated. A large font was discovered, sufficient in size for the faithful to be completely immersed, and above it a painting of Christ as the Good Shepherd. The other walls contained scenes from the Bible, including: David and Goliath, the Samaritan Woman at the Well, the Healing of a Lame Man, and Jesus and Peter Walking on Water. Useful comparisons may be made with portrayals of episodes from the Buddha's lives (known as *jatakas*), in Kushan sculpture (see fig. 47).

One of the most important finds from the period of Roman occupation was made by Franz Cumont at the Tower of Archers, beside the Temple of the Palmyrene Gods. The tower was so named because of the large number of arrows found at the site and a shield, made from wood and leather, represents an early notion of a map. The shield had been decorated with a ship and a list of stations between the Black Sea and Syria and it is clear that the owner was a legionary soldier who had kept a record of each stage of his campaign marches.

The religious and cultural diversity of Dura Europos is reflected in the finds at the necropolis. There were two types of mausoleum at Dura- towers similar to those at Palmyra and underground tombs. The items found in these tombs provide a clear picture of life for the citizens of Dura. They wore clothes of wool and cotton, some with coloured borders, and on rare occasions Chinese silk. Their shoes were of leather or straw and both men and women wore bronze, silver and gold jewellery. During the Parthian period green-glazed pottery was imported in large quantities but during the Roman period, apart from a large silver vase with a bacchanalian motif, there are relatively few imported items. It is clear, therefore, that economic activity had fallen to a fairly modest level by the Roman era.

Dura's history was short and its end both sudden and violent. In 253 the city seems to have been captured and held for a brief period by the Sasanian King Shapur I. The occupation appears to have been brief and the inhabitants subsequently reinforced the city's fortifications. The Sasanians returned in 256 and dug mines beneath the walls, in particular beneath the defensive towers. A desperate attempt was made to defend the city: near Tower 19 attackers and defenders had dug tunnels towards each other and where they met had engaged in subterranean hand-to-hand combat. The tunnel had then collapsed, entombing both sides. With its defensive wall breached, the city surrendered

and was put to the torch. Archaeologists found few skeletons at Dura, apart from those in the mine, and no trace of habitation after the city's fall. It therefore seems likely that the victors took off the inhabitants to be sold into slavery.

The old caravan trail across the Syrian Desert from Dura Europos to Palmyra was still in use as recently as 50 years ago but has now fallen into disuse. Merchants struck out over 210 km of arid wasteland and if they made it – and many did not – they came to the oasis of Palmyra, situated at an altitude of 600 metres on the northeastern slope of Jebel al-Muntar. The oasis is watered by a spring that runs from Jebel al-Muntar and has been a caravan stop on the road between the Mediterranean and Mesopotamia for at least four millennia.

Palmyra

'Palmyra, a town famous for its situation, the richness of its soil and its agreeable waters, is surrounded by a vast belt of sand. Virtually cut off by nature from the rest of the world, she enjoys independence though lying between the two powerful empires of both Rome and Parthia. When there is discord the first thoughts of both of these are for her.'

(Pliny the Elder, *Natural History*)

Palmyra's correct name is actually Tadmor, a Semitic word still in use today and apparently meaning, 'to protect'. The city is referred as Palmyra in Greco-Latin sources, probably because of the large number of date palms in the area. The earliest reference to Tadmor was in a cuneiform document from Mari on the Euphrates, dated to the eighteenth century BC but apart from a few pottery shards in the courtyard of the Temple of Bel, very little from this early date has been found at the site. There is a mention in the Bible of the founding of 'Tadmor in the wilderness' by Solomon (2 Chronicles, chapter 8), but a different Tadmor – a town near the Dead Sea – is thought to have been the place to which the writer was referring. By 64 BC Syria had become a province of Rome but it was many decades before they gained control of the inland, desert region and Palmyra seems to have continued to enjoy a degree of independence. The Roman triumvir Marcus Antonius advanced on the city in 41 BC in search of loot but its inhabitants fled eastwards across the Euphrates, taking their valuables with them. Marcus eventually retreated empty handed. Pliny the Elder's reference to the city (see above) reflects the widely held belief that the town was vulnerable to attack and by the first century AD, it appears to have succumbed to Roman control. A Roman garrison was firmly entrenched in Palmyra by the reign of Emperor Trajan (r. 98–117 AD) and Palmyrene archers and cavalrymen fought for their new masters in campaigns right across the empire.

Fig. 410 **Overall view of Palmyra, Syria**
The Mamluk era Fakhr al-Din ibn Ma'ani Citadel is visible in the distance (see below). The great caravan road from Dura enters the city from the east and runs along this magnificent colonnaded avenue, 11 metres wide and 1.1 km in length.

In 106 AD the town of Petra (in today's Jordan) fell to Trajan and Palmyra replaced it as the greatest commercial centre in the region. Much of the caravan traffic between Rome and Arabia, Persia and India passed through the town and its merchants grew rich. Most of Palmyra's grandest monuments date to the first and second centuries AD when wealth poured into the city. In about 129 AD, Emperor Hadrian visited Palmyra and declared it a free city with the power to collect taxes and run its own financial affairs. There are several dozen Palmyrene, or dual Palmyrene-Greek inscriptions from this period referring to the activities of merchants on Corinthian columns ranged along the city's main thoroughfares. On the columns are ledges for the statues to which the inscriptions refer. One example, dated 193 AD, typifies the great respect accorded the town's merchants:

> *'This statue is that of Taimarsu son of Taima son of Moqimu Garba, chief of the caravan, which has been made for him by the members of the caravan who came up with him from Charax, because he saved them (their) expenses, three hundred denarii of gold, ancient currency, and was well pleasing to them: to his honour, and to the honour of Yannai and Abdibol his sons. In the month Nisan, the year 504' (193 AD)*

(Quoted in Meyers, 1997)

The first two centuries of the Christian era were the period of Palmyra's greatest prosperity. Based on inscriptions it appears that during this period, Palmyrene merchants favoured the route that went across the Syrian Desert to Dura Europos and passed down the Euphrates – either by boat* of by camel – to Charax Spasini, just south of Basra at the head of the Persian Gulf. On the way down the Euphrates the merchants of Palmyra stopped at Vologesias, a town founded near Ctesiphon in the first century AD. They would then sail from Charax to India, often in their own fleets of ships, shunning the land route across Persia as too dangerous. Caravans were financed and sent out from Palmyra by individual merchants, by groups of investors or, on occasion, by the city authorities. Caravan leaders (*synodiarchs*) appear to have come, for the most part, from one clan: a number of inscriptions refer to men of different generations of the same family setting out with goods. A tariff of customs duties levied by the Palmyrene authorities is preserved in the Hermitage Museum. Dated 137 AD, it states, among other things, that caravans returning without a load will be taxed at the rate of one *denarius*; and that butter carried in alabaster vessels was charged 25 *denarii* while butter conveyed in skins was charged only 13 d*enarii*. Other local taxes (listed in Stark, 1966) were levied upon water consumption, hides and furs, leather tanning, slaves and prostitutes.

* Many of the traditional vessels used for ferrying goods down the Euphrates were in use until very recently and some are still in use today. The basic types include *muhaylahs* and *safinahs*, sailing craft of up to 25 metres in length; *kalaks* (a timber raft supported by goatskins); b*alams* (narrow, flat-bottomed boats), and huge coracles known as *gufas*.

Fig. 411 **White limestone funerary reliefs of a Palmyrene merchant or noble and his wife**
2nd century AD
(Palmyra Museum. Photos by Edward Gibbs)
Palmyra's limestone sculptures comprise three types – civic, religious and funerary – and reveal influences from the Greek and Roman worlds, from Parthian Iran and also from India.

By the first century AD it had been discovered that the monsoon winds could be used to make the round trip to India: they blow steadily from the southwest across the Indian Ocean from March to September and from the northeast from November to January. This phenomenon, believed to have been discovered by a Greek mariner named Hippalus, enabled ships to strike out across the Indian Ocean instead of following the coastline, thereby shaving months off the journey. By the end of the first century, Roman ships were trading as far as the Malay Archipelago and the Mekong Delta. Roman coins and other artefacts were unearthed at Oceo in Vietnam's Mekong Delta during the 1940's by Louis Malleret. Oceo was the likely capital of the Funan kingdom and Malleret's discoveries are evidence of a high level of commercial activity between the two states. In 166 AD, a merchant representing himself as an envoy of the Roman emperor Marcus Aurelius arrived at the Indochinese port of Tonkin with what the Chinese annals refer to rather sniffily as containing 'no precious stones whatever'. A Roman glass bowl, discovered in the Chinese province of Guangdong in 1954, is further evidence of extensive trade links from an early date (fig. 96), although in this instance it is possible that the bowl made its way through many pairs of hands along land routes.

One of the most important sources of information about the ports and products of Roman sea trade with the East is *The Periplus of the Erythraen (Red) Sea*, a handbook for merchants, apparently written by an Egyptian Greek mariner during the first century AD. It describes the maritime routes through the Red Sea and Indian Ocean and outlines some of the merchandise carried. From the *Periplus* and other sources, it is clear that the Romans* (including their vassals the Pamyrenes), were now able to trade independently without relying on the Parthians who had up to this point both dominated land based commerce and extracted hefty brokerage fees from its participants. Roman ships carried tin, copper, glass, amber, coral, wool, silver and gold plate, and large numbers of coins eastwards while drugs and spices, silks†, cottons, exotic animals, furs, pearls, ivory, tortoiseshell, precious and semi-precious stones came west. The Kushans were energetic consumers of Roman products and they also secured the lion's share of Chinese and Central Asian goods for export from their ports. The Kushans' main port was at Barbaricum on the Indus and a number of Kushan coins have been found at Charax Spasini.

In addition to Barbaricum, the *Periplus* lists the following trading ports around the coast of India to which Roman ships are said to have gone on a regular basis. Roman coins of gold and silver, a small amount of glass and a quantity of pottery (including Mediterranean amphorae) have been found at various sites around the coast of India, evidence of extensive commercial relations:

BARYGAZA   (modern Bharuch, Gujarat)
CALLIENA   (Kalyan, near Bombay)
MUZIRIS   (probably Cranganore, Kerala- near Cochin on the Malabar Coast)
NELCYNDA   (exact location unknown, but also apparently near Cochin on the Malabar Coast)
CAMARA   (exact location unknown)

* The crews of these 'Roman ships' were unlikely to have included many men from Italy. They were more likely, in the words of Mortimer Wheeler, to 'have been manned by Frisians, Greeks, Levantines, Arabs and others who, like Kipling's Parnesius, had 'never seen Rome except in a picture.' (Wheeler, 1954). For the sake of brevity, when we refer to 'Roman' merchants, it can be taken to mean all those who served on the ships of the empire.
† Chinese silk was found among the clothes worn by Palmyra's dead and a few fragments of the precious material can also be seen in Palmyra's museum.

Fig. 412 The Temple of Bel (also called the 'Temple of the Sun'), Palmyra.
1st century AD with later additions and alterations. Bel was Palmyra's main deity, associated with the Greek god Zeus and the Roman god Jupiter. The courtyard is 200 metres by 200 metres and a Bel temple probably occupied the site at least as far back as the Hellenistic period.

PODOUKE   (Arikamedu,† just south of Pondicherry on the Coromandel Coast)

SOPATMA   (possibly Markanam, north of Pondicherry on the Coromandel Coast)

MASALIA   (possibly Masulipatam on the Bay of Bengal)

During the early part of the third century AD, under the Roman Emperor Septimius Severus (a man of part Syrian descent), Palmyra reached its greatest size – about 12 km in diameter. Severus's son Caracalla elevated the city to the rank of Roman Colony, thereby granting the inhabitants an exemption from the payment of taxes and stimulating commerce still further. .The foundation of the Sasanian Dynasty in 224 threatened to bring trade to a halt. Its founder Ardashir I blocked access to the mouths of the Tigris and Euphrates, severing the Palmyrenes' favoured route to India via Charax. From this point onwards the more northerly branches of the Silk Road became prominent and inscriptions honouring the achievements of Palmyrene merchants become scarce.

Under threat from Persia, the rulers of the city sought to preserve its commercial power by edging towards independence from a weak and unstable Rome. Around 251 AD an Arabian clan, led by Odainat, succeeded in establishing a more or less independent state with Pamyra as its capital, while at the same time preserving the interests of Rome. By 258 Odainat had been appointed Governor of the Roman province of Syria and, in 262 and 267, after the capture of Emperor Valerian, he led campaigns against the Sasanian capital at Ctesiphon. After Rome appointed him 'Chief General of the Armies of the East' Odainat proclaimed himself 'King of Kings' but his ambitions came to an abrupt

† The extensive remains of a Roman settlement have been discovered at Arikamedu.

end during campaigns in Cappadocia in 267–68, when both he and his son and heir were assassinated. His wife Zenobia assumed power on behalf of his second son- then too young to ascend the throne. Zenobia was one of the most charismatic, beautiful and headstrong women in history but the mixture of legend and fact that surrounds her has become difficult to penetrate. What is known is that she was beautiful, with pale skin and dark eyes, was well versed in history and politics and was an accomplished horsewoman who rode with her armies. During the minority of her son Wahballat Zenobia became regent, giving herself the title of 'Queen' while her son acquired the titles of his father. Palmyrene armies soon conquered all of Syria and occupied Anatolia and Egypt; Zenobia proclaimed her son Augustus and herself Augusta- rulers of the entire Roman Empire. Emperor Aurelian retaliated by attacking and defeating the Palmyrene army at Antioch and Emesa (Homs) and Zenobia withdrew to Palmyra.

Zenobia quickly reinforced the city's fortifications but within a week the Romans had arrived and before long had stormed the walls. Zenobia escaped with a small party of followers and set off eastwards to seek help from the Sasanian king Shapur. As she was about to cross the Euphrates she and her cortège were captured and, in August 272 AD, the beleaguered inhabitants of Palmyra surrendered to Aurelian. Although a small number of Zenobia's counsellors were executed the city was spared serious looting. Aurelian started for Rome with Zenobia and several of her sons secured, it is said, with golden chains. The histories vary as to Zenobia's fate- some say that she died on the way to Rome of disease or from refusing to eat, while others relate that she was exiled to Tivoli and married a Roman senator. Aurelian had left a fairly modest garrison at Palmyra and the city quickly rose up and massacred its new masters. In the spring of 273 AD Aurelian returned and re-entered the city unopposed, and this time it was looted and partially destroyed.

In 297 AD, Emperor Diocletian signed a peace treaty with the Sasanians and demarcated the border of Syria along the Kabur River. Palmyra became a Roman garrison, the hub of a vast network of roads and defensive lines known as *limites* (singular *limes*). The main road between Damascus and the Euphrates was the *Strata Diocletiana* and, under Roman protection, trade once again flowed along it. Christianity gained a secure foothold in Palmyra during the fourth century and a number of its temples were converted to use as churches, including the city's largest and finest monument – the great Temple of Bel (fig. 412).

Excavations of the city's four necropolises – all situated beyond the city walls to the north, west, southwest and southeast – have provided a wealth of detail, not only about the funerary practices of its citizens but also about its political and commercial life. There are two types of tomb at

Palmyra – above ground tomb towers and underground sepulchres. Tomb towers began to be used at Palmyra around the first century BC. The later ones- from the early centuries of the Christian era- were more ornate and decorated with Corinthian pilasters and elaborate friezes. The Valley of the Tombs, beyond the Camp of Diocletian to the west of the city, contains a large number of tomb towers each built for a specific family (fig. 413). As many as 400 people were interred within a single tower, each contained within a burial slot, sealed (in most cases) with a limestone portrait bust of the deceased. The notion that high places are sacred has been identified with the original, Semitic inhabitants of Palmyra but it also exists throughout the ancient world.

During the first century AD an increasing number of underground tombs (*hypogea*) began to appear, eventually replacing the tower as the preferred method of interment. The façades of these *hypogea* were in Roman or Parthian style with interior walls of stone or plaster and decorated with mythological scenes, episodes from early life and portraits of the deceased. The best *hypogea* are in the southwestern necropolis.

During the reign of the Byzantine Emperor Justinian I (527–65), the city's fortifications were expanded and its irrigation system improved. The Arabs occupied the city in 634 and, although its name reverted to *Tadmor* and some of its old lustre dimmed, it was still an important centre for Silk Road trade. During the thirteenth to fifteenth centuries under the Mamluks the city revived with evidence that glass and pottery manufacture were occurring. The Temple of Bel was fortified during this period with its *cella* (central sanctuary chamber) converted for use as a mosque. The Mamluks also appear to have erected the Castle of Fakhr al-Din Ibn Ma'ani, although the emir from whom the citadel takes its name was active during the seventeenth century. In 1401 the city was pillaged by a detachment from Timur's army and under the Ottomans, it fell into ruin. European travellers and writers of the eighteenth and nineteenth centuries, fascinated by both the architecture of the city and the legends surrounding Queen Zenobia, ensured that Palmyra was not entirely forgotten, however, and it is still one of the Silk Road's most impressive and enduring monuments.

The caravan roads beyond Palmyra wind out westwards through Homs (Emesa) to the coast and southwestwards to Damascus. Homs is located close to the Orontes River about 160 km north of Damascus and has occupied an important crossroads for about three millennia. During the Roman era the city was ruled by a succession of priest-kings, custodians of the temple dedicated to the Sun God Baal. A marriage between Julia Domna, daughter of one of the priest-kings, to the Roman Emperor Septimius Severus in 187 AD ushered in the city's golden age. Severus expanded the network of roads linking the town to other cities in the empire and trade

Fig. 413 **The Valley of the Tombs, Palmyra**

flourished, but there is little to be seen of this period among the chemical plants and oil refineries of modern Homs.

Sixty-five kilometres west of Homs is the towering immensity of the Krak Des Chevaliers (the Castle of the Knights, or *Qalaat al-Hosn*). Krak has been described, by T. E. Lawrence among others, as the finest castle in the world and its ingenious design meant that it stayed in the hands of the Crusaders for more than 160 years – from 1109 until 1271. Its highest point is 750 metres above sea level and dominates a strategic pass called the Homs Gap, in the Orontes Valley. This gap is the only significant pass in the mountain range that runs along much of the Syrian coast and the castle therefore controlled the movement of both people and trade goods to and from the Mediterranean.

The road to Damascus has been walked since biblical times. Paul, Apostle to the Gentiles, was born Saul of Tarsus, a vociferous opponent of the early Christian church. He was born to a devoutly Jewish family and was one of those involved in the persecution of Christians that followed the death of Jesus. He experienced a blinding light on the road to Damascus that led to his conversion, and spent his remaining years as a missionary, spreading the new faith throughout the Mediterranean world. After years of travel, including sojourns in Damascus, Antioch and Greece, he was eventually arrested and sent to Rome where he spent his remaining years under house arrest before being executed for his faith. His surviving letters, preserved in the New Testament, are the earliest extant writings of the Christian faith. Christianity can therefore be included in the list of intellectual and spiritual phenomena to have reached the West via the Silk Road.

There was a direct route south from Damascus to Petra, passing through Gerasa (Jerash) and Philadelphia (modern Amman). These three southern towns, all now in Jordan, were important commercial centres- especially during the Roman era- but a lack of space precludes further discussion of their importance here. Damascus, capital of modern Syria, is one of the oldest and most important cities of the Silk Road. Despite centuries of political and religious upheavals, invasions and wars that have continued into modern times, many of its great monuments have survived.

Fig. 414 **The Bab al-Barid, one of the propylae to the Temple of Jupiter**
Roman, ca. 3rd century AD
Damascus, Syria

Damascus

The town sits within a fertile oasis at 660 metres above sea level, overlooking the Barada River. It first gains mention in Egyptian texts from around 1500 BC when it is referred to as Dimeshq- more or less identical to its modern Arabic name which means, 'the northern'. During the early first millennium BC it became a regional capital of the Aramaic states and has retained the status of capital to some degree ever since. Over the next millennium it fell under Assyrian, Babylonian, Achaemenian, Greek, Seleucid and Nabataean control but did not emerge as an imperial capital until the Roman conquest of Syria in 64 BC. Septimius Severus declared the city a Roman Colony during the second century AD and commerce flourished. There are still a few Roman remains in the city, the most striking of which are the monumental gates (known as *propylae*) at the east and west entrances to the Great Umayyad Mosque. The mosque is set within the sacred enclosure (*temenos*) of the original Roman Temple of Jupiter, itself built on the site of a much earlier Aramaean temple. The main entrance to the Roman temple and now to the mosque is the Bab Jairun on the eastern side. The western gate, the Bab al-Barid, stands at the eastern end of the Souq al-Hamadiyyeh, one of Damascus's principal markets (fig. 414). Its Corinthian columns and decorated lintel are now draped with electric cables but are still a splendid reminder of the city when it was part of the Roman Empire.

Before the construction of the Great Umayyad Mosque, the *temenos* walls enclosed a basilica dedicated to St John the Baptist, built after 395 when the city was under Byzantine control. A process that began with the arrival in Damascus of St Paul the Apostle around 31 AD, culminated during the Byzantine era when it became a Christian city with numerous churches and monasteries. A few inscriptions above the southern entrance to the *temenos* and a colonnade beside the north gate are all that remain of the Byzantines' tenure. There is still a shrine to John the Baptist's head in the southeast corner of the enclosure but the Umayyad Caliph Al-Walid (r. 705–15) levelled the last of the original Roman and Byzantine structures within the *temenos* during the construction of the mosque during the early eighth century. The only surviving Byzantine church in Damascus is in the old city- the Ananias (Hanani) Chapel is at the eastern end of the Street Called Straight, just inside the city walls and close to the Bab Sharqi (the Eastern Gate). The elegantly named Street Called Straight was the main east-west thoroughfare (*Decumanus*) of Roman times and all the wealth of the ages passed along it.

During the sixth century Syria became increasingly remote from the Byzantine capital at Constantinople and war with the Sasanians of Persia left the country economically and politically exhausted. With the rise of Islam during the seventh century, the inhabitants of

Fig. 415 **The Great Umayyad Mosque, Damascus**
Built in 705, with many later additions

Damascus welcomed their new masters with open arms. The city was taken by the Arabs in 635 and became capital of the Umayyad Caliphate in 661. For the next hundred years, until 750, Damascus was the sun around which the world revolved and was the destination for much of Asia's caravan trade. The only surviving monument from the Umayyad era is the Great Umayyad Mosque, mentioned briefly above (fig. 415). It was begun in 705 by Caliph Al-Walid who had set his heart on building nothing less than the finest mosque in all of Islam. As we have seen, he demolished the Roman and Byzantine remains within the enclosure but the old traditions did not disappear entirely. Byzantine craftsmen were used to build the mosque and elements of Byzantine church architecture abound. On the west wall of the courtyard are fabulous mosaics showing scenes from Paradise, installed by the Umayyads but heavily influenced by Byzantium.

In 750 the Umayyad dynasty fell to the Abbasids and the centre of power shifted to a new capital, Baghdad. For the next 400 years Damascus was to remain in the shadows, divided into segregated quarters for its Muslim, Christian and Jewish inhabitants. The city's fortunes revived in 1154 when Nur al-Din Zangi (r. 1146–74), sultan of the Zangids

(nominal vassals of the Seljuks), seized Damascus and made it his capital. During Nur al-Din's rule the Fatamid Caliphate was defeated and both Syria and Egypt brought under Zangid control. Damascus enjoyed a new lease of life and new religious and civic buildings were erected. Between 1174 and 1177 the Zangid dynasty was overthrown by Salah al-Din (Saladin, d. 1193), scourge of the Crusaders and founder of the Ayyubid dynasty. The Ayyubids ruled Damascus until 1260 when it endured a brief but bloody occupation by the Mongols. The Mamluk Sultan Baybars (r. 1260–77) defeated the Mongols and Damascus became the second city of the new empire after Cairo. Under Mamluk rule, commerce revived and Damascene artisans produced inlaid metalwork, glass, ceramics and silk of superlative quality for export to the cities of the Middle East and Europe.

During the later years of the Mamluk Empire Timur pillaged the city and many of its best craftsmen were taken to work in the Timurid capital of Samarkand. This did not end the city's prosperity, however. The old monuments were repaired and new ones were erected and even after the Ottoman Turks took control of the city in 1516, it continued to flourish, albeit as a centre for regional rather than global trade.

Fig. 416 **Drawing by David Roberts showing a general view of Tyre, Lebanon**
Drawn in 1839

'I have seen old ships sail like swans asleep
Beyond the village which men still call Tyre,
With leaden age o'ercargoed, dipping deep
For Famagusta and the hidden sun
That rings black Cyprus with a lake of fire;'

(James Elroy Flecker [1884–1915] 'The Old Ships')

The Mediterranean ports along the Turkish, Syrian and Lebanese coast (known collectively as the Levant), marked the *de facto* end of the Silk Road for those merchants who elected to load their goods aboard ships bound for the markets of Rome. Three of the key Roman ports were Brindisi, on the Adriatic coast and linked to Rome by a highway known as the Appian Way; and Ostia and Civitavecchia (*Centumcellae*), both on the country's western seaboard and within a short distance of the capital. The second-century AD Greek orator Aelius Aristides wrote approvingly of the goods flowing into Rome by land and sea:

'If someone should need to see all the products of the
world, he should travel the entire universe or come to your
town, for all that grows, all that is made in every country,
is always here in abundance. The laden ships bring these
products here from everywhere, every year both in the
high season and at the return of autumn. And the town is
like a common market for the whole earth.'

(Aelius Aristides, 'In Praise of Rome' XXVI)

Probably the two richest and most important anchorages of the eastern Mediterranean were the great Phoenician port cities of Tyre and Sidon, both situated on the Lebanese coast.

Tyre and Sidon

'Phlebas the Phoenician, a fortnight dead,
Forgot the cry of gulls, and the deep sea swell
And the profit and loss.
A current under sea
Picked his bones in whispers. As he rose and fell
He passed the stages of his age and youth
Entering the whirlpool.
Gentile or Jew
O you who turn the wheel and look to windward,
Consider Phlebas, who was once handsome and tall as you.'

(T. S. Eliot [1888–1965]. 'The Waste Land', 1922)

The land known today as Lebanon consists of a narrow, fertile, forested plain with a line of seaports along its coast. Its inhabitants were a Semitic people, the Canaanites, known to the Greeks as 'Phoenicians' apparently because of the purple dye (*phoinikies*) that they manufactured and sold. The Phoenician coastal cities were semi-autonomous and run by a democratically elected council of elders. Byblos (from where the Bible takes it name) and Berytus (Beirut) were centres for trade and religion while Tyre and Sidon were commercial ports. By the third millennium BC, Phoenician mariners were already exporting olive oil, wine and cedar-wood to Egypt and importing gold, copper and turquoise. Phoenician scholars are also credited with the invention of the alphabet, an innovation that augmented their commercial skills still further.

Egypt was conquered by Semitic nomads known as the Hyksos during the seventeenth century BC and sea trade was interrupted. Egypt did not finally shake off Hyksos domination until the reign of the Pharaoh Thutmose III (1490–1436 BC). Syria (including modern-day Lebanon) was invaded by Thutmose and absorbed into the Egyptian empire. In the twelfth century BC, Phoenicia regained its independence and for the next three centuries was the greatest sea power in the Mediterranean. Phoenician colonies were established on the North African coast at Carthage (near Tunis) and in Cyprus, Crete and Rhodes. The Phoenicians were skilled metalworkers and jewellers and much of their expansion appears to have been driven by a need to find new sources of silver, tin and copper for their workshops. Tyre was already an important city by the fifteenth century BC and, at the height of the Phoenicians' economic boom during the tenth century BC, it appears to have been considerably enlarged. The city is located on two sandstone reefs about 2 km off the southern Lebanese coast and the two islands were enlarged at this time and new harbours and temples constructed. The skill of Tyrian architects was renowned in the ancient world, and the Bible tells us that they were invited to Jerusalem to build the Temple of Solomon and the Palace of King David.

Commercial treaties and strategic marriages took place with neighbouring states: the latter represented most famously in the Bible's account of Jezebel, princess of Tyre, to King Ahab of Israel.

> *'The tribute of the seacoast- from the inhabitants of Tyre, Sidon, Byblos, Malhallata, Maiza, Kaiza, Amurru and [of] Arvad which is [an island] in the sea, [consisting of]: gold, silver, tin, copper, copper containers, linen garments with multi-coloured trimmings, large and small monkeys, ebony, boxwood, ivory from walrus tusk- [thus ivory] a product of the sea- [this] their tribute I received and they embraced my feet.'*

(Assyrian inscription, ca. 877 BC. Quoted in Jidejian, 1971)

The period of Assyrian rule (883–612 BC) began with the imposition of heavy taxes and demands for tribute on the Phoenician ports and, after a series of rebellions, Tyre was besieged and subjugated in 721 BC. This did not put paid to the unrest, however. During the seventeenth century BC, Sidon rebelled and was eventually destroyed. A new city was built on the site but by the end of the seventh century BC Assyria had fallen to Babylonia and Tyre became a reluctant vassal of the new regime.

In 539 BC, Babylon fell to the Achaemenians under Cyrus the Great (r. 559–529 BC), and Phoenicia came under Persian control. The Persians encouraged the continuation of trade and the Phoenician fleet supported their endeavours to conquer Greece during the fifth century BC. Around 450 BC, coins were introduced to the Phoenician ports and this greatly enhanced the opportunities for trade but it was not to last. During the 4th century BC a series of rebellions took place in the cities along the Lebanese coast against the heavy tributes demanded by the Persians. The desire of the Phoenicians to rid themselves of Persian rule left the way open for the conquest of their cities by Alexander the Great. Tyre fell to Alexander in 332 BC, after a seven-month siege and the construction of a causeway from the mainland.* The Phoenicians were absorbed into the Greek empire but, as resilient as ever, they quickly adopted Greek ways and trade soon resumed. The ancient Greeks do not appear to have held the Phoenicians in very high regard:

> *'Thither came the Phoenicians, men famed for their ships, greedy knaves, bringing countless trinkets in their black ship.'*

(Homer (fl. ca. 800 BC), *The Odyssey*)

Under the Seleucids, the cities continued to prosper and by the time the Roman general Pompey had absorbed Syria and Lebanon into their empire in 64 BC, Tyre was one of the richest metropolises of the East.

Many of the important buildings still standing in Tyre were built during the Roman and Byzantine eras; a long paved avenue leading across from the mainland and entering the city through a great archway. Tyre's main street has recently been reconstructed and gives a sense of how the city looked during its heyday. Beside the street was an aqueduct that carried the city's water supply from the mainland; and Roman baths and a colossal 60,000-seat hippodrome served the needs of its citizens. As with Damascus, Christianity came early to Tyre and there are the remains of a cathedral from the fourth century that was said to have been the most magnificent edifice of its day.

As Roman citizens, the merchants of the Levantine port cities enjoyed both the protection of Rome and access to its markets. Pottery, glass and purple dye were manufactured in the coastal cities and goods from Syria, Persia and the East were transshipped through its ports. Perfumes, rare woods, jewellery and wine were exported to Roman ports and, as wealth flowed in, civic buildings and private mansions were constructed and a network of roads linked the coastal towns. By the end of the fourth century, the Roman Empire had split into two – the western part with its capital in Rome and the eastern part (the Byzantine Empire), based in Constantinople. The port cities continued to flourish under the Byzantines but during the sixth century, earthquakes destroyed Beirut, Sidon and the temples of Baalbek, marking the beginning of a period of great upheaval. Corruption, religious disagreements and excessive demands for tribute created dissent among the populace and when the seeds of Islam were scattered in the region during the sixth century they fell on fertile ground. The Byzantine forces were defeated in 636, at the Battle of Yarmuk on the Syrian-Jordanian border, and 700 years of Roman rule came to an abrupt end. Under the Arabs prosperity quickly returned to the coastal cities and Tyre continued to produce textiles (including silks), ceramics, glass and the ubiquitous purple dye for export throughout the Middle East and the Mediterranean. Between about 660 and about 870, under the Umayyads and the early years of the Abbasids, Persian and Arab mariners were the best in the world. The Chinese pilgrim I-Ching refers to the Po-sse (Persian) ship that conveyed him from Guangzhou (Canton) to Sumatra and the Tang annals refer to the Ta-shih (Arab) and Po-sse who attacked Guangzhou in 758.

During the twelfth and thirteenth centuries, the knights of the Crusades ranged along the Syrian and Lebanese coast capturing and frequently destroying the port cities. Tyre was besieged in 1124 and despite putting up a stubborn resistance it was eventually captured. It remained a Crusader city until 1291 and became, once again, a flourishing port. Merchants flocked to Tyre to buy its glassware, pottery and cane-sugar products, none more so than the Venetians who controlled one third of the city. Although the Crusades ended with the fall of Acre to the Mamluks in 1291, the city was left in ruins and never fully regained its former glory.

* During the Roman era sea currents deposited sand against the causeway and the city is now on an isthmus.

Fig. 417 **Drawing by David Roberts showing the causeway and Crusader citadel (sea castle) at Sidon, Lebanon.**
Drawn in 1839

Throughout the centuries Sidon has been somewhat overshadowed by Tyre – its neighbour to the south – but it is just as ancient and its commercial and religious significance was just as great. The Greek geographer Strabo, writing in the 1st century AD in his description of the world 'The Geography', remarks upon the rivalry that had existed between the two cities from the remotest period of antiquity:

'At any rate, both cities have been famous and illustrious, both in early times and at the present time; and no matter which of the two one might call the metropolis of the Phoenicians, there is a dispute in both cities.'

(Strabo, 1st century AD. Quoted in Jidejian, 1971)

Sidon was built on a promontory with an anchorage sheltered by an island and its men and ships, along with those of Tyre, served the Achaemenians of Persia during their campaigns against the Greeks during the fifth century BC. In return the Phoenician kings of Sidon were accorded great status and built palaces and great temples, including a Temple dedicated to the god of healing, Eshmun and one to Mithra that still functioned during the Byzantine era. During the halcyon days of the Phoenicians, Sidon's prinicipal industries were the production of glass and purple dye manufacture. Some scholars have ascribed the invention of glass blowing to Sidon and so many *Murex trunculus* shellfish were used to produce the purple dye that an immense artificial hill was created.

In 332 BC Sidon fell to Alexander the Great but it quickly revived and came to rival Tyre during the Roman, Byzantine and Caliphate periods. The Crusaders, led by Baldwin I ruler

of Jerusalem, laid siege to the city in 1111 and for the next 180 years it passed back and forth, from Christian to Muslim. One of the very few Crusader structures to have survived in Sidon is the sea castle, built on a rocky outcrop and linked to the mainland by means of a bridge (fig. 417). A network of Crusader sea castles once guarded the harbours of the Levantine coastal cities but most were destroyed after Acre fell to the Mamluks in 1291. After Acre's fall, the city served as a port for Damascus but by then, the fortunes of the Silk Road in general and the port-cities of the Levant in particular were waning.

The north-south section of the Silk Road that runs to the east of the Levantine coast leads up from Petra, through Damascus and Homs to Syria's second largest city, Aleppo. At Aleppo the road intersects with the great highway that leads across from the upper reaches of the Euphrates to Antioch.

Aleppo

Because of it position at the intersection of two important commercial routes, Aleppo (*Halab* in Arabic) has flourished throughout very nearly all of its recorded history. It is equidistant (about 100 km), from both the Mediterranean and the Euphrates, and has acted as a conduit for caravan-traffic between the eastern territories and the seaports. Aleppo is first mentioned in texts of the 3rd millennium BC and, during the eighteenth century BC, was capital of the Amorite kingdom of Yamhad. It was fought over by Hittites, Egyptians and Mitannians before emerging as a semi-autonomous Hittite city-state around 1200 BC. It fell to the Assyrians during the eighth century BC and was under Achaemenian control from the sixth to the fourth century BC. During these years it possessed little commercial or political significance and its chief role was as a centre for the worship of the storm god Hadad. The Seleucids revived Aleppo during the third century BC, rebuilding it as a Greek city and renaming it Beroea. Under the Greeks and then the Romans it was an important commercial centre, particularly after the destruction of Antioch in 40 AD. It continued to flourish under Byzantine rule but was attacked and burned by the Sasanian king Khusrau I (r. 532–79) in 540 AD. It fell to the Arabs in 636 AD and reverted to its Arab name, Halab, but the focus of the Islamic world was then on Damascus and the city fell on hard times. The most important structure of the Umayyads was the city's Great Mosque, built around 715 as a smaller version of the Damascus mosque, but nothing of it survives today.

Aleppo's fortunes revived during the tenth century when was under the sway of the Hamdanid dynasty of the Upper Tigris. A brief, brilliant cultural renaissance occurred under the Hamdanids but within twenty years the town had fallen to a Byzantine army and most of its population taken into captivity. During the eleventh and twelfth centuries it was

Fig. 418 **The Al-Qalgha or Citadel, Aleppo, Syria**
Early 13th century, with remains dating to at least the 1st millennium BC

fought over by the Byzantines, the Fatimids and by a succession of Arab tribes. It was then besieged by the Crusaders in 1124–25 and trade virtually ceased. The Crusaders had withdrawn by 1146 and a new period of prosperity ensued under the short-lived Ayyubid dynasty, founded by the illustrious Saladin. New districts were laid out beyond the city walls, the town's fortifications were strengthened and the city's most famous landmark – the Al-Qalgha or Citadel, acquired its present form (fig. 418).

During the first half of the thirteenth century the city forged trade links with Europe – most notably with Venice – but in 1260 the Mongols attacked and destroyed the town, assassinating the last Ayyubid king and precipitating a period of decline. Aleppo was under somewhat shaky Mamluk control for the next stage of its history and calamities continued to occur. In 1348 an epidemic decimated its population and in 1400 Timur sacked the town but a period of revival was at hand. In 1516 Aleppo became a part of the Ottoman Empire and trade with Turkey and the

countries of Europe ensued. The old sections of the town still contain many reminders of the boom years of the sixteenth and seventeenth century: merchants' houses, richly decorated caravanserais (known as *khans*), and a labyrinthine network of souqs with covered stalls extending over 15 km , all still grace the city.

The 100 kilometres or so that link Aleppo with Antioch (Antakya in Turkey) traverse harsh, arid terrain but the whole area contains as many as 700 ruined settlements, known collectively as the Dead Cities. The ruins date mostly from the early Byzantine period until the advent of Islam, a period when Antioch was one of the richest cities of the eastern Mediterranean. The highway between Aleppo and Antioch contains some of the best-preserved sections of Roman road still in existence.

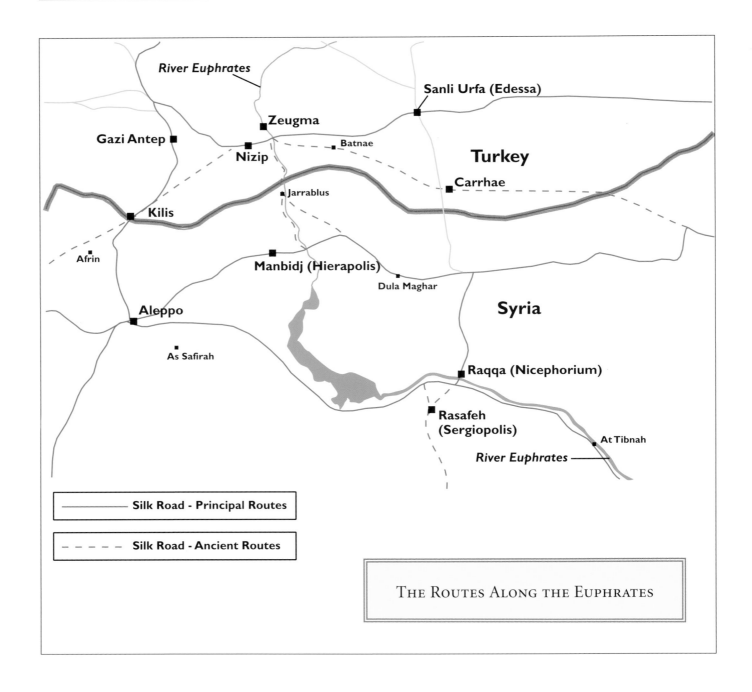

THE ROUTES ALONG THE EUPHRATES

THE ROUTE ALONG THE EUPHRATES TO ZEUGMA

Before leaving Syria, we should briefly examine the old caravan road along the upper reaches of the Euphrates that connected Zeugma (Seleucia on the Euphrates) with Ctesiphon and Seleucia on the Tigris. The post-stops on this route are outlined in detail in the 'Parthian Stations', but with the pre-eminence of Palmyra during the first and second centuries AD the route fell out of favour. It did continue to be used as an alternative to the Tigris route and the Palmyra- Dura Europos route in times of trouble, however. The route passed through Raqqa (formerly Nicephorium or Callinicum), a town founded by Greeks but which did not attain its apogee until the Abbasid period.

Caliph Al-Mansur established a city there in 772, with the same circular plan as his beloved Baghdad. His grandson Harun Al Rashid made Raqqa his summer capital and built an opulent residence known as the 'Palace of Peace' (Qasr as-Salam). Raqqa was a centre for pottery manufacture during the thirteenth century – possibly as a consequence of potters displaced by the Mongols' advance on Ray – but it did not survive their conquest of Syria. A few structures still survive, nevertheless. Parts of Al-Mansur's Grand Mosque still stand, as do sections of the city walls and one of the original Abbasid portals- the Baghdad Gate erected around 772. There are caravan trails from Raqqa to Aleppo and also to Palmyra and, about 35 km to the southwest, the walls of Rasafeh (Sergiopolis) – one of the most atmospheric of Syria's caravan cities – rise above the flat void of the desert (fig. 419).

Fig. 419 **Rasafeh, Syria**
Byzantine period, 4th to
6th centuries
The entrance to one of
its water cisterns is visible
in the foreground.

Rasafeh

During its early history the town of Rasafeh was a little known stopping place, well off the main Raqqa-Aleppo and Raqqa-Palmyra routes. Around 303 AD, during the reign of the Emperor Diocletian, a Christian officer in the Roman legions by the name of Sergius was tortured and murdered by his fellow soldiers for his beliefs. The Christian communities of Syria were appalled by Sergius's death and a shrine was erected above his tomb in Rasafeh. Rasafeh became a place for pilgrimage and the town was eventually renamed Sergiopolis in honour of the (by then) canonised St Sergius. During the fifth and sixth centuries, under the Christian rulers of Byzantium, Rasafeh was built up as a garrison town and as a sacred site. The town's water supply was assured by the construction of immense underground cisterns that can still be seen today. Its principal building, the Basilica of St Sergius, was also constructed during this period under the patronage of Emperor Anastasius I (r. 491–518). The city walls are still relatively intact and encompass an area of about 400 by 550 metres with a gate on each side. The northern gate is a masterpiece of Byzantine architecture, embellished with multiple arches supported by acanthus-topped columns.

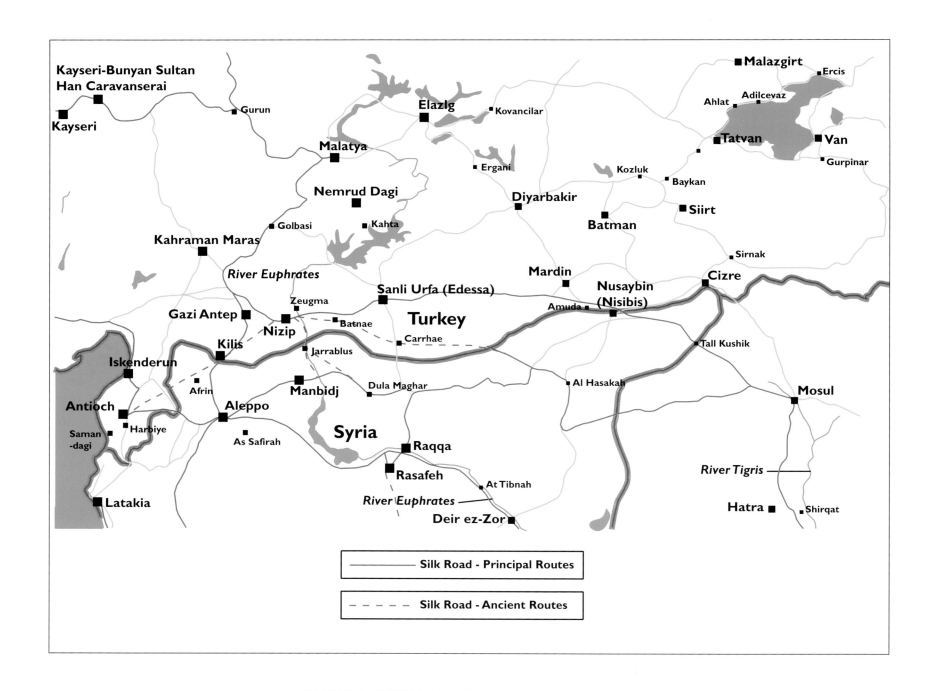

Silk Road - Principal Routes

----- Silk Road - Ancient Routes

TRADE ROUTES IN THE UPPER
EUPHRATES AREA

CHAPTER TWENTY SIX

THE SILK ROAD THROUGH TURKEY

We will look briefly at the two important Silk Road cities of Zeugma and Antioch, both located on highways originating in the upper Euphrates, before resuming our examination of the east-west route from Tabriz (see p. 347).

Zeugma

Zeugma ('the Bridge') is located northeast of Aleppo on both banks of the Euphrates, near the tiny village of Belkis, 10 km from the Turkish town of Nizip, in the foothills of the Taurus Mountains. One of many highways connected Zeugma and Aleppo, passing through the important caravan city of Hierapolis (partly comprising modern Manbidj in Syria). Zeugma was founded by Seleucus I Nicator (r. 312–281 BC) and takes its name from the bridge of boats that once spanned the river. Trajan replaced the boats with a stone bridge and Zeugma grew as one of the most important crossing places on the river- a customs-post at the frontier of the Roman and Parthian worlds. The Romans called it Seleucia on the Euphrates (not to be confused with Seleucia on the Tigris), and garrisoned the town with 5000 soldiers who intermarried with the local population. It grew rich as a result of the caravan trade between Mesopotamia and Anatolia, surpassing Pompeii in size, but its wealth made it a target for raids. The Parthians attacked Zeugma on a number of occasions and in 252 AD the Sasanians sacked and burnt it. It partially recovered and remained a centre of Christianity for several more centuries. Justinian surrounded it with high walls during the sixth century but this did not prevent its capture by the Arabs in 637. The last mention of Zeugma occurs in 1048. The site is renowned for its exquisite mosaic pavements and for its statuary, but in the autumn of 2000 the site was partially inundated by the reservoir created by the Birecik Hydroelectric Dam.

There was a network of excellent roads leading to and from Zeugma in all directions. The best roads were those built by the Romans for both military and commercial reasons, to allow the expeditious movement of men and goods across their eastern provinces. Two roads ran east to the Tigris and on to Persia – one through Edessa and the other through Batnae (modern Sürüc, where an annual fair was held offering goods from China), and Carrhae. One of the main northwesterly routes led through Caeserea

(Kayseri) – the former capital of Cappadocia* – to Constantinople, and another ran straight to the Mediterranean to Antioch and its port at Seleucia Pieria (modern Samandagi).

Antioch

The coastal highways, the roads from the north and the caravan trails from Mesopotamia all converge on Antioch (modern Antakya), situated about 20 km northwest of the Syrian border. The city occupies a particularly favourable position, at the southwestern edge of the Amluk Plain beneath the 506-metre Mt Silpius, at the point where the Orontes River cuts though the mountains to the sea. It is yet another of the cities founded by Seleucus I Nicator around 300 BC, chosen as the western capital of the Seleucid Empire on account of its strategic position and abundant water supply. It appears that Seleucus first intended that Seleucia Pieria should be the capital but about twenty years later, during the reign of Antiochus I (280–261 BC), the capital became firmly established at Antioch- possibly because of a fear of attack from the sea.

From 64 BC onwards Antioch was capital of Roman Syria but this state of affairs was soon interrupted. In 40 BC the Parthians seized most of Syria, including Antioch, and remained in the city until 39 BC when the Romans drove them out. The earliest settlement appears to have been on the east bank of the Orontes River, laid out according to a grid plan with its main, 3 km colonnaded street running parallel to the Orontes along a northeast-southwest axis. At the northeastern end of this street was the Beroea (Aleppo) Gate and at the opposite end was the Daphne Gate, the entrance to the city's main residential suburb. Daphne (modern Harbiye) is about 8 km south of Antioch and sits on a fertile plateau above the city, watered by springs that also fed Antioch itself through a series of aqueducts. At times, Antioch received far more water than it would have wished to receive- winter torrents from Mount Silpius cascaded down through a ravine in the northeastern part of the city before pouring into the Orontes and the city has been deluged on many occasions. The torrent was called *Parmenius* or *Onopnictes* ('Donkey Drowner') and was only one of the disasters that afflicted the city during its long

* For more on Cappadocia see p. 349.

history. Earthquakes, fires, invading armies and the plundering of its stone for building materials have expunged much of the city's past and parts of the Roman town, for example, are now buried as much as 9 metres beneath its surface.

Much of what is known about Antioch's past has been gleaned from ancient sources and from excavations by a joint French-American expedition between 1932 and 1939. The city enjoyed its greatest period of prosperity from the second to seventh centuries AD. According to a number of early sources the Orontes was navigable as far the sea in antiquity, and goods were brought by boat from the both the port at Seleucia Pieria and from the hinterland right into the city. The celebrated philosopher and orator Libanius (314–93 AD) wrote effusively about Antioch during the fourth century when its population was as much as half a million. His references to trade are somewhat vague but it appears that Seleucia Pieria received produce from Egypt and exported goods to Italy and Constantinople, although the land route appears to have been favoured. The city made money from the transit of goods en route for the markets of Rome and it also exported products of its own- wine, olive oil, woollen and linen cloth are all mentioned.

Fourth-century Antioch was a cosmopolitan city in which Christian and Jews lived – though not always peacefully – side by side with followers of Egyptian, Roman and Near Eastern pagan cults. Libianus did not state clearly his own beliefs but they tended, it seems, towards paganism. His pupils, on the other hand, included St. John Chrysostom who was one among a community of 100,000 Christians living in the city at the time. The presence of Christians in Antioch goes back much further than the fourth century: Sts Peter and Paul both lived in Antioch in the years immediately after Christ's death and the *Senpiyer Kilisesi* ('Cave Church of St Peter') in the northeastern part of town is claimed not only to be the world's first cathedral, it is also said to be the place where the phrase 'Christian' was first used. Until Constantine's reign the Christians of Antioch were subjected to campaigns of persecution but with his construction of the Golden Octagon – the Great Church begun by him in 327 and completed by his son in 341 – Christianity became the state religion. Consistent with its name, the church was octagonal in shape with a central domed roof, and was gilded and ornamented with gold and bronze. It was built in a large open area with a square in front, surrounded by a portico and was dedicated to

Fig. 420 **Mosaic depicting the Drinking Contest of Dionysos and Herakles**
Early 3rd century AD
H. 183.5 cm, W. 186.42 cm
From the 'House of the Drinking Contest', Antioch (Antakya), Turkey
(Worcester Art Museum, Massachusetts)
In this mosaic a kneeling Herakles looks distinctly the worse for wear while a relaxed figure of the god of wine, Dionysos appears to have gotten the better of him.

'Harmony, the Divine Power which unites the Universe, the Church, and the Empire'. It may well have been the prototype for later Roman churches.

The following remarks by Libianus, from an oration delivered at the opening of the Olympic games at Antioch in 356, could just as well be applied to other Silk Road capitals such as Xian or Samarkand:

'If a man had the idea of travelling all over the earth with a concern not to see how cities looked, but to learn their individual ways, Antioch would fulfil his purpose and save him journeying. If he sits in our market-place, he will sample every city: there will be so many people from each place with whom he can talk…'

During the sixth century Antioch was struck by a series of catastrophic events- a devastating fire in 525 was followed by an earthquake in 526, a further earthquake in 528 and the investment of the city by Persians in 540. The earthquake of 526 is said to have killed a quarter of a million people including the city's Patriarch, Euphrasius. The city's Great Church, first begun by Constantine the Great in 327, and almost every other building in the city was destroyed and people from the countryside entered the city to rob the dead. The then emperor, Justin, ordered the immediate rebuilding of the city but in 528 a second earthquake destroyed what was left as well, it seems, as any reconstruction that had occurred by then. The new emperor, Justinian, provided funds to begin rebuilding the city a second time and its name was changed to Theoupolis ('City of God'), perhaps as an act of supplication. The prayers of the inhabitants were to no avail, however: in June 540 a Sasanian army under Khusrau I (r. 532–79) captured the city and looted the treasure stored in the city's Great Church. The church itself, only recently rebuilt after the 526 earthquake, was spared but a large part of Antioch was summarily torched. The city bought off the Persians with a large cash payment and the promise of annual tribute and they departed for home, taking a number of captives with them.

The Byzantine historian Procopius (d. ca. 565) has left a vivid account of the aftermath of the Persian assault on Antioch:

'Everything was everywhere reduced to ashes and levelled to the ground, and since many mounds of ruins was all that was left standing of the burned city, it became impossible for the people of Antioch to recognise the site of each person's house…and since there were no longer public stoas or colonnaded courts in existence anywhere, nor any market place remaining, and since the side streets no longer marked off the thoroughfares of the city, they did not any longer dare to build any house.'

(Procopius [d. ca. 565], 'On Buildings')

Justinian rebuilt the city once again, on a smaller scale and with a considerably reduced population but its agonies were far from over. In 542 bubonic plague arrived and decimated the population, followed by earthquakes in 551 and 557, a cattle plague in 553 and a further outbreak of bubonic plague in 560. Persian raids in 557 and the persecution of pagans throughout the 560s added to the city's woes and the city was occupied once again in 611, this time by Khusrau II. When the Arabs took possession of the city in 638, what they were acquiring was a mere shadow of what it had once been. The Byzantine Emperor Nicephorus II (r. 963–69) recaptured the city in 969, followed by the Seljuks in 1084 and the Crusaders in 1098. The city remained under Crusader control until 1268 as the 'Frankish principality of Antioch' but its trade had withered away and, under the Mamluks, even its great harbour at Seleucia Pieria became blocked with silt. It was damaged further in 1401 by the army of Timur and from then on was little more than a backwater.

The site of ancient Antioch was not fully explored until a joint French-American expedition in 1932–39. Discoveries at the site are dispersed between American museums, the Antakya museum and the Louvre. The most spectacular finds were its floor mosaics, dating from the early second to the early sixth centuries, and a small number of sculptures made from imported marble. The mosaics come from houses, baths, and tombs and (with later examples), from churches. The earliest examples reveal strong Hellenistic influences and the later ones contain a number of Persian motifs such as confronting rams' heads and parrots with ribbons. Mythological motifs are plentiful and one of the best known mosaics- part of the extensive collection in the Worcester Art Museum, Massachusetts- follows just such a theme (fig. 420).

Very little sculpture has survived from Antioch- a result of earthquakes, the recycling of materials and the destruction of pagan images by the Christians of the later Byzantine era. The absence of local marble meant that the stone had to be imported and with the material came influences from the Greco-Roman world. The most famous of Antioch's statues is known only in legend- a bronze figure of the Tyche of Antioch was seated on a rock that represented Mount Silpius, wearing a turreted diadem representing the city wall and with a youthful river god at her feet representing the Orontes. This sculpture was made for the city at the end of the third century BC, not long after it was founded by Eutychides of Sicyon. Although the Tyche of Antioch now exists only as a description in ancient sources, a number of copies were made including a marble example now in the Vatican.

There is space here for only one example of Antioch's sculpture and it comes from the second century AD when the city prospered under the Romans (fig. 421).

Fig. 421 **Marble sculpture of Hygieia, Goddess of Health**
2nd century AD
H. 178.8 cm
Found at the site of a public baths, Antioch, Turkey
(Worcester Art Museum, Massachusetts)

344

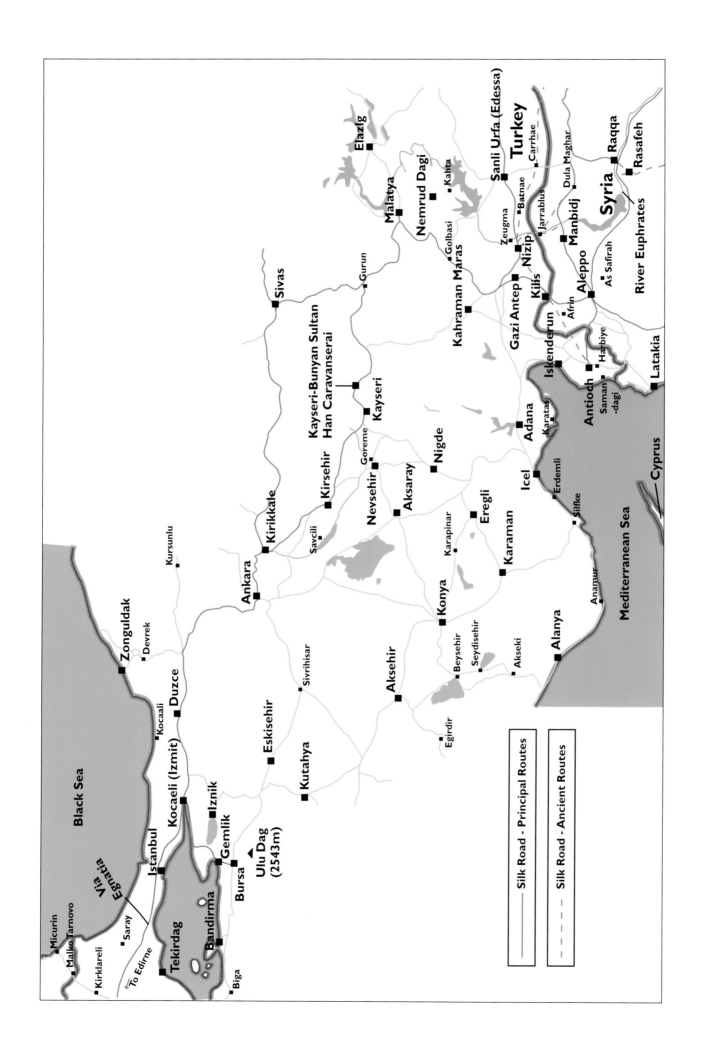

TRADE ROUTES BETWEEN
ANTIOCH AND BYZANTIUM

Silk Road - Principal Routes

Silk Road - Ancient Routes

THE MAIN ROAD BETWEEN ANTIOCH AND BYZANTIUM

Under the Romans, a complex network of well-maintained roads connected the major cities of Syria and Turkey. The main road between Antioch and Byzantium is shown above and leads northeast to Malatya (Melitene under the Romans), then west to the Cappadocian city of Kayseri (or Caeserea Mazaca), then northwest through Ankara (Ancyra), the modern Turkish capital. About 100 km southeast of Malatya, in the vicinity of Adyaman in southeastern Anatolia, is Mount Nemrut or Nemrud Dagi.

Nemrud Dagi

'And whoever, in the long time to come, takes over this reign as king or dynast, may he, if he observes this law and guards my honour, enjoy, through my intercession, the favour of the deified ancestors and all the gods. But if he, in his folly of mind, undertakes measures contrary to the honour of the gods, may he, even without my curse, suffer the full wrath of the gods.'

(Part of a Greek inscription by Antiochus I of Commagene [ca. 69–36 BC] on the reverse of the Apollo-Mithras-Helios on the West Terrace at Nemrud Dagi)

At 2,150 metres, Nemrud Dagi is one of the highest mountains in the Anti-Taurus range and its summit is visible in all directions. On top of the mountain is the *hierothesion* ('the temple-tomb and common dwelling place of all the gods'), of the late Hellenistic king Antiochus I of Commagene (ca. 69–36 BC). For thirty years Antiochus performed a precarious balancing-act between Rome and Parthia and was largely successful until 36 BC, when the Romans deposed him. The kingdom of Commagene lingered on until 72 AD when it was absorbed into the Roman Empire and Nemrut Dagi became yet another monument to a fallen civilization.

A 50-metre high tumulus made from crushed limestone dominates the site and on the north, east and west sides of this mound are terraces cut from the same rock. Processional routes lead up to the summit from the valleys below and along the East and West Terraces are colossal enthroned statues of Antiochus and his protective deities. These statues were once 8 or 9 metres high but they have been decapitated, or felled entirely, by two millennia of earthquakes (fig. 422). The statues come from an extensive pantheon of Greco-Persian deities and include Apollo-Mithras-Helios-Hermes, as well as Zeus-Oromasdes. On the backs of the thrones are Greek inscriptions, called *nomos* or 'sacred laws' that outline the rituals that must be performed – both now and in the

Fig. 422 **The East Terrace, Nemrud Dagi, Turkey**
1st century BC
(Photo by Edward Gibbs)

future – in honour of the gods. On both the East and West Terraces can also be seen the massive, shattered portraits of Antiochus's Persian, Macedonian and Commagenian forebears – both real and imagined – including Darius the Great and Alexander. An additional feature on the West Terrace is a stone relief, 2.4 by 1.75 metres, carved with a lion horoscope- the oldest such representation known. The surface of the lion's body contains a constellation of nineteen stars that have been variously calculated to show the configuration of the planets on 7 July, 62 BC or 14 July, 109 BC. Antiochus's tomb probably lies within the tumulus but despite numerous attempts it has never been located. The architecture and sculpture at Nemrud Dagi reflect the concerns of a man immersed in three cultures: Greek, Roman and Persian.

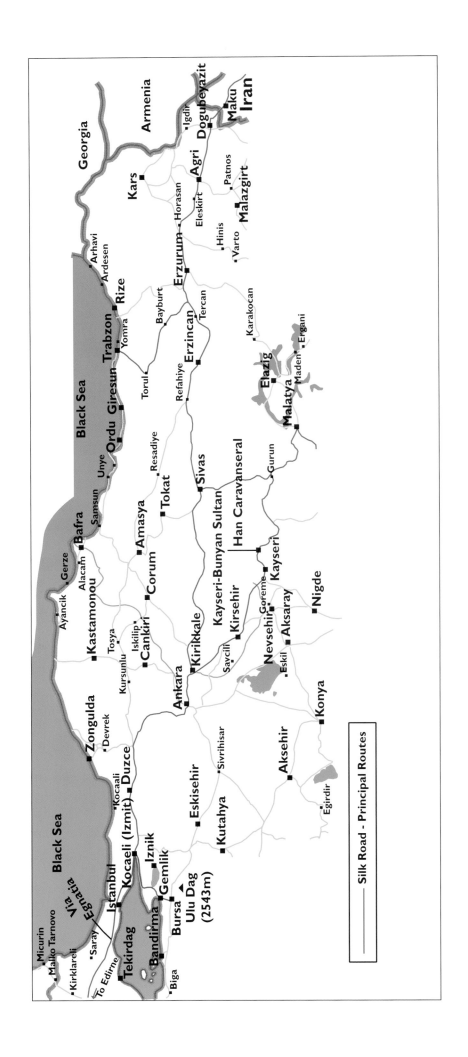

THE EAST-WEST ROUTE
ACROSS TURKEY

Fig. 423 **The Ishak Pasha Saray with the Silk Road beyond**
Begun in 1685, completed 1784 This fortified palace mosque was built by Ishak Pasha, governor of Eastern Anatolia, in 1685 and combines Persian and Ottoman architectural styles with borrowings from the Seljuk era. There are Urartian remains nearby from around the ninth century BC, suggesting that the location has been strategically important for centuries.

THE EAST-WEST ROUTE ACROSS TURKEY

As we saw at the end of the section on Iran, the other great east-west branch of the Silk Road leads across northwestern Iran, from Tabriz to the modern frontier with Turkey at Bazargan, close to Mount Ararat (Agri). Mount Ararat (5,137 metres) is a colossal, ice-capped volcano that towers above the border area. Among the many legends attached to Ararat is the belief that the mountain is the last resting place of Noah's ark although no conclusive evidence of this has ever been produced.

The great trans-Anatolian highway from the Iranian border to Ankara passes through Dogubeyazit, Agri, Erzurum, Erzincan and Sivas. Dogubeyazit is about 40 km from the border and occupies an important strategic position on the old highway. A few kilometres to the east of the town the Ishak Pasha Saray, one of the most beautiful buildings in Turkey, presides over the road (fig. 423).

Erzurum, about 260 km further along the highway, is the largest city in eastern Anatolia and sits on a high plateau at about 1,900 metres. It was an important centre on the old caravan route to Persia and enjoyed its greatest prosperity under the Byzantines, around the fifth century AD. At that time the city was called Theodosiopolis and the Byzantine walls and citadel (the *kale* or *kala*) still survive. The city fell to the Arabs in 653 and to the Seljuks in 1071. A branch of

the Seljuks survived in Anatolia, even after their defeat at the hands of the Khorezmshahs in 1194. The Seljuk state (the sultanate of Rum or Konya), continued until the Mongols subjugated it in 1243, its existence laying the foundations for the Ottoman Empire. The Seljuks revived the city's fortunes and built some of its finest buildings, of which the Ulu Mosque (built in 1179), the Cifte Minareli Madrassah (built in 1253) and the thirteenth-century Yakutiye Madrassah are but three. Erzurum came under Ottoman control in 1515 and the Lala Mustafa Pasha Mosque of 1563 was erected during that period by the renowned architect Sinan (see p. 363). Erzurum's name derives from *Arzan ar-Rum*, or *Arz ar-Rum* ('Land of the Romans'), a descriptive appellation applied to the city by the Arabs.

A highway branching off to the northwest through the Pontic Mountains connects Erzurum with the Black Sea port of Trabzon (Trebizond). During ancient times the city was known as Trapezus and was an important commercial centre for more than two millennia. It came into its own after the capture of Constantinople by the Crusaders in 1204, becoming an offshoot of the Byzantine Empire. It grew rich from duties on trade goods that passed though its port en route to and from Iran and from its own exports- including silver, iron, alum, cloth and wine. Trabzon continued to flourish until the Ottomans annexed it in 1461.

About 450 km west of Erzurum is the central Anatolian city of Sivas, sitting at an altitude of 1,275 metres on the Kizil Irmak River at the crossroads of ancient trade routes from Persia and Baghdad. With its old Roman name of Sebastea it

Fig. 424 **Kayseri-Bunyan Sultan Han Caravanserai**
Seljuk period, 1232–36
Near Kayseri, Cappadocia, Turkey

commercial centre and witnessed the construction of many of its great monuments. The oldest of the city's major structures is the Ulu Cami ('great mosque') of the Danismend Emirate, built in the late twelfth century. One of the most outstanding examples of Seljuk architecture is the Izzeddin Keykavus Sifahanesi ('the house of recovery') built, as its name suggests, as a hospital and medical school. It was erected in 1217 and is renowned for its tilework. The Cifte Minare Medresse ('seminary of the twin towers') is opposite the Izzeddin Keykavus Sifahanesi and has a towering central portal. It was built in 1271, along with the Gok Medresse ('Blue Seminary') and the Buruciye Medresse, all three built in Seljuk style but actually erected by the viziers of the Mongol Il-Khans.

On the old Sivas-Kayseri highway stands one of the finest caravanserais of the entire Silk Road. The Kayseri-Bunyan Sultan Han was built in 1232–36 by the Seljuk ruler Ala ad-Din Keykubat I. It covers an area of 3,900 square metres and contains its own mosque; its massive walls and turrets giving it the appearance of a castle (fig. 424).

was capital, under Emperor Diocletian (r. 284–305), of the province of Armenia Minor. Under the Byzantine Emperor Justinian I (r. 527–65) the city's fortifications were extended and it became a thriving centre for caravan trade. In 1021 Sennacherib-John (r. 1003–21), the Armenian king of Vaspurakan (the area around Lake Van) submitted to Byzantine rule and was rewarded with the viceroyalty of Sebastea. His descendants continued to rule the area until the arrival of the Turkmen Danismend Emirs (ca. 1071–1178), who controlled the city from about 1080 until the advent of the Seljuks in 1171.

Under the sovereignty of the Seljuk Turks the city acquired its modern name, continued to flourish as a

About 45 km to the southwest is the town of Kayseri, situated on a flat plain beneath Mt Erciyes (ancient Mount Argaeus), an extinct volcano of almost 4,000 metres in height. Kayseri sits on the main highway across Anatolia and is only 260 km from Ankara. It was originally called Mazac but was renamed Caesarea Cappadociae during the first century AD and became capital of the Roman province of Cappadocia. The city was a centre for Christian worship

Fig. 425 **'The Fairy Chimneys'**
Rock cut dwellings near Goreme, Cappadocia

until the advent of Islam in the seventh century. The Seljuks acquired the city in 1084 and held it until the arrival of the Mongols in 1243. The Seljuks expanded the town's Byzantine-era citadel, built of black stone and still standing today. They also constructed a number of octagonal and circular tomb towers (*türbes*), at least part of the city's Great Mosque, a seminary – the Sahibiye Medresse (now a book bazaar) – and a medical school.

Cappadocia

When Kayseri became capital of the Roman province of Cappadocia in 17 AD, its new masters controlled a vast area extending across the plateau to the north of the Taurus Mountains. They also controlled the mountain passes and the trade routes that passed through them and the area grew rich from commerce. Christianity arrived early in Cappadocia – by the second century AD it was already well entrenched – and the inhabitants cut dwellings, churches and monasteries into the region's soft, volcanic tufa stone. At Kandovan, south of Tabriz in Iran, there are similar dwellings cut into the rocks but Cappadocia has vast numbers, particularly around Goreme, Soganli and Zelve (fig. 425).

Some of the area's rock-cut churches and monasteries date back as early as the seventh century but most were constructed from the ninth to the eleventh centuries. The fact that so many have survived the Arab invasions of the eighth and ninth centuries, the Seljuks in the eleventh and even the Mongols in the thirteenth century is nothing less than miraculous. There are as many as 500 churches in Cappadocia and many are extensively decorated with wall paintings applied to a surface of plaster or lime and plaster. Paintings were created with locally obtained pigments such as iron oxide, haematite and chalk but imported colours were also used- mercury dust and sulphur from Asia Minor and Afghan lapis among them. The subject matter of these paintings is incredibly diverse- monumental portraits of Christ and the Virgin Mary and scenes of the Crucifixion and Ascension predominate during the early period (mid-sixth to early eighth century). The Byzantine Empire experienced a period of Iconoclasm from about 726 until 843 and non-figurative motifs such as crosses set against classically influenced vine-scrolls (rinceaux) make their appearance. The ninth to eleventh centuries, when the great majority of paintings were executed, bore witness to the full flowering of Byzantine art. The subject matter of paintings from this period includes episodes from the life of Christ and portraits of Byzantium's rulers.

The next major city on the route west from Kayseri is Ankara, 330 km away in a semi-desert region of Central Anatolia. Along the route are the remains of the caravanserais (*hans*) that once provided sanctuary to the merchants who frequented this section of the Silk Road.

Ankara

The central Anatolian town of Ankara has always sat at the crossroads of the north-south and east-west routes and has therefore been an important commercial centre throughout its history. The city dates back at least to Hittite times and when Augustus absorbed the ancient territory of Galatia into the Roman Empire in 25 BC it became a provincial capital. The city flourished under the Romans but it declined in later years and, until it became the national capital in 1923, it was a small, somnolent Anatolian town known chiefly for the soft angora wool to which it gives its name.

The *Monumentum Ancyranum*, a bilingual Greek-Latin inscription from Ankara's temple of Augustus and Rome, is one of the most important records of ancient times. The original version was inscribed on two bronze pillars in front of Augustus' tomb in Rome and copies were distributed throughout the provinces. Most of it was written by Augustus himself and included in this long list of his various accomplishments is a reference to the skill and fortitude of Roman mariners:

> '*My fleet made an ocean voyage from the mouth of the Rhine to the region where the sun rises, even as far as the borders of the Cimbrians,* where no Roman had gone before either by land or by sea; and the Cimbrians, the Charydes, the Semnones† and the other German peoples of that region sought my friendship and that of the Roman people through ambassadors*'.

The last major town on the highway between Ankara and Istanbul is Bursa, the next to last stop on the great Silk Road and a city famous since the Byzantine period for its silk.

Bursa

Only 90 km to the south of Istanbul, Bursa sits in the northern foothills of the Ulu Dag (the ancient Bithynian Olympus). The Romans and Byzantines called the city Prusa and Emperor Justinian I (r. 527–65) constructed a palace and baths in a city already famous for its thermal springs. The Byzantines are believed to have discovered the Chinese secret of silk production during Justinian's reign- a group of monks arrived from Khotan in about 550 with silkworm eggs concealed in their hollowed-out staffs (see p. 182). Bursa became an important centre for silk production and until very recently, silk cocoons were traded in the Koza Han ('Silk Cocoon Caravanserai') every June and July. Silks are still produced in Bursa and sold at the Bedesten (covered bazaar) but, as we saw at Kashgar, synthetic fabrics and cheap imports threaten the continued existence of the industry.

Bursa fell to the Seljuks at the end of the eleventh century but beginning with the first Crusade in 1095, possession of the city passed back and forth between Muslim and

* i.e. the edge of the known world
†Tribes of the Elbe Valley and the Jutland Peninsula (an ancient source of amber).

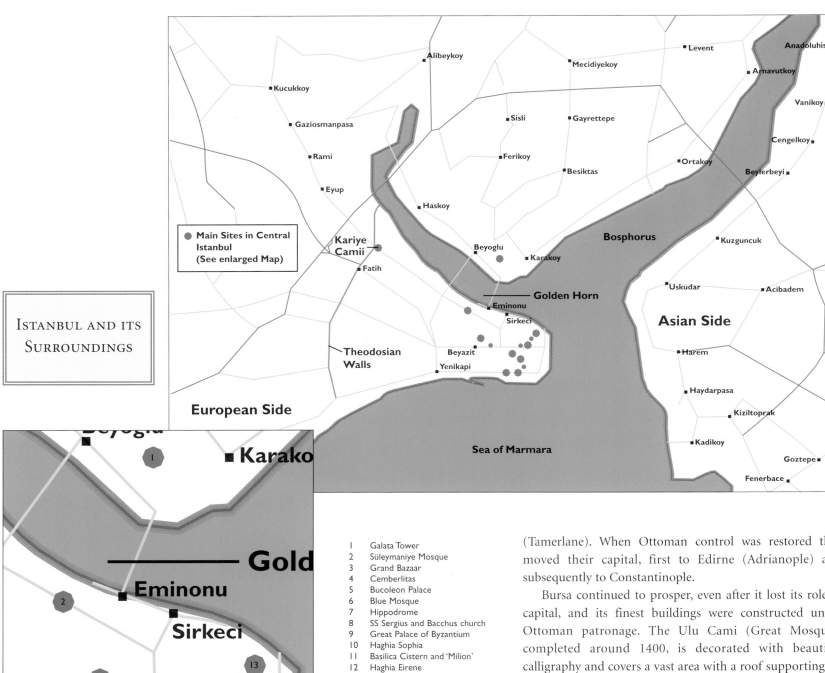

ISTANBUL AND ITS
SURROUNDINGS

1	Galata Tower
2	Süleymaniye Mosque
3	Grand Bazaar
4	Cemberlitas
5	Bucoleon Palace
6	Blue Mosque
7	Hippodrome
8	SS Sergius and Bacchus church
9	Great Palace of Byzantium
10	Haghia Sophia
11	Basilica Cistern and 'Milion'
12	Haghia Eirene
13	Topkapi Saray

(Tamerlane). When Ottoman control was restored they moved their capital, first to Edirne (Adrianople) and subsequently to Constantinople.

Bursa continued to prosper, even after it lost its role as capital, and its finest buildings were constructed under Ottoman patronage. The Ulu Cami (Great Mosque), completed around 1400, is decorated with beautiful calligraphy and covers a vast area with a roof supporting no fewer than twenty domes. It was commissioned by Beyazit I ('The Thunderbolt', r. 1389–1402) whose tomb and mosque complex are on a hill to the east of the city. The architecture of the Yesil Cami (Green Mosque), finished in 1424, marks the advent of a pure Turkish style and takes its name from its exquisite tilework. In addition to the mosque the complex contains a madrassah (theological college), kitchen, bath, and the tomb of its founder – Sultan Mehmet I (d. 1421).

The Muradiye Complex is the city's other great set of royal buildings. Its mosque, completed around 1426 by Sultan Murad II (r. 1421–51), replicates the style of other Bursa mosques and the twelve tombs beside it contain the sultan and a number of his relatives. The highway from Bursa skirts the shores of the Sea of Marmara and arrives at the terminus of the trans-Asian Silk Road, the city of Istanbul.

Christian. After the fall of Constantinople (Istanbul) to the Crusaders in 1204 Bursa became an outpost of Byzantine rule and so it remained until 1326 when the Ottoman Sultan Orhan (r. 1324–60) seized the town and made it the first capital of the new empire. After a brief period as capital of the Ottomans the city was invested, in 1402, by Timur

Constantinople (Istanbul)

'Once out of nature I shall never take
My bodily form from any natural thing,
But such a form as Grecian goldsmiths make
Of hammered gold and gold enamelling
To keep a drowsy Emperor awake;
Or set upon a golden bough to sing*
To lords and ladies of Byzantium
Of what is past, or passing, or to come.'

(From William Butler Yeats [1865–1939], 'Sailing to Byzantium'.* Emperor Theophilus of Byzantium [r. 829–42] had a taste for life's finer things and is said to have installed a tree of gold and enamel, complete with mechanical singing birds, in his sumptuous palace in Constantinople)

The city's aspect and early history

'All those who have seen Constantinople are agreed that this city is in the finest situation that there is in the world, so that it seems as if nature has made it to dominate and command the whole earth.'

(From Jean de Thévenot [1633–67], *The travels of Monsieur de Thévenot into the Levant.* Quoted in Drège and Bührer, 1989)

The metropolitan part of modern Turkey's largest city occupies Europe's most southeasterly point but its suburbs are in Asia, the two halves separated by the Bosphorus, the straits that join the Black Sea with the Sea of Marmara. The European half of Istanbul is further bisected by one of the world's great natural harbours- a long estuary known as the Golden Horn (see map). The point where the Golden Horn and the Bosphorus meet has been occupied since at least the seventh century BC, and possibly even earlier. Greeks from Argos and Megara led, according to legend, by one *Byzos*, built a settlement on the site known as Byzantium (in Greek, Byzantion) on or near the location of the present-day Topkapi Palace. The Greek city was surrounded by stone walls and boasted grand palaces, temples and squares. Until the end of the second century AD the city flourished as a result of both maritime and terrestrial commerce. The Greeks collected tolls on ships passing through the Bosphorus, and also derived income from fishing and the sale of produce from the surrounding agricultural districts. The city's prosperity came to an abrupt end in 196 AD when it was captured by the Roman Emperor Septimius Severus. Severus pulled down the city's walls and killed off many of its administrators but, apparently at the urging of his son, he soon rebuilt and expanded it in a Roman style, literally laying the foundations for the work of Emperor Constantine in later years. Now renamed Antonina after Severus's son, the city was ideally positioned at the terminus of the two great Roman roads across the Balkans – the Via Egnatia and the *Via Militaris* (for more on these roads see p. 365). The Antonina of the Roman era consisted of a walled city extending from Sirkeci to the Cemberlitas district and east to the Sea of Marmara. Within its walls were civic buildings, baths, temples and an acropolis on a hill at the eastern edge of the peninsula. The acropolis contained temples dedicated to Artemis, Aphrodite, Poseidon and the Sun and also had a theatre on its eastern side. The city's necropolis was to the west of the main residential and business area, between Cemberlitas and Beyazit. A large square, known as the Tetrastoon, was situated in the space now flanked by the Blue Mosque and the Haghia Sophia church. The main street, known as the Mese ('central street') and lined with columns, ran from the Tetrastoon to the city gate and marked the terminus of the great highway known as the Via Egnatia that continued on via Thessalonica (once the Byzantine Empire's second city) and Dyrrhachium (modern Durrës in Albania) to Rome itself. The Mese followed the approximate course of today's Divanyolu Caddesi. Septimius Severus built the greatest monuments of this period, including the Zeuxippos Baths, the Hippodrome and the Kynegion – an arena for performances with wild beasts – although little of his work now remains. A possible exception is a stone pillar in a park beside the Topkapi Saray known as the Column of the Goths. The column celebrates the victory of the Romans over the Goths and may be associated with Severus.

The third century AD was a period of turbulence for the Roman Empire, during which barbarian tribes threatened its borders and a succession of weak, ephemeral rulers presided over a decline in both trade and population. Emperor Diocletian (r. 284–305 AD) attempted to resolve the crises facing Rome by dividing the empire into western and eastern spheres- with an emperor for each. The logical capital of the western half was Rome but the capital of the east – comprising the Balkans, Asia Minor, Syria and Egypt – was initially not at Istanbul but at Nicomedia, the site of the modern city of Kocaeli (Izmit). When Diocletian and his co-emperor Maximian both abdicated in 305 more chaos followed, with warfare erupting between Maximinus and Licinius. Constantine, the son of Emperor Constantius (d. 306), defeated Maximian's son Maxentius in 312 at the Milvian Bridge near Rome and became western emperor, while Maximinus and Licinius shared the eastern empire. By 313 Licinius had defeated Maximinus and seized the east but in 324 Constantine defeated Licinius in two battles, both in modern Turkey – Adrianople (modern Edirne, near the Greek border) and Chrysopolis (Uskudar, opposite Istanbul) – and became emperor of the entire Roman Empire.

Constantinople and the Byzantine Empire

Before the Battle of the Milvian Bridge Constantine is said to have seen a vision that impelled him to paint the monogram of Christ on the shields of his troops, and his religious convictions appear to have been a major factor in the the military and political success that he enjoyed throughout his life. The Edict of Milan, agreed with Licinius in 313, ended his predecessor's persecution of Christians and in 325 at Nicaea (Iznik) Constantine addressed the first ecumenical council of the Christian church. Constantine's reign, from 324 until his death in 337, was not particularly long but the number and diversity of his accomplishments mark him out as one of history's greatest figures. Soon after his victory over Licinius, Constantine began work to transform the Greek city of Byzantium as the site for the new capital of the Roman Empire. The choice of Byzantium as capital was made for military, political and economic reasons- the city could be easily defended from attack by the Sasanians to the east and could also provide a base from which to defend Roman territories in Egypt, Syria and the Holy Land. Politically, the city was free of the taint of corruption attached to

Fig. 427 **The base of the Egyptian Obelisk**
From the reign of Emperor Theodosius I (r. 379–95), Istanbul, Turkey
The scene to the left shows the erection of the obelisk and the one to the right depicts captives paying homage to the emperor.

Rome and economically it could be expected to thrive as a result of sea and land based commerce. Constantine brought Romans to the city, where they mingled with the Greeks who had arrived during the time of Byzos, and for the next eleven centuries it was the seat of one of the richest and most powerful empires of the entire Silk Road.

Constantine built upon and expanded the work begun by Septimius Severus and on 11 May 330 the new city – now renamed Constantinople ('the city of Constantine') – was inaugurated in a sacred ceremony. Constantine tripled the extent of the city's walls and rebuilt the Zeuxippos Baths, the Hippodrome and the Tetrastoon. Around the Tetrastoon new buildings were erected including the Great Palace, the Senate, and the four-arched triumphal gateway known as the Milion. A heavily damaged stone column is all that remains of the Milion, situated close to Haghia Sophia at the end of Divanyolu Caddesi, but the arch once marked the terminus of the Via Egnatia and was the point from which distances to all points of the empire were measured (fig. 426).

Fig. 426 **The remains of the triumphal arch known as the Milion**
4th century AD
Istanbul, Turkey

Mary Magdalene's alabaster jar and some of the loaves used by Christ to feed the multitude, were said to have been deposited at its base.

These sparse reminders of early Byzantium are supplemented by the existence of more than twenty ancient churches, many of which have been converted to mosques. Many people still worshipped the ancient gods of the Greek world: Constantine's nephew Julian the Apostate (r. 361–63) attempted to restore pagan worship during his own reign but after his death Christianity became firmly entrenched as the state religion. The people of Byzantium, from the emperor downwards, expressed their devotion by lavishing gifts in the form of precious vessels and manuscripts, icons and even land upon the Church. By the tenth century, treasures from the Silk Road were flowing into the churches of Constantinople and the clergy wore robes of silk and velvet, trimmed with embroidery, jewels and enamels. Ascetic practices also prevailed among the clergy, however; ideas that came from Egypt but also acquired, perhaps, from the Buddhist monks of the East. Perhaps the most extreme examples of ascetic practice in Byzantium occurred among the Anchorites – men who lived in caves or trees and survived on berries and bark. Among these, the most fervent were the 'Stylites' – Christians who spent years standing atop pillars. One of the most famous of the Stylites in the fifth century, a man called Daniel, ascended a column at the age of thirty-three and remained standing upon it until his death some fifty years later!

One of the first churches to be built by Constantine was Haghia Eirene ('Church of the Divine Peace'), which now stands within the Topkapi Saray complex. The original church was destroyed during the Nika Rebellion of 532, when two of the city's factions attacked public buildings and

Fig. 428 **Cemberlitas, Constantine's Column at the site of the ancient Forum**
4th century
Istanbul, Turkey

Fig. 429 **Haghia Sophia Church, Istanbul**
Completed in December 537 and built on the site of two earlier churches

The Hippodrome is to the southwest of the Milion and was once the venue for the city's grandest spectacles. Constantine expanded upon Severus's original plan to create a stadium large enough to hold 100,000 people. The outline of the racetrack is still discernible and the central line of the stadium still contains columns and obelisks brought to the city from Greece and Egypt. The Serpentine Column, dating to 479 BC, was brought from Delphi and beside it is the 3,500-year-old Egyptian Obelisk- carried from Luxor and standing upon a base carved on four sides with scenes from the life of Emperor Theodosius I (r. 379–95, fig. 427).

Constantine's circular Forum stood beside the Mese ('central street') and once contained the Senate house and a column of red porphyry topped with a statue of the great man in the guise of Apollo. The column still stands – despite fires, earthquakes and invasions – and is today known as Cemberlitas (the hooped or burned column) after the iron rings that now reinforce it (fig. 428). Christian relics, including the crosses of the two thieves crucified with Christ,

demanded the dismissal of officials of the emperor, Justinian I (r. 527–65). Justinian rebuilt the church, only to see it heavily damaged by fire during the final years of his reign. Haghia Eirene was destroyed by earthquakes and rebuilt many times over the following centuries and under the Ottomans, it saw service as an armoury and a museum. Today it is used for concerts.

Another expression of Constantine's Christian heritage is to be found in Haghia Sophia (the 'Church of Divine Wisdom' or 'The Great Church'), one of the greatest buildings on earth (fig. 429).

The original church – of which nothing now remains – was built on the site of a pagan temple and is variously ascribed to Constantine's reign or, if the contemporary church historian Socrates is to believed, to that of his son Constantius II (r. 337–61). Socrates tells us that the church was consecrated in February 360 but the original structure survived for little more than forty years: it was set on fire during a riot in 404. The church was rebuilt during the reign of Theodosius II (r. 408–50), formal dedication occurring in 415, but like Haghia Eirene it was destroyed during the Nika Rebellion of 532. Of the second (415) structure, the west portico and atrium were uncovered in 1935, together with several columns and capitals, and a cornice carved with sheep. As soon as the Nika revolt had been put down, Justinian I began work on the structure that still survives today. The architects were Isidore of Miletus and Anthemius of Tralles, and craftsmen and materials were brought to the city from all parts of the empire. The church was completed in less than six years. Through the centuries the building has been damaged and repaired many times: repeated earthquakes weakened the structure causing parts of the dome to fall in 559, 868 and 989 but each time it was restored to its former glory. Three of Christianity's holiest relics are said to have been stored in the church: the spear and the sponge from the Crucifixion and, for a short period, the True Cross itself – liberated from the Sasanians in 628 and held briefly before being returned to Jerusalem. A reverential description of the great cathedral survives from around the time of Justinian I's rededication ceremony in 562:

> 'Thus through the spaces of the great church come rays of light, expelling clouds of care, and filling the mind with joy. The sacred light cheers all: even the sailor guiding his bark on the waves, leaving behind him the unfriendly billows of the raging Pontus, and winding a sinuous course amidst creeks and rocks, with heart fearful at the dangers of his nightly wanderings…. Yet not only does it guide the merchant at night, like the rays from the Pharos on the coast of Africa, but it also shows the way to the living God.'

(From a description of Haghia Sophia by Paul the Silentiary, ca. 563. Quoted in Kelly, 1987)

The men of the Fourth Crusade, back by the Doge of Venice, captured the city in 1204 and were not dislodged until 1261. Many of Byzantium's greatest treasures were carried off to Venice and the Vatican and Haghia Sophia was singled out for pillage on a grand scale:

> '… a free scope was allowed to their avarice, which was glutted, even in the holy week, by the pillage of Constantinople. The right of victory, unshackled by any promise or treaty, had confiscated the public and private wealth of the Greeks; and every hand, according to its size and strength, might lawfully execute the sentence and seize the forfeiture. A portable and universal standard of exchange was found in the coined and uncoined metals of gold and silver, which each captor, at home or abroad, might convert into the possessions most suitable to his temper and situation. Of the treasures, which trade and luxury had accumulated, the silks, velvets, furs, the gems, spices, and rich movables, were the most precious, as they could not be procured for money in the ruder countries of Europe…
>
> In the cathedral of St. Sophia, the ample veil of the sanctuary was rent asunder for the sake of the golden fringe; and the altar, a monument of art and riches, was broken in pieces and shared among the captors. Their mules and horses were laden with the wrought silver and gilt carvings, which they tore down from the doors and pulpit; and if the beasts stumbled under the burden, they were stabbed by their impatient drivers, and the holy pavement streamed with their impure blood. A prostitute was seated on the throne of the patriarch; and that daughter of Belial, as she is styled, sung and danced in the church, to ridicule the hymns and processions of the Orientals. Nor were the repositories of the royal dead secure from violation: in the church of the Apostles, the tombs of the emperors were rifled; and it is said, that after six centuries the corpse of Justinian was found without any signs of decay or putrefaction. In the streets, the French and Flemings clothed themselves and their horses in painted robes and flowing head-dresses of linen; and the coarse intemperance of their feasts insulted the splendid sobriety of the East.'

(Edward Gibbon [1737–94], The History of the Decline and Fall of the Roman Empire)

By the time the city had reverted to Byzantine rule in 1261, Haghia Sophia was falling down. It was rebuilt during the fourteenth century but sustained further damage during an earthquake in 1344, suffered a partial collapse of its dome in 1346 and was finally restored completely in 1354. Haghia Sophia is justly renowned for its mosaics, although of those from Justinian's time only the non-figurative ones survive; the rest were destroyed during the Iconoclast period of

Fig. 430 **Mosaic depicting Leo VI prostrated before Christ**
Reign of Leo VI (the Wise),
r. 886–912
H. 230 cm, W. 470 cm
Above the Imperial (West) Gate, Haghia Sophia, Istanbul
This mosaic depicts Christ seated upon a jewelled throne between medallions of the Virgin Mary and the Archangel Gabriel. The book he holds is inscribed in Greek with the caption, 'Peace be with you. I am the light of the world'. Before him kneels Emperor Leo VI.

726–843, when Byzantium's emperors forbade the use of icons. After the Ottoman conquest, the city's new master began to cover Haghia Sophia's mosaics with plaster and by the eighteenth century they had disappeared completely. They were not revealed again until the nineteenth century and, even today, have not been fully restored. They are composed from fragments of gold, silver, pottery, marble and glass and the depictions are of Christ, the Virgin Mary and the emperors and empresses of Byzantium. The last are portrayed in aspects of humility but they are, nonetheless, God's representatives on earth (fig. 430).

A somewhat later mosaic from the South Gallery shows Christ making a gesture of benediction to Empress Zoe and her third husband, Constantine IX Monomachus (r. 1042–55, fig. 431).

By the time the victorious Ottoman army entered the city on 29 May 1453, the empire of Byzantium barely extended beyond the city walls. The new master of Constantinople, Sultan Mehmet II (the Conqueror, r. 1451–81), was as awe struck by Haghia Sophia as every generation had been before him, and it was spared. It was converted to use as a mosque – a symbol of the triumph of Islam over Christianity in the Eastern Roman Empire:

'By his command the metropolis of the Eastern church was transformed into a mosque: the rich and portable·

instruments of superstition had been removed; the crosses were thrown down; and the walls, which were covered with images and mosaics, were washed and purified, and restored to a state of naked simplicity. On the same day, or on the ensuing Friday, the muezin, or crier, ascended the most lofty turret, and proclaimed the ezan, or public invitation in the name of God and his prophet; the imam preached; and Mahomet and Second [Mehmet II] performed the namaz of prayer and thanksgiving on the great altar, where the Christian mysteries had so lately

Fig. 431 **Mosaic depicting Christ blessing Empress Zoe and Constantine IX Monomachus (r. 1042–55)**
Probably completed during the reign of Empress Zoe's first husband, Emperor Romanus III (r. 1028–34) with subsequent alterations
H. 224 cm; W. 240 cm
South Gallery, Haghia Sophia, Istanbul
Both the inscription and the faces of the two rulers have been altered and it appears that the mosaic has been modified to reflect changes in Empress Zoe's marital circumstances. It also appears that the empress, who spent her days blending perfumes and was inordinately fond of Indian herbs, took the opportunity while updating the mosaic to give herself a face lift!

* The denunciation of the Nestorian sect occurred during the reign of Theodosius II (r. 408–50). At the Council of Ephesus in 431, the Nestorians were condemned for their belief in the human nature of Christ. The remnants of the sect migrated east, first to Persia and eventually to Central Asia and China (see p. 90).

Fig. 432 **The City Walls, Istanbul**
Built by Theodosius II (r. 408–50) with later additions and repairs

been celebrated before the last of the Cæsars. From St. Sophia he proceeded to the august, but desolate mansion of a hundred successors of the great Constantine, but which in a few hours had been stripped of the pomp of royalty. A melancholy reflection on the vicissitudes of human greatness forced itself on his mind; and he repeated an elegant distich of Persian poetry: 'The spider has wove his web in the Imperial palace; and the owl hath sung her watch-song on the towers of Afrasiab.'

(Edward Gibbon (1737–94), *ibid.*)

Constantine's successors continued to add new buildings to the city. Emperor Valens (r. 364–78) built the magnificent aqueduct that still stands today but his reign was cut short in 378, when he and his armies were overrun and slaughtered by the Goths at Adrianople. The desire of Gratian, emperor in the west, to stabilise the military situation in the east led him to appoint a ruler who was to become one of the most capable of all Byzantine regents. Theodosius I (r. 379–95) was a man of Spain and a devout Christian*. He and his descendants increased the rate of urban development-building at least one new forum (the Forum of Theodosius or Forum Tauri), additional fortifications, a new harbour and a new public bath. The city's new walls were erected during the reign of Theodosius II (r. 408–50) and still stand today, despite being rebuilt and occasionally breached over the centuries (fig. 432). They extend for 6.5 km from the Golden Horn to the Sea of Marmara, protecting the landward side of the city from invasion. At the southern end of the walls is the Golden Gate, the point at which a returning emperor would begin his triumphal procession through the city.

* The city of Alexandria was founded in 331 by Alexander the Great, on a ridge between the Mediterranean and Lake Mareotis at the mouth of the Nile. After Alexander's death in 323 BC, the city became the capital of Ptolemaic Egypt and flourished as a multi-cultural, multi-ethnic centre of Hellenic scholarship and science. In its day it was the greatest city in the world with twin harbours dominated by the Pharos Lighthouse, one of the Seven Wonders of antiquity. Ptolemy I established the *Mouseion* (Museum) during the third century BC – a fraternity of scholars led by a priest of the Muses. The *Mouseion* contained one of the most celebrated libraries in history and was not finally destroyed until the civil war of 272 AD. Alexandria fell under Roman control in about 30 BC and was afflicted by anti-Jewish riots and a series of revolts that were ruthlessly put down. The city was attacked by Sasanians in 619, Arabs in 641 and was eventually superseded by Cairo. By the time Napoleon saw it in 1798 it was a fishing village of a few thousand souls.

By the fifth century Constantinople was a thriving, full-developed metropolis with a population of between 300,000 and 600,000. The remarkable mosaic floors of the Great Palace of Byzantium, built on high ground close to the Hippodrome, date to this period. The original building was begun by Constantine the Great but was destroyed, along with many other structures, during the Nika Revolt of 532. The palace courtyard, together with its extensive mosaic decoration, is all that remains. The mosaics date to the late fifth or early sixth century and contain many elements from the Classical world, each rendered with a new freshness. Their subject matter includes scenes from rural life, hunting, wild and mythical animals, and children at play (figs. 433 and 434).

The palace mosaics may well date to the reign of Justinian I (r. 527–65), an emperor whose long tenure was marred by wars, plague, scandal and rebellion but who was nonetheless one of Byzantium's greatest rulers. In two texts attributed to the Byzantine historian Procopius (d. ca. 565) – 'On Buildings' and 'Secret History' – Justinian's

Figs. 433 and 434 **Mosaics from the courtyard of the Great Palace of Byzantium**
Late 5th or early 6th century
Istanbul
The upper scene shows a tiger hunt and the lower, boys riding a dromedary. In the latter scene a servant leads the camel and the boy at the front wears a laurel wreath and carries a tame bird.

accomplishments and foibles are outlined in great detail. He regained North Africa, Italy and southern Spain for the western part of the empire and rebuilt many of the buildings destroyed during the Nika Revolt on an even grander scale, but the public behaviour of his spirited wife Theodora (a former actress) and intermittent conflict with the Sasanians of Persia have tarnished his reputation. Although much of Justinian's territory (including most of Italy) was lost soon after his death, Constantinople was for a time the capital of a vast empire extending from Spain to North Africa, to the eastern limits of the Black Sea and to Syria and Egypt.

Justinian's reign was also accompanied by a burgeoning of commerce, both with the countries of the Silk Road and with Europe. Sericulture appears to have begun in Byzantium during Justinian's reign (see p. 182). Silk worms were raised along the southern shores of the Black Sea and the Caspian and cocoons were then sent to Egypt and Syria to be spun and woven into lengths of cloth. Two of the key centres for Byzantine silk production were Alexandria* and Tyre although Chinese silks continued to be imported as well. By the seventeenth century the main centre for production had been shifted to Constantinople and the industry had become a state monopoly. Lengths of silk were produced in the imperial workshops of the Great Palace and were marked with the emperor's name or monogram. Silk textiles from the imperial looms could not be exported and could only be purchased at the 'House of Lamps'- the imperial saleroom in the Great Palace. During Justinian's reign, Byzantine silk textiles were often woven with gold and silver threads or embellished with pearls or jewels. The motifs of silks from the early period were influenced by Greece and Rome, by Sasanian Persia and, in later years, by the Islamic world. The ruling family wore purple and gold while the nobility wore reds, greens and yellows. By the ninth century court dress included jewelled brocades, often dyed in deep reds and purples, while the imperial family also wore a length of gold brocade wrapped around the body. Silks were also used for church hangings and to decorate the homes of the rich. The story of Liutprand of Cremona (c. 920-72), the Holy Roman Emperor Otto I's ambassador to Byzantium, illustrates just how strict were the controls on the export of silks. During his stay Liutprand was granted permission to purchase lengths of silk but, when he tried to export them, they were confiscated by customs officials. Byzantine silks not from the imperial looms could generally be exported and were prized by the Muslim states to the east and the countries of Europe. Antioch, Aleppo and Trebizond are all mentioned as centres for this trade and exotic goods like spices, ivory and aromatics were imported to Byzantium in exchange.

Byzantium's other principal industries were metal-working and jewellery manufacture. Until the seventh century when both cities fell under Arab control, Antioch

and Alexandria were the key centres for metalwork, with the former also renowned for its fine jewellery. Thereafter both trades were centred upon Constantinople. Those engaged in jewellery production pursued very precise occupations so that, for example, different people would manufacture the gold wire, apply the granulation, apply enamel or set the semi-finished item with gems. Metalworkers were engaged in the manufacture of ecclesiastical vessels or produced state-regalia and insignia. Gold and silversmiths were engaged in very different, distinct occupations while other craftsmen produced more prosaic items like kitchen utensils, architectural fixtures and even anchors and chains. The very best artisans produced objects for the imperial household – the finest of which were the automata dscribed elsewhere in this section. Silver vessels produced in the imperial workshops were, like the silks described above, stamped with the name or monogram of the monarch.

Aqueducts of the type built by Emperor Valens during the fourth century had supplied the city with its water but it was eventually realized that these structures were vulnerable to attack. To solve the problem Justinian built vast underground cisterns where water could be stored against sieges or drought. The best known of these, the Basilica Cistern (Yerebatan Saray), was constructed around 532, close to Haghia Sophia, and has the same sense of cathedral grandeur. The existence of the cistern was forgotten over time and it was not rediscovered until the sixteenth century when a Frenchman, Peter Gilles, noticed that some of the city's residents drew water and even caught fish through the floors of their houses. The cistern's roof is supported by 336 8-metre high columns, two of which rest upon colossal Medusa heads plundered by the Byzantines from earlier monuments (fig. 435).

Among Justinian's other achievements was the SS Sergius and Bacchus Church, now a mosque and built just before Haghia Sophia around 527. It was constructed as a rectangle

Fig. 435 **The Basilica Cistern (Yerebatan Saray), Istanbul**
Built ca. 532 during the reign of Justinian I (527–65)

* One of the most remarkable
trade routes of this era was the
Varangian Road, controlled by
the Vikings, and linking the
Baltic and the Middle East via
Russia. The principal wares
carried along this route were furs
and slaves, but livestock,
goatskins, hawks, honey, nuts,
beeswax, corn, (Baltic) amber,
walrus ivory, weapons and
armour are also mentioned in
contemporary sources. Scarlet
cloth, silks, fine weapons, spices,
gold and silver all found their
way back north with returning
merchants. Large numbers of
Middle Eastern coins, fragments
of Chinese silk and Persian glass
have all been unearthed in
Scandinavia and attest to the
extent of this trade. Perhaps the
most extraordinary artefact to
have travelled north is a bronze
Buddha, found in the 1950's in
the ruins of a Viking longhouse
on Helgö Island, Sweden. The
sixth or seventh century Buddha
originated in the Swat Valley of
northern Pakistan and was
discovered with an Egyptian
(Coptic) bronze ladle of similar
date. A number of Vikings are
recorded as having lived in
Constantinople and by the 11th
century Scandinavians, Russians
and Anglo-Saxons from England
were serving as mercenaries in
the 'Varangian Guard' of the
Byzantine emperors. The most
famous of the Varangian
bodyguards was Harald Hadrada,
king of Norway (r. 1045-66), who
served the Byzantine Emperor
Michael IV (r. 1034-41) during
his youth. He was eventually
killed by the English King Harold
in 1066 at Stamford Bridge,
shortly before the latter's own
defeat and death at the Battle of
Hastings. A rare fragment of
Viking verse, extolling the glories
of Constantinople, has come
down to us. It was written by Jarl
Rognvald of Orkney, perhaps the
last of the northerners to visit
Constantinople, who set sail from
Bergen in 1151 with a fleet of
fifteen ships. By that time most
of the Vikings were Christians
and their destination was the
Holy Land. The old ways were
not entirely forgotten, however:
'Let us ride on the sea-king's steed;
no plough from the field shall
we need;
our soaked prows shall furrow
the sea,
and to Miklagard we go.
Serve the prince for our pay and so
into clash of conflict we go,
To redden the wolf's jaws
and bring
back gold from the glorious king.'
(Jarl Rognvald of Orkney, ca. 1151.
Quoted in Davidson, 1976.
Miklagard is 'the great town',
Constantinople)

containing a domed octagon, with a columned and galleried Byzantine interior, and Justinian's dedicatory inscription is still visible around the dome's base. The architect has overcome the problem of placing a dome atop a somewhat oddly shaped rectangular building by the use of *pendentives* (spherical triangles that fill the space between the corner of the rectangle and the base of the dome) a device used on an immense scale at Haghia Sophia. Sergius and Bacchus were soldiers in the Roman army on the Syrian frontier and were martyred for their Christian beliefs (see p. 339). A few hundred metres to the east of SS Sergius and Bacchus Church, overlooking the Sea of Marmara, is Justinian's other legacy – the Bucoleon Palace – the only section of the Great Palace still standing.

Justinian's codification of Roman law, the *Corpus Juris Civilis* ('Body of Civil Law'), has proved to be as enduring as the buildings he erected. It encompasses collections of past laws and extracts from the opinions of the great Roman jurists, as well as outlining the emperor's own new laws. From the eleventh century onwards, in European cities like Bologna, the *Corpus Juris Civilis* was studied at length and ultimately became the inspiration for the legal systems of more or less every European nation.

Justinians' empire fell away after his death and the following years brought great change to Byzantium. The Sasanian ruler Khusrau II (r. 591–628) pursued a war against Byzantium, his armies reaching Chalcedon (modern Kadikoy, on the eastern shore of the Bosphorus opposite Constantinople), and capturing Antioch, Damascus and Jerusalem. In the north, Byzantine territories were threatened by invasions of Slavs, Avars and Bulgars. Emperor Heraclius (r. 610–41) made peace with the Avars and took the fight to the Persians. He defeated the Persian armies at Nineveh, occupying Ctesiphon and regaining the Byzantine's lost territories. Heraclius reorganized Asia Minor into military districts known as 'themes' and it seemed for a while that peace had been restored. The rise of Islam soon led to a series of military reverses, however, and by the 670s Syria, Palestine and Egypt had been lost for good and the Arab navy threatened Constantinople itself. After five consecutive years of attacks between 674 and 678, the Arabs eventually withdrew without capturing the city, thanks in part to the Byzantine's use of 'Greek Fire' (a highly flammable mixture of naphtha and saltpetre) against their ships. The last ruler of the Heraclian dynasty was Justinian II Rhinotmetus ('the noseless', r. 685–95 and 705–11), a vigorous builder who recovered parts of Macedonia from the Slavs, only to then lose the Byzantine territories in Armenia to the Arabs. Justinian was deposed by a revolt in 695, his nose was cut off and he was banished to the Crimean Peninsula. After the new Byzantine emperor threatened to arrest him he sought refuge with the Khazars- a confederation of Turkic tribes and one of the Silk Road's major trading powers, who occupied what is now the southeastern part of European Russia (see also p. 243). He subsequently fled Khazaria and sought help from the Khan of the Bulgars. With Bulgar's help Justinian returned to Byzantium in 705 and seized back power but, despite success in resolving longstanding theological differences with the papacy in Rome, the main preoccupation of the second part of his reign seems to have been a campaign of revenge against his enemies. He was overthrown for a second time in 711, and this time he and his family were assassinated.

The eighth century brought internal troubles, in large part due to the attack on the use of icons in Christian worship begun by Leo III (r. 717–41). During the ensuing period of iconoclasm, lasting until 843, churches and monasteries were ransacked and monks and artists fled to Italy. Constantinople was soon under siege again by the Arabs (called Saracens by the Byzantines); a sustained attack was repulsed in 718, perhaps aided by outbreaks of plague and famine among the invaders. At this time Christianity was far from entrenched in Europe and had little more than a toehold in Russia and the Balkans: many historians believe that, had Constantinople fallen to the Saracens, Islam would have quickly swept through Europe. Leo III's son and successor Constantine V (r. 741–75) continued his father's policy of iconoclasm but he was also an accomplished military tactician, enjoying successes against the Umayyads in Northern Syria, and winning a series of battles against the Bulgars before he was finally slain. During the reigns of Leo III and Constantine V the capital was struck by a series of natural disasters: earthquakes in 732 and 740, an outbreak of plague from 745–47, and a vicious winter in 763 that saw pack ice drifting down from the Black Sea. Finally, in 766, the city was struck by a terrible drought.

The daughter-in-law of Constantine V, Empress Irene, had her son Constantine VI blinded and deposed in 797 and for the next five years ruled the Byzantine Empire, the first female to do so. Her attempts to court popularity by reducing taxes were a disaster for the economy and she faced military threats from two sides- from the Abbasid armies of Harun Al Rashid and from the Bulgars. In 800 Charlemagne (r. 800–814), King of the Franks, was crowned emperor of the West and proposed a strategic marriage with Irene in order to unify the empire but she had been deposed before the message arrived. With the exception of part of Spain, southern Italy and the British Isles, Charlemagne had conquered all of Europe but he did not achieve recognition from Byzantium until 812, long after Empress Irene's death. One consequence of Charlemagne's rule was the revival of pan-European road links after centuries of disuse.* Irene had been deposed in 802 by Nicephorus- a financial official

---

† This practice recalls the treatment of the king of the Yuezhi, defeated and killed by the Xiongnu leader Maodun in the second century BC (see p. 33).

of her court; but his reign, as Nicephorus I (r. 802–11), was brief. He took immediate steps to reform the economy and to counter the threat from both the Arabs and the Bulgars but his efforts ended in disaster- the Arabs captured Heraclea and Tyana in 806 and Nicephorus was forced to agree to pay annual tribute to Caliph Harun. Worse still were his campaigns against the Bulgars; he invaded Bulgaria in 811 but he and his armies were ambushed and massacred. The Bulgar Khan Krum, following ancient nomadic traditions, had Nicephorus's skull lined with silver and made into a drinking cup.[†]

By 813 the Bulgars were threatening Constantinople itself and disaster was only averted by the death of Krum in 814. A treaty was secured with Krum's successors, resulting in a period of peace that would last for the next eighty years, and by the 860s the Bulgars had begun to convert to Christianity. During the reign of Theophilus (r. 829–42) the Byzantine coffers, replenished by the fiscal reforms of Nicephorus I, were used to erect new civic buildings and fortifications in Constantinople and other cities. Many of Theophilus's buildings still bear laudatory inscriptions, celebrating his achievements. He also brought about a renaissance of the arts and revived the capital's university under the rectorship of the eminent scholar Leo the Mathematician. Despite continuing conflict with the Arabs, now under the leadership of Caliph Al Muhtasim (r. 833–42), Theophilus was a noted Islamophile and many of the buildings he erected reveal Muslim influences. He was also fond of roaming about the capital incognito to hear the views of his subjects, and of mechanical toys. His toys, at least some of which were invented by Leo the Mathematician, included the mechanical birds immortalized by Yeats, as well as the golden lions that guarded his throne and would let out a roar and beat the ground with their tails.

Theophilus was the last iconoclast ruler and his death in 842 ushered in a new golden age for Byzantium, known as the Middle Byzantium period (843–1261). Diplomatic links were forged with both Islamic states and with the countries of Europe and Byzantine political influence extended from Kievan Rus (occupied by parts of today's Ukraine, Belarus and Western Russia), Norman Sicily and Southern Italy to Egypt and the Holy Land. The official language became Greek and religious icons in ivory, paint and mosaic filled innumerable new churches built under imperial patronage. The final schism of the Catholic and Orthodox churches occurred in 1054, when a delegation from Rome and the Patriarch of Constantinople argued so violently over doctrine that anathemas were pronounced by and upon both sides. This event marks the commencement of the Great Schism that still divides the Eastern and Western churches.

A dynasty of Macedonian rulers began in 867 with Basil I (r. 867–86), the son of a peasant, who had the emperor murdered as he slept off a drinking binge. The rule of Basil's son, the scholarly Leo VI ('the Wise', r. 886–912), was marred by conflict with the Arabs and Bulgars but these were halcyon days for merchants and artists alike. His laws regulating the activities of Constantinople's twenty-two professional guilds – contained in a text known as the 'Book of the Prefect' – still exists today and provide a wealth of information about the commercial life of the city. The regulations contained in the text are concerned with such matters as restricting membership of guilds, the prevention of profiteering and the attempt to contain each commercial activity within a particular locality. Syrian silks, for example, could only be sold in one section of the bazaar and could remain in the capital for no longer than three months. Cyril Mango (Mango, 1994) summarises some of the restrictions placed on members of the textile trade. Textile workers were especially tightly regulated and divided into six different categories: the vestiopratai (traders in precious stuffs), the prandiopratai (dealers in Syrian imports), metaxopratai (raw silk traders), the katartarioi (who worked the silk), serikarioi (who sewed the silk) and the othoniopratai (linen traders). Members of one occupation were not permitted to switch to another, transactions over a certain amount had to be declared and certain goods – the purple cloth of the imperial family for example – could not be exported. The metaxopratai were not permitted to buy their merchandise outside of city or to sell them to Jewish merchants who would then export them. Leo's other great accomplishment was his completion of the canon of imperial laws, begun by his father, which became the legal code of the empire. Despite four marriages, Leo failed to produce an heir and was succeeded by his brother and co-emperor Alexander. Leo is immortalized in one of Haghia Sophia's most outstanding mosaics, above the West Gate (see fig. 430).

Macedonians ruled Byzantium for the next two centuries during which territory was acquired from the Armenians, the Arab threat was contained and Byzantine influence in the Balkans and Russia was increased. The Bulgars were finally defeated in 1014 by Basil II (r. 976–1025), an outstanding ruler known as 'the Bulgar Slayer'. Basil II died without an heir and, although his relatives managed to preserve the Macedonian line for another 56 years, Byzantium was ruled by a succession of weak hedonists who squandered the empire's resources and paid insufficient attention to its frontiers. From the time of Basil's death in 1025 to the accession of Alexius I of the Comnenus family in 1081, there were no fewer then thirteen rulers of Byzantium, including Basil's nieces, Zoe and Theodora who each ruled both jointly and individually. The vain, ambitious Zoe (r. 1028–50) was married to three different emperors: Romanus III Argyrus (ruled 1028-34), Michael IV (1034-41), and to Constantine IX Monomachus (1042–55). The machinations of Empress Zoe, who is still to be seen in one of Haghia Sophia's mosaics (fig. 431), were manifold and complex. She poisoned at least one of her husbands (the first), had his successor (Michael V, r. 1041–42) deposed and blinded, and engaged in intrigues that were truly *Byzantine.*

Throughout these years Byzantium seemed oblivious to the relentless rise in the east of the Seljuks, Turkic peoples of the Oguz (Ghuzz) tribe of Central Asia. The Seljuks had captured northern Persia around 1040, Baghdad in 1055 and had ventured as far as Kayseri (Caesarea) by 1067. The Byzantine Emperor Romanus IV Diogenes (r. 1067–71) assembled an immense army in 1071 and met the Seljuks at Manzikert (modern Malazkirt, north of Lake Van in eastern Anatolia). Romanus was defeated and captured by the Seljuk army of Sultan Alp Arslan and was not released until a large ransom had been paid. During his incarceration he had been deposed by his stepson Michael VII (r. 1071–78). When he finally returned to Constantinople Romanus was blinded and died in exile the following year. After the Battle of Manzikert the Byzantine Empire began a slow process of disintegration and Anatolia was opened up to Turkish conquest and settlement, a process that would ultimately lead to the foundation of the Ottoman Empire.

A degree of stability returned in 1081, when the new emperor Alexius I Comnenus (r. 1081–1118) ushered in a century of Comnenus family rule. Alexius faced a raft of problems, including a continuing Seljuk threat, advances by the Normans under Robert Guiscard in southern Italy and a new menace from yet another group of Turkic nomads – the Pechenegs – who had moved south from their lands to the north of the Black Sea and, in the winter of 1090–91, laid siege to Constantinople itself. Alexius sought help from another nomadic tribe, the Kumans, and in April 1091, the Pechenegs were attacked and virtually annihilated.

The Norman threat was also dispelled, with the assistance of the Venetians, in exchange for trade concessions, marking the beginning of Venice's commercial activity in the East. In 1095 Pope Urban II responded to Alexius's call for help against the forces of Islam and his rallying cry brought the knights of the First Crusade to the Holy Land. Feudal lords like Godfrey of Bouillon, Duke of Lower Lorraine, and Robert, Duke of Normandy (the son of William Conqueror) who led a force with thousands of knights and infantrymen, answered the call to arms but there were also visionaries like Peter the Hermit, who arrived in 1096 with a ragtag army of ill-armed followers. The Crusaders recaptured Antioch in 1098 and Jerusalem in 1099 and colonized the Syrian and Palestinian coast but, although a limit was placed on Seljuk expansion, relations with Byzantium quickly deteriorated and remained fraught from that time onward. In 1142, Raymond – ruler of the Crusader principality of Antioch – refused to cede his territories to the then emperor of Byzantium, John II Comnenus (r. 1118–43). After John's untimely death in 1143, Raymond made a brief, unsuccessful attempt to invade Cilicia (a

district of southern Anatolia). The new emperor Manuel I Comnenus (r. 1143–80) endeavoured to regain the Byzantine territories in Italy from the Normans but was defeated at Brindisi in 1156. He was more successful in his campaigns in Cilicia and, in 1159, also forced the Latin rulers of Antioch and Jerusalem to accept Byzantine suzerainty.

The Second Crusade passed through Asia Minor in 1146 but the intemperate behaviour of its armies generated great resentment amongst the populace. A perpetual shifting of loyalties between the various powers in the region marked Manuel I's long reign. This process culminated in 1176 after Frederick I Barbarossa, German king and Holy Roman emperor (r. 1152–90), had urged the Seljuk Sultan Kilidj Arslan to march on Constantinople. Manuel I counter-attacked, leading a vast army into Seljuk territory, but it was outflanked and routed at Myriokephalon, southeast of modern Ankara. Further disasters were to follow- in 1185, Sicilian Normans led by William II invaded Greece and occupied Thessalonica, the second city of the Byzantine Empire. The Normans were soon driven out but the populace of Constantinople turned on Andronicus I (r. 1183–85), the last of the Comnenian rulers and put him to death. In 1186 there was a revolt among the Bulgars and in 1187, Jerusalem fell to Saladin- an event that brought about the Third Crusade. Frederick Barbarossa, whose publicly stated aim was now the conquest of Byzantium, led the crusade but his plans were thwarted by events. After defeating the Seljuks, Barbarossa's Crusaders made for the Levant but he was drowned while crossing a river. In 1191, his successor Richard I 'the Lion-Heart' of England captured Byzantine-held Cyprus as well as Acre from the Saracens and secured a peace treaty with Saladin that would hold for the next five years.

After the Comnenus dynasty ended in 1185, its first successors – Isaac II Angelus (r. 1185–95 and 1203–04) and his brother Alexius III (r. 1195–1203) – were unable to regain any of the lost territories or to check the growing threat to Byzantium's borders. Despite a victory over the Serbs in 1190, their armies were beaten in 1195 and 1196 by the Bulgarians and Henry VI, successor to Frederick Barbarossa, was only prevented from attacking Byzantium when its rulers agreed to pay an annual tribute of 1,600 pounds of gold. Henry died in 1197 but the Doge of Venice, Enrico Dandolo, saw an opportunity to secure commercial dominance for the Venetians in the Eastern Mediterranean. Plans for a Fourth Crusade began to grow, encouraged by both the Doge and by a new Pope – Innocent III – who sought to drive the Muslims from the Holy Land for good and to integrate the Catholic and Orthodox churches.

The knights of the Fourth Crusade assembled at Venice in 1201 and in June 1203 their fleet arrived off Constantinople. They first captured the suburb of Galata, on the north side of the Golden Horn, and on Good Friday 1204 entered the main part of the city. Constantinople endured three days of pillage with much of its populace fleeing to the provinces. On 16 May Baldwin of Flanders was crowned as Latin Emperor of Byzantium, the beginning of more than half a century of Crusader rule. Edward Gibbon's description of the looting of Haghia Sophia (p. 354) is but one illustration of a glorious city at its nadir. Robert de Clari, a participant in the Fourth Crusade, has left a first-hand account of the treasures discovered in the Bucoleon Palace:

'And the palace of Boukoleon [Bucoleon] was very rich… Within this palace, which was held by the marquis, there were fully five hundred halls, all connected with one another and all made with gold mosaic. And in it there were full thirty chapels, great and small, and there was one of them which was called the Holy Chapel, which was so rich and noble that there was not a hinge nor a band nor any other part such as is usually made of iron that was not all of silver, and there was no column that was not of jasper or porphyry or some other rich precious stone… Within this chapel were found many rich relics. One found there two pieces of the True Cross as large as the leg of a man and as long as half a toise, and one found there also the iron of the lance with which Our Lord had His side pierced and two of the nails which were driven through His hands and feet, and one found there in a crystal phial quite a little of His blood, and one found there the tunic which He wore and which was taken from Him when they led Him to the Mount of Calvary, and one found there the blessed crown with which He was crowned, which was made of reeds with thorns as sharp as the points of daggers. And one found there a part of the robe of Our Lady and the head of my lord St. John the Baptist and so many other rich relics that I could not recount them to you or tell you all the truth.'

(Robert de Clari from *The Conquest of Constantinople*, ca. 1204. Translated by E. H. McNeal. Quoted in Kelly, 1987)

The fifty years of Latin rule in Byzantium had a profound effect upon Western culture, with many of Constantinople's holiest relics and some of its greatest artistic creations finding their way to Europe. Perhaps the best known of the plundered relics was the Crown of Thorns, referred to by Robert de Clari. Baldwin II, the last Latin ruler of Byzantium, sold it to Louis IX of France, who built the Church of Sainte Chapelle in Paris to house it. In addition, merchants and returning Crusaders brought Byzantine literary works and ideas with them when they returned home. The commercial structure of the Eastern Mediterranean was also changed forever. The main beneficiaries were the Venetians, who were able to establish a vast network of trading stations and acquired a number of Aegean islands- most notably Crete.

The Byzantine Empire was not completely extinguished by the loss of Constantinople. Small Byzantine states were founded at Nicaea (Iznik), Epirus (in northern Greece) and Trebizond on the Black Sea but Constantinople remained under Latin control until 1261. The Byzantine principality of Nicaea grew to become a powerful commercial and political centre in the region and in 1261 a Nicaean general, Michael Palaeologus, finally recaptured Constantinople from its Latin rulers. As Emperor Michael VIII Palaeologus (r. 1261-82) he established the Palaeologian dynasty, which ruled the empire of Byzantium for the last two centuries of its existence. Michael VIII acquired a city that had suffered extensive damage by fire, had been abandoned by most of its population and many of whose great buildings lay in ruins. His efforts, and those of his successors, to rebuild the city were limited in scale and hampered by lack of funds but there took place what has been termed the Palaeologian Renaissance when artists, scholars and builders resumed their activities. The ruined columns that had once lined the city's streets were replaced with trees and efforts were made to entice back the populace. Michael VIII's greatest achievement was the restoration of the city's churches – in particular the Church of St Saviour in Chora (Kariye Camii), situated beside the city walls in the Edirnekapi section of the city. The embellishments for which the Chora church is renowned today – its frescoes and mosaics – were added at the beginning of the fourteenth century, long after Michael's death. They were added by the talented government minister, poet and astronomer Theodore Metochites (ca. 1260–1332), between about 1315 and 1321, and include a superb depiction of the man himself presenting a model of the church to Christ (fig. 436).

The Turkish style of Theodore Metochite's turban introduces the final chapter of Byzantine history- a twilight

Fig. 436 **Mosaic depicting Theodore Metochites presenting the Church of St Saviour in Chora to Christ** Executed during the reign of Andronicus II Palaeologus (r. 1282–1328)

period overshadowed by civil war and by the rise of the Ottomans. From 1321–28, 1341–47 and 1376–79, disputes over succession resulted in civil wars that raged through the Byzantine Empire and left it vulnerable to the relentless advance of the Turks. In 1326, they seized Bursa (Prusa) and made it their capital; in 1331 they took Nicaea and in 1337, Nicomedia was lost. By now the Asiatic hinterland of the Byzantine Empire consisted of little more than a small strip of land facing Constantinople and, in 1365, when Edirne (Adrianople) fell to the Turks, the former's total domains comprised only their capital and a few outposts. The cost of defending the empire and the decline in trade placed a great strain on the Byzantine economy. A new low point was reached in 1369, when Emperor John V Palaeologus (r. 1341–91) – much of whose troubled reign was spent as a near-vassal of the Turks – journeyed to Italy to propose a union of the Catholic and Orthodox churches. On the way home he was detained by the Venetian authorities for failing to pay his travel expenses, despite mortgaging some of the gems from his crown.

In 1347, the Black Death had arrived in Constantinople, one of the first European cities to be afflicted. It is believed to have begun in a famine-affected area of northern China and was contracted from fleas feeding on infected rats. It had been first passed to Europeans earlier in 1347, during a siege by Kipchak Turks of the Genoese port of Caffa in the Crimea. When some of the besiegers fell ill with the plague, they are said to have catapulted the corpses of their comrades into the town. Within five years one third of Europe's population – about twenty-five million people – lay dead and there were further outbreaks throughout the fourteenth century.

As if this was not enough, the Byzantines' hold on commerce in what remained of their empire was weakened by the Genoese and Venetians, both of whom enjoyed lucrative trade concessions and were exempted from customs duties. The Venetians had gained a virtual monopoly on Constantinople's retail activities and the Genoese, by now, were stronger still. In 1261 the Genoese had given assistance to the Byzantines, in the shape of a fleet of warships, to help them regain control of Constantinople from its Latin rulers. As their reward they were allowed to settle wherever they liked in the city and were subsequently granted the right to settle in Galata, although not on a permanent basis. This caveat did not deter the Genoese, who set about building a series of fortifications that eventually enclosed the entire Galata district. During the declining years of the Byzantine Empire Galata flourished as the principal commercial centre on the trade routes across the Black Sea to Central Asia. The fortified, 62-metre high Galata Tower in what is now the Beyoglu section of Istanbul was erected in 1348 by the Genoese and stands as a testament to their commercial power. A number of travellers who passed through Constantinople around 1400 relate that the Genoese district of Galata was one of the few sections of the city that had not fallen into decay. Among them was Ruy Gonzalez de Clavijo, representative of King Henry III of Castile, who saw Constantinople in 1403 en route to Samarkand. He observed that most of her great buildings were in ruins, the harbours on the Marmara coast were silted up and there were open fields in the heart of the city.

In 1394 the Ottoman Sultan Bayezit I (nicknamed the 'Thunderbolt', r. 1389–1402) began a blockade of Constantinople. A new crusade led by the Hungarians began in 1396 with the aim of countering the Ottoman threat to the Balkans and Central Europe, but its army was surrounded and annihilated at Nicopolis in northern Bulgaria. The beleaguered rulers of Byzantium received a brief respite in 1402 with the arrival of Timur (Tamerlane). His army engaged the Ottomans near Ankara in July 1402; the Turks were routed and Sultan Bayezit captured. The Ottomans were left in disarray and withdrew from Constantinople and for a time there was peace, but the succession of Sultan Murad II in 1421 was followed by a new wave of expansionism. In 1422 Murad began a new blockade of Constantinople. This attempt failed but the end was now inevitable for the rulers of Byzantium. In 1430 Thessalonica, by now ceded to the Venetians, was captured and even though the Catholic and Orthodox churches finally patched up their differences and united in 1439, no concerted military assistance was forthcoming from the countries of Europe.

The final siege of Constantinople began in the spring of 1453. The defenders included Venetians and Genoese but they were vastly outnumbered and, on this occasion the city's walls proved to be no match for the new innovation of cannon. The chain that was used to block the entrance to the Golden Horn was circumvented by the Turks, who dragged their ships overland from the Bosphorous up over the hill of Galata. The final assault occurred on 29 May and Constantine XI Palaeologus (r. 1449–53), the last of eleven centuries of Byzantine emperors, died during hand-to-hand fighting as the city fell. The last flicker of Byzantium – the Empire of Trebizond (Trabzon) – sputtered on until 1461 when it, too, fell to the Ottomans.

After the customary three days of looting order was quickly restored and Sultan Mehmet II set about rebuilding the city. Large numbers of Turks came to settle but there were also Greeks, Jews and Armenians brought in from the provinces to replace those who had fled or died during the siege. During the years after the Ottoman conquest many of the great buildings of the city were built. The whole metropolis, including both the European and Asian parts of the city, came to be known as Istanbul, possibly derived from the Greek *eis stin poli* ('to the city') or, perhaps, from the Turkish *Islamboul* ('full of Islam'). Officially, however, it remained *Qustantiniya* (the 'city of Constantine') and though Islam held sway and its churches were converted to mosques, Istanbul was a cosmopolitan, multi-faith city that, by 1600, numbered about half a million inhabitants. The first buildings to be erected by Mehmet II were the Yediküle Fortress near the Golden Gate, the Eski Saray ('old palace') in the centre of the city, the Fatih Mosque (almost completely destroyed by an earthquake in 1766), and the Grand Bazaar.

Mehmet II quickly replaced the Eski Saray Palace with a vast series of pavilions contained within four courtyards, which were built between 1459 and 1465 and became known as the Topkapi Saray (the Seraglio). The Topkapi Palace remained the residence of the Ottomans until the middle of the nineteenth century. The Topkapi's oriental porcelain collection, now contained in the royal kitchens, contains over 10,000 pieces of mainly Chinese ceramics. Among the collection are celadons from the Song dynasty (960–1279), and blue and white and polychrome porcelains from the Yuan to the Qing dynasties (1279–1911). Few of these items came along the terrestial Silk Road; they arrived by sea or as booty from the Ottomans' military campaigns in the Middle East.

Mehmet II's reign was marked by continuing wars of conquest with Serbia, Greece, the Crimea, Albania and the island of Rhodes but trade links were also forged with the Venetians and Genoans. The Ottomans rebuilt the post-stations on the Via Egnatia and one of Mehmet II's first projects after their capture of Constantinople was the establishment of the Grand Bazaar (fig. 437).

Despite its solid, stone structure the Grand Bazaar, like many of Istanbul's great buildings, has been damaged on numerous occasions by fire. One of the worst conflagrations began in May 1756 and, before it was finally extinguished two months later, it had consumed 1,000 shops and 200 mosques. It was quickly rebuilt, however, and the 4,000 shops of the largest covered market in the world have remained the focus of the city's commercial activities ever since:

'We walked through the splendid bazaars which form the centre of Stamboul. It was a pure labyrinth built solidly in stone in the Byzantine style and a vast place of shelter from the heat of the day. Huge galleries, some arched, others with ribbed vaulting, with sculpted pillars and colonnades, are each devoted to a particular kind of wares. Above all we admired the clothing and the Turkish slippers of the women, the worked and embroidered fabrics, the cashmere, the carpets, the furniture inlaid with gold, silver and mother of pearl, the jewellery, and especially the shining weaponry gathered in that part of the bazaar that is called the bezesteen.'

(From Gerard de Nerval [1805–55], 'Journey to the Orient'. Quoted in Drège and Bührer, 1989)

Fig. 437 **The Grand Bazaar, Istanbul**
Begun after 1453 by Mehmet II (r. 1451–81) and rebuilt many times

Many of Istanbul's grandest palaces and mosques were erected in the sixteenth century, during the reign of Sultan Süleyman the Magnificent (r. 1520–66). The renowned architect Sinan (ca. 1491–1588) was responsible for more than 300 mosques, palaces, medresses (theological colleges) and civic buildings throughout the empire. More than eighty of his edifices still stand in Istanbul, including the city's largest and most important mosque, Süleymaniye (1550–57), but by Sinan's day the sea lanes between Europe and the Orient were filled with sailing ships and the Silk Road was little more than a memory.

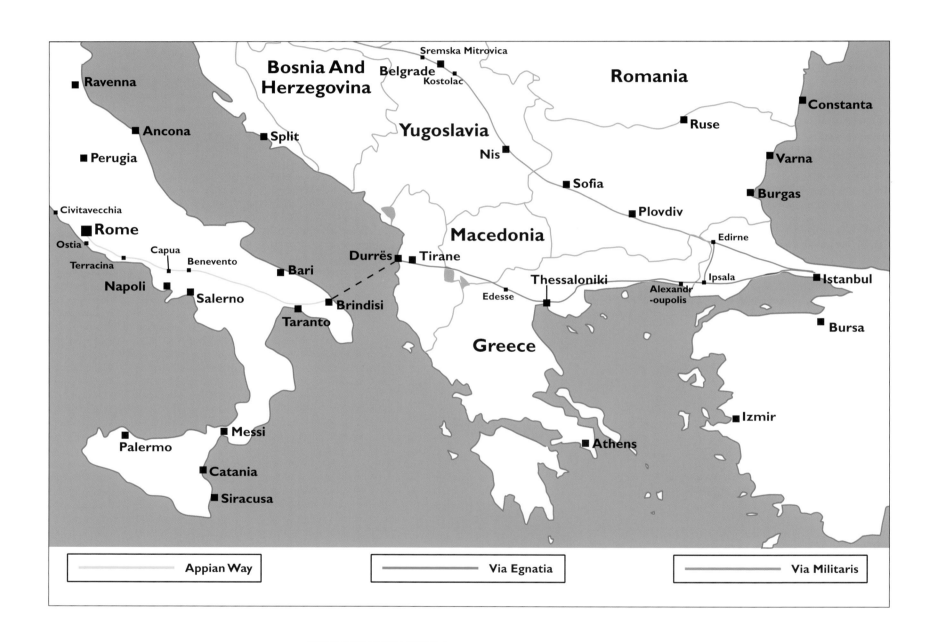

Appian Way	Via Egnatia	Via Militaris

THE VIA EGNATIA, THE
VIA APPIA AND OTHER ROMAN ROUTES

CHAPTER TWENTY SEVEN

ALL ROADS LEAD TO ROME

The principal route westwards from Byzantium, the Via Egnatia, was the first substantial road to be built by the Romans outside Italy. It was constructed sometime between 146 BC and 120 BC on the foundations of earlier roads built during the fifth century BC by the kings of Macedonia. Its purpose was at first military- to enable the Romans to consolidate their rule in the East- and later served as a commercial conduit for goods heading to and from Rome. The precise length of the road is a matter of dispute but was about 750 km in all. It ran from Dyrrhachium (modern Durrës in Albania), across Greece to Byzantium and Asia Minor, where it joined the ancient Royal Road of the Persians (see p. 297). The Romans built their roads by laying large stones on a layer of gravel and cement- the latter made from a mixture of volcanic ash and lime. They were adept at both cambering the surface of their roads and providing efficient drainage and had a penchant for straightness. Milestones were placed at intervals of about a mile (1.6 km) and were marked with distances as well as the name of the nearest way station. The Via Egnatia figures in the accounts of the missionary journeys of St Paul the Apostle and was quite clearly the main route across Greece in antiquity.

A second road, the Via Militaris, led across the Balkan Peninsula and was one of many *viae militares* (military roads) that criss-crossed the Roman Empire. It has its origins in the late third century BC, a time when the Romans began to penetrate deep into the Balkans in search of copper and iron, precious metals and slaves. It took a further three centuries before the region was entirely subjugated and the Roman provinces of Moesia, Dacia, Pannonia and Dalmatia established. The Via Militaris ran in a west-east direction, passing through Sirmium (Sremska Mitrovica), Singidunum (Belgrade) and Viminacium (Kostolac) to Byzantium and was protected by a series of forts. The road continued to be used by merchants, long after Roman influence in the Balkans had fallen away. The towns along the route changed hands with every incursion of Goths, Bulgars, Avars and other tribes and eventually came under Byzantine control.

The 563 km long Via Appia (Appian Way) was the principal Roman highway to the East and was laid down in 312 BC by Appius Claudius Caecus, to connect Rome with Capua (just to the northeast of Naples). It was subsequently extended to Beneventum (modern Benevento), Tarentum (Taranto) and Brundisium (Brindisi). There were sea connections between Brindisi and Dyrrhachium (Durrës), the point at which the Via Egnatia began. Large stretches of the Appian Way still exist, as do some of its monuments: Trajan's Arch, erected in Benevento in 114 AD, still stands, as do some of the funerary monuments and mileposts that used to flank the highway. At the old Roman seaport of Ostia, just to the south of Rome, the remains of storehouses can still be seen with mosaics depicting the occupations of the various merchants. Thus a mosaic of an elephant denotes a trader in ivory while another of fish is attached to a dealer in aquatic products.

CHAPTER TWENTY EIGHT

THE END OF THE OF THE ROAD: THE SILK ROAD IN DECLINE

'The cloud-capp'd towers, the gorgeous palaces,
The solemn temples, the great globe itself,
Ye all which it inherit, shall dissolve…'

(William Shakespeare, 'The Tempest'. Act IV, Scene 1)

The death in 1449 of Ulugh Beg, grandson of Timur, was one of a number of events that brought about the final decline of the Silk Road. After Ulugh Beg's passing the Timurid Empire finally disintegrated as town after town fell to the Uzbeks and the absence of centralized control in Central Asia meant that the safety of merchants along the trade routes could no longer be guaranteed. Caravans were forced to hire an armed escort, resulting in higher costs. To the west, Constantinople fell to the Ottoman Turks in 1453, bringing the Byzantine Empire to an end and bringing the eastern Mediterranean under Muslim control. All east-west trade was now compelled to pass through Ottoman territory and this resulted in an additional financial burden on merchants in the form of tolls and taxes. The European trading powers began to seek ways to evade the Ottoman monopoly and to reduce these costs, ushering in an era of maritime exploration that would transform the way in which trade would be conducted during the coming centuries. The first voyages had already begun during the early part of the fifteenth century, sponsored by Prince Henry 'The Navigator' of Portugal, to seek gold, ivory and slaves and in 1415, the Portuguese captured the Moorish city of Ceuta on the northern coast of Africa. Emboldened by their success they began to explore the African coastline and, in 1487, Bartolomeu Dias became the first European to round the Cape of Good Hope; he was actually blown round it in a storm. He was followed in 1497–98 by Vasco da Gama, discoverer of the maritime route to India and in 1510 the Portuguese captured Goa, quickly followed in 1511 by the Malay port of Malacca- both becoming important bases for trade with the East. Under the newly founded Mughal Empire the Portuguese were granted trading rights and by the 1540s they were engaged in commerce with Thailand, Burma, Cambodia and Japan. For more than a century the Portuguese dominated trade with Africa and India while the Spanish raced to colonize the New World, a process that had begun in 1492 with the voyage of Christopher Columbus.

The irony of Columbus's voyage was that, by sailing west, he too hoped to reach *Cipangu* (Japan) and India. Columbus, believing that the earth was round but miscalculating its circumference, believed until his death that he had reached Asia during his voyage instead of the Bahamas.

The great age of maritime exploration was not confined to the European powers. During the early years of the Ming dynasty (1368–1644) Chinese emperors launched a number of expeditions led by the incomparable Admiral Zheng He (1371–1434). Zheng, the son of a Muslim from Yunnan province, began his career at the age of twelve as a court eunuch. He distinguished himself in a number of military posts and became a favourite of Emperor Yongle (r. 1403–24). Yongle restored China to a position of economic and military strength and selected Zheng to lead a series of maritime expeditions to unite the countries of South and Southeast Asia under Chinese hegemony. Between 1405 and 1433, under the Emperors Yongle and Xuande (r. 1425–35), with a brief suspension of operations under Hongxi (r. 1425), Zheng led seven different voyages. They were truly epic in both scale and reach: the first, in 1405, involved more than sixty ships – the largest 130 metres in length – carrying 27,000 men. The flotilla left Suzhou and travelled for two years, exploring the coastlines of Vietnam, Java, Sumatra, Malacca, Sri Lanka and southwestern India but his subsequent voyages were even more noteworthy. His fourth expedition, from 1413–15, was a round trip of 12,000 km, stopping at Hormuz on the Persian Gulf. Part of the fleet then sailed down the Arabian coast as far as Dhofar and Aden and went on to explore the east coast of Africa, almost as far south as Mozambique, some eighty years ahead of the Portuguese. Part of the expedition even made a detour by land to visit Mecca and Egypt. When the fleet returned to China in 1415 they brought envoys from more than thirty countries to pay homage to the Chinese court and a rich cargo that included a giraffe. His final expeditions all revisited the Persian Gulf and the east African coastline and, although the voyages did not result in the establishment of permanent settlements in the places he visited, they undoubtedly contributed to the diaspora of Chinese to the countries of Southeast Asia that occurred in later years. Zheng's voyages also sought to advance China's commercial interests: his ships carried cargoes that included raw and embroidered silks, porcelain, pearls, musk, camphor, precious metals, rice, millet and beans. He returned to China with spices, gems, medicines, pigments and exotic animals-both as tribute and as the proceeds of barter with the countries along the route.

Zheng died in 1434 and China's status a great sea power was lost as the country began to fold in on itself. Chinese merchants continued to trade but without official approval. The Portuguese arrived on the coast of Southern China in 1517 and, despite being regarded with undisguised contempt by the Chinese, succeeded in establishing a trading port at Macau in 1557. From their bases at Goa and Macau, the Portuguese controlled most of the maritime trade with the East but the Spanish sought access as well. Their efforts, ironically, were assisted by the Portuguese navigator Ferdinand Magellan. Magellan approached the king of Portugal with a scheme to sail around the coast of South America but, unable to arouse interest in the plan, was eventually commissioned by King Charles I of Spain to sail west in search of spices. After rounding Cape Horn Magellan traversed the Pacific and reached the Philippines. He was killed in the Philippines in 1521 but this did not prevent the establishment of trading ports at Manila and in the Moluccas Islands in Indonesia. From these bases the Spanish conducted a lucrative trans-Pacific trade via Mexico and Peru to Europe. Goods were carried overland from one side of Mexico to the other where, at the port of Veracruz, they were put on ships bound for Spain. The Portuguese continued to dominate trade across the Indian Ocean but from 1624 onwards, Chinese merchants also traded with the Dutch in Formosa (Taiwan). In 1580 Portugal was annexed by Spain but Spanish ambitions to dominate trade with the East were shortlived. Sir Francis Drake's defeat of the Spanish Armada in 1588 put paid to Spanish control of the seas and ushered in the era of the great English and Dutch trading companies. Throughout this period the cities of the Silk Road, starved of revenue from land-based commerce, began to wither and die.

CONCLUSION

'I sometimes think of the saga of East and West as if it were music- an orchestrated symphony with solos,
mostly sad, here and there, flashes and discords: and ever in the background heard in its quieter moments,
moving in a rough repeated harmony, the padding footsteps of the caravans.'

(Freya Stark, 1966)

So what is there left to say about the Silk Road? Perhaps it is this: that the men and women who tramped the grand old road – whether they were princes or paupers; whether they built palaces or tore them down; whether they grew rich or starved; whether they died in bed or in a ditch; whether they were artisans, or merchants, or kings, or conquerors – all were threads in the long, luxuriant fabric of the greatest trade route that mankind has ever known. They have all left their traces and the woman of today, resplendent in a silk dress; the child captivated by a firework display; the astronomer on a starlit night; the boatman who opens a canal lock gate or the stricken yachtsman in the Southern Ocean, saved by the watertight compartments of his vessel- all are participants in the heritage of the Silk Road and all are beneficiaries of its gifts.

In a section from 'Leaves of Grass', the American poet Walt Whitman speaks eloquently of the thousands of generations who have preceded us and of the legacy that they have left behind. He is not writing of the Silk Road but what he has to say about these, the inhabitants of the past, is a fitting and appropriate way to conclude this journey:

'Nations ten thousand years before These States,
and many times ten thousand years before These States;
Garner'd clusters of ages, that men and women like us
grew up and travel'd their course, and pass'd on;
What vast-built cities-what orderly republics-
what pastoral tribes and nomads;
What histories, rulers, heroes,
perhaps transcending all others;
What laws, customs, wealth, arts, traditions;
What sort of marriage-what costumes-
what physiology and phrenology;
What of liberty and slavery among them-
what they thought of death and the soul;
Who were witty and wise-who beautiful and poetic-
who brutish and undevelop'd;
Not a mark, not a record remains-

And yet all remains.
O I know that those men and women were not for nothing,
any more than we are for nothing;
I know that they belong to the scheme of the world
every bit as much as we now belong to it,
and as all will henceforth belong to it.
Afar they stand-yet near to me they stand,
Some with oval countenances, learn'd and calm,
Some naked and savage-
Some like huge collections of insects,
Some in tents-herdsmen, patriarchs, tribes, horsemen,
Some prowling through woods-
Some living peaceably on farms, laboring, reaping,
filling barns,
Some traversing paved avenues, amid temples, palaces,
factories, libraries, shows, courts, theatres, wonderful
monuments.
Are those billions of men really gone?
Are those women of the old experience of the earth gone?
Do their lives, cities, arts, rest only with us?
Did they achieve nothing for good, for themselves?
I believe of all those billions of men and women that fill'd
the unnamed lands, every one exists this hour, here or elsewhere,
invisible to us, in exact proportion to what he or she grew from
in life,
and out of what he or she did, felt, became, loved, sinn'd, in life.
I believe that was not the end of those nations, or any person of
them,
any more than this shall be the end of my nation, or of me;
Of their languages, governments, marriage, literature, products,
games, wars, manners, crimes, prisons, slaves, heroes, poets,
I suspect their results curiously await in the yet unseen world-
counterparts of what accrued to them in the seen world.
I suspect I shall meet them there,
I suspect I shall there find each old particular of those unnamed
lands.'

('Unnamed Lands', from Walt Whitman's 'Leaves of Grass', 1900)

CHRONOLOGIES

CHINA

NEOLITHIC CULTURES	ca. 6500–1900 BC

EARLY DYNASTIES
Shang	ca. 1500–1050 BC
Western Zhou	1050–771 BC
Eastern Zhou	
Spring and Autumn	770–475 BC
Warring States	475–221 BC

IMPERIAL CHINA
Qin	221–207 BC
Han	
Western Han	206 BC–9 AD
Xin (Wang Mang interregnum)	9–23 AD
Eastern Han	25–220 AD
Three Kingdoms	
Shu Han	221–63 AD
Wei	220–65 AD
Wu	222–80 AD

Period of Disunity:
Southern dynasties (Six Dynasties)
Western Jin	265–316
Eastern Jin	317–420
Liu Song	420–79
Southern Qi	479–502
Liang	502–57
Chen	557–89

Sixteen Kingdoms
[Chinese appellation for period when a succession of nomadic groups fought for control of northern China]
	304–439

Northern dynasties
Northern Wei	386–534
Eastern Wei	534–50
Western Wei	535–57
Northern Qi	550–77
Northern Zhou	557–81
Sui	589–618
Tang	618–907
Five Dynasties	907–960
Liao	907–1125
Song	
Northern Song	960–1126
Southern Song	127–1279
Jin	1115–1234
Yuan	1279–1368
Ming	1368–1644
Qing	1644–1911

REPUBLICAN CHINA
Republic	1912–49
People's Republic	1949–Present

PRE-ISLAMIC STATES OF WESTERN AND CENTRAL ASIA

Achaemenian Empire	ca. 550–330 BC
Alexander the Great	336–323 BC
Seleucid Empire	ca. 312–64 BC
Parthian Empire	ca. 256 BC– 226 AD
Mauryan Empire	ca. 4th–2nd century BC
Greco–Bactrian kingdom	ca. 3rd–2nd century BC
Scythians	ca. 2nd–1st century BC
Xiongnu confederation	ca. 4th century BC– ca. 1st century AD
Kushan Empire	ca. 1st century BC– 4th century AD
Sasanian Empire	224–651 AD
Hepthalites ('White Huns')	ca. 4th–6th century AD
Sogdian states	ca. 2nd–8th century AD
Western Turks	ca. 5th–7th century AD

ISLAMIC STATES

Arabian Peninsula:
Rule of the Rightly Guided Caliphs in Arabia	632–61
Umayyad Caliphate	661–750
Abbasid Caliphate	749–1258

Egypt:
Tulunid dynasty	868–904
The Ikhshidids	935–69
The Fatimids	909–1171
The Ayyubids	1168–1260
The Mamluks	1252–1517

Persia and Transoxiana:
The Samanids	875–999
The Tahirids	821–73
The Saffarids	867–908
The Seljuks	1037–1194
The Kharakhanids	992–1211
The Kharakhitai (Non–Muslim state)	ca. 1124–1210
The Khorezmshahs	1157–1231
The Zangids	1127–77
The (Mongol) Il–Khans	1256–1335
The Timurids	1370–1506
The (Uzbek) Shaibanids	1428–1599
The Safavids	1502–1722

Turkey:
Seljuk Sultanate of Rum	1194–1243
Ottoman Sultanate	1300–1924

Afghanistan and India:
Ghaznavids	977–1186
Ghurids	1100–1215
Mughal Empire	1526–1857

EMPERORS OF BYZANTIUM
(Adapted from Kelly, 1987)

Constantine dynasty
Constantine I	r. 324–37 AD
Constantius II	337–31
Julian	361–63

Non–dynastic emperors
Jovian	363–64
Valens	378

Theodosian dynasty
Theodosius I	379–95
Arcadius	395–408
Theodosius II	408–50
Pulcheria	450–53
Marcian	450–57

Leonine dynasty
Leo I	457–44
Zeno	474–91
Leo I	474
Anastasius	518

Justinian dynasty

Justin I	518–27
Justinian I	565
Justin II	578
Tiberius	582
Maurice (married Tiberius's daughter)	582–602

Non–dynastic emperor

Phocas	602–10

Heraclian dynasty

Heraclius	610–41
Constantine II	641
Constantine III	641–68
Constantine IV	668–85
Justinian II	685–95 and 705–11

Usurpers during reign of Justinian II

Leontius	695–98
Tiberius	698–705

Non–dynastic emperors

Philippicus Bardanes	711–13
Anastasius II	713–16
Theodosius II	716–17

Syrian dynasty

Leo III	717–41
Constantine V	741–75
Leo IV	775–80
Constantine VI	780–97
Irene (as Regent and then Empress)	780–802

Non–dynastic emperors

Nicephorus I	802–11
Stauracius	811
Michael I	811–13
Leo V (the Armenian)	813–20

Phrygian dynasty

Michael II (the Stammerer)	820–29
Theophilus (the Unfortunate)	829–42
Michael III (the Drunkard)	842–67

Macedonian dynasty

Basil I	867–86
Leo VI (the Wise)	886–912
Alexander	886–913
Constantine VII (Porphyrogenitus)	913–59

Usurpers during and after reign of Constantine VI

Romanus	919–44
Romanus II	959–63
Nicephorus II	963–69
John Tzimisces	969–76

Macedonian dynasty continued

Basil II (the Bulgar–slayer)	976–1025
Constantine VIII	1025–28
Zoe	1028–1050
Romanus III	1028–34
Michael IV	1034–41
Michael V	1041–42
Zoe and Theodora (jointly)	1042
Constantine IX Monomachus	1042–55
Theodora (as sole Empress)	1055–56

Non–dynastic emperors

Michael VI Stratioticus	1056–57
Isaac I Komnenos	1057–59
Constantine X Dukas	1059–67
Romanus IV Diogenes	1067–71
Michael VII Parapinakes	1071–78
Nicephorus III Botaniates	1078–81

Comnenus dynasty

Alexius I	1081–1118
John II	1118–43
Manuel I	1143–80
Alexius II	1180–83
Andronicus I	1183–85

Angeli dynasty

Isaac II Angelus	1185–95 and 1203–04
Alexius III	1195–1203
Alexius IV	1203–04

Usurping emperor

Alexius V Dukas	1204

Latin emperors installed by the Crusaders

Baldwin of Flanders	1204–05
Henry of Flanders	1206–16
Peter de Courtnay (never ruled)	1217
Yolande	1217–19
Robert II of Courtnay	1221–28
Baldwin II	1228–61
John de Brienne (Regent)	1229–37

Byzantine emperors exiled at Nicaea during the Latin occupation of the city

Theodore I Lascaris	1204–22
John III Dukas Vatatzes	1222–54
Theodore II	1254–58
John IV	1258–61

Byzantine emperors restored: Palaeologian dynasty

Michael VIII	1261–82
Andronicus II	1282–1328
Michael IX	1295–1320
Andronicus III	1328–41
John V	1341–91

Usurping emperor

John VI Cantacuzenos	1341–54

Palaeologian dynasty continued

Andronicus IV	1376–79
John VII	1390
Manuel II	1391–1425
John VIII	1425–48
Constantine XI	1449–53

Ottoman sultans immediately after the capture of the city in 1453

Mehmet II the Conqueror (Fatih)	1453–81
Beyazit II	1481–1512
Selim I the Grim	1512–20
Süleyman the Magnificent	1520–66
Selim II	1566–74
Murad III	1574–95
Mehmet III	1595–1603

GLOSSARY

abhayamudra Hand position indicating freedom from fear, or reassurance; the hand raised with the palm pointing towards the viewer.

agora (Greek 'meeting place') In ancient Greek cities, an open space that served as a meeting place for various activities of the citizens. Typically the central marketplace, the equivalent of the Roman forum.

Amitabha Buddha (Sanskrit; Japanese: Amida) The Buddha of infinite light, ruler of the pure land known as the Western Paradise.

Ananda First cousin and devoted companion of the Buddha.

apsaras or Apsara (Sanskrit) Female semi–divinity, or celestial nymph.

Aramaic. One of the major systems of writing in the Middle East during the first millennium BC. It derived from Semitic script and became the *lingua franca* of merchants in the region.

arhat (Sanskrit; Chinese: Lohan; Japanese: Rakan) A Buddhist holy figure who has gained insight into the true nature of existence and has achieved nirvana (q.v.).

Ariadne (Greek mythology) The daughter of Pasiphae and the Cretan king Minos, inamorata of the Athenian hero Theseus.

Athena (Greek mythology) The Goddess of War and city protectress, identified by the Romans with Minerva .

Atlas (Greek mythology) Son of the Titan Iapetus and the nymph Clymene, and brother of Prometheus. In Homer's works he supported the pillars that separated heaven and earth.

avadanas (Sanskrit 'Noble Deeds') The Buddha's explanations of events by means of an individual's worthy deeds in a previous life. The most important Avadana is an account of miraculous events in the life and former lives of the Buddha himself.

Avalokitesvara (Sanskrit) A celestial bodhisattva (q.v.), the archetype of universal compassion. In his female form, he is associated with Tara and Guanyin (q.v.)

balbals Grave-markers, once erected by nomadic Turks above the graves of their companions to designate how many of the enemy the occupant had slain.

bodhisattva One destined for Buddhahood, eligible to enter nirvana, but who elects to remain a bodhisattva in order to help living beings attain salvation.

Brahma Hindu deity, a member of the *puranic* trinity (the *Trimurti*), associated with creation.

Brahmins (Hindu priests) The priestly caste of Hindus (although not all Brahmins are priests).

caitya (Sanskrit 'that which is worthy to be gazed upon') A sacred place or shrine, especially a Buddhist prayer-hall, often with a votive stupa at one end.

caliph (Arabic *Khalifah*: 'successor'– to Muhammad) A ruler of the Muslim community.

caravanserai A public building, often fortified, used for sheltering caravans, merchants and other travelers.

cella (central sanctuary chamber) The main body of a temple containing the image of the deity.

chaikana (or chaihana) A teahouse.

chakra (or Cakra. Sanskrit 'wheel') A wheel or disc attribute of Vishnu.

chiaroscuro (Italian 'light and shade', or 'dark') In painting, the modelling of volume by bold contrast of light and shade.

cleruchs (Greek) War veterans, given grants of land in dependent countries of the Greek Empire.

Corinthian A type of pillar, one of the three classical orders of Greek architecture, characterized by a fluted column, topped by a capital decorated with acanthus leaves.

cozbo (Kharosthi script) An official or functionary.

Da Qin (Chinese 'Great Qin') The Chinese name for Rome or the Roman Empire.

decumanus. (Latin 'Main Road'). The main east-west thoroughfare in a Roman city.

deva (Sanskrit 'The Shining One', female: devata). A deity or god, an inhabitant of the heavenly realms.

dharmachakramudra The gesture signifying the 'turning the wheel of the law', in which both hands are held at chest level. The tips of the thumb and forefinger of the right hand form a circle and are touched by the left hand.

dhyanamudra. The gesture of meditation, where the hands of a seated figure are placed in the lap, one above the other, with palms facing upwards.

Dionysos (Greek mythology) Known to the Romans as Bacchus – the God of Wine and altered states (or religious ecstasy).

Doric A type of column, one of the three classical orders of Greek architecture. It is characterized by the absence of a base, a simple tapering column and a plain capital.

Durga (Sanskrit 'Difficult to Penetrate') A Hindu goddess, the female counterpart of Siva (q.v.) and slayer of the buffalo demon.

dvarapala Heroic door guardian or keeper of the Buddhist faith, placed in pairs at the entrances to temples.

Eros (Greek Mythology) Known to the Romans as Cupid, the God of Love.

farsakh (Persian, also *parasang* or *farsang*) The distance that a laden mule will walk in an hour, varying from about 5 to 6 km.

Fravashis In the Zoroastrian religion, the Fravashis (singular: Fravartin) are guardian angels or protecting spirits who guide the souls of the departed to heaven. The Fravashis assisted Ahura Mazda, the supreme Zoroastrian divinity, in the creation of the world and are also the defenders of heaven.

gandharvas (Sanskrit) Male celestial deities, sometimes known as musicians of the gods.

Ganesha The elephant-headed son of the Hindu god Siva (q.v.)

Garuda (Sanskrit) Mythical bird, often depicted in part human form. Garuda is the mortal enemy of the nagas (q.v.) and is also the mount of the Hindu god Vishnu. (q.v.).

ghat (Hindi) A landing-place with steps on the banks of a river. A flat area at the top of the steps, used by Hindus as a place for cremation, is known as a burning ghat.

ghazal A short lyric love poem, often treated symbolically.

Gigaku dancing (also called *kure–uta* or 'Wu singing') Comic dances performed with masks and closely associated with Buddhist temple ritual. Gigaku is the earliest form of Japanese theatrical entertainment and was introduced in 612 AD from southern China.

girikh ('Persian Knots') Geometrical arabesque decoration in Islamic architecture.

gonbad (Persian) Dome.

Guanyin (Chinese; Japanese: Kannon) The bodhisattva of compassion, portrayed in female form and identified with the bodhisattva Avalokitesvara (q.v.).

hadiths (Arabic 'news or story') Collection of traditions or sayings of the Prophet Muhammad, regarded by Muslims as source of moral guidance. The authority of the hadiths is second only to that of the Koran.

hamsa (Sanskrit) A mythical semi-divine goose; the mount of the Hindu god Brahma (q.v.)

Harpocrates (Greek 'Horus the Child') The Greeks' name for the Egyptian sky god Horus, represented as a small boy with his finger held to his lips. Harpocrates was regarded as the God of Silence and was popular throughout the Roman Empire.

haveli In India, a mansion or small palace.

Herakles (Greek mythology) Known as Hercules to the Romans, Herakles was the illegitimate offspring of Zeus and Alkmene, granddaughter of Perseus. He was honoured as a hero throughout the Greek world and after his death by poisoning was granted immortality among the gods.

Hermes (Greek mythology) Son of Zeus and Maia, the daughter of the Titan Atlas, Hermes is identified with the Roman god Mercury. He is worshipped as the God of Fertility, as the protector of travelers and roads and as the conveyor of souls to the underworld. He was also the messenger of the gods and is often depicted wearing winged sandals or a winged hat.

hierothesion (Greek 'the temple-tomb and common dwelling place of all the gods') A sacred tomb sanctuary.

Hinayana (Sanskrit 'lesser path' or 'vehicle') Older school of Buddhism, popular in Sri Lanka, Thailand and Burma, in which the routes to salvation are more limited than those of the rival, Mahayana school (q.v.) Also known as the Theravada ('path of the elders') school.

Hu (Chinese, poss. derives from *rou*– 'meat'– or *yue*–'moon') General name applied in ancient China to the peoples living along the country's northern frontier.

hypogeum (Latin, plural hypogea) An underground burial chamber.

intaglio 'Hollow relief' carving, commonly used for engraved seals and gems, in which a positive imprint is formed when pressed onto heated wax.

Ionic A type of column, one of the three classical orders of Greek architecture. Ionic columns generally have a fluted shaft and a capital usually decorated with two scroll–like designs (volutes).

iwan A covered or vaulted hall, open at one end, in a mosque or palace.

jatakas Birth stories, episodes from the historical Buddha's prior lives, intended as moral lessons.

kala (Turkish) A fortified settlement.

karaburan (Turkish). A strong, warm wind that blows over Central Asia. It often carries fine-grained soil which is deposited as loess (q.v.).

kariz (Persian– also called kyariz or qanats) Underground water conduits for irrigation.

Kasyapa An Indian ascetic who converted to Buddhism late in life and, along with Ananda (q.v.), became one of the Buddha's key disciples.

Khagan (or Khan) King or ruler.

khan A lodging place or inn for travellers and merchants. They are analogous to caravanserais (q.v.) but are generally located within towns.

Kharosthi. Writing system used in northwestern India before about 500, probably derived from Aramaic script (q.v.) and influenced by another Indian script, Brahmi.

khuriltay (Mongolian) Proceedings attended by all minor and major Mongol leaders, as well as shamans, to appoint a new Great Khan.

kirttimukha (Sanskrit ' Face of Glory') A horned, demon or lion mask used as a decorative device above temple doors and windows.

Kubera. In Hinduism, the king of nature spirits, or yakshas (q.v.) and the God of Wealth. Known as Jambhala in Buddhism.

Kufic. The earliest form of Arabic script, characterized by an angular style and used in inscriptions on Islamic buildings and coins.

kurgan (Turkish and Russian) Barrow, artificial burial mound.

lalitasana (Sanskrit) The position of 'royal ease', in which one leg is placed parallel to the ground and the other is pendant.

li (Chinese) A *li* is equivalent to about 0.45 km. In Chinese literature, phrases such as 'a hundred thousand *li*' or 'ten thousand *li*' simply mean a distance beyond imagining.

limes (Latin 'path', plural limites) Originally a strip of open land used by Roman troops to advance into hostile territory. The word subsequently came to be used to mean a military road, strengthened with a line of watchtowers and fortifications, or a natural or artificial frontier.

loess Wind-born dust from desert or vegetation-free areas at the margins of ice sheets. Loess deposits in Northwest China can exceed 150 metres in depth and have created vast fertile areas.

lokapala (Sanskrit and Pali) A 'heavenly king' who protects one of the four cardinal directions.

madrassah. A Muslim religious school.

Mahayana (Sanskrit 'greater vehicle' or 'path') The school of Buddhism most prevalent from Nepal to Japan and therefore also known as Northern Buddhism, in contrast to the older, 'Southern' Hinayana form (q.v.) Its principal tenet is that salvation is open to all and may be attained rapidly with the assistance of bodhisattvas (q.v.).

Maitreya (Sanskrit 'friendliness'; Japanese: Miroku) The Buddha of the Future, now residing as a bodhisattva in Tushita heaven, but who will become incarnate when the teachings of Sakyamuni (q.v.) have become forgotten.

mandala (Sanskrit 'disk' or 'circle') In Hinduism and Buddhism, a cosmic diagram, used as an aid for meditation. A mandala is essentially a representation of the universe, a collection point of universal forces.

Manichaeism A religion influenced by both Gnosticism (a religious movement of the early Christian era rooted in paganism and magic), and Christianity itself. It originated in Persia around 230 AD, founded by Mani (216, or 217–76 AD) and spread across Asia and the Roman Empire, surviving in the far west of China until the thirteenth century. It is based on the struggle between the forces of Light (the Spirit) and Darkness (the Flesh).

Manjusri (Sanskrit; Chinese: Wenshu; Japanese: Monju) In Mahayana Buddhism, the bodhisattva (q.v.) personifying supreme wisdom.

mantra (Sanskrit) A sound expressing the deepest essence of understanding, the recitation of which is believed to evoke a state of enlightenment or intense positive energy.

Mara The 'Lord of the Senses' who attempted to distract the Buddha as he sat beneath the Bo tree awaiting enlightenment.

masnavi (Arabic 'the doubled one') A continuous narrative poem with rhyming couplets.

mawali (Arabic) Clients or subjects – non-Arab converts to Islam, often treated as second–class citizens.

mehrab (Arabic) A niche in the wall of a mosque that indicates the direction of Mecca.

minai Islamic pottery with polychrome enamel painting, and sometimes gilding, on a white ground.

minqi (Chinese 'objects or articles of the spirit') Objects placed in tombs, deposited in the belief that they would enable the deceased to carry his wealth and his favourite possessions with him to the afterlife.

mise (Chinese 'secret colour') Green glazed ceramics from the Tang and Five Dynasties periods in China.

Mithra, Mithraism Pre–Zoroastrian religion in ancient Persia, involving the worship of Mithra, God of Light, justice and war. Mithra's slaying of the cosmic bull appears frequently in the art of the classical world. Mithra was associated with the Greek sun god Helios and often appears with Anahita, Goddess of the Waters.

muezzin (Arabic *muaddin*) In Islam, the official who proclaims the call to prayer.

mullah (Arabic *mawla*, or *mawlay* 'Protector') In different parts of the Islamic world it may denote a king, sultan, scholar or religious leader. The most common usage is for religious leaders, scholars of Islam and teachers in religious schools.

naga (Sanskrit 'snake') A snake deity or spirit, often depicted in part-human form.

Naskhi Cursive style of Islamic script.

Nestorius, Nestorianism Early Christian doctrine, named after Nestorius, Roman Catholic patriarch of Constantinople, who was expelled from the church in 432 for heresy. It held that Christ has two natures – one human and one divine. His followers took Nestorianism eastwards from the sixth century onwards and it survived in parts of China until the fourteenth century.

Nike (Greek mythology) The winged goddess of victory.

nirvana (Sanskrit 'blowing out' or 'extinction'). Extinction of the fires of greed, hatred and ignorance, when perfect knowledge is attained and the cycle of earthly rebirths ceases.

ostraka Inscribed tile or pottery fragments.

pagoda A brick, stone or wood tower of several storeys, erected to house relics of the Buddha. It evolved from the stupas (q.v.) of India.

paizi (or gerege) Metal plaques of gold, silver or iron issued by the Mongols as badges of office and to travellers on state business.

Parinirvana. (Sanskrit) The moment when the Buddha finally exits this world and enters nirvana (q.v.).

Parthian Shot A cavalry tactic, also popular as an artistic motif, in which a hunter shoots backwards from a galloping horse.

pendentive An architectural device consisting of a spherical triangle that fills the space between the corner of the rectangle and the base of the dome.

Phrygian cap A conical wool or felt headdress with a pointed crown, originating in Phrygia in Asia Minor.

pipa (Chinese) A four–stringed lute.

pishtaq A formal gateway or monumental portal.

propylae The entrance gates to an enclosure (usually to the precincts of a temple).

purnaghata Vase-of-plenty, often used as a decorative element.

putto (plural putti) Chubby, cherub-like young boys, frequently depicted with wings, appearing in paintings and sculpture.

qebla Direction of prayer – the side of a mosque facing the Black Stone in the Ka'ba in Mecca.

qilin (Chinese 'male' plus 'female') A Chinese mythical beast resembling a unicorn.

qin (Chinese) A type of Chinese zither.

rabat (or ribat) A fortified monastery or frontier post, with both religious and military functions, found throughout the Muslim Empire.

rhyta or rhytons (Greek) An animal or horn-shaped vessel for libations.

rubaiyat (Persian 'quatrains') In Persian poetry, rhyming quatrains most famously used by Omar Khayyam (c. 1048– c. 1125).

Sakyamuni Title of the historical Buddha.

sancai (Chinese) Three-coloured, usually lead-glazed earthenware pottery fired at low temperature. Its colours were typically yellow, white, green, brown and blue.

sangharama (or vihara) A Buddhist monastery.

Seres (Latin 'country of silk') The name given by the Romans to China.

Serindia Term deriving from 'Seres' (q.v.), referring to the region of Chinese Central Asia traversed by the Silk Road and influenced by the cultures of both China and India.

Sevener Shi'ites A subsect of the Ismaili Shi'ites who believed that Ismail (the seventh descendant of the Prophet's son in law Ali) was also the seventh and last imam. They also believed that Mohammad at-Tamm, the son of Ismail, would return at the end of time as the Chosen One (*al -mahdi*).

sgrafitto (Italian) Decoration applied by first covering the body of the vessel with a white slip and then creating the design by scratching through it with a sharp point to create a line drawing.

shahristan The old inner part of a town.

shanyu (Chinese) High chieftain among the nomads of the Ordos region of China's northern frontier.

Siddhartha The personal name of the historical Buddha.

Silenus. (Greek mythology) An elderly Satyr (male fertility spirit), companion to Dionysos (q.v.).

Siva (or Shiva, Sanskrit 'Beneficent one') One of the principal Hindu deities, a member of the trinity known as the *Trimurti*, characterized by a cosmic energy that manifests itself as both a destructive and creative force.

squinch An arch that spans each corner of a square building to facilitate the transition from a square to a round or polygonal base for a dome.

stupa A Buddhist structure of Indian invention in the form of a mound or dome, built to house relics of the Buddha.

Surya (Sanskrit) The Hindu god of the sun, often depicted as a charioteer.

sutra. (Sanskrit 'thread') A category of Buddhist scripture, believed to have been the words of the Buddha himself.

synodiarch A merchant in charge of a caravan.

Tantric Buddhism (Tantra is Sanskrit for 'loom') Also called Esoteric or Vajrayana ('Diamond Vehicle') Buddhism, a form of Mahayana Buddhism (q.v.) developed in Tibet and making use of mystic and astrological texts, mantras and mandalas (q.v.).

temenos (Greek) A sacred temple enclosure.

themes (Latin) Large military districts created by the Byzantines as a buffer against Islamic expansion.

Theravada See Hinayana.

tiraz (Persian 'embroidery') Textiles embroidered with an inscription in silk thread, usually a laudatory message referring to the name, accomplishments and regnal dates of the caliph or other ruler.

Togatus (Latin 'toga wearer') A Roman philosopher or statesman.

torana (Sanskrit) In Indian architecture, a gateway, especially to a Buddhist stupa (q.v.).

Transoxiana (In Arabic *Mawana'an nahr*: 'what is beyond the river') Important historical region in Central Asia, the lands between the Amu Darya (Oxus) River and the Syr Darya (Jaxartes) River.

ulus (Mongolian) Territory or dominion of the Mongol khans.

urna (Sanskrit) A tuft of hair between the eyebrows, often represented as a dot, that denotes a great man– particularly with regard to the Buddha.

usnisha (Sanskrit 'that which is on top') A raised chignon or cranial bump indicative of princely origins and superior wisdom, particularly with regard to the Buddha.

Vairocana (Sanskrit) The most important of the five cosmic Buddhas, often represented at the centre of a mandala (q.v.).

Vajrapani (Sanskrit 'thunderbolt bearer' or 'diamond bearer') A celestial bodhisattva (q.v.), the manifestation of Aksobhya, Buddha of the East.

vihara (Sanskrit) A Buddhist monastery or a hall in a monastery.

Vimalikirti Indian sage, renowned for his skill in debate.

Vishnu Along with Siva and Brahma (q.v.), one of the three members of the Hindu trinity (the *Trimurti*), who appears as ten different avatars or manifestations, most notably Rama and Krishna.

Yaksha (Sanskrit, female: yakshi) Nature or fertility deities found in both Hinduism and Buddhism.

Zeus (Greek mythology) Supreme god in the Greek pantheon, the protector and ruler of humankind, identified by the Romans with Jupiter.

Zoroastrianism A pre-Islamic religion, founded in ancient Persia during the sixth century BC by Zoroaster (or Zarathustra). Its basic beliefs concern the struggle between good and evil, light and darkness**.**

BIBLIOGRAPHY

General

Ancient Trades and Cultural Contacts in Southeast Asia. Bangkok: National Culture Commission, Bangkok, 1996.

Anderson, G. L. *Masterpieces of the Orient.* New York: W. W. Norton & Co., 1961.

Babur, Zahiru'din Muhammad. *The Babur–nama in English (Memoirs of Babur).* Trans. by A. S. Beveridge, London: Luzac and co., 1921.

Bamborough, P. *Treasures of Islam.* Poole: Blandford Press, 1976.

Boardman, J. *The Diffusion of Classical Art in Antiquity.* London: Thames and Hudson, 1995.

Boisselier, Jean. *The Wisdom of the Buddha.* Trans. by Carey Lovelace. London: Thames and Hudson, 1994.

Boulnois, Luce. *The Silk Road.* Trans. by Dennis Chamberlain, New York: E. P. Dutton and Co., 1966.

Branigan, K. (ed.), *The Atlas of Archaeology.* London: Macdonald & Co., 1982.

Brooks, Noah. *The Story of Marco Polo.* London: John Murray, 1898.

Byron, Robert. *The Road to Oxiana.* London: Macmillan and Co. Ltd, 1937.

Collins, R. *East to Cathay: The Silk Road.* New York: McGraw–Hill, 1968.

Dawood, N. *Tales from the Thousand and One Nights.* London: Book Club Associates, 1977.

Drège, J–P and Bührer, E. M. *The Silk Road Saga.* New York, Oxford: Facts on File, 1989.

Elisseeff, V. (ed.). *The Silk Roads: Highways of Culture and Commerce.* New York: Berghahn Books; Paris: UNESCO Pub., 2000.

Falk, Toby (ed.). *Treasures of Islam.* London: Philip Wilson Ltd/ Sotheby's, 1985.

Foltz, R. *Religions of the Silk Road.* Basingstoke: Macmillan, 1999.

Fox, Robin Lane. *Alexander the Great.* London: Futura Publications, 1973.

Franck, Irene and Brownstone, David. *The Silk Road: A History.* New York, Oxford: Facts on File, 1986.

Gerasimov, Mikhail Mikhailovich. *The Face Finder (Ich suchte Gesichter).* Trans. by Alan Brodrick, London: Hutchinson, 1971.

Grube, E. J. *Landmarks of the World's Art. The World of Islam.* London: Paul Hamlyn, 1966.

Gumilev, L. N. *Searches for an Imaginary Kingdom: The Legend of the Kingdom of Prester John.* Trans. by R. E. F. Smith, Cambridge: Cambridge University Press, 1987.

Hillenbrand, R. *Islamic Art and Architecture.* World of Art Series, London: Thames and Hudson, 1999.

Hourani, G. F. *Arab Seafaring In the Indian Ocean in Ancient and Early Medieval Times,* Rev. by J. Carswell, Princeton: Princeton University Press, 1995.

Ibn Battuta, M. *Travels in Asia and Africa 1325–1354.* Trans. by H. A. R. Gibb, London: The Broadway Travellers, George Routledge and Sons, 1929.

Kunst des Buddhismus entlang der Seidenstrasse. Exhibition catalogue, München: Staatliches Museum für Völkerkunde, 1992.

Lee, Sherman E. *A History of Far Eastern Art.* London: Thames and Hudson, 1964.

Liu, Xinru. *Silk and Religion: An Exploration of Material Life and the Thought of People, AD 600–1200.* Delhi, Oxford: Oxford University Press, 1996.

Mandeville, Sir John. *The travels and voyages of Sir John Mandevile, Knt.: containing an exact description of the way to Hierusalem, Great Caan, India, the country of Preston–John, and many other eastern countries: with an account of many strange monsters and whatever is curious and remarkable therein / carefully collected from the original manuscript, and illustrated with variety of pictures.* London: printed for J. Osborne et al, ca.1700.

Meyers, E. M. (ed.). *The Oxford Encyclopedia of Archaeology in the Near East.* Vols 1–5, New York: O.U.P., 1997.

Mitchener, M. *Oriental Coins and Their Values: The Ancient and Classical World.* London: Hawkins Publications, 1978.

NHK (ed.) *Shiruku Rodo* (The Silk Road). 12 vols., Tokyo: NHK, 1975–81.

Ortiz, G. *In Pursuit of the Absolute. Art of the Ancient World. The George Ortiz Collection.* Revised hard cover edition, Bern 1996.

Pal, P. et al. *Light of Asia: Buddha Sakyamuni in Asian Art.* Los Angeles: L. A. County Museum of Art, 1984.

Polo, Marco. *The Travels of Marco Polo The Venetian.* Trans. by William Marsden, New York: Doubleday and Co., 1948.

Rice, D. Talbot. *Islamic Art.* (Revised edition), World of Art Series, London: Thames and Hudson, 1996.

Rice, E. E. *Alexander the Great.* Beijing, 1997

Rtveladze, E. *The Great Silk Road.* (in Russian). Tashkent: Uzbek National Encyclopedias, 1999.

Scott, Phillippa. *The Book of Silk.* London: Thames and Hudson, 1993.

Sérinde, Terre de Bouddha : dix siècles d'art sur la Route de la Soie. Exhibition catalogue, Galeries nationales du Grand Palais, Paris : Réunion des musées nationaux, 1995.

Shiruku Rodo dai bunmei ten. Shiruku rodo, oashisu to sogen no michi, (The Grand Exhibition of Silk Road civilizations). 3 vols., Exhibition catalogue, Nara National Museum. Nara: Nara Kokuritsu Hakubutsukan, 1988.

Shiruku Rodo no iho: kodai chusei no tozai bunka koryu (Cultural Contacts between East and West in Antiquity and Middle Ages from U.S.S.R.). Exhibition Catalogue, Tokyo National Museum and Museum of Art, Osaka. Tokyo: Nihon Keizai Shinbunsha, 1985.

Slessarev, V. *Prester John– The Letter and the Legend.* Minneapolis: University of Minnesota Press, 1959.

Snellgrove, David L. (ed.), *The Image of the Buddha.* Paris: UNESCO, 1978.

Spink and Son. *Treasures from the Silk Road: Devotion, Conquest and Trade Along Ancient Highways.* Exhibition catalogue, London, 1999.

Tait, Hugh (ed.). *Five Thousand Years of Glass.* London: British Museum Press, 1991.

Tanabe, K. *Silk Road Coins: The Hirayama Collection.* Kamakura: Institute of Silk Road Studies, 1993.

The Koran. Trans. by N. J. Dawood, London: Penguin, 1999.

Tilden, J. (ed.). *Silk & Stone: the art of Asia.* Hali annual III, London: Hali, 1996.

Vollmer, J. E., Keall, E. J. and Nagai-Berthrong, E. *Silk Road China Ships.* Toronto: Royal Ontario Museum, 1983.

Walker, Annabel. *Stein: pioneer of the Silk Road.* London: John Murray, 1995.

Watt, J. and Wardwell, A. *When Silk Was Gold: Central Asian and Chinese Textiles.* New York: Metropolitan Museum, 1997.

Wheeler, (ed.), M. *Splendours of the East: Temples, Tombs, Palaces and Fortresses of Asia.* London: Weidenfeld and Nicolson, 1965.

Whitfield, S. *Life Along the Silk Road.* London: John Murray, 1999.

Wood, F. *Did Marco Polo go to China?* London: Secker and Warburg, 1995.

Yaldiz, M, Gadebusch, R. D. et al, *Magische Götterwelten: Werke aus dem Museum für Indische Kunst Berlin.* Berlin: Staatliche Museen zu Berlin–Preußischer Kulturbesitz, 2000.

Yule, Sir Henry. *Cathay and the Way Thither.* Vol. III, rev. by H. Cordier, London: Hakluyt Society, 1914.

BIBLIOGRAPHY   377

India, Pakistan and Afghanistan

Ali, M. *The Afghans*. Kabul: Kabul University, 1969.

Barthoux, J. J. *Les Fouilles de Hadda*. Vols. 1 and 3, Paris: Éditions d'art et d'histoire, 1930–1933.

Chandra, P. *The sculpture of India: 3000 B.C. – 1300 A.D.* Washington DC: National Gallery of Art, 1985.

Czuma, S. J. *Kushan Sculpture: Images from Early India*. Cleveland: Cleveland Museum of Art, 1985.

Dani, Ahmad Hasan. *Chilas: The City of Nanga Parvat (Dyamar)*. Islamabad: Quaid–I–Azam University, 1983.

Dani, Ahmad Hasan. *Guide to the Karakorum Highway*. Islamabad: Quaid-I-Azam University.

Dani, Ahmad Hasan. *Human Records on the Karakorum Highway*. Lahore: Sang-e-Meel Publications, 1995.

Dani, Ahmad Hasan. *The Historic City of Taxila*. Lahore: Sang-e-Meel Publications, 1999.

Dupree, A. et al, *A Guide to the Kabul Museum*. Kabul: Afghan Tourist Organization, 1968.

Dupree, N. H. *The Road to Balkh*. Kabul: Afghan Tourist Organization, 1967.

Dupree, N. H. *An Historical Guide to Afghanistan*. Kabul: Afghan Tourist Organization, 1977.

Dupree, N. H. et al. *The National Museum of Afghanistan: An Illustrated Guide*. Kabul: Afghan Tourist Organization, 1974.

Errington, E. and Cribb, J. (eds.). *The Crossroads of Asia*. Exhibition Catalogue, Cambridge: Ancient India and Iran Trust, 1992.

Gardner, P. *The Coins of the Greek and Scythic Kings of Bactria and India in the British Museum*. London: Trustees of the British Museum, 1886.

Hackin, J. *Nouvelles recherches archéologiques à Begram*. 2 vols., Paris: Imprimerie Nationale, 1954.

Hallade, H. *The Gandhara Style and the Evolution of Buddhist Art*. London: Thames and Hudson, 1968.

Harle, J. C. *The Art and Architecture of the Indian Subcontinent*. London: Penguin, 1986.

Huntington, S. *The Art Of Ancient India*. New York: Weatherhill, 1985.

Ingholt, H. and Lyons, I. *Gandharan Art in Pakistan*. New York: Pantheon Books, 1957.

Jettmar, K. et al (eds.) *Antiquities of Northern Pakistan: reports and studies*. Mainz : Zabern, 1989–1994.

Klimburg-Salter, D. *Buddha in Indien: Die frühindische Skulptur von König Asoka bis zur Guptazeit*, Exhibition catalogue, Milan and Vienna: Skira editore and Kunsthistorisches Museum, 1995.

Kurita, I. *Gandharan Art*. 2 vols., Tokyo, 1988.

Marshall, Sir John. *A Guide to Taxila*. Calcutta: Superintendent Government Printing, 1918.

Marshall, Sir John. *Taxila: an illustrated account of archaeological excavations carried out at Taxila under the orders of the Government of India between the years 1913 and 1934*. Cambridge, 1951.

Mousavi, S. A. *The Hazaras of Afghanistan: An Historical, Cultural, Economic and Political Study*. Richmond, Surrey: Curzon Press, 1998.

Mukhtarov, Akhror. *Balkh in the Late Middle Ages.*

Papers on Inner Asia No. 24. Trans. by R. D. McChesney, Bloomington (Indiana): Research Institute for Inner Asia Studies, Indiana University, 1993.

Pal, P. *Indian Sculpture*. 2 vols., Los Angeles, Berkeley and London: Los Angeles County Museum of Art in association with University of California Press, 1986 and 1988.

Pal, P. *The Ideal Image: The Gupta Sculptural Tradition and Its Influence*. New York: Asia Society and John Weatherhill, 1978.

Rice, F. Mortimer and Rowland, B. *Art in Afghanistan: Objects from the Kabul Museum*. Miami: University of Miami Press, 1971.

Rosenfield, J. M. *The Dynastic Arts of the Kushans*. Berkeley: University of California Press, 1967.

Rowland, Benjamin *Ancient Art from Afghanistan: Treasures from the Kabul Museum*. Exhibition catalogue, New York: Asia Society, 1976.

Rowland, Benjamin. *The Wall Paintings of India, Central Asia & Ceylon: A Comparative Study*. Boston: Merrymount Press, 1938.

Sariandi, V. *Bactrian Gold from the Excavations of the Tillya Tepe Necropolis in Northern Afghanistan*. St. Petersburg: Aurora Art Publishers, 1985.

Sharma, R. C. *Buddhist Art: Mathura School*. New Delhi: Wiley Eastern Press, 1995.

Wolfe, N. H. *The Valley of Bamiyan*. Kabul: Afghan Tourist Organization, 1963.

Zwalf, W. *A Catalogue of the Gandhara Sculpture in the British Museum*. London: British Museum Press, 1996.

Zwalf, W. *The Shrines of Gandhara*. London: British Museum Publications, 1979.

China, Japan and Korea

'Treasures of Chang'an. Capital of the Silk Road.' Exhibition catalogue, Hong Kong Museum of Art and the Overseas Exhibitions Department, Cultural Bureau of Shaanxi. Xian: Xianggang shi zheng ju, 1993.

A Grand View of Xinjiang's Cultural Relics and Historic Sites. Urumqi, 1999.

Agnew, Neville (ed.). *Conservation of Ancient Sites On The Silk Road: Proceedings of an international conference on the conservation of grotto sites*. Los Angeles: Getty Conservation Institute, 1997.

Akiyama, T. and Matsubara, S. *Arts of China: Buddhist Cave Temples– New Researches*. Vol. 2, Tokyo: Kodansha International, 1969.

Alley, Rewi. *Selected Poems of the Tang and Song Dynasties*. Hong Kong: Hai Feng Publishing Co., 1981.

Andrews, F. H. *Wall Paintings from Ancient Shrines in Central Asia recovered by Sir Aurel Stein*. London: Oxford University Press, 1948.

Barber, E. W. *The Mummies of Urumqi*. London: Macmillan, 1999.

Barfield, T. J. *The Perilous Frontier: Nomadic Empires and China*. Oxford: Basil Blackwell, 1989.

Baumer, C. *Southern Silk Road: In the Footsteps of Sir Aurel Stein and Sven Hedin*. Bangkok: Orchid Press, 2000.

Bhattacharya, C. *Art of Central Asia: With Special Reference to wooden objects from the Northern Silk

Route*. Delhi: Agam Prakashan, 1977.

Birrell, Anne. *Popular Songs and Ballads of Han China*. London: Unwin Hyman Ltd, 1988

Blunden, C. and Elvin, M. *Cultural Atlas of China*. Oxford: Time Life Books, 1983.

Bonavia, J. *The Silk Road from Xi'an to Kashgar*. Hong Kong: Odyssey Publications, 1988. (Reprinted 1999).

Burrow, T. *A Translation of the Kharosthi Documents from Chinese Turkestan*. London: Royal Asiatic Society, 1940.

Bynner, W. *The Jade Mountain. A Chinese Anthology: Being 300 Poems of the Tang Dynasty*. New York: Alfred A. Knopf, 1930.

Cable, M. and French, F. *Through Jade Gate and Central Asia*. London: Hodder and Stoughton, 1927.

Cable, M., French, E., and French, F. *A Desert Journal: Letters from Central Asia*. London: Constable and Co. Ltd, 1934.

Cable, M. and French, F. *The Gobi Desert*. London: Hodder and Stoughton, 1942.

Cable, M. and French, F. *China: Her Life and Her People*. London: University of London Press, 1946.

Capon, E. *Tang China: Vision and splendour of a golden age*. London: Macdonald Orbis, 1989.

Capon, E. and Macquitty, W. *Princes of Jade*. London: Nelson, 1973.

Che, Muqi. *The Silk Road: Past and Present*. Beijing: Foreign Languages Press, 1989.

Chen, Yu. *Tales from Dunhuang*. Trans. by Li Guishan, Beijing: New World Press, 1989.

China Cultural Relics Promotion Center. *Treasures: 300 Best Excavated Antiques from China*. Beijing: New World Press, 1992.

China's Buried Kingdoms. Virginia: Time Life Books, 1993.

Chuka Jinmin Kyowakoku Shiruku Rodo bunbutsu ten; The exhibition of ancient art treasures of The People's Republic of China: archaeological finds of the Han to T'ang dynasty unearthed at sites along the Silk Road. Exhibition catalogue, Tokyo: Yomiuri Shinbumsha, 1979.

Daily Life of Aristocrats in Tang China. Exhibition catalogue, Hong Kong: Regional Council, 1993.

Duan, Wenjie (ed.). *The Cream of Dunhuang Art*. Dunhuang Research Academy, 1994.

Dubs, Homer. *History of the Former Han by Pan Ku (Han Shu)*. 3 vols., Baltimore: Waverly Press, 1938.

Dubs, Homer. *A Roman City in Ancient China?* London, 1957.

Dunhuang Research Inst. (ed.). *The Mogao Grottoes of Dunhuang*. Hong Kong: Polyspring Co., 1993.

Emmerick, R. E. *A Guide to the Literature of Khotan*. Studia Philologica Buddhica, Tokyo: The Reiyukai Library, 1979.

Fa Xian. *A Record of Buddhistic Kingdoms, Being an Account of the Chinese Monk Fâ–Hien*. Trans. by James Legge, Oxford: Clarendon Press, 1886.

Feng, Fei. *The Nude Art of the Qiuci Grottoes*. Hong Kong: Xinjiang Fine Arts and Photographing Press/Educational and Cultural Press Ltd., 1992

Feng, Zhao and Zhiyong, Yu (eds.). *Legacy of the Desert King: Textiles and Treasures Excavated at Niya on the Silk Road*. Exhibition catalogue,

Chinese National Silk Museum, Hangzhou and Xinjiang Institute of Archeology, Urumqi, 2000.

Fong, Weng C. and Watt, James C.Y. *Possessing the past: treasures from the National Palace Museum, Taipei.* Exhibition catalogue, New York: Metropolitan Museum of Art, 1996.

Fontein, Jan and Wu, Tung. *Unearthing China's Past.* Boston: Museum of Fine Arts, 1973.

Gao, Feng and Sun, Jianjun. *Zhongguo deng ju jian shi.* Beijing: Beijing gong yi mei shu chu ban she, 1992

Gernet, Jacques. *A History of Chinese Civilisation.* Trans. by J. R. Foster, Cambridge: C.U.P., 1982.

Gernet, Jacques. *Buddhism in Chinese Society: An Economic History From the Fifth to the Tenth Centuries.* Trans. by F. Verellen, New York: Columbia University Press, 1995.

Gernet, Jacques. *Daily Life in China on the Eve of the Mongol Invasion, 1250–1276.* Trans. by H. M. Wright, London: Allen and Unwin, 1962.

Giès, Jacques (ed.). *The Arts of Central Asia: The Pelliot Collection in the Musée Guimet.* 3 vols., London: Serindia Publications, 1994–96.

Giles, Lionel. *Six Centuries at Tunhuang: A Short Account of the Stein Collection of Chinese MSS. in the British Museum.* London: China Society, 1944.

Grotto Art of Pazikelik Buddhist Caves in Turpan. Xinjiang Peoples' Publishing Press, 1990.

Hambis, M. Louis. *L'Asie Centrale: Histoire et Civilisation.* Paris: Imprimerie nationale, 1977.

Harada, Jiro *English Catalogue of Treasures in the Imperial Repository Shosoin.* Tokyo: Imperial Household Museum, 1932.

Haussig, Hans Wilhelm. *Archäologie und Kunst der Seidenstrasse.* Darmstadt: Wissenschaftliche Buchgesellschaft, 1992.

Hayashi, Ryoichi. *The Silk Road and the Shoso-in.* New York and Tokyo: Weatherhill/Heibonsha, 1975.

He, Zhenghuang (ed.). *Xian: An Ancient Capital of China.* Beijing: Foreign Languages Press, 1990.

Hedin, Sven. *My Life as an Explorer.* New York: Garden City Publishing, 1925.

Hedin, Sven. *The Silk Road.* Trans. by F. H. Lyon, New York: Dutton, 1938.

Hinton, D. *The Selected Poems of Li Po.* London: Anvil Press, 1996.

Hopkirk, P. *Foreign devils on the Silk Road: the search for the lost cities and treasures of Chinese Central Asia.* London: John Murray, 1980.

Huang, Zuan et al. *Die Antike Seidenstrasse.* Beijing: China Im Bild, 1987.

Hui Li. *The Life of Hiuen–Tsiang.* Trans. by Samuel Beal, London: Kegan Paul et al, 1914.

Juliano, A. and Lerner, J. *Monks and Merchants: Silk Road Treasures from Northwest China.* New York: Harry N. Abrams Inc. with the Asia Society, 2001.

Karetzky, Patricia. *Arts of the Tang Court.* Hong Kong: O.U.P., 1996.

Keller, D and Schorta, R (eds.). *Fabulous Creatures from the Desert Sands: Central Asian Woolen Textiles from the Second Century BC to the Second Century AD.* Riggisberg: Abegg–Stiftung, 2001.

Knauer, E.R. *The Camel's Load in Life and Death: iconography and ideology of Chinese pottery figurines from Han to Tang and their relevance to trade along the silk routes.* Zurich: Akanthus, 1998.

Krahl, R. *Chinese Ceramics from the Meiyintang Collection.* London: Azimuth Editions, 1994.

Kyongju National Museum. *Kyongju and the Silk Road.* Kyongju, 1991.

Lattimore, Owen. *Pivot of Asia: Sinkiang and the Inner Asian Frontiers of China and Russia.* Boston: Little, Brown and co., 1950.

Le Coq, A. von. *Buried treasures of Chinese Turkestan: an account of the activities and adventures of the second and third German Turfan expeditions.* Trans. by Anna Barwell, London: George Allen & Unwin, 1929.

Lee, Sherman E. *China– 5000 years: Innovation and Transformation in the Arts.* Exhibition catalogue, New York: Guggenheim Museum, 1998.

Li, Guo and Gao, Guo Xiang (eds.). *The Treasure House of Dunhuang.* 1993.

Li, Wei et al. *Women of the Tang Dynasty.* Exhibition catalogue, Shaanxi History Museum, Hong Kong: Pacific Century, 1995.

Li, Zhengyu et al (ed.), *Dunhuang Art Relics Collected in the State Hermitage Museum, Russia.* Vols. I & II, Shanghai, 1998.

Liao, Jingdan (dir.). *The Great Treasury of Chinese Fine Arts and Crafts.* Vol. 10, Beijing: The People's Fine Arts Publishing House, 1988.

Liu, Wenmin. *The Silk Road: An Ancient Road to Central Asia.* Trans. by Jiang Ying, Beijing: China Three Gorges Publishing House, 1993.

Loewe, M. *Everyday Life in Early Imperial China during the Han Period, 202 BC–AD 220.* London: Carousel Books, 1973.

Ma, Yue and Yan, Zhongyi et al (eds.). *Xian: Legacies of Ancient Chinese Civilization.* Beijing: Morning Glory Publishers, 1992.

Mair, Victor H. *Tun-huang Popular Narratives.* Cambridge: Cambridge University Press, 1983.

Mallory, J. P. and Mair, V. H. *The Tarim Mummies: Ancient China and the Mystery of the Earliest Peoples from the West.* London: Thames and Hudson, 2000.

Mancheng Han mu fa jue bao gao, 2 vols. Beijing: Wen wu zhu ban she: Xin hua shu dian fa xing, 1980.

Medley, M. *Tang Pottery and Porcelain.* London: Faber and Faber, 1981.

Metropolitan Museum of Art, New York and Museum für Indische Kunst, Berlin. *Along the Ancient Silk Routes: Central Asian Art from the West Berlin State Museums.* Exhibition catalogue, New York: Metropolitan Museum of Art, 1982.

Michaelson, Carol. *Gilded Dragons: Buried Treasures From China's Golden Ages.* London: British Museum, 1999.

Mission Paul Pelliot. I & II (M. Paul–David, M. Hallade and L. Hambis). *Toumchouq.* 2 vols., Paris: Académie des Inscriptions et Belles-Lettres, 1961–64.

Mission Paul Pelliot. III & IV (M. Hallade, S. Gaulier and L. Courtois). *Douldour–Aqour et Soubachi.* 2 vols., Paris: Imprimerie nationale, 1967–1982.

Mission Paul Pelliot. XIII (Krishna Riboud, G. Vial and M. Hallade). *Tissus de Touen–houang conservés au Musée Guimet et a la Bibliothèque nationale.* Paris, 1970.

Mission Paul Pelliot. XIV & XV *Bannières et Peintures de Touen–Houang conservées au Musée Guimet.* 2 vols., Paris, 1974–1976

Mu, Shunying et al. *The Ancient Art in Xinjiang, China.* Xinjiang Fine Arts and Photo Publishing House, 1994.

National Museum of Chinese History. *A Journey into China's Antiquity.* 4 vols., Beijing: Morning Glory Publishers, 1997.

National Museum of Chinese History. *Exhibition of Chinese History.* Beijing: Morning Glory Publishers, 1998.

Needham, Joseph. *Science and Civilisation in China. Vol.1, Introductory orientations.* Cambridge: Cambridge University Press, 1954.

Pal, P. (ed.). *The Flowering of a Foreign Faith: New Studies in Chinese Buddhist Art.* Mumbai: Marg Publications, 1998.

Paludan, Ann. *Chronicle of the Chinese Emperors: the reign-by-reign record of the rulers of imperial China.* London: Thames and Hudson, 1998.

Paludan, Ann. *The Chinese Spirit Road: The Classical Tradition of Stone Tomb Statuary.* New Haven & London: Yale University Press, 1991.

Pelliot, Paul. *Trois Ans dans La Haute Asie.* Paris: Bulletin de Comité de Asie française, 1910.

Piotrovsky, M. (ed.), *Lost Empire of the Silk Road: Buddhist Art from Khara Khoto (X–XIIIth century).* Lugano : Thyssen-Bornemisza Foundation, 1993.

Prodan, M. *The Art of the Tang Potter.* London: Thames and Hudson, 1960.

Qi, Xiaoshan and Wang, Bo (eds.). *A Collection of Important Historical Sites and Relics in the Western Regions.* Urumqi: Xinjiang People's Publishing Press, 1999.

Qian, Hao et al. *Out of China's Earth: Archeological Discoveries in the People's Republic of China.* London: Frederick Muller; Beijing: China Pictorial, 1981.

Rawson, Jessica (ed.). *Mysteries of Ancient China: New Discoveries from the Early Dynasties.* London: British Museum, 1996.

Research Center for Silk Roadology. *Space Archeology.* Silk Roadology 1. Nara: 1995.

Rhie, Marilyn Martin. *Early Buddhist Art of China and Central Asia.* Vol. 1, Leiden, Boston: Brill, 1999.

Rodzinski, Witold. *The walled kingdom: a history of China from 2000 BC to the present.* London: Fontana, 1984.

Roran okoku toyukyu no bijo (The Kingdom of Loulan and the Eternal Beauty). Exhibition catalogue, Tokyo: Asahi Shinbunsha, 1992.

Schafer, Edward. *The golden peaches of Samarkand: a study of T'ang exotics.* Berkeley and London: University of California Press, 1963.

Schafer, Edward. *The Vermilion Bird. T'ang Images of the South.* Berkeley and Los Angeles: University of California Press, 1967.

Schloss, Ezekiel. *Ancient Chinese Ceramic Sculpture. From Han Through Tang.* Vol. I, Stamford: Castle Publishing, 1977.

Schloss, Ezekiel. *Foreigners in Ancient Chinese Art.* Exhibition catalogue, New York: China Institute in America, 1969.

Seth, Vikram. *Three Chinese Poets.* London: Faber and

Faber, 1992.

Shao, Menglong (ed.). *Precious Cultural Relics in the Crypt of Famen Temple.* Xian: Shaanxi People's Fine Arts Publishing House, 1989.

Shipton, Diana. *The Antique Land.* London: Hodder and Stoughton, 1950.

Sickman, Laurence and Soper, Alexander. *The Art and Architecture of China.* Harmondsworth: Penguin, 1988.

Sima, Qian *Records of the Grand Historian: Shij.* 2 vols., trans. by Burton Watson, New York: Columbia University Press, 1993.

Sinor, Denis (ed.). *The Cambridge History of Early Inner Asia.* Cambridge: Cambridge University Press, 1990.

Skrine, Sir Clarmont. *Chinese Central Asia.* London: Methuen, 1926.

So, Jenny F. and Bunker, Emma C. *Traders and raiders on China's northern frontier.* Exhibition Catalogue, Seattle: Arthur M. Sackler Gallery in association with the University of Washington Press, 1995.

Stein, M. Aurel. *A Third Journey of Exploration in Central Asia, 1913–16.* From *The Geographical Journal.* London: Aug/Sept 1916.

Stein, M. Aurel. *Ancient Khotan: Detailed report of archaeological explorations in Chinese Turkestan.* 2 vols., Oxford: Clarendon Press, 1907.

Stein, M. Aurel. *Innermost Asia– Detailed report of explorations in Central Asia, Kan-su and Eastern Iran.* Oxford: Clarendon Press, 1928.

Stein, M. Aurel. *On Central Asian Tracks.* New York: Pantheon, 1964.

Stein, M. Aurel. *Ruins of Desert Cathay.* 2 vols., London: Macmillan, 1912.

Stein, M. Aurel. *Sand–Buried Ruins of Khotan.* London: Hurst and Blackett Ltd, 1904.

Stein, M. Aurel: *Serindia– Detailed Report of Explorations in Central Asia and Westernmost China.* Oxford: Clarendon Press, 1921.

Sullivan, Michael. *The Cave Temples of Maichishan.* London: Faber and Faber, 1969.

Sun, Yifu (ed.). *The Silk Road on Land and Sea.* Beijing: China Pictorial Publications, 1989.

Swann, Peter C. *Chinese Monumental Art.* London: Thames and Hudson, 1963.

Tang, Z. C. *Poems of Tang.* San Rafael California: T. C. Press, 1969

The Chinese Bronzes of Yunnan. London : Sidgwick and Jackson; Beijing: Cultural Relics Publishing House, 1983.

The Silk Road and the World of Xuanzang. Asahi Shimbun 120th Anniversary Commemorative Exhibition, Osaka: Asahi Shimbun, 1999.

Ting, Joseph (ed.). *The Maritime Silk Route: 2000 years of Trade on the South China Sea.* Hong Kong: Urban Council, 1996.

Tomb Treasures from China: The Buried Art of Ancient Xian. Exhibition catalogue, Asian Art Museum of San Francisco and Kimbell Art Museum, Fort Worth, 1994.

Treasures of Dunhuang Grottoes. Hong Kong: Polyspering Co. Ltd, 1999.

Turfan Museum Guide. Urumqi: Xinjiang Fine Arts and Photo Publishing House, 1992.

Twitchett, Denis (ed.). *The Cambridge history of China. Vol.6, Alien Regimes and Border States, 710–1368.* Cambridge: Cambridge University Press, 1993.

Twitchett, Denis and Fairbank, John K. (eds.). *The Cambridge history of China. Vol.1, The Ch'in and Han Empires, 221 B.C.–A.D. 220.* Cambridge: Cambridge University Press, 1986.

Twitchett, Denis and Fairbank, John K. (eds.). *The Cambridge history of China. Vol.3, Sui and T'ang China, 589–906. Part 1.* Cambridge: Cambridge University Press, 1979.

Waley, A. D. *The Secret History of the Mongols and other pieces.* London: George Allen and Unwin, 1963.

Waley, Arthur. *A Catalogue of Paintings Recovered from Tun–huang by Sir Aurel Stein, K.C.I.E.* London: British Museum, 1931.

Waley, Arthur. *Translations from the Chinese.* New York: Alfred A. Knopf inc., 1941.

Waley, Arthur. *The Real Tripitaka and Other Pieces.* London: Allen and Unwin, 1952.

Wang, Zhongshu. *Han Civilisation.* Trans. by K.C. Chang, New Haven, Connecticut and London: Yale University Press, 1982.

Warner, Langdon. *The Long Old Road in China.* New York: Doubleday, Page & Co., 1926.

Watson, B. *The Columbia Book of Chinese Poetry.* New York: Columbia University Press, 1984.

Watson, W. *Tang and Liao Ceramics.* London: Thames and Hudson, 1984.

Watson, W. *The Art of Dynastic China.* London: Thames and Hudson, 1981.

Watson, W. *The genius of China.* Exhibition catalogue, Royal Academy of Arts, London: Times Newspapers, 1973.

Wei, Cuiyi and Luckert, K.W. *Uighur Stories From Along The Silk Road.* Lanham, Maryland: Univesity Press of America, 1998.

White, J. and Bunker, E. *Adornment for Eternity: Status and Rank in Chinese Ornament.* Exhibition catalogue, Denver: Denver Art Museum, 1994.

Whitfield, R. and Farrer, A. *Caves of the Thousand Buddhas. Chinese Art from the Silk Route.* London: British Museum, 1990.

Whitfield, R. *The Art of Central Asia: The Stein Collection in the British Museum.* Vols. 1–3, Tokyo: Kodansha, 1985.

Whitfield, R., *Dunhuang: Caves of the Singing Sands. Buddhist Art from the Silk Road.* London: Textile & Art Publications, 1996.

Wong, Grace. *The Silk Road. Treasures of Tang China.* Exhibition catalogue, Singapore: Landmark Books, 1991.

Wong, How Man and Dajani, Adel A. *Islamic Frontiers of China. Silk Road Images.* London: Scorpion Publishing, 1990.

Wriggins, S. H. *Xuanzang: A Buddhist Pilgrim on the Silk Road.* Boulder, Colorado: Westview Press, 1996.

Xian Forest of Stone Tablets Museum Guide, Xian, 2000.

Xinjiang: the land and its people. Beijing: New World Press, 1989.

Xu, Huatian et al. *A Guide to the Scenic Spots and Historical Sites in Xinjiang China.* Urumqi Xinjiang People's Publishing House, 2000.

Xu, Yuan Zhong. *300 Tang Poems– A New Translation.* Beijing: 1987.

Xu, Yuan Zhong. *Golden Treasury of Chinese Poetry from Han to Sui (206BC– AD 618).* Beijing: Peking University Press, 1996

Xuanzang. Si–yu-ki: *Buddhist Records of the Western World,* by Hiuen Tsiang. Trans. by Samuel Beal, 2 vols. in 1, London: Kegan Paul et al, 1884.

Yamanobe, T. *Fabrics from the Silk Road: The Stein Collection, National Museum, New Delhi.* Kyoto: Shikosha, 1979.

Yang, Xiaoneng (ed.). *The Golden Age of Chinese Archaeology.* New Haven; London: Yale University Press, 1999.

Yap, Yong and Cotterell, A. *The Early Civilisation of China.* London: Weidenfeld and Nicolson, 1975.

Yung, Peter. *Bazaars of Chinese Turkestan: Life And Trade Along The Old Silk Road.* Oxford: O.U.P., 1997.

Zhang, Xuerong (ed.). *A Series of Books of Maijishan Grottoes.* Vol. 1, Tianshui: Gansu People's Fine Arts Publishing House,1997.

Zhou, Xuejun and Song, Weimin (eds.). *Archaeological Treasures of the Silk Road in Xinjiang Uygur Autonomous Region.* Exhibition catalogue, Shanghai Museum, Shanghai: Shanghai Translation Publishing House, 1998.

Zheng, Zhenduo (ed.). *Bingling si shi ku.* Beijing: Zhongyang ren min zheng fu wen hua bu wen hua si ye guan li ju, 1953.

Zou, Zongxu. *The Land Within the Passes: A History of Xian.* Trans. by Susan Whitfield, London and New York: Viking, 1991.

Central Asia, Mongolia, Steppe Peoples

Abdullaev, K. A. et al (ed.). *Culture and Art of Ancient Uzbekistan.* Exhibition catalogue, 2 vols., Moscow, 1991.

Afrasiab History Museum. *Wall Paintings of Afrasiab (Reconstruction).* Samarkand, 1997.

Alder, Garry. *Beyond Bokhara: The Life of William Moorcroft.* London: Century Publishing, 1985.

Azarpay, G. *Sogdian Painting: The Pictorial Epic in Oriental Art.* Berkeley: University of California Press, 1981.

Barthold, W. *Turkestan Down to the Mongol Invasion.* Karachi: Indus Publications, 1981. (First published in Russian 1900, first English edition 1928).

Basilov, Vladimir N. (ed.). *The Nomads of Eurasia.* University of Washington Press, 1989.

Berger, P. and Tse Bartholomew, T. *Mongolia: The Legacy of Chingis Khan.* Exhibition catalogue, Asian Art Museum of San Francisco. London: Thames and Hudson, 1995.

British Museum. *Frozen Tombs: The Culture and Art of the Ancient Tribes of Siberia.* London, 1978.

Buryakov, Y. F. et al, *The Cities and Routes of the Great Silk Road (On Central Asian Documents).* Tashkent: 'SHARG' Publications, 1999.

Bussagli, Mario. *Painting of Central Asia.* Geneva: Editions d'Art Albert Skira, 1963.

Central Asian Research Centre. *Cities of Central Asia.*

London, 1961.

Clavijo, Don Ruy Gonzalez de. *Embassy to Tamerlane 1403–1406.* Trans. by Guy Le Strange, London: Routlege and Sons, 1928.

Cleaves, F. W. (ed. and trans.). *The Secret History of the Mongols.* Vol. I, Harvard–Yenching Institute, 1982.

Fabritsky, B. and Shmeliov, I. *Khiva.* Leningrad: Aurora Art Publishers, 1973.

Frumkin, G. *Archaeology in Soviet Central Asia.* Leiden/Köln: E. J. Brill, 1970.

Frye, R. N. *The Heritage of Central Asia From Antiquity to the Turkish Expansion.* Princeton: Markus Wiener Publishers, 1997.

Gombos, K. *The Pearls of Uzbekistan: Bukhara, Samarkand, Khiva.* Trans. by I. Kemenes, Budapest: Corvina Press, 1976.

Grousset, R. *The Empire of the Steppes: A History of Central Asia.* Trans. by Naomi Walford, New Brunswick: Rutgers University Press, 1970.

Hambly, G. *Central Asia.* New York and London: Dell/Weidenfeld and Nicolson,1969.

Harmatta, János (ed.). *History of civilizations of Central Asia. Vol.II. The development of sedentary and nomadic civilization.* Paris: UNESCO Publishing, 1994.

Heissig, W. and Dumas, D. *The Mongols.* Innsbruck: Pinguin Verlag, 1995.

Hrbas, M. and Knobloch, E. *The Art of Central Asia.* London: Paul Hamlyn, 1965.

International Merv Project. *The Ancient Cities of Merv, Turkmenistan.* London: University College, 1996.

Invernizzi, A. (ed.). *In the Land of the Gryphons: Papers on Central Asian archaeology in antiquity.* Firenze: Casa Editrice Le Lettere, 1995.

Jettmar, Karl. *Art of the Steppes: The Eurasian Animal Style.* London: Methuen, 1967.

Kalter, Johannes. *The Arts and Crafts of Turkestan.* London: Thames and Hudson, 1984.

Kessler, A. T. *Empires Beyond the Great Wall: The Heritage of Genghis Khan.* Natural History Museum of L. A. County, 1993.

Kirichenko, O. (ed.). *Bukhara– An Oriental Gem.* Tashkent: 'Sharq' Publications, 1997.

Kirichenko, O. (ed.). *Khiva– The City of A Thousand Domes.* Tashkent: 'Sharq' Publications, 1997.

Klimburg–Salter, D. *The Silk Route and the Diamond Path: Esoteric Buddhist Art on the Trans–Himalayan Trade Routes.* Los Angeles, 1982.

Knobloch, E. *Beyond the Oxus: Archaeology, Art and Architecture of Central Asia.* London: Ernest Benn Ltd, 1972.

Lawton, J. *Samarkand and Bukhara.* London: Tauris Parke Books,1991.

Litvinsky, B. A. (ed.). *History of civilizations of Central Asia. Vol.III. The crossroads of civilizations AD 250 to 750.* Paris: UNESCO Publishing, 1996.

Macleod, C. and Mayhew, B. *Uzbekistan: The Golden Road to Samarkand.* Hong Kong: Odyssey Publications, 1999.

Manz, Beatrice. *The Rise and Rule of Tamerlane.* Cambridge University Press, 1989.

Masson, M. E. and Pugacenkova, G. A. *The Parthian Rhytons of Nisa.* Trans. by C. M. Breton Bruce, Florence: Le Lettere-Licosa, 1982.

Naumkin, V. *Caught in Time: Great Photographic Archives. Samarkand.* Reading: Garnet Publishing Ltd, 1992.

Pugachenkova, G. A. *Le Trésors de Dalverzine–Tépé.* Leningrad: Editions D'Art Aurore, 1978.

Pugachenkova, G. A. (ed.). *Antiquities of Southern Uzbekistan.* Tashkent and Tokyo: Khamza Fine Arts Research Centre/ Soka University Press, 1991.

Ratchnevsky, P. *Genghis Khan: His Life and Legacy.* Trans. by T. N. Haining, Oxford U.K. and Cambridge U.S.A: Blackwell Publishers, 1991.

Rice, Tamara Talbot. *Ancient Arts of Central Asia.* London: Thames and Hudson, 1965.

Royal Geographical Society: *The Country of the Turkomans: An anthology of exploration from the Royal Geographical Society.* London: Ogus Press and the R.G.S., 1977.

Rtveladze, E. *Pre-Muslim Coins of Chach.* Silk Road Art and Archaeology 5, Journal of the Institute of Silk Road Studies, Kamakura, 1997–98.

Rudenko, S. I. *Frozen Tombs of Siberia: The Pazyryk Burials of Iron Age Horsemen.* Trans. by M.W. Thompson, London: Dent, 1970.

Skrine, F. H. and Ross, E. D. *The Heart of Asia: A History of Russian Turkestan and the Central Asian Khanates from the Earliest Times.* London: Methuen & Co., 1899.

State Museum of History and Regional Ethnography, Ministry of Culture, Turkmenian SSR: *Marble Sculpture of Nisa, Parthian Ritons of Nisa, Treasures of Parthian Kings, Athena from Nisa.* 4 vols., Ashkabad, 1991.

Teague, Ken. *Metalcrafts of Central Asia.* Princes Risborough: Shire Publications, 1990.

Tudev, L. and Natsagdorj, Sh (eds.). *Ancient Karaq–Korum.* Ulan Bator, 1995.

UNESCO, *Amir Temur in World History.* Paris, 1996.

UNESCO. *Mongolia's Tentative List: Cultural and Natural Heritage,* 1996.

Iran

Arberry, A. J. (ed.). *Persian Poems: An Anthology of Verse Translations.* London: J. M. Dent, 1954.

Boyle, J.A. (ed.). *Persia: History and Heritage.* London: Henry Melland, 1978.

Browne, Edward G. *A Literary History of Persia.* Vols. 1 and 2, London: T. Fisher Unwin Ltd, 1906.

Curtis, John. *Ancient Persia.* London and Tehran: British Museum Publications and Karang Publishing,.

Dieulafoy, M. *L'Art Antique de la Perse.* Paris: Librairie centrale d'Architecture, 1884.

Ferdowsi. *The Epic of the Kings: Shah-Nama.* Trans. by Reuben Levy, London: Routledge & Kegan Paul, 1967.

Ferrier, R. W. (ed.). *The Arts of Persia.* New Haven and London: Yale University Press, 1989.

Firouz, L. *Origins of the Oriental Horse.* Institute for Ancient Equestrian Studies, Conference in Petrovpavlovsk, Kazakhstan, 1995.

Fisher, W.B. (ed.). *The Cambridge History of Iran Vol.1: The Land of Iran.* London: Cambridge University Press, 1968.

Frye, R. N. *The Heritage of Persia.* London: Cardinal (Sphere Books Ltd), 1976 (first published 1962).

Frye, R. N. *The Golden Age of Persia.* London: Phoenix Press, 1975.

Frye, R. N. *The History of Ancient Iran.* München: C. H. Bek'sche, 1983.

Ghirshman, R. *Iran: From the earliest times to the Islamic conquest.* Harmondsworth, London: Penguin, 1954.

Ghirshman, R. *Iran: Parthians and Sassanians.* The Arts of Mankind Series. London: Thames and Hudson, 1962.

Godard, A. *The Art of Iran.* Trans. by Michael Heron, London: Allen and Unwin Ltd, 1965.

Harper, Prudence Oliver. *The Royal Hunter: Art of the Sasanian Empire.* New York: Asia Society, 1978.

Hutt, A. and Harrow, L. *Islamic Architecture: Iran 1.* London: Scorpion Publications, 1977.

Hutt, A. and Harrow, L. *Islamic Architecture: Iran 2.* London: Scorpion Publications, 1978.

Kai Ka'us Ibn Iskandar. *A Mirror for Princes: The Qabus Nama.* Trans. by Reuben Levy, London: Cresset Press, 1951.

Kiani, M.Y. and Kleiss, W. *Iranian Caravanserais.* Tehran: Cultural Heritage Organization of Iran, 1995.

Kritzeck, James (ed.). *Anthology of Islamic Literature.* London: Pelican, 1964.

Matheson, Sylvia. *Persia: An Archaeological Guide.* New Jersey: Noyes Press, 1973.

Michell, George (ed.). *Architecture of the Islamic World.* London: Thames and Hudson, 1978. Stevens, Sir Roger. *The Land of the Great Sophy.* London: Methuen & Co. Ltd, 1962.

Nizami of Ganja. *The Haft Paikar (The Seven Beauties).* Trans. by C.E. Wilson, 2 vols., London: Probsthain & Co., 1924.

O'Kane, B. *Studies in Persian art and architecture.* Cairo: American University in Cairo Press, 1995.

Pope, Arthur Upham. *Persian architecture.* London: Thames and Hudson, 1965.

Pope, Arthur Upham and Ackerman, Phyllis (eds.). *A survey of Persian art from prehistoric times to the present.* Vol. 3, Architecture, London and New York: Oxford University Press, 1964–65. (Originally published by O.U.P.London, 1938–39).

Porada, Edith. *Ancient Iran: The Art of Pre-Islamic Times.* London: Methuen, 1965.

Sarre, Friedrich. *Die Kunst Des Alten Persien.* Berlin: Bruno Cassirer Verlag, 1922.

Yarshater, Ehsan (ed.). *The Cambridge History of Iran Vol. 3: The Seleucid, Parthian and Sasanian Periods'.* London: Cambridge University Press, 1983.

Yassavoli, J. et al. *The Fabulous Land of Iran: Colourful and Vigorous Folklore.* Tehran: Farhang-Sara, 1993.

Iraq

Al–Duri, Khidr Jasmin. *Society and Economy of Iraq Under the Seljuqs (1055–1160 AD) With Special Reference to Baghdad.* Ann Arbor, Michigan: University Microfilms International, 1971.

Al–Salithi, Dr. W. I. *Hatra.* London: Iraqi Cultural Centre, 1978.

Al–Shawi, N. A. *Sculptures of Hatrans: A Study of Costume and Jewelry.* Ann Arbor, Michigan: University Microfilms International, 1986.

Fathi, Ihsan. *The Architectural heritage of Baghdad.*

Exhibition catalogue, London: Iraqi Cultural Centre Gallery, 1979.

Le Strange, G. *Baghdad during the Abbasid Caliphate*. London: O.U.P., 1924 (first edition 1900). Levy, Reuben. *A Baghdad Chronicle*. Cambridge: Cambridge University Press, 1929.

Metz, Helen Chapin (ed.). *Iraq: A Country Study*. Washington DC: Library of Congress, 1990.

Osborn, R. D. *Islam Under the Khalifs of Baghdad*. London: Seeley, Jackson and Halliday, 1878.

Roux, Georges. *Ancient Iraq*. London: Pelican, 1966.

Simons, Geoff. *Iraq: From Sumer to Saddam*. London: Macmillan, 1994.

Vattioni, F. *Le Iscrizioni di Hatra*. Naples: Istituto Orientale Di Napoli, 1981.

Wiet, Gaston. *Baghdad: Metropolis of the Abbasid Caliphate*. Trans. by Seymour Feiler, University of Oklahoma Press, 1971.

Syria and Lebanon

Ball, Warwick. *Syria: A Historical and Architectural Guide*. Essex: Scorpion Publishing, 1994.

Bounni, A. and Al-As'ad, K. *Palmyra: History, Monuments and Museum*. Damascus, 1997.

Drijvers, H. J. W. *The Religion of Palmyra*. Institute of Religious Iconography, State University Groningen, Leiden: E.J. Brill, 1976.

Eiselen, F. C. *Sidon: A Study in Oriental History*. New York: AMS Press Inc., 1966.

Higuchi, T. and Izumi, T. (eds.). *Tombs A and C– Southeast Necropolis, Palmyra, Syria*. Nara, Japan: Research Center for Silk Roadology, 1994.

Hopkins, Clark. *The Discovery of Dura-Europos*. New Haven and London: Yale University Press, 1979.

Jidejian, Nina. *Sidon through the Ages*. Beirut: Dar El-Machreq Publishers, 1971.

Jidejian, Nina. *Tyre through the Ages*. Beirut: Dar El-Machreq Publishers, 1969.

Khayyata, M. Wahid. *Aleppo in World History*. (Publication date unknown.)

Matheson, Susan B. *Dura Europos: The Ancient City and the Yale Collection*. Yale University Art Gallery, 1982.

Perkins, Ann. *The Art of Dura-Europos*. London: O.U.P., 1973.

Rostovtzeff, M. *Caravan Cities*. Oxford at the Clarendon Press, 1932.

Rostovtzeff, M. *Dura-Europos and its Art*. Oxford at the Clarendon Press, 1938.

Stark, Freya. *Rome on the Euphrates: The Story of a Frontier*. London: John Murray, 1966.

Sultan Muhesen, Dr. et al (eds.). *Palmyra and the Silk Road*. Activities of the International Colloquium, 7–11 April 1992, Damascus, 1996.

Syrian Arab Republic Ministry of Culture. *Syria: The First Discoveries in History*. Expo Seville 92, Directorate General of Antiquities and Museums, Damascus, 1992.

Turkey and Byzantium

Aksit, Ilhan. *The Museum of Chora: Mosaics and Frescoes*. Istanbul: Aksit Kultur Turizm Sanat Ajans Ltd, 2001.

Begley, V. and De Puma, R. D. (eds.). *Rome and India: The Ancient Sea Trade*. Madison, Wisconsin: University of Wisconsin Press, 1991.

Browning, Robert. *The Byzantine Empire*. London: Weidenfeld and Nicolson, 1980.

Davidson, H. R. Ellis. *The Viking Road to Byzantium*. London; George Allen and Unwin Ltd, 1976.

Davison, R. H. *Turkey: A Short History*. Huntingdon: Eothen Press, 1988.

Downey, Glanville. *A History of Antioch in Syria from Seleucus to the Arab Conquest*. Princeton, New Jersey: Princeton University Press, 1961.

Grabar, A. *Byzantium: Byzantine Art in the Middle Ages*. London: Methuen, 1966.

Jobst, Werner. *Istanbul: The Great Palace Mosaic*. Istanbul: Arkeoloji Ve Sanat Yayinlari, 1997.

Kelly, Laurence. *Istanbul: A Traveller's Companion*. London: Constable, 1987.

Krahl, R. *Chinese Ceramics in the Topkapi Saray Museum, Istanbul*. 3 vols., London : Sotheby's in association with the Directorate of the Topkapi Saray Museum, 1986.

Liebeschuetz, J. H. W. G. *Antioch: City and Imperial Administration in the Later Roman Empire*. Oxford: Clarendon Press, 1972.

Luke, Sir Harry. *The Old Turkey and the New: From Byzantium to Ankara*. London: Geoffrey Bles, 1955. (First published by Macmillan, London, 1936).

Maclagan, M. *The City of Constantinople*. Ancient Peoples and Places series, London: Thames and Hudson, 1968.

Mango, Cyril. *Byzantium: The Empire of the New Rome*. London: Phoenix Giant, 1994. (First published by Weidenfeld and Nicolson, London, 1980).

Metzger, H. *Anatolia II: First Millennium BC to the end of the Roman period*. Translated by James Hogarth, Ancient Civilisations series, Geneva: Nagel Publishers, 1969.

Museum Associations Guide. *Hagia Sophia, Hagia Eirene et al*. Ankara (Publication date unknown.)

Norwich, John Julius. *A Short History of Byzantium*. London: Penguin, 1998.

Pasinli, Alpay. *Guide to the Istanbul Archeological Museum*. Istanbul: A Turizm Yayinlari, 1999.

Rice, D. Talbot. *Art of the Byzantine Era*. London: Thames and Hudson, 1963.

Rice, D. Talbot. *The Byzantines*. Ancient Peoples and Places series, London: Thames and Hudson, 1962.

Rice, Tamara Talbot. *Everyday Life in Byzantium*. London: B. T. Batsford Ltd, 1967.

Runciman, Steven. *Byzantine style and civilisation*. Harmondsworth, London: Penguin, 1975.

Stoneman, R. *A Traveller's History of Turkey*. Gloucestershire: Windrush Press, 1993.

Wheeler, Sir Mortimer. *Rome Beyond the Imperial Frontiers*. London: G. Bell and Sons, 1954.

Zachariadou, E (ed.). *The Via Egnatia Under Ottoman Rule (1380–1699)*. Institute for Mediterranean Studies. Rethymnon: Crete University Press, 1996.

Periodicals

Various issues of:

Arts of Asia
Hali
Marg
National Geographic
Oriental Art
Orientations

INDEX